THE HISTORY OF
MARKETING SCIENCE

World Scientific–Now Publishers Series in Business

ISSN: 2251-3442

World Scientific – Now Publishers Series in Business: **Vol.3**

THE HISTORY OF MARKETING SCIENCE

Editors

Russell S. Winer
New York University, USA

Scott A. Neslin
Dartmouth College, USA

Published by

World Scientific Publishing Co. Pte. Ltd.

5 Toh Tuck Link, Singapore 596224

USA office: 27 Warren Street, Suite 401-402, Hackensack, NJ 07601

UK office: 57 Shelton Street, Covent Garden, London WC2H 9HE

and

now publishers Inc.
PO Box 1024
Hanover, MA 02339
USA

Library of Congress Cataloging-in-Publication Data
The history of marketing science / [edited] by Russell S. Winer and Scott A. Neslin.
    pages cm. -- (World scientific-now publishers series in business, ISSN 2251-3442 ; vol. 3)
    Includes index.
    ISBN 978-9814596473 -- ISBN 978-9814619479 (pbk)
    1. Marketing research--History. 2. Marketing--Management--History. 3. Marketing--Study and
teaching--History. I. Winer, Russell S. II. Neslin, Scott A., 1952–
    HF5415.2.H55 2015
    381'.109--dc23

    2014009472

British Library Cataloguing-in-Publication Data
A catalogue record for this book is available from the British Library.

In-house Editors: Chitralekha Elumalai/Philly Lim

Typeset by Stallion Press
Email: enquiries@stallionpress.com

Printed in Singapore

To the trailblazers who founded the field of Marketing Science

Contents

About the Editors

 **Russell S. Winer** is the William Joyce Professor and Chair of the Department of Marketing at the Stern School of Business, New York University. He received a BA in Economics from Union College and an MS and PhD in Industrial Administration from Carnegie Mellon University. He has been on the faculties of Columbia and Vanderbilt universities and the University of California at Berkeley. Professor Winer has been a visiting faculty member at M.I.T., Stanford University, Cranfield School of Management (UK), the Helsinki School of Economics, the University of Tokyo, École Nationale des Ponts et Chausées, Henley Management College (UK), and the Indian School of Business. He has written three books, *Marketing Management, Analysis for Marketing Planning* and *Product Management*, and a research monograph, *Pricing*. He has authored over 70 papers in marketing on a variety of topics including consumer choice, marketing research methodology, marketing planning, advertising, and pricing. Professor Winer has served two terms as the editor of the *Journal of Marketing Research*. He is the past co-editor of *Journal of Interactive Marketing*, an Associate Editor of the *International Journal of Research in Marketing*, and is on the editorial boards of the *Journal of Marketing*, the *Journal of Marketing Research*, and *Marketing Science*. He is a past Executive Director of the Marketing Science Institute in Cambridge, Massachusetts. Professor Winer is a founding Fellow of the INFORMS Society for Marketing Science and is the 2011 recipient of the American Marketing Association/Irwin/McGraw-Hill Distinguished Marketing Educator award.

Scott A. Neslin is the Albert Wesley Frey Professor of Marketing at the Tuck School of Business, Dartmouth College. He has been at Tuck since completing his PhD in 1978 at the Sloan School of Management, MIT. He was a visiting associate professor at MIT (1984) and a visiting scholar at the Yale School of Management (1989–1990), the Fuqua School of Business, Duke University (2002), as part of Duke's Teradata Center for CRM, and Columbia Business School (2009–2010).

Professor Neslin's expertise is in the measurement and analysis of marketing productivity. His focus is on database marketing, sales promotion, and advertising. He has published on these and other topics in journals such as *Marketing Science, Journal of Marketing Research, Management Science, Journal of Marketing,* and *Journal of Interactive Marketing.* In the field of database marketing, he is co-author with Robert C. Blattberg and Byung-Do Kim of *Database Marketing: Analyzing and Managing Customers* (2008, Springer). He is also co-editor, with Kristof Coussement and Koen W. De Bock of *Advanced Database Marketing* (2013, Gower). In the database marketing area, he has investigated the application of predictive modeling to cross-selling, forecasting customer churn, and optimal customer management. He has analyzed issues in multichannel customer management including research shopping, customer channel migration, channel choice, and cross-channel effects of advertising. In the sales promotion area, he is co-author with Robert C. Blattberg of the book, *Sales Promotion: Concepts, Methods, and Strategies* (1990, Prentice-Hall), and author of the monograph *Sales Promotion* (2002, Marketing Science Institute). His work on promotions includes studies of the impact of promotions on stockpiling, consumption, repeat purchasing, and factors that determine promotion effectiveness, as well as strategic issues related to store brands, optimal promotion planning, and corporate-wide shifts in promotion policy.

Professor Neslin is an Associate Editor for *Marketing Science,* and is on the editorial boards of the *Journal of Marketing Research, Journal of Marketing, Journal of Interactive Marketing, Journal of the Academy of Marketing Science,* and *Marketing Letters.* He served as President of the INFORMS Society for Marketing Science (ISMS) and is an ISMS Fellow. Website: http://mba.tuck.dartmouth.edu/pages/faculty/scott.neslin/.

About the Contributors

Kusum L. Ailawadi is the Charles Jordan 1911 TU'12 Professor of Marketing at the Tuck School at Dartmouth. She received her MBA from the Indian Institute of Management in Bangalore, India, and her PhD from the University of Virginia. She examines the impact of promotions and store brands on the performance of manufacturers and retailers, and studies consumer, competitor, and retailer response to major marketing policy changes.

Kusum is a recipient of the Davidson, Maynard, and Little best paper awards, the winner of the *Marketing Science Institute/Journal of Marketing Research* competition for academic-practitioner collaborative research, and a finalist for the O'Dell and Paul Green awards and the ISMS Practice Prize. She serves on the editorial boards of *JMR*, *Marketing Science*, *JAMS*, and *Journal of Retailing* and is an area editor for *JM* and *IJRM*. She is also an academic trustee of the Marketing Science Institute and AiMark, organizations in the US and Europe respectively that bring together academics and practitioners to facilitate research and idea exchange.

Tulin Erdem is the Leonard N. Stern Professor of Business Administration and Professor of Marketing at the Stern School of Business, New York University. She served there as the Co-Director of Center for Digital Economy Research and the Director of Stern Center for Measurable Marketing.

Before joining Stern in 2006, Tülin Erdem has also been the E.T. Grether Professor of Business

Administration and Marketing at the Haas School of Business, University of California at Berkeley, where she served also as the Associate Dean for Academic Affairs and the Marketing Group Chair, and the PhD Director at the Haas School of Business.

Her research interests include advertising, brand management and equity, consumer choice, decision-making under uncertainty, econometric modeling, and marketing mix effectiveness. She has published several papers in top field journals. She has received best paper awards, as well as major research grants, including two major National Science Foundation (NSF) grants. She has served as an Area Editor at *Marketing Science*, Associate Editor at *Quantitative Marketing and Economics* and *Journal of Consumer Research*. She has been on the editorial boards of *Journal of Marketing Research, International Journal of Research in Marketing, Journal of the Academy of Marketing Science and Marketing Letters*.

Tülin Erdem served as the President of INFORMS Marketing Society (ISMS). She was also the editor-in-chief of *Journal of Marketing Research* during 2009–2012.

Tülin Erdem has a BA (Boğaziçi University) and MA in Economics and PhD in Business Administration (University of Alberta).

Peter S. Fader is the Frances and Pei-Yuan Chia Professor of Marketing at the Wharton School of the University of Pennsylvania. His expertise centers around the analysis of behavioral data to understand and forecast customer shopping/purchasing activities. He serves as co-director of the Wharton Customer Analytics Initiative, a research center that serves as a "matchmaker" between leading-edge academic researchers and top companies that depend on granular, customer-level data for key strategic decisions. Professor Fader believes that marketing should not be viewed as a "soft" discipline, and he frequently works with different companies and industry associations to improve managerial perspectives in this regard. His work has been published in (and he serves on the editorial boards of) a number of leading journals in marketing, statistics, and the management sciences. He has won many awards for his teaching and research accomplishments.

Peter N. Golder is a Professor of Marketing at the Tuck School of Business at Dartmouth. His research on market entry timing, new products, long-term market leadership, and quality has won more than 10 best paper or best book awards including William F. O'Dell (*Journal of Marketing Research*), Harold H. Maynard (*Journal of Marketing*), INFORMS Long Term Impact Award (*Marketing Science*), Frank M. Bass (*Marketing Science*), and Berry Book Prize (*American Marketing Association*). His research has also been featured in numerous mass-media outlets including *The Wall Street Journal*, *The Financial Times*, *The Economist*, and *Advertising Age*. He holds a PhD in Business Administration from the University of Southern California and a BS in mechanical engineering from the University of Pennsylvania.

Sunil Gupta is the Edward W. Carter Professor of Business at the Harvard Business School. His research interests include digital marketing, customer management, pricing, and return on marketing investment.

His articles in these areas have won several awards including the O'Dell (1993, 2002, and 2009) and the Paul Green (1998, 2005) awards for the *Journal of Marketing Research*, and the best paper awards for the *International Journal of Research in Marketing* (1999) and Marketing Science Institute (1999, 2000, and 2003). His book, *Managing Customers as Investments*, won the 2006 annual Berry-AMA book prize for the best book in marketing.

Sunil holds a Bachelors degree in Mechanical Engineering from the Indian Institute of Technology, an MBA from the Indian Institute of Management, and a PhD from Columbia University.

Dominique M. Hanssens is the Bud Knapp Distinguished Professor of Marketing at the UCLA Anderson School of Management. From 2005 to 2007 he served as Executive Director of the *Marketing Science Institute*. A Purdue University PhD graduate, Professor Hanssens's research focuses on strategic marketing problems, in particular marketing productivity, to which he applies his expertise in data-analytic methods such as econometrics and time-series analysis. He has served or is serving in various editorial capacities with *Marketing Science, Management Science, Journal of Marketing Research*, and *International Journal of Research in Marketing*. Five of his articles have won Best Paper awards, in *Marketing Science* (1995, 2001, 2002), *Journal of Marketing Research* (1999, 2007) and *Journal of Marketing* (2010), and eight were award finalists. The second edition of his book with Leonard Parsons and Randall Schultz, entitled *Market Response Models* was published in 2001 and translated in Chinese in 2003. In 2010, he was elected a Fellow of the INFORMS Society for Marketing Science. He is a founding partner of MarketShare, a global marketing analytics firm headquartered in Los Angeles.

Bruce G. S. Hardie is a Professor of Marketing at London Business School. He holds BCom and MCom degrees from the University of Auckland (New Zealand), and MA and PhD degrees from the University of Pennsylvania.

His primary research interests lie in the development of data-based models to support marketing analysts and decision makers, with a particular interest in models that are easy to implement. Most of his current projects focus on the development of probability models for customer-base analysis.

Eunkyu Lee is a Professor and Chair of the Marketing Department at the Whitman School of Management, Syracuse University. He is a graduate of Seoul National University, and received his MBA and PhD from Duke University. He has also taught at Seattle University and the University of British Columbia.

His primary research area is quantitative modeling for the investigation of distribution channel management and marketing strategy issues. His research has been published in various academic journals including *Journal of Marketing Research, Marketing Science, Management Science, Marketing Letters,* and *Quantitative Marketing and Economics.* In the recent years, his research has been focused on game theoretic analysis of strategic interactions among distribution channel members over issues such as store brand strategy, product line design, motion picture distribution, and online/offline mixed distribution channel structures.

Donald R. Lehmann is the George E. Warren Professor of Business at Columbia University Graduate School of Business. He has a BS degree in mathematics from Union College, Schenectady, New York, and an MSIA and PhD from the Krannert School of Purdue University.

His research interests include modeling choice and decision making, meta-analysis, the introduction and adoption of innovations, and the measurement and management of marketing assets (customers and brands). He has taught courses in marketing, management, and statistics at Columbia, and has also taught at Cornell, Dartmouth, and New York University. He has published in and served on the editorial boards of *Journal of Consumer Research, Journal of Marketing, Journal of Marketing Research, Management Science,* and *Marketing Science,* and was the founding editor of *Marketing Letters* and editor of the *International Journal of Research in Marketing.* In addition to numerous journal articles, he has published several books: including *Market Research and Analysis,*

Analysis for Marketing Planning, Product Management, Meta Analysis in Marketing, and *Managing Customers as Investments.* He has won best paper awards from several journals, multiple lifetime achievement awards, and is a Fellow of both the Association for Consumer Research and the Informs Society for Marketing Science. Professor Lehmann has served as Executive Director of the Marketing Science Institute and as President of the Association for Consumer Research.

Gary L. Lilien is a Distinguished Research Professor at Penn State and co-founder and Research Director of the Institute for the Study of Business Markets (isbm.org). He is the author or co-author of 15 books and over 100 professional articles. He is an inaugural Fellow of INFORMS, of ISMS, and of the European Marketing Academy. He is former president of The Institute of Management Sciences, was departmental editor for Marketing for *Management Science,* is former editor-in-chief and is currently Area Editor for *Interfaces,* and is Area Editor at *Marketing Science.* His honors include inaugural INFORMS Fellow, EMAC Fellow, ISMS Fellow, Morse Lecturer, Kimball Medal, and honorary doctorates from three universities. He received the 2008 Educator of the Year Award from the American Marketing Association and the award for the best applied work in marketing science is named the Gary Lilien ISMS-MSI Practice Prize in his honor.

Murali K. Mantrala is the Sam M. Walton Distinguished Professor of Marketing at the University of Missouri, Columbia (MU). Murali holds a PhD in Marketing from Northwestern University; and MBAs from the University of Minnesota, Minneapolis, and Indian Institute of Management, Calcutta. Before joining MU, Murali was Manager at ZS Associates (1999–2003), a global sales consulting firm headquartered in Evanston, Illinois. Earlier in his career, Murali was at Sandoz

Pharmaceuticals, India, managing its sales force in Tamil Nadu for several years. His sales research papers have appeared in the *Journal of Marketing Research* and *Marketing Science* among other journals. He currently serves as an Associate Editor of the *Journal of Retailing* and on the editorial boards of *Journal of Marketing* and *Journal of Personal Selling and Sales Management*. In 2010, Murali received the Humboldt Research Award, Alexander von Humboldt Foundation for his past and ongoing research in sales with German scholars.

Wendy W. Moe is an Associate Professor of Marketing and Director of the MS in Marketing Analytics at the Robert H. Smith School of Business, University of Maryland. She is a recognized expert in online marketing and social media and is the author of Social Media Intelligence. Professor Moe has been on the faculty at the University of Maryland since 2004. Prior to that, she was on the faculty at the University of Texas at Austin. She holds a PhD, MA, and BS from the Wharton School at the University of Pennsylvania as well as an MBA from Georgetown University. In addition to her academic work, Professor Moe has consulted for numerous corporations and government agencies, helping them develop and implement state-of-the-art statistical models in the context of web analytics, social media intelligence and forecasting.

Eitan Muller has a joint appointment at the Stern School of Business at New York University and the Arison School of Business at Interdisciplinary Center (IDC) Herzliya. He earned a BSc (with distinction) in Mathematics from the Technion, Israel Institute of Technology, an MBA (with distinction) in Marketing, and a PhD in Managerial Economics from the Kellogg Graduate School of Management, Northwestern University.

The main research interest of Professor Muller is in the diffusion of innovations, social networks, and new product pricing.

He has published extensively in journals in marketing, business, and economics, with more than 11,000 citations in Google Scholar. He has won several awards including the Harold Maynard award for significant contribution to marketing theory and thought.

He is the co-editor-in-chief of the *International Journal of Research in Marketing*, and is a member of the editorial boards of the *Journal of Marketing*, and the *Journal of Marketing Research*.

Scott A. Neslin is the Albert Wesley Frey Professor of Marketing at the Tuck School of Business, Dartmouth College. He has been at Tuck since completing his PhD in 1978 at MIT. He has visited at MIT (1984), Yale School of Management (1989–1990), the Fuqua School of Business (2002), and Columbia Business School (2009–2010).

Professor Neslin's research focuses on customer relationship management, sales promotion, and advertising. In the CRM area, he is co-author of *Database Marketing: Analyzing and Managing Customers* (2008, Springer) and co-editor of *Advanced Database Marketing* (2013, Gower). In the promotions area, he is co-author of *Sales Promotion: Concepts, Methods, and Strategies* (1990, Prentice-Hall), and author of *Sales Promotion* (2002, MSI). He is an Area Editor for *Marketing Science*, and on the editorial boards several journals including the *Journal of Marketing Research* and *Journal of Marketing*. He is former President of the INFORMS Society for Marketing Science (ISMS) and an ISMS Fellow.

Website: http://mba.tuck.dartmouth.edu/pages/faculty/scott.neslin/.

Vithala R. Rao is the Deane Malott Professor of Management and Professor of Marketing and Quantitative Methods, Johnson, Cornell University, Ithaca, New York. He is well known for his scholarly contributions to several topics including conjoint analysis and multidimensional scaling, promotions, pricing, market structure, corporate acquisition, brand equity, and Internet recommendation systems. His numerous papers have appeared in such journals as *Journal of Marketing Research*,

Marketing Science, Journal of Marketing, Journal of Consumer Research, and *Management Science.* He serves on the editorial boards of various top journals in marketing.

Professor Rao received the 2008 Charles Coolidge Parlin Marketing Research Award presented by the American Marketing Association Foundation. In 2012, he was elected Fellow of the INFORMS Society of Marketing Science. He is the co-author or editor of five books in marketing including *Pricing Research in Marketing* and a forthcoming book, *Applied Conjoint Analysis.* He has worked for several corporations in the US and abroad as an Advisor and Seminar Leader.

Gary J. Russell is the Henry B. Tippie Research Professor of Marketing at the Tippie College of Business, University of Iowa. His primary research interest is the application of scanner-data-based choice models to substantive marketing issues. His work has addressed sales response to advertising, market structure definition, brand equity measurement, and brand price competition. Recent work is concerned with multiple category promotion response, fusion methodologies for linking panel and store-level scanner data, and spatial aspects of choice. His work appears in such journals as *Journal of Consumer Research, Marketing Science, Marketing Letters, Journal of Marketing Research, Journal of Retailing, International Journal of Research in Marketing,* and *Management Science.* He serves on the editorial board of *Journal of Marketing Research* and is an Associate Editor of *Marketing Science.*

David A. Schweidel is an Associate Professor of marketing at Emory University's Goizueta Business School and co-director of the Emory Marketing Analytics Center (EmoryMAC). He received his BA in mathematics, MA in statistics, and PhD in marketing from the University of Pennsylvania. His research focuses on the development and application of statistical models to understand customer behavior and inform managerial decisions. His current research focuses on the use of social media, both as a complement to marketing research tools and as part of an organization's marketing strategy.

Subrata Sen is the Joseph F. Cullman Professor of Marketing at the School of Management at Yale University. He has also served on the faculties of the University of Texas at Austin, University of Chicago, and the University of Rochester.

Sen holds a Bachelor's degree in Electrical Engineering from the Indian Institute of Technology at Kharagpur, and a PhD in Industrial Administration from Carnegie-Mellon University.

He has served as Editor of Marketing Science and has been on the Editorial Boards of the *Journal of Marketing* and the *Journal of Marketing Research*.

Sen's research has been published in journals such as *Marketing Science, Management Science, Journal of Marketing Research, Journal of Marketing, Journal of Consumer Research*, and the *American Political Science Review*. His current research interests relate to the pricing of product bundles, cross-country diffusion of new products, the effectiveness of anti-drug advertising, and the value of celebrity endorsements. He has been an expert witness in several legal cases and has served as a consultant to a variety of firms such as Citibank, Ford, IBM, Eastman Kodak, and Xerox.

Steven M. Shugan is the McKethan-Matherly Eminent Scholar and Professor at the University of Florida. His PhD in Managerial Economics is from Northwestern University. Formerly a full professor at University of Chicago (13 years) and assistant professor at University of Rochester (2 years), he has taught marketing, econometrics (Chicago), statistics (Florida) and computer science (Northwestern). He was editor-in-chief of *Marketing Science* (6 years), editor of *Journal of Business* and associate editor of *Management Science* and served on over 10 editorial boards including the *Journal of Consumer Research and Journal of Marketing Research*. He has numerous publications and made over 100 professional presentations in over 24 countries. He is an INFORMS fellow as well as an Inaugural Fellow of the Society for Marketing Science. He won several best paper awards (including twice — *Marketing Science, Journal of Marketing, Journal of Retailing*, finalist — *Journal of Service Research*, finalist — *Journal of Marketing Research*) and best teaching awards. He has consulted for over 30 different organizations (most recently for Apple Inc. and Oracle Inc.).

Richard Staelin is the Edward and Rose Donnell Professor of Business Administration at the Fuqua School of Business, Duke University. He graduated from the University of Michigan and taught at Carnegie-Mellon University for 13 years prior to his arrival at Duke in 1982. Since then he has been Deputy Dean (twice), Associate Dean of Executive Education, Executive Director for the Teradata Center for CRM and the initial Managing Director of GEMBA at Duke. He has taught in every program ever offered by Duke. He has published over 80 papers in academic journals and has received best paper awards at JMR, JM, and Marketing Science and the Outstanding Educator award and the Converse award from the AMA. He also served on the editorial boards of Marketing Science, JMR, JM, IJRM, and JCR and was the editor of Marketing Science for three years and the Consulting Editor for JM's special issue on CRM. Staelin has served on over 40 PhD committees and is Chairman of the Board of Directors for a small biotech firm (BioElectronics). He was elected an inaugural Fellow in ISMS and a Fellow in INFORMS.

Joffre Swait received his PhD in 1984 from the Transportation Systems Division, Department of Civil Engineering, Massachusetts Institute of Technology. He has extensive consulting experience in North and South America in Transportation, Telecommunications, Packaged Goods, Financial Services, Computer Hardware, and Tourism. He has been a faculty member of the Instituto Tecnológico de Aeronáutica (ITA) and the Universidade Federal do Rio de Janeiro (COPPE) in Brazil; the University of Florida (USA); the University of Alberta (Canada); and the University of

Technology, Sydney. He is Co-Director of the Center for the Study of Choice (CenSoC) and Research Professor at the Faculty of Business, University of Technology Sydney. He is also a partner of Advanis Inc., a Canadian market research firm.

Gerard J. Tellis (PhD Michigan) is a Professor of Marketing and Management, Neely Chair of American Enterprise, and Director of the Global Innovation Center, at the USC Marshall School of Business. Dr Tellis is an expert in innovation, new product growth, emerging markets, advertising, and global market entry. He has published 5 books and over 100 papers (http://www.gtellis.net) that have won over 20 awards. His new book, *Unrelenting Innovation*, explains how transforming culture can enable firms to stay relentlessly innovative. His book *Will and Vision* (co-authored with Peter Golder) was cited as one of the top 10 books by the *Harvard Business Review* and was the winner of the AMA Berry Award. His book *Effective Advertising* integrates over 50 years of research on advertising.

Dr Tellis is a Distinguished Professor of Marketing Research, Erasmus University, Rotterdam, a Research Professor at the Judge Business School, Cambridge University, and a Fellow of Sidney Sussex College, Cambridge University, UK. He is an Associate Editor of *Marketing Science* and *Journal of Marketing Research*. He is Vice-President of External Relations for the Informs Society of Marketing Science and was a Trustee of the Marketing Science Institute. Formerly he was Sales Development Manager at Johnson & Johnson.

Russell S. Winer is the William Joyce Professor and Chair of the Department of Marketing at the Stern School of Business, New York University. He received a BA in Economics from Union College and an MS and PhD in Industrial Administration from Carnegie Mellon University. He has authored over 70 papers and 3 books in marketing on a variety of topics including consumer choice, marketing research methodology, marketing planning, advertising, and pricing. Professor Winer is currently a Senior Editor for *Marketing Science* and has served two terms as the editor of the *Journal of Marketing Research*. He is a past Executive Director of the Marketing Science Institute in Cambridge, Massachusetts. Professor Winer is a founding Fellow of the INFORMS Society for Marketing Science and is the 2011 recipient of the American Marketing Association/Irwin/McGraw-Hill Distinguished Marketing Educator award.

Chapter 1

The History of Marketing Science: Beginnings

Scott A. Neslin and Russell S. Winer

1.1 Introduction

The field of marketing science has a rich history of modeling marketing phenomena using the disciplines of economics, statistics, operations research, and other related fields. Since it is roughly 50 years from its origins, we feel that it is timely to review the accomplishments of marketing scientists in a number of research areas.

This history has not gone previously unnoticed. A number of fascinating retrospective articles about the origins of the field of marketing science authored by some of its pioneers appeared in a special section of the Fall 2001 issue of *Marketing Science*. An article by Steckel and Brody (2001) highlighted the importance of understanding the history of any field. They noted three reasons: (1) understanding our history is just simply interesting as would be finding our genealogical roots, (2) history helps us to better understand how a field evolves and why it is where it is now, and (3) history also aids our predictions of where a field is headed.

An excellent example of the first reason is to wonder at the evolution of the kind of data that have become available to researchers. If you were modeling consumer choice behavior in the 1960s and 1970s, you were pretty much limited to a few diary panel datasets. This evolved to the now-famous IRI scanner panel coffee data in the 1980s and 1990s. In the 21st century, we have almost unlimited data from comScore on e-commerce choice behavior. Similarly, advertising effects research has moved from a few publicly available datasets on cigarettes and the Lydia Pinkham Company's "vegetable compound" to multi-channel advertising data including online and mobile advertising exposure.

In this introductory chapter to the book, we provide a brief summary of the history of the field. An excellent historical overview of the field by David Montgomery can be found in the Fall 2001 Special Section of *Marketing Science*. Here, we update and broaden Montgomery's review. In addition, the chapter also acts as a foreword to the book by providing our goals and dedications.

1.2   The origins of marketing science

The earliest contributions to what we today call marketing science came from outside the field, usually from faculty trained in operations research/management science and residing in engineering departments, not business schools. Some of the papers were published in marketing journals such as the *Journal of Marketing*. An example is "Application of Operations Research to Marketing and Related Management Problems" (Magee, 1954), but most were published in journals like *Operations Research* or *Management Science* (see, for example, Anshen, 1956; Brown, Hulswitt, and Kettelle, 1956; Vidale and Wolfe, 1957).

There is general agreement that a Ford Foundation report written in 1959 by UC Berkeley economist Robert Gordon and Stanford professor James Howell sharply critical of American business education provided the catalyst for bringing a more rigorous approach to research in marketing conducted by faculty in business schools. This report, *Higher Education for Business*, coincided with a Ford Foundation-supported entity called the Institute of Basic Mathematics for Application to Business that was jointly run by the Harvard Business School and MIT's then-named School of Industrial Management. Ford provided fellowships for interested business school faculty to take one-year sabbaticals to improve their skills in quantitative analysis and the social sciences. The goal of these programs was to "raise teachers' and students' receptivity for quantitative methods to such a point that these methods will be incorporated, wherever appropriate, into the teaching of production, marketing, accounting, finance, and other recognized areas of business" (Carroll, 1958).

Fortunately for the field of marketing, five of the attendees who took advantage of the Institute were Frank Bass (Purdue), Edgar Pessemier

(Purdue), Robert Buzzell (Harvard), Ronald Frank (Chicago), and Philip Kotler (Northwestern). These founding "fathers" were complemented by a number of other prominent early marketing scientists including John Little (MIT), Paul Green (Wharton), Alfred Kuehn (CMU), William Massy (CMU, Stanford), Al Silk (Northwestern, Chicago), Glen Urban (MIT), David Montgomery (MIT, Stanford), Don Morrison (Columbia), and John Farley (Chicago, CMU). While this group produced many seminal contributions to the field, important contributions were also made by marketing science textbooks that were influential in doctoral programs. These included *Mathematical Models and Methods in Marketing* by Bass *et al.* (1961), *Mathematical Models and Marketing Management* by Buzzell (1964), *Quantitative Techniques in Marketing Analysis* by Frank, Kuehn, and Massy (1962), *Marketing Models: Quantitative Applications* by Day and Parsons (1970), *Management Science in Marketing* by Montgomery and Urban (1969), *Stochastic Models of Buyer Behavior* by Massy, Montgomery, and Morrison (1970), and *Marketing Decision Making* by Kotler (1971). Fortunately, most of these highly influential scholars are still alive and providing valuable counsel to their younger colleagues.

Key topics of the day included the following:

- Bayesian decision theory
- Multivariate analyses, e.g., factor, cluster, etc.
- Markov brand switching and learning models
- Probability models of brand choice
- Simultaneous-equation regressions
- Latent structure modeling
- Linear programming in media selection
- Dynamic programming.

1.3 The Marketing Science Institute

Soon after the release of the Ford Foundation report in 1962, the Marketing Science Institute (MSI) was founded in Philadelphia by Thomas McCabe Sr., the former President of Scott Paper Company, with the assistance of Professors Wroe Alderson (Wharton), John Howard (Columbia), and Albert Wesley Frey (Pittsburgh). The original goals of MSI were stated by McCabe (Wind, 2011):

> Our progress in the science of marketing in my opinion has not kept pace with our evolution in the physical sciences ... we lack the knowledge necessary to meet the sales challenges that face us ... the time has never been more appropriate, the need never greater for the establishment of an independent institute to accelerate the rate at which scientific techniques are being applied to marketing activities.

Twenty-nine companies signed up for five-year charter memberships.

Although not stated explicitly, from the beginning, MSI's objective was to bridge the gap between academia and practice while maintaining rigor and relevance in research. Some titles of monographs produced in the 1960s demonstrate that MSI was successful in achieving its goals:

- *Promotional Decisions Using Mathematical Models* by Kuehn and Rohloff.
- *Experiments on the Value of Information in Simulated Marketing Environments* by Fitzroy, Green, and Robinson.
- *Advertising Measurement and Decision Making* by Robinson, Dalbey, Gross, and Wind.
- *Promotional Decision Making: Practice and Theory*, by Robinson and Luck.

It should be noted that the definition of "scientific techniques" included rigorous experimental work based on theories from psychology, and was not limited to mathematical models.

In 1968, MSI moved from Philadelphia to Cambridge and established a formal relationship with Harvard Business School. Its publication emphasis shifted from monographs to working papers and to the funding of projects in areas that needed new research perspectives. Examples of these projects included work on market segmentation (James Taylor), product life cycles (Victor Cook), new product development (Pessemier), market definition (George Day and Allan Shocker), and the well-known PIMS (Profit Impact of Marketing Strategy) project (Buzzell) Figure 1.1.

1959 – Ford Foundation report, *Higher Education for Business*

1961 – Marketing Science Institute founded

1964 – First issue of the *Journal of Marketing Research*

1966 – Purdue University: Applications of the Sciences on Marketing Management

1967 – TIMS College of Marketing formed

1968 – AMA Summer Educators Conference Workshop "Management Science in Marketing"

1969 – Departmental Editor in Marketing for Management Science

1978 – Stanford "Marketing Measurement and Analysis" conference

1982 – First issue of *Marketing Science*

2002 – INFORMS Society for Marketing Science (ISMS) founded

Fig. 1.1   Timeline of important events in the history of marketing science

A major shift in its approach to supporting academic research was initiated in the mid-1970s when MSI instituted a bi-annual research priorities program to focus its support for academic research toward marketing problems that trustees from its member companies indicated were of current importance. The first five priorities developed by the then Executive Director, Stephen Greyser, were Marketing Management (e.g., market structure), Marketing and Economics (e.g., study of advertising/promotion elasticities), Marketing Models and Methods (e.g., new methods for measuring effectiveness of TV commercials), Communications and Consumer Behavior (e.g., prediction of consumer purchase behavior), and Distribution (e.g., current developments in electronic point-of-sale terminals and retail inventory controls).

MSI has had an enormous impact on both the marketing science and consumer behavior communities (Low, 2011). As can be seen from the data in Figure 1.2, a published article receiving prior MSI support has about 75% more citations than the average non-MSI-supported article. Areas that MSI has been particularly successful in supporting have been services, channels, strategy, and pricing. In addition, a time-series analysis of the impact of the research priorities shows a significant lagged impact of the priorities on

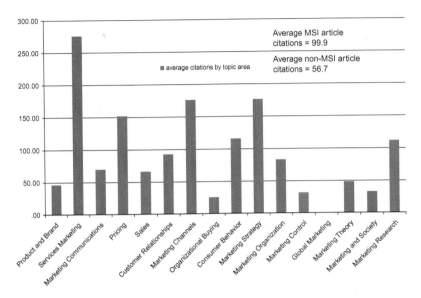

Fig. 1.2   Citation data from MSI-sponsored research

Source: George Low (2011).

MSI working papers and, importantly, publications based on those working papers.

1.4   The TIMS Marketing College[1]

The TIMS Marketing College was founded in 1967 as the professional organization for academicians and practitioners interested in the "application of scientific methods to marketing problems" (Montgomery, 1967). The founding of the "TIMS College" was the confluence of three forces: (1) growth in the number of marketing articles appearing in *Management Science*, which was published by The Institute for Management Science (TIMS); (2) growth in the intellectual capital of the field, represented not only by articles but also by significant

---

[1]This section on the TIMS College draws heavily on the series of articles referred to earlier in the Fall 2001 issue of *Marketing Science*. These include articles by Bass (2001), Little (2001), Montgomery (2001), Morrison (2001), and Wittink (2001). We also thank David Montgomery for information provided by personal communications.

books such as those mentioned earlier; (3) the budding link between academia and industry in the development of scientific methods for marketing.

The link between academia and industry was fundamental and pervasive. For example, Buzzell's book documents the application of linear programming to media selection, the measurement of advertising effects, and cases representing industry practice. As noted above, MSI had been founded to bridge industry and practice. Senior academicians entering the field had a distinct managerial orientation; *implementation* was of high priority. It was no wonder that the 1968 census of the TIMS College membership identified 71 members from industry among the total of 148 members.

While the ingredients for a professional organization of academicians *and* practitioners were present, it took human effort to mix the ingredients together. David Montgomery, then a junior faculty member at MIT, was a key contributor, encouraged by John Little. Paul Green, George Haines, James Heskett, John Little, William Massy, Al Silk, Martin Starr, Leonard Simon, as well as David Montgomery comprised the Planning Board for launching the TIMS College. Numerous others provided encouragement, time, and effort. The culture of "stepping up", which to this day characterizes the INFORMS Society for Marketing Science (ISMS) membership, was firmly rooted in this formative period.

The TIMS College undertook several initial activities, perhaps the most important of which was the organization of the marketing track of sessions at the TIMS meetings. The TIMS College also published a newsletter to keep its members informed.

As the years progressed, so did the field. During the period 1966–1972, the number of marketing articles in *Management Science* increased from 5 to 10 in the previous seven-year periods to 37. Included among these papers were the now classic "A New Product Growth Model of Consumer Durables" (Bass, 1969), and "Models and Managers: the Concept of a Decision Calculus" (Little, 1970). These and other articles published in this era clearly were scientific and simultaneously linked to practice. The culmination of this was the 1971 Special Issue of *Management Science* which included nine marketing papers, several of which focused on sales force management.

The stage was now set for the two seminal contributions of the TIMS Marketing College: the annual Marketing Science conference, and the founding of the *Journal Marketing Science.*

The first Marketing Science conference was held in the spring of 1979 at Stanford, with David Montgomery and Dick Wittink serving as chairs. The conference was titled, "Marketing Measurement and Analysis" (there was perhaps hesitation that some might perceive "Marketing Science" as an oxymoron).[2] The conference drew 120 attendees, with 11 of the 40 papers authored by practitioners, and several practitioner panels. The conference was a huge success in the quality of the work presented and in the "buzz" it created. Hosts quickly lined up for follow-ups, and included UT Austin, NYU, Wharton, USC, and Chicago. The conference was formally titled "The Marketing Science Conference" in 1983 when it was hosted at USC. Attendance soon increased to the 300s–400s.

As the field grew, it became apparent to the TIMS college leaders that the supply of good work was exceeding capacity of *Management Science* as well as *Operations Research* and *JMR*, which also published marketing science papers. Frank Bass and John Little asked Donald G. Morrison to chair a committee for investigating the feasibility of a new journal. Working during 1979, the committee concluded that a new journal was warranted, to be entitled *Marketing Science.* Donald Morrison was appointed Editor, with Seenu Srinivasan, Subrata Sen, and Jerry Wind as area editors. In Morrison's words, "we wish to publish high-quality quantitatively oriented papers in the areas of marketing models, measurement, theory, and applications."[3] Submissions started arriving in late 1980, and the first issue was published in 1982. The lead article was "NEWS: A Decision Oriented Model for Product Analysis and Forecasting," by Lew Pringle, Dale Wilson, and Ed Brody. The next two articles were "A Marketing Decision Support System for Retailers," by Len Lodish, and "Maximum Likelihood Estimation for an Innovation Diffusion Model of New Product Acceptance," by Dave Schmittlein and Vijay Mahajan. The marriage of science and practice was clearly evident in these articles.

---

[2]See Wittink's article in the Fall 2001 issue of *Marketing Science.*

[3]"Launching Marketing Science," Donald G. Morrison, Preface to the inaugural issue of *Marketing Science*, 1982.

An important institutional development along the way was the merger of TIMS and ORSA (Operations Research Society of America). While the TIMS College was obviously a part of TIMS, ORSA also sponsored a quantitative journal — *Operations Research* — that had a long history of publishing marketing articles and overlapped with TIMS in other subject areas as well. During 1970–1990, the two organizations began to sponsor joint meetings (the ORSA/TIMS conference) as well as joint journals (*Marketing Science* was in fact co-published by TIMS and ORSA). Eventually, two governing bodies became burdensome and redundant. ORSA and TIMS merged in 1995; the new organization was called "The Institute for Operations Research and Management Science": INFORMS. The TIMS Marketing College was now the INFORMS College on Marketing.

1.5 The INFORMS society for marketing science

January 25, 2002, marked a seminal event in the creation of ISMS as we know it today. Joel Steckel, then President of the TIMS College, convened a meeting of the College's officers and others, including Ed Brody, Naveen Donthu, Scott Fay, Jim Hess, Barbara Kahn, Gary Lilien, John Little, Peter Popkowski Leszczyc, Jagmohan Raju, Steve Shugan, and Bart Weitz. Among the topics discussed was the need to elevate from an INFORMS college to an INFORMS society.[4] INFORMS societies are the flagships of the INFORMS communities: "The societies are significantly larger than the sections, chapters, or fora, and focus on a common theme."[5]

The group saw four advantages from moving to society status: (1) a seat on the INFORMS council, so that the interests of marketing science could be more directly represented, (2) prestige, which would translate to higher membership and more weight to the respect for awards, *Marketing Science*, and other activities, (3) a stimulus for expanding the college's infrastructure so as to link more directly to members' needs and the organization's activities, and (4) by expanding the infrastructure, providing more opportunities for more people to get involved with governance. The infrastructure was important. At the time, the College governance consisted

---

[4]We thank Joel Steckel for providing the minutes from this meeting.
[5]https://www.informs.org/Participate-In-a-Community/Societies-and-Sections.

of six officials: President, President-Elect, Secretary/Treasurer, Conference Coordinator, Past President, and Newsletter Editor. The new ISMS board would consist of 11 officials: President, President-Elect, Past-President, Secretary, Treasurer, Newsletter Editor, and Vice Presidents of Electronic Communication, Meetings, Practice, Education, and Membership. Another VP position — External Relations — would be added later. In addition, the President would appoint up to three Advisory Board members, non-voting but important voices to be heard at board meetings.

INFORMS approved the College's application for society status in 2002, and John Hauser announced the formation of the ISMS at the 2002 Marketing Science conference hosted by the University of Alberta. Joel Steckel was the first President of ISMS, to be followed by Jagmohan Raju, Tülin Erdem, Rick Staelin, Scott Neslin, Kannan Srinivasan, and now John Hauser. The mission of ISMS is stated in its by-laws, to "foster the development, dissemination, and implementation of knowledge, basic and applied research, and science and technologies that improve the understanding and practice of marketing."[6] One sees the mix of science and application that are the roots of the organization.

ISMS built upon its predecessor and expanded its activities. The major ones include the following:

- *Marketing Science Conference*: ISMS continues to sponsor the conference, which topped 900 in attendance at the 2012 conference hosted by Boston University. The 2013 conference in Istanbul topped 600.
- *Doctoral Consortium*: ISMS continues to sponsor this gathering of 90–100 PhD students, held the day before the beginning of the Marketing Science Conference.
- *Doctoral Dissertation Proposal Competition*: ISMS recognizes up to five dissertation proposals annually as the best dissertation proposals on important marketing issues. Each award carries with it $5,000 in support. One of the awards is funded by the Vithala R. and Saroj V. Rao Endowment. Another has recently been supported by the Sheth Foundation.

---

[6]https://www.informs.org/Community/ISMS/Archived-Documents/By-Laws.

- *Practice Prize Competition*: ISMS sponsors a competition to recognize "outstanding implementation of marketing science concepts and methods."[7]
- *Journal Support*: Originally, the TIMS College, and subsequently ISMS, provided financial support for the journal *Marketing Science*. Once *Marketing Science* became self-sustaining, this support was no longer needed. However, ISMS occasionally supports special efforts such as the *Management Science* special issue, "Marketing within the Enterprise and Beyond" (2011), and provided funding for *Journal of Marketing Research* to temporarily expand its capacity to expedite the publication of accepted papers.[8]

The above activities clearly map the development, dissemination, and implementation of marketing science. In addition, ISMS reinforces the work that best exemplifies this mission through the following awards:

- *John D.C. Little Award* for the best marketing paper published in *Marketing Science* or *Management Science*.
- *Frank M. Bass Dissertation Award* for the best marketing paper derived from a PhD thesis.
- *Gary L. Lilien ISMS-MSI Practice Prize* for the winner of the Practice Prize competition.
- *Fellow Award* recognizes cumulative individuals' long-term contributions to the mission of ISMS.
- *Long Term Impact Award* to a marketing paper published in *Marketing Science, Management Science*, or another INFORMS journal, which is viewed to have made a significant long-run impact on the field of Marketing.
- *Dissertation Proposal Award* to the winners of the Dissertation Proposal Competition.
- *Buck Weaver Award* for lifetime contribution to theory and practice in the development of rigor and relevance in marketing science.

---

[7]Lilien, G. L. (2004). The inaugural ISMS practice prize competition, *Management Science*, 23(2), Spring, 180–191.

[8]Erdem, T. State of the journal, *Journal of Marketing Research*, 47(6), 997.

1.6 Looking ahead

ISMS now serves as the organizational face of the growing field of marketing science. The evidence is that this growth has indeed been abetted by the efforts of ISMS and its predecessor, the TIMS College. Several challenges remain. Two big ones are encouraging international growth and fostering interdisciplinary research. The Marketing Science Conference is currently held in a non-North American site every third year. This certainly draws new people to the field. However, there may be more ISMS can do such as tutorials, doctoral student mentoring, and encouraging work on emerging markets. Marketing science readily draws on economics, psychology, statistics, stochastic processes, and optimization. These comprise marketing science's discipline base. As marketing becomes more intertwined with other business functions — operations, finance, R&D, etc. — marketing science needs to collaborate with these areas as well.

Another challenge is to re-engage our roots in science *and* practice. Some believe that marketing science research, at least the published academic research, has lost the intimate relationship with practice that defined the field in the 1960s. In contrast to the early days of the TIMS College, ISMS clearly is now dominated by academicians. The question is complex. Today's data and modeling capabilities lend themselves to more academic-leaning work. However, these same data and capabilities are being applied by businesses such as Google and any number of consulting firms. The potential for collaboration would apparently be greater than ever. However, due to intellectual capital concerns, businesses may be reluctant to join with academicians in an official capacity. Academicians may be quite content with focusing more on the science and implement the science through consulting and teaching. However, *implementation* is part of the ISMS mission and ultimately ISMS must ask itself whether it is fulfilling that mission.

1.7 This book

We have three goals for this book:

(1) Provide a road map for the development of 16 areas of marketing science, which not only is useful from a historical perspective but also

identifies the important gaps in the literature, which can provide an impetus for future research.

(2) Provide a resource for the main consumers of the academic marketing research literature: doctoral students, faculty, and marketing science practitioners in consulting firms and companies.

(3) Emphasize both the role and the importance that pioneers in marketing science have had in the rapid development of the field over the past approximately 50 years. This book honors those contributions.

In order to achieve these goals, the chapters share several characteristics. First, they are not intended to be reviews of the literature in the specific area. Instead, authors were instructed to select the most important research that advanced the area at different points in time. As a result, the literature references are selective and not comprehensive. Second, each chapter has a graphic with a timeline for the key developments in the area covered by the chapter or, in some cases, by sub-area. This "genealogical" chart is a key part of each chapter and an important takeaway and summary. Third, each chapter is intended to be brief and largely qualitative with relatively few equations. While this is in stark contrast to articles in *Marketing Science*, the *Journal of Marketing Research*, and other journals publishing marketing science papers, our objective was to make it highly readable and easy to digest and thus reach as many people as possible, including those readers with backgrounds outside of economics, statistics, operations research, etc. We hope we have created a book that has achieved these goals and gives marketing scientists and other interested readers a good sense of the development of the field and its main contributors.

We would like to acknowledge a number of people. First, we are greatly appreciative of now publishers and, in particular, Zac Rolnik whose enthusiasm for the project created a tremendous amount of momentum for it. Second, we thank the authors of the chapters for responding amicably to our cajoling and comments on the chapters. They responded quickly to our comments and worked hard to improve their chapters. We particularly appreciate a number of people who pitched in either as authors or co-authors at late dates to rescue some of the chapters.

Finally, this book honors those early colleagues who took a field that had been subject to disdain in the 1950s to one that has sponsored a highly successful journal, holds an annual conference that attracts nearly

1,000 participants from around the world, and has gained the respect of many colleagues in the disciplines upon which marketing science is built. Most of them are mentioned either in this chapter or in another chapter. This book is dedicated to them.

References

Anshen, M. (1956). Management science in marketing: Status and prospects, *Management Science*, 2(April), 222–231.

Bass, F. M. (1969). A new product growth model for consumer durables, *Management Science*, 15, 215–227.

Bass, F. M. (2001). Some of history of the TIMS/INFORMS college on marketing as related to the development of marketing science, *Marketing Science*, 20(Fall), 360–363.

Bass, F. M., R. D. Buzzell, M. R. Greene, W. Lazer, E. A. Pessemier, D. R. Shawver, A. Schuchman, C. A. Theodore, and G. W. Wilson, eds. (1961). *Mathematical models and methods in marketing*, Homewood, Illinois: Richard D. Irwin.

Brown, A. A., F. T. Hulswit, and J. D. Kettelle (1956). A study of sales operations, *Operations Research*, 4(June), 296–308.

Buzzell, R. D. (1964). *Mathematical models and marketing management*, Boston, Massachusetts: Harvard University Press.

Carroll, T. (1958). Ford Foundation activities in the field of business education, Ford Foundation Archives, No. 002970, December 27.

Day, R. L. and L. J. Parsons (1970). *Marketing models: Quantitative applications*, Scranton, Pennsylvania: Intext Educational Publishers.

Frank, R. E., A. A. Kuehn, and W. F. Massy (1962). *Quantitative techniques in marketing analysis*, Homewood, Illinois: Richard D. Irwin.

Gordon, R. A. and J. E. Howell (1959). *Higher education for business*, New York: Columbia University Press.

Kotler, P. (1971). *Marketing decision making: A model building approach*, New York: Holt, Rinehart and Winston.

Little, J. D. C. (1970). Models and managers: The concept of a decision calculus, *Management Science*, 16(April), B466–B485.

Little, J. D. C. (2001). The history of the marketing college is a work in progress, *Marketing Science*, 29(Fall), 364–372.

Low, G. (2011). MSI – 50 years of knowledge generation. Presentation available at http://www.msi.org/publications/publication.cfm?pub=1843.

Magee, J. F. (1954). Application of operations research to marketing and related management problems, *Journal of Marketing*, 18(April), 361–369.

Massy, W. F., D. B. Montgomery, and D. G. Morrison (1970). *Stochastic models of buying behavior*, Cambridge, Massachusetts: MIT Press.

Montgomery, D. B. (1967). College on marketing proposed, *Management Science: Series C-Bulletin*, 13(6), C130–C132.

Montgomery, D. B. (2001). Management science in marketing: Prehistory, origin, and early years of the INFORMS marketing college, *Marketing Science*, 4(Fall), 337–348.

Montgomery, D. B. and G. L. Urban (1969). *Management science in marketing*, Englewood Cliffs, New Jersey: Prentice-Hall.

Morrison, D. G. (2001). Founding marketing science, *Marketing Science*, 4(Fall), 357–359.

Steckel, J. H. and E. Brody (2001). 2001: A marketing odyssey, *Marketing Science*, 4(Fall), 331–336.

Vidale, M. L. and H. B. Wolfe (1957). An operations-research study of sales response to advertising, *Operations Research*, 5(June), 370–381.

Wind, Y. (2011). MSI – The Philadelphia story, presentation made at a celebration honoring the 50th anniversary of the founding of the Marketing Science Institute.

Wittink, D. R. (2001). Marketing measurement and analysis: The first 'marketing science' conference, *Marketing Science*, 20(Fall), 349–356.

Part I

Methods

Chapter 2

Brand Choice Models

Gary J. Russell

2.1 Introduction

The theory of brand choice is one of the fundamental elements of marketing science. Virtually all decisions made by marketing managers involve assumptions — explicit or implicit — about how consumers make purchase decisions and how strategic marketing variables (such as price, advertising, and distribution) impact these decisions. To support this effort, the goal of research in brand choice is to create models that both reflect the behavioral realities of consumer choice and allow accurate forecasts of future choice behavior.

The history of research in brand choice is a complex blend of research drawn from psychology, economics, and statistics. Because brand choice covers a large number of distinct topics, it is best to think of the area in terms of a slow evolution from fundamental research in psychology in the 1950s to applied micro-economic theory in the 2000s. In Figure 2.1, we have organized this evolution under six general research themes: Theoretical Foundations, Single Choice, Consumer Heterogeneity, Multiple Decisions, Economic Theory, and Choice Dependence. These headings are listed in rough chronological order, with arrows denoting paths of influence. For the most part, the arrows are intended to show the relationships between subtopics, not between individual articles. However, it should be understood that chronology is important: earlier work almost always informs later work. For example, research on logit models (in the 1980s) and on consumer response parameter heterogeneity (in the 1990s) made possible later work on spatial choice (in the 2000s).

G. J. Russell

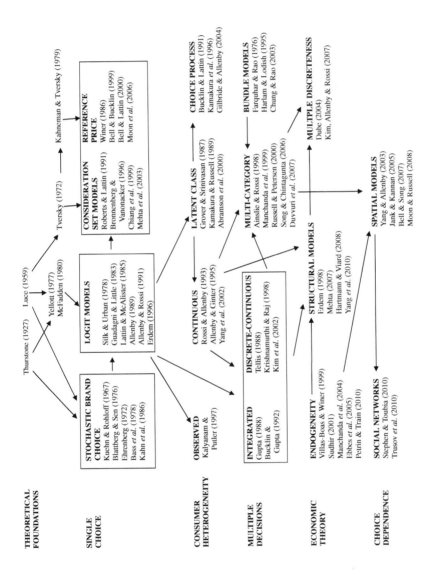

Fig. 2.1   History of choice modeling in marketing

This chapter is not a detailed review of work in brand choice over the last 50 years. Readers interested in detailed discussions of early work in brand choice should consult Massy, Montgomery, and Morrison (1970) (stochastic brand choice) and Corstjens and Gautschi (1983) (economics and psychology). Readers interested in a comprehensive examination of the impact of economic theory on the evolution of choice modeling should consult Chandukala *et al.* (2007).

This chapter is organized as follows. Using Figure 2.1 as a guide, we first review (in chronological order) the six general research themes in brand choice. Within each theme, we discuss various subfields, noting interrelationships. As will be seen, this discussion illustrates the fact that improvements in data availability and statistical tools have repeatedly stimulated new work in choice theory and new application areas. We conclude with a brief discussion of possible future developments in brand choice.

2.2 Theoretical foundations

Brand choice models rest upon key assumptions about how consumers make purchase decisions. In contrast to research in marketing by psychologists, theories in choice modeling are not intended to be process models detailing how the organization of the human brain leads to choice outcomes. Rather, theories in choice modeling are *artificial* in the sense of Simon (1969): they are paramorphic ("as if") representations of choice behavior designed to improve our understanding of the impact of environmental influences (such as the marketing mix) on choice decisions. In this section, we review pioneering work in psychology that set the stage for future developments.

2.2.1 *Definition of a choice model*

We define a choice model in the following manner. A consumer is presented with the task of selecting one of N alternatives, denoted $A(1), \ldots, A(N)$. For each alternative, there exists a mapping from the characteristics of each alternative to a real-valued number $V(A(i)) = V(i)$. The consumer constructs $U(V(i)) = U(i)$, called preference (psychology) or utility (economics), which allows an ordering of the alternatives on a one-dimensional continuum. Using the $U(i)$ values, the consumer selects one alternative by employing some type of decision rule. The decision rule assigns a probability of choosing alternative i as $\Pr(i) = F(U(1), \ldots, U(N))$ where $0 < \Pr(i) < 1$ and $F(\cdot)$ is some multivariate function with N arguments. That is, the choice process is assumed to be *inherently stochastic*: there is no alternative with $\Pr(i) = 0$ or $\Pr(i) = 1$.

Although this definition may seem needlessly formal, it provides the researcher important guidelines for developing a choice model. Clearly, three elements are needed: a set of choice alternatives, a set of corresponding $U(i)$ preference scale values, and a decision rule. The history of brand choice can be viewed as an evolving understanding of how these components ought to be specified in marketing applications.

2.2.2 *Thurstone model*

The starting point for brand choice is the work of Louis Thurstone, a psychologist interested in psychophysics (the human perception of physical stimuli such as the intensity of light). His experiments required subjects to determine which of two stimuli was more intense (e.g., which light was brighter). His key insight, reported in his Theory of Comparative Judgment (Thurstone, 1927), reprinted in Thurstone (1959), is that humans do not perceive a stimulus in the same fashion on different occasions, even though the stimulus object has not changed. Using our earlier notation, Thurstone postulated a *discriminal process* of the form

$$U(i) = V(i) + e(i), \qquad (2.1)$$

where $V(i)$ is the true intensity of $A(i)$, and $e(i)$ is a normally distributed random variable with mean zero. That is, $U(i)$ is the sensation of intensity that is perceived by the individual and is used to decide which stimulus has higher intensity. Thurstone argued that the choice rule is simple: the subject selects the stimulus with the higher $U(i)$ value. Because the $e(i)$ error varies across stimuli and over time, Thurstone's model implies that judgments of intensity made by one individual will be inconsistent, particularly when the true $V(i)$ values are similar. As such, a researcher can only predict the probability that a certain alternative will be judged to be most intense.

In a brand choice setting, $V(i)$ is interpreted as the long-run average preference value of the alternative and $e(i)$ is a situation-specific random effect that masks the relationship between the true $V(i)$ value and perceived $U(i)$. Following Thurstone (1927), researchers in marketing assume that the consumer always chooses the alternative with the highest perceived $U(i)$. This combination of a randomly generated $U(i)$ value coupled with a (deterministic) maximum $U(i)$ choice rule is today known as a *random utility theory* (RUT) model. Choice probabilities for a RUT model are obtained by writing down the N-dimensional multivariate distribution defined by Eq. (2.1) and then computing the probability $\Pr(i) = \Pr\{U(i) = \max[U(1), \ldots, U(N)]\}$. (See Train (2003) for details.) When the $e(i)$ are normally distributed (as assumed by Thurstone (1927)), the resulting choice process is known as a *probit choice model*.

2.2.3 *Luce model*

Luce (1959) proposed an alternative theory of choice based upon certain assumptions about choice probabilities. Let $\Pr(i \mid S)$ denote the probability of selecting item i from S, a set of alternatives including both item i and another item j. Let S^* be another set of items, also including both i and j. Luce's choice axiom takes the form

$$\Pr(i|S)/\Pr(j|S) = \Pr(i|S^*)/\Pr(j|S^*). \qquad (2.2)$$

In words, the choice axiom states that the ratio of choice probabilities is a fixed quantity that does not depend upon the choice set. Choice models with this property are said to exhibit *independence from irrelevant alternatives*.

Luce (1959) shows that Eq. (2.2) is sufficient to derive an explicit expression for the choice probabilities. If the choice axiom holds, then there exists a ratio-scaled preference value $Q(i)$ for each item. Moreover, relative to a set of alternatives $S = \{A(1), \ldots, A(N)\}$,

$$\Pr(i|S) = Q(i)/\{Q(1) + \cdots + Q(N)\}. \qquad (2.3)$$

Luce (1959) argues that $Q(i)$ represent psychologically real preference values that are fixed over time. Accordingly, the stochasticity of choice (and the need for choice probabilities) is due to errors made in the decision process. The probability function in Eq. (2.3) is called *a logit choice model* in academic marketing.

Logit models dominated the choice theory literature in marketing science during the 1980s. One key reason is that the model is computationally tractable, even for large choice sets. However, an equally important reason is that logit models are also RUT models. Yellott (1977) showed that logit choice probabilities are consistent with a RUT model in which the $e(i)$ are independent draws from an extreme value distribution. Relative to Eq. (2.1), the Luce preference values depend upon RUT utilities according to the expression $Q(i) = \exp(V(i))$, where $\exp(\cdot)$ denotes the exponential function. Moreover, McFadden (1980) showed that the logit model can also be derived using a micro-economic argument based upon RUT. (In the economic interpretation of the logit model, the $e(i)$ errors represent variables that impact choice, but are not observed by the researcher.) The popularity of the logit model is due in large part to these connections to theories in both psychology and economics.

2.2.4 Tversky models

Amos Tversky made major contributions to choice theory that stimulated considerable subsequent work in marketing science. Tversky (1972) proposed the Elimination by Aspects (EBA) model, a choice process based upon a lexicographic choice rule. In contrast to Thurstone and Luce, Tversky assumes that each choice alternative can be subdivided into aspects (characteristics) that are used sequentially to prune the choice set until only one alternative remains. EBA can be viewed as a generalized Luce choice model and is consistent with RUT. The model stimulated later work in marketing on multi-attribute utility models (such as conjoint measurement (see, e.g., Louviere, Hensher, and Swait, 2000)) and consideration set formation.

Drawing upon findings from laboratory choice experiments, Kahnemann and Tversky (1979) argued that linear utility models (often used in marketing) ignore important elements of the choice decision. Their utility model, known as Prospect Theory, assumes that individuals construct a reference point and then evaluate alternatives in terms of losses and gains relative to the reference point. Individuals are assumed to be risk-averse in such a way that losses impact utility more strongly than gains. As will be seen, this work has stimulated research in which a Prospect Theory utility expression is embedded in a logit or probit model formulation.

2.3 Single choice

Building upon these foundations, early work in brand choice was focused on applying the various theories to real world choice behavior. These models assume that the consumer constructs a choice set, examines all alternatives, and then selects one item. To distinguish this type of model from the multiple decision models of the 1990s, we refer to these early models as *single choice* models. In this section, we trace the development of single choice models, taking up each subtopic in Figure 2.1 roughly in chronological order.

2.3.1 *Stochastic brand choice*

The earliest choice models in marketing were constructed on datasets with limited information on marketing mix variables. Stochastic brand choice models acknowledge the inherent stochasticity of choice (by forecasting choice probabilities), but make weak assumptions about the underlying choice process. Although there exist a wide variety of models (see Massy, Montgomery, and Morrison (1970) for a review), two model specifications are most prominent: NBD and Markov.

The NBD model (Ehrenberg, 1972) assumes that the number of packages of a particular brand purchased by one household over some time period follows a Poisson distribution with an idiosyncratic mean equal to $\lambda(h)$. Further, the $\lambda(h)$ parameters vary across the household population as a Gamma distribution. By analytically "mixing" the household-level Poisson distributions using the Gamma household population distribution, Ehrenberg obtained a market-level forecasting model: the negative binomial distribution or NBD.

Strictly speaking, the NBD model is a count model, not a single choice model. Nevertheless, the NBD model has two important links to previous and subsequent work in brand choice. First, Bass, Jeuland, and Wright (1978) showed analytically that a heterogeneous population of consumers, each making choices according to the Luce choice axiom, will have a long-run purchase count histogram that approximates an NBD distribution. Second, the NBD model can be viewed as an early attempt to model consumer-level heterogeneity with respect to model parameters. This modeling approach, today known as *unobserved heterogeneity*, was elaborated in considerable detail by other researchers in the 1990s.

Early work in stochastic brand choice was also dominated by Markov models. A zero-order Markov model can be regarded as a logit model. A first-order Markov model assumes that choice probabilities on each purchase occasion are defined by a logit model whose parameters depend upon the brand purchased on the previous choice occasion. Higher order Markov models, such as the linear learning model (Kuehn and Rohloff, 1967), allow for dependence upon a longer string of purchase decisions.

Early studies employed Markov models to study differences in decision rules across the consumer population. Blattberg and Sen (1976) used different parameterizations of first-order Markov models (different types of loyalty and switching patterns) to argue that consumers within the same product category exhibit a wide variety of decision rules. Kahn, Kalwani, and Morrison (1986) used different parameterizations of zero-order, first-order, and second-order Markov models to analyze consumer tendency to either repeat buy (inertia) or switch away from (variety seeking) the previous brand purchased. They found that inertia and variety seeking varies both across brands and across product categories, suggesting that consumers use different choice rules in different product categories. This work anticipated the later literature on *choice process heterogeneity*.

2.3.2 *Logit models*

Most brand choice research in the 1980s was dominated by applications of the logit model. As noted earlier, the model has theoretical justifications in psychology and economics. Moreover, relative to the probit model, the logit model was much easier to calibrate using the standard optimization software of this time period.

The ASSESSOR new product model of Silk and Urban (1978) was a transitional study, incorporating both a Markov model (to measure repeat buying) and a logit model (to measure shifts in buying behavior due to the introduction of the new product). The logit model is calibrated in two stages. First, the authors create a ratio-scaled brand preference scale using self-reported brand ratings and the Luce choice axiom. Second, using reported purchase behavior, the authors calibrate a logit model that includes the brand preference values as independent variables. The authors argue that the logit model is necessary because unknown factors cause observed choice probabilities to deviate from the probabilities predicted by the Luce model.

Probably, the most influential study in this stream of research is Guadagni and Little (1983). This was the first research that showed how to specify a logit model using scanner data purchase histories. One of their most important contributions was the creation of a so-called *loyalty variable* based upon past purchase behavior. From a theoretical perspective, the loyalty variable shifts purchase probabilities toward a small set of brands that the consumer buys on a regular basis. In effect, the loyalty variable allows for differences in the choice set across consumers. Guadagni and Little (1983) reported that about half of the explained variation in choice behavior is due to the loyalty variable.

All subsequent work in this area builds upon the Guadagni and Little (1983) framework in some manner. We note a few representative studies. Lattin and McAlister (1985) built a specialized logit model to measure consumer variety seeking by allowing current purchase probability to depend upon past choices. Allenby (1989) analyzes brand price competition using the nested logit model, a generalization of the logit model that allows brands to be clustered into homogeneous submarkets. Within each submarket, a simple logit model governs choice, but globally (across submarkets) choice probabilities do not obey the independence from irrelevant alternatives property found in Luce models (see, e.g., Ben-Akiva and Lerman, 1985). Allenby and Rossi (1991) use the logit model as a platform to build a non-homothetic utility model linking brand quality to price-induced brand switching patterns. Erdem (1996) builds a logit model to analyze the dynamics of market structure. This study, which allows for variability in response parameters across consumers, is an early example of the choice modeling literature on *continuous heterogeneity*.

2.3.3 *Consideration set models*

Tversky's (1972) work on the EBA model suggested that consumers may prune a large set of brands to a smaller set, which is then given close scrutiny.

Consideration set models assume that a standard choice model (such as the logit) applies within a consumer's idiosyncratic consideration set. The key question, then, is how consideration set membership is determined.

The pioneering study by Roberts and Lattin (1991) argued that the same utilities that determine choice also determine product consideration. In this model, the consumer first creates a consideration set by adding products until the change in the expected maximum utility of the set is not justified by the increased cognitive costs of choice set evaluation. A logit choice model determines the final choice, conditional upon the consideration set. In an application to Australian breakfast cereals, the authors show that brand positioning impacts both the likelihood of consideration and the probability of choice.

Subsequent work has emphasized the role of the marketing mix in brand consideration. Bronnenberg and Vanhonacker (1996) allow price level and other variables to determine whether the brand is considered. Mehta, Rajiv, and Srinivasan (2003) build a structural (economic) model assuming that consumers learn about brand quality and use quality perceptions to assemble a consideration set. Chiang, Chib, and Narasimhan (1999) use Bayesian methods to infer the probability that a given consumer will have any particular consideration set. All these studies conclude that measures of consumer reaction to price and promotion are seriously biased if consideration sets are ignored.

2.3.4 *Reference price models*

Prospect Theory (Kahneman and Tversky, 1979) stimulated research on consumer reactions to price. Winer (1986), in a pioneering analysis, argued that consumers react to the difference between observed price and a reference price ("sticker shock") in making choice decisions. He proposed two models of reference price formation, both drawn from economic theory. Bell and Bucklin (1999) develop a reference price model that allows reference price to impact both category incidence and brand choice. They find evidence for asymmetric reactions to losses and gains, consistent with Prospect Theory. Bell and Lattin (2000), in an important methodological paper, show that consumer response parameter heterogeneity may be mistaken for reference price effects under some circumstances. Moon, Russell, and Duvvuri (2006) use a latent class analysis (see Sec. 2.4.2) that permits consumers to have different mechanisms for generating reference price points. They find evidence for both internal (memory-based) and external (shopping-environment-based) reference price processes. The reference price literature is an excellent example of logit choice models being used to empirically test psychological theory in a real-world purchase setting. Readers interested in a detailed discussion of reference price models should consult Winer (2014).

2.4 Consumer heterogeneity

As the logit choice literature evolved in the 1980s, researchers became concerned that models did not adequately represent market segmentation. For purposes of our discussion, a market segment is a group of consumers, each of whom has the same choice model with the same response parameters. Models of consumer heterogeneity provide the researcher with several benefits: understanding segmentation structure, correcting for parameter bias induced by aggregation, and uncovering differences in decision rules across consumers.

2.4.1 *Observed heterogeneity*

Observed heterogeneity refers to models that allow response parameters to depend on observed variables such as consumer demographics and past purchase history. The Guadagni and Little (1983) loyalty variable is an early example of this approach. Although all consumers have the same set of parameters, the coding of the loyalty variable implies that brand intercepts (baseline brand preferences) vary by consumer (and over time, within a consumer). Another interesting example is Kalyanam and Putler (1997), which uses economic theory to argue that price sensitivity should depend on consumer income and that baseline preferences for different package sizes should depend on demographics related to the rate of product consumption.

2.4.2 *Unobserved heterogeneity: Latent class*

In practice, it is very difficult for researchers to assemble a rich-enough set of demographics to permit the observed heterogeneity approach to be used. In contrast, unobserved heterogeneity models require the statistical algorithm to uncover the pattern of parameter heterogeneity by analyzing only the consumer purchase histories. In a latent class model, the researcher assumes that there are a finite number of segments. The resulting statistical algorithm amounts to a likelihood-based cluster analysis.

The pioneering application of latent class analysis in choice modeling is Grover and Srinivasan (1987). Their analysis of brand switching patterns essentially assumed that each consumer follows a simple Luce Model, but that different segments have different brand preferences. Kamakura and Russell (1989) built upon this approach by developing a latent class mixture of logit models. This model allows a segmented analysis of scanner panel choice histories, essentially generalizing the Guadagni-Little (1983) logit model. Because the latent class logit model implies differential price response across consumer segments, Kamakura and Russell (1989) were able to empirically investigate patterns of competition between national and private label brands. Numerous extensions of latent class models have appeared in the marketing science literature. See Wedel and Kamakura (2000) for a detailed review and discussion.

An important early use of latent class modeling was the correction of *spurious state dependence* in choice models. Similar to a first-order Markov process, state dependence refers to carryover effects in which the purchase of a particular brand in one time period impacts the choice probabilities in a subsequent period. Abramson *et al.* (2000) demonstrated that carryover effects will be overstated unless consumer preference heterogeneity is adequately modeled by the researcher. This work has important practical implications for measuring the dynamic impact of promotions (Neslin and van Heerde, 2008).

2.4.3 *Unobserved heterogeneity*: *Choice process models*

A special application of latent class analysis is choice process heterogeneity, the study of differences in choice rules across consumers. Choice process heterogeneity amounts to rewriting the standard latent class model to allow for variation in both type of choice rule and vector of response parameters. Again, the total number of consumer groups (a crossing of choice rule and parameter vector) must be finite. As noted earlier, work by Blattberg and

Sen (1976) and Kahn, Kalwani, and Morrison (1986) anticipated this stream of research.

An early example of choice process heterogeneity is Bucklin and Lattin (1991). Using a latent class analysis based upon the nested logit model, they provide evidence that consumers who prepare a shopping list (called planners) are not sensitive to marketing mix elements in the retail environment. Kamakura, Kim, and Lee (1996) used different types of nested logit models to argue that some consumers first consider brand name (Yoplait) and then flavor (blueberry); others consider flavor first, then brand name. Gilbride and Allenby (2004), in a Bayesian generalization of latent class analysis, develop a method of assigning different types of choice rules (conjunctive, disjunctive and compensatory) to consumers.

2.4.4 *Unobserved heterogeneity: Continuous*

Another type of response parameter heterogeneity assumes that the variation of parameters across the consumer population follows some multivariate distribution (such as multivariate normal). This so-called *random parameter* approach can be interpreted as allowing idiosyncratic parameters for each consumer, and so is a limiting case of a latent class model as more and more segments are added. Because the likelihood function for a choice model with random coefficients involves multiple integrals, these types of models were considered impractical until the 1990s. Models of this sort became practical because techniques were developed to simulate integrals: maximum simulated likelihood for classical statistical inference (Train, 2003) and Markov Chain Monte Carlo for hierarchical Bayes inference (Allenby and Rossi, 1999).

The number of applications of continuous heterogeneity in choice modeling is too large to attempt a survey here. Rossi and Allenby (1993) develop an interesting application of empirical Bayes techniques, which avoids the computation of integrals. Erdem (1996) is a good example of the maximum simulated likelihood approach. Allenby and Ginter (1995) employ Gibbs sampler technology (a Markov Chain Monte Carlo technique) to estimate individual level parameters in a conjoint measurement study. Yang, Allenby, and Fennell (2002), in a study using psychological theory to motivate data collection and model specification, estimate a hierarchical Bayes model that allows consumer response heterogeneity to vary across consumers and choice occasions, depending upon the choice environment and the consumer motivations.

2.5 Multiple decisions

The work on logit models and consumer heterogeneity provided the basic tools needed to undertake more ambitious models. We define a multiple decision response model as choice model that predicts several outcome variables simultaneously. All research studies discussed below are attempts to generalize earlier work on choice models to address more complex and more realistic problems.

2.5.1 *Discrete-continuous models*

Discrete-continuous models are designed to answer two questions: which brand will be chosen, and how much will be purchased. Most models in this area are adaptations of the *selection bias* literature in econometrics (Train, 1993). The essential idea is the following. For a set of N brands, we have $2N$ utility equations, arranged in two blocks. The utilities in the first block form a RUT model and thereby determine the probability of brand purchase. The second block of utilities determine purchase quantity (a ratio-scaled continuous measure). These quantity utilities are positively correlated with the corresponding brand's RUT model utility. However, the researcher sees only the outcome of the quantity utility process for the chosen brand. All other quantity utility outcomes are censored. Because this structure embeds a RUT model (such as logit or probit), it can be viewed as a generalized single-choice response model.

Two rigorous treatments of the brand-choice purchase-quantity problem appeared in the literature almost simultaneously. Tellis (1988), using a two-step procedure, showed that advertising in one category impacts purchase quantity, but not choice. Krishnamurthi and Raj (1988), using a slightly more complex approach, showed that the price elasticities for the choice decision are elastic, while the price elasticities for the quantity decision are inelastic. Subsequent studies have generalized the basic framework to deal with other types of discrete-continuous problems. For example, Kim, Allenby, and Rossi (2002) used a special type of linear utility function to predict the purchase of a basket of yogurt flavors. For each flavor, the model forecasts the probability of purchase along with the expected purchase quantity. Thus, the model can be seen to involve multiple discrete-continuous problems, all determined jointly by one global utility process.

2.5.2 *Integrated choice models*

Discrete-continuous models are related to integrated choice: models that specify whether or not a choice is made at a given time. By defining non-choice as one nest in a nested logit model, it is possible to relate marketing activity to both product category incidence and brand choice (see, e.g., Bucklin and Gupta, 1992). Gupta (1988) takes this logic a step further by decomposing the choice decision into three components: purchase timing (Erlang-2 distribution), brand choice (logit) and purchase quantity (ordered logit). Using data from the coffee category, he shows that the impact of promotion (measured in terms of elasticities) is mostly due to brand switching (84%), followed by purchase time acceleration (14%) and stockpiling (2%). (Subsequent research due to Van Heerde, Gupta, and Wittink (2003) shows that brand switching is a relatively minor effect of promotions when promotional impact is measured in terms of changes in unit sales.) Although the technical details of these models are very different from RUT discrete-continuous models discussed above, the research motivation is the same: to link the brand choice decision to other decisions (quantity and/or purchase incidence) made at the same time.

2.5.3 *Bundle models*

An important problem is forecasting the purchase of a collection (bundle) of products purchased simultaneously. Research in this area makes two assumptions. First, there exists a consideration set of bundles. Second, there exists a common set of attributes such that each product in a bundle can be evaluated in terms of these attributes. These assumptions imply that the classical statement of a choice problem (stated earlier) is applicable.

The most challenging aspect of bundle models is specifying the utility function for a bundle. To address this issue, Farquhar and Rao (1976) proposed the balance model, a utility function that codes each attribute in terms of "more is better" (maximize the bundle mean) or "heterogeneity is better" (maximize the bundle variance). Chung and Rao (2003) extend the balance model to non-comparable attributes and develop a hierarchical Bayes model calibration approach. Harlam and Lodish (1995) draw upon the balance model logic, but assume that the bundle is assembled sequentially, with the probability of choosing the next product contingent on the products already selected.

2.5.4 *Multi-category models*

Multi-category models assume that the consumer enters the store and then selects a subset of the total number of categories to buy. This is known as *pick-any response* data: the consumer can select none, all or some of the categories. There are two challenges in this type of research. First, for a store with N categories, there are 2^N possible baskets of categories — an extremely large choice set, even for modest values of N. Second, in contrast to bundle models, the researcher does not have access to information on global attributes that are common to all categories. The challenge is to build N binary choice models that take into account the fact that the N choices are not independent.

Two different solutions to this problem were proposed at about the same time. Manchanda, Ansari, and Gupta (1999) develop a *multivariate probit* (MVP) model for market basket choice. The MVP model consists of N binary probit models whose errors are mutually correlated. Cross-price demand effects are built into the deterministic portion of the utility expression using price variables for all N categories. Russell and Petersen (2000) develop a *multivariate logistic* (MVL) model for market basket choice. The model can be regarded as a multinomial logit model defined over all possible market baskets. Because the MVL model implies that the choice of one category depends upon all other categories in the market basket, the pattern of cross-price demand effects is generated by the model structure. Song and Chintagunta (2006) propose a variant of the MVL model that allows the prediction of both category incidence and brand choice using aggregate sales data.

Another way of viewing the multi-category decision is to assume that each category choice is independent, conditional upon the consumer's set of model parameters. Cross-category dependence is then created by allowing model parameters to be correlated across categories. Ainslie and Rossi (1998) propose a random effect model that restricts cross-category parameter correlations to be positive. Duvvuri *et al.* (2007) extend this work by developing a multivariate probit model that allows for unrestricted patterns of cross-category parameter correlation. Their analysis provides evidence that consumers identify focal categories that drive purchases in complementary categories.

2.6 Economic theory

Although economic theory has always played a role in the specification of choice models, research that draws heavily on the economic paradigm began in earnest during the early 2000s. Two developments in marketing science encouraged this trend. First, the multiple decisions research stimulated researchers to examine more complex choice problems. Second, the Bayesian computational revolution made the calibration of probit choice models practical. We provide a sketch of some important contributions below.

2.6.1 *Endogeneity*

An important paper by Villas-Boas and Winer (1999) alerted researchers to the fact that the traditional one-equation choice model paradigm, which dominated work in the years 1970–2000, could generate misleading results. Endogeneity refers to the fact that typical purchase history dataset captures the actions of two types of economic actors. Consumers, of course, make decisions in response to marketing variables such as price and promotion. However, these marketing variables are not exogenously determined; rather, marketing variables are typically controlled by manufacturers and retailers. If the decision rules of manufacturers and retailers (called "the firm" in the text that follows) are ignored, the estimated parameters of the consumer's choice rule can be biased.

The correction of endogeneity is a complex topic in econometrics. The *limited information* approach, advocated by Villas-Boas and Winer (1999), involves the joint estimation of a system of two equations, one for the consumer and the other for the firm. The firm equation is a statistical expression linking the marketing mix variables to exogenously determined variables called instruments. Their empirical work demonstrates that ignoring endogeneity leads to an understatement of consumer price sensitivity. Recent work by Ebbes *et al.* (2005) (latent instrumental variables) and Petrin and Train (2010) (control function method) provide additional ways of implementing the limited information approach.

In contrast, the *full information* approach involves deriving an optimal rule for setting the value of marketing mix variables. For example, Sudhir (2001) examines consumer choice in a market in which both manufacturers and retailers engage in a strategic game of price setting. He finds evidence for retailers optimizing category profitability in determining shelf prices. The full information approach may be problematic in a marketing context because the assumption of optimality implies that the researcher cannot suggest improvements in managerial decision making. However, Manchanda, Chintagunta, and Rossi (2004) show that a model of limited managerial rationality can be constructed, which both corrects endogeneity and allows for policy recommendations.

2.6.2 *Structural models*

Structural models are choice models whose specification relies on economic assumptions of optimality: utility maximization for consumers and profit maximization for firms (Chintagunta *et al.*, 2006). This definition is broad enough that logit models built on economic assumptions (e.g., Allenby, 1989; Allenby and Rossi, 1991) can be regarded as structural models. The use of structural models in marketing science is connected with the philosophy of science notions of causality. Economic theory provides a way of understanding the workings of a complex system of interactions among economic actors. Accordingly, predictions of consumer reactions to changes in marketing policies (called *counterfactuals*) may be more valid if a structural model is adopted. An excellent overview of the structural approach to choice model specification is provided by Chintagunta and Nair (2011).

We briefly highlight a few examples of structural models in the context of brand choice. Mehta (2007) develops a special utility structure that allows the study of category incidence and brand choice in the context of market basket analysis. This work uses an indirect utility approach (the dual of the consumer utility maximization problem) to make the specification computationally tractable. Yang *et al.* (2010) use a variant of the MVL choice model to model the television watching behavior of members of the same household (father, mother, and child). The authors argue that the interlocking conditional distributions implied by the MVL model constitute an economic equilibrium that takes into account the behavioral interactions of family members.

Dynamic structural models are particularly interesting. These models assume that actions taken by the consumer alter particular states (variables or parameters) which, in turn, impact future behavior. Erdem (1998) assumes that consumers learn about product quality using an (optimal) Bayesian information-updating mechanism. Her empirical work provides support for the notion that umbrella branding (using the same brand across product categories) allows consumers to transfer quality perceptions across products in a dynamic learning process. Hartmann and Viard (2008) analyze consumer response to a rewards program, taking into account the role of switching costs in driving repeat purchase behavior. Because consumers have rational forward expectations, the probability of purchase rises as the consumer nears the awarding of a reward.

2.6.3 *Multiple discreteness*

Even within a product category of close substitutes such as soft drinks or yogurt, consumers may select an assortment of products on one shopping trip. A model of multiple discreteness explains the choice of a single-category assortment as the outcome of a utility process in which consumers simultaneously choose items and quantities. Dube (2004) argues that consumers anticipate future consumption occasions and accordingly maximize a utility function defined across these occasions. The consumer's maximization problem yields a mixture of interior (positive quantity) and corner (no consumption) solutions — in other words, a bundle of products. Kim *et al.* (2007) develop an alternative approach to the multiple discreteness problem in which product characteristics are projected onto the utility space. Both studies can be viewed as structural model extensions of the marketing science literature on bundling and multi-category choice.

2.7   Choice dependence

Classical choice models have the implicit assumption that consumers make purchase decisions without outside influence. Even if two consumers have the same choice process (such as logit), face the same environment factors, and have the same response parameters, the choice outcomes of the two consumers will be independent. Models of choice dependence view the world as one of interdependence, in which the choices of one consumer can impact the decisions of other consumers. We consider two types of choice dependence: spatial models and social networks.

2.7.1   *Spatial models*

Spatial choice models require three ingredients: a map, a distance metric, and a choice outcome. Consumers are placed in various locations on the map, and it is assumed that choice outcomes of nearby consumers are more similar (*positive spatial correlation*). In the spatial statistics literature, the map is geographical and distances are typically Euclidian measures. However, in marketing science, the map and the associated distance metric are best viewed as a way of expressing consumer similarity. Spatial models in marketing imply some type of dependence among consumers during the choice process.

The literature in this area continues to grow. Yang and Allenby (2003) construct a Bayesian spatial autoregressive model of automobile purchases. Their empirical work suggests that consumers who are physically near each other and also share demographic similarities will have similar preferences. Jank and Kannan (2005) develop a spatial multinomial logit for online purchases assuming that geographically similar consumers share similarities in preferences and in reaction to price. Moon and Russell (2008) develop a new product recommendation model using a spatial choice model based upon a pick-any psychometric map. In all these applications, spatial dependence is probably due to *homophily*, similarity in purchase behavior due to similarities in lifestyle. In contrast, Bell and Song (2007) construct a spatial model of new product adoption that links the probability of adoption to the number of neighboring consumers who have already adopted the product. The most likely explanation in this case is *social influence*, that is, interactions between consumers that drive changes in purchase behavior.

2.7.2 *Social networks*

The growing importance of social media has stimulated research into the behavior of consumers in a social network. A network consists of a group of consumers, each of whom occupies a node in a graph of linkages. The linkages specify the relationships — and the intensity of these relationships — between consumers. If we also have information on choice outcomes of each consumer, then the social network can be considered a map and a spatial choice model may be used. For example, the MVL model (Russell and Petersen, 2000; Yang *et al.*, 2010) was originally developed by spatial statisticians to model binary outcomes on a lattice (Cressie, 1993). Accordingly, the MVL model could be applied to a network of consumers, each of whom decides whether or not to buy a particular product. The close connection between multi-category models and spatial models implies that other generalizations of multi-category models to network data are possible.

Marketing science research in social networks is in its infancy. However, two recent papers are illustrative of work designed to measure network effects. Stephen and Toubia (2010) analyze a network of online firms and determine that sellers who gain most benefit from the network are often not centrally located. Trusov, Bodapati, and Bucklin (2010) propose a Bayesian Poisson model framework that identifies the set of consumers who most influence a given consumer's online behavior. Although neither of these models is properly a choice model, the studies point the way toward future work on the role of social influence in online purchase behavior.

2.8 Conclusions

The history of choice modeling in marketing science is a meandering path, informed by work in psychology, economics and statistics. Early work by Thurstone (1927), Luce (1959), Tversky (1972), and McFadden (1980) provided the theoretical foundations for the analysis of scanner panel data using the multinomial logit model. Advances in computational power and simulation estimation technology allowed researchers to build more realistic models incorporating consumer parameter heterogeneity, multiple decisions, economic logic, and choice dependence.

It is difficult to predict the future evolution of choice modeling in marketing. Nevertheless, there is growing awareness that the classical RUT model framework may be inadequate. Because choice models evolved from psychophysical research on human judgments of stimulus intensity, RUT models make two key assumptions. First, the deterministic portion of utility of an alternative depends only on the attributes of that alternative (see Eq. (2.1)). Second, the consumer makes choices in isolation, without any influence of other consumers.

In fact, marketing science already includes studies that violate these assumptions. For example, the extensive literature on reference price mechanisms (based upon the Prospect Theory of Kahneman and Tversky (1979)) contains examples in which the reference price point is constructed from the prices of all brands, thus violating the first RUT assumption. Recently, Steenburgh (2008) argued that RUT models make the unreasonable prediction that changes in all marketing mix variables (such as price and advertising) lead to the same substitution patterns. This can only be corrected by allowing the utility of a given alternative to depend on the attributes of all alternatives in the choice set — again violating the first RUT assumption.

Further attacks on the RUT framework arise from attempts to relate work in consumer behavior to work in marketing science. Kivetz, Netzer, and Srinivasan (2004) develop a model of the *compromise effect*, a behavioral regularity in which the choice share of a product is increased when it is viewed as an intermediate quality option as opposed to when it is viewed as an extreme option. A standard RUT model cannot explain this type of choice behavior. Stuttgen, Boatwright, and Monroe (2012) argue that consumers commonly engage in *satisficing* behavior: a choice process in which a consumer searches until a product that is "good enough" is located. Using both eye-tracking data and choice data from an online conjoint analysis task, they empirically show that a model based upon satisficing dominates the utility maximization behavior predicted by RUT.

The second RUT assumption (that consumers make decisions in isolation) is clearly violated by the recent literature on spatial models and social networks. From a technical point of view, choice dependence does not necessarily mean that RUT models are entirely useless. For example, the Yang *et al.* (2010) application of the MVL model envisions a group of RUT individuals interacting in a way that results in a stable economic equilibrium. Nevertheless, the larger point remains that the behavior of the individual depends upon the choice context created by other individuals.

The way forward in choice modeling may well be the development of a context-dependent theory of choice that allows for attribute spillover across alternatives and interactions among consumers. Although such models will face considerable technical challenges, context-dependent models have the potential to explain some of the prediction errors currently attributed to stochasticity in choice and unobserved parameter heterogeneity. Moreover, from a conceptual point of view, context dependence may be a more valid way of viewing consumer choice in an increasingly information-rich and interactive world.

References

Abramson, C., R. L. Andrews, I. S. Currim, and M. Jones (2000). Parameter bias from unobserved effects in the multinomial logit model of consumer choice, *Journal of Marketing Research*, 37(November), 410–426.

Ainslie, A. and P. E. Rossi (1998). Similarities in choice behavior across product categories, *Marketing Science*, 17(2), 91–106.

Allenby, G. (1989). A unified approach to identifying, estimating and testing demand structures with aggregate scanner data, *Marketing Science*, 8(Summer), 265–280.

Allenby, G. and J. L. Ginter (1995). Using extremes to design products and segment markets, *Journal of Marketing Research*, 32(November), 392–403.

Allenby, G. and P. Rossi (1991). Quality perceptions and asymmetric switching between brands, *Marketing Science*, 10(Summer), 185–204.

Allenby, G. and P. E. Rossi (1999). Marketing models of consumer heterogeneity, *Journal of Econometrics*, 89, 57–78.

Bass, F. M., A. Jeuland, and G. W. Wright (1978). Equilibrium stochastic choice and market penetration theories: Derivations and comparisons, *Management Science*, 22(June), 1051–1063.

Ben-Akiva, M. and S. R. Lerman (1985). *Discrete choice analysis: Theory and application to travel demand*, Cambridge, MA: MIT Press.

Bell, D. R. and R. E. Bucklin (1999). The role of internal reference points in the category purchase decision, *Journal of Consumer Research*, 26(September), 128–143.

Bell, D. R. and J. M. Lattin (2000). Looking for loss aversion in scanner panel data: The confounding effect of price response heterogeneity, *Marketing Science*, 19(Spring), 185–200.

Bell, D. R. and S. Song (2007). Neighborhood effects and trial on the internet: Evidence from online grocery retailing, *Quantitative Marketing and Economics*, 5, 361–400.

Blattberg, R. and S. K. Sen (1976). Market segments and stochastic brand choice models, *Journal of Marketing Research*, 13(February), 34–45.

Bronnenberg, B. J. and W. R. Vanhonacker (1996). Limited choice sets, local price response, and implied measures of price competition, *Journal of Marketing Research*, 23(May), 163–173.

Bucklin, R. E. and S. Gupta (1992). Brand choice, purchase incidence, and segmentation: An integrated modeling approach, *Journal of Marketing Research*, 29(May), 201–215.

Bucklin, R. E. and J. M. Lattin (1991). A two-stage model of purchase incidence and brand choice, *Marketing Science*, 10(Winter), 24–39.

Chandukala, S. R., J. Kim, T. Otter, P. E. Rossi, and G. M. Allenby (2007). Choice models in marketing: Economic assumptions, challenges and trends, *Foundations and Trends in Marketing*, 2(2), 1–88.

Chiang, J., S. Chib, and C. Narasimhan (1999). Markov Chain Monte Carlo and models of consideration set and parameter heterogeneity, *Journal of Econometrics*, 89, 223–248.

Chintagunta, P. K., T. Erdem, P. E. Rossi, and M. Wedel (2006). Structural modeling in marketing: Review and assessment, *Marketing Science*, 25(November–December), 604–616.

Chintagunta, P. K. and H. S. Nair (2011). Discrete-choice models of consumer demand in marketing, *Marketing Science*, 30(November–December), 977–996.

Chung, J. and V. R. Rao (2003). A general choice model for bundles with multiple category products: Application to market segmentation and pricing of bundles, *Journal of Marketing Research*, 40(May), 115–130.

Corstjens, M. and D. A. Gautschi (1983). Formal choice models in marketing, *Marketing Science*, 2(Winter), 19–56.

Cressie, N. A. C. (1993). *Statistics for spatial data*, New York: John Wiley and Sons.

Dube, J.-P. (2004). Multiple discreteness and product differentiation: demand for carbonated soft drinks, *Marketing Science*, 23(Winter), 66–81.

Duvvuri, S., A. Ansari, and S. Gupta (2007). Consumers' price sensitivities across complementary product categories, *Management Science*, 53(December), 1933–1945.

Ebbes, P., M. Wedel, U. Bockenholt, and T. Steerneman (2005). Solving and testing for regression-error (in)dependence when no instrumental variables are available: With new evidence for the effect of education on income, *Quantitative Marketing and Economics*, 3, 365–392.

Ehrenberg, A. S. C. (1972). *Repeat buying: Theory and applications*, London: North Holland.

Erdem, T. (1996). A dynamic analysis of market structure based on panel data, *Marketing Science*, 15(4), 359–378.

Erdem, T. (1998). An empirical analysis of umbrella branding, *Journal of Marketing Research*, 35(August), 339–351.

Farquhar, P. H. and V. R. Rao (1976). A balance model for evaluating subsets of multiattributed items, *Management Science*, 22(January), 528–539.

Gilbride, T. J. and G. M. Allenby (2004). A choice model with conjunctive, disjunctive, and compensatory screening rules, *Marketing Science*, 23(Summer), 391–406.

Grover, R. and V. Srinivasan (1987). A simultaneous approach to market segmentation and market structuring, *Journal of Marketing Research*, 24(May), 139–153.

Guadagni, P. M. and J. D. C. Little (1983). A logit model of brand choice calibrated on scanner data, *Marketing Science*, 2(Summer), 203–238.

Gupta, S. (1988). Impact of sales promotions on when, what and how much to buy, *Journal of Marketing Research*, 25(November), 342–355.

Harlam, B. A. and L. M. Lodish (1995). Modeling consumers' choices of multiple items, *Journal of Marketing Research*, 32(November), 404–418.

Hartmann, W. R. and V. B. Viard (2008). Do frequency reward programs create switching costs? A dynamic structural analysis of demand in a reward program, *Quantitative Marketing and Economics*, 6, 109–137.

Jank, W. and P. K. Kannan (2005). Understanding geographical markets of online firms using spatial models of customer choice, *Marketing Science*, 24(Fall), 632–634.

Kahn, B. E., M. U. Kalwani, and D. G. Morrison (1986). Measuring variety-seeking and reinforcement behavior using panel data, *Journal of Marketing Research*, 23(May), 89–100.

Kahneman, D. and A. Tversky (1979). Prospect theory: An analysis of decision under risk, *Econometrica*, 47(2), 263–291.

Kalyanam, K. and D. S. Putler (1997). Incorporating demographic variables in brand choice models: An indivisible alternatives framework, *Marketing Science*, 16(2), 166–181.

Kamakura, W. A. and G. J. Russell (1989). A probabilistic choice model for market segmentation and elasticity structure, *Journal of Marketing Research*, 26(November), 379–390.

Kamakura, W. A., B.-D. Kim, and J. Lee (1996). Modeling preference and structural heterogeneity in consumer choice, *Marketing Science*, 15(2), 152–172.

Kim, J., G. M. Allenby, and P. E. Rossi (2002). Modeling consumer demand for variety, *Marketing Science*, 21(Summer), 229–250.

Kim, J., G. M. Allenby, and P. E. Rossi (2007). Product attributes and models of multiple discreteness, *Econometrica*, 138, 208–230.

Kivetz, R., O. Netzer, and V. Srinivasan (2004). Alternative models for capturing the compromise effect, *Journal of Marketing Research*, 41(August), 237–257.

Krishnamurthi, L. and S. P. Raj (1998). A model of brand choice and purchase quantity sensitivities, *Marketing Science*, 7(Winter), 1–20.

Kuehn, A. and A. C. Rohloff (1967). Evaluating promotions using a brand switching model, in Patrick J. Robinson, ed., *Promotional decisions using mathematical models*, Reading, MA: Allyn and Sons, pp. 50–85.

Lattin, J. M. and L. McAlister (1985). Using a variety-seeking model to identify substitute and complementary relationships among competing products, *Journal of Marketing Research*, 22(August), 330–339.

Louviere, J. J., D. A. Hensher, and J. D. Swait (2000). *Stated choice methods: Analysis and application*, Cambridge: Cambridge University Press.

Luce, R. D. (1959). *Individual choice behavior: A theoretical analysis*, New York: John Wiley and Sons.

Manchanda, P., A. Ansari, and S. Gupta (1999). The shopping basket: A model for multicategory purchase incidence decisions, *Marketing Science*, 18(2), 95–114.

Manchanda, P., P. K. Chintagunta, and P. E. Rossi (2004). Response modeling with non-random marketing mix variables, *Journal of Marketing Research*, 41(November), 467–478.

Massy, W. F., D. B. Montgomery, and D. G. Morrison (1970). *Stochastic models of buying behavior*, Cambridge, MA: MIT Press.

McFadden, D. (1980). Econometric models of probabilistic choice, in Charles F. Manski and Daniel McFadden, eds., *Structural analysis of discrete data with econometric applications*, Cambridge, MA: MIT Press, 198–272.

Mehta, N. (2007). Investigating consumers' purchase incidence and brand choice decisions across multiple product categories: A theoretical and empirical analysis, *Marketing Science*, 26(March–April), 196–217.

Mehta, N., S. Rajiv, and K. Srinivasan (2003). Price uncertainty and consumer search: A structural model of consideration set formation, *Marketing Science*, 22(Winter), 58–84.

Moon, S. and G. J. Russell (2008). Predicting product purchase from inferred customer similarity: An autologistic model approach, *Management Science*, 54(January), 71–82.

Moon, S., G. J. Russell, and S. D. Duvvuri (2006). Profiling the reference price consumer, *Journal of Retailing*, 82(1), 1–11.

Neslin, S. and H. J. Van Heerde (2008). Promotion dynamics, *Foundations and Trends in Marketing*, 3(4), 177–268.

Petrin, A. and K. Train (2010). A control function approach to endogeneity in consumer choice models, *Journal of Marketing Research*, 47, 3–13.

Rossi, P. E. and G. M. Allenby (1993). A Bayesian approach to estimating household parameters, *Journal of Marketing Research*, 30(May), 171–182.

Roberts, J. H. and J. M. Lattin (1991). Development and testing of a model of consideration set composition, *Journal of Marketing Research*, 28(November), 429–440.

Russell, G. J. and A. Petersen (2000). Analysis of cross category dependence in market basket selection, *Journal of Retailing*, 76(3), 367–392.

Silk, A. J. and G. L. Urban (1978). Pre-test market evaluation of packaged goods: A model and measurement methodology, *Journal of Marketing Research*, 15(May), 171–191.

Simon, H. A. (1969). *The sciences of the artificial*, Cambridge, MA: MIT Press.

Song, I. and P. K. Chintagunta (2006). Measuring cross-category price effects with aggregate store data, *Management Science*, 52(October), 1594–1609.

Steenburgh, T. J. (2008). The invariant proportion of substitution property (IPS) of discrete choice models, *Marketing Science*, 27(March–April), 300–307.

Stephen, A. and O. Toubia (2010). Deriving value from social commerce networks, *Journal of Marketing Research*, 47(April), 215–228.

Stuttgen, P., P. Boatright, and R. T. Monroe (2012). A satisficing choice model, *Marketing Science*, 31(November–December), 878–899.

Sudhir, K. (2001). Structural analysis of manufacturer pricing in the presence of a strategic retailer, *Marketing Science*, 20(Summer), 244–264.

Tellis, G. J. (1988). Advertising exposure, loyalty, and brand purchase: A two-stage model of choice, *Journal of Marketing Research*, 25(May), 134–144.

Thurstone, L. (1927). Psychophysical analysis, *American Journal of Psychology*, 37, 368–389.

Thurstone, L. L. (1959). *The measurement of values*, Chicago: University of Chicago Press.

Train, K. (1993). *Qualitative choice analysis: Theory, econometrics, and an application to automobile demand*, Cambridge, MA: MIT Press.

Train, K. (2003). *Discrete choice methods with simulation*, New York: Cambridge University Press.

Trusov, M., A. Bodapati, and R. Bucklin (2010). Determining influential users in internet social networks, *Journal of Marketing Research*, 47(August), 643–658.

Tversky, A. (1972). Choice by elimination, *Journal of Mathematical Psychology*, 9, 341–367.

Van Heerde, H. J., S. Gupta, and D. Wittink (2003). Is 75% of the sales promotion bump due to brand switching? No, only 33% is, *Journal of Marketing Research*, 40(November), 481–491.

Villas-Boas, M. J. and R. S. Winer (1999). Endogeneity in brand choice models, *Management Science*, 45(October), 1324–1338.

Wedel, M. and W. A. Kamakura (2000). *Market segmentation: Conceptual methodological foundations*, 2nd edn., Boston: Kluwer Academic Publishers.

Winer, R. S. (1986). A reference price model of brand choice for frequently purchased products, *Journal of Consumer Research*, 13(September), 250–256.

Winer, R. (2014). Pricing, in R. Winer and S. A. Neslin, eds., *History of marketing science*, Hanover, MA: Now Publishers, Chapter 6.

Yang, S. and G. M. Allenby (2003). Modeling interdependent consumer preferences, *Journal of Marketing Research*, 40(August), 282–294.

Yang, S., G. M. Allenby, and G. Fennell (2002). Modeling variation in brand preference: The role of objective environment and motivating conditions, *Marketing Science*, 21(Winter), 14–31.

Yang, S., Y. Zhao, T. Erdem, and Y. Zhao (2010). Modeling the intra-household behavioral interaction, *Journal of Marketing Research*, 47(June), 470–484.

Yellott, J. I. (1977). The relationship between Luce's choice axiom, Thurstone's law of comparative judgment, and the double exponential distribution, *Journal of Mathematical Psychology*, 15, 109–144.

Chapter 3

Conjoint Analysis

Vithala R. Rao

3.1 Introduction

Several interdependent decisions such as product design and positioning, communication, and pricing are involved in the formulation of a marketing strategy for a brand (of a product or service). These decisions will need to be made in the wake of uncertain competitive reactions and a changing environment. For a business to be successful, the decision process must include a clear understanding of how customers will choose among (and react to) various competing alternatives, each described usually as profiles on multiple attributes. While choosing, consumers typically make trade-offs among the attributes of a product or service. Conjoint analysis (CA) is a set of techniques ideally suited to studying customers' choice processes and determining trade-offs.

CA is probably the most significant development in marketing research methodology over the last 40 years or so. In its original incarnation introduced to marketing researchers in 1971 (Green and Rao, 1971), this method was called "conjoint measurement." The theory for this method is concerned with the conditions under which there exist measurement scales for both the evaluative score (dependent variable) and functions of each attribute level (independent variables), and pre-specified composition rules; these rules are based on a formal axiomatic system formulated by Krantz *et al.* (1971). Some of these axioms are consistency, transitivity, attribute independence, etc. The evaluative score can be categorical, ordinal, or interval-scaled. Several representations such as additive, polynomial functions could be employed in the decomposition.

In the course of implementing conjoint measurement methods to applied business problems, as encountered in marketing, the emphasis on theoretical aspects of measurement has given way to more pragmatic issues of design of studies and analyzing data. This is due to various intricacies in testing[1] whether the axioms are satisfied in the data collected. The testing procedures require extensive data and are highly complicated even for a small number of respondents. This process became frustrating for applied researchers. The methodology that has evolved to handle these problems is popularly called "conjoint analysis" to reflect the stated distinction. The terminology of CA,[2] introduced in 1978 by Green and Srinivasan (1978), refers to any decompositional method that estimates the structure of a consumer's preferences[3] in terms of the levels of attributes of the alternatives. The methodology uses, quite heavily, statistical experimental design and parameter estimation methods.

CA has been successfully applied in several thousand applied marketing research projects for tackling several marketing decisions such as optimal design of new products, target market selection, pricing a new product, and competitive reactions. A significant advantage of the method has been the ability to answer various "what if" questions using market simulators; these simulators are based on the results from a conjoint study for hypothetical and real choice alternatives.[4]

Five different features of CA have contributed to its versatility for tackling marketing managerial problems: (i) it is a measurement technique for quantifying buyer trade-offs and values, (ii) it is an analytical technique

---

[1] See Corstjens and Gautschi (1983) for detailed methods for testing these axioms.

[2] The differences between conjoint measurement (with its psychometric origins and axioms) and conjoint analysis (a more pragmatic methodology) are important from a theoretical perspective, but will not be delved into here. See Rao (1977) for a discussion of conjoint measurement.

[3] This method is quite similar to preference analysis in multidimensional scaling which focuses on estimating the ideal points for or weights on perceptual dimensions. These functions will be described in the next section.

[4] It will be useful to review some terms used in conjoint analysis. Attributes are (mainly) physical characteristics that describe a product; levels are the number of different values an attribute takes; profile is a combination of attributes, each attribute at a particular level, presented to a respondent for an evaluation (or stated preference); choice set is a pre-specified number of profiles presented to a respondent to make a pseudo-choice (stated choice).

for predicting buyers' likely reactions to new products/services; (iii) it is a segmentation technique for identifying groups of buyers who share similar trade-offs/values, (iv) it is a simulation technique for assessing new product service ideas in a competitive environment; and (v) it is an optimization technique for seeking product/service profiles that maximize share/return (Green, Krieger, and Wind, 2001).

Against this brief background, this chapter will provide a historical account[5] of how this methodology has evolved over the years and will identify some research issues. Section 3.2 will describe the basics of conjoint models and estimation, and will provide a simplified illustration of one approach. Section 3.3 will describe the origins of this methodology using a genealogy chart and identify two different approaches (ratings-based and choice-based) identifying principal types of CA in vogue in marketing research. Sections 3.4–3.6 will present an overview of the variety of applications of the conjoint method. Sections 3.7 and 3.8 will enumerate a series of recent developments and future directions with limited elaboration.

3.2 Basics of conjoint models

Conjoint methods are intended to "uncover" the underlying preference function of a product in terms of its attributes.[6] Figure 3.1 lays out some basic steps involved in the design of a conjoint study.

Assume that there are J products profiles each described on R attributes. A general product profile for the jth product can be written as $(x_{j1}, x_{j2}, \ldots, x_{jR})$ where x_{jr} is the level for the jth profile on the rth attribute $(r = 1, 2, \ldots, R; j = 1, 2, \ldots, J)$. While there exist several ways for specifying the preference functions in CA, researchers usually start with an additive conjoint model; but, the theory extends to models with interactions as well. The preference score[7] for the jth product profile, y_j

---

[5]For a previous such review, see Carroll and Green (1995).

[6]For an introduction to conjoint analysis, see Orme (2006).

[7]This exposition considers a ratings-based conjoint analysis where respondents provide preference ratings for a number of product profiles. The same will apply to the v-function in the choice-based conjoint analysis.

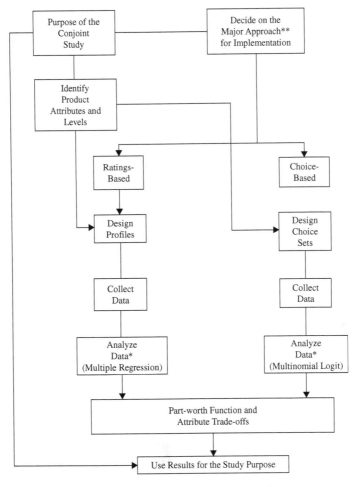

Fig. 3.1   Major steps in a conjoint study

*One method for each is shown among several alternatives.
**Several alternatives exist here.
Source: Rao, V.R. (2008). Developments in Conjoint Analysis, in B. Wierenga, ed., *Handbook of marketing decision models*, New York: Springer Science + Business Media, LLC.

for one respondent additive conjoint model is:

$$y_j = U_1(x_{j1}) + U_2(x_{j2}) + \cdots + U_r(x_{jR}),$$

where $U_r(\bullet)$ is the component utility function specific to the rth attribute (also called part-utility function or part-worth function). No constant term is specified, but it could be included in any one of the U-functions or assumed to be zero (without any loss of generality.) The specification of the U-function for any attribute will depend upon its type (categorical and quantitative). In practice, a conjoint study may contain both types of attributes.

Brand names or verbal descriptions such as high, medium or low are examples of a categorical attribute; here the levels of the attribute are described by words. A quantitative attribute is one measured by either an interval scale or ratio scale; numbers describe the "levels" of such an attribute; examples are the weight of a laptop and speed of the processor.

The levels of a categorical attribute can be recoded into a set of dummy variables (one less than the number of levels) and a part-worth function is specified as a piecewise linear function in the dummy variables. In this case, the component-utility function for a categorical attribute (tth for example) will be:

$$U_t(x_{jt}) = D_{t1}U_{t1} + D_{t2}U_{t2} + \cdots + D_{tr_t}U_{tr_t},$$

where r_t is the number of discrete levels for the tth attribute (resulting from the construction of the profiles or created expost); D_{tk} is a dummy variable taking the value 1 if the value x_{jt} is equivalent to the kth discrete level of x_{jt} and 0 otherwise; and U_{tk} is the component of the part-worth function for the kth discrete level of x_{jt}. In practice, only $(r_t - 1)$ — one less the number of discrete levels of the attribute — dummy variables are necessary for estimation.

A quantitative attribute can be used in a manner similar to a categorical attribute by coding its values into categories or used directly in the specification of the part-worth function for the attribute. In the latter case, the function can be specified as linear (vector model) or non-linear; one example of a non-linear function is the ideal point model. Mathematically, the component-utility function can be specified as:

$$U_t(x_{jt}) = \begin{cases} w_t x_{jt} & \text{for the vector model; and} \\ w_t(x_{jt} - x_{0t})^2 & \text{for the ideal point model;} \end{cases}$$

where w_t is a weight (positive or negative); and x_{0t} is the ideal point on the tth attribute.

A linear function is appropriate for an attribute deemed to be desirable (e.g., speed of a laptop computer) or undesirable (e.g., weight of a laptop computer); such a function is called a vector model for which the utility increases (or decreases) linearly with the numerical value of the attribute. The ideal point model is appropriate for an attribute for which preference either increases (or decreases) with increasing value of the attribute; if the function is like an inverted U-shape, it is called a positive ideal point model and if it is a U-shape, it is called a negative ideal point model. An example of an attribute with a negative ideal point is the temperature of tea, where ice tea is preferred and hot tea is preferred but not tepid tea.

As mentioned above, with suitable redefinitions of variables, the preference function can be written as $y = X\beta + \varepsilon$; where ε is the random error of the model assumed to be normally distributed with zero mean and variance of σ^2 and y is the rating on a given profile and X is the corresponding set of p dummy (or other) variables. The β is a $p \times 1$ vector of part-worths among the levels of attributes. Such a formulation is typical for a ratings-based approach to CA and regression methods are employed for estimating the parameters.

In the choice-based conjoint (CBC) methods, the respondent is given a number of choice sets, each choice set consisting of a small number (typically 4 or 5) profiles, and is asked to indicate which profile will be chosen, and the task is repeated for several choice sets. For analyzing such choice data, a random utility model is employed. According to this model, the utility for an object consists of two parts — a deterministic component and a random component — and an individual chooses an object among a choice set according to the maximum random utility. When an Extreme Value Type-I distribution is assumed for the random component, the resulting choice can be described by the multinomial logit model (MNL); accordingly, the probability of choosing profile j in choice set $C = \exp(v_j) / \sum \exp(v_k)$ where the summation is taken over all the profiles in the choice set C and v_j is the deterministic component of the utility for the profile j (McFadden, 1974). The deterministic utility function v can be specified as a linear combination analogous to the function for y in the ratings methods. The parameters of the v-function are estimated using maximum likelihood methods. A variety of extensions and alternatives exist for analyzing stated choice data. The estimated coefficients will be used in computing the part-worth values for the attributes.

Table 3.1   Alternatives for selected features of conjoint analysis

Representation of stimuli	Formats of data collection	Nature of data collection	Estimation methods
Verbal descriptions	Full profile evaluations	One-shot	Regression-based methods
Pictorial descriptions	Partial profile evaluations	Adaptive Multiple times*	Random utility models
Videotapes and supporting materials	Stated preferences		Direct computation based on self-explicated importances
Virtual proto-types	Stated choices Self-explicated methods		Hierarchical Bayes estimation*
Combinations of physical models, photographs and verbal descriptions	Configurators*		Methods based on new optimization methods* analytic center estimation, support-vector machines, genetic algorithms

*These are newer methods.
Source: Adapted from Hauser and Rao (2004) and Rao (2008).

Current approaches for implementing a CA project differ in terms of several features; some main features are stimulus representation, formats of data collection, nature of data collection, and estimation methods. Table 3.1 lays out some alternatives for these features. There is no clear agreement as to which data collection format is the best and all the ones shown in Table 3.1 are in vogue and more are being developed as well.

At this point, it will be useful to indicate the software available for designing and implementing conjoint studies. These are:

- Sawtooth Software (ACA, CBC, etc.; probably the most complete solution) (www.sawtooth.com).
- SPSS (useful for preference-based approach) (http://www.ibm.com/software/analytics/spss/academic).
- SAS (OPTEX for design and several general-purpose programs for data analysis) (www.sas.com).
- STATA (A general-purpose package for analyzing data) (www.stata.com).

- LIMDEP/NLOGIT (useful for analyzing data of various types; Greene (2012)).
- Bayesm package in R (developed by Rossi, Allenby, and McCulloch (2005)).
- MATLAB (one needs to develop specific program code); can also consult Prof. Ken Train's MATLAB codes on his website.

It is important to become highly familiar with any of the software before implementing the method for an applied or basic research project.

3.3 Genealogy of CA

Figure 3.2 shows the genealogy of CA methodology, as practiced today, and labeled as "ratings-based" and "choice-based" methods. Their historical origins are quite distinct; one is derived from the axiomatic measurement (Krantz *et al.*, 1971; Luce and Tukey, 1964) and the other from the theory of Thurstone's Law of Comparative Judgment (Thurstone, 1927).

The ratings-based methods can be traced back to the Mathematical Analysis of Perceptions and Preferences (MAPP) project of Paul Green sponsored by the Marketing Science Institute (Green and Rao, 1972; Green and Wind, 1973; Carroll, 1973). These methods of CA became prominent to tackle the problem of reverse mapping in multi-dimensional scaling applications (i.e., determining values of objective/physical characteristics of a product to yield a predetermined position in the space of perceptual dimensions). The main issue is how to design a new product's attributes (mainly physical characteristics) relevant to a specific location in a positioning map. This problem is quite complicated due to the potential for multiple solutions (see DeSarbo and Rao, 1986). However, the researcher can determine a function that relates physical characteristics to preference (or perceptions) for a new product with relative ease. With the knowledge of the preference function, a researcher can determine the attributes of a product to reach a given preference level using simulation or optimization methods. Given this relative ease, the methodology of CA has become quite popular in marketing research;[8] in this methodology, a utility function for a choice alternative is directly

---

[8]This point was discussed at the conference held at the Wharton School, the University of Pennsylvania in May 2002 to honor Paul E. Green.

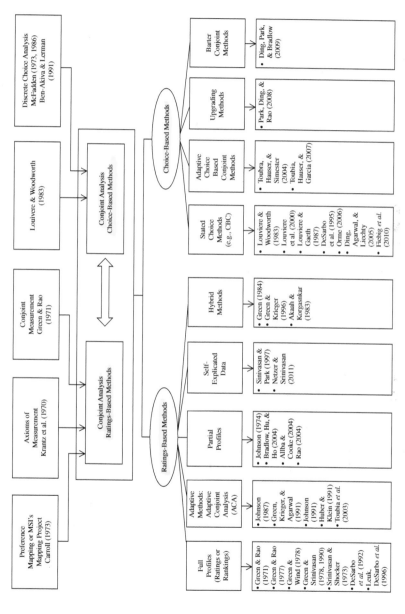

Fig. 3.2   Conjoint analysis in marketing: A genealogy chart (does not address the issues of design of profiles and choice sets)

specified in terms of attributes and estimated with appropriate methods; accordingly, no reverse mapping is necessary. Over time, several developments have occurred in the ratings-based methods which are elaborated below.

The choice-based methods are based on the behavioral theory of random utility maximization (McFadden, 1974); the origin of this approach is the Law of Comparative Judgment development by Thurstone (1927). This approach decomposes an individual's random utility for an object into two parts: deterministic utility and random part. Depending on the distributional assumptions for the error part, a number of alternative models are developed to describe the probability of choice of an object. The most popular one is the MNL that uses the Type-I extreme value distribution for the error term. These methods belong to the family of discrete choice analysis methods. Louviere and Woodworth (1983) introduced these methods to marketing researchers. An excellent volume that elaborates on these stated choice methods is by Louviere, Hensher, and Swait (2000) (see also Ben-Akiva and Lerman (1991) for several theoretical developments). As with the ratings-based methods, various researchers have introduced enhancements to these methods; some of these are described below.

3.4 Ratings-based methods

Over the past several years, various researchers have contributed to the ratings-based methods (see Green and Srinivasan (1978, 1990) for excellent reviews of this approach). Five types of ratings-based CA can be identified: (i) full profile method (CA) that utilizes all the attributes in describing a stimulus; (ii) adaptive methods (ACA), developed in part to handle the issue of large number of attributes, which elicit preferences gradually to reduce respondent's task burden; (iii) partial profiles method that shows a subset of attributes at a time; (iv) self-explicated CA; and (v) hybrid methods, which use a combination of the previous methods. The first three of these can be called decompositional methods because the stated preference or stated choice data are decomposed to obtain part-worth functions. The fourth one (self-explicated method) is a bottom-up method and called compositional method because it composes a preference score from ratings of scores on attribute levels and relative importances of attributes. A brief description of developments in each of these follows:

3.4.1 *Full profile method*

The full profile method is the traditional CA; in this method, a researcher collects preferences (judgments) for profiles of hypothetical products each described on the entire set of attributes selected for the conjoint study. These profiles are called full profiles. However, when one concatenates levels of all attributes, the complete set of full profiles (or full factorial design) will in general be very large. A respondent will be unduly burdened when asked to provide preference judgments on all profiles. Typically, a smaller set of full profiles, selected according to an experimental design, are used in a conjoint study (see Green (1974) for such experimental designs). An individual's overall stated preferences are decomposed into separate and compatible utility values corresponding to each attribute typically using regression-based methods (see Green and Rao (1971) and Green and Wind (1975) for illustrations of this approach). These separate functions are called attribute-specific part-worth functions. In most cases, the preference functions can be estimated at the individual level. This estimated preference function can be deemed as an indirect utility function. When the responses are obtained as ranks, linear programming methods are utilized as shown by Srinivasan and Shocker (1973) in addition to monotone regression methods (Green and Rao, 1971).

The full-profile approach has been typically applied at the individual level, and part-worth functions are estimated for each individual in the sample. Typically, clusters of respondents with relatively homogeneous part-worth estimates to identify segments among respondents; such a step is useful both for description and design of strategies aimed at each segment. However, this approach becomes infeasible when the number of attributes (and the number of levels of the attributes) becomes large; in such cases, the number of profiles will be too many (beyond 20 or so) depending on the fractional experimental designs employed and it is extremely difficult to obtain reliable data from respondents due to fatigue, boredom, and other factors. This "large number of attributes" problem had led to the development of other methods of data collection and analysis (i.e., adaptive methods, partial profiles methods, self-explicated methods, and hybrid methods), which are elaborated below.

An alternative for individual-level analysis of ratings conjoint data is the use of latent class analysis introduced to the conjoint literature by DeSarbo et al. (1992), which is essentially an extension of the regression approach. The latent classes are akin to segments of respondents mentioned above. The basic idea is to identify simultaneously subgroups of individuals in the sample who have similar part-worth functions and their sizes. For this purpose, let us assume that the responses are assumed to follow a normal distribution. If we let y_i represent a (J × 1) vector of ratings (responses) to the J conjoint product profiles given by the ith individual in the sample and X represent the ($J \times L$) matrix of L independent variables (coded from the attribute profiles). Let Θ represent the parameters (mean vector and variance–covariance matrix) of the probability distribution for y_i, vector Θ_g represent a similar vector for the gth group and α_g be the size of the gth group. Further let Prob (., ., .) denote the probability distribution of y_i. With this notation, the latent class model with G groups is:

$$\text{Prob}(y_i, \Theta, X) = \sum_{g=1}^{G} \alpha_g \text{Prob}(y_{ig}, \Theta_g, X)$$

$$\text{Subject to } 0 < \alpha_g < 1; \quad \text{and} \quad \sum_{g=1}^{G} \alpha_g = 1.$$

The parameters Θ_g and α_g are estimated using maximum likelihood methods. The number of latent classes is determined using fit criteria such as the Akaike information criterion or the Bayesian information criterion (BIC) (also called Schwarz criterion); these fit criteria are based on the value of the likelihood adjusted for the number of parameters estimated in the latent class model. The DeSarbo et al. (1992) paper contains a nice illustration of this approach.

A second alternative to individual-level analysis of ratings data is the use of hierarchical Bayesian (HB) methods introduced to the conjoint literature by Lenk et al. (1996). This approach estimates relationships between individual-level part-worth parameters to characteristics of individuals rather than estimating parameters for each individual. An advantage of this method is the ability to estimate part-worth values for individuals not included in the study sample. Further, this approach can be employed even when a small number of product profiles are employed in the conjoint study (in a way tackling the large number of attributes issue). For the linear HB model, the conjoint model for the ith individual level is written as: $Y_i = X_i\beta_i + \varepsilon_i$; for $i = 1, \ldots, n$, where $Y_i =$ is a vector of m_i responses (ratings); note that the number of responses can vary over individuals (due to such reasons as incompleteness of data). Further, the subjects' part-worths are described in terms of a set of covariates (usually background variables) as $\beta_i = \Theta z_i + \delta_i$ for $i = 1, \ldots, n$. Here, z_i is a $q \times 1$ vector of characteristics (or covariates) and Θ is a $(p \times q)$ matrix of regression coefficients which represent the relationships between the part-worths and subject covariates. The error terms $\{\varepsilon_i\}$ and $\{\delta_i\}$ are assumed to be mutually independent and distributed as multivariate normal with zero means and covariance matrices $\{\sigma_i^2 I\}$ and Λ respectively, where Λ is a $p \times p$ matrix. The error variances $\{\sigma_i^2\}$ are assumed to have prior distributions of inverse gamma distribution. Using these assumptions, one can work out the posterior distributions for the β_i parameters. The various parameters are estimated using the MCMC method and the Metropolis algorithm.

3.4.2 *Adaptive methods*

To deal with the problem of large number of attributes in a conjoint study, researchers have also developed adaptive conjoint methods which are called adaptive conjoint analysis (ACA) (Johnson, 1987). Strictly speaking, this method is a type of hybrid[9] model approach. The method involves first a self-explicated task (i.e., eliciting data on attribute importances and attribute-level desirabilities using ranking and subsequent rating) followed by preference ratings for a set of partial profile descriptions, two at a time using a graded, paired comparison scale. The partial profile descriptions are tailored to each respondent based on the data collected in the self-explicated task. Both the tasks are administered by computer. This method does alleviate the difficulty of a respondent in evaluating full profiles with a large number of attributes. The comments by Green *et al.* (1991) and

---

[9]Hybrid models involve a combination of several tasks aimed to increase the "efficiency" of data collection in conjoint studies usually for large number of attributes. See Green (1984) for a review of these methods; see *also* Green and Krieger (1996) for individualized hybrid models.

response by Johnson (1991) illuminate the issues involved with this method such as scale comparability between phases, construction of partial profiles, updating part-worth values, and holding out predictive validity, and will form an interesting reading. The method is now much more developed. Further, the paper by Huber and Klein (1991) deals with a related problem of how individuals adapt acceptable minimum attribute levels (cut-offs) in a choice environment. It is easy to see why the adaptive methods helped tackle the problem of large number of attributes in the ratings-based studies. It is difficult to categorically state as to how many attributes can be handled in the adaptive methods, but a reasonable guess is that the number can be as high as 10 or 12; but this depends on the number of levels of the attributes. Additionally, Toubia *et al.* (2003) have developed polyhedral methods based on mathematical programming to design profiles for collecting adaptive conjoint data and have shown that they fare better in terms of predictive ability.

3.4.3 *Partial profiles method*

One way to deal with the "large number of attributes" issue is to present a number of profiles on a reduced number of attributes; this method is called partial profiles, first introduced by Johnson (1974). This method does reduce the respondent burden but it involves some kind of imputation of values of missing attributes as additional partial profiles are presented to a respondent. This problem is tackled by Bradlow, Hu, and Ho (2004), who develop a learning-based method of imputing missing attribute levels in partial conjoint profiles. The method is based on the premise (and empirical finding) that respondents learn to impute missing levels of the attributes over the course of the conjoint task. Further, the relative importance of their attribute part-worths can shift when they evaluate these partial profiles, suggesting that intrinsic part-worths (and hence preferences) can be influenced by the conjoint task and are thus sensitive to the order in which the profiles are presented. Additionally, the respondent's learning process can be further influenced by manipulating the prior information they have about the product category. To explain the imputation model behind the proposed method, some illustrative notation is needed. Suppose there are H respondents (denoted by $i = 1, \ldots, H$) in the (ratings-based) conjoint experiment. Each respondent rates T product profiles (denoted by $M_i(t)$, $t = 1, \ldots, T$), each product profile has J attributes (denoted by $j = 1, \ldots, J$) and each attribute j has two levels, with attribute level $x_{ij}(t) = 1$ or 0. Respondent i's rating for profile $M_i(t)$ is given by $y_i(t)$. The model assumes that each respondent does not ignore a missing attribute level but constructs an imputed value for it based on some prior information. If $x'_{ij}(t)$ denotes this imputed value and I is the indicator variable, then:

$$x'_{ij}(t) = \begin{cases} x_{ij}(t) & \text{if } r_{ij}(t) = 1 \\ Ix_{ij}(t) & \text{if } r_{ij}(t) = 0 \end{cases}.$$

Estimation of the part-worths of the attributes is done via the following regression:

$$y_i(t) = \alpha_i + \sum_{j=1}^{J} [\beta'_{ij}x'_{ij}(t) + \beta'_{ij}x_{ij}(t)] + \varepsilon_i(t).$$

One advantage of the proposed method is that it can infer not only missing attribute levels from prior levels presented of the same attribute, but from prior levels of other attributes as well. (See the comments by Alba and Cooke (2004) and Rao (2004) on this approach, who suggest opportunities for future research in incorporating behavioral inference processes in descriptive CA models.)

3.4.4 *Self-explicated methods*

In contrast, the compositional approach based on the multi-attribute attitude models (see Wilkie and Pessemier, 1973 for a broader discussion) estimates preferences from judged values of the components (importances and desirabilities) that contribute to preference. In the compositional approach, individuals are asked to evaluate the desirability of each level of all the attributes as well as the relative importances assigned to the attributes. Then, the preference for any product concept is estimated as a weighted sum of the desirabilities for the specific levels of attributes describing that concept; the weights are the relative importances. This approach is called the "self-explicated" method (see Green and Srinivasan, 1978, for more details). Studies have shown that the self-explicated method is surprisingly quite robust (Srinivasan and Park, 1997). More recently, Netzer and Srinivasan

(2011) developed an adaptive self-explicated method for handling a large number of attributes in this approach and showed impressive results.

3.4.5 *Hybrid methods*

Hybrid methods have been developed to deal with the problem of handling large number of attributes (and levels) in a conjoint study. This problem was tackled by combining the two approaches of the self-explicated method and the full profile approach.

Essentially, the hybrid approach involves two phases. In Phase I, the respondent is asked to provide data on attribute desirabilities and attribute importances in a manner quite similar to the self-explicated approach. In Phase II, the respondent is given a limited number of profiles for evaluation rather than administering all profiles as done in a full profile approach. The limited number of profiles administered is drawn from a master design, constructed according to an orthogonal main effects plan or some other experimental design. The final estimation of part-worth functions in this approach is at the level of a subgroup. The software needs to be tailor-made specific to the situation on hand. While this approach originally meant for estimating conjoint parameters at the subgroup-level, methods are now available estimating parameters at the individual level for the hybrid approach (see Green and Krieger (1996)). The reader may refer to Akaah and Korgaonkar (1983) for a comprehensive empirical comparison of several ratings-based methods with the general conclusion that traditional (full profile) and hybrid methods outperform other methods (such as the self-explicated methods).

3.5 Choice-based methods

One significant development in conjoint methodology is the use of data on stated choices elicited under hypothetical scenarios that mimic the marketplace and the possibility of estimating part-worth functions from such data using primarily multinomial logit methods; these methods are labeled choice-conjoint methods (CBCA or CBC), and have become popular in the early 1990s and are now probably the most widely used methods. As noted earlier, these methods are based on behavioral theory of random utility maximization. There are four methods under this category, which cover a wide range of variants: (i) stated choice methods; (ii) adaptive CBC methods; (iii) upgrading methods; and (iv) barter conjoint methods. Even though the data collection methods vary, the analysis tends to use Bayesian approaches. The Bayesian CBC method has achieved prominence due to a number of factors such as sound theoretical basis, availability of software for collecting and analyzing data and increasing familiarity of researchers with this approach (despite the need for some statistical sophistication in using these methods). The general shift toward choice-based methods is likely to persist due the same reasons.

3.5.1 *Stated choice methods*

The paper by Louviere and Woodworth (1983) introduced these methods to marketing researchers, which are designed to collect choice data that are consistent with random utility theory-based choice models. They have the advantage of simulating choices that are made in a way very similar to the actual marketplace choices. Rather than collecting evaluations on hypothetical attribute profiles and estimating utility models to predict choices for new products as in the ratings-based approaches, this approach collects stated choice data directly and develops a model giving the probability of choice of an alternative in terms of a set of attributes and their respective attribute levels. To emulate the idea that individuals make choices in the marketplace among a subset of products, this approach involves presenting several choice sets of hypothetical profiles, each set consisting of a few product profiles described by a finite number of attributes.

A major advantage of this method is that it deals with choices rather than ratings for measuring preferences. Standard statistical methods such as the multinomial logit can be employed for analyzing choice conjoint data at the aggregate level or at the subgroup level. More recently, advanced methods using HB techniques enable estimation of parameters at the individual level (Allenby *et al.*, 1995). Details of these HB methods are quite similar to those described above for the ratings approaches except that the choice variable is the outcome of a probability function. In all these analyses, interactions among attributes can be included if deemed necessary.

It is important to stress that CBC methods provide additional advantages such as the ability to value brand-based attributes, an ability to assess competitive effects on choice, an ability to assess price sensitivity to price differences, and ease in using the estimated model to predict real marketplace choices. The disadvantages of this method are that the design of a CBC study is far more complex due to the intricacies of generating an "efficient" series of choice sets. The OPTEX procedure in the SAS system developed by Kuhfeld (2000) can be also be a good solution. Also, some respondents may find making a choice within some choice sets to be difficult.

An issue in the data collection in conjoint studies (in general and in CBC studies in particular) is whether respondents experience strong incentives to expend their cognitive resources (or devote adequate time and effort) in providing responses (ratings or choices) to hypothetical stimuli presented as profiles or in choice sets. The literature on experimental economics suggests that data collected without such incentive-compatibility may be inconsistent, erratic, and possibly, untrustworthy. Incentive compatibility can be implemented using the BDM procedures (Becker, DeGroot, and Marschak, 1964). In a recent paper, Ding, Grewal, and Liechty (2005) provide experimental evidence to strongly indicate that conjoint choice data collected which are incentive-aligned[10] outperform those without such alignment in terms of out-of-sample predictive power. Wertenbroch and Skiera (2002) also show that willingness to buy estimates for products using contingent evaluation procedures are lower when the incentive-compatibility constraint is not imposed. This stream of research has obvious implications for collecting conjoint data in practice. See Ding (2007) for a more complete discussion of a truth-telling mechanism for conjoint applications.

As noted earlier, the MNL method with several enhancements is the workhorse for analyzing the stated choice data. In this method, several issues such as heterogeneity for scale of the error term and the parameters of the model need to be carefully addressed; readers should consult the recent paper by Fiebig *et al.* (2010) for these technical matters.

Similar to the ratings methods, DeSarbo, Ramaswamy, and Cohen (1995) developed latent class models for CBC data. Their model for

---

[10]One should note that for some contexts, incentive-alignment is not easy to accomplish; for example, consider a conjoint study in which hypothetical movies are evaluated.

the probability of a respondent choosing jth product profile in a choice set C_n is:

$$P(j \in C_n) = \sum_{g=1}^{G} \alpha_g P_g(j \in C_n); \quad \text{where } 0 < \alpha_g < 1; \text{ and } \sum \alpha_g = 1.$$

The probability of a respondent choosing jth item in the choice set C_n is given by:

$$P_g(j \in C_n) = \frac{\exp\left(\beta_{0jg} + \sum_{k=1}^{K} X_{jk}\beta_{kg}\right)}{\sum_{a \in C_n} \exp\left(\beta_{0ag} + \sum_{k=1}^{K} X_{ak}\beta_{kg}\right)},$$

where the β_s-parameters represent the intercept and coefficients for the X-attributes (K variables) specific to the G groups (or latent classes). The authors estimate this model using maximum likelihood methods. As before, the number of groups is determined using various fit criteria such as AIC. Their empirical application for a major packed-foods firm shows that the latent class model offers benefits in identifying segments, not generally feasible in the CBC analysis (which is essentially an aggregated analysis).

3.5.2 *Adaptive CBC methods*

Johnson (1987, 1991) had developed adaptive CBC methods (similar to those for the adaptive ratings-based methods) and these were implemented in the Sawtooth Software under the CBC software (Orme, 2006). Toubia, Hauser, and Simester (2004) developed polyhedral methods for CBC analysis and for adaptive CBC analysis. These methods involve designing questions that quickly reduce the sets of part-worths that are consistent with the respondent's prior choices using the interior point algorithms and estimating part-worth values. The authors conduct several simulations that suggest that the polyhedral question design does well in many domains, particularly when the part-worth values are heterogeneous; they also present an empirical application for the design of executive programs. The authors have recently extended this approach to probabilistic polyhedral methods (see Toubia, Hauser, and Garcia, 2007). The predictive validity with the polyhedral approaches is somewhat mixed.

3.5.3 *Upgrading methods*

The upgrading method (Park, Ding, and Rao, 2008) is a new web-based method that collects incentive-aligned conjoint data. This method combines the merits of the conjoint approaches of self-explicated method and choice-based method. Briefly, the upgrading method first endows a subject with a product profile and a budget, and allows her to upgrade it, one attribute at a time, to a more desirable product configuration. During the process, she states her bid or willingness to pay (WTP) for each potential upgrade (or more desirable levels of an attribute) she is interested in. Subsequent application of the BDM procedure (Becker, DeGroot, and Marschak, 1964) ensures that it is in the best interest of a subject to state truthfully her WTP. Each subject will receive her upgraded product after the rounds of upgrading by the end of the study. The authors have implemented this procedure on the Web in an empirical implementation with digital cameras. They analyze the data collected using Bayesian methods to come up with WTP estimates for each attribute using a random-coefficients HB logit model, similar to the model specified by Allenby, Arora, and Ginter (1995). Their model for the probability that the ith subject chooses the kth alternative from the jth pair (including the profiles before and after the upgrading auction) is:

$$p_{ij}^k = \frac{\exp\left(\beta_i^T x_{ij}^k\right)}{\sum_l \exp\left(\beta_i^T x_{ij}^l\right)},$$

where x_{ij}^k (including an intercept and bid amount where applicable) describes the kth digital camera by the ith subject from the jth pair, and β_i is a vector of the part-worths for the ith subject. The authors assume a hierarchical shrinkage specification for the individual part-worths, where a priori, $\beta_i \sim N(\bar{\beta}, \Lambda)$. This specification allows for individual-level part-worth estimates β_i but still permits estimation of the aggregate or average part-worth $\bar{\beta}$, as well as of the amount of heterogeneity (Λ). They assume average bids for each attribute level as slightly informative but use vague priors to ensure proper posteriors but also allow the data to primarily govern the inferences. They assess the convergence properties of the Markov Chain Monte Carlo analysis to ensure that the algorithm converged properly. They demonstrate that this procedure significantly improves the predictive validity compared to self-explicated methods for in-sample and holdout prediction tasks for hypothetical and actual product profiles.

3.5.4 *Barter conjoint methods*

Ding, Park, and Bradlow (2009) developed an interesting method for collecting conjoint data from individuals, which enables reduction of "wear-out" and uses a natural way people trade with each other. This approach called "Barter Conjoint Method" collects a large amount of data from any individual and enables exchange of information among participants in a natural environment. Very briefly, this method involves endowing each respondent in a sample with a product profile and allowing him or her to make an offer to exchange the endowed profile, revealing this information of offers made, responses to the offers and allowing each individual in the sample (or market) to acquire a final product (using simulated/random market mechanisms). The authors conducted experiments to demonstrate this method and showed significant improvements in predictive validity relative to the incentive-aligned choice-based conjoint (CBC) method.

In the choice-conjoint methods, the respondent is given a number of choice sets, each choice set consisting of a small number (typically 4 or 5) profiles and is asked to indicate which profile will be chosen.

One notable development is the use of HB estimation methods which enable an analyst to incorporate prior knowledge in the part-worth values as monotonic or other types of order constraints in the estimation process (Allenby, Arora, and Ginter, 1995) (see also Lenk *et al.* (1996)). Further, part-worth functions are estimated at the aggregate (or subgroup) level or at an individual level. Researchers have also used finite mixture methods (DeSarbo *et al.*, 1992) to "uncover" segments of respondents based on the preference or choice data collected in conjoint studies; see also Andrews, Ansari, and Currim (2002). The variety of recently developed techniques for estimation of part-worth functions is very impressive and is beyond the scope of this chapter. For a recent discussion of conjoint methods see Hauser and Rao (2004) and Rao (2008).

3.6 Applications

Since its introduction, conjoint methods have been applied in a large number of applied marketing research projects. There is no recent estimate of the number of applied studies but one may conjecture that its use is increasing tremendously. The conjoint methodology has been applied in several areas; these include consumer nondurable products (bar soaps, carpet cleaners, lawn chemicals etc.), industrial goods (copying machines, portable computer terminals, personal computer design etc.), other products (car batteries, ethical drugs, pesticides, etc.), financial services (branch bank services, auto insurance policies, credit card features etc.), transportation (domestic airlines, electric car design etc.), and other services (hotel design, car rental agencies, telephone pricing etc.). The method has been applied successfully for tackling several marketing decisions such as optimal design of new products, target market selection, pricing a new product, and studying competitive reactions. Some highprofile applications of these techniques include the development of Courtyard Hotels by Marriott (Wind *et al.*, 1989) and the design of the E-Z Pass Electronic Toll Collection System in New Jersey and neighboring States in the US (Green, Krieger, and Vavra, 1997). A significant advantage of the conjoint method has been the ability to answer various "what if" questions using market simulators; these simulators are based on the results of an analysis of conjoint data collected on hypothetical and real choice alternatives.

3.7 Some recent developments

At the risk of omitting some, the following eight developments[11] in CA seem significant:

(1) *Shift from ratings-based methods to CBC methods*: It is becoming quite common to utilize CBC analysis in most situations; this is due to various reasons including the appeal of dealing with choice rather than preference. Even when one deals with preference data, it becomes necessary to convert utility estimates into probability of choice. This step is essentially eliminated in the choice-based methods. However, the choice-based methods may not have the same flexibility as ratings-based methods.

(2) *Shift from regression methods to HB regression methods*: Independent of which approach is used for collecting conjoint data (ratings or choices), there is a trend to utilize HB methods for estimation. As

---

[11]This section draws from Rao V. R. (2008). Developments in conjoint analysis, in B. Wierenga, ed., *Handbook of marketing decisions models*, Springer.

we have seen, the HB methods enable incorporating heterogeneity and yield individual-level estimates of part-worths.

(3) *Tendency to utilize ACA methods*: Given the availability of commercial software for implementing CA, applied studies in industry seem to utilize adaptive conjoint methods.[12] An example of such software is available from Sawtooth Software (http://www.sawtoothsoftware.com).

(4) *Beginnings of multi-period (dynamic) conjoint studies*: As CA is used for a diversity of problems, the issue of understanding dynamics of consumer choice behavior will become significant. The idea of estimating demand for new products even before they diffuse in the marketplace becomes important for both practice and research. The concepts of information acceleration can be utilized for such estimation problems. It is at least in this context that the dynamic conjoint studies will become extremely essential.

(5) *Shift from focus on prediction to focus on understanding of choice process*: The primary focus in CA has so far been on developing models and procedures that enhance predictive ability. As noted in the discussion on partial profiles, there is some shift toward incorporating some postulates of choice process. This shift is expected to become more significant as conjoint modelers begin to incorporate learnings from behavioral research on information processing and choice. This writer also thinks that such a shift will be highly worthwhile.

(6) *Pragmatic approaches to theoretically sound methods (e.g., incentive-aligned)*: Despite the fact that the origins of CA were in the axiomatic development of conjoint measurement, current practice seems to have largely been on developing pragmatic approaches for data collection and estimation. However, recent trends indicate that conjoint

---

[12]The adaptive conjoint analysis (ACA) approach involves presenting two profiles that are as nearly equal as possible in estimated utility measured on a metric scale and developing new pairs of profiles sequentially as a respondent provides response to previous questions. There has been considerable amount of research on this approach. In a recent paper, Hauser and Toubia (2005) found that the result of the metric utility balance used in ACA leads to part-worth estimates to be biased due to endogeneity. The authors also found that these biases are of the order of response errors and suggest alternatives to metric utility balance to deal with this issue. See also, Liu, Otter, and Allenby (2007) who suggest using the likelihood principle in estimation to deal with the endogeneity bias in general.

researchers are concerned about theoretical bases of the data collected in conjoint studies. An example of this is the development of incentive-aligned methods for data collection. This trend will continue and future data collection efforts will begin to incorporate assumptions normally made to develop consumer utility functions (e.g., budget constraints and separability).

(7) *Simpler models to richer methods and models*: The trend toward technically advanced methods of estimation and data collection is here to stay. In particular, the HB methods will continue to be part of the standard arsenal of a conjoint analyst.

(8) *Mainly product design domain to varied domains*: A dominant application of CA has been product/service design. The methods are now being applied to a varied set of domains such as tourism, health care, corporate acquisitions and the like. This trend is likely to continue.

3.8 Future outlook

In one sentence, CA is alive, well, and growing. The preceding discussion of recent trends is an indication of the potential future for CA. Theory and practice have exploded to address a myriad of issues.[13] As this field continues to be vibrant for many years to come, new challenges will appear. Several researchers in CA have identified new research directions in this thriving methodology of CA.

In addition to the HB methods for data analysis, there have been several developments; these include methods for dealing with a positive part-function for price (Rao and Sattler, 2003), and modeling choices for bundles (Bradlow and Rao, 2000; Chung and Rao, 2003), experimental designs based on new criteria such as utility balance (Huber and Zwerina, 1996; Hauser and Toubia, 2005), continuous CA (Wittink and Keil, 2003; Su and Rao, 2006), and measuring reservation prices (WTP) for single products and bundles (Jedidi and Zhang, 2002; Jedidi et al., 2003). These are but only a few examples of continuous developments in CA research.

There have been papers that identify ideas for future research in this methodology; these include Netzer et al. (2008), Hauser and Rao

---

[13] See also the forthcoming book, Rao, V.R. (2014). *Applied conjoint analysis*, Springer.

(2004), Bradlow (2005), and Rao (2008). Broadly, there are three types of challenges: (i) pragmatic issues involve an analysis of trade-offs between complexity of method, cost, and managerial application; (ii) conceptual issues relate to the development of suitable conjoint models that include roles of price, diffusion of information on attributes, competition, and behavioral processes; (iii) methodological issues involve the development of newer methods of data collection and estimation. Further, future conjoint studies will go beyond individual or organizational consumers and be employed for other stakeholder groups, such as stockholders, employees, suppliers, and governmental organizations. In conclusion, one might say that CA is alive and well!

References

Akaah, I. P. and P. K. Korgaonkar (1983). An empirical comparison of the predictive validity of self-explicated, huber-hybrid, traditional conjoint, and hybrid conjoint models, *Journal of Marketing Research*, 20(May), 187–97.

Alba, J. W. and A. D. J. Cooke (2004). When absence begets inference in conjoint analysis, *Journal of Marketing Research*, 41(November), 382–387.

Allenby, G. M., N. Arora, and J. L. Ginter (1995). Incorporating prior knowledge into the analysis of conjoint studies, *Journal of Marketing Research*, 37(May), 152–162.

Andrews, R. L., A. Ansari, and I. Currim (2002). Hierarchical Bayes versus finite mixture conjoint analysis models: A comparison of fit, prediction, and part-worth recovery, *Journal of Marketing Research*, 39(February), 87–98.

Becker, G. M., M. H. DeGroot, and J. Marschak (1964). Measuring utility by a single-response sequential method, *Behavioral Science*, 9(July), 226–232.

Ben-Akiva, M. and S. R. Lerman (1991). *Discrete choice analysis*, Cambridge, MA: MIT Press.

Bradlow, E. T. (2005). Current issues and a 'Wish List' for conjoint analysis, *Applied Stochastic Models in Business and Industry*, 21, 319–323.

Bradlow, E. T. and V. R. Rao (2000). A hierarchical Bayes model for assortment choice, *Journal of Marketing Research*, 37(May), 259–268.

Bradlow, E. T., Y. Hu, and T.-H. Ho (2004). A learning-based model for imputing missing levels in partial conjoint profiles, *Journal of Marketing Research*, 41(November), 369–338 and 392–396.

Carroll, J. D. (1973). Models and algorithms for multidimensional scaling, conjoint measurement, and related techniques, in P. E. Green and Y. Wind, eds.,

Multiattribute decisions in marketing, Hinsdale, IL: Dryden Press, pp. 335–337 and 341–348.

Carroll, J. D. and P. E. Green (1995). Psychometric methods in marketing research, Part I: Conjoint analysis, *Journal of Marketing Research*, 32(November), 385–391.

Chung, J. and V. R. Rao (2003). A general choice model for bundles with multiple category products: Application to market segmentation and optimal pricing for bundles, *Journal of Marketing Research*, 40(May), 115–130.

Corstjens, M. and D. A. Gautschi (1983). Formal choice models in marketing, *Marketing Science*, 2(Winter), 19–56.

DeSarbo, W. S. and V. R. Rao (1986). A constrained unfolding methodology for product Positioning, *Marketing Science*, 5(Winter), 1–19.

DeSarbo, W. S., V. Ramaswamy, and S. H. Cohen (1995). Market segmentation with choice-based conjoint analysis, *Marketing Letters*, 6(2), 137–147.

DeSarbo, W. S., M. Wedel, M. Vriens, and V. Ramaswamy (1992). Latent class metric conjoint analysis, *Marketing Letters*, 3(3), 273–288.

Ding, M. (2007). An incentive-aligned mechanism for conjoint analysis, *Journal of Marketing Research*, 44(May), 214–223.

Ding, M., R. Grewal, and J. Liechty (2005). Incentive aligned conjoint analysis, *Journal of Research*, 42(February), 67–82.

Ding, M., Y.-H. Park, and E. T. Bradlow (2009). Barter markets for conjoint analysis, *Management Science*, 55(6) (June), 1003–1017.

Farquhar, P. H. and V. R. Rao (1976). A balance model for evaluating subsets of multiattributed items, *Management Science*, 22(January), 528–539.

Fiebig, D. G., M. P. Keane, J. Louviere, and N. Wasi (2010). The generalized multinomial logit model: Accounting for scale and coefficient heterogeneity, *Marketing Science*, 29(3) (May–June), 393–421.

Green, P. E. (1974). On the design of choice experiments involving multifactor alternatives, *Journal of Consumer Research*, 1(September), 61–68.

Green, P. E. (1984). Hybrid models for conjoint analysis: An expository review, *Journal of Marketing Research*, 21(May), 155–169.

Green, P. E. and A. M. Krieger (1996). Individualized hybrid models for conjoint analysis, *Management Science*, 42(June), 850–867.

Green, P. E. and V. R. Rao (1971). Conjoint measurement for quantifying judgmental data, *Journal of Marketing Research*, 8(August), 355–363.

Green, P. E. and V. R. Rao (1972). *Applied multidimensional scaling: A comparison of alternative approaches and algorithms*, New York: Holt, Rinehart and Winston, Inc.

Green, P. E. and V. R. Rao (1977). Nonmetric approaches to multivariate analysis marketing, in J. N. Sheth, ed., *Multivariate methods for market and survey research*, Chicago, IL: American Marketing Association.

Green, P. E. and V. Srinivasan (1978). Conjoint analysis in consumer research: Issues and outlook, *Journal of Consumer Research*, 5(September), 103–123.

Green, P. E. and V. Srinivasan (1990). Conjoint analysis in marketing: New developments with implications for research and practice, *Journal of Marketing*, 54(October), 3–19.

Green, P. E. and Y. Wind (1973). *Multiattribute decisions in marketing*, Hinsdale, IL: Dryden Press.

Green, P. E. and Y. Wind (1975). New way to measure consumers' judgments, *Harvard Business Review*, 53(July–August), 107–117.

Green, P. E., A. M. Krieger, and M. K. Agarwal (1991). Adaptive conjoint analysis: Some caveats and suggestions, *Journal of Marketing Research*, 28(May), 215–222.

Green, P. E., A. M. Krieger, and T. G. Vavra (1997). Evaluating new products, *Marketing Research*, 9(Winter) 12–19.

Green, P. E., A. M. Krieger, and Y. Wind (2001). Thirty years of conjoint analysis: reflections and prospects, *Interfaces*, 31(May–June), S56–S73.

Greene, W. H. (2012). *Econometric Analysis*, 7th edn., Boston: Prentice-Hall.

Hauser, J. R. and V. R. Rao (2004). Conjoint analysis, related modeling, and applications, in Yorum Wind and Paul E. Green, eds., *Marketing research and modeling: progress and prospects: A tribute to Paul E. Green*, Norwell, MA: Kluwer Academic Publishers.

Hauser, J. R. and O. Toubia (2005). The impact of utility balance and endogeneity in conjoint analysis, *Marketing Science*, 24(3), 498–507.

Huber, J. and K. Zwerina (1996). On the importance of utility balance in efficient designs, *Journal of Marketing Research*, 33(August), 307–317.

Huber, J. and N. Klein (1991). Adapting cut-offs to the choice environment: The effects of attribute correlation and reliability, *Journal of Consumer Research*, 18(December), 346–357.

Jedidi, K. and Z. J. Zhang (2002). Augmenting conjoint analysis to estimate consumer reservation price, *Management Science*, 48(10), 1350–1368.

Jedidi, K., S. Jagpal, and P. Manchanda (2003). Measuring heterogeneous reservation prices for product bundles, *Marketing Science*, 22(1), 107–130.

Johnson, R. M. (1974). Trade-off analysis of consumer values, *Journal of Marketing Research*, 11(May), 121–127.

Johnson, R. M. (1987). Adaptive conjoint analysis, Sawtooth Software Conference on Perceptual Mapping, Conjoint Analysis, and Computer Interviewing, Ketchum, ID: Sawtooth Software, Inc., 253–265.

Johnson, R. M. (1991). Comment on adaptive conjoint analysis: Some caveats and suggestions, *Journal of Marketing Research*, 28(May), 223–225.

Krantz, D. H., R. D. Luce, P. Suppes, and A. Tversky (1971). *Foundations of measurement Volume I: Additive and polynomial representations*, New York and London: Academic Press.

Kuhfeld, W. F. (2000). Experimental design, efficiency, coding, and choice designs. Chapter (TS-722C). Available at: https://support.sas.com/techsup/tnote_stat.htm;#market.

Lenk, P. J., W. S. DeSarbo, P. E. Green, and M. R. Young (1996). Hierarchical Bayes conjoint analysis: Recovery of part-worth heterogeneity from reduced experimental designs, *Marketing Science*, 15(2), 173–191.

Liu Q., T. Otter, and G. M. Allenby (2007). Investigating endogeneity bias in marketing, *Marketing Science*, 26(September/October), 642–650.

Louviere, J. J. and G. J. Gaeth (1987). Decomposing the determinants of retail facility choice using the method of hierarchical information integration: A supermarket illustration, *Journal of Retailing*, 63, 25–48.

Louviere, J. J. and G. Woodworth (1983). Design and analysis of simulated choice or allocated experiments: An approach based on aggregated data, *Journal of Marketing Research*, 20(November), 350–467.

Louviere J. J., D. A. Hensher, and J. Swait (2000). *Stated Choice Methods*, Cambridge, New York: Cambridge University Press.

Luce, D. and J. Tukey (1964). Simultaneous conjoint measurement: A new type of fundamental measurement, *Journal of Mathematical Psychology*, 1(1964), 1–27.

McFadden, D. (1974). Conditional logit analysis of qualitative choice behavior, in P. Zarembka, ed., *Frontiers in econometrics*, New York: Academic Press, pp. 105–142.

McFadden, D. (1986). The choice theory approach to market research, *Marketing Science*, 5(4), 275–297.

Netzer, O. and V. Srinivasan (2009). Adaptive self-explication of multi-attribute preferences, *Journal of Marketing Research*, 48(February), 140–156.

Netzer, O., O. Toubia, E. T. Bradlow, E. Dahan, T. Evgeniou, F. M. Feinberg, E. M. Feit, S. K. Hui, J. Johnson, J. C. Liechty, J. B. Orlin, and V. R. Rao (2008). Beyond conjoint analysis: Advances in preference measurement, *Marketing Letters*, 19(December), 337–354.

Orme, B. (2006). *Getting started with conjoint analysis: Strategies for product design and pricing research*, Madison, WI: Research Publishers LLC.

Park, Y.-H., M. Ding, and V. R. Rao (2008). Eliciting preference for complex products: A web-based upgrading method, *Journal of Marketing Research*, 45(November), 562–574.

Rao, V. R. (1976). Conjoint measurement in marketing analysis, in J. N. Sheth, ed., *Multivariate methods in market and survey research*, Chicago: American Marketing Association.

Rao, V. R. (2004). Comments on conjoint analysis with partial profiles, *Journal of Marketing Research*, 41(November), 388–389.

Rao, V. R. (2008). Developments in conjoint analysis, in B. Wierenga, ed., *Handbook of Marketing Decision Models*, Springer, 23–55.

Rao, V. R. and H. Sattler (2003). Measurement of price effects with conjoint analysis: Separating informational and allocative effects of price, in A. Gustafsson, A. Herrmann and F. Huber, eds., *Conjoint Measurement: Methods and Applications*, 3rd edn., Berlin: Springer.

Rossi, P. E., G. M. Allenby, and R. McCulloch (2005). *Bayesian statistics and marketing*, West Sussex, England: John Wiley & Sons Ltd.

Srinivasan, V. and C. S. Park (1997). Surprising robustness of self-explicated approach to customer preference structure measurement, *Journal of Marketing Research*, 34(2), 286–291.

Srinivasan, V. and A. D. Shocker (1973). Linear programming techniques for multidimensional analysis of preferences, *Psychometrika*, 38, 337–369.

Su, M. and V. R. Rao (2006). A continuous conjoint analysis for preannounced new products with evolutional attributes, Working Paper, Johnson School, Cornell University.

Thurstone, L. (1927). A law of comparative judgment, *Psychological Review*, 34, 273–286.

Toubia, O., J. R. Hauser and R. Garcia (2007). Probabilistic polyhedral methods for adaptive choice-based conjoint analysis: Theory and application, *Marketing Science*, 26(5) (September–October), 596–610.

Toubia, O., J. R. Hauser, and D. I. Simester (2004). Polyhedral methods for adaptive conjoint analysis, *Journal of Marketing Research*, 42(February), 116–131.

Toubia, O., D. I. Simester, J. R. Hauser, and E. Dahan (2003). Fast polyhedral adaptive conjoint estimation, *Marketing Science*, 22(3), 273–303.

Wertenbroch, K. and B. Skiera (2002). Measuring consumers' willingness to pay at the point of purchase, *Journal of Marketing Research*, 39(May), 228–241.

Wilkie, W. and E. A. Pessemier (1973). Issues in marketing's use of multi-attribute attitude models, *Journal of Marketing Research*, 10(4) (November), 428–441.

Wind, Y., P. E. Green, D. Shifflet, and M. Scarbrough (1989). Courtyard by Marriott: Designing a hotel with consumer-based marketing, *Interfaces*, 19(January–February), 25–47.

Wittink, D. R. and S. K. Keil (2003). Continuous conjoint analysis, in Gustafsson, Anders, Andreas Herrmann and Frank Huber, eds., *Conjoint measurement: Methods and applications*, 3rd edn., Berlin: Springer, pp. 541–564.

Chapter 4

Innovation Diffusion

Eitan Muller

4.1 Introduction

Innovation diffusion has recently been defined as:

> The process of the market penetration of new products and services, which is driven by social influences. Such influences include all the interdependencies among consumers that affect various market players with or without their explicit knowledge.[1]

As a field in marketing innovation, diffusion began with Frank Bass's 1969 paper, and — as the author often mentioned in private communications — was largely ignored until criticized by Bernhardt and Mackenzie in 1972, who were "skeptical about (its) immediate practical value." Refinements of the Bass model began shortly thereafter by Dodson and Muller (1978); Horsky and Simon (1983); and Peterson and Mahajan (1978); and the first review paper was published in 1979 by Mahajan and Muller, having been rewritten thrice since then.

A representative genealogy is presented in Figure 4.1, describing the main advances in the field, partitioned into issues and methodology. The main issues investigated involved successive generations of a base technology; inclusion of decision variables and their optimal allocation; international and cross-country diffusion; and the effect of competition at the brand level on the diffusion of new products. In terms of methodology,

---

[1]This chapter refers to and extends the manuscripts by Muller, Peres, and Mahajan (2009) and Peres, Muller, and Mahajan (2010).

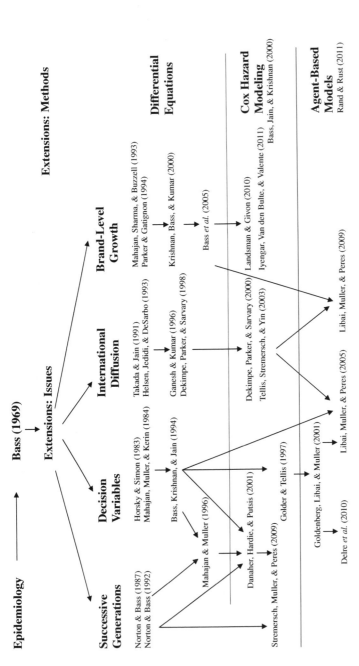

Fig. 4.1   Innovation diffusion representative genealogy*

*A vertical line such as the one leading from Norton and Bass (1992) to Stremersch, Muller, and Peres (2009) implies that both deal with the same issue (successive generations) and that the latter directly relied on the former for its conceptual, theoretical, modeling, and/or empirical aspects. Two diagonal lines such as the ones leading to Danaher, Hardie, and Putsis (2001) imply that the latter paper deals with both issues of the preceding papers, in this case with decision variables in successive generations of a base technology. The figure is representative in that in each case, one or two papers are chosen as representative(s) of a much larger body of research. A full genealogy is of course not feasible given the thousands of citations of the Bass paper and the hundreds in marketing journals.

early papers used the tools of differential equations almost exclusively. While elegant and simple, differential equations gave way to more flexible modeling methods, both empirical and simulation, e.g., Cox (proportional) hazard models and agent-based models. Referring to Figure 4.1, Sec. 4.2 describes the evolution of the field, while Sec. 4.3 tries to identify promising future directions for innovation diffusion.

4.2   The evolution of innovation diffusion research

Under the assumption that the Bass model is sufficiently known (in 2004, it was chosen as one of the 10 most influential papers in *Management Science*'s first 50 years (see Bass, 2004)), this chapter will concentrate on its extensions.

4.2.1 *Successive generations*

While the basic Bass diffusion process terminates when all consumers in the specified market potential have bought the product, the reality is that old products are substituted with newer generations, and so consumers do not stop purchasing, but instead upgrade to a new generation of the same base technology. The first to deal with generational substitution was Frank Bass (1987) in a paper he wrote together with one of his doctoral students, John Norton. The model therein assumed that sales are proportional to cumulative adoption, and while the first-generation growth follows a simple Bass model, the second comprises new adopters and upgraders. In this paper as well as its (1992) extension, Norton and Bass showed that the model performs best under the assumption that the growth parameters (p and q of the Bass model) are constant across generations, while market potential grows. These assumptions caused a lively debate on two aspects of the model. First, the fact that sales are proportional to cumulative adoption implies that the product in question is a repeat-purchase product or a service, but not a durable. Thus, later efforts such as that of Mahajan and Muller (1996) were aimed at durables, while others, such as that of Kim, Chang, and Shocker (2000) extended the model where it applied to services.

The assumption of equal growth parameters across generations has practical importance for forecasting, as projections regarding the growth of advanced generations of a product must often be made during the early stages of product penetration or before launch, and are thus based on using diffusion parameters from previous generations. Theoretically, this matter is important, since it deals with dependency within a sequence of diffusion processes and, more broadly, with rigidity of the social system across generations. Does the social system learn to improve its adoption skills across generations, or does it begin each diffusion process a new? If it has learning capabilities, how strong and how category-specific are they?

As Stremersch, Muller, and Peres (2009) pointed out, the literature offers contradicting answers to the question of whether diffusion accelerates across technology generations. The key finding (or assumption) of several studies across multiple product categories is that growth parameters are constant across technology generations (Norton and Bass, 1992, 1987; Mahajan and Muller, 1996; Kim, Chang, and Shocker, 2000). Exceptions to this premise were provided by Islam and Meade (1997) and Pae and Lehmann (2003).

Contradicting the stability of growth parameters across generations, a large body of evidence suggests that the overall temporal pattern of diffusion of innovation accelerates over time (Kohli, Lehmann, and Pae, 1999; Van den Bulte and Stremersch, 2004). A recent analysis by Van den Bulte (2000) found conclusive evidence that such acceleration does indeed occur. These two research branches form an intriguing paradox. It appears that, in the same economy, an acceleration of the diffusion of innovations over time should be reflected in acceleration of diffusion of technology generations that succeed one another; however, the diffusion rates of sequential technology generations remain constant.

A resolution to the paradox was suggested recently by Stremersch, Muller, and Peres (2009), who noted constant growth parameters across generations, yet a shorter time to take off for each successive generation. They investigated whether the faster take-off of successive generations is due to the passing of time, or to the generational effect. They defined "technology generation" as a set of products similar in customer-perceived characteristics, and "technology vintage" as the year when the first model of a specific technology generation was launched commercially. Using a discrete proportional hazard model in 12 product categories, Stremersch, Muller, and Peres found that acceleration in time to take off is due to the passing of time, and not to generational shifts. Thus, time indeed accelerates early growth, whereas generational shifts do not.

4.2.2 Decision variables

The first major paper to tackle normative issues within the Bass framework was co-authored by Dan Horsky (a doctoral student of Frank Bass) and Len Simon (1983). The issue that they investigated was simple: If the Bass model's external coefficient summarizes the firm's advertising effort, then it should be under the control of the firm. They found that if indeed the external coefficient is a concave function of advertising, then advertising declines over time. Intuition is the one that guides all normative papers on innovation diffusion: Early on, the value of adopters to the firm is higher. This is so not only due to the time value of money, but also because early adopters begin the word-of-mouth process, and the earlier they adopt, the viral chain that emanates from these adopters is longer. Thus it is worth subsidizing the early adopters in terms of an advertising blitz, lower prices, or giving the product away to a select seed of individuals.

The fact that the price is often declining in new high-tech products is due to supply-side considerations such as economies of scale, economies of scope, and learning by doing. Demand-side consideration would have a price lowest in the introductory stage of the product life cycle. This is well documented in Robinson and Lakhani (1975) — the first paper to deal with optimal pricing in the Bass framework — who showed that even in the presence of economies of scale and learning by doing, which reduced the average costs to a tenth of the original, optimal price is still increasing because it is still worth subsidizing early adopters.

The fact that the Bass model does not contain marketing mix variables raises a conceptual conflict, since the model provides a high level of fit and forecasting power even without incorporating marketing mix. Bass, Krishnan, and Jain (1994) proposed a resolution to this conflict by introducing the Generalized Bass Model (GBM) that assumes that the marketing mix variables' effect is multiplicative (i.e., both growth parameters are affected equally), and that advertising and pricing are measured as percentage change rather than absolute values. When the percentage change in price and advertising is constant, the GBM reduces to the original Bass model. Studies that compared the performance of the GBM to that of the original Bass model concluded that both models provide a similar fit (e.g., Danaher, Hardie, and Putsis, 2001). The GBM's limitations — the marketing mix variables do not influence diffusion via their absolute level but via changes in their levels — were noted later by the same authors (Bass, Jain, and Krishnan, 2000). The GBM's normative aspects were also recently criticized by Fruchter and Van den Bulte (2012).

A considerable number of normative studies on marketing mix influences have explored optimal allocations under various market conditions: While work in the 1980s dealt mainly with advertising, most work from the 1990s onwards investigates the influence of price. Additional marketing mix variables such as channels, strategies, and word-of-mouth seeding campaigns began in the 2000s.

Pricing decisions were also studied in the context of successive generations of a base technology (Padmanabhan and Bass, 1993 or Lehmann and Esteban-Bravo, 2006). In a study on the cellular industry in Europe, Danaher, Hardie, and Putsis (2001) found an interesting non-symmetrical interaction between generations in the response to price.

The power and effect of seeding strategies, including sampling and product demonstrations, were studied by Libai, Muller, and Peres (2005), and Jain, Mahajan, and Muller (1995); and more recently of seeding programs in social networks (Hinz et al., 2011).

Despite the frequent use of marketing channels in innovation marketing, the topic of diffusion through marketing channels is still under-researched. Take, for example, a typical channel model such as that used by Mesak and Darrat (2002), where the growth process is a double-diffusion model: The product has to be diffused first among retailers, and only afterwards among the final consumers. Similarly, Lehmann and Weinberg (2000) introduced technological substitution into the distribution channel. They examined the issue of sequential channels through the question of the optimal timing of the video release of a movie. Usually video release pushes box office sales down to zero; thus, there is a trade-off between an early video release, which enhances video revenues, and a later video release, which is better for box office revenues. Their empirical observation was that films are usually released to video later than optimal.

The normative issue of optimal timing was investigated in the context of technological substitution with respect to the release of a new generation. The prevailing wisdom among practitioners is that the firm should introduce the product as soon as it is available. This rule of thumb is supported by two main studies in the field, which indicate that the firm should introduce the new generations either as soon as they are available or not at all (Wilson and Norton, 1989), or at maturity of the old generation (Mahajan and Muller, 1996). Inclusion of factors such as cannibalization of market potentials and competition among brands might alter these results. Studies in the entertainment industry have investigated optimal timing of the release of a new movie (Lehmann and Weinberg, 2000; Mahajan, Muller, and Kerin 1984).

4.2.3 *International diffusion*

One of the first influential papers to deal with international diffusion was co-authored by two of Frank Bass's students, Hirokazu Takada and Dipak Jain (1991). Therein, they established what became one of the major findings to date on cross-country influences, and called it *lead–lag effect* (with few exceptions such as Elberse and Eliashberg, 2003), In other words, the entry-time lag has a positive influence on the diffusion process, i.e., countries that introduce a given innovation later show a faster diffusion process (Tellis, Stremersch, and Yin 2003; Ganesh and Kumar, 1996) and a shorter time to take off (Van Everdingen, Fok, and Stremersch, 2009).

Cross-country effects can be the result of two types of influence mechanisms: weak ties, and signals. Weak ties come from adopters in one country who communicate with non-adopters from other countries (Wuyts *et al.*, 2004). However, even without communicating with or imitating other individuals, non-adopters are influenced by diffusion in other countries. In other words, the level of acceptance of the innovation in one country acts as a *signal* for customers in other countries, reducing their perceptions of risk and increasing the legitimacy of using the new product. While several studies have stated explicitly that the dominant effect was due to communication (Putsis *et al.*, 1997), others explored the effect without relating it to a specific mechanism (e.g., Dekimpe, Parker, and Sarvary, 2000b, 2000c).

Understanding cross-country influences is also valuable in the context of normative managerial decisions in multinational markets. Some studies have explored entry strategies, i.e., the question of whether a firm should enter all its markets simultaneously (a "sprinkler" strategy), or sequentially (a "waterfall" strategy). Kalish, Mahajan, and Muller (1995) suggested that the waterfall strategy is preferred when conditions in foreign markets are unfavorable (slow growth or low innovativeness), competitive pressure is low, the lead–lag effect is high, and fixed entry costs are high. Libai, Muller, and Peres (2005) extended this question to explore responsive budgeting strategies where firms dynamically allocate their marketing efforts as per developments in the market. Many other questions still await answers, and issues such as regulation (addressed by Stremersch and Lemmens, 2009), international competition, and the optimal marketing mix of growing international markets can be further explored.

A large number of studies in the last two decades have focused on explaining inter-country differences in new product adoption. These studies generally focused on differences in the diffusion parameters p and/or q (Van den Bulte and Stremersch, 2004), time to take off (Tellis, Stremersch, and Yin, 2003), and duration of the growth stage (Stremersch and Tellis, 2004). The salient result of all these papers is that diffusion processes vary greatly among countries, even for the same products or within the same continent (Helsen, Jedidi, and DeSarbo, 1993). In addition to measuring the differences between growth processes, these studies also investigated country-specific sources that generated these differences. These underlying factors can be divided into *cultural* sources and *economic* sources.

4.2.3.1 *Cultural sources*

Cultural sources relate to the country's cultural characteristics and values. Takada and Jain (1991) found that the diffusion parameter q is higher in countries that are high-context and homophilous (such as Asian Pacific countries) relative to countries such as the US, which are low-context and heterophilous. *High-context* refers to a culture where much of the information conveyed through a communication resides in the context of the communication rather than in its explicit message; and *homophilous* implies that communication takes place among individuals who share certain characteristics. Similarly, Dekimpe, Parker, and Sarvary found — regarding cellular phones (2000b) and industrial digital telephone switches (2000c) — that population heterogeneity has a negative effect on both time to adoption and the probability of transition from non-adoption to partial or full adoption in a country. Van den Bulte and Stremersch (2004) used Hofstde's dimensions of national culture and found that the importance of word-of-mouth (relative to advertising) is higher in collectivistic cultures and in cultures with high power distance and masculine values.

4.2.3.2 *Economic sources*

The influences of many macroeconomic variables have been studied, yielding two main empirical generalizations: First, the **wealth** of the country (usually measured by gross domestic product (GDP) per capita and also by lifestyle, health status, and urbanization) has a positive influence on diffusion (Desiraju, Nair, and Chintagunta, 2004). It should be noted that wealth is not necessarily equivalent to general welfare. For example, Van den Bulte and Stremersch (2004) found a positive relationship between the Gini index for inequality and the importance of word-of-mouth. A second generalization is that **access to mass media** (usually operationalized by the penetration of TV sets) has a positive influence on the diffusion parameter p (Talukdar, Sudhir, and Ainslie, 2002; Stremersch and Tellis, 2004).

4.2.4 *Brand-level growth*

The interplay between category and brand level growth raises the question of whether competition enhances or delays category growth. Generally, competition has been found to have a positive effect on diffusion parameters (e.g., Van den Bulte and Stremersch, 2004; Dekimpe, Parker, and Sarvary, 1998). An exception was observed by Dekimpe, Parker, and Sarvary (2000c), who showed that an existing installed base of an old technology negatively affected the growth of new technologies. Krishnan, Bass, and Kumar (2000) studied the impact of late entrants on the diffusion of incumbent brands. Using data on diffusion of minivans and cellular phones in several US states, they found that the effect varied across markets. In some markets, the market potential and the internal communication parameter q increased with the entry of an additional brand, whereas in other markets, only one of these parameters increased. These studies do not provide explanations of the mechanisms underlying the acceleration. One potential explanation is that acceleration results from heavier marketing pressure on the target market. Kim, Bridges, and Srivastava (1999) implicitly suggested that the number of competitors constitutes a signal for the product's quality and long-term potential, which may result in acceleration. Alternatively, the positive effect may be a result of reduction in network externalities (Van den Bulte and Stremersch, 2004).

Constructing a brand-growth model requires discussing several conceptual issues. A basic question is the extent to which internal influence mechanisms operate at brand level. Some regard brand adoption as a two-stage process in which consumers first adopt the category, and then choose the brand (Hahn *et al.*, 1994; Givon, Mahajan, and Muller, 1995) based on factors other than internal communication such as promotion activities, price deals, and special offers. Despite the intuitive rationale of this approach, only rare attempts have been made to use it, partially because it requires high-quality, individual-level data.

The development of service markets and increased use of customer relationship management (CRM) systems by service providers can facilitate data availability and promote the use of these types of models. Landsman and Givon (2010) used banking data to investigate the growth of financial products; and Weerahandi and Dalal (1992) used business-to-business data to study fax penetration. Another approach was used by Iyengar, Van den Bulte, and Valente (2011), who investigated the growth of pharmaceuticals and noted that the adoption decision of a brand by a physician is not enough; prescription volume has to be added in order to meaningfully investigate the diffusion of a new drug.

Although the relationships between brand-level and category-level adoption have not yet been clearly identified, the main body of literature has assumed that internal dynamics are important at the brand level, and therefore, a Bass-type model can be used to model brand choice. Mapping the communications flow in the market, one can say that a potential customer adopts the focal brand as an outcome of the combination of two alternative communication paths: *within-brand communication* with adopters of the focal brand; and *cross-brand communication* with adopters of other brands. Cross-brand communication can influence a consumer's choice of a brand in two ways: The consumer may receive negative information about the competing brands; or s/he may receive information about the category from adopters of other brands and subsequently adopt the focal brand because its marketing mix is most appealing. Two studies — Parker and Gatignon (1994) and Libai, Muller, and Peres (2009a) — tried to examine systematically the distinction between within- and cross-brand communication. Measuring for consumer goods and cellular services, both studies concluded that both within-brand and cross-brand influences exist. A similar communication breakdown can be conducted vis-à-vis generic and brand advertising (Bass *et al.*, 2005).

A conceptual issue exists in the modeling of brand-level diffusion vis-à-vis market potential. Some have assumed that the diffusion process operates in separate markets in which each firm draws from its own market potential, while others have assumed that both firms compete for the same market potential. The former assumption requires careful treatment and interpretation — if we assume that the market potentials of the two brands do not overlap, then the brands do not compete for the attention and wallets of the same potential consumers. On the other hand, if we assume that the market potentials of the brands do overlap, and the total market potential is the summation of the individual potentials, then this overall market potential overestimates the true potential, since the intersections should be subtracted from the overall count. Mahajan, Sharma, and Buzzell (1993) investigated the market potential issue through Polaroid's lawsuit against Kodak, the latter having been accused of patent violation and attracting Polaroid's customers to a new brand of digital camera. By dividing the non-adopter pool into sub-pools according to the market potential of each brand, it was possible to filter out the effects of cannibalization vs. market expansion.

Within- and cross-brand influences occur even among brands that do not directly compete. Joshi, Reibstein, and Zhang (2009) consider a brand extension of a high-status market that comes up with a new, lower-status version of the product. According to that study, while the existing high-status market has a positive influence on the new market, the reciprocal social influence of the new, low-status market on the old market is negative. The example given is Porsche's entry into the SUV market. The target customers of the SUV Porsche were metrosexual males, who were negatively influenced by the profile of the category's existing adopters, i.e., suburban soccer moms.

In addition to competing for market potential, firms can compete for one another's existing customers for multi-purchase products such as services, or a combination of products and services such as hardware/software in which both defection and network externalities exist either at the category level (Goldenberg, Libai, and Muller, 2010) or at the brand level (Binken and Stremersch, 2009). Attrition and its consequences have been discussed in the CRM literature on mature markets. However, recent studies demonstrated that customer attrition can have a substantial effect on growing markets. Since most of the studies in the diffusion literature deal with durable goods, researchers have generally modeled the diffusion of services as if they were durable goods, and have not examined customer attrition. The exceptions are a few studies that attempted to incorporate churn into the diffusion framework (Hahn *et al.*, 1994; Libai, Muller, and Peres, 2009b).

4.2.5 *On methodology*

In terms of methodology, early papers used the tools of differential equations almost exclusively. While elegant and simple, differential equations gave way to more flexible modeling methods, both empirical and simulation, and included Cox (proportional) hazard models and agent-based models. There are two ways to integrate hazard modeling into innovation diffusion. The first is to reinterpret the Bass model as a hazard model by noting that the conditional probability of adoption given that the consumer has not adopted (the hazard rate) is linear in the number of previous adopters. A detailed explanation of this equivalence and how the marketing mix variables are added to the hazard model is given in Bass, Jain, and Krishnan (2000). The second way is to use the hazard model for discrete events in the product life cycle such as take-off or saddles (Golder and Tellis, 1997, 2004; Goldenberg, Libai, and Muller, 2002).

Golder and Tellis (1997) defined take-off as "the time at which a dramatic increase in sales occurs, which distinguishes the cut-off point between the introduction and growth stage of the product life cycle." The importance of take-off time to the firm is quite clear — a rapid increase in sales requires substantial investments in production, distribution, and marketing, which most often involve considerable lead time to put into place successfully. Golder and Tellis applied a proportional hazard model to data that included 31 successful innovative product categories in the US between 1898 (automobiles) and 1990 (direct broadcast satellite media). They found that the average time to take off for categories introduced after World War II was six years, and that average penetration at take-off was 1.7% of market potential. Later studies investigated factors that influence time to take off. Factors that have been found to accelerate take-off include price reduction, product category (entertainment products take off faster than do white goods), and cultural factors such as a low level of uncertainty avoidance (Tellis, Stremersch, and Yin, 2003).

While a hazard model does provide several advantages including the ability to handle data right censoring, it is still an aggregate approach, while increasingly the data are on the disaggregate level, such as data from social networks. One well-known approach for describing individual adoption decisions and tying them to aggregate outcomes is agent-based modeling. As Rand and Rust (2011) note, if one looks at new products, the patterns of growth in the market that result from the interaction of many consumers might be much more complex than the adoption rules of these individuals. The advantage of the agent-based approach is that the modeling is conducted at the individual level, and does not require knowledge of or assumptions regarding the macro-dynamics.

Agent-based models describe the market as a collection of individual units (*agents*) interacting with each other through connections (*links*). The adoption behavior of each individual unit is determined by a decision rule. Neural networks, cellular automata, and small-world models are examples of agent-based modeling techniques. A typical agent-based model is the cellular automata of Goldenberg, Libai, and Muller (2001) where the individual consumer is an agent that receives a value of "0" if it has not yet adopted the product, and "1" if it has. Potential adopters adopt due to a combination of external influences and internal influences in a pattern similar to that of the Bass framework. Network structure can vary considerably depending on the issue at hand. It can also take the form of an actual social network on which the agent-based model simulates the growth of a new product. In the last decade, agent-based models are increasingly being used in the marketing literature, particularly to examine issues related to new product growth (Garber *et al.*, 2004; Delre *et al.*, 2010). For more on agent-based modeling, its validation and verification, see Rand and Rust (2011).

4.3 What is next?

The overall economic outcomes of diffusion processes are usually measured at the aggregate level. However, marketing activities of firms often take place at the individual level and are increasingly aimed at influencing the internal dynamics of the market such as influential programs and buzz campaigns. Maximizing or even just measuring their effectiveness requires a transition from aggregate-level to individual-level perspective both in practice as well as in research. This transition appears to be the main driver in diffusion research as elaborated in this section.

The structure of the social network is the first factor taken into account when modeling individual-level decisions, since it directly influences the speed and spatial pattern of diffusion, and in turn, the firm's marketing decisions. If, for example, the social system is comprised of isolated "islands" that hardly communicate with one other, the firm should launch the product separately in each such island in order to create global diffusion; whereas for other network structures, the firm might be better off enhancing internal communications.

A notable marketing phenomenon of recent note is firms' attempts to impact their customers' word-of-mouth processes via word-of-mouth agent campaigns, referral reward programs, and viral marketing campaigns. The complex nature of word-of-mouth dynamics, including difficulties in following the spread of the effect of word-of-mouth and the lack of established ways to measure the effect, makes the financial justification for word-of-mouth programs a pressing issue, especially since such initiatives compete for resources with traditional marketing efforts.

Using agent-based modeling, along with empirical verification via actual social networks, researchers are beginning to investigate approaches to quantifying the effects of word-of-mouth seeding programs. One potential means of quantifying the value of a member in such a program is to observe and measure that individual's ripple effect, i.e., the number of others that s/he affects directly, as well as and second- and third-degree "infections". Thus far, little has been done in terms of empirically measuring the effects of such programs in general, and as regards social networks in particular.

An additional network-related issue that we believe merits more research attention is network externalities. One of the surprising findings in the empirical literature thereon is the lack of empirical evidence on individuals' adoption threshold levels. For adoption to occur in the presence of network externalities, a potential adopter has to overcome two barriers. First, the consumer has to be convinced via the communication process that the product provides good value and fit. Second, s/he must be assured that the number of other adopters is such that the network product will indeed supply its potential value, i.e., it surpasses the consumer's individual threshold level. The shape of the thresholds' distributions within a population is of utmost importance to the speed of diffusion. Given that social threshold modeling is already well grounded in the sociological literature on collective action, one would imagine that the issue of threshold distribution is by now well established. Unfortunately, this is not the case, and empirical evidence in that sense is missing.

As for technological substitution, while models for the diffusion of technology generations have been around for a while, major questions remain unanswered. The first question relates to the substitution process — according to traditional approaches, the new generation eventually replaces the older generation. However, this is no longer the case. For many products, old and new generations co-exist for a long time. In the mobile phone industry, the number of users of analog phones continued to increase long after digital technologies became available. Use of older handset types in emerging economies challenges manufacturers to cope simultaneously with multiple technology generations. The current models of technological substitution are restrictive in their treatment of the co-existence of multiple generations. They also provide little insight into other substitution issues such as leapfrog behavior, and the differences between adopter groups (e.g., new customers joining the category vs. upgraders). Moreover, generational shift at the brand level has not yet been tackled.

Current demographic changes are affecting cross-country influences and raising new challenges for global marketers. Diffusion of innovations in emerging economies is of increasing managerial interest, especially in industries such as telecommunications, where market potential in the developed world is about to approach its limit, while emerging economies present rapidly growing potential markets for innovations.

As competitive structures become complex, brand-level decision making becomes important in optimizing managerial decision making. Consider the scope of competition. Is there a single market potential from which all brands draw, or is it a reasonable working hypothesis that each brand has its own market potential? Since having a distinct market from which to draw customers implies that competitive pressures are relatively low, it would seem that when competition is intense, the common market potential hypothesis is more reasonable. Second is the question of the influence of competition along the distribution chain. In the mobile phone industry, for example, while competing service providers distribute the same handset model, third parties offer customers real-time auto-selection of the network with the best rate, so that customers use the services of multiple service providers. Extending the basic diffusion model to include both multiple layers and competition would improve descriptive and normative investigations of this matter.

Third is the still-open question regarding whether brand choice is a one- or a two-stage process. If brand choice is a two-stage process in which consumer interactions are dominant in category choice, and special offers and advertising are dominant in choosing the brand, then straightforward application of a standard diffusion model on brand-level data is problematic. Although some insights into the brand choice process will derive from behavioral studies, diffusion modeling can combine choice and individual-level decisions and estimate their relative importance at each stage. Insights from such combined models might be striking in terms of marketing mix decisions.

The fourth issue deals with the nature of consumer interactions under competition. For example, the launch of the iPhone by Apple that relied heavily on word-of-mouth communication lifted not only iPhone, but the entire smart phone industry. While the distinction between consumer interactions at the category level and the brand level has received scant attention so far, it is crucial for managing the growth process.

References

Bass, F. M. (1969). A new product growth model for consumer durable, *Management Science*, 15(1), 215–227.

Bass, F. M. (1994). Why the Bass model fits without decision variables, *Marketing Science*, 13(3), 203–223.

Bass, F. M. (2004). Comment on a new product growth model for consumer durables, *Management Science*, 50(22), 1833–1840.

Bass, F. M., T. V. Krishnan, and D. C. Jain (1994). Why the Bass model fits without decision variables, *Marketing Science*, 13(3), 203–223.

Bass, F. M., D. C. Jain, and T. V. Krishnan (2000). Modeling the marketing mix in new-product diffusion, in V. Mahajan, E. Muller, and Y. Wind, eds., *New-product diffusion models*, New York: Kluwer Academic Publishers.

Bass, F. M., A. Krishnamoorthy, A. Prasad, and S. P. Sethi (2005). Generic and brand advertising strategies in a dynamic duopoly, *Marketing Science*, 24(4), 556–568.

Bernhardt, I. and K. D. MacKenzie (1972). Some problems in using diffusion models for new products, *Management Science*, 19(2), 187–200.

Binken, J. L. G. and S. Stremersch (2009). The effect of superstar software on hardware sales in system markets, *Journal of Marketing*, 73(2), 88–104.

Danaher, P. J., B. G. S. Hardie, and W. P. Putsis (2001). Marketing-mix variables and the diffusion of successive generations of technological innovation, *Journal of Marketing Research*, 38(4), 501–514.

Dekimpe, M. G., P. M. Parker, and M. Sarvary (1998). Staged estimation of international diffusion models: An application to global cellular telephone adoption, *Technological Forecasting and Social Change*, 57, 105–132.

Dekimpe, M. G., P. M. Parker, and M. Sarvary (2000b). Global diffusion of technological innovations: A coupled-hazard approach, *Journal of Marketing Research*, 37(1), 47–59.

Dekimpe, M. G., P. M. Parker, and M. Sarvary (2000c). Globalization: Modeling technology adoption timing across countries, *Technological Forecasting and Social Change*, 63, 25–42.

Delre, S. A., W. Jager, T. H. A. Bijmolt, and M. A. Janssen (2010). Will it spread or not? The effects of social influences and network topology on innovation diffusion, *Journal of Product Innovation Management*, 27(2), 267–282.

Dodson, J. A. and E. Muller (1978). Models of new product diffusion through advertising and word of mouth, *Management Science*, 24(15), 568–578.

Elberse, A. and J. J. Eliashberg (2003). Demand and supply dynamics for sequentially released products in international markets: The case of motion pictures, *Marketing Science*, 22(3), 329–354.

Fruchter, G. E. and C. Van den Bulte (2011). Why the generalized Bass model leads to odd optimal advertising policies, *International Journal of Research in Marketing*, 28(3), 218–230.

Ganesh, J. and V. Kumar (1996). Capturing the cross-national learning effect: An analysis of industrial technology diffusion, *Journal of the Academy of Marketing Science*, 24, 328–337.

Garber, T., J. Goldenberg, B. Libai, and E. Muller (2004). From density to destiny: Using spatial analysis for early prediction of new product success, *Marketing Science*, 22, 419–428.

Givon, M., V. Mahajan, and E. Muller (1995). Software piracy: Estimation of lost sales and the impact on software diffusion, *Journal of Marketing*, 59(1), 29–37.

Goldenberg, J., B. Libai, and E. Muller (2001). Talk of the network: A complex system look at the underlying process of word of mouth, *Marketing Letters*, 12(3), 211–223.

Goldenberg, J., B. Libai, and E. Muller (2002). Riding the saddle: How cross-market communications can create a major slump in sales, *Journal of Marketing*, 66(2), 1–16.

Goldenberg, J., B. Libai, and E. Muller (2010). The chilling effects of network externalities, *International Journal of Research in Marketing*, 27(1), 4–15.

Golder, P. N. and G. J. Tellis (1997). Will it ever fly? Modeling the takeoff of really new consumer durables, *Marketing Science*, 16, 256–270.

Golder, P. N. and G. J. Tellis (2004). Growing, growing, gone: Cascades, diffusion, and turning points in the product life cycle, *Marketing Science*, 23, 207–218.

Hahn, M., S. Park, L. Krishnamurti, and A. A. Zoltners (1994). Analysis of new product diffusion using a four-segment trial-repeat model, *Marketing Science*, 13(3), 224–247.

Helsen, K., K. Jedidi, and W. S. DeSarbo (1993). A new approach to country segmentation utilizing multinational diffusion patterns, *Journal of Marketing*, 57(4), 60–71.

Hinz, O., B. Skiera, C. Barrot, and J. U. Becker (2011). Seeding strategies for viral marketing: An empirical comparison, *Journal of Marketing*, 75(3), 55–71.

Horsky, D. and L. S. Simon (1983). Advertising and the diffusion of new products, *Management Science*, 2(1), 1–18.

Islam, T. and N. Meade (1997). The diffusion of successive generations of a technology: A more general model, *Technological Forecasting and Social Change*, 56, 49–60.

Iyengar, R., C. Van den Bulte, and T. Valente (2011). Opinion leadership and social contagion in new product diffusion, *Marketing Science*, 30(2), 195–212.

Jain, D., V. Mahajan, and E. Muller (1995). An approach for determining optimal product sampling for the diffusion of new products, *Journal of Product Innovation Management*, 12(2), 124–135.

Kalish, S., V. Mahajan, and E. Muller (1995). Waterfall and sprinkler new-product strategies in competitive global markets, *International Journal of Research in Marketing*, 12(2), 105–119.

Kim, N., D. R. Chang, and A. D. Shocker (2000). Modeling intercategory and generational dynamics for a growing information technology industry, *Management Science*, 46, 496–512.

Kim, N., E. Bridges, and R. K. Srivastava (1999). A simultaneous model for innovative product category sales diffusion and competitive dynamics, *International Journal of Research in Marketing*, 16(2), 95–111.

Kohli, R., D. R. Lehmann, and J. Pae (1999). Extent and impact of incubation time in new product diffusion, *Journal of Product Innovation Management*, 16, 134–144.

Krishnan, T. V., F. M. Bass, and V. Kumar (2000). The impact of a late entrant on the diffusion of a new product/service, *Journal of Marketing Research*, 37(2), 269–278.

Landsman, V. and M. Givon (2010). Service diffusion augmented by brand choice, *Quantitative Marketing and Economics*, 8(1), 91–121.

Lehmann, D. R. and C. B. Weinberg (2000). Sale through sequential distribution channels: An application to movies and videos, *Journal of Marketing*, 64(3), 18–33.

Lehmann, D. R. and M. Esteban-Bravo (2006). When giving some away makes sense to jump-start the diffusion process, *Marketing Letters*, 17, 243–254.

Libai, B., E. Muller, and R. Peres (2005). The role of seeding in multi-market entry, *International Journal of Research in Marketing*, 22(4), 375–393.

Libai, B., E. Muller, and R. Peres (2009a). The influence of within-brand and cross-brand word of mouth on the growth of competitive markets, *Journal of Marketing*, 73(2), 19–34.

Libai, B., E. Muller, and R. Peres (2009b). The diffusion of services, *Journal of Marketing Research*, 46(2), 163–175.

Mahajan, V. and E. Muller (1979). Innovation diffusion and new product growth models in marketing, *Journal of Marketing*, 43(4), 55–68.

Mahajan, V. and E. Muller (1996). Timing, diffusion, and substitution of successive generations of technological innovations: The IBM mainframe case, *Technological Forecasting and Social Change*, 51, 109–132.

Mahajan, V., E. Muller, and Roger A. Kerin (1984). Introduction strategy for new products with positive and negative word of mouth, *Management Science*, 30, 1389–1404.

Mahajan, V., S. Sharma, and R. D. Buzzell (1993). Assessing the impact of competitive entry on market expansion and incumbent sales, *Journal of Marketing*, 57, 39–52.

Mesak, H. I. and A. F. Darrat (2002). Optimal pricing of new subscriber services under interdependent adoption processes, *Journal of Service Research*, 5(3), 140–153.

Muller, E., R. Peres, and V. Mahajan (2009). *Innovation diffusion and new product growth*, Marketing Science Institute, Cambridge, MA: Relevant Knowledge Series.

Norton, J. A. and F. M. Bass (1987). A diffusion theory model of adoption and substitution for successive generations of high-technology products, *Management Science*, 33, 1069–1086.

Norton, J. A. and F. M. Bass (1992). The evolution of technological generations: The law of capture, *Sloan Management Review*, 2, 66–77.

Padmanabhan, V. and F. M. Bass (1993). Optimal pricing of successive generations of product advances, *International Journal of Research in Marketing*, 10, 185–207.

Pae, J. H. and D. R. Lehmann (2003). Multigeneration innovation diffusion: The impact of intergeneration time, *Journal of the Academy of Marketing Science*, 31, 36–45.

Parker, P. and H. Gatignon (1994). Specifying competitive effects in diffusion models: An empirical analysis, *International Journal of Research in Marketing*, 11(1), 17–39.

Peres, R., E. Muller, and V. Mahajan (2010). Innovation diffusion and new product growth: A critical review and research directions, *International Journal of Research in Marketing*, 27(2), 91–106.

Peterson, R. A. and V. Mahajan (1978). Multi-product growth models, in J. N. Sheth, ed., *Research in marketing*, Greenwich, CT: JAI Press, pp. 201–231.

Putsis, W. P., S. Balasubramanian, E. H. Kaplan, and S. K. Sen (1997). Mixing behavior in cross-country diffusion, *Marketing Science*, 16(4), 354–370.

Rand, W. and R. T. Rust (2011). Agent-based modeling in marketing: Guidelines for rigor, *International Journal of Research in Marketing*, 28(3), 181–193.

Robinson, B. and C. Lakhani (1975). Dynamic price models for new-product planning. *Management Science*, 21(10), 1113–1122.

Stremersch, S. and A. Lemmens (2009). Sales growth of new pharmaceuticals across the globe: The role of regulatory regimes, *Marketing Science*, 28(4), 690–708.

Stremersch, S., E. Muller, and R. Peres (2009). Does growth accelerate across technology generations? *Marketing Letters*, 21, 103–120.

Stremersch, S. and G. J. Tellis (2004). Understanding and managing international growth of new products, *International Journal of Research in Marketing*, 21(4), 421–438.

Takada, H. and D. Jain (1991). Cross-national analysis of diffusion of consumer durable goods in Pacific Rim countries, *Journal of Marketing*, 55(2), 48–54.

Talukdar, D., K. Sudhir, and A. Ainslie (2002). Investigating new product diffusion across products and countries, *Marketing Science*, 21(1), 97–116.

Tellis, G. J., S. Stremersch, and E. Yin (2003). The international takeoff of new products: The role of economics, culture, and country innovativeness, *Marketing Science*, 22(2), 188–208.

Van den Bulte, C. (2000). New product diffusion acceleration: Measurement and analysis, *Marketing Science*, 19, 366–380.

Van den Bulte, C. and S. Stremersch (2004). Social contagion and income heterogeneity in new product diffusion: A meta-analytic test, *Marketing Science*, 23, 530–544.

Van Everdingen, Y. M., D. Fok, and S. Stremersch (2009). Modeling global spillover in new product takeoff, *Journal of Marketing Research*, 46(5), 637–652.

Weerahandi, S. and S. R. Dalal (1992). A choice-based approach to the diffusion of a service: Forecasting fax penetration by market segments, *Marketing Science*, 11(1), 39–53.

Wilson, L. O. and J. A. Norton (1989). Optimal entry timing for a product line extension. *Marketing Science*, 8(1), 1–17.

Wuyts, S., S. Stremersch, C. Van den Bulte, and P. H. Franses (2004). Vertical marketing systems for complex products: A triadic perspective, *Journal of Marketing Research*, 41(4), 479–487.

Chapter 5

Econometric Models

Dominique M. Hanssens

5.1 Introduction: Why econometric models in marketing?

The discipline of econometrics came into existence in the 1940s, pioneered by twice-Nobel Laureate Jan Tinbergen of Erasmus University, Rotterdam. In its simplest form, econometrics sits at the intersection of economics (which supplies subject-matter theory), mathematics (which supplies functional forms to quantify the theories), and statistics (which estimates the relevant parameters). Econometrics has become both a highly respected academic discipline, and a frequently used tool to support economic policy making. For example, the Federal Reserve Board employs a large staff of econometricians whose models help set important monetary policy.

Marketing adopted econometric thinking in the 1960s, with the pioneering work on the advertising–sales relationship by Kristian Palda (1964). Similar to its evolution in macro-economics, econometrics in marketing enjoys both academic respect and industry application. The main reason for this is its sustained focus on *market response models*, i.e., models that quantify how marketing investments such as sales calls, advertising, and product innovation impact business performance (mainly sales and market share). Quantifying marketing impact is intellectually challenging (with respect to academic interest) and managerially relevant (with respect to application in practice). Indeed, given their focus on *business performance* variables such as sales revenues, econometric marketing models are used both for *marketing resource allocation* and for *performance forecasting*. These two tasks are intrinsically interrelated for managers, but few marketing science techniques have been sufficiently successful in both to earn widespread industry adoption. The few include conjoint measurement and econometric modeling (often called marketing-mix modeling in industry). The first is reviewed in the chapter by Professor Vithala Rao, and requires primary data sources, i.e., consumer surveys. The second relies on secondary data sources, both within the firm (i.e., its marketing decisions) and outside the firm (i.e., the socio-economic environment, seasonality and competition).

This chapter will describe, in sequence, the milestone developments in representing important marketing phenomena with econometric models since the 1960s. I will focus, in turn, on marketing-substantive innovations and methodological innovations, acknowledging that several of those were fueled by the arrival of new marketing data sources. These advances were published in leading journals such as *Marketing Science, Management Science, Journal of Marketing Research, Journal of Marketing, International Journal of Research in Marketing* and *Quantitative Marketing and Economics.* In addition, a few influential research monographs appeared at various points in this evolution, starting with Parsons and Schultz' *Marketing Models and Econometric Research* (1976). Subsequent books include the works by Naert and Leeflang (1978), Cooper and Nakanishi (1988), Hanssens, Parsons, and Schultz (1990, 2001), Leeflang *et al.* (2000) and Rossi, Allenby, and McCulloch (2005).

5.2 Major marketing phenomena

The key development in marketing thinking, which enabled subsequent econometric modeling, was Neil Borden's concept of the *marketing mix,* i.e., the notion that marketing decisions can be organized in four distinct areas, viz., product, price, place, and promotion (Borden, 1964). In most cases, metrics that quantify these decisions are readily available, for example number of product stock-keeping units (SKUs), list prices, number of stores, and advertising dollars or gross rating points (GRPs). These quantifications form the basis for econometric marketing models. In addition, because costly marketing resources are involved (for example, investments in advertising and sales calls alone average about 10% of company revenues), management interest in the results runs high: how much to invest in various forms of marketing continues to be a challenging question for executives, all the way up to the C-suite.

Foundation: the marketing mix (Borden, 1950s)

Marketing Phenomena	New Data Sources	Econometric Methods
Sales & Market Share Response (Figure 5.2A) (1970s)	Time-series and cross-sectional sales and marketing data (1960s)	Functional Form Specification (Figure 5.3A) (1970s)
Competitive Response (Figure 5.2A) (1970s)		Distributed Lags (Figure 5.3A) (1960s)
	Scanner data (1980s)	
Optimal Marketing (Figure 5.2A) (all decades)		Evolution and Long-Term Effects (Figure 5.3A) (1990s)
Customer Equity (Figure 5.2B) (1990s)	CRM data (1990s)	Data Disaggregation & Heterogeneity (Figure 5.3B) (1980s)
Investor Response (Figure 5.2B) (2000s)		Endogeneity (Figure 5.3B) (1960s)
	Digital marketing data (2000s)	
Internet Behavior (Figure 5.2B) (2000s)		Unobserved Assets (Figure 5.3B) (2000s)
		Structural Models (Figure 5.3B) (1990s)

Fig. 5.1   Overall evolution of econometric models in marketing

Both sales prediction and effective marketing resource allocation require knowledge of the *sales response function*. In order to gain marketing realism, several important marketing phenomena must be represented by such functions. These phenomena represent the substantive field of marketing, and have been hypothesized and tested using concepts from economics, psychology, and management strategy. They are in no particular order: category vs. brand-level response, competitive response, optimal marketing, customer equity, investor response, and internet behavior. In what follows, I will review the evolution of marketing econometric thinking in each of these important aspects, along with some more recent areas of development. For each area, I indicate the decade in which most of the original contributions were made. This evolution is also represented graphically in Figure 5.1. A more complete coverage, at least for the 20th century, of these and other issues in market response modeling may be found in Hanssens, Parsons, and Schultz (2001). Their implications for the management of the marketing mix are discussed in this book in the chapters by Professors Tellis, Gupta, Winer, Lehmann, Staelin, and Coughlin.

5.2.1   Brand sales, category sales, and market share (1970s, see Figure 5.2A)

Early market response models focused on explaining variations in individual brand sales. For example, Palda (1964) included one marketing variable

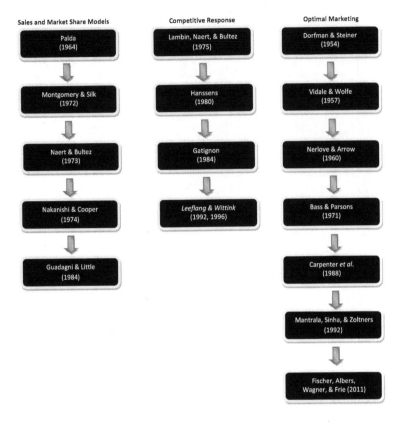

Fig. 5.2A   Marketing phenomena

(advertising), and Montgomery and Silk (1972) considered multiple advertising media. Soon thereafter, it was recognized that these sales impacts could originate from category-expanding effects (e.g., bringing new customers to the category) as well as market-share effects (e.g., inducing existing category customers to switch to a marketed brand) (e.g., Lambin, Naert, and Bultez, 1975). The fundamental identity relationship:

$$\text{Brand Sales} = \text{Category Demand} \times \text{Brand Market Share} \qquad (5.1)$$

leads to the connection between response elasticities e with respect to marketing:

$$e(\text{Brand Sales}) = e(\text{Category Demand}) + e(\text{Brand Market Share}). \qquad (5.2)$$

This identity has been used on a number of occasions. It is particularly useful as one can expect category demand effects of marketing to be less susceptible to competitive retaliation than share-stealing marketing (Hanssens, 1980). In addition, market leaders often favor marketing that expands the category, as they expect to capture the lion share of the incremental category sales. Notwithstanding these preferences, category-expansion effects of marketing are typically the exception rather than the rule. For example, price promotions cause only temporary shifts in aggregate demand (e.g., Nijs *et al.*, 2001), and advertising impact is often subject to share-of-voice effects (e.g., Little, 1979). The relevance of market-share effects of marketing has led to some important econometric research on market-share models, starting with Naert and Bultez (1973), and Nakanishi and Cooper (1974). The econometric challenge is to produce logically consistent models, i.e., market-share specifications that always produce non-negative market shares and that sum to one across market participants. While several analytical options exist, the *multinomial logit* (MNL) *model* and the *multiplicative competitive interaction* (MCI) *model* have emerged as the most useful. These are discussed in detail in Cooper and Nakanishi (1988).

In the early 1980s, a data revolution occurred in marketing practice (see Figure 5.1): consumer purchasing became tractable at the individual transaction level through the use of scanner data (mainly in relatively low-priced categories such as food, health, personal care and cleaning products). Academically, this data revolution led to the specification of *individual-level choice models,* in particular the MNL (e.g., Guadagni and Little, 1984). The main difference between and the aggregate models is that the dependent variable takes on only two values: zero (no purchase) and one (purchase). The rich choice-modeling literature that emerged, reviewed in this book by Professor Gary Russell, is the logical adaptation of the pre-existing market-share models to these new, individual-level databases. Furthermore, the MNL model was later expanded to include category-demand effects by including an "outside good" or a "no-purchase option" in the consumers' choice set (Berry, Levinsohn, and Pakes, 1995). This development led to the adoption of structural models in marketing, discussed in Sec. 5.3.7.

In conclusion, the marketing econometrics literature has recognized early the importance of distinguishing between category-level and share-level marketing effects. The distinction has led to several empirical generalizations about sales response to marketing. In addition, the resulting methodological advances in estimating market-share models became the precursors of the choice modeling frameworks that were enabled by the advent of individual-transaction-level scanner data in the 1980s.

5.2.2 *Competitive reactions (1970s, see Figure 5.2A)*

Marketing activities do not occur in a vacuum, and in many cases they lead to competitive reactions that have an impact on their ultimate effect. This was recognized by Lambin, Naert and Bultez (1975) in their theoretical and empirical extension of the Dorfman–Steiner (1954) optimal marketing spending rules to various competitive-reaction scenarios. A notable contribution in this area is Gatignon's (1984) demonstration that the nature of competitive reaction determines if advertising spending by one brand leads either to the brand gaining market power (with decreasing price sensitivity) or to consumers gaining power from increased information (with rising price sensitivity).

Excellent reviews of the competitive-reaction literature and findings may be found in Leeflang and Wittink (1992, 1996). Econometrically, competitive reaction may be gauged by the so-called reaction functions. In addition, one may theorize about optimal competitive action and postulate models that represent Nash equilibrium (i.e., simultaneous profit–optimizing decisions across all competitors), collusion, or leader–follower behavior. Again, econometric methods may be used to determine which type of competitive behavior is best represented by the data. For example, Roy, Hanssens, and Raju (1994) used time-series analytic methods to derive that competitive pricing behavior in one US automotive category was of the Stackelberg leader–follower type. Research on competitive conduct has been explored mainly by NEIO (new empirical industrial organization) applications in marketing since the mid-1990s, which are discussed in Section 5.3.7.

5.2.3 *Optimal marketing (all decades, see Figure 5.2A)*

The managerial relevance of marketing models becomes apparent when they are used to improve the quality of marketing decisions, for example, better budgeting and better allocation across the marketing mix or across different market segments. The foundations for addressing these questions were provided by key profit-maximization methods developed in economics and operations research. Among the most used in marketing are the profit-maximizing marketing-mix rules in Dorfman and Steiner (1954), the consideration of saturation effects in Vidale and Wolfe (1957), and the treatment of advertising as a capital investment in Nerlove and Arrow (1962).

Starting with the advertising optimization in Parsons and Bass (1971), a large number of applications of profit-maximizing marketing have been reported, and many more go unreported as the data and decision contexts are too proprietary for public dissemination. As computing power has increased, the optimization algorithms have gained in complexity and relevance, for example, from single-period to multi-period optimization and from monopolistic models to models with competition. For example, Carpenter *et al.* (1988) derived optimal marketing spending and pricing rules for 11 brands of laundry detergent under different competitive scenarios. We have also learned important new marketing concepts such as the *flat maximum principle* in marketing resource allocation (Mantrala, Sinha, and Zoltners, 1992). This principle states that marketing budgets are relatively profit-insensitive to deviations from optimum. On the other hand, deviations from optimal allocations of these budgets can be highly profit-sensitive.

Organizations that bridge the marketing academic and practitioner worlds such as the *Marketing Science Institute (MSI)* and the *Institute for the Study of Business Markets (ISBM)* have been instrumental in diffusing the findings on optimal marketing from academic journals. One specific and important initiative is the biennial *ISMS Practice Prize competition*, recently renamed the *Lilien Practice Prize competition*. The majority of Practice Prize winners and finalists in these competitions have been based on econometric modeling, typically combined with optimization methods. A recent example is an entry titled, "Dynamic marketing budget allocation across countries, products, and marketing activities at Bayer" by Fischer *et al.* (2011).

5.2.4 *Customer equity (1990s, see Figure 5.2B)*

Market response models are typically estimated on transactions data, such as unit sales or revenue. However, as the economies of advanced

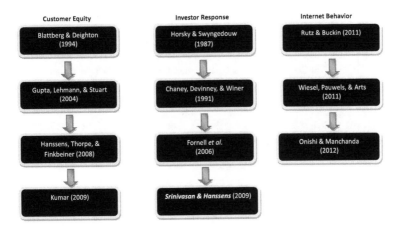

Fig. 5.2B   Marketing phenomena

*Figures 5.2 and 5.3 list pioneering papers, major substantive contributions, *literature review* papers or *books* (in italics) and examples of application papers. Specifics are discussed in the text.

nations gradually become more focused on service, the *quality of a firm's customer relationships* is becoming an increasingly important metric of business performance. At the same time (see Figure 5.1), customer and prospect databases have become widely available, leading to a new branch of customer relationship management (CRM) analytics described in Blattberg, Kim, and Neslin (2008) and reviewed by Professor Scott Neslin in this book.

This evolution has led marketing econometricians to propose and estimate marketing effects on *customer equity*, defined as the net present value of expected future income streams due to a firm's customer relationships. The concept was first formalized by Blattberg and Deighton (1996) and its implications are described in Gupta, Lehmann, and Stuart (2004). From an econometric perspective, different response equations are specified for new customers (quantifying acquisition) and existing customers (quantifying customer retention and customer up- and cross-selling). In combination, the results reveal how different marketing investments enhance (or sometimes diminish) customer equity, which is a key indicator of the future financial health of the enterprise. A few articles have presented detailed applications of customer equity modeling in selected industries, such as financial services (Hanssens, Thorpe, and Finkbeiner, 2008), telecommunications and information technology (e.g., Kumar, Venkatesan, and Reinartz, 2008).

5.2.5 *Marketing and investor response (2000s, see Figure 5.2B)*

When a firm makes a good decision, e.g., one that increases demand and profitability, it may become a more attractive target for investors and thus its stock price (assuming the firm is publicly listed) may be impacted as well. This simple and important possibility introduces the notion of an *investor response function*, a logical extension of market response modeling to the investor domain. The first investor response functions were reported by Horsky and Swyngedouw (1987), who examined the impact of brand-name changes on stock prices, and by Chaney, Devinney, and Winer (1991), who studied the investor effects of new-product introductions. Since then, a sizeable number of econometric papers have opened up a new interdisciplinary research area sometimes called the *marketing–finance interface*.

The founding principle is that, in a well-functioning market, resources will flow to enterprises that simultaneously satisfy customer needs (a marketing objective) and investor needs (a financial objective). However, there is some doubt that the actions of Wall Street also serve the needs of Main Street, especially in light of the global economic upheavals of the 2000s. Translated in marketing-econometric terms, some questions that require scientific scrutiny include the following: Do investors recognize the importance of customer satisfaction as a performance metric? Similarly, do they recognize the difference between companies' base revenue vs. revenue that is captured under temporary price-promotional conditions? Does advertising impact investor perceptions of brand value above and beyond its impact on sales?

The typical starting point of an investor response model is the *stock-return response model*, augmented with the firm's financial results and marketing actions in order to test hypotheses on their impact on expected future cash flows. These are expressed in unanticipated changes, i.e., deviations from past behaviors that are already incorporated in investor expectations. The stock-return response model is defined as

$$R_{it} = ER_{it} + \beta_1 U\Delta REV_{it} + \beta_2 U\Delta INC_{it} + \beta_3 U\Delta CUST_{it}$$
$$+ \beta_4 U\Delta OMKT_{it} + \beta_5 U\Delta COMP_{it} + \varepsilon_{i2t}, \qquad (5.3)$$

where R_{it} is the stock return for firm i at time t, ER_{it} is the expected return from the well-known Fama–French model in finance. A test of "value relevance" of unexpected changes to firm and competitive results and actions is a test for significance of the β coefficients in Eq. (5.3); significant values imply that these variables provide incremental information in explaining stock returns.

A sizable number of findings on marketing impact on stock returns have been published. Many of these are reviewed in a Special Section of the *Journal of Marketing* on *Marketing Strategy and Wall Street* (November 2009), and in a review article by Srinivasan and Hanssens (2009). These findings can be classified as either *marketing action effects* (e.g., the effect of an advertising campaign on stock returns) or *marketing asset effects* (e.g., the impact of brand equity on stock price). Overall, the results support the notion that investor markets are *reasonably efficient*, in the sense that relevant marketing assets and good marketing decisions are incorporated in investor valuations. However, there are a number of exceptions that point to possible improvements in investor resource allocations: sometimes, investors are *slow* to respond to important marketing developments, and sometimes they *overreact* to such developments. The marketing–finance interface is an important area for future research in which market response models play a major role.

5.2.6 *Internet behavior (2000s, see Figure 5.2B)*

The "digital revolution" that started in the 1990s has had major impact on marketing practice and on econometric models in marketing (see Figure 5.1). On the one hand, *new metrics* became available that provide much more detailed tracking of customer pre-purchase behaviors, including search, blog, and sentiment metrics. On the other hand, *customer interactivity* increased dramatically, i.e., the voice of the customer can be heard and tracked in direct response to various marketing activities. As a result, models of internet behavior need to recognize multiple stages in market response (e.g., through different equations in a response model). On the marketing practice side, the concept of *media* was expanded to include owned media (e.g., company websites), paid media (e.g., advertising), and earned media (e.g., customer product ratings, customer recommendations).

A detailed review of internet marketing models is provided in the chapter by Professors Sismeiro and Bucklin. From an econometric perspective, three major areas of contribution have emerged: (1) modeling the effects of paid vs. natural search, and branded vs. generic search (e.g., Rutz and Bucklin, 2011), (2) representing the complete purchase funnel, including off-line and on-line marketing impacts (e.g., Wiesel, Pauwels, and Arts, 2011, and (3) modeling the effects of social media such as consumer blogging (e.g., Onishi and Manchanda, 2012). Overall, the modeling of internet behaviors has barely started and many new contributions may be expected to go forward.

5.3 Methodological developments

The second part of this historical overview focuses on methodological advances that have enabled the study of the marketing phenomena summarized in the previous sections. Most of these developments came from the econometrics discipline, while some originated in statistics, time-series analysis, and, more recently, computer science. I will discuss, in turn, functional form specification, distributed lags, evolution vs. stationarity, endogeneity, heterogeneity, unobservable assets, and structural modeling.

5.3.1 *Functional form specification (1970s, see Figure 5.3A)*

Market response modelers have recognized early on that marketing effects cannot be linear, i.e., every dollar invested in marketing cannot have the same impact across spending levels. Indeed, if linear effects were the rule, and net marginal revenues were positive, firms would spend an infinite amount on their marketing. But, if not linear, what is the shape of the response function?

Two rival hypotheses have been proposed — a concave response function (diminishing returns to scale) and an S-shaped function (increasing,

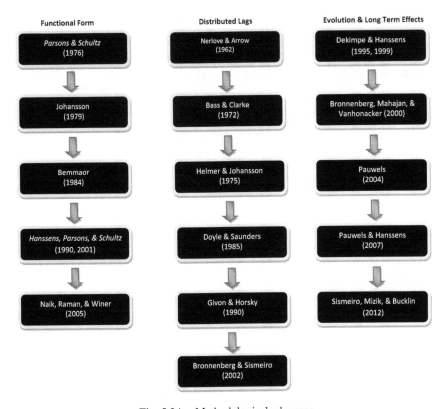

Fig. 5.3A   Methodological advances

then diminishing returns) — both of which can be explained on marketing conceptual grounds. All else equal, higher marketing spending is expected to increase sales for a variety of reasons, such as acquiring previously unaware prospects, increasing purchase quantities, increasing brand switching in favor of the marketed brand, and retaining a larger fraction of the existing customer base. At the same time, we expect there to be *diminishing returns* to these effects, again for several reasons. Consumers cease to be responsive once they have learned the basic message contained in the marketing (saturation effect), markets deplete as successful marketing induces purchasing which then removes the buyers from the market (market-depletion effect) and, finally, there are natural ceilings to the number or percent of target customers that can be reached (ceiling effect). While sales can still increase with increases in marketing support, each additional unit of marketing brings less in incremental sales than the previous unit did.

Several contributions have been made on this important topic. Perhaps the most influential is that of Johansson (1979), who proposed a maximum-likelihood test on the choice of S-shaped vs. concave response. A substantial number of test applications have revealed, over the years, that the concave response function is dominant, i.e., the first marketing dollars generally yield larger returns than the subsequent ones. Since Johansson's test, additional approaches to functional form specification have been developed. For example, Bemmaor (1984) proposed a regime-switching model to represent response threshold effects.

A second, fundamental property of sales response is that of *interaction* among the marketing-mix effects. For example, the marginal impact of an advertising campaign depends on the prevailing level of sales support in the field. While several forms of interaction can be specified, the most common form has been the *multiplicative* model, for example

$$S_t = e^c \, A_t^\beta \, X_t^\gamma \, Z_t^\delta \, e_t^u, \tag{5.4}$$

where S_t refers to sales or another performance metric in period t (for example, week t), A_t is the advertising support in that week, X_t refers to another element of the marketing mix, Z_t corresponds to an environmental factor, and u_t is an error term. For simplicity of exposition, we list only one X and one Z variable. The base response model may be estimated across time periods t, but could also be specified over cross-sectional units $i = 1, \ldots, I$, or both. We expect $0 < \beta < 1$ in estimation, a condition which results in concavity. Note that variables that can logically assume zero values (such as advertising spend) need to be rescaled prior to parameter estimation. Of course, more complex interaction patterns can be investigated. For example, Naik, Raman, and Winer (2005) included strategic foresight effects in their interactive model specification.

The multiplicative function is particularly appealing as it recognizes that marketing-mix effects interact with each other (i.e., the marginal sales effect of an incremental advertising dollar depends on the other elements in the equation). In addition, taking logarithms linearizes the model, making it more easily estimable. Finally, the response parameters are easily interpreted as response elasticities. These elasticities provide an important *benchmark* for comparing marketing-mix impacts across studies, leading to various empirical generalizations of marketing impact (e.g., Bass and Wind, 1995; Hanssens, 2009).

The base model (5.4) implies that, with infinite advertising comes infinite sales. In practice, however, there will be a limit or *ceiling* (K) to sales, usually determined by prevailing market conditions and/or supply limits. Furthermore, if the response is S-shaped, the base model (5.4) can readily be extended to an "odds" model that allows for S-shaped response, as demonstrated by Johansson (1979):

$$(S_t - I)/(K - S_t) = c\, A_t^{\beta}\, X_t^{\gamma}\, Z_t^{\delta}\, e_t^{u}, \tag{5.5}$$

where I is the minimum sales level (e.g., the level at zero marketing spend), and K is the ceiling level. For example, if sales is expressed in relative terms (i.e., market shares), I could be set at 0% and K at 100%. For advertising response parameters $0 < \beta < 1$, model (5.5) is still concave, but for $\beta > 1$, the function is S-shaped. Johansson (1979) discusses the formal estimation of (5.5) with maximum-likelihood methods, as well as an easy approximation based on ordinary least squares.

In conclusion, research on the shape of the response function has focused on interaction effects and on concavity vs. S-shaped response. The econometric literature has formulated several useful empirical generalizations in this context. For example, most marketing actions have concave response effects, with two notable exceptions: distribution effects on sales are often S-shaped and price effects, including temporary price promotions, are convex, i.e., their elasticities are typically greater than one in absolute value (see Hanssens, 2009).

5.3.2 *Distributed lags (1960s, see Figure 5.3A)*

Even the pioneering articles in marketing econometrics of the 1960s recognized that marketing's impact is not restricted to the period in which the effort is expended. For example, a sales call in week t may lead to a purchase order in week $(t + 2)$. Thus, marketing econometric models should accommodate *lags* in response, sometimes called *carryover* effects. However, there is little marketing theory on response lag structure, so the question is largely empirical. A comprehensive article by Bass and

Clarke (1972) laid out the econometric choices for distributed-lag modeling. Among these, the most popular has been the Koyck model, which implies geometrically declining marketing effects over time. A more flexible model, first proposed by Helmer and Johansson (1977) is the *transfer function model*, which offers an empirical search procedure for determining lag structure (of which the Koyck model is a special case), i.e., what is the initial-impact period, what is the longest impact period and what is the pattern between the two?

Searching for response lag structures can be time-consuming and subject to collinearity among lagged regressors. An alternative approach, inspired by the well-known Nerlove and Arrow (1962) goodwill decay model and often favored in industry applications, is the use of a lag-combination variable, sometimes called *adstock* in the case of advertising. However, it is not clear *a priori* what the adstock weights should be. A more comprehensive approach was offered by Givon and Horksy (1990): they disentangle carryover effects due to lagged response vs. those due to brand loyalty. Their empirical results show that the latter are much more influential than the former, adding evidence that marketing communication effects are inherently short-lived, i.e., they are better at inducing trial than repeat purchase behavior. These results are corroborated when the sales data can be divided into first-purchase vs. repeat-purchase quantities (Deighton, Henderson, and Neslin, 1994).

Distributed lag models have been extended to the geo-spatial domain by modeling spatial correlations in function of the distance between geographical units (such as cities or states). This approach is especially useful when the data quality of some geographical units is poor or even absent (Bronnenberg and Sismeiro, 2002). In combination, both temporal and geographical adjacency can now be fully utilized to improve the performance of market response models.

Overall, while the literature has continued to offer alternative ways to model lagged effects of marketing, the basic findings have shown to be remarkably robust. In particular, marketing communications (mainly sales calls and advertising) show short-term effects that gradually dissipate, while the effects of marketing offers (mainly product, price and distribution) are virtually instantaneous. In addition, temporary price cuts can have negative leads and lags, i.e., sales may decline *in anticipation of* a promotion, and decline again after the promotion as a consequence of consumer forward buying (Doyle and Saunders, 1985; Van Heerde, Leeflang, and Wittink, 2000). Overall, the availability of good data and advanced econometric techniques have largely solved the distributed-lag question in marketing, at least theoretically.

5.3.3 *Endogeneity (1960s, see Figure 5.3B)*

Marketing decisions are made in real business settings, not in a laboratory. Thus, the modeling of their effects on business performance should recognize that observed decision levels (for example a price point, the breadth of a product line) are not chosen at random, but instead may be related to past or future (i.e., expected) business outcomes. This gives rise to simultaneity in the marketing–sales relationship, also known as *endogeneity* or *reverse causality*.

Early evidence of endogeneity was provided by Bass and Parsons (1969) in their study of cigarette advertising and sales. Corrections for

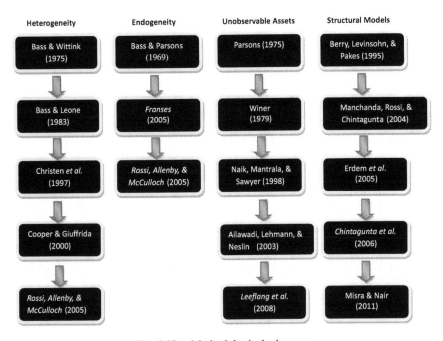

Fig. 5.3B   Methodological advances

endogeneity have largely followed the econometric literature on the subject, including the use of the Hausman–Wu test and advanced estimation methods using instrumental variables (e.g., two and three-stage least-squares, generalized methods of moments). As an illustration of the relevance of endogeneity correction, Elberse and Eliashberg (2003) find that advertising impacts motion-picture attendance with an elasticity of 0.58 in an uncorrected equation. However, when controlling for screen (distribution) endogeneity, the estimated advertising impact drops to 0.20. By contrast, the impact of movie reviews increases from 0.55 to 0.75 when controlling for screen endogeneity. Thus, the consideration that movie exhibitors anticipate movie demand and adjust their screen allocations accordingly results in a different picture of advertising vs. product-quality impact than would otherwise be found. Several recent contributions in the area of simultaneity in market response models will be discussed under the more general heading of modeling demand and supply behaviors. A detailed discussion of endogeneity issues in marketing may be found in Franses (2005). Furthermore, endogeneity within the context of individual consumer choices is discussed in Professor Gary Russell's chapter on "Choice Models" in this book.

5.3.4 *Data disaggregation and heterogeneity* *(1980s, see Figure 5.3B)*

Much of the evolution in marketing econometric modeling may be explained by evolution in marketing and customer databases available for research (see Figure 5.1). In particular, databases have become more disaggregated, both cross-sectionally (e.g., store-level or individual consumer-level data) and over time (e.g., from monthly to weekly to daily observations). This has not only resulted in a tremendous gain in degrees of freedom for modelers, but also raised new econometric challenges, notably in the detection and treatment of *aggregation bias*. For example, response elasticities derived from monthly data may be substantially different from those derived from daily data. This has led to procedures for *de-biasing* response estimates at more aggregate levels (e.g., Bass and Leone, 1983; Russell, 1988; Christen *et al.*, 1997). At the cross-sectional level, much progress has been made in estimating random-coefficient response models that recognize territorial or individual consumer differences in response, especially with the advent of simulation-based Bayesian estimation methods (e.g., Rossi, Allenby, and McCulloch, 2005). I refer to the chapter by Professor Gary Russell for more discussion of individual-level response estimation.

Another consequence of data disaggregation is the advent of computer science techniques to measure marketing impact. These so-called data mining methods rely on massive computation, as distinct from marketing-driven model specification, to detect replicable patterns in the data. Data mining methods are sometimes viewed as competitors to the econometric approach. However, they need not be and could be used in conjunction with each other. For example, Cooper and Giuffrida (2000) used data mining on the *residuals* of a market-share response model to represent additional determinants of promotional impact that could not be detected by the econometric response model. Overall, data disaggregation has led to the recognition of *big data* as a new business asset. Marketing econometric models, along with other techniques, continue to play a major role in monetizing that asset.

5.3.5 *Evolving environments and long-term marketing effects (1990s, see Figure 5.3A)*

Market conditions change for a variety of reasons, and the existence of these changes enables market response modelers to trace their impact econometrically. However, some changes are of a temporary nature (i.e., change, followed by return to the mean), while others are more permanent in character (i.e., change that initiates evolution, which is the opposite of mean reversion). In the 1990s, researchers started to make such formal distinctions in marketing, and then ask the natural follow-up question: do marketing initiatives result in temporary or permanent changes in business performance?

The statistical basis for this stream of research is unit-root testing (see e.g., Dekimpe and Hanssens, 1995a). Consider the simple case where the over-time behavior of the variable of interest (e.g., a brand's sales S_t) is described by a first-order autoregressive process:

$$(1 - \phi L)S_t = c + u_t, \qquad (5.6)$$

where ϕ is an autoregressive parameter, L the lag operator (i.e., $L^k S_t = S_{t-k}$), u_t a residual series of zero-mean, constant-variance (σ_u^2), and uncorrelated random shocks, and c a constant. Note that Eq. (5.6) may also be written in the more familiar form

$$S_t = c + \phi S_{t-1} + u_t,$$

which corresponds to a simple regression model of S_t on its own past. Applying successive backward substitutions allows us to write Eq. (5.6) as

$$S_t = [c/(1 - \phi)] + u_t + \phi u_{t-1} + \phi^2 u_{t-2} + \cdots,$$

in which the present value of S_t is explained as a weighted sum of random shocks. Depending on the value of ϕ, two scenarios can be distinguished. When $|\phi| < 1$, the impact of past shocks diminishes and eventually becomes negligible. Hence, each shock has only a temporary impact. In that case, the series has a fixed mean $c/(1 - \phi)$ and a finite variance $\sigma_u^2/(1 - \phi^2)$. Such a series is called stable. When $|\phi| = 1$, however, (5.6) becomes:

$$S_t = (c + c + \cdots) + u_t + u_{t-1} + \cdots,$$

implying that each random shock has a permanent effect on the subsequent values of S. In that case, no fixed mean is observed, and the variance increases with time. Sales do not revert to a historical level, but instead wander freely in one direction or another, i.e., they *evolve*. Unit-root tests verify whether the parameter ϕ in Eq. (5.6) is smaller than or equal to one. When combined time-series cross-sectional data are available, unit-root tests are expanded to so-called panel-unit root tests.

The distinction between stationary and evolving environments has led to the conclusion that most sales variables are evolving, but most market shares are stationary (Dekimpe and Hanssens, 1995b). This finding has an important strategic implication — if marketing is to have long-term (i.e., permanent) effects, it must operate in an evolving environment, for example a product category whose primary demand is still growing. Once the category is well-defined (e.g., a soft-drink category in an advanced economy), market shares of the major players tend to be stationary, thus any of their marketing actions can at most have temporary share-lifting effects.

The results of unit-root tests reveal to what extent a marketing eco-system — such as the performance and marketing spending behavior of the major brands in a category — is evolving or stationary. The modeling of such a system then proceeds in levels of variables (stationary), changes in variables (evolving), or a mixture of the two. Vector-autoregressive (VAR) models have been used to represent such a system. In some cases, they are augmented by long-term equilibrium conditions among the variables, resulting in error-correction models. This systems approach has resulted in a remarkable demonstration that the effects of an effective marketing campaign can be amplified by a factor of five over the long run when marketers use decision rules that reinforce the initial impact (Pauwels, 2004).

From a strategic perspective, a marketing eco-system may be in a state of equilibrium, continued evolution, hysteresis, or escalation (Dekimpe and Hanssens, 1999). Furthermore, these states may go through sequences over time in mature markets, with relatively long periods of stationarity alternating with short but important periods of evolution (Pauwels and Hanssens, 2007). As a recent illustration of this principle, consider the marketing strategies employed by pharmaceutical companies (Sismeiro, Mizik, and Bucklin, 2012). On the demand side, some customers (prescribing physicians) are in a response-equilibrium state (e.g., they oscillate between prescribing brand A and brand B). Others are still establishing their brand preferences and are highly responsive to temporary marketing efforts (hysteresis). On the supply side, some brands may be escalating their marketing spending in an effort to grow or protect their prescription base (escalation). Finally, some brands and doctors may be continually evolving their behavior over time (co-evolution). The authors proposed a segmentation scheme along these four categories and then diagnosed the position of each brand using VAR models.

Another illustration is the study of the evolution in market shares among major brands of iced tea (Bronnenberg, Mahajan, and Vanhonacker, 2000), and how it led to the formation of an eventual market structure. The evolution is the result of the bi-directional relationships between consumer preference and retail distribution, and the authors carefully model the time window when the industry is still evolving, versus the time when it has reached stability. Both examples illustrate how combined time-series econometric methods can be used to diagnose evolution and quantify its determinants.

5.3.6 *Unobservable assets (2000s, see Figure 5.3B)*

Most variables in market response models are directly observable, such as records of sales, prices, and marketing investments. A few are not, and they include some strategically important concepts such as *brand strength* (health) and *performance baseline.* While the former is broader in scope, and includes many contributions from psychology, they are similar in terms of financial value to the firm. In particular, the baseline in a marketing econometric model, i.e., the sales revenue when marketing investments are set to zero, is often viewed as an indicator of brand strength. Thus, it is important to know what percent of realized revenue is "base". In addition, we wish to know if and how marketing builds the base, i.e., do marketing-induced sales lifts translate into increases in the base?

State-space models such as Kalman filters have been proposed as an elegant approach to answer these questions. State-space models augment the usual observation equations, e.g., for sales, with state equations, e.g., for the baseline or intercept of sales (Naik, Mantrala, and Sawyer, 1998). Then marketing initiatives can be evaluated, both for their impact on temporary sales lift and their ability to improve baseline sales, which is a longer-term objective. A comprehensive overview of such models may be found in Leeflang *et al.* (2009). Note that an early precursor to state-space models in marketing was the application of time-varying response models (e.g., Parsons, 1975; Winer, 1979). These models recognized that consumer response to marketing changes over the life cycle of a product, which has important consequences for marketing resource allocation.

When cross-sectional comparisons can be made, for example, of different brands in the same category, brand strength may be assessed as a *revenue premium* (Ailawadi, Lehmann, and Neslin, 2003). Indeed, strong brands either sell more or charge a price premium, or both, relative to their weaker competitors. The authors demonstrate the econometric measurement of the revenue premium on a number of brands in different consumer product categories. Thus, the use of econometric techniques has enabled us to quantify important but inherently unobservable constructs such as brand strength.

5.3.7 *Structural models (1990s, see Figure 5.3B)*

Starting in the mid-1990s, efforts have been made to increase the behavioral realism of market response models by focusing on the economic and marketing assumptions that led to model specification, in particular, assumptions on the *supply side*, i.e., marketing decision making (Bronnenberg, Rossi, and Vilcassim, 2005). This evolution is sometimes referred to as structural modeling, and mirrors the development of NEIO in economics. An excellent overview may be found in Chintagunta *et al.* (2006).

Two important marketing phenomena in particular have received the attention of structural modelers: forward-looking decision making by consumers (using dynamic programming techniques) and joint models of supply and demand (using assumptions about the behavior of individual consumers and marketers). Structural models are often based on the demand function derived by Berry, Levinsohn, and Pakes (1995). They postulate that individual consumers maximize their utility and represent this with a multinomial logit choice model (including a "no purchase" option). They also recognize that consumers' response parameters are heterogeneous. They then aggregate the logit-derived choices across a heterogeneity distribution. As such they are able to estimate aggregate-level demand models based on individual-level structural assumptions.

On the supply side, the typical assumption made by structural modelers is that of profit-maximizing firms. Such an assumption allows the modeler to impose an equilibrium condition (on the supply side) on the market response model. For example, sales response to advertising (a demand function) is estimated under the assumption that the observed advertising spending levels are the result of firms maximizing their profits (a supply function). To date, most applications of this nature have assumed short-term profit maximizing behavior, as long-term maximization is considerably more complex to model. A notable exception is the structural model for pharmaceutical sales call allocation decisions used by Manchanda, Rossi, and Chintagunta (2004). They only assume that managers use information about likely physician responsiveness in making their sales contact decisions. One interesting finding is that physicians are not detailed optimally. Instead, high-volume prescribers receive a disproportionally high number of sales calls, even though they may be unresponsive.

Overall, structural models improve the practice of market response modeling by enhancing our understanding of the underlying behavioral mechanisms. For example, if sales are state-dependent (i.e., current sales depend on previous sales), a structural model can explain why that is the case, e.g., is it due to consumer habit formation, or switching costs or learning? By contrast, while a reduced-form econometric model can measure the extent of state-dependency, it can generally not pinpoint its causes.

The cost of structural modeling is *complexity* and *assumption-dependency*, i.e., the models are generally more complex mathematically and therefore more difficult to parameterize. In addition, the results rest on assumptions on firm and consumer behavior that may or may not hold in any given application. For these reasons, the adoption of structural models in applied settings is still limited. With the advent of new and better data sources, and vastly increased computational power, new opportunities arise to make structural models more relevant and applicable to real marketing problems. For example, structural models of salesforce effort that include forward-looking behavior have been estimated and used for the purpose of improving salesforce quota and compensation plans (Misra and Nair, 2011). Another example is in high-technology markets, where it has been shown that estimated price elasticities increase when the impact of a price change on future price expectations is incorporated (Erdem, Keane, and Strebel, 2005).

In sum, at this juncture, marketing econometrics is witnessing a healthy co-evolution along two dimensions: (1) better data allow for stronger empirical specifications, so the models are becoming econometrically more precise and (2) the use of economic and psychological theory around the behavior of marketers and consumers increases the behavioral realism of the models.

5.4 Conclusion

This chapter has described the history of econometric marketing models in over half a century (the oldest reference is 1954, the most recent is 2012).

Over that period, this subfield of marketing has thrived, both academically and in terms of marketing practice. In particular, econometric marketing models have shown remarkable resilience in light of advances in data sources and computing power. The field also adapts itself well to advances in behavioral theories that lead to more elaborate model specifications and estimation methods.

In the last few years, the advent of digital data sources such as clickstreams and online buzz data has opened up a new set of opportunities for marketing insight generation through econometric modeling. These are reviewed in the chapter by Professors Bucklin and Sismeiro. One important development is that online data sources may become substitutes for costly and infrequently collected data on consumer attitudes such as brand awareness and consideration set. Then, econometric models can be built to gauge the impact of changing customer attitudes on business performance in virtually real time. In that way, an important reconciliation can be engineered between the domains of consumer attitudes and business transactions.

A second important development is that digital marketing platforms make marketing experimentation (i.e., test and control designs) much faster and less expensive to execute than in the past. Incorporating such experimental-design results in econometric models can help resolve the endogeneity problem and provide reliable estimates of marketing effects without prior history. Finally, various data mining techniques developed in the computer science field will augment econometric models on "Big Data", especially in areas where little or no prior theory is available. Combining the power of econometric models, experimental designs and data mining methods will offer unparalleled opportunity for scholars and for managers to understand and predict market response and to improve marketing practice.

References

Ailawadi, K. L., D. R. Lehmann, and S. A. Neslin (2003). Revenue premium as an outcome measure of brand equity, *Journal of Marketing*, 67(October), 1–17.

Bass, F. M. and D. G. Clarke (1972). Testing distributed lag models of advertising effect, *Journal of Marketing Research*, 9(August), 298–308.

Bass, F. M. and R. P. Leone (1983). Estimation of bimonthly relations from annual data, *Management Science*, 29(January), 1–11.

Bass, F. M. and L. J. Parsons (1969). A simultaneous equation regression analysis of sales and advertising, *Applied Economics*, 1(May), 103–124.

Bass, F. M. and J. Wind (1995). Introduction to the special issue: Empirical generalizations in marketing, *Marketing Science*, 14, G1–G5.

Bemmaor, A. C. (1984). Testing alternative econometric models on the existence of advertising threshold effect, *Journal of Marketing Research*, 21(August), 298–308.

Berry, S., J. Levinsohn, and A. Pakes (1995). Automobile prices in market equilibrium, *Econometrica*, 63, 841–890.

Blattberg, R. C. and J. Deighton (1996). Manage marketing by the customer equity test, *Harvard Business Review*, (July–August), 136–144.

Blattberg, R. C., B.-D. Kim, and S. A. Neslin (2008). *Database marketing: Analyzing and managing customers*, Springer, New York, NY.

Borden, N. H. (1964). The concept of the marketing mix, *Journal of Advertising Research*, 4(1) (January), 7–12.

Bronnenberg, B. J., V. Mahajan, and W. R. Vanhonacker (2000). The emergence of market structure in new repeat-purchase categories: The interplay of market share and retailer distribution, *Journal of Marketing Research*, 37(1), 16–31.

Bronnenberg, B. J. and C. Sismeiro (2002). Using multimarket data to predict brand performance in markets for which no or poor data exist, *Journal of Marketing Research*, 39(February), 1–17.

Bronnenberg, B. J., P. E. Rossi, and N. Vilcassim (2005). Structural modeling and policy simulation, *Journal of Marketing Research*, 42(February), 22–26.

Carpenter, G. C., L. G. Cooper, D. M. Hanssens, and D. F. Midgley (1988). Modeling asymmetric competition, *Marketing Science*, 7(Fall), 393–412.

Chaney, P. K., T. M. Devinney, and R. S. Winer (1991). The impact of new product introductions on the market value of firms, *Journal of Business*, 64(4), 573–610.

Chintagunta, P., T. Erdem, P. E. Rossi, and M. Wedel (2006). Structural modeling in marketing: Review and assessment, *Marketing Science*, 25(6) (November–December), 604–616.

Christen, M., S. Gupta, J. C. Porter, R. Staelin, and D. R. Wittink (1997). Using market level data to understand promotional effects in a nonlinear model, *Journal of Marketing Research*, 34(3) (August), 322–334.

Cooper, L. G. and M. Nakanishi (1988). *Market share analysis: Evaluating competitive marketing effectiveness*, Boston: Kluwer Academic Publishers.

Cooper, L. G. and G. Giuffrida (2000). Turning data mining into a management science tool: New algorithms and empirical results, *Management Science*, 46(2) (February), 249–264.

Deighton, J., C. M. Henderson, and S. A. Neslin (1994). The effects of advertising on brand switching and repeat purchasing, *Journal of Marketing Research*, 31(February), 28–43.

Dekimpe, M. G. and D. M. Hanssens (1995a). The persistence of marketing effects on sales, *Marketing Science*, 14(1), 1–21.

Dekimpe, M. G. and D. M. Hanssens (1995b). Empirical generalizations about market evolution and stationarity, *Marketing Science*, 14(3 Suppl. 2), G109–G121.

Dekimpe, M. G. and D. M. Hanssens (1999). Sustained spending and persistent response: A new look at long-term marketing profitability, *Journal of Marketing Research*, 36(4), 397–412.

Dorfman, R. and P. O. Steiner (1954). Optimal advertising and optimal quality, *American Economic Review*, 44(December), 826–836.

Doyle, P. and J. Saunders (1985). The lead effect in marketing, *Journal of Marketing Research*, 22(February), 54–65.

Elberse, A. and J. Eliashberg (2003). Demand and supply dynamics for sequentially released products in international markets: The case of Motion Pictures, *Marketing Science*, 22(3), 329–354.

Erdem, T., M. Keane, and J. Strebel (2005). Learning about computers: An analysis of information search and technology choice, *Quantitative Marketing and Economics*, 3(3), 207–247.

Fischer, M., S. Albers, N. Wagner, and M. Frie (2011). Dynamic marketing budget allocation across countries, products, and marketing activities, *Marketing Science*, 30(4) (July/August), 568–585.

Franses, P. H. (2005). Diagnostics, expectations and endogeneity, *Journal of Marketing Research*, 48(February), 27–29.

Gatignon, H. (1984). Competition as a moderator of the effect of advertising on sales, *Journal of Marketing Research*, 21(November), 387–398.

Givon, M. and D. Horsky (1990). Untangling the effects of purchase reinforcement and advertising carryover, *Marketing Science*, 9(2) (Spring), 171–187.

Guadagni, P. M. and J. D. C. Little (1983). A logit model of brand choice calibrated on scanner data, *Marketing Science*, 2(Summer), 203–238.

Gupta, S., D. R. Lehmann, and J. A. Stuart (2004). Valuing customers, *Journal of Marketing Research*, 59(February), 7–18.

Hanssens, D. M. (1980). Market response, competitive behavior, and time-series analysis, *Journal of Marketing Research*, 17(November), 470–485.

Hanssens, D. M., L. J. Parsons, and R. L. Schultz (1990). *Market response models*, Boston, Massachusetts: Kluwer Academic Publishers.

Hanssens, D. M., L. J. Parsons, and R. L. Schultz (2001). *Market response models*, 2nd edn., Boston, Massachusetts: Kluwer Academic Publishers.

Hanssens, D. M., D. Thorpe, and C. Finkbeiner (2008). Marketing when customer equity matters, *Harvard Business Review*, 86(5) (May), 117–125.

Hanssens, D. M. (ed.) (2009). *Empirical generalizations about marketing impact*, Marketing Science Institute, Cambridge, MA, Relevant Knowledge Series.

Helmer, R. M. and J. K. Johansson (1977). An exposition of the Box-Jenkins transfer function analysis with application to the advertising-sales relationship, *Journal of Marketing Research*, 14(May), 227–239.

Horsky, D. and P. Swyngedouw (1987). Does it pay to change your company's name? A stock market perspective, *Marketing Science*, Fall, 320–235.

Johansson, J. K. (1979). Advertising and the S-curve: A new approach, *Journal of Marketing Research*, 16(August), 346–354.

Kumar, V., R. Venkatesan, and W. Reinartz (2008). Performance implications of adopting a customer focused sales campaign, *Journal of Marketing*, 72(September), 50–68.

Lambin, J.-J., P. A. Naert, and A. Bultez (1975). Optimal marketing behavior in oligopoly, *European Economic Review*, 6, 105–128.

Leeflang, P., D. R. Wittink, M. Wedel, and P. A. Naert (2000). *Building models for marketing decisions*, Boston: Kluwer.

Leeflang, P. and D. R. Wittink (1992). Diagnosing competitive reactions using (aggregated) scanner data, *International Journal of Research in Marketing*, 9(1) (March), 39–57.

Leeflang, P. and D. R. Wittink (1996). Competitive versus consumer response: Do managers overreact? *International Journal of Research in Marketing*, 13(2) (April), 103–119.

Leeflang, P., T. Bijmolt, J. van Doorn, D. Hanssens, H. van Heerde, Peter Verhoef, and J. Wierenga (2009). Creating lift versus building the base: Current trends in marketing dynamics, *International Journal of Research in Marketing*, 26(1) (March), 13–20.

Little, J. D. C. (1979). Aggregate advertising models: The state of the art, *Operations Research*, 27(July–August), 629–667.

Manchanda, P., P. E. Rossi, and P. K. Chintagunta (2004). Response modeling with nonrandom marketing-mix variables, *Journal of Marketing Research*, 59(November), 467–478.

Mantrala, M. K., P. Sinha, and A. A. Zoltners (1992). Impact of resource allocation rules on marketing investment-level decisions and profitability, *Journal of Marketing Research*, 29(2) (May), 162–175.

Misra, S. and H. Nair (2011). A structural model of sales-force compensation dynamics: Estimation and field implementation, *Quantitative Marketing and Economics*, 9(3) (September), 211–225.

Montgomery, D. B. and A. J. Silk (1972). Estimating dynamic effects of market communications expenditures, *Management Science*, 18, B485–B501.

Naert, P. A. and A. V. Bultez (1973). Logically consistent market share models, *Journal of Marketing Research*, 10(August), 334–340.

Naert, P. A. and P. S. H. Leeflang (1978). *Building implementable marketing models*, Leiden: Martinus Nijhoff.

Nakanishi, M. and L. G. Cooper (1974). Parameter estimation for a multiplicative competitive interaction model least squares approach, *Journal of Marketing Research*, 11(August), 303–311.

Naik, P. A., M. K. Mantrala, and A. G. Sawyer (1998). Planning media schedules in the presence of dynamic advertising quality, *Marketing Science*, 17(3), 214–235.

Naik, P. A., K. Raman, and R. S. Winer (2005). Planning marketing-mix strategies in the presence of interaction effects, *Marketing Science*, 24(1) (Winter), 25–34.

Nijs, V. R., M. G. Dekimpe, J.-B. Steenkamp, and D. M. Hanssens (2001). The category effects of price promotions, *Marketing Science*, 20(1) (Winter), 1–22.

Nerlove, M. and K. J. Arrow (1962). Optimal advertising policy under dynamic conditions, *Economica*, 29(May), 129–142.

Onishi, H. and P. Manchanda (2012). Marketing activity, blogging, and sales, *International Journal of Research in Marketing*, 29(3) (September), 221–234.

Palda, K. S. (1964). *The measurement of cumulative advertising effects*, Englewood Cliffs, NJ: Prentice Hall.

Parsons, L. J. and F. M. Bass (1971). Optimal advertising expenditure implications of a simultaneous-equation regression analysis, *Operations Research*, 19(May–June), 822–831.

Parsons, L. J. (1975). The product life cycle and time-varying advertising elasticities, *Journal of Marketing Research*, 12(November), 476–480.

Parsons, L. J. and R. L. Schultz (1976). *Marketing models and econometric research*. New York: North Holland.

Pauwels, K. (2004). How dynamic consumer response, competitor response, company support, and company inertia shape long-term marketing effectiveness, *Marketing Science*, 24(4) (Fall), 596–610.

Pauwels, K. and D. M. Hanssens (2007). Performance regimes and marketing policy shifts, *Marketing Science*, 26(3) (May–June), 293–311.

Rossi, P. E., G. M. Allenby, and R. McCulloch (2005). *Bayesian statistics and marketing*, London: Wiley.

Roy, A., D. M. Hanssens, and J. S. Raju (1994). Competitive pricing by a price leader, *Management Science*, 40(7) (July), 809–823.

Russell, G. J. (1988). Recovering measures of advertising carryover from aggregate data: The role of the firm's decision behavior, *Marketing Science*, 7(Summer), 252–270.

Rutz, O. J. and R. E. Bucklin (2011). From generic to branded: A model of spillover effects in paid search advertising, *Journal of Marketing Research*, 48(February), 87–102.

Sismeiro, C., N. Mizik, and R. E. Bucklin (2012). Modeling coexisting business scenarios with time-series panel data: A dynamics-based segmentation approach, *International Journal of Research in Marketing*, 29(June), 134–147.

Srinivasan, S. and D. M. Hanssens (2009). Marketing and firm value: Metrics, methods, findings and future directions, *Journal of Marketing Research*, 46(June), 293–312.

Van Heerde, H., P. S. H. Leeflang, and D. R. Wittink (2000). The estimation of pre- and postpromotion dips with store-level scanner data, *Journal of Marketing Research*, 37(August), 383–395.

Vidale, M. L. and H. B. Wolfe (1957). An operations research study of sales response to advertising, *Operational Research Quarterly*, 5(June), 370–381.

Wiesel, T., K. Pauwels, and J. Arts (2011). Marketing's profit impact: Quantifying online and off-line funnel progression, *Marketing Science*, 30(4) (July–August), 604–611.

Winer, R. S. (1979). An analysis of the time varying effects of advertising: The case of Lydia Pinkham, *Journal of Business*, 52(October), 563–576.

Chapter 6

Market Structure Research

Steven M. Shugan

6.1 Introduction

This chapter provides history and perspective on past research in defining the market structure. There were several approaches taken and each approach adopted a slightly different definition of market structure analysis. However, market structure usually refers to the empirical, conceptual, or pictorial representation of competing products or services in a market where the definition of the market and the definition of competition vary depending on the approach. "The early turning points" (see Figure 6.1) illustrates a few of the many milestones in the literature.

Prior to 1965, for example, industry practice dictated market definition in a marketing area where industry participants defined their markets and their competitors. There was only a concept of sub-markets based on readily observable factors. For example, Ferber and Wales (1951) compared prefabricated housing to competitive sub-markets. Industry practice defined the competitive sub-markets as standard housing and rental apartments. The comparison included objective differences between the sub-markets, how consumer awareness varied across sub-markets, how consumer attitudes varied across sub-markets, and brand preferences across sub-markets. There was, however, research in economics (e.g., Hotelling, 1929) and psychometrics (e.g., Clark, 1957; Luce, 1959) which would later influence many researchers in marketing.

In the 1950s, most researchers in marketing favored a data-based approach (Shugan, 2002). For example, Ferber (1951) stated that "many, if not most, marketing studies require an analysis of statistical data at

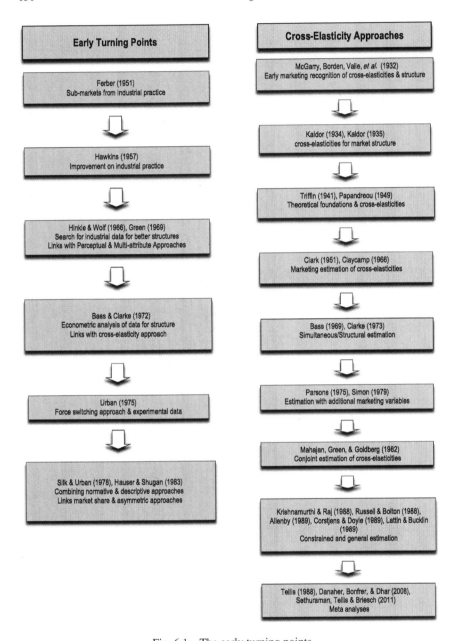

Fig. 6.1   The early turning points

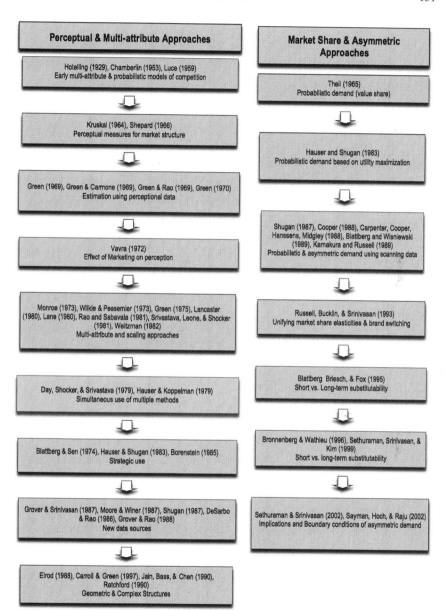

Fig. 6.1 *(Continued)*

some stage or other." Ferber (1951) recommended a consulting relationship with the firms to obtain necessary data. Without a direct consulting relationship, academic researchers needed to rely on secondary data that already assumed particular market structures. Hinkle and Wolf (1966) stated that "Quantitative research by marketing faculties and graduate students is hampered by a shortage of attainable data and by lack of knowledge about available reliable data." It was (and still is) to everyone's best interest to embrace the market definition that already constrains available data. However, industrial classifications often lacked important information necessary for defining a market structure (Hawkins, 1957). For example, if two television programs attracted exactly the same viewers during the same time slot, the two programs competed for the same advertising dollars. If two television programs attracted very different viewers, the two programs probably competed in different sub-markets despite government and industry classifications to the contrary. Similarly, Storey and Farris (1964) did a detailed analysis of the market structure for the baking industry. Farley (1964) used the market structure to predict brand loyalty but the market structure again followed industry practice (e.g., canned peas, rice, tuna, etc.).

Although, later research in marketing recognized the importance of correctly defining market structures, early research in marketing recognized a fact that is sometimes forgotten in current research. Early research recognized that market structures change over time. For example, one seminal article by Smith (1956) states that "it is the obligation of those responsible for sales and marketing administration to keep the strategy mix in adjustment with the market structure at any point in time and to produce in marketing strategy at least as much dynamism as is present in the market."

During the mid-1960s, Volney Stefflre advocated a research methodology that he called "market structure analysis." His methods were not published in scholarly journals but parts of these methods could be found in several book chapters. Generally, his methods broke down products into their attributes, their usage situations, and the benefits that those products provided (Haley, 1968; Stefflre 1968). Stefflre was primarily interested in new products, how market structures could predict which new products might be successful, and how those new products would impact incumbent products.

Around that same time, Clevenger, Lazier, and Clark (1965) used semantic differential and factor analysis to measure corporate images or a market structure consisting of a perceptual space. Their analysis considered issues of stability, robustness, and generality. Their research study used a geometric space that produced a visual representation of a market structure. Also at that time, Frank and Green (1968) introduced and advocated methods for numerical classification that could classify products and, subsequently, determine a market structure or, at least, sub-markets. Green, Halbert, and Robinson (1966) added canonical analysis to the emerging tools for defining a market structure. Then in the last years of the 1960s, research studies began considering market structures consisting of products existing as points in a multidimensional space that exhibited the properties of a geometric space. For example, proximity in the space represented competitive substitutability. The points in the space were functions of the product attributes measured through some scaling procedure. Green, Carmone, and Robinson (1968) published a book on the analysis of marketing behavior using non-metric scaling and related techniques. Neidell (1969) showed how a market could be structured in the same way that a map of the United States could be estimated from only data on the distances between the cities. Green and Rao (1969) theoretically and empirically compared 10 types of proximity measures advocated by various researchers for classifying products and creating a market structure. Morrison (1969) explained how to interpret the output of these multivariate analyses. Green and Carmone (1969) traced the history of scaling and reported an empirical comparison of three computer programs. The programs provided different market structures because they employed different weightings. The research in the 1960s led to the research stream depicted in Figure 6.2 as the "perceptual and multi-attribute approach". The figure also provides an example of a market structure derived using this approach.

In the 1970s, the number of research studies on market structures grew dramatically. However, although many methods emerged for defining the market structure, rather than focusing on the foundation and theory underlying market structures, most books and articles during the 1970s failed to develop a theory for defining market structures. Moreover, unlike economists, who were focused on the market structure for anti-trust policy, many research studies in marketing focused on the methodology rather than

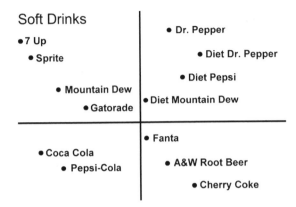

Fig. 6.2   Market structure using perceptual approach (multidimensional scaling) inspired by: Maiera, A., Z. Vickersa, and J. Inman (2007). Sensory-specific satiety, its crossovers, and subsequent choice of potato chip flavors, *Appetite*, 49(2), 419–428

the underlying objectives. For example, Myers and Tauber (1977) provided an excellent review of the literature on the market structure in 1977. However, the book classified methods for defining a market structure based on the statistical tool (e.g., factor analysis, discriminant analysis, conjoint analysis, multidimensional scaling, and benefit analysis) rather than based on any theory of market structure. Other books and articles during the 1970s focused on the data availability and data requirements. For example, Day, Shocker, and Srivastava (1979) classified methods for defining market structures into two approaches based on the type of required data. The first approach used observed consumer purchase or usage data. The second approach used customer judgment data usually found in consumer surveys. Fortunately, in the 1970s, survey data and purchase diaries both became accepted sources of data (O'Dell, 1962; Wind and Lerner, 1979) so research could proceed on multiple fronts. Perhaps, progress only occurs when very different approaches are allowed to compete. Combined with the wide availability of statistical software, research on defining market structures could rely on many sources of information. Unfortunately, ease of publication can be related to the popularity of particular data sources which can inhibit the benefit of research on multiple fronts.

In the 1970s, a few researchers adopted a less normative approach. Rather than embracing a consulting paradigm, they embraced a scientific paradigm focused on understanding market structures. For example,

Bass and Clarke (1972) advocated a scientific philosophy when doing econometric research in marketing. Bass and Clarke (1972) stated that "the basic idea is to deduce specific implications from explicit premises; if the premises are true, one can make predictions about the data. If the predictions are not fulfilled, the data are not consistent with the theory (model) and it is discredited. In attempting to discriminate among alternative models, predictive testing may eliminate some of the candidates. Then if a model survives the tests, even sharper restrictions and premises may be established as a basis for further testing until, hopefully, only one theory survives." "... the concept is not widely understood or practiced in econometrics." Of course, very few researchers accomplished both tasks with some notable exceptions (e.g., Urban, 1975; Silk and Urban, 1978). Unfortunately, secondary data was not always well-suited for testing marketing theories on market structure as required by a scientific paradigm. These research studies eventually led to the research stream depicted in the "cross-elasticity approach" (see Figure 6.3). The figure also provides an example of a market structure derived using this approach.

In the late 1970s, there was a movement toward analyzing scanning data (or scanner data) from supermarkets (Wind, 1978). These data were obtained from scanning the universal product code of trade items at the point of sale. That research led to the research stream depicted in the "market

	Aim	Aquafresh	Babool	Close-Up	Colgate	Crest	Gleem	Ipana
		Average cross-elasticities for TOOTH PASTE brands on all others						
Aim	−2.08	0.17	−0.14	−0.50	0.21	0.12	−0.34	−0.35
Aquafresh	−0.05	−2.83	0.06	−0.07	−0.37	−0.22	0.28	−0.30
Babool	0.01	−0.03	−3.64	−0.32	−0.01	−0.02	0.49	0.02
Close-Up	0.27	−0.09	−0.31	−1.71	−0.17	0.45	0.27	0.23
Colgate	0.01	−0.40	−0.44	−0.20	−3.32	−0.15	0.28	0.25
Crest	0.24	0.33	0.08	0.41	−0.05	−4.00	0.35	0.45
Gleem	0.02	0.25	−0.03	−0.33	0.30	−0.49	−3.88	−0.15
Ipana	0.27	−0.45	−0.15	−0.40	−0.29	−0.21	0.18	−3.90
Kiss-my-face	0.11	0.14	0.49	0.45	0.29	0.41	0.33	−0.44
Marvis	0.38	0.05	0.40	−0.37	−0.30	0.13	−0.41	0.27
Nature's Gate	−0.17	0.46	−0.46	0.18	0.19	−0.28	−0.26	−0.41
Peelu	0.46	0.05	−0.30	0.01	0.49	−0.04	0.21	0.26
Pepsodent	0.31	0.05	0.10	0.37	−0.24	0.07	0.27	0.13
Sensodyne	0.12	−0.12	−0.39	−0.07	0.17	−0.16	0.06	0.44
Tom's	0.26	0.04	0.50	0.10	0.23	0.07	0.16	0.24
Tom's of Maine	−0.14	−0.45	0.08	0.17	0.09	−0.50	0.44	0.24
Xyliwhite	0.40	−0.23	−0.15	−0.21	0.46	−0.15	−0.36	0.06

Fig. 6.3   Market structure using sales cross-elasticity approach inspired by: Kamakura and Kang (2007). Chain-wide and store-level analysis for cross-category management, *Journal of Retailing*, 82(2), 159–170

Average cross-elasticities for Price Tiers (TOILET PAPER)

	Quilted	White Cl	KleenexU	Kirkland	Walmart	Charmin	Simply S	Kleenex
Quilted NorthernUltra	-1.63	0.62	0.78					
White CloudUltra	0.89	-2.79	0.77					
Kleenex CottonelleUltra	0.62	0.67	-3.79					
Kirkland Signature				-3.62	0.70	0.65		
Walmart White Cloud				0.84	-3.60	0.62		
Charmin Sensitive				0.64	0.88	-3.49		
Simply Soft							0.62	0.82
Kleenex Cottonelle							-3.42	0.67
Charmin Basic							0.76	-4.04
Marcal							0.68	0.61
Simply 5000							0.62	0.64
Viti							0.92	0.78
Flen							0.67	0.66

Fig. 6.4   Market structure using market shares with asymmetry inspired by: Blattberg and Wisniewski (1989)

share and asymmetric approaches" (see Figure 6.4). The figure also provides an example of a market structure derived using this approach.

As usual, advancing technology and data availability inspired scholarly research (Shugan, 2004). That process is good provided it does not hinder either traditional scientific theory testing, problem-driven research, or research employing other data sources.

Of course, regardless of the type of numerical data, the quantity of that data or the particular statistical tool used to analyze those data; these are not the key differences between research studies on market structures. The key difference is the underlying theory for market structures. Certainly, the implementation of the theory needs to be sound, but it is the underlying theory that is being tested. It is the underlying theory that dictates the potential applicability of the resulting market structures and the limits of the resulting market structures. The theory should dictate the method and implementation, not the other way around. Therefore, it seems more reasonable to classify research studies in this chapter based on their underlying theory of the market structure rather than the specific data being employed or the statistical tools being used. Often, these factors are correlated, but they still differ.

For example, consider two research studies. The first study employs a factor analysis of cross-elasticity data. The second study employs a cluster analysis of cross-elasticity data. It seems that these two research studies are adopting the same theory of market structure (based on cross-elasticities) even though they are employing different statistical tools (i.e., factor analysis versus cluster analysis). In contrast, consider two research studies that both use factor analysis. One research study derives a market structure from consumer perceptions of similarity and the other research study derives a market structure from stated preference data. Those market structures are very different even though both studies employ survey data and both employ the same statistical tool. Hence, classifying the research study based on the statistical tools seems superficial.

Consequently, this chapter is organized around the underlying theoretical foundations for defining market structures. In that way, we can better group research studies that have similar theoretical underpinnings rather than grouping research studies based on more superficial differences such as the source of the data or the research study's final choice of a statistical tool.

6.2 History of market structures using cross-elasticities in economics

This section considers the theoretically correct method for defining market structures. From early research in economics to the beginning of marketing science, the concept of a cross-elasticity became the theoretical foundation for market structures. It might be difficult to understand why cross-elasticities are so conceptually important. Estimating cross-elasticities was never the most popular way to define a market structure in marketing. In fact, historically, most research studies estimated cross-elasticities only after defining the market structure. However, many factors beyond theory influenced popularity including practicality, objectivity, and data availability.

It is difficult to find the true origin of any idea because good and bad ideas often inspire still other related ideas before the idea is precisely articulated in a seminal publication. Sometimes, ideas (such as the "marketing mix") first appear in speeches or out-of-print books. Regarding cross-elasticities, Kaldor (1934, 1935) was one of the first researchers to advocate the use of cross-elasticities to define the market structure and publish a seminal article on the topic. Triffin (1941) was also an early advocate of the cross-elasticity approach. Triffin (1941) argued that "all commodities are more or less substitutable" and that "the boundaries of the industries become a hindrance rather than a help." He concluded that because all products were substitutes to some degree, defining a markets structure was equivalent to measuring the product differentiation between each pair of products in the market. Moreover, the appropriate measure of the differentiation or substitutability between two products was a cross-elasticities measure or coefficient of interdependence.

Parenthetically, although these arguments may be theoretically correct, it was difficult for a marketing manager, regulator, or policy maker to consider all goods as substitutes. As Day (1977) stated: "the strategically relevant product-market definition lies in stretching the company's perceptions appropriately far enough so that significant threats and opportunities are not missed, but not so far as to dissipate information gathering and analysis efforts on long shots."

Triffin (1941), Papandreou (1949), and many other economists believed that, although the concept of a single market of products or services might be useful for empirical analyses, it was not theoretically sound. From a theoretical viewpoint, every product competes with every other product. This view was consistent with the early work in marketing that recognized that the physical product itself or its physical appearance was not the critical part of the product or the marketing of a product. Product and services provided benefits and marketing needed to focus on those benefits (Levitt, 1960; Haley, 1968; Kotler and Levy, 1969). Parenthetically, early researchers in marketing also recognized that elasticities were an important part of marketing but, for various reasons, failed to apply the concept of a formal cross-elasticity (McGarry et al., 1932).

The theoretical concept was that market structure depends on marketing actions. For example, if a firm were to change some marketing mix variable (e.g., price, advertising, features, service, etc.), that action potentially changed the sales of every other product. The greater the impact of those changes on any particular product in the market, the greater was the substitutability between the two products. Hence, the impact of a potential change in a marketing mix variable determined market structure.

To put it simply, a firm's competitors were those sellers whose marketing actions affected the firm's sales. A firm's competitors were those sellers whose own sales were impacted by the firm's actions. A cross-elasticity was a measure of the potential intensity of that competition. Before discussing the cross-elasticity method in more detail, let us briefly review the precise calculation and precise interpretation of a cross-elasticity.

For a focal firm, a cross-elasticity provided the impact of a change in a competitor's marketing mix variable (price, expenditures on any activity, change in the product attributes, etc.) on some quantitative measure of the focal firm's performance (usually unit demand). For example, a cross-price elasticity of demand measured the change in demand for one firm's product given a change in the price of a potentially competitive firm's price. Measurement of the marketing mix variable was usually in dollars and the measurement of demand was usually in unit sales. For example, consider the cross-elasticity with respect to a competitor's price. This elasticity was the percent change in the unit sales of one firm divided by the percent change in another firm's price. Precisely, the cross-price elasticity of demand for product i with respect to the change in price for product j was the percent change in sales (i.e., the quantity demanded) for product i divided by the percent change in product j's price. Conceptually, the concept of change embodies the true nature of competition. Competition occurs when the actions of one firm impact the sales of another firm. To observe that impact, we must observe an action by one firm. Only when one firm takes some action, can we determine whether that firm competes with other firms.

6.3 History of market structures using cross-elasticities in marketing

This section provides a brief history of research in marketing that defined market structures using cross-elasticities. Given that the cross-elasticity approach measures the impact of a change, it was logical to focus on pricing decisions because price was the marketing mix variable that changed most often. Advertising changed but change occurred less often. Product attribute levels, distribution channels, levels of service, capacity, and many other decision variables also changed, but change was less often still. Finally, there was change that involved the introduction of new products, the introduction of new channels of distribution, and the introduction of entirely new features but those changes were very rare compared to price changes.

Consequently, there have been numerous research studies in marketing that developed the use of cross-price elasticities to understand and define market structures. Some research studies in marketing used cross-price elasticities to define a market structure from the set of products that comprise the household budget, but those research studies were rare. Most research studies took prevailing wisdom in industry regarding historic market structures and tested that structure using cross-price elasticities. Some research studies tested whether the market structure could be summarized by a series of sub-markets where competition within the sub-market was greater than competition between the sub-markets. Some research studies determined that cross-price elasticities correlated with surrogate measures for cross-price elasticities such as similar product features. However, all these research studies embraced the fundamental concept underlying the cross-price elasticity approach including the requirement of observing a change in price.

In one early, but hardly noticed, article in marketing, Clark (1951) estimated the elasticity and cross-price elasticity of the demand for gasoline. His analysis revealed that the estimated elasticity of demand for gasoline, based on county data, was increased by large cross-elasticities across regions. When many drivers lived near neighboring counties, they bought in the county that had the lower price. This analysis indicated a geographic market structure where proximity was a surrogate measure for cross-price elasticity. Claycamp (1966) used a multiple regression to analyze both dynamic cross-price elasticities and the carry-over effect on like grades of gasoline at competing service stations. The analysis revealed several interesting findings regarding cross-price elasticities and the market structure. For example, only current price differentials between gas stations determined current sales. Past price differentials were irrelevant.

One of the first articles, and probably the seminal article, on estimating demand systems in marketing was that of Bass (1969). Bass (1969) used a simultaneous equation regression to analyze limited time-series data for sales and advertising. The analysis revealed that advertising elasticity for filter brands was substantially greater than that for non-filter brands. The research study provided support for a market structure with different sub-markets for filter and non-filter brands. Clarke (1973) analyzed the effect of one brand's advertising on the sales of another brand. The analysis indicated that cross-advertising elasticities were very large. Hence, the advertising of one brand affected the sales of other brands. It appeared that cross-advertising elasticities implied a more homogenous market structure than cross-price elasticities did. Parsons (1975) estimated a regression model using data on a quality household cleanser in cake form where advertising expenditures were limited by insufficient funds. The analysis revealed that that demand elasticities changed over the product life cycle. The analysis provided evidence that market structures can change over time. Years later, Danaher, Bonfrer, and Dhar (2008) confirmed the earlier findings and provided a new finding related to cross-advertising elasticities. Also years later, Sethuraman, Tellis, and Briesch (2011) conducted a meta-analysis of direct-to-consumer brand advertising for research studies published between 1960 and 2008 and found that there was a decline in the advertising elasticity over time but advertising elasticities were higher for durable goods than for non-durable goods.

Simon (1979) estimated a brand life cycle model to analyze elasticities, carryover effects, and obsolescence with time-varying price responses. The analysis revealed that cross-price elasticities change over time indicating that market structures may change over time. This finding suggested that the market structures for differentiated brands might differ from market structures for commodities. Surprisingly, elasticities were greater during the introductory phase of a brand probably because buyers had not yet settled on a favorite brand. Perhaps, sub-markets develop over time.

Mahajan, Green, and Goldberg (1982) used conjoint analysis to estimate cross-price elasticities. The modeling "trick" was to characterize each brand as a separate price-related factor. Respondents indicated their subjective likelihood of buying a set of J brands, each priced at some experimental level. Although the research study did not identify specific sub-markets, the study provided an easy method for accomplishing the first and most difficult step in that process.

Krishnamurthi and Raj (1988) argued that consumer decisions often involved a discrete choice (which) and a continuous (how much) outcome. Their research study considered both cross-choice elasticities that determine which brand was chosen and own-quantity elasticities that determine how much was purchased. Consequently, the market structure might depend on the quantities purchased. There might be a different market structure, for example, for heavy and light users. That idea was not necessarily inconsistent with the idea of cross-price elasticities being different for heavy and light users.

Tellis (1988) provided a meta-analysis that included 367 estimated price elasticities from about 220 different brands. The results indicated that price elasticity appeared relatively homogeneous across data sources, functional forms, the numbers of observations, and the number of parameters. However, estimated elasticities were very sensitive to the level of aggregation as well as the exclusion of promotions, lagged price, advertising, and quality. The omission of quality from market share models biased the price elasticities toward zero. So, managers who used these estimates would believe their markets were less price-sensitive than they actually are. This disturbing result indicated that omitted variables are critical because they were correlated with observed prices. When estimating cross-price elasticities, the omission of variables could provide support for incorrect market structures. Moreover, detecting flaws related to relevant omitted variables was and remains difficult, in part, because all research studies omit many more variables than they include.

Russell and Bolton (1988) analyzed data using a method that constructs a direct relationship between market structure and elasticity structure. The analysis decomposed the elasticities into market share, inter-brand variation in the marketing mix, and consumer propensities to switch within and between market partitions in response to marketing actions. The analyses revealed why actual price elasticities do not always correspond to managerial intuition. This finding suggested that market structures based on industry practice might be incorrect and a healthy skepticism was justified.

Allenby (1989) developed a one-to-one map between a specific demand structure and a restricted cross-elasticity matrix using a random utility model. The resulting demand structure could be summarized with a visual representation of the market structure. Lattin and Bucklin (1989) showed that, when consumers were exposed to pricing and promotional activity by frequently purchased packaged goods, they may have developed expectations about future prices and promotions. Their analysis accounted for consumer expectations. The research study showed clear differences between promotional elasticities, non-promotional price elasticities, and reference effects. Their analysis suggested that market structure could differ in non-promotional periods and promotional periods. For example, a price promotion by a brand and a change in the regular price of that brand might have different effects on the same competitive brand.

Corstjens and Doyle (1989) estimated the space elasticity for a retailer. Their analysis revealed, for example, that retailers should replace merchandise in mature sub-markets with merchandise in new faster growing sub-markets. Initially, profits decline because of the negative cross-elasticity relationships with the newer sub-markets. However, in the long run, there are very significant profit improvements from optimally balancing the benefits of replacing products in profitable (but mature) sub-markets with new products in growing sub-markets, despite a loss in immediate profitability. This analysis was consistent with earlier suggestions that the market structure is dynamic and, at least, sub-markets change over time.

6.4 History of market structures based on asymmetric competition

This section provides a brief history of research in marketing on market structures employing asymmetric competition (market structures where one product's actions affect a second product's sales but the second product's actions may not affect first product's sales). The theoretical implications of asymmetry remain unclear because symmetry is a critical assumption underlying most other approaches. Moreover, asymmetric cross-price elasticities are possibly inconsistent with market structures using symmetric cross-elasticity matrices or multidimensional spatial representations. However, price-scaling can capture asymmetries (Hauser and Shugan, 1983) because product positions change differently for different price changes. Hence, asymmetries may be a function of simultaneous price and positioning optimizations.

Classical demand theory implies symmetric cross-price elasticities after adjusting for income effects. For example, consider the case when the proportion of income spent on two products is the same. According to demand theory, the cross-price elasticities should reflect symmetric competition between the two products. Mathematically, the cross-price elasticity for the first product with the second product should equal the cross-price elasticity for the second product with the first product. When the proportion of incomes spent differs between the two products, then the ratio of the cross-price elasticities should equal the ratio of the proportions of income spent on the two products. This symmetry implies that the effect of a price change for the first product on the second product's sales is the same as the effect of an equal price change of the second product on the first product's sales when the usage rates for the two products are roughly equal.

Cooper (1988) was one of the first research studies to consider asymmetric cross-price elasticities and the implications for multidimensional representations of the market structure. The research study used a special case of three-mode factor analysis to portray the systematic structure underlying asymmetric cross-elasticities for a broad class of market-share attraction models. One set of brand positions portrayed how brands exert influence over the competition. The other set of points portrayed how brands are influenced by others. Similar to Shugan (1987), the angles between the brands provided direct measures of competitive effects. Of course, it is important to distinguish between asymmetric cross-price elasticities and asymmetric effects that only violate the constant ratio property in Logit models (Carpenter *et al.*, 1988). Logit models impose additional constraints on the market structure well-beyond those constraints imposed by economic theory. For example, Logit models assumed that as the market share of any one brand increases, the market shares of the other brands will decrease according to a specific relationship. Economic theory made no assumption about that relationship. Hence, Logit models implicitly assumed specific market structures.

Probably, one of the most famous seminal articles on asymmetric competition was Blattberg and Wisniewski (1989). That article estimated a model derived from a basic utility formulation using 28 brands across 4 product categories. The analysis revealed a market structure consisting of price-tiers where sub-market consists of brands with similar prices. The analysis also revealed a specific asymmetric pattern of price competition implying a specific market structure for frequently purchased packaged goods. Lower-price, lower-quality brands took sales from their own tier and lower tiers, but did not steal significant share from higher tiers. This type of asymmetry was missing from most research studies on market structures. In fact, most research studies implicitly assumed that if one product competed with a second product, then the converse was true.

Kamakura and Russell (1989) analyzed brand switching data by partitioning the market into consumer segments differing in both brand preference and price sensitivity. The analysis provided a unified description of the market structure that linked the pattern of brand switching to the magnitudes of own- and cross-price elasticities. Kamakura and Russell (1989) confirmed the asymmetric price-tier market structure proposed by Blattberg and Wisniewski (1989). This research finding was possibly problematic for some approaches to the market structure because it suggested that competition may not be symmetric. For example, each product in the market might see a different market structure because the market structure depended on which product is taken as the focal product. However, these cross-price elasticities may have been unequal (i.e., asymmetric) because of a scaling artifact. The base market shares and prices were often unequal across brands (Russell, Bucklin, and Srinivasan, 1993). Moreover, most of these research studies failed to correctly adjust for income effects. Income effects must be included when estimating cross-elasticities (Theil, 1965). Nevertheless, many research studies have subsequently verified asymmetries.

A 1995 review article (Blattberg, Briesch, and Fox, 1995) concluded that cross-promotional effects are generally asymmetric. Promoting higher quality brands impacts weaker brands (and private label products) disproportionately. Bronnenberg and Wathieu (1996) provided empirical findings showing asymmetric relationship between positioning and promotion that goes beyond Blattberg and Wisniewski's price-tier effect. The asymmetric relationship can create conceptual problems for some definitions of market structure because it might imply that two products are only in the same market from one product's perspective but not the other. Later, a meta-analysis in Sethuraman, Srinivasan, and Kim (1999) revealed that national brands do impact store brands more than the reverse when the cross-effect was measured in elasticities. Moreover, the asymmetric relationship disappeared with absolute effects (the change in market share of a competing brand for a unit price change of the focal brand). Sethuraman and Srinivasan (2002) verified, in a more general case, that absolute cross-price effects reversed the cross-price elasticity asymmetries. Sayman, Hoch, and Raju (2002) estimated cross-price effects in 19 product categories, and found that only in categories with high-quality store brands did the store brands compete with the leading national brands. That competition was more intense than the competition with the secondary national brands. Their analysis suggested that quality dictated the market structure rather than whether the brand was national or not.

6.5 History of market structures using multi-attribute demand theory

This section provides a brief history of research in marketing that defined market structures using multi-attribute demand theory that defined products as bundles of attributes. From the first uses of cross-elasticities, economists were aware of the problems related to their usefulness for defining market structures. One major problem with the cross-price elasticity approach for defining market structures was that the resulting market was defined in terms of the products or brands rather than their physical attributes (e.g., features, durability, reliability, etc.) or psychological dimensions (e.g., ease-of-use, perceived quality, effectiveness). Some of the previous research studies made assumptions about the product attributes. For example, research studies often grouped products by attribute before estimating the cross-elasticities. Some previous research studies made inferences about product attributes after estimating the cross-elasticities. For example, some research studies assumed that some particular attributes (e.g., high versus low quality) explained the observed pattern of cross-elasticities. However, most of the previous research studies made no formal attempt to directly infer a particular simplified market structure or multidimensional product space from the estimated cross-elasticities. Of course, for many marketing objectives, it was useful to summarize the matrix of cross-elasticities in terms of a simplified product attribute representation. The simplified representation should reveal direct relationships between the likely outcomes of marketing actions by each product and the outcomes on every competitive product. Usually, that simplified representation took the form of a spatial map where products were located in some multidimensional space and their proximity in the multidimensional product space summarized the competitive relationship between the products. Sometimes, that summary took the form of a hierarchical tree structure where products are on branches of the tree and their proximity (e.g., number of nodes apart) summarized the competitive relationship among the products. Hence, spatial maps and hierarchical trees were convenient simplified visual representations of the market structure.

Summarizing the cross-elasticity matrix in this way was not necessary for all applications. For example, economists do use market structures for public policy decisions involving antitrust and monopoly power. For those applications, knowing the relationships among the products or brands may be sufficient. However, in marketing, managers and academics often use inferences about market structures for decisions that do not involve price. For example, market structures were and are used to identify opportunities for launching new products (Srivastava, Leone, and Shocker, 1981). Market structures were and are used to predict cannibalism for new products. Most of the early applications of the market structure analysis involved decisions that were attempts to possibly change the market structure rather than merely change prices. Hence, it was useful to understand why some pairs of products were more substitutable than other pairs of products. It was necessary to decompose the cross-elasticity matrix and often infer a multi-dimensional product space that unambiguously captures differences in the product attributes. Some research studies constrained the cross-elasticity matrix based on the Luce (1959) assumption that the ratio of market shares should remain constant across every choice subset in the market. This assumption is not compatible with asymmetric market structures like Shugan (1987) because utility maximization would violate this assumption when consumers have different weights for different brand attributes.

Hair *et al.* (2009) summarized the two past approaches for decomposing any pairwise matrix into a multidimensional product space. The first approach was called decompositional and the second approach was called compositional. Decompositional methods start with aggregate relationships such as the cross-elasticities or similarities between pairs of products. These methods then summarize that pairwise data into dimensions such as sportiness, luxuriousness, and economy. Compositional methods start with disaggregate data such as product attributes and summarize that data to form a market structure. For example, a compositional method could start with the many attributes of an automobile (miles per gallon, weight, acceleration, breaking, horse-power, torque, etc.) and summarize those many attributes into dimensions such as sportiness, luxuriousness, and economy.

However, from a theoretical perspective, both approaches are mathematically doing similar tasks. Both approaches are reducing a large, possibly unconstrained, set of relationships among the products to a simple Euclidian spatial map or hierarchical tree structure with the minimum loss of information. To be specific, most past and present decompositional approaches to the market structure start with a matrix of numbers that describe the pairwise relationships between the products in the market and derive a simplified spatial structure that obey some intuitive laws. For example, the matrix could consist of cross-elasticities for each pair of products where the diagonal of the matrix would be own-price elasticities.

The matrix could also consist of pairwise similarities or the matrix could consist of preferences for each pair of products. In all these cases, the approach is decompositional (because attributes must be inferred). When the matrix consists of correlations involving attributes or preferences, the approach was compositional (because attributes are known). However, whether the approach is decompositional or compositional, the matrix is still reduced to a Euclidian spatial map or a hierarchical tree (Rao and Sabavala, 1981). Both the decompositional and the compositional approaches to defining market structures are conceptually similar.

Note that reducing or summarizing the matrix is often a problem of properly summarizing the data so as to retain as much information (i.e., variance) as possible while reducing complexity (i.e., the number of parameters). The reduction of the data differs from regression-like approaches that partition the variables into dependent and independent variables. The dependent variables define the market structure and the independent variables establish a causal relationship that links the market structure to marketing actions. However, classifying variables into two sets (i.e., dependent and independent) was unnecessary when the market structure only summarizes the data. For example, factor analysis can summarize a matrix of cross-elasticities or similarities by rotating the matrix. The rotation is done by multiplying by a rotational matrix. By transforming the original matrix in this way, factor analysis moves the variance (i.e., information) from the last columns of the matrix to the first columns of the matrix. No information is lost. Information is merely moved. It is analogous to walking around a theater. The observer's perspective and view of the stage might dramatically improve, but none of the objects in the room actually move. The research study might proceed to ignore the columns of the matrix with little variance losing as little information as possible. It might also rotate the remaining columns to improve interpretation (i.e., move information back to the other remaining columns). Although it is possible to interpret this procedure as exploratory because no hypothesis testing takes place, the procedure essentially produces a market structure by simplifying the original matrix whether the matrix consists of cross-elasticities, similarities, distances, or any other data.

Hence, despite their very different approaches, compositional and decompositional methods are still both data reduction tools. Remember, there are an extraordinary large number of cross-elasticities. There is a cross-elasticity for every pair of products in the market including every brand, every item, every color, every model number, and so on. The cross-elasticities might differ for different prices and different levels of advertising expenditures. Moreover, there are cross-elasticities for every different marketing mix variable (e.g., price, service) and every marketing action (e.g., new product introductions, changes in features). There are cross-price elasticities, cross-advertising elasticities, cross-feature elasticities, and so on. There could be an infinite number of different cross-elasticities for every pair because the elasticity could be different for every price level. One goal of every model is simplification. As Shugan (2007) noted: "Models are only useful because they remove the irrelevant aspects of reality." "We require assumptions to reduce a vast quantity of numerical data points to a very small meager set of summary statistics or estimated parameters. It is impossible to add value to a dataset by ignoring parts of it, unless ignoring parts of it reveals the predictive or explanatory power of the assumptions." We already have reality and we already have the raw data. Models reduce reality and the raw data to a few estimated parameters or summary statistics that are more useful than the raw data. By definition, models reduce the available information because it is possible to go from the data to the estimated parameters but it is never possible to recover the raw data from the estimated parameters. However, summary statistics and estimated parameters supposedly capture all the relevant information in the data. A market structure should accomplish that task. Hence, it is necessary to somehow summarize all these many elasticities into a simple manageable representation of the market structure.

Hauser and Shugan (1983) provided one early theory that imposed a structure on the cross-elasticity matrix. Hauser and Shugan (1983) developed a market structure model to determine how a firm should adjust its marketing expenditures and its price to defend its position in an existing market from attack by a competitive new product. Hauser and Shugan (1983) developed a model (sometimes referred to as "Defender") similar to economic models being developed at the time using a model where consumers maximized their utility. The consumer utility was modeled as a function of the product attributes. However, consumers were heterogeneous. Different consumers valued different attributes more than others. Those differences were captured by a probability distribution. The percent of consumers purchasing a product was determined by integrating the probability distribution of consumer preferences over the region where that product dominated all other products. The percent of consumers purchasing a product was equivalent to the market share for the product when each consumer had the same usage rate. Of course, the distribution could also reflect the usage rates. Hauser and Shugan (1983) explored different probability distributions and showed how defensive strategies changed for different distributions.

Hauser and Shugan (1983) provided a market structure model that translated consumer positions in a perceptual space into market shares. However, the required utility maximization revealed that product market shares depended on product attributes divided by product prices. This is a result of the way prices impact consumer choice decisions in economic models when the utility function is a function of the product attributes. Hence, Hauser and Shugan (1983) analysis suggested that product positioning maps that define the market structure should be price-scaled.

There was a basic problem with the market structure model in Hauser and Shugan (1983). Like other classical economic models with heterogeneity (Hotelling, 1929; Chamberlin, 1953) and early multi-attribute models (Lancaster, 1980; Lane, 1980) at that time, products were located over a finite interval. Unlike other classical economic models, Hauser and Shugan (1983) did consider non-uniform distributions. However, their analysis still assumed that products were located on an interval which had endpoints. These endpoints create a great deal of mathematical complexity. To remedy that problem, Hauser and Shugan (1983) used a trigonometric analysis where products were all positioned in the positive quadrant where attributes were all non-negative. Within that quadrant, the consumer preference distribution was defined over the angle with the abscissa (consistent with the economic utility maximizing framework). Hence, Hauser and Shugan (1983) showed mathematically that the angles that the products formed with the abscissa would predict a unique market share for each product given a probability distribution for consumer preferences over the attribute space. This type of model leads to complex trigonometric equations. See Ratchford (1990) for a review of the state-of-the-art during that time period.

Subsequent economic models adopted circular preferences which avoided the endpoints in a finite interval model (Schmalensee, 1978;

Weitzman, 1982; Borenstein, 1985). By assuming the products are located on a circle, there are no endpoints. This type of model avoided much of the mathematical complexity associated with trigonometric models of the market structure. However, circular models are still rare in modern-day applications that seek to define market structures.

The market structure model in Hauser and Shugan (1983) had the property that the market structure depended on the relative prices of the products. For relatively small changes in price, only adjacent products should have positive cross-price elasticities. For larger changes in price, more distant products would have positive cross-price elasticities. Hence, the model based on consumer utility maximization and a preference distribution for the population, suitably constrained the cross-elasticity matrix to a relatively small number of parameters.

Shugan (1987) proved that in a two-dimensional space, the observed price changes and the corresponding changes in market share in the Hauser and Shugan (1983) model imply unique positions in the two-dimensional space for every product. This uniqueness was rarely observed because most two-dimensional representations of the market structure in other models are unique only to either a monotonic or positive-linear transformation. The uniqueness was a property of constraining the space to the positive quadrant.

Shugan (1987) estimated the Hauser and Shugan (1983) market structure model with data obtained from supermarket scanning data. As a result of that estimation, per dollar multidimensional brand maps are obtained from aggregate sales and price time-series data. The estimation procedure allowed the derivation of the map from observed choice behavior and predicted the direct effect of both a brand's price and a brand's position on that brand's sales. It integrated the traditional cross-price elasticity interpretation of substitutability with perceptual mapping. It also reproduced the asymmetric cross-price elasticities from a theoretical framework. Actual spatial maps for the market structure were estimated for three product categories.

Urban, Johnson, and Hauser (1984), around the same time, developed one of the most novel, theoretically sound models and easy-to-implement procedures for testing market structures. Moreover, unlike many other previous procedures, their procedure was based on the scientific method by using data to test different hypothesized market structures suggested by managers or previous exploratory studies. For example, hypothesized market structures might be based on different product attributes (e.g., brand, form, size), usage situations (e.g., coffee in the morning versus coffee at dinner), or user characteristics (e.g., heavy versus light users). Their goal was to collect data that would empirically test whether a particular market structure was present. Consumers were asked to choose products from different consideration sets. Their preferred products were subsequently eliminated to reveal second choices. The market structure, if correct, should predict the second choice. The research study derived a statistical test to determine whether the theoretical predictions were consistent second choices. With this procedure, "sub-markets" were said to exist when consumers were statistically more likely to buy again in that "sub-market" than would be predicted based on an aggregate "constant ratio" model.

Also in the 1980s, other researchers were simultaneously and subsequently developing methods for inferring market structure from choice data, purchase data (including quantities purchased) and aggregate sales data. Moore and Winer (1987) used commonly available consumer diary panel data to construct a time-series of joint space maps and then integrated these maps into market structures that predicted response to changes in the marketing mix. Grover and Srinivasan (1987) used panel data to simultaneously segment and define market structures. Jain, Bass, and Chen (1990) improved on this approach to define market structures. Elrod (1988) developed method for inferring a product-market map from panel data. The method combined the parsimony of stochastic choice models, the rationale of random utility models, and the ability of multidimensional scaling procedures to simultaneously infer both brand positions and consumer preferences from preference (choice) data. The method assumed that consumers have stationary purchase probabilities for the observational period. Hence, the model was best suited to frequently-bought mature product categories. Neither experimental nor survey data was required.

6.6 History of market structures using psychometric theories

This section provides a brief history of research in marketing that defined market structures using psychometric theory (i.e., the theory of psychological measurement). It is important to realize that there was a very fundamental difference between product substitutability measured with psychological measurement and product substitutability measured with cross-elasticities. It was the same fundamental difference that existed between statistics and psychometrics. Most classical statistical measures are based on correlations. Correlations, like economic cross-elasticities, are functions of change.

In contrast, psychometric approaches tend to emphasize absolute values rather than change. For example, if two test scores are close together in magnitude, psychometric approaches tend to group the test-takers into the same group. In contrast, a statistical or economic approach might only group the test-takers together if there is a correlation between the scores of the two test-takers across multiple tests regardless of the absolute scores. Better yet, a statistical or economic approach might only group the test-takers together if the test-takers responded similarly to a control variable (for example, hours spent studying).

Psychometric approaches, therefore, often start with absolute measures rather than measures of change. For example, rather than using a variable like the cross-elasticity to describe a pair of products, a variable like similarity might be employed. Another example of an absolute measure might be the difference in preference between a pair of products (e.g., a strong preference versus a weak preference). The psychometric approaches also emphasized the use of survey data. Although cross-elasticities, choice data, purchase data (including frequency and quantity), sales (aggregate quantities), inter-purchase times (Grover and Rao, 1988), and other observable behaviors are naturally linked to sales, survey data is arguably far richer than purchase data. The primary argument in favor of survey data is that survey data is experimental in the sense that consumers can consider hypothetical or counterfactuals. Without experimental data, it is necessary to assume that different periods are replications of a single period or use statistical controls to eliminate any differences between the time periods beyond changes in the observed marketing mix. Obviously, many factors change from period to period and controlling for those factors may require still more assumptions. Moreover, all the problems associated with non-experimental data (selection bias, omitted variable bias, aggregation bias, etc.) must be overcome. When one firm changes its decisions, other firms respond and it is necessary to make strong assumptions about the nature of that response in order to predict the outcome that would have resulted had there been no response. When one firm changes its decisions, other firms might change because a common unobserved event has caused both firms to change their actions. In the worst case, all firms are in equilibrium and we never observe sufficient variation from the equilibrium to estimate the partial derivatives. Finally, unless there is a real variation in long-term prices and other marketing variables over time (that is not caused by common factors affecting all brands), many weeks or years of observations contain no more and probably less information than a single experiment where prices are varied across matched markets.

We should not confuse large quantities of data with abundant information. Information, in statistics, is related to variation. Information in decision making is related to newness. Unless the data has variation and tells us something that we do not already know, that data has no information. For example, even when we observe prices every second of the day, we may obtain no more information than observing prices every week. Unless we observe prices and quantities outside of equilibrium, it is extremely difficult to predict the outcome of an unobserved unilateral action without assuming it.

As noted earlier, compositional methods start with individual level data and aggregate that data to obtain a market structure (Hair *et al.*, 2009). There were two early streams of research in psychometrics that probably spawned the development of compositional approaches for defining a market structure. First, there was the idea of representing the structure between objects as distances in a Euclidean space (Young and Householder, 1938). Second, there was an idea by Louis Leon Thurstone (1931) that was based on Charles Edward Spearman's early work (Spearman, 1914). Thurstone's idea was that a large number of variables could be summarized with a small set of variates that were linear combinations of the original variables.

Some of the subsequent development of this research focused on transforming ordinal data into metric information (Coombs, 1958; Kruskal, 1964). This research was based on the idea that respondents might only be able to provide ordinal data even though their underlying preferences had metric properties. For example, respondents could only indicate that one product was preferred to another product but be unable to communicate the intensity of that preference. Hence, respondents could not provide metric information. Consequently, much of the complexity in early compositional methods focused on determining the latent metric values underlying ordinal responses. To a large extent, this objective was unrelated to defining a market structure even though it became a central part of research on market structures.

The history of inferring a concealed structure, latent factors, or unobserved dimensions predates research studies in marketing. For example, Spearman (1914) developed a factor analysis procedure that could find two common factors from a matrix of inter-correlations. Thurstone (1931) developed a more general method for factor analysis which had no restrictions regarding the number of group factors. Richardson's (1938) was the first or one of the first applications of multidimensional scaling. In its early days, cluster analysis was sometimes referred to as grouping. For example, Cox (1957) proposed condensing multivariate observations (with a focus on normally distributed variates) into a small number of groups where the grouping intervals were chosen to retain as much information as possible. Fisher (1958) devised a practical procedure for grouping a set of arbitrary numbers so that the variance within groups is minimized. Ward (1963) provided a procedure for forming hierarchical groups of mutually exclusive subsets, each of which has members that are maximally similar with respect to specified characteristics. Shepard (1966) showed that ordered data (e.g., ordering of objects) was sometimes sufficient to fix the positions of those objects on a numerical scale. Shepard (1966) used both mathematical and "Monte Carlo" results to show how metric information could be extracted from purely ordinal data for two multidimensional cases.

Hence, by the mid-1960s, mathematical psychologists had developed many techniques for summarizing data that provided the capability of identifying common underlying structures in the data. Beyond summarizing the data, many of these techniques claimed to summarize ordinal data (i.e., only providing an ordering the objects) with some type of metric summary (e.g., numerical distances). Within that context, many psychometricians were interested in transforming ordinal data into a special representation that had metric properties. Products would exist in that spatial representation as points and the proximity of those points in the space would represent similarity or substitutability (most of this research equated similarity measures with measures of substitutability). For example, Green (1969, 1975) followed a stream of literature including Richardson (1938),

Torgerson (1952), and Shepard (1962) to develop methods that described products as points in a multidimensional space based on product attributes (Wilkie and Pessemier, 1973). See Day, Shocker, and Srivastava (1979) for other examples of related methods employing customer judgment.

Within marketing, the problem became how to adapt those techniques to marketing problems. That adaptation included developing survey instruments, modifying the techniques to different marketing settings, and linking the numerical output from these techniques to marketing decisions. One seminal article on this topic was Green and Rao (1969). That article theoretically and empirically compared 10 types of proximity measures advocated by various researchers interested in clustering and related techniques. Green and Carmone (1969) described the basic concepts of multidimensional scaling of similarities and preference data and provided a short description of its historical development to 1969. The research study also provided an empirical comparison of three computer programs and found that differences among the resulting market structures reflect the influence of differential preference weightings of the perceptual dimensions. Green (1970) reviewed the progress in the 1960s in measurement theory, multidimensional scaling, and non-metric methods that are useful in defining market structure and marketing in general.

Measurement theory and psychometric approaches emphasized the need to understand consumer perceptions which might differ from firm perceptions even for objective quantities such as the price of the product. For example, the seminal article by Monroe (1973) concluded that to focus on price alone and assume as constant all context variables was "a grave error" because "a number of psychological and other contextual factors may lead to a perception of price by the buyer that was different from the perception assumed by the price setter."

Perceptual mapping was an ideal approach for analyzing consumer perceptions and became a popular tool for doing so. For example, Vavra (1972) provided a procedure that extended factor analysis to the description of changes in subject perceptions of a product after their exposure to an advertisement for the product. Hauser and Koppelman (1979) provided an extensive review and evaluation of the use of perceptual mapping for defining market structures. The research study presented theoretical arguments and empirical evidence suggesting that factor analysis was superior to discriminant analysis and similarity scaling with respect to predictive ability, managerial interpretability, and ease of use.

By 1979, there were many methods, techniques, and conceptual approaches for defining a market structure using psychometric methods. Day, Shocker, and Srivastava (1979) provided a review that compared and contrasted different methods for defining a market structure according to whether they were consistent with a conceptual definition of a product market and their ability to yield diagnostic insights. DeSarbo and Rao (1986) developed market structures using unfolding methodology to repositioning products, design new products, and target consumer segments. Years later, Carroll and Green (1997) combined exploratory multidimensional scaling and confirmatory conjoint analysis to create a constrained procedure for estimating a market structure. The dimensions of the perceptual dimensions were constrained to be linear or non-linear functions of a set of fixed external variables. Finally, Ghose (1998) noted that spatial and tree representations of market structures employ different distance patterns.

6.7 Directions for future research

This chapter suggests that although there is a market structure, that structure must be conditioned on many factors which could include the decision-variable, the point-in-time, and the measure of substitutability. Research on these factors will probably continue. In addition, future research might also address the following issues.

(1) Past market structure applications have focused on the special problems relating to keeping new products from cannibalizing existing products. The unique problems of other applications lack sufficient attention. Market structure applications awaiting future research include defining markets for co-branding strategies, evaluating antitrust complaints, litigation involving patent infringement, mergers and acquisitions, distribution strategies into different markets, brand equity, and the life-time-value of consumers (e.g., which consumers are in the market).

(2) Despite numerous empirical articles on market structures, there are surprisingly few published generalizations. It would be useful to determine which findings appear to be consistent across industries

and which findings are not. Perhaps, a meta-analysis type approach is warranted.

(3) Given a large literature on market structure, there are surprisingly few published theories. Every empirical analysis seems to begin from scratch. The past literature has focused on developing tools and, as technology has changed, tools have changed. Although tools are useful, the literature fails to reveal why some markets have many sub-markets (and some not), why some markets are dominated by a small number of firms (and some not), why some markets change over time (and some not) and why some markets have different structures for different consumers while others have a single well-defined structure. There is no marketing theory regarding how market structures develop, what influences their development, what causes market structures to change (if they do), and what variables determine the ultimate market structure in an industry. Future research should focus on theory development with empirical tests of those theories.

(4) Finally, distribution channels are rapidly changing. The internet, international transport, smart phones, GPS, just-in-time inventory, and other emerging technologies are having a dramatic effect on marketing activities. Future research might consider their impact on market structures.

References

Allenby, G. M. (1989). A unified approach to identifying, estimating and testing demand structures with aggregate scanner data, *Marketing Science*, 8(3), 265–280.

Bass, F. M. (1969). A simultaneous equation regression study of advertising and sales of cigarettes, *Journal of Marketing Research*, 6(3), 291–300.

Bass, F. M. and D. G. Clarke (1972). Testing distributed lag models of advertising effect, *Journal of Marketing Research*, 9(3), 298–308.

Blattberg, R. C. and K. J. Wisniewski (1989). Price-induced patterns of competition, *Marketing Science*, 8(4), 291–309.

Blattberg, R. C., R. Briesch, and E. J. Fox (1995). How promotions work, *Marketing Science*, 14(3), G122–G132.

Blattberg, R. C. and S. K. Sen (1974). Market segmentation using models of multidimensional purchasing behavior, *Journal of Marketing*, 38(4), 17–28.

Borenstein, S. (1985). Price discrimination in free-entry markets, *The RAND Journal of Economics*, 16(3), 380–397.

Bronnenberg, B. J. and L. Wathieu (1996). Asymmetric promotion effects and brand positioning, *Marketing Science*, 15(4), 379–394.

Carpenter, G. S., L. G. Cooper, D. M. Hanssens, and D. F. Midgley (1988). Modeling asymmetric competition, *Marketing Science*, 7(4), 393–412.

Carroll, J. D. and P. E. Green (1997). Psychometric methods in marketing research: Part ii, multidimensional scaling, *Journal of Marketing Research*, 34(2), 193–204.

Chamberlin, E. H. (1953). The product as an economic variable, *The Quarterly Journal of Economics*, 67(1), 1–29.

Clark, L. (1951). The elasticity of demand for Tennessee gasoline, *Journal of Marketing Science*, 15(4), 399–414.

Clarke, D. G. (1973). Sales-advertising cross-elasticities and advertising competition, *Journal of Marketing Research*, 10(3), 250–261.

Clarke, F. R. (1957) Constant-ratio rule for confusion matrices in speech communication, *Journal of the Acoustical Society of America*, 29(6), 715–720.

Claycamp, H. J. (1966). Dynamic effects of short duration price differentials on retail gasoline sales, *Journal of Marketing Research*, 3(2), 175–178.

Clevenger, T. Jr., G. A. Lazier, and M. L. Clark (1965). Measurement of corporate images by the semantic differential, *Journal of Marketing Research*, 2(1), 80–82.

Coombs, C. H. (1958). An application of a nonmetric model for multidimensional analysis of similarities, *Psychological Reports*, 4(1), 511–518.

Cooper, L. G. (1988). Competitive maps: The structure underlying asymmetric cross elasticities, *Management Science*, 34(6), 707–723.

Corstjens, M. L. and P. Doyle (1989). Evaluating alternative retail repositioning strategies, *Marketing Science*, 8(2), 170–180.

Cox, D. R. (1957). Note on grouping, *Journal of the American Statistical Association*, 52(280), 543–547.

Danaher, P. J., A. Bonfrer, and S. Dhar (2008). The effect of competitive advertising interference on sales for packaged goods, *Journal of Marketing Research*, 45(2), 211–225.

Day, G. S. (1977). Diagnosing the product portfolio, *Journal of Marketing*, 41(2), 29–38.

Day, G. S., A. D. Shocker, and R. K. Srivastava (1979). Customer-oriented approaches to identifying product-markets, *Journal of Marketing*, 43(4), 8–19.

DeSarbo, W. and V. Rao (1986). A constrained unfolding methodology for product positioning, *Marketing Science*, 5(1), 1–19.

Elrod, T. (1988). Choice map: Inferring a product-market map from panel data, *Marketing Science*, 7(1), 21–40.

Farley, J. U. (1964). Why does "brand loyalty" vary over products? *Journal of Marketing Research*, 1(4), 9–14.

Ferber, R. (1951). On teaching statistics to marketing students, *Journal of Marketing*, 15(3), 340–343.

Ferber, R. and H. G. Wales (1951). The market for prefabricated housing, *Journal of Marketing*, 16(1), 18–28.

Fisher, W. D. (1958). On grouping for maximum homogeneity, *Journal of the American Statistical Association*, 53(28), 789–798.

Frank, R. E. and P. E. Green (1968). Numerical taxonomy in marketing analysis: A review article, *Journal of Marketing Research*, 5(1), 83–94.

Ghose, S. (1998). Distance representations of consumer perceptions: Evaluating appropriateness by using diagnostics, *Journal of Marketing Research*, 35(2), 137–153.

Green, P. E. (1969). Multidimensional scaling: An introduction and comparison of nonmetric unfolding techniques, *Journal of Marketing Research*, 6(3), 330–341.

Green, P. E. (1970). Measurement and data analysis, *Journal of Marketing*, 34(1), 15–17.

Green, P. E. (1975). Marketing applications of mds: Assessment and outlook, *Journal of Marketing*, 39(1), 24–31.

Green, P. E. and F. J. Carmone (1969). Multidimensional scaling: An introduction and comparison of nonmetric unfolding techniques, *Journal of Marketing Research*, 6(3), 330–341.

Green, P. E., F. J. Carmone, and P. J. Robinson (1968). *Analysis of marketing behavior using non-metric scaling and related techniques*, Boston: Marketing Science Institute.

Green, P. E., M. H. Halbert, and P. J. Robinson (1966). Canonical analysis: An exposition and illustrative application, *Journal of Marketing Research*, 3(1), 32–39.

Green, P. E. and V. R. Rao (1969). A note on proximity measures and cluster analysis, *Journal of Marketing Research*, 6(3), 359–364.

Grover, R. and V. Srinivasan (1987). A simultaneous approach to market segmentation and market structuring, *Journal of Marketing Research*, 24(2), 139–153.

Grover, R. and V. R. Rao (1988). Inferring competitive market structure based on a model of interpurchase intervals on a model of interpurchase intervals, *International Journal of Research in Marketing*, 5(1), 55–72.

Hair, J. F., B. Black, B. Babin, and R. E. Anderson (2009). *Multivariate data analysis*, New Jersey: Prentice Hall.

Haley, R. I. (1968). Benefit segmentation: A decision-oriented research tool, *Journal of Marketing*, 32(3), 30–35.

Hauser, J. R. and F. S. Koppelman (1979). Alternative perceptual mapping techniques: Relative accuracy and usefulness, *Journal of Marketing Research*, 16(4), 495–506.

Hauser, J. R. and S. M. Shugan (1983). Defensive marketing strategies, *Marketing Science*, 2(4), 319–360.

Hawkins, E. R. (1957). Methods of estimating demand, *Journal of Marketing*, 21(4), 428–438.

Hinkle, C. L. and J. S. Wolf (1966). Academic research and the data drought dilemma, *Journal of Marketing Research*, 3(2), 196–198.

Hotelling, H. (1929). Stability in competition, *The Economic Journal*, 39(15), 41–57.

Jain, D., F. M. Bass, and Y.-M. Chen (1990). Estimation of latent class models with heterogeneous choice probabilities: An application to market structuring, *Journal of Marketing Research*, 27(1), 94–101.

Kaldor, N. (1934). Mrs. Robinson's "Economics of Imperfect Competition", *Economica*, 1(3), 335–341.

Kaldor, N. (1935). Market imperfection and excess capacity, *Economica*, 2(5), 33–50.

Kamakura, W. A. and G. J. Russell (1989). A probabilistic choice model for market segmentation and elasticity structure, *Journal of Marketing Research*, 26(4), 379–390.

Kotler, P. and S. J. Levy (1969). Broadening the concept of marketing, *Journal of Marketing*, 33(1), 10–15.

Krishnamurthi, L. and S. P. Raj (1988). A model of brand choice and purchase quantity price sensitivities, *Marketing Science*, 7(1), 1–20.

Kruskal, J. B. (1964). Multidimensional scaling by optimizing goodness of fit to a nonmetric hypothesis, *Psychometrika*, 29(1), 1–27.

Lancaster, K. (1980). Competition and product variety, *The Journal of Business*, 53(3), S79–S103.

Lane, W. J. (1980). Product differentiation in a market with endogenous sequential entry, *The Bell Journal of Economics*, 11(1), 237–260.

Lattin, J. M. and R. E. Bucklin (1989). Reference effects of price and promotion on brand choice behavior, *Journal of Marketing Research*, 26(3), 299–310.

Levitt, T. (1960). Marketing myopia, *Harvard Business Review*, 38(4), 45–56.

Luce, R. D. (1959). Individual choice behavior: A theoretical analysis, New York: Wiley.

Mahajan, V., P. E. Green, and S. M. Goldberg (1982). A conjoint model for measuring self- and cross-price/demand relationships, *Journal of Marketing Research*, 19(3), 334–342.

McGarry, E. D., N. H. Borden, R. S. Vaile, J. E. Boyle, D. R. Cowan, H. E. Agnew, J. F. Pyle, and W. A. Sherman (1932). Elasticity of demand as a useful marketing concept, *American Economic Review*, 22(1), 117–127.

Monroe, K. B. (1973). Buyers' subjective perceptions of price, *Journal of Marketing Research*, 10(1), 70–80.

Moore, W. L. and R. S. Winer (1987). A panel-data based method for merging joint space and market response function estimation, *Marketing Science*, 6(1), 25–42.

Morrison, D. G. (1969). On the interpretation of discriminant analysis, *Journal of Marketing Research*, 6(2), 156–163.

Myers, J. H. and E. Tauber (1977). Market structure analysis, Chicago: American Marketing Association.

Neidell, L. A. (1969). The use of nonmetric multidimensional scaling in marketing analysis, *Journal of Marketing*, 33(4), 37–43.

O'Dell, W. F. (1962). Personal interviews or mail panels? *Journal of Marketing*, 26(4), 34–39.

Papandreou, A. G. (1949). Market structure and monopoly power, *American Economic Review*, 39(5), 883–897.

Parsons, L. J. (1975). The product life cycle and time-varying advertising elasticities, *Journal of Marketing Research*, 12(4), 476–480.

Rao, V. R. and D. J. Sabavala (1981). Inference of hierarchical choice processes from panel data, *Journal of Consumer Research*, 8(1), 85–96.

Ratchford, B. T. (1990). Commentary: Marketing applications of the economics of product variety, *Marketing Science*, 9(3), 207–211.

Richardson, M. W. (1938). Multidimensional psychophysics, *Psychological Bulletin*, 35(9), 659–660.

Russell, G. J., R. E. Bucklin, and V. Srinivasan (1993). Identifying multiple preference segments from own- and cross-price elasticities, *Marketing Letters*, 4(1), 5–18.

Russell, G. J. and R. N. Bolton (1988). Implications of market structure for elasticity structure, *Journal of Marketing Research*, 25(3), 229–241.

Sayman, S., S. J. Hoch, and J. S. Raju (2002). Positioning of store brands, *Marketing Science*, 21(4), 378–397.

Schmalensee, R. (1978). Entry deterrence in the ready-to-eat breakfast cereal industry, *The Bell Journal of Economics*, 9(2), 305–327.

Sethuraman, R., G. J. Tellis, and R. A. Briesch (2011). How well does advertising work? Generalizations from meta-analysis of brand advertising elasticities, *Journal of Marketing Research*, 48(3), 457–471.

Sethuraman, R. and V. Srinivasan (2002). The asymmetric share effect: An empirical generalization on cross-price effects, *Journal of Marketing Research*, 39(3), 379–386.

Sethuraman, R., V. Srinivasan, and D. Kim (1999). Asymmetric and neighborhood cross-price effects: Some empirical generalizations, *Marketing Science*, 18(1), 23–41.

Shepard, R. N. (1962). The analysis of proximities: Multidimensional scaling with an unknown distance function, 27(1), 125–139.

Shepard, R. N. (1966). Metric structures in ordinal data, *Journal of Mathematical Psychology*, 3(2), 287–315.

Shugan, S. M. (1987). Estimating brand positioning maps using supermarket scanning data, *Journal of Marketing Research*, 24(1), 1–18.

Shugan, S. M. (2002). In search of data: An editorial, *Marketing Science*, 21(4), 369–377.

Shugan, S. M. (2004). The impact of advancing technology on marketing and academic research, *Marketing Science*, 23(4), 469–475.

Shugan, S. M. (2007). It's the findings, stupid, not the assumptions, *Marketing Science*, 26(4), 449–459.

Silk, A. J. and G. L. Urban (1978). Pre-test-market evaluation of new packaged goods: A model and measurement methodology, *Journal of Marketing Research*, 15(2), 171–191.

Simon, H. (1979). Dynamics of price elasticity and brand life cycles: An empirical study, *Journal of Marketing Research*, 16(4), 439–452.

Smith, W. R. (1956). Product differentiation and market segmentation as alternative marketing strategies, *Journal of Marketing*, 21(1), 3–8.

Spearman, C. E. (1914). The theory of two factors, *Psychological Review*, 21(2), 101–115.

Srinivasan, T. C. and R. S. Winer (1994). Using neoclassical consumer-choice theory to produce a market map from purchase data, *Journal of Business & Economic Statistics*, 12(1), 1–9.

Srivastava, R. K., R. P. Leone, and A. D. Shocker (1981). Market structure analysis: Hierarchical clustering of products based on substitution-in-use, *Journal of Marketing*, 45(3), 38–48.

Stefflre, V. J. (1968). Market structure studies: New products for old markets and new markets, in Frank M. Bass, *et al.*, eds., *Applications of the sciences to marketing management*, New York: John Wiley & Sons.

Storey, D. A. and P. L. Farris (1964). Market performance in the baking industry, *Journal of Marketing*, 28(1), 19–25.

Tellis, G. J. (1988). The price elasticity of selective demand: A meta-analysis of econometric models of sales, *Journal of Marketing Research*, 25(4), 331–341.

Theil, H. (1965). The information approach to demand analysis, *Econometrica*, 33(1), 67–87.

Thurstone, L. L. (1931). Multiple factor analysis, *Psychological Review*, 38(5), 406–427.

Torgerson, W. S. (1952). Multidimensional scaling: I. Theory and method, *Psychometrika*, 17(4), 401–419.

Triffin, R. (1941). Monopoly in particular-equilibrium and in general-equilibrium economics, *Econometrica*, 9(2), 121–127.

Urban, G. L. (1975). Perceptor: A model for product positioning, *Management Science*, 21(8), 858–871.

Urban, G. L., P. L. Johnson, and J. R. Hauser (1984). Testing competitive market structures, *Marketing Science*, 3(2), 83–112.

Vavra, T. G. (1972). Factor analysis of perceptual change, *Journal of Marketing Research*, 9(2), 193–199.

Ward, J. H., Jr. (1963). Hierarchical grouping to optimize an objective function, *Journal of the American Statistical Association*, 58(301), 236–244.

Weitzman, M. L. (1982). Increasing returns and the foundations of unemployment theory, *The Economic Journal*, 92(36), 787–804.

Wilkie, W. L. and E. A. Pessemier (1973). Issues in marketing's use of multi-attribute attitude models, *Journal of Marketing Research*, 10(4), 428–441.

Wind, Y. (1978). Issues and advances in segmentation research, *Journal of Marketing Research*, 15(3), 317–337.

Wind, Y. and D. Lerner (1979). On the measurement of purchase data: surveys versus purchase diaries, *Journal of Marketing Research*, 16(1), 39–47.

Young, G. and A. S. Householder (1938). Discussion of a set of points in terms of their mutual distances, *Psychometrika*, 3(1), 19–22.

Chapter 7

Stochastic Models of Buyer Behavior

Peter S. Fader, Bruce G. S. Hardie and Subrata Sen

7.1 Introduction

"Winwood Reade is good upon the subject," said Holmes. "He remarks that, while the individual man is an insoluble puzzle, in the aggregate he becomes a mathematical certainty. You can, for example, never foretell what any one man will do, but you can say with precision what an average number will be up to."

Sir Arthur Conan Doyle, *The Sign of Four*

Buyer behavior is a complex phenomenon. We can safely assume that the actual data-generating process that lies behind any observed measure(s) of buyer behavior (e.g., the brands chosen across a series of purchase occasions, the number of times a product is purchased in a certain time period, the time at which a new product is first purchased) embodies a huge number of factors. Even if the actual process were completely deterministic, it would be impossible to measure all the variables that determine an individual's buying behavior in any setting. As such, any account of buyer behavior should be expressed in probabilistic/random/stochastic terms so as to account for our ignorance regarding (and/or lack of data on) all the determinants.

Rather than trying to tease out the effects of various marketing, personal, and situational variables, a stochastic model of buyer behavior acknowledges the fact that we can never completely describe the actual data-generating process. Thus, we completely embrace the notion of stochasticity, viewing the behavior of interest as the outcome of one or more probabilistic processes. (This does not imply that we think the individual is truly purchasing "at random". Rather it simply reflects our uncertainty regarding the factors that influence buying behavior; the probabilistic process captures the net effect of all the influences not explicitly considered in the model.) A stochastic model of buyer behavior typically has two components. First, the individual behavior of interest (e.g., brand chosen, number of purchases) is characterized in terms of a probability distribution (or several distributions in the case of a more complex model), with the parameters of this distribution reflecting the individual's underlying behavioral propensities. Second, differences in these underlying behavioral propensities across individuals are captured by an additional probability distribution (or distributions).[1] These two components result in a *mixture distribution*, which characterizes the behavior of a randomly chosen individual.

While such models do not give us any insights as to "how" or "why" consumers behave the way they do, they still have a number of uses. Such models are primarily used to summarize and interpret patterns of market-level behavior and predict behavior in future periods, be it at the aggregate or at a more granular level (e.g., conditional on past behavior). As such, they can be used as benchmarks against which actual behavior can be compared. They can also serve as a basis for testing some "structural" hypotheses (e.g., from economic or psychological theories) about the underlying nature of buyer behavior.

Stochastic models of buyer behavior have been part of the marketing science literature from the very beginning. Magee (1953) is the first published application of management science and operations research techniques to a marketing problem (Montgomery, 2001); he developed a stochastic model to characterize buyer behavior as part of a tool for determining the level and allocation of promotional effort. While such models received the attention of many researchers in the 1960s

---

[1]While an explicit accounting for cross-sectional heterogeneity has been an integral part of stochastic models of buyer behavior right from the beginning, some early models did not include the second component (i.e., they implicitly assumed homogeneity in the individual-level behavioral propensities).

and 1970s, they lost favor in 1980s. However, the rising popularity of customer analytics — and the associated improvements in data richness and computational power — in recent years has drawn many researchers (and practitioners) back toward these models. Thus, this review considers how developments in the collection of customer data have been associated with the "birth," "death," and current "resurrection" of stochastic models of buyer behavior in marketing.[2]

7.2 Birth

In the beginning there was . . . data.

The practice of "public opinion polling," be it for political or commercial purposes, was well established by the 1930s. This decade saw the emergence of the so-called panel technique: "Instead of taking a new sample for each poll, repeated interviews with the same group of people have been tried" (Lazarsfeld and Fiske, 1938, p. 596). Two well-known early examples are the *Woman's Home Companion* panel of readers (Lazarsfeld and Fiske, 1938) and the BBC's Drama Panel (Silvey, 1974).

These early panels were custom panels set up by a given organization to study company-specific problems. In 1941, the Industrial Surveys Company founded its National Consumer Index panel (later called the National Consumer Panel), which saw a panel of 2,000 households being given diaries, collected once a month, to record their purchases of certain categories of consumer goods (Stonborough, 1942). In 1944, the company switched to a weekly diary (Shaffer, 1955). Across the pond, Attwood Statistics Ltd founded its consumer panel service in the United Kingdom in 1948. In 1951, Industrial Surveys Company acquired (and then changed its name to) the Market Research Corporation of America (MRCA) (Jones and Tadajewski, 2011). Another well-known operation from this era was the *Chicago Tribune* panel, which covered the Chicago market area.

These new data sources quickly caught the attention of market researchers. It was now practical to answer questions that previous research methods (such as the store audit, doorstep interview, pantry inventory

---

[2]As this review is an historical overview and not a technical recitation, it is equation-free. We refer the reader to the cited works for the mathematical details.

and garbage-pail analysis) could not answer (Stonborough, 1942, p. 130):
"How many people continue buying the same brand? What brands do
they switch to when they stop repeating? How many times do they repeat
before switching? How many customers has the brand lost? How many
has it gained? What did the new buyers purchase previously? What are
the lost buyers purchasing now? How many people are exclusive buyers of
one brand? How many are non-exclusive buyers? Are exclusive buyers
more loyal than non-exclusive buyers? Which of the two groups buys
more?"

During the 1940s and early 1950s, the analyses of panel data were
limited to various tabulation procedures. The 1950s saw operations research
move beyond its military roots, with mathematical models being used
to address problems faced by both public and private organizations —
including marketing problems (Magee, 1954; Howard, 1955; Anshen,
1956). At the same time, psychologists and sociologists were starting to use
mathematical models in their studies of social phenomena (e.g., Lazarsfeld,
1954; Bush and Mosteller, 1955). It was simply a matter of time before
researchers working with the panel operators started to develop new
mathematical models of buyer behavior that were "custom-made" for
consumer panel data. Motivated by specific business issues, this resulted in
stochastic models for *brand choice*, *purchase counts*, and *purchase timing*.
These basic choice, counting and timing "building-block" models were later
combined to develop richer models of buyer behavior. We now review these
consumer-panel-data-based models, summarizing the key developments in
Figure 7.1.

7.2.1   *The emergence of models for choice data*

The earliest applications of panel data in marketing focused on the measurement and tracking of brand loyalty and brand switching (e.g., Churchill,
1942; Womer, 1944). In 1952 and 1953, Brown (1952a–1952i, 1953)
published a series of articles in *Advertising Age* in which he examined
buying behavior in nine product categories using data from the *Chicago
Tribune* panel for 1951. This work, along with Cunningham's (1956)
study, brought widespread attention to the topic of brand loyalty and
stimulated research on the development of mathematical models that could

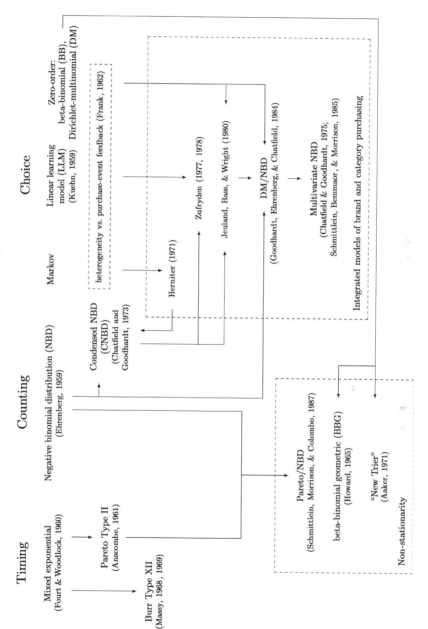

Fig. 7.1 A concise genealogy of the key stochastic models of buyer behavior

help managers understand the dynamics of brand switching and brand loyalty.

Kuehn's (1958) PhD dissertation titled "An Analysis of the Dynamics of Consumer Behavior and its Implications for Marketing Management" was one of the first attempts to describe brand-choice behavior using a stochastic model. In an analysis of sequences of five purchases using panel data for the frozen orange juice category, Kuehn noted strong frequency and recency effects. For example, (i) someone who had purchased a given brand four times was more likely to buy the same brand on the fifth purchase occasion than someone who had purchased it three times, and (ii) someone who had purchased the focal brand three times with the last purchase occurring on the fourth purchase occasion was more likely to buy the same brand on the fifth purchase occasion than someone who purchased the focal brand three times with the last purchase occurring on the third purchase occasion. While he briefly considered the possibility of using a Markov chain model to describe such behavior, he concluded that the patterns observed were more consistent with a modified version of the stochastic learning model developed by Bush and Mosteller (1955).

At the heart of a learning model (as applied to brand choice) is the idea that the purchasing of a given brand increases the probability that the customer will buy the product at the next purchase occasion. (Similarly, failure to purchase a given brand decreases the probability that the customer will buy the product at the next purchase occasion.) The cumulative effect of this process implies that the probability of purchasing a given brand on any purchase occasion is a function of the individual's entire purchase history.

There are two interesting aspects to note about Kuehn's initial work. First, he did not formally specify the learning model. Second, he did not fit the model to the data; he simply noted that the patterns observed in his purchase sequence analysis were consistent with the learning model. The model, which later became known as the linear learning model (LLM), was formally specified in Kuehn (1961, 1962), but no formal details of how to estimate the model parameters were provided.

In the following years, a number of researchers addressed the issue of parameter estimation and proposed variants of, and extensions to, Kuehn's LLM (e.g., Carman, 1966; McConnell, 1968; Haines, 1969; Herniter and

Howard, 1964; Massy, Montgomery, and Morrison, 1970; Lilien, 1974; Lawrence, 1975; Srinivasan and Kesavan, 1976; Wierenga, 1978; Leeflang and Boonstra, 1982). One notable application was Kuehn and Rohloff's (1967) use of the LLM to provide a baseline for promotion evaluation.

Around the same time that Kuehn was studying brand choice using learning models, other researchers were starting to use Markov chains to model the same behavior. In an address to the Advertising Research Foundation annual conference, Lipstein (1959) introduced the idea of modeling brand-switching behavior using a Markov model. He discussed how measures of brand loyalty could be derived from such a model, and provided some insight as to how these models could be used in practice. For example, rather than estimating a single transition matrix for all customers, the panel could be split into predominantly hard-core buyers (e.g., 75% of purchases devoted to a single brand) and predominantly switchers, with separate transition matrices estimated for each group. These ideas were presented more formally in Harary and Lipstein (1962).

Independent of Lipstein, Maffei (1960, 1961) explored how Markov chains could be used to explore the effects of advertising on brand preferences; Maffei (1960) provided a mathematical treatment of the subject, while Maffei (1961) documented the results from a series of field experiments. Herniter and Magee (1961) examined how the characterization of buying behavior as a Markov process could be used, amongst other things, as a basis of developing optimal promotional strategies. Other early applications of Markov models include Baum and Dennis (1961), Longton and Warner (1962), Barclay (1963), and Styan and Smith (1964).[3] Markov models were not enthusiastically received by all, with Ehrenberg (1965) presenting a rather negative appraisal of the framework. (Also see Massy and Morrison, 1968; Morrison, 1978).

Both the linear-learning and Markov models assume that past brand choices affect future brand choices. In the case of a first-order Markov

---

[3]It is interesting to note the role played by practitioners in the application of Markov models to marketing problems: Lipstein worked at the New York advertising agency Benton and Bowles, Inc., Herniter and Magee at Arthur D. Little, Inc., Baum and Dennis at the Attwood Group of Companies, Barclay at the Chicago advertising agency Needham, Louis and Brorby, Inc., and Smith at Procter and Gamble Company.

model, brand-choice probabilities at the current purchase occasion depend on the brand chosen on the most recent purchase occasion. In the case of the LLM, brand-choice probabilities are a function of an initial probability of purchase and the individual's entire purchase history. (While not immediately obvious in the early mathematical representations of the LLM, the first-order Markov model is actually nested within the basic LLM.)

Commenting on the LLM, Frank (1962) suggested that this dependence of brand-choice probabilities on past purchases was in fact an example of "spurious contagion resulting from the aggregation of many customers with different and constant probabilities of purchasing" (p. 50). In other words, the non-zero-order nature of brand choice observed by researchers using the linear-learning and Markov models was simply an artifact of unobserved heterogeneity; brand choice could be characterized by a heterogeneous Bernoulli (i.e., zero-order) process. (Note that the initial studies assumed a homogeneous specification of both the linear-learning and Markov models.)

This was formalized as a statistical model by Morrison (1966) who captured heterogeneity in the brand-choice probabilities using the beta distribution (i.e., the beta-Bernoulli model). Seemingly unaware of this work being undertaken by US researchers, a British economist proposed "a model of brand loyalties" (Pyatt, 1970). For his two-brand model, the number of times an individual chooses a focal brand across n category purchases is characterized by the binomial distribution (i.e., repeated Bernoulli trials) with the probability of choosing the focal brand varying between households according to the beta distribution. In other words, brand choice is modeled using the beta-binomial (BB) distribution (Pearson, 1925; Skellam, 1948). His proposed "index of loyalty" is better known as the polarization index (Sabavala and Morrison, 1977).

Pyatt generalized the model for the case where there are more than two brands in the category. The binomial generalized to the multinomial distribution, with heterogeneity captured by a "generalized beta" distribution (i.e., the Dirichlet distribution), resulting in what we now call the Dirichlet-multinomial (DM) distribution (Ishii and Hayakawa, 1960; Mosimann, 1962). No justification was provided for the Dirichlet; Chatfield and Goodhardt (1975) and Bass, Jeuland, and Wright (1976) provided independent "theoretical justifications" based on the relationship between gamma random variables and the beta/Dirichlet distributions.

Morrison proposed two heterogeneous first-order Markov models for a two-brand market (Morrison, 1966; Massy, Montgomery, and Morrison, 1970), the brand loyal (BL) model and last purchase loyal (LPL) model, where heterogeneity was captured by a beta distribution. Building on this work, Jeuland (1979) proposed a first-order model of multibrand choice that captured the notion of brand-choice inertia (i.e., the extent to which past purchasing behavior is likely to be repeated), with heterogeneity captured by a Dirichlet distribution.[4]

All these heterogeneous models of brand choice assumed the same behavioral mechanism for the whole population. Jones (1973) proposed a model that allows individuals to have different behavioral mechanisms. His model of brand choice for a two-brand market, applied to several datasets by Givon and Horsky (1979), assumes that the behavior of a proportion of the population can be characterized by a heterogeneous Bernoulli model, the behavior of another proportion of the population by a heterogeneous LLM, with the behavior of the rest of the population characterized by a heterogeneous first-order Markov model. Blattberg and Sen (1975, 1976) extended this idea of different segments of customers being represented by different models. They allowed for a number of segments, each characterized by a constrained zero-order or first-order model, with customers being allocated to a segment (i.e., a model that best describes their brand choices) using a Bayesian model discrimination procedure.

Another approach taken by several researchers to assess the order of the brand-choice process was to test sequences of purchases by individual households using, say, a runs test (e.g., Frank, 1962; Massy, 1966; Wierenga, 1974; Bass *et al.*, 1984). While the idea of such an approach is attractive, the need for long sequences of brand choices for each household is a problem. As a result, we can only consider heavy purchasers of the category or we have to look at purchases over a long period of time (which brings into question the assumption of stable/stationary preferences over the time

---

[4]The "mirror image" of Jeuland's inertia model is Givon's (1984) variety-seeking model in which a consumer's desire for "variety" means that their probability of making a repeat purchase is lower than that associated with the absence of such variety-seeking behavior; also see Kahn, Kalwani, and Morrison (1986).

period being considered). Although the results of these studies are mixed, the general conclusion is that while households tend to differ in the order of their choice processes, the behavior of a large proportion of households is consistent with a zero-order process.[5]

Herniter (1973) proposed a model of brand choice which started with the assumption that customers make their choices according to a multinomial process. However, rather than specifying a parametric distribution for the brand-choice probabilities, he derived the distribution that maximized the entropy of the system. A unique characteristic of this model is that it is completely determined by the market shares; no additional data are required. As noted by Bass (1974), the major weakness of this approach is that brand switching is determined entirely by the market shares; two very different categories with the same pattern of market shares must have the same patterns of brand switching. Bass proposed a non-entropy-based model that has an additional parameter (which he called the product-class brand-loyalty factor), thereby allowing for different patterns of loyalty (and therefore brand switching) for a given set of market shares.[6]

Another model (apparently) based on the concept of entropy is the Hendry model developed by the Hendry Corporation. Publicly available details of the underlying model were both very limited and opaque. Given the attention this model received from major manufacturers, a number of researchers examined the model and were critical (Armstrong and Shapiro, 1974; Ehrenberg and Goodhardt, 1974; Herniter, 1974). From a managerial perspective, one of the important aspects of the Hendry model is its notion of partitioning the market according to a hierarchical structure (Kalwani and Morrison, 1977; Rubinson, Vanhonacker, and Bass, 1980). While the Hendry model provides a means of discriminating between hypothesized market structures, other approaches have found favor in the literature (e.g., Grover and Dillon, 1985; Urban, Johnson, and Hauser, 1984).

---

[5]Panel data are typically collected at the household level, yet most of the inferences about buyer behavior are at the level of the individual. Kahn, Morrison, and Wright (1986) examined the effects of within household aggregation, finding that household purchasing looks more zero order than that of the typical individual family member.

[6]If we assume that heterogeneity in brand-choice probabilities is captured by a beta or Dirichlet distribution, this factor is equivalent to the polarization index. See Bass, Jeuland, and Wright (1976) for the development of these ideas.

From an historical perspective, one of the primary legacies of the early work on the modeling of brand choice is the recognition that what appears to be purchase-event feedback (i.e., past brand choices affecting future brand choices via a learning or Markov process) can be an artifact of unobserved heterogeneity.[7] While there is heterogeneity in the order of the brand-choice processes, the behavior of the majority of people is consistent with a zero-order process. As such, heterogeneous zero-order models such as the BB and DM provide a good characterization of aggregate brand choice and switching behaviors in many frequently purchased consumer product categories.

7.2.2 *The emergence of models for count data*

In the late 1950s, Attwood Consumer Panel had the problem that its panel was reporting too many purchases relative to factory shipment data for a major client. Was this due to the panel having too many heavy buyers? One of the company's statisticians, Andrew Ehrenberg, was asked to fit a theoretical distribution to data on the number of people who had bought the product 0, 1, 2, 3, ... times, with a view to using this to "clean up" the data. The traditional distribution for such count data, the Poisson, did not fit the data. In his studies at Cambridge, this statistician had seen the negative binomial distribution (NBD) applied in a number of social and biological settings. He fitted this distribution to the data and found that it provided an excellent fit (Ehrenberg, 2004). Was this good fit mere chance, or did the NBD provide a good characterization of the purchasing of other products? Further research suggested that it was surprisingly robust, leading to the publication of "The Pattern of Consumer Purchases" (Ehrenberg, 1959).

Ehrenberg's characterization of the NBD was as a gamma mixture of Poissons, a formulation originally proposed by Greenwood and Yule (1920). This assumes that the number of purchases made by an individual

---

[7]Within the econometrics literature, this has become known as the problem of *spurious state-dependence* (Heckman, 1981). Over the years, a number of researchers have developed sophisticated models of brand choice that control for the effects of marketing activities and unobserved heterogeneity in the search for purchase-event feedback effects (or state dependence); see Neslin and van Heerde (2008) for a review of this research in the context of sales promotions.

in a given time period can be characterized by a Poisson distribution, and that mean buying rates vary across individuals according to a gamma distribution. This is but one of a number of chance mechanisms that yield the NBD. For example, the NBD can also be derived as a Poisson-stopped sum of logarithmic distributions (Quenouille, 1949). Under this formulation, purchase occasions are assumed to be characterized by a Poisson distribution, which is the same for all individuals, and the amount purchased per purchase occasion (1, 2, 3, ... units) is characterized by a logarithmic distribution (also assumed to be the same for all individuals). The NBD can also be derived as a contagion process where individuals start out the same and an individual's probability of buying the product changes each time they make a purchase (e.g., Irwin, 1941).

For any situation where the NBD provides a good fit to count data, we cannot prove that one story that leads to the NBD is more correct than another. We can, however, appeal to logic. The notion of heterogeneity is fundamental to marketing, as manifest in the concept of market segmentation. Moreover, we know from casual observation that, on average, some people tend to buy and consume more of a product than others. As such, we favor the story in which individuals are assumed to be different (i.e., the gamma mixture of Poissons derivation as used by Ehrenberg).

While Ehrenberg was the first to apply a mixed Poisson model to diary panel data, he was not the first to use such a model in a marketing setting; that honor goes to Magee (1953), working at Arthur D. Little, Inc. Working in a B2B setting, he proposed that the number of cases of the focal product ordered per month by a dealer could be characterized by a Poisson distribution, with inter-dealer heterogeneity captured by an exponential distribution (i.e., a gamma distribution with the shape parameter set to one).

Early applications of the NBD to the modeling of customer buying behavior assumed that the number of purchases of a particular pack size of the focal brand made by an individual in a given time period could be characterized by a Poisson distribution. As the model was used by other researchers, its poor fit in some settings, along with the challenges of how to model the purchasing of a brand with multiple pack sizes that may not be integer multiples of the smallest pack size (e.g., Grahn, 1969) or the purchasing of products such as gasoline led to a seemingly minor yet fundamental shift in the nature of the count phenomenon being modeled (Ehrenberg, 1988), from the number of *purchases* to the number of *purchase occasions* (or transactions). It is now standard to think of the NBD as the fundamental model for characterizing the distribution of the number of transactions across a group of individuals for a given time period.

As we know from any introductory stochastic processes book, the assumption that the number of events occurring in a given time period is characterized by the Poisson distribution is equivalent to assuming that inter-event times are distributed exponential. The fact that the mode of the exponential is at zero is troubling for many: Is anyone really likely to buy again immediately?

As a remedy for this seemingly counter-intuitive assumption, Herniter (1971) proposed the use of an Erlang-k interpurchase-time distribution (which has a non-zero mode for $k > 1$) coupled with the exponential distribution to capture heterogeneity in mean buying rates. (The Erlang collapses to the exponential when $k = 1$.) Chatfield and Goodhardt (1973) assumed that interpurchase times are characterized by an Erlang-2 distribution, which yields what they called the *condensed Poisson distribution.* Assuming that the heterogeneity in the mean buying rates is captured by the gamma distribution results in the condensed NBD (or CNBD) model. Their empirical comparison of the NBD and CNBD models found that the difference in the fit of the two models is small. The one situation where the CNBD provides a better fit is where there is a very low proportion of buyers in the dataset being analyzed.

Banerjee and Bhattacharyya (1976) assumed an inverse Gaussian interpurchase-time distribution, with heterogeneity in this two-parameter distribution captured by a bivariate distribution with a left-truncated t-distribution and modified gamma distribution as marginals. Their limited empirical analysis indicated that the proposed model provided a marginal improvement in fit over that of the NBD, especially when analyzing purchasing in very short time periods.

Few researchers have sought to explain why we would see deviations from the NBD assumption of exponential interpurchase times. Notable exceptions are Kahn (1987), who developed a theoretical model of interpurchase times based on assumptions of how the individual consumes the product, and Kahn and Morrison (1989), who considered the impact of the phenomenon of weekly shopping trips on the apparent distribution of interpurchase times for a given product.

A number of statisticians have challenged the NBD assumption that heterogeneity in the mean of the Poisson is distributed according to a gamma distribution, proposing Poisson-based models with alternative mixing distributions. For example, Holla (1966) proposed the inverse Gaussian distribution, which results in a model that is more right skewed than the NBD for a given mean and variance (Willmot, 1987). Sichel (1982) found that the inverse Gaussian Poisson model provided a better fit than either the NBD or CNBD to the two datasets he considered. Another approach is to replace the continuous mixing distribution with a finite number of homogeneous subgroups (called components), resulting in a *finite mixture model* (e.g., Dillon and Kumar, 1994).

One possible rationale for wanting to replace the gamma with some other mixing distribution is that the data may have a large number of zero counts and, in an effort to account for these zeros, the NBD under-fits the right tail of the count distribution. If it can be argued that there exists a group of individuals in the population who will never buy the product (i.e., *hard-core non-buyers*), the NBD's mixing distribution can be replaced with one that assumes a fraction of the population has a mean buying rate of zero and that the mean buying rates of the rest of the population are captured by the gamma distribution (Morrison, 1969). Such a model is now typically called the *zero-inflated NBD*. When using such a model, the fundamental question is whether there really exists a group of hard-core non-buyers (Ehrenberg, 1970). As Morrison noted, if this is the case, the estimate of the fraction of the population that are "never buyers" should be independent of the time period used for model calibration (e.g., three versus six versus twelve months).

One application of the NBD model proposed by Goodhardt and Ehrenberg (1967) was that of *conditional trend analysis*, in which any observed changes in buying behavior over two non-overlapping periods (for the same set of households) are evaluated by comparing them to the patterns that would be expected given the assumption of no change in underlying buyer behavior (while acknowledging the inherent randomness in an individual's purchasing around their underlying mean buying rate).

In particular, predictions of repeat buying in the second period are made conditional on the number of purchases made in the first period. One particular prediction of interest is the *conditional expectation*, which is the expected number of purchases in the second period given that x purchases were made in the first period. This idea was first explored by Magee (1953) using his exponential mixture of Poissons model. Goodhardt and Ehrenberg derived their results using a bivariate extension of the NBD, while Morrison (1968) presented an alternative derivation using Bayes' theorem (thereby introducing what are now called *parametric empirical Bayes* methods to the marketing literature). Equivalent results for the CNBD and the zero-inflated NBD were derived by Schmittlein and Morrison (1983) and Morrison (1969), respectively. Drawing on the work of Robbins (1977), Morrison and Schmittlein (1981) presented results for Poisson purchasing with an arbitrary heterogeneity distribution. (See Morrison and Schmittlein (1988) for a examination of how violations of the assumptions underlying the NBD affect the conditional expectations.)

An alternative approach to modeling the number of times a product is purchased in a given time period is to divide the time period into n discrete periods and model whether or not a purchase occurs in each of these smaller periods. The number of purchases is therefore modeled using the BB (Chatfield and Goodhardt, 1970; Pyatt, 1970).[8] The example given in Chatfield and Goodhardt (1970) was to model the purchasing of a product not in terms of the number of purchases made by an individual in a 24-week period but rather in terms of the number of weeks (out of 24) in which an individual purchased the product. Easton (1980) used the BB to characterize purchasing in an industrial setting, commenting that using a discrete purchase interval is a useful way of overcoming the problem of determining exactly when a purchase is deemed to have occurred in such a setting.

From an historical perspective, Ehrenberg (1959) was the start of a rich stream of research on developing models that characterize how many times a behavior of interest occurs in a given time period. While many

---

[8]Note that the NBD is the limiting case of the BB as the number of discrete periods into which the given time period is divided (i.e., n) goes to infinity (e.g., Greene and Stock, 1971).

extensions to the basic model have been proposed, the NBD is a very robust model of buyer behavior (Ehrenberg, 1988; Morrison and Schmittlein, 1988) and should be the starting point whenever one needs to characterize count data.

7.2.3 *The emergence of models for timing/duration data*

One of the early applications of consumer panel data was monitoring the success of new grocery products, with analysts examining quantities such as penetration (i.e., the percentage of households that have made a first/trial purchase by a given point in time) and the first repeat buying ratio (i.e., the percentage of triers making a first repeat purchase) (Womer, 1944). By the late 1950s, researchers on both sides of the Atlantic were working on the problem of forecasting the sales of a new product given consumer panel data on early purchasing behavior. Fourt and Woodlock (1960) summarized the initial efforts by researchers at MRCA, while Baum and Dennis (1961) reported on work undertaken at Attwood.

Fourt and Woodlock noted that cumulative trial curves exhibit two general patterns: (i) successive increments in cumulative trial decline, and (ii) the cumulative curve approaches a penetration limit of less than 100% of the households in the panel. Their proposed model is equivalent to assuming that (i) the population can be divided into two groups, "ever triers" and "never triers" and (ii) the distribution of the time to trial purchase (from the launch date) for any member of the "ever triers" group is characterized by a (common) geometric distribution. Alternatively, we can talk of a randomly chosen household's time to trial as being characterized by a geometric distribution with heterogeneity in the parameter of the geometric distribution being captured by a constrained two-segment discrete mixing distribution with one of the mass points located at zero, the size of which represents 100 minus the penetration limit. The continuous-time equivalent of this model (i.e., replacing the geometric with its continuous-time analogue, the exponential distribution) was proposed by Anscombe (1961), who considered the problem of estimating the model parameters.

Fourt and Woodlock found that the predictions based on this model tend to be too low for later time periods (i.e., the empirical trial curve does not level off as quickly as the model predicts), with the actual cumulative percentage of households making a trial purchase exceeding the estimated size of the "ever trier" segment in a longitudinal holdout period. This phenomenon was attributed to heterogeneity in consumer buying rates: Heavy category buyers are likely to be the earlier triers and the model picks up the levelling off of their purchases, ignoring the lighter buyers who have yet to try the product (but eventually will). The proposed solution was to include a linear "stretch" factor that allowed the cumulative trial ceiling to increase over time.

The linear "stretch" factor is rather ad-hoc in nature, and suffers from the problem that predicted cumulative trial can exceed 100%. Given that the motivation for this factor was heterogeneity in trial rates, Anscombe (1961) suggested that the constrained two-segment discrete mixing distribution be replaced by a continuous mixing distribution, with the natural choice being the gamma distribution.[9] The empirical analysis presented in Hardie, Fader, and Wisniewski (1998) indicates that this is a very robust model for trial purchasing in a controlled test-market environment. (The gamma mixture of exponentials is also known as the Pareto Type II distribution, and was used previously by Silcock (1954) in the analysis of job duration data. This distribution also characterizes the time to the first observed purchase in a setting where the number of purchases is modeled using the NBD.)

A defining property of the geometric and exponential distributions is that they are *memoryless*. In the context of new product trial, this means that the probability of an individual making a trial purchase in the next week given they have yet to try the new product is independent of the length of time it has been on the market. Massy (1968, 1969) relaxed this assumption by assuming that, at the level of the household, time to trial is characterized by a Weibull distribution, which allows for the probability of an individual making a trial purchase in the next week given they have yet to try the new product to increase, decrease, or be independent of the length of time it has

---

[9]Its discrete-time analogue is the beta-geometric distribution. First proposed by Potter and Parker (1964), it has a long history in the population studies and biostatistics literature. However, it was ignored by marketing researchers as a timing model for many years. It was proposed by Fader and Hardie (2007) as a model for how long an individual remains a customer of a firm in a contractual business setting.

been on the market. Cross-sectional heterogeneity was captured using the gamma distribution.[10]

As noted above, panel data analysts decompose the total sales of a new product into its trial and repeat components. Repeat sales can be further decomposed into depth-of-repeat components (i.e., how many people have made one repeat purchase, two repeat purchases, etc.). The probability models used to characterize how long it takes (from time of launch) for someone to make their first-ever (i.e., trial) purchase of a new product have also been used to model how long after their trial purchase someone makes their first repeat purchase, how long after their first repeat purchase they make their second repeat purchase, and so on. Massy (1968, 1969) used a gamma mixture of Weibulls to characterize the time it takes to transition from one depth-of-repeat class to the next, Eskin (1973) used Fourt and Woodlock's geometric with "never triers + stretch factor" model, and Kalwani and Silk (1980) also considered the gamma mixture of exponentials.

From an historical perspective, the primary legacy of the early efforts to develop models for forecasting the sales of new products is the introduction to marketing of two simple stochastic models for timing data. The Pareto Type II and generalized Burr Type XII distributions are robust models for characterizing and forecasting the time to the occurrence of a single event, both in marketing and other settings (e.g., Morrison and Schmittlein, 1980).

7.2.4 *Integrated models of buyer behavior*

The basic counting, timing, and choice models discussed above can be used to characterize a number of different buying behaviors. Nevertheless, some behaviors are better characterized as the combined outcome of several counting, timing, and/or choice processes. For example, the total number of units of a product purchased in a given time period can be viewed as the outcome of two counting processes, one that characterizes the number of shopping occasions on which the product was purchased, the

---

[10]A gamma mixture of Weibulls is also known as generalized Burr Type XII distribution (Dubey, 1968) and reduces to the Pareto Type II when the shape parameter of the Weibull equals one.

other characterizing the number of units purchased per purchase occasion. Similarly, the number of shopping occasions on which a particular brand is purchased can be viewed as the combined outcome of a counting process that characterizes the number of category purchases made in a given time period, and a choice process to characterize the number of times the brand was chosen given the number of category purchases.

As noted earlier, the nature of the count phenomenon modeled using the NBD shifted from the number of units purchased to the number of purchase occasions (or transactions). But suppose we wish to model the number of units purchased by an individual in a given period of time. Morrison and Perry (1970) proposed a model based on the assumption that the number of purchase occasions made by each customer is distributed Poisson and the number of units purchased on any given purchase occasion is distributed geometric. Heterogeneity in the Poisson mean is assumed to be gamma distributed, while heterogeneity in the parameter of the geometric distribution is assumed to be distributed beta; these two distributions are assumed to be independent. The resulting unconditional distribution of the number of units purchased in a given time period is a doubly mixed Pólya–Aeppli distribution (Huang, 2002). Paull (1978) developed a "generalized NBD" model in which the number of purchase occasions is modeled using the NBD and the number of units purchased per purchase occasion modeled using either a regular regression or an ordered logit, with panelist demographics and purchase occasion-specific factors such as time since last purchase, brand purchased, etc. as covariates.

Almost as soon as researchers started using Markov models to charac-terize brand switching, there was a discussion of the fact that these models could not provide predictions of buying behavior in calendar time (e.g., on a week-by-week basis) as they modeled sequences of brand choices given category purchases: "A manufacturer is not nearly so much interested in what brand a customer will buy on his nth purchase as he is in the combination of this information with a knowledge of when the nth purchase will be made" (Howard, 1963, p. 39). One "solution" was to remove this conditioning on category purchasing by including a "no purchase" state and using the Markov model to characterize "brand" purchasing in discrete time, with no category purchasing in any given discrete-time interval being captured by the "purchase" of the "no purchase" brand (e.g., Draper and

Nolin, 1964). However, this approach cannot account for multiple purchases in the discrete time interval. Howard (1963) and Herniter and Howard (1964) proposed that brand-to-brand transitions be captured using a Markov model with the time between the brand-to-brand transitions treated as a random variable, resulting in a semi-Markov process. Such an approach was taken by Herniter (1971) in the first joint model of category purchasing and brand choice. Category purchasing was assumed to be characterized by a zero-inflated exponential mixture of Erlang interpurchase times while brand choice was characterized by a homogeneous stationary first-order Markov process.

Zufryden (1977, 1978) developed what he called the CNBL model, in which category purchasing is characterized by the CNBD and brand choice by a heterogeneous LLM. In a study that compared the performance of the six joint models formed by the assumption of NBD versus CNBD category purchasing and BB versus homogeneous stationary first-order Markov versus heterogeneous LLM brand choice, Zufryden (1983) found that the CNBL generally performed best in predictive tasks. Jeuland, Bass, and Wright (1980) developed a model in which category purchasing is characterized by a gamma mixture of Erlang distributions (Erlang-2 in their empirical analysis, and therefore CNBD) and brand choice by the DM distribution.

The best-known joint model of category purchasing and brand choice is Goodhardt, Ehrenberg, and Chatfield's (1984) NBD-Dirichlet model, which assumes category purchasing is characterized by the NBD and brand choice by the DM. (This is obviously a special case of Jeuland, Bass, and Wright's (1980) model.) This model describes the patterns of buying behavior observed in many product categories (Ehrenberg, 1988) including duplication of purchases, growth in the penetration of a brand, and the property of "double jeopardy" (Ehrenberg, Goodhardt, and Barwise, 1990).

The NBD is used widely as a model of brand purchasing, yet the NBD-Dirichlet uses it as a model of category purchasing. This begs the question: Can both brand and category purchasing be characterized by the NBD? Schmittlein, Bemmaor, and Morrison (1985) showed that the answer is "yes" when the shape parameter of the category-level NBD equals the sum of the parameters of the DM brand choice model. This is in fact Chatfield and Goodhardt's (1975) multivariate NBD model, extended by Wagner and Taudes (1986, 1991), in which the purchases of each brand are distributed NBD with a common scale parameter, and total category purchases are distributed NBD with the same common scale parameter and shape parameter equal to the sum of the brand-specific shape parameters.

All these joint models of category and brand purchasing assume that the distribution of brand preferences is independent of the distribution of category purchasing rates. As such, the conditional expectation of future brand purchasing under the NBD-Dirichlet, given the observation that the brand was purchased x times out of n category purchases in a previous period, is simply the NBD conditional expectation of the number of category purchases in the second period given n category purchases in the first period times the mean of the posterior distribution of the probability of purchasing the focal brand given it was purchased x times out of n in the first period. Extending the results of Robbins (1977), Dalal, Lee, and Sabavala (1984) considered the problem of making conditional expectations when the NBD-Dirichlet individual-level assumptions of Poisson category purchasing and Bernoulli brand choice of the focal brand are coupled with an arbitrary joint (and possibly dependent) distribution for brand-choice probabilities and category purchasing rates.

The assumption of independence is one of convenience, since allowing for dependence between the two processes was deemed impractical from a computational perspective when these models were developed. In their examination of the relationship between brand choice and purchase frequency, Shoemaker *et al.* (1977) rejected this assumption and proposed the use of a modified Dirichlet distribution in which the Dirichlet parameters are a function of the observed number of category purchases. They called the resulting distribution the frequency-dependent Dirichlet. The problem with this approach is that individual choice probabilities (which are unobserved) are a function of the realization of another random process (i.e., the number of category purchases). Ideally we want there to be a correlation between the brand-choice probabilities and mean category purchase rates, all of which are unobserved. One common way to accommodate this is through the use of finite mixture models (e.g., Böckenholt, 1993).

7.2.5   *Relaxing the assumption of stationarity*

The majority of the stochastic models of buyer behavior discussed above are of the form where an individual's behavior is characterized by a probability distribution and heterogeneity in a parameter of this distribution (e.g., Bernoulli choice probability, Poisson mean) is assumed to vary across individuals according to a mixing distribution (e.g., beta and gamma, respectively). The key assumption is that the value of this parameter remains constant over time for any given individual; this is the assumption of stationarity. The success of these models suggests that this may not be too problematic an assumption. Nevertheless, several researchers have proposed models that allow the individual parameters to vary over time according to an additional stochastic process.

It is important to note that when we talk about non-stationarity, we are not talking about the probability of the behavior changing as a function of purchase-event feedback or the short-term changes due to a firm's promotional activities (e.g., Lenk, Rao, and Tibrewala, 1993). Rather, we are talking about an underlying parameter changing over time. For example, under a standard first-order Markov model of brand choice, an individual's probability of purchasing a brand changes from occasion to occasion depending on which brand they purchased on the previous purchase occasion. But these state-specific probabilities themselves do not change over time (i.e., we have a stationary transition matrix). A non-stationary Markov process would see the state transition probabilities changing over time (e.g., Lipstein, 1965, 1968).

Howard (1965) proposed a stochastic mechanism (which he called the "dynamic inference" process and which we now call a change-point process) by which the individual-level parameter(s) can change at discrete points in time. The specific example developed by Howard is what he called the Bernoulli-beta-geometric model, now called the beta-binomial-geometric (BBG) model. Here the observed behavior of interest (e.g., brand choice) is characterized by a Bernoulli distribution with heterogeneity in the Bernoulli probability of success captured by a beta distribution. At each discrete point in time (i.e., purchase occasion), each individual changes (or "renews," to use Howard's terminology) their Bernoulli probability of success (i.e., buying the focal brand) according to another homogeneous Bernoulli process. (This means that the length of time an individual behaves according to a given value of their Bernoulli probability of success is characterized by a homogeneous geometric distribution.) When an individual renews their Bernoulli probability of success, they draw another value from the same beta distribution. Nagano (1972) found that this model provides a good fit to brand-choice data; Sabavala and Morrison (1981) used it to characterize TV viewing and magazine readership.

While an individual's Bernoulli probability of success can change (multiple times) under the BBG model, the market-level mean is constant as each renewal represents a draw with replacement from the same beta distribution. Aaker (1971) proposed a variant of this model in which the market-level mean can change over time, using it to describe the acceptance of a new product. His "new-trier" model allows just one (geometrically distributed) renewal per person. The new Bernoulli probability of success is drawn from a second beta distribution that has a mass point at zero, with the drawing of a value of zero representing the individual's rejection of the new product.

Under Howard's model, changes in brand-choice probabilities occur at discrete points in time and the new probability is independent of the old probability. Montgomery (1969) proposed a heterogeneous non-stationary zero-order model of brand choice in which the probabilities change over time according to a diffusion process (i.e., evolve in a continuous manner). Jones (1970a, 1970b, 1971) extended this model to account for the possibility of purchase-event feedback.

An increasingly popular way of accommodating non-stationarity is the hidden Markov model (HMM). This was introduced to the marketing literature by Poulsen (1983, 1990), who called it the latent Markov model. In a model of brand choice, heterogeneity is captured using a finite mixture model. On any purchase occasion, an individual belongs to one of the components (or states) and their behavior reflects the brand-choice probabilities associated with that state. Individuals switch between states according to a latent (i.e., hidden) stationary transition matrix.

One motivation for wishing to account for non-stationarity in models of buyer behavior is an observed "slowing down" in total purchasing. While this can be accommodated by a generalization of Howard's dynamic inference model along the lines of that proposed by Aaker, an alternative approach was proposed by Schmittlein, Morrison, and Colombo (1987).

They assumed that a customer buys according to a heterogeneous stationary process (i.e., a gamma mixture of Poissons, or NBD) and then "dies" at an unobserved (and unobservable) as-if random point in time (characterized by a gamma mixture of exponentials, or Pareto Type II), resulting in the Pareto/NBD model. This simple "buy till you die" structure, representing an extreme form of non-stationarity, has proven to be very effective in many empirical settings.

A common characteristic of these models is that there is no attempt to explain why the change in the probability of the behavior occurs. We would assume that it is the result of some external influence (other than past purchases). However, the set of possible external influences (e.g., a change in financial circumstances, children leaving home, the emergence of new competing products) is very large, and different influences will impact different people. As such, their effect is treated as-if random and modeled using a stochastic process that captures the non-stationarity in the underlying model parameter(s) of interest.

7.3 Death

> A historic moment came at 8.01 am on 26 June 1974 when Clyde Dawson, director of research and development for Marsh Supermarkets, bought a 10-pack of Wrigley's Chewing Gum in his company's store in Troy, Ohio — the first purchase made in the first store to be fully equipped with scanners which could read the new Uniform Product Codes (UPC).
>
> Morton, 1994, p. 101

The overwhelming majority of stochastic models of buyer behavior developed from the late 1950s to the 1980s ignored the effects of marketing actions on buyer behavior. The reason for this was simple: It was prohibitively expensive to get reliable data on the prices and promotional activities for all the brands in the store in which each purchase was made. Data collected via services such as the Nielsen Food Index were simply too aggregated to be of any real use.

This lack of marketing-mix data disappeared with the widespread adoption of the uniform product code (UPC) by manufacturers and the associated scanners by retailers. The primary drivers of this adoption were the desires to increase productivity at the checkout and provide detailed sales data (Morton, 1994). This new data-collection method was quickly used by market research firms to create consumer panels in which data on panelists' purchasing, initially collected by panel members presenting a special identification card to the checkout clerk (which meant the details of the purchases were recorded in a special database), were merged with data on the in-store environment (extracted from each store's computer systems and collected by field auditors employed by the research firm). This "scanner panel data" meant that researchers now had data that they could use to understand how price and promotional activities affected individual buying behavior. There had always been an interest in understanding the effects of marketing efforts; it was simply the case that the required data had not been available.

Many of the established stochastic models of buyer behavior could not be adapted to answer the questions managers and researchers were now asking given this new data source. For example, the DM, the primary model of multibrand choice, cannot be modified easily to accommodate the effects of time-varying covariates (e.g., price and promotion for each week) on choice probabilities. Guadagni and Little (1983) published their seminal paper in which they modeled brand choice using McFadden's (1974) "conditional logit model," with its utility-maximizing foundations, calibrated on scanner panel data. At the same time, both ACNielsen and Information Resources, Inc. released scanner panel datasets for use by academic researchers. "There followed an academic feeding frenzy" (Guadagni and Little, 2008, p. 27) and the rest is history. (See Russell (this volume) for a review of this literature.)

Similarly, models for count data, such as the NBD, cannot be modified easily to accommodate the effects of time-varying covariates, and therefore fell out of favor. However, models for timing/duration data did not suffer the same fate, as it is relatively easy to incorporate the effects of time-varying covariates into such models using proportional hazards regression. (See Helsen and Schmittlein (1993) for an early expository review of hazard rate models in marketing.) Gupta (1991) and Jain and Vilcassim (1991) modeled the effects of marketing actions on interpurchase times at the product-category level using such a modeling framework. Drawing on the work of Howard (1965), Fader, Hardie, and Huang (2004) developed a non-stationary variant of these models as a model of new product sales. Vilcassim and Jain (1991) formulated a semi-Markov model of purchase timing and brand choice in which the effects of marketing actions on transition rates were captured using a proportional hazards model. Helsen and Schmittlein (1994) used a multiple-spell hazard rate model to study how the effectiveness of consumer price promotions changes as an individual gains more experience with a new product (i.e., passes through higher and higher depth-of-repeat levels).

Despite this work on the modeling of interpurchase times, the sheer dominance of the multinomial logit model (and its extensions) was universal; by the beginning of the 21st century, anyone questioning marketing doctoral students about Kuehn/Ehrenberg/Fourt and Woodlock/etc. or beta mixtures of binomials would have largely been met by blank stares. The stochastic models of buyer behavior that were so central to the emerging field of marketing science in the 1960s and 1970s were "dead" and but a fading memory for the majority of marketing academics. Models of buyer behavior were expected to be derived from economic primitives — however tenuous the link — and had to include marketing-mix variables for all the brands that make up the product category.

7.4 Resurrection?

On 6 August 1991, Tim Berners-Lee posted a short note on the `alt.hypertext` newsgroup in which he described the WorldWideWeb (WWW) project he had been working on at CERN, noting that it "merges the techniques of information retrieval and hypertext to make an easy but powerful global information system."

Aaron Montgomery Ward is widely considered to be the father of the mail-order catalog industry, founding Montgomery Ward & Company in 1872. Over the next 100 years, the mail-order industry and its "direct mail" sibling flourished. These firms were in a position to track the purchasing of individuals in a way that firms selling their products through traditional channels could only dream of. Similarly, those firms that had a contractual/subscription-based business model, such as many magazine publishers and insurance firms, were able to build customer information files.

The challenge faced by all such firms was the cost of collecting, storing, and processing this customer data.[11] The information technology revolution of 1970s and 1980s saw these costs plummet. New books on direct marketing (e.g., David Shepard Associates, 1990; Roberts, Lou, and Berger, 1989) and database marketing (e.g., Hughes, 1991) appeared, talking about ideas such as customer lifetime value, which had previously been discussed in industry-specific publications or obscure academic articles (e.g., Deming and Glasser, 1968). By the mid-1990s, the idea that firms could now create customer transaction databases and "value" individual customers was becoming mainstream (e.g., Hallberg, 1995; Jenkinson, 1995; Pearson, 1996). The commercialization of the web and the subsequent explosion of e-commerce meant that these databases were a reality for many firms.

Prior to 2000, the task of developing models of buyer behavior that made use of such data sources received little attention from marketing academics. The best-known papers from that era are Morrison *et al.* (1982) and Schmittlein, Morrison, and Colombo (1987), the latter presenting the Pareto/NBD model (as discussed in Sec. 7.2.5). However, the Pareto/NBD model was largely ignored in the decade following its publication; according to Google Scholar, it received a total of 12 citations over that period, with Schmittlein and Peterson (1994) the only published application.

As academics started working with these new databases in the late 1990s, they quickly realized that the dominant models of the 1980s and 1990s were of limited use. While the firm's transaction database contained extremely rich data on the purchasing of its own products, it contained no information on the marketing activities of its competitors or its customers' purchasing of competing products; as such, the multinomial logit and its extensions were not appropriate. Some researchers turned to the forgotten stochastic models of buyer behavior for inspiration. Reinartz and Kumar (2000) used the Pareto/NBD model in their analysis of customer profitability, while Fader and Hardie (2001) used the beta-geometric to model repeat purchasing at an e-commerce site.

---

[11] See, for example, Howard's (1978) description of operations at Sears, Roebuck and Company in the late 1950s.

As interest in topics such as customer lifetime value (CLV) developed, so did the interest in simple stochastic models that could generate the predictions of future buying behavior required for any serious CLV computation exercise. (See Fader and Hardie (2009) for a review of this work. Also see Neslin (this volume) for a review of the broader literature on database marketing.) The Pareto/NBD has proven to be a seminal model. For example, Fader, Hardie, and Lee (2005b) extended the Pareto/NBD, which models the flow of transactions, to account for spend per transaction, developing a model for the computation of CLV that requires just three pieces of information for each customer: The time of the last transaction (recency), the number of transactions in a given time period (frequency), and the average spend per transaction (monetary value).

An attractive feature of these probability models is that, in contrast to many of the state-of-the-art models developed by marketing scientists these days, they have closed-form expressions for many of the key quantities of interest. While it may have been challenging to evaluate the associated mathematical functions 30–40 years ago, it is now practical to do so on the most basic of personal computers. For example, building on the counting, timing, and choice foundations laid in the 1960s, Fader and Hardie (Fader and Hardie, 2001, 2007, 2010; Fader, Hardie, and Lee, 2005a; Fader, Hardie, and Shang, 2010) have developed a number of models of buyer behavior that make use of data from a firm's customer transaction databases. The defining characteristic of these models is that they can be built from scratch in an Excel spreadsheet. This drastically lowers the barriers to implementation for anyone wanting to use the models. Furthermore, these models are often very scalable. For example, with the BG/BB model (Fader, Hardie, and Shang, 2010), computation time depends on the length of the model calibration period. It is independent of the number of customers in the database, taking the same time to estimate the model on data for 1,000 customers as it does for data on 10 million customers. As such, these models are being used by analysts working in firms such as Amazon, Google, and McKinsey, as well as other lesser-known firms.

Reflecting on the gap between what marketing scientists create and what managers use, Urban and Karash (1971, p. 62) proposed an evolutionary approach to the development of marketing models: "The introduction of models as an evolutionary development from simple to more complex but related ones would foster managerial acceptance, encourage an orderly development of data and analysis systems, and reduce risks of failure." This new generation of stochastic models of buyer behavior can be viewed as "simple models" (Fader and Hardie, 2005) that represent the starting point for the evolutionary development of a firm's customer analytics capabilities.

The price of this simplicity can be a lack of completeness (Little, 1970). For example, the absence of marketing-mix covariates in these models means they cannot be used to support resource allocation decisions (e.g., for acquisition and retention). The models do not accommodate the richness of new data sources (such as connection information in a social network) or more realistic as-if stories of buyer behavior (e.g., relaxing the "buy till you die") assumption of the Pareto/NBD to accommodate different levels of customer engagement. The desire for more complete models is a natural development of the adoption of these simple stochastic models of buyer behavior and represents exciting opportunities for researchers.

Only time will tell whether or not this represents a full-scale resurrection of the stochastic models of buyer behavior developed in the 1960s and 1970s, or merely a brief revival. Our hope is that the renewed interest in these types of models will get researchers thinking more carefully about the data-generating process underlying the behavioral phenomena of interest. While different kinds of data structures have waxed and waned in popularity, the fundamental behavioral components have not changed: The timing, counting, and choice primitives are as relevant as ever. Coupled with the simulation-based estimation methods now available to researchers (be it maximum simulated likelihood or hierarchical Bayes approaches), there are many interesting research opportunities that will allow researchers to continue in the same stochastic modeling traditions associated with the creation of the field of "marketing science" in the first place.

Acknowledgments

The authors thank Kinshuk Jerath for bringing the excellent Sherlock Holmes quote to their attention, and Don Morrison and Dave Montgomery for their helpful comments on an earlier draft.

References

Aaker, D. A. (1971). The new-trier stochastic model of brand choice, *Management Science*, 17(April), B435–B450.

Anshen, M. (1956). Management science in marketing: Status and prospects, *Management Science*, 2(April), 222–231.

Anscombe, F. J. (1961). Estimating a mixed-exponential response law, *Journal of the American Statistical Association*, 56(September), 493–502.

Armstrong, J. S. and A. C. Shapiro (1974). Analyzing quantitative models, *Journal of Marketing*, 38(April), 61–66.

Banerjee, A. K. and G. K. Bhattacharyya (1976). A purchase incidence model with inverse Gaussian interpurchase times, *Journal of the American Statistical Association*, 71(December), 823–829.

Barclay, W. D. (1963). A probability model for early prediction of new product market success, *Journal of Marketing*, 27(January), 63–68.

Bass, F. M. (1974). The theory of stochastic preference and brand switching, *Journal of Marketing Research*, 11(February), 1–20.

Bass, F. M., M. M. Givon, M. U. Kalwani, D. Reibstein, and G. P. Wright (1984). An investigation into the order of the brand choice process, *Marketing Science*, 3(Fall), 267–287.

Bass, F. M., A. Jeuland, and G. P. Wright (1976). Equilibrium stochastic choice and market penetration theories: Derivations and comparisons, *Management Science*, 22(June), 1051–1063.

Baum, J. and K. E. R. Dennis (1961). The estimation of the expected brand share of a new product, *VIIth ESOMAR/WAPOR Congress*, Baden–Baden.

Blattberg, R. C. and S. K. Sen (1975). A Bayesian technique to discriminate between stochastic models of brand choice, *Management Science*, 21(February), 682–696.

Blattberg, R. C. and S. K. Sen (1976). Market segments and stochastic brand choice models, *Journal of Marketing Research*, 13(February), 34–45.

Böckenholt, Ulf (1993). Estimating latent distributions in recurrent choice data, *Psychometrika*, 58(3), 489–509.

Brown, G. H. (1952a). Less than 15% of Chicago margarine users are loyal to one brand: Half buy four or more brands, *Advertising Age*, June 9, 53–56.

Brown, G. H. (1952b). Almost half of Chicago toothpaste users are loyal to one brand: Contrasts with margarine buying, *Advertising Age*, June 30, 45–47.

Brown, G. H. (1952c). Coffee buyers are loyal to brands, yet two-thirds buy four or more brands in a year, *Advertising Age*, July 14, 54–56.

Brown, G. H. (1952d). 99% of flour buyers definitely favor one brand: 44% buy one brand only, *Advertising Age*, July 28, 46–48.

Brown, G. H. (1952e). 75% of Chicago families buy shampoo: Brand loyalty difficult to assess, *Advertising Age*, August 11, 56–58.

Brown, G. H. (1952f). Brand loyalty is rare among cereal buyers, *Advertising Age*, September 1, 44–48.

Brown, G. H. (1952g). Headache remedy brand loyalty analysis turns up two unsuspected problems, *Advertising Age*, September 22, 80–82.

Brown, G. H. (1952h). Study finds brand loyalty low among buyers of soaps and sudsers, *Advertising Age*, October 6, 82–86.

Brown, G. H. (1952i). Study finds changing purchase patterns are a major factor in the concentrated orange juice market, *Advertising Age*, December 1, 76–79.

Brown, G. H. (1953). Brand loyalty — Fact or fiction? *Advertising Age*, January 26, 75–76.

Bush, R. R. and F. Mosteller (1955). *Stochastic models for learning*, New York: John Wiley & Sons, Inc.

Carman, J. M. (1966). Brand switching and linear learning models, *Journal of Advertising Research*, 6(June), 23–31.

Chatfield, C. and G. J. Goodhardt (1970). The beta-binomial model for customer purchasing behaviour, *Applied Statistics*, 19(3), 240–250.

Chatfield, C. and G. J. Goodhardt (1973). A consumer purchasing model with Erlang inter-purchase times, *Journal of the American Statistical Association*, 68(December), 828–835.

Chatfield, C. and G. J. Goodhardt (1975). Results concerning brand choice, *Journal of Marketing Research*, 12(February), 110–113.

Churchill, H. L. (1942). How to measure brand loyalty, *Advertising & Selling*, August 24, 70–72.

Cunningham, R. M. (1956). Brand loyalty — What, where, how much? *Harvard Business Review*, 34(January–February), 116–128.

Dalal, S. R., J. C. Lee, and D. J. Sabavala (1984). Prediction of individual buying behavior: A Poisson–Bernoulli model with arbitrary heterogeneity, *Marketing Science*, 3(Fall), 352–367.

David Shepard Associates (1990). *The new direct marketing*, Homewood, IL: Business One Irwin.

Deming, W. E. and G. J. Glasser (1968). A Markovian analysis of the life of newspaper subscriptions, *Management Science*, 14(February), B283–B293.

Dillon, W. R. and A. Kumar (1994). Latent structure and other mixture models in marketing: An integrative survey and overview, in R. P. Bagozzi, ed., *Advanced methods of marketing research*, Oxford: Blackwell, pp. 295–351.

Draper, J. E. and L. H. Nolin (1964). A Markov chain analysis of brand preferences, *Journal of Advertising Research*, 4(3), 33–38.

Dubey, S. D. (1968). A compound Weibull distribution, *Naval Research Logistics Quarterly*, 15(June), 179–188.

Easton, G. (1980). Stochastic models of industrial buying behaviour, *OMEGA*, 8(1), 63–69.

Ehrenberg, A. S. C. (1959). The pattern of consumer purchases, *Applied Statistics*, 8(March), 26–41.

Ehrenberg, A. S. C. (1965). An appraisal of Markov brand-switching models, *Journal of Marketing Research*, 2(November), 347–362.

Ehrenberg, A. S. C. (1970). A note on never-buyers, *Journal of Marketing Research*, 7(November), 536–538.

Ehrenberg, A. S. C. (1988). *Repeat-buying*, 2nd edn., London: Charles Griffin & Company Ltd.

Ehrenberg, A. (2004). My research in marketing: How it happened, *Marketing Research*, 16(Winter), 36–41.

Ehrenberg, A. S. C. and G. J. Goodhardt (1974). The Hendry brand switching coefficient, *ADMAP*, 10(August), 232–238.

Ehrenberg, A. S. C., G. J. Goodhardt, and T. P. Barwise (1990). Double jeopardy revisited, *Journal of Marketing*, 54(July), 82–91.

Eskin, G. J. (1973). Dynamic forecasts of new product demand using a depth of repeat model, *Journal of Marketing Research*, 10(May), 115–129.

Fader, P. S. and B. G. S. Hardie (2001). Forecasting repeat sales at CDNOW: A case study, *Interfaces*, 31(May–June), S94–S107.

Fader, P. S. and B. G. S. Hardie (2005). The value of simple models in new product forecasting and customer-base analysis, *Applied Stochastic Models in Business and Industry*, 21(July–October), 461–473.

Fader, P. S. and B. G. S. Hardie (2007). How to project customer retention, *Journal of Interactive Marketing*, 21(Winter), 76–90.

Fader, P. S. and B. G. S. Hardie (2009). Probability models for customer-base analysis, *Journal of Interactive Marketing*, 23(January), 61–69.

Fader, P. S. and B. G. S. Hardie (2010). Customer-base valuation in a contractual setting: The perils of ignoring heterogeneity, *Marketing Science*, 29(January–February), 85–93.

Fader, P. S., B. G. S. Hardie, and C.-Y. Huang (2004). A dynamic changepoint model for new product sales forecasting, *Marketing Science*, 23(Winter), 50–65.

Fader, P. S., B. G. S. Hardie, and K. L. Lee (2005a). "Counting your customers" the easy way: An alternative to the Pareto/NBD model, *Marketing Science*, 24(Spring), 275–284.

Fader, P. S., B. G. S. Hardie, and K. L. Lee (2005b). RFM and CLV: Using iso-value curves for customer base analysis, *Journal of Marketing Research*, 42(November), 415–430.

Fader, P. S., B. G. S. Hardie, and J. Shang (2010). Customer-base analysis in a discrete-time noncontractual setting, *Marketing Science*, 29(November–December), 1086–1108.

Fourt, L. A. and J. W. Woodlock (1960). Early prediction of market success for new grocery products, *Journal of Marketing*, 25(October), 31–38.

Frank, R. E. (1962). Brand choice as a probability process, *The Journal of Business*, 35(January), 43–56.

Givon, M. (1984). Variety seeking through brand switching, *Marketing Science*, 3(Winter), 1–22.

Givon, M. and D. Horsky (1979). Application of a composite stochastic model of brand choice, *Journal of Marketing Research*, 16(May), 258–266.

Goodhardt, G. J. and A. S. C. Ehrenberg (1967). Conditional trend analysis: A breakdown by initial purchasing level, *Journal of Marketing Research*, 4(May), 155–161.

Goodhardt G. J., A. S. C. Ehrenberg, and C. Chatfield (1984). The Dirichlet: A comprehensive model of buying behaviour, *Journal of the Royal Statistical Society, Series A (General)*, 147(5), 621–655.

Grahn, G. L. (1969). NBD model of repeat-purchase loyalty: An empirical investigation, *Journal of Marketing Research*, 6(February), 72–78.

Greenwood, M. and G. U. Yule (1920). An inquiry into the nature of frequency distributions representative of multiple happenings with particular reference to the occurrence of multiple attacks of disease or of repeated accidents, *Journal of the Royal Statistical Society*, 83(March), 255–279.

Greene, J. D. and J. S. Stock (1971). A rate-frequency model of behavior, *Journal of Advertising Research*, 11(August), 9–19.

Grover, R. and W. R. Dillon (1985). A probabilistic model for testing hypothesized hierarchical market structures, *Marketing Science*, 4(Fall), 312–335.

Guadagni, P. M. and J. D. C. Little (1983). A logit model of brand choice calibrated on scanner data, *Marketing Science*, 2(Summer), 203–238.

Guadagni, P. M. and J. D. C. Little (2008). A logit model of brand choice calibrated on scanner data: A 25th anniversary perspective, *Marketing Science*, 27(January–February), 26–28.

Gupta, S. (1991). Stochastic models of interpurchase time with time-dependent covariates, *Journal of Marketing Research*, 28(February), 1–15.

Haines, G. H., Jr. (1969). *Consumer behavior: Learning models of purchasing*, New York, NY: The Free Press.

Hallberg, G. (1995). *All consumers are not created equal*, New York: John Wiley & Sons, Inc.

Harary, F. and B. Lipstein (1962). The dynamics of brand loyalty: A Markovian approach, *Operations Research*, 10(January–February), 19–40.

Hardie, B. G. S., P. S. Fader, and M. Wisniewski (1998). An empirical comparison of new product trial forecasting models, *Journal of Forecasting*, 17(June–July), 209–229.

Heckman, J. J. (1981). Statistical models for discrete panel data, in C. F. Manski and D. McFadden, eds., *Structural analysis of discrete data with econometric applications*, Cambridge, MA: The MIT Press, pp. 114–178.

Helsen, K. and D. C. Schmittlein (1993). Analyzing duration times in marketing: Evidence for the effectiveness of hazard rate models, *Marketing Science*, 12(Fall), 395–414.

Helsen, K. and D. C. Schmittlein (1994). Understanding price effects for new nondurables: How price responsiveness varies across depth-of-repeat classes and types of consumers, *European Journal of Operational Research*, 76(2), 359–374.

Herniter, J. (1971). A probabilistic market model of purchase timing and brand selection, *Management Science*, 18(December), P102–P113.

Herniter, J. D. (1973). An entropy model of brand purchase behavior, *Journal of Marketing Research*, 10(November), 361–375.

Herniter, J. D. (1974). A comparison of the entropy model and the Hendry model, *Journal of Marketing Research*, 11(February), 21–29.

Herniter, J. D. and R. A. Howard (1964). Stochastic marketing models, in D. B. Hertz and R. T. Eddison, eds., *Progress in operations research*, Vol. II, New York: John Wiley & Sons, Inc., pp. 33–96.

Herniter, J. D. and J. F. Magee (1961). Customer behavior as a Markov process, *Operations Research*, 9(January–February), 105–122.

Holla, M. S. (1966). On a Poisson-inverse Gaussian distribution, *Metrika*, 11, 115–121.

Howard, J. A. (1955). Operations research and market research, *Journal of Marketing*, 20(October), 143–149.

Howard, R. A. (1963). Stochastic process models of consumer behavior, *Journal of Advertising Research*, 3(3), 35–42.

Howard, R. A. (1965). Dynamic inference, *Operations Research*, 13(September–October), 712–733.

Howard, R. A. (1978). Comments on the origin and application of Markov decision processes, in M. L. Puterman, ed., *Dynamic programming and its applications*, New York: Academic Press, pp. 201–205.

Huang, C.-Y. (2002). *An integrated stochastic model for the analysis of web site visiting behaviors*, unpublished PhD thesis, University of London.

Hughes, A. M. (1991). *The complete database marketer*, Chicago, IL: Probus Publishing Company.

Irwin, J. O. (1941). Discussion on Chambers and Yule's paper, *Supplement to the Journal of the Royal Statistical Society*, 7(2), 101–107.

Ishii, G. and R. Hayakawa (1960). On the compound binomial distribution, *Annals of the Institute of Statistical Mathematics*, 12(February), 69–80.

Jain, D. and N. Vilcassim (1991). Investigating household purchase timing decisions: A conditional hazard function approach, *Marketing Science*, 10(Winter), 1–23.

Jenkinson, A. (1995). *Valuing your customers*, London: McGraw-Hill Book Company.

Jeuland, A. P. (1979). Brand choice inertia as one aspect of the notion of brand loyalty, *Management Science*, 25(July), 671–682.

Jeuland, A. P., F. M. Bass, and G. P. Wright (1980). A multibrand stochastic model compounding heterogeneous Erlang timing and multinomial choice processes, *Operations Research*, 28(March–April), 255–277.

Jones, D. G. B. and M. Tadajewski (2011). Percival White (1887–1970): Marketing engineer, *Marketing Theory*, 11(4), 455–478.

Jones, J. M. (1970a). A dual-effects model of brand choice, *Journal of Marketing Research*, 7(November), 458–464.

Jones, J. M. (1970b). A comparison of three models of brand choice, *Journal of Marketing Research*, 7(November), 466–473.

Jones, J. M. (1971). A stochastic model for adaptive behavior in a dynamic situation, *Management Science*, 17(March), 484–497.

Jones, J. M. (1973). A composite heterogeneous model for brand choice behavior, *Management Science*, 19(January), 499–509.

Kahn, B. E. (1987). A theoretical model of interpurchase times, *Applied Stochastic Models and Data Analysis*, 3(2), 93–109.

Kahn, B. E., M. U. Kalwani, and D. G. Morrison (1986). Measuring variety-seeking and reinforcement behaviors using panel data, *Journal of Marketing Research*, 23(May), 89–100.

Kahn, B. E. and D. G. Morrison (1989). A note on "random" purchasing: Additional insights from Dunn, Reader, and Wrigley, *Applied Statistics*, 38(1), 111–114.

Kahn, B. E., D. G. Morrison, and G. P. Wright (1986). Aggregating individual purchases to the household level, *Marketing Science*, 5(Summer), 260–268.

Kalwani, M. U. and D. G. Morrison (1977). A parsimonious description of the Hendry system, *Management Science*, 23(January), 467–477.

Kalwani, M. U. and A. J. Silk (1980). Structure of repeat buying for new packaged goods, *Journal of Marketing Research*, 17(August), 316–322.

Kuehn, A. A. (1958), *An analysis of the dynamics of consumer behavior and its implications for marketing management*, unpublished PhD dissertation, Graduate School of Industrial Administration, Carnegie Institute of Technology.

Kuehn, A. A. (1961). A model for budgeting advertising, in F. M. Bass *et al.*, eds., *Mathematical models and methods in marketing*, Homewood, IL: Richard D. Irwin, Inc., pp. 315–348.

Kuehn, A. A. (1962). Consumer brand choice as a learning process, *Journal of Advertising Research*, 2(4), 10–17.

Kuehn, A. A. and A. C. Rohloff (1967). Consumer response to promotions, in P. J. Robinson, ed., *Promotional decisions using mathematical models*, Boston, MA: Allyn and Bacon, Inc., pp. 50–85.

Lawrence, R. J. (1975). Consumer brand choice: A random walk?' *Journal of Marketing Research*, 12(August), 314–324.

Lazarsfeld, P. F. (ed.) (1954). *Mathematical thinking in the social sciences*, Glencoe, IL: The Free Press.

Lazarsfeld, P. and M. Fiske (1938). The "panel" as a new tool for measuring opinion, *The Public Opinion Quarterly*, 2(October), 596–612.

Leeflang, P. S. H. and A. Boonstra (1982). Some comments on the development and application of linear learning models, *Management Science*, 28(November), 1233–1246.

Lenk, P. J., A. G. Rao and V. Tibrewala (1993). Nonstationary conditional trend analysis: An application to scanner panel data, *Journal of Marketing Research*, 30(August), 288–304.

Lilien, G. L. (1974). A modified linear learning model of buyer behavior, *Management Science*, 20(March), 1027–1036.

Lipstein, B. (1959). The dynamics of brand loyalty and brand switching, in A. H. Johnson, Chair, *Proceedings of the Fifth Annual Conference of the Advertising Research Foundation*, New York, NY, pp. 101–108.

Lipstein, B. (1965). A mathematical model of consumer behavior, *Journal of Marketing Research*, 2(August), 259–265.

Lipstein, B. (1968). Test marketing: A perturbation in the market place, *Management Science*, 14(April), B437–B448.

Little, J. D. C. (1970). Models and managers: The concept of a decision calculus, *Management Science*, 16(April), B466–B485.

Longton, P. A. and B. T. Warner (1962). A mathematical model for marketing, *Metra*, 1(3), 297–310.

Maffei, R. B. (1960). Brand preferences and simple Markov processes, *Operations Research*, 8(March–April), 210–218.

Maffei, R. B. (1961). Advertising effectiveness, brand switching and market dynamics, *The Journal of Industrial Economics*, 9(April), 119–131.

Magee, J. F. (1953). The effect of promotional effort on sales, *Journal of the Operations Research Society of America*, 1(February), 64–74.

Magee, J. F. (1954). Application of operations research to marketing and related management problems, *Journal of Marketing*, 18(April), 361–369.

Massy, W. F. (1966). Order and homogeneity of family specific brand-switching processes, *Journal of Marketing Research*, 3(February), 48–54.

Massy, W. F. (1968). Stochastic models for monitoring new-product introduction, in F. M. Bass, C. W. King and E. A. Pessemier, eds., *Applications of the sciences in marketing management*, New York: John Wiley & Sons, Inc., pp. 85–111.

Massy, W. F. (1969). Forecasting the demand for new convenience products, *Journal of Marketing Research*, 6(November), 405–412.

Massy, W. F., D. B. Montgomery and D. G. Morrison (1970), *Stochastic models of buyer behavior*, Cambridge, MA: The MIT Press.

Massy, W. F. and D. G. Morrison (1968). Comments on Ehrenberg's appraisal of brand-switching models, *Journal of Marketing Research*, 5(May), 225–228.

McConnell, J. D. (1968). Repeat-purchase estimation and the linear learning model, *Journal of Marketing Research*, 5(August), 304–306.

McFadden, D. (1974). Conditional logit analysis of qualitative choice behavior, in P. Zarembka, ed., *Frontiers in econometrics*, New York: Academic Press, pp. 105–142.

Montgomery, D. B. (1969). A stochastic response model with application to brand choice, *Management Science*, 15(March), 323–337.

Montgomery, D. B. (2001). Management science in marketing: Prehistory, origin, and early years of the INFORMS marketing college, *Marketing Science*, 20(Fall), 337–348.

Morrison, D. G. (1966). Testing brand-switching models, *Journal of Marketing Research*, 3(November), 401–409.

Morrison, D. G. (1968). Analysis of consumer purchase data: A Bayesian approach, *Industrial Management Review*, 9(Winter), 31–40.

Morrison, D. G. (1969). Conditional trend analysis: A model that allows for nonusers, *Journal of Marketing Research*, 6(August), 342–346.

Morrison, D. G. (1978). The use and limitations of brand switching models, in H. L. Davis and A. J. Silk, eds., *Behavioral and management science in marketing*, New York: John Wiley & Sons, Inc., pp. 5–11.

Morrison, D. G., R. D. H. Chen, S. L. Karpis, and K. E. A. Britney (1982). Modelling retail customer behavior at Merrill Lynch, *Marketing Science*, 1(Spring), 123–141.

Morrison, D. G. and A. Perry (1970). Some data based models for analyzing sales fluctuations, *Decision Sciences*, 1(July), 258–274.

Morrison, D. G. and D. C. Schmittlein (1980). Jobs, strikes, and wars: Probability models for duration, *Organizational Behavior and Human Performance*, 25(April), 224–251.

Morrison, D. G. and D. C. Schmittlein (1981). Predicting future random events based on past performance, *Management Science*, 27(September), 1006–1023.

Morrison, D. G. and D. C. Schmittlein (1988). Generalizing the NBD model for customer purchases: What are the implications and is it worth the effort? *Journal of Business and Economic Statistics*, 6(April), 145–159.

Morton, A. Q. (1994). Packaging history: The emergence of the uniform product code (UPC) in the United States, 1970–1975, *History and Technology*, 11(1), 101–111.

Mosimann, J. E. (1962). On the compound multinomial distribution, the multivariate β-distribution, and correlations among proportions, *Biometrika*, 49(June), 65–82.

Nagano, S. (1972). An empirical comparison of brand choice models, *Bulletin of University of Osaka Prefecture, Series D, Sciences of Economy, Commerce and Law*, 16, 55–66.

Neslin, S. A. and H. J. van Heerde (2008). Promotion dynamics, *Foundations and Trends in Marketing*, 3(4), 177–268.

Paull, A. E. (1978). A generalized compound Poisson model for consumer purchase panel data analysis, *Journal of the American Statistical Association*, 73(December), 706–713.

Pearson, E. S. (1925). Bayes' theorem, examined in the light of experimental sampling, *Biometrika*, 17(December), 388–442.

Pearson, S. (1996), *Building brands directly*, London: Macmillan Press.

Potter, R. G. and M. P. Parker (1964). Predicting the time required to conceive, *Population Studies*, 18(July), 99–116.

Poulsen, C. S. (1983), *Latent structure analysis with choice modeling applications*, unpublished PhD dissertation, University of Pennsylvania.

Poulsen, C. S. (1990). Mixed Markov and latent Markov modelling applied to brand choice behaviour, *International Journal of Research in Marketing*, 7(1), 5–19.

Pyatt, G. (1970). A model of brand loyalties, in M. G. Kendal, ed., *Mathematical model building in economics and industry, second series*, London: Charles Griffin & Company Ltd., 81–99.

Quenouille, M. H. (1949). A relation between the logarithmic, Poisson, and negative binomial series, *Biometrics*, 5(June), 162–164.

Reinartz, W. and V. Kumar (2000). On the profitability of long-life customers in a noncontractual setting: An empirical investigation and implications for marketing, *Journal of Marketing*, 64(October), 17–35.

Robbins, H. (1977). Prediction and estimation for the compound Poisson distribution, *Proceeding of the National Academy of Sciences, USA*, 74(July), 2670–2671.

Roberts, M. L. and P. D. Berger (1989). *Direct marketing management*, Englewood Cliffs, NJ: Prentice Hall.

Rubinson, J. R., W. R. Vanhonacker, and F. M. Bass (1980). On a parsimonious description of the Hendry system, *Management Science*, 26(February), 215–226.

Sabavala, D. J. and D. G. Morrison (1977). A model of TV show loyalty, *Journal of Advertising Research*, 17(December), 35–43.

Sabavala, D. J. and D. G. Morrison (1981). A nonstationary model of binary choice applied to media exposure, *Management Science*, 27(June), 637–657.

Schmittlein, D. C., A. C. Bemmaor, and D. G. Morrison (1985). Why does the NBD model work? Robustness in representing product purchases, brand purchases and imperfectly recorded purchases, *Marketing Science*, 4(Summer), 255–266.

Schmittlein, D. C. and D. G. Morrison (1983). Prediction of future random events with the condensed negative binomial distribution, *Journal of the American Statistical Association*, 78(June), 449–456.

Schmittlein, D. C., D. G. Morrison, and R. Colombo (1987). Counting your customers: Who are they and what will they do next? *Management Science*, 33(January), 1–24.

Schmittlein, D. C. and R. A. Peterson (1994). Customer base analysis: An industrial purchase process application, *Marketing Science*, 13(Winter), 41–67.

Shaffer, J. D. (1955). The reporting period for a consumer purchase panel, *Journal of Marketing*, 19(January), 252–257.

Shoemaker, R. W., R. Staelin, J. B. Kadane, and F. R. Shoaf (1977). Relation of brand choice to purchase frequency, *Journal of Marketing Research*, 14(November), 458–468.

Sichel, H. S. (1982). Repeat-buying and the generalized inverse Gaussian–Poisson distribution, *Applied Statistics*, 31(3), 193–204.

Silcock, H. (1954). The phenomena of labour turnover, *Journal of the Royal Statistical Society, Series A (General)*, 117(4), 429–440.

Silvey, R. (1974). *Who's listening? The story of BBC audience research*, London: George Allen & Unwin Ltd.

Skellam, J. G. (1948). A probability distribution derived from the binomial distribution by regarding the probability of success as variable between the sets of trials, *Journal of the Royal Statistical Society, Series B*, 10(2), 257–261.

Srinivasan, V. and R. Kesavan (1976). An alternate interpretation of the linear learning model of brand choice, *Journal of Consumer Research*, 3(September), 76–83.

Stonborough, T. H. W. (1942). Fixed panels in consumer research, *Journal of Marketing*, 7(October), 129–138.

Styan, G. P. H. and H. Smith, Jr. (1964). Markov chains applied to marketing, *Journal of Marketing Research*, 1(February), 50–55.

Urban, G. L., P. L. Johnson, and J. R. Hauser (1984). Testing competitive market structures, *Marketing Science*, 3(Spring), 83–112.

Urban, G. L. and R. Karash (1971). Evolutionary model building, *Journal of Marketing Research*, 8(February), 62–66.

Vilcassim, N. and D. Jain (1991). Modeling purchase-timing and brand-switching behavior incorporating explanatory variables and unobserved heterogeneity, *Journal of Marketing Research*, 28(February), 29–41.

Wagner, U. and A. Taudes (1986). A multivariate Polya model of brand choice and purchase incidence, *Marketing Science*, 5(Summer), 219–244.

Wagner, U. and A. Taudes (1991). Microdynamics of new product purchase: A model incorporating both marketing and consumer-specific variables, *International Journal of Research in Marketing*, 8(3), 223–249.

Wierenga, B. (1974). *An investigation of brand choice processes*, Rotterdam: Rotterdam University Press.

Wierenga, B. (1978). A least squares estimation method for the linear learning model, *Journal of Marketing Research*, 15(February), 145–153.

Willmot, G. E. (1987). The Poisson-inverse Gaussian as an alternative to the negative binomial, *Scandinavian Actuarial Journal*, (3–4), 113–127.

Womer, S. (1944). Some applications of the continuous consumer panel, *Journal of Marketing*, 9(October), 132–136.

Zufryden, F. S. (1977). A composite heterogeneous model of brand choice and purchase timing behavior, *Management Science*, 24(October), 121–136.

Zufryden, F. S. (1978). An empirical evaluation of a composite heterogeneous model of brand choice and purchase timing behavior, *Management Science*, 24(March), 761–773.

Zufryden, F. S. (1983). An empirical evaluation of alternative composite brand choice-purchase incidence models, in J. N. Sheth, ed., *Research in marketing*, 6, 259–282.

Part II

Management

Chapter 8

Advertising Effectiveness

Gerard J. Tellis

8.1 Introduction

Advertising is probably as old as selling or marketing. As far back in history as when individuals or organizations sought to sell goods or services to others, they resorted to advertising in one form or another to inform buyers of their offerings. Advertising got a boost in the US when the country won its independence from Great Britain. There was a tremendous burst in commercial activity, as citizens strove to make the newly liberated United States independent from Britain in all goods and service. Producers of these goods and services then needed advertising to inform buyers of their offerings.

Advertising got its second big boost after the civil war with the confirmation of the United States and the opening up of the West. There was a tremendous drive to mass manufacturing in the emerging mass market of the United States. This move was unparalleled anywhere in the then developed world of Western Europe. One of the first mass produced goods in the US was Procter and Gamble's (P&G) soap. In 1875, when P&G succeeded in manufacturing a soap that was as pure as the best imported soap of that time, Castile, they wanted to advertise that fact to the then rapidly expanding markets of the US to increase demand for it. P&G called the soap "Ivory" and launched an advertising campaign on the theme, "99 and 44/100% pure." That campaign probably marks the birth of modern advertising in the US and may be even in the world.[1] Since then, advertising has grown tremendously to become an over US$300 billion industry in the US and a US$1.3 trillion industry in the world.

Since the birth of modern advertising, researchers have sought to ascertain its effectiveness. These researchers were motivated in informing advertisers about how much they should spend on advertising, in what media, with what content, and over what time period. These fundamental questions about advertising research have persisted till today. These questions have spawned a massive literature on advertising. Researchers have published their findings in journals of advertising, consumer behavior, business, economics, marketing, management, and psychology. As such, they have spawned a vast, rich body of knowledge on various aspects of advertising. It would be fascinating to review this literature and distill what we have learned. But the task is too big for the confines of one chapter. So I focus only on studies which try to estimate the (a) effects of advertising on (b) sales or market share in (c) real markets. Most if not all of these studies fall within the general rubric of "marketing science" rather than the rubric of "consumer behavior" or "lab studies." The simple reason is that research in marketing science tends to study real markets in order to better describe and predict real market phenomena and better control optimal advertising expenditures. Research in consumer behavior tends to focus on tight laboratory experiments in order to arrive at precise theories to explain why and how advertising works.

Knowledge about advertising's effects in real markets has grown rapidly in the last 50 years after researchers began to use sophisticated econometric and statistical methods to estimate advertising effectiveness. Prior to the 1960s and for some decades after that, research on advertising was published primarily in the economics journals. Since the 1960s, research took different paths in different disciplines. Research on the economic effects of advertising as a competitive activity appeared in economics journals. Research on theories of how individuals processed advertising messages in their minds appeared primarily in advertising and consumer behavior journals. Research on the effectiveness of advertising in

---

[1]Tellis, G. J. (1998). *Advertising and sales promotion strategy*, Addison-Wesley.

real markets appeared primarily in marketing journals. The latter research will be the focus of this chapter.

The modeling paradigm has primarily examined the effects of advertising intensity on market behavior. Advertising intensity has been measured by a brand's advertising expenditure, gross rating points (GRP), frequency, or ad exposures delivered to the market. Market behavior has been measured by a brand's unit sales, revenues, choices, or market share (in units or revenues). The method of analysis has been econometric models and field experiments. Because econometric models typically use real market data, which may not be easily controlled, they are strong on relevance but weak on ascertaining causality. To tighten the estimates of how advertising causes sales, these studies have resorted to increasingly complex econometric models. Because field experiments control some market conditions and the timing of the advertising, they are stronger on causality but less realistic. They also represent their findings through relatively simple analyses.

Neither the laboratory experiment nor the econometric approach is universally superior by itself. However, the market experiment represents a nice hybrid. If properly designed, it can combine the strengths of the laboratory experiment and the econometric model without being straddled with their limitations. A hybrid approach also has the strength of determining advertising's impact on the mental processes (to help copy design) and on sales (to help budgeting). This chapter reviews the findings from studies that have used econometric models or market experiments and have all been carried out in real markets. These studies can be classified into the following five streams of research: (1) Models of Ad Elasticity, (2) Models of Ad Carryover and Dynamics, (3) Models of Ad Frequency, (4) Models of Ad Content, (5) Field Experiments of Ad Effectiveness. Figure 8.1 traces the genealogy of studies in these five areas and how these areas relate to each other as well as prior disciplines.

What is common to all these five streams of research are the following:

- Use of advertising as independent variable
- Use of sales or market share as dependent variables
- Focus on the effect of advertising
- Carried out with real market data.

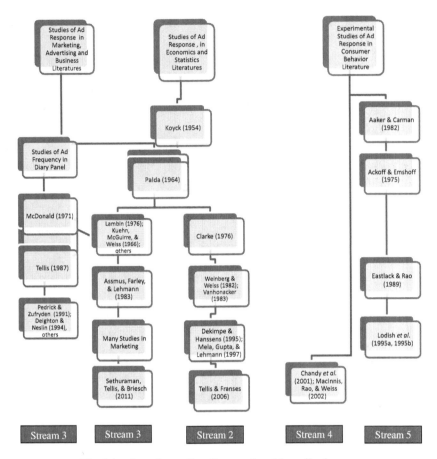

Fig. 8.1   Genealogy of studies on advertising effectiveness

What distinguishes these streams from each other are the following issues:

- The effects of advertising, measured primarily as expenditure in the current period (Stream 1).
- The effects of advertising over time captures as duration or dynamics (Stream 2).
- The effects of advertising, measured as exposures or frequency (Stream 3).
- The effects of advertising content (Stream 4).
- The effect of advertising measured in field experiments (Stream 5).

The next five sections discuss each of these streams of research.[2]

8.2 Stream 1: Models of advertising elasticity

This stream of research focuses on estimating the effect of advertising during the same period as that of the advertising. Studies in the stream measure advertising with aggregate metrics such as total expenditure or total GRP. They measure sales as units or monetary revenues or market share. The most common and useful metric for capturing this effect is the advertising elasticity.

Advertising elasticity is the percentage change in sales (or market share) for a one-percent change in the level of advertising. Because the numerator and denominator are in percentages, elasticity is unit-free (i.e., independent of the units of sales or advertising). Technically, the appropriate name is the **elasticity of sales to advertising** but researchers refer to it simply as the advertising elasticity. Researchers estimate advertising elasticity by analyzing the differences in sales or market share due to differences in advertising budget from period to period within a time frame.

Studies of advertising elasticity determine the shape and strength of the advertising response function. Typically, researchers express this shape as a particular mathematical function, and the strength as an elasticity. To do so, researchers use some econometric models of the effect of advertising on sales or market share (see Chapter 5 by Hanssens). Sections 8.2.1 and 8.2.2 cover important studies in this stream and important generalizations.

8.2.1 *History of important studies*

A pioneering study on advertising effectiveness was by Christian Palda (1964) based on the author's 1963 award-winning dissertation. Palda laid out the philosophy and theory of the econometric model and how it could be used to estimate the effectiveness of advertising on sales. He estimated the effect of advertising on sales as the advertising elasticity. Moreover, he emphasized that one had to consider not only the current effects of

---

[2]The review of specific studies borrows from Tellis (2004).

advertising but also its dynamics or carryover effect, which occurred in subsequent periods. To do so, he established the logic of using real historical market data. In particular, he used data from the company, Lydia Pinkham. These data covered advertising and sales data of the company's vegetable compound from 1908 to 1935, which became public due to court litigation. He contacted the company and got additional data from 1936 to 1960.

Palda's actual estimates of advertising elasticity are way off for reasons of data aggregation, which we will discuss in Sec. 8.3. However, Palda's contribution lies in the four essential principles of estimating advertising elasticity, which he espoused and which have persisted till today and include use of the econometric model, focus on the coefficient of advertising in the model, incorporation of dynamic effects, and estimation on real market data. Subsequent researchers took the analysis in a variety of directions, including alternate functional forms for capturing the advertising response, alternate methods for estimating the elasticity, alternate specifications for estimating dynamics, alternate levels of data aggregation, and alternate data covering a variety of categories, brands, stages of the life cycle, calendar time periods, and countries.

In pursuing these variations, perhaps the biggest contribution in the estimation of advertising elasticity was made by Jean Jacques Lambin (1976). His study is impressive in scope and the range of issues he sought to address. The data for his study cover four stages of the product life cycle, 16 product categories, 107 brands, and 8 Western European countries although a large fraction of the data is from Belgium. He included at least two marketing variables besides advertising, used three methods of estimation, and adopted at least two specifications of advertising carryover. Given this richness in context, he obtained 176 estimates of elasticities. From the results, Lambin derived 24 findings or preliminary generalizations. A review of these findings indicates that about 20 of them still hold.

Following Lambin, researchers continued in the research for the most accurate estimate of advertising elasticity by the use of more sophisticated models and estimation methods. The wealth of estimates naturally led other researchers to try to determine generalizations about advertising elasticity. The most sophisticated of the methods for ascertaining generalizations is the meta-analysis. A meta-analysis is a scientific study that treats the advertising elasticities from original studies as dependent observations, which are then pooled together and analyzed by the characteristics of those original studies. In contrast, a traditional literature review briefly describes each original study and summarizes the results across studies.

8.2.2 *Generalizations*

There are at least two major reviews and two major meta-analyses of the effects of advertising on sales. I review only the two meta-analyses, for one important reason.[3] The two meta-analyses are comprehensive enough that they encompass the scope and findings of the two reviews.

The first meta-analysis of advertising elasticity is by Assmus, Farley, and Lehmann (1984). They conducted a meta-analysis of 128 econometric models from primary studies that analyzed the impact of advertising on sales or market share. Their major findings were the following (Tellis, 2004):

- The grand mean for the advertising elasticity was 0.2.
- The grand mean for the carryover elasticity of advertising was 0.5.
- Short-term elasticities were much lower in models that incorporated a carryover coefficient (a lagged dependent variable) than in models without one.
- Models that contained exogenous variables had smaller short-term elasticities than those that did not.
- Elasticities in linear additive models were higher than those in multiplicative models (see Chapters 3–5 for different types of models).
- Pooled data involving cross-sectional observations in addition to time series observations, yielded higher elasticities.
- Food products have an elasticity that is 0.1 higher than other products.
- Elasticities were significantly higher for Europe relative to the US.
- Elasticities did not differ by measure of the dependent variable (sales or market share), by product or brand, or by type of estimation method.

Recently, a new meta-analysis by Sethuraman, Tellis, and Briesch (2010) attempted to update the original one by Assmus, Farley, and Lehmann

---

[3]The two reviews of econometric studies that are not covered here are Aaker and Carman (1982) *op. cit.*, and Leone and Schultz (1980), "A study of Marketing Generalization," *Journal of Marketing*, 44(Winter), 10–18.

(1984) to ascertain what findings about advertising elasticity have changed over the more recent 20-year period and what findings have remained the same and are truly enduring. Sethuraman, Tellis, and Briesch (2010) covered 751 short-term and 402 long-term advertising elasticities estimated in 56 studies published between 1960 and 2008. The study found several new empirical generalizations about advertising elasticity.

- The average short-term advertising elasticity is 0.1, which is half the prior meta-analytic mean of 0.2 (Assmus, Farley, and Lehmann, 1984).
- The advertising elasticity has declined over time.
- The advertising elasticity is higher

  (a) for durable goods than non-durable goods
  (b) in the early stage of the life cycle than in the mature stage
  (c) for yearly data than for quarterly data.
  (d) when advertising is measured in GRP than in monetary terms.

- The mean long-term advertising elasticity is 0.24, which is much lower than the implied mean in the prior meta-analysis (0.41) of Assmus, Farley, and Lehmann (1984).
- Many of the results for short-term elasticity hold for long-term elasticity, with a few exceptions.

The great strength of this stream of research spanning over half a century is that it has yielded a lot of specific knowledge about how advertising works. This knowledge has been tested across a variety of research contexts as explained above. At the same time, the above stream of research is limited in that it has generally relied on temporally aggregate data, used mostly sales or market share rather than consumer choices as the dependent variable, focused on advertising dollars or GRP rather than advertising exposures, and estimated by naturally occurring data rather than experiments. Each of the other four streams of research described in Sections 8.3–8.6 address one or more of these limitations.

8.3 Stream 2: Models of advertising carryover and dynamics

This stream of research focuses on the size and duration of the effects of advertising that occur beyond the same period as that of the advertising. Like the prior stream of research, studies in this stream measure advertising with aggregate metrics such as total expenditure or total GRP. They measure sales as unit or monetary revenues or market share. The metric used for capturing the effect of advertising is again the elasticity. The metric for the duration of the effect is the number of time periods in which the data are collected.

It is a well-known fact that the effect of advertising is not instantaneous but carries over from the moment of advertising to subsequent periods. The analysis of advertising carryover is important for several reasons (Tellis, 2004). First, the total effect of advertising depends on the instantaneous effect plus any carryover. If the carryover is substantial, then ignoring this component can grossly underestimate the true effect of advertising. Second, if a pulse of advertising has some carryover effect, it may suggest that the next pulse need not be scheduled until the effect of first pulse decays. Third, the duration of the effects of advertising may have implications for whether firms should treat advertising as an expense or an investment and whether the government should allow it to be tax-deductible or not. Fourth, the duration of advertising's effect may determine to what extent advertising is a barrier to entry or advertising creates long-terms habits (such as smoking). This section covers the modeling of carryover, the data aggregation problem and solution, other studies on advertising dynamics, and generalizations.

8.3.1 *History of the problem and solution of data aggregation*

How can one estimate such carryover effects of advertising's, especially if one adopted an econometric model? The most obvious solution is to include lagged variables for various values of advertising as additional independent variables. However, doing so creates two problems: (1) the lagged values of advertising tend to be highly correlated leading to non-sense estimates of the coefficients of lagged advertising. (2) It is unclear how many lags the researcher should use.

A pioneering solution to this problem was obtained by Koyck (1954). Koyck showed that an econometric model with infinite lags of the key independent variable would reduce to one with only one lag of the dependent variable, under the assumption that the effect of advertising was constant over the time period but declined monotonically following a smooth geometric decay. Koyck (1954) showed this via the Koyck transformation, by which a moving average model of infinite order can be reduced to an auto-regressive-moving-average model each of single order. The derivation is simple and nifty and solved a major problem in econometric modeling.

Palda (1964) used the Koyck model in his attempt to estimate the carryover effect of advertising. The two assumptions of the Koyck model seemed reasonable in the context of advertising because one could assume that the effect of advertising itself would not change over time but that its effects would decline smoothly and monotonically because memory decays at that rate. However, in retrospective, the estimates of advertising carryover that Palda got were too large, leading to non-sense estimates of how long the effects of advertising lasted. Initially, no one realized this problem. Accordingly, a large number of primary econometric studies attempted to estimate the size and duration of the carryover effect of advertising using the Koyck model.

A critically important contribution to this stream of research was made by Clarke (1976), who surveyed the results of 28 studies that analyzed the effects of advertising on sales or market share. From those, he derived 69 different estimates of the carryover effects of advertising. He found that these estimates gave widely different estimates of how long it took for most (90%) of advertising's effects to last or dissipate. Estimates varied from a low of 0.8 of a month to a high of 1368 months, or 113 years! On closer analysis, he found that a key factor, which affected the estimates of the duration of advertising carryover, was the level of data aggregation. This term refers to the level at which data on sales and advertising is collected and analyzed. In the sample of original studies Clarke (1976) surveyed, this aggregation could be in weeks, months, quarters, or years. His major finding was that the higher the data aggregation, the longer the *estimated* (but not necessarily true) duration of advertising's carryover.

Clarke (1976) assumed that the appropriate data interval was the *purchase frequency* — the average frequency with which consumers purchase the product being studied. Based on that, he estimated that the duration of the effects of advertising on sales for the sample of categories he surveyed was between 3 and 15 months. Clarke's (1976) major assumption — the appropriate data interval is the purchase frequency — is probably not warranted.

A large number of subsequent studies sought to ascertain why there was this aggregation bias and what could be done to correct it if the true data interval were known (e.g., Weinberg and Weiss (1982); Vanhonacker (1983)). However, none of the studies attempted to ascertain what the true data interval should be. So which data interval is the right one?

Leone (1995a) computed the duration of the carryover effect from past studies. In particular, he used as input the 114 estimates of the carryover effect of advertising collected by Assmus *et al.* (reviewed above). To compute the duration of the carryover effect, Leone (1995) used the principle established by Clarke (1976). Leone (1995) found that the average carryover effect of advertising was 0.69. Based on this figure, he found that 90% of the effect of advertising would last 6 months. This time period is a little shorter than that determined by Clarke (1976) but also based on an erroneous assumption about the true data interval.

Tellis, Chandy, and Thaivanich (2000) tried to answer this question, with a model of advertising response at a highly disaggregate level of hours in the day when advertising occurred. They used a distributed lag model, which can be considered a segmented Koyck model. A key feature of the model is that it captured the effects of individual ads, channels, and time of day. Data for the empirical testing was gathered for 5 markets in the US. In contrast to most past studies, the authors found that the carryover effect of advertising was fairly short. Over the 5 markets studied, the average carryover effect was 8 hours. Critics argued that this number might seem unreasonably short and that the study of Tellis, Chandy, and Thaivanich suffered from disaggregation bias. However, consider that consumers receive hundreds of messages a day. The new messages could well erase the effect of the old messages. Nevertheless, the issue still remained, what was the true data interval?

This problem was solved by Tellis and Franses (2006). By a nifty use of the lag operator, these authors proved that the appropriate data interval is not the frequency of the purchase interval as previously believed. Rather, the appropriate data interval is the unit-exposure time. This interval is the largest period in which advertising exposure occurs at the most once and then at the same time every period. This interval is probably in days, hours, or minutes because advertising frequency is typically quite disaggregate. Thus, the duration of advertising's effects would probably be much shorter than that estimated by Clarke (1976) and may well be close to that estimated by Chandy, Tellis, and Thaivanich (2001).

8.3.2 *Other studies on advertising dynamics*

Three other studies on the dynamic effects of advertising deserve mention (Tellis, 2004).

Lodish *et al.* (1995a) found that in general, the effects of advertising did not die out immediately after a campaign stopped. When advertising was effective, 76% of the initial increase persisted for a year later, *after the campaign ended*, and another 28% persisted for a third year. So the total carryover effect could equal the current effect (computed in the first year). In these cases, there was also a small (about 6%) carryover effect in category volume. Advertising effectiveness was also more persistent over time for new products than for mature products. Note, that the findings of this study seem to conflict sharply with those of Clarke (1976) who found that advertising carryover is from 3 to 9 months, and those of Tellis, Chandy, and Thaivanich (2000) who found that advertising carryover lasts only about 8 hours. One solution to this conflict comes from considering the time frame. The findings of Lodish *et al.* (1995) about advertising carryover is different from that computed in all prior studies reviewed so far in this chapter. The prior studies try to estimate the average carryover effects of advertising in separate time periods or separate ads while the campaign is progressing. In contrast, Lodish and his associates (1995) estimate the carryover effect of an *entire campaign after it ends*. Thus, even though many authors have tried to compare the two types of findings and draw generalization, no simple comparison is valid. The two sets of findings must be treated as complementary findings about the carryover effects of advertising.

Dekimpe and Hanssens (1995) sought to determine the long-term or persistent impact of advertising using vector auto-regressive models (see Chapter 5). They tested their model on monthly sales of a chain of home improvement stores from 1980 to 1986. The authors find that sales and total advertising spending have a long-run or evolving component, for two reasons: (a) repeat purchases from those who bought due to advertising and (b) purchases from those who heard about the product from those who saw the advertising. They argue that these higher sales feed back into higher advertising as managers set ad budgets based on sales figures. They thus suspect that the evolving pattern they find is due to such a chain reaction. The authors' most important and ambitious claim is that while some of the effect of advertising dissipates in the short term, some of it lasts or persists, even when the advertising is stopped. They estimate that an extra dollar in advertising updates the long-run sales forecast by US$1.09 and the long-run advertising forecast by US$0.49. On the other hand, the authors find that even though advertising has a positive persistent effect, it does not have a positive persistent profit impact.

Mela, Gupta, and Lehmann (1997) examined the "long-term" effects of promotion and advertising on consumer's brand choice. This study is probably one that focused on the longest time horizon — $8\frac{1}{4}$ years. As such, the title of "long-term" is probably justified. The authors analyzed single-source data in one product category — a frequently purchased non-food packaged product. During the time period of the study, the authors found that advertising had declined while promotions had increased. The author's most important finding was that advertising reduces consumers' price sensitivity while promotion increases consumers' price and promotion sensitivity. They found that these effects were significantly larger for a price-sensitive segment than for a loyal segment. Subsequent analysis of profitability on the same dataset indicated that advertising could be more profitable than promotions or price discounting (Jedidi, Mela, and Gupta, 1999).

Dekimpe and Hanssens used a Vector Auto-Regressive (VAR) model. As such, it would suffer from aggregation bias just as the Koyck model. As yet, no one has estimated the degree of aggregation bias in VAR models. The studies of Mela, Gupta, and Lehmann (1997) and Lodish (1995) represent alternate methods of estimating the dynamics of advertising to the standard Koyck model.

8.3.3 *Generalizations*

Research on advertising dynamics leads to the following tentative generalizations:

- Advertising does have a carryover effect which seems to be as large as the current effect. Thus, the total effect of advertising is twice the current effect.

- Researchers need to be careful in estimating the carryover effects of advertising via Koyck or VAR models because they lead to an aggregation bias.
- Data at the frequency of advertising scheduling (not at that of purchases) is necessary for estimating the carryover effects of advertising. In precise terms, the optimal data interval is the largest interval in which advertising occurs just once and at the same time within that interval.
- The duration of advertising's effects is likely to be quite short. However, no precise estimates are available as of now because none of the prior studies have properly taken this rule for the appropriate data interval in computing the duration of advertising's effects.

8.4   Stream 3: Models of ad frequency

This stream of studies focuses on the effect of individual exposures of advertising. In contrast to the prior two streams of research, this stream of research focuses on disaggregate measures of advertising. The prior stream of research used aggregate measures of advertising such as total expenditure or total GRP. Advertising normally works through its effects on individual consumers. Thus, the advertising budget in a time period ultimately translates into a sequence of individual exposures targeted at one or more consumers. Similarly, sales may be considered an aggregate of consumers' choices about individual brands. The term, **frequency**, refers to the number of ad exposures each consumer receives in a particular time period. **Effective frequency** refers to the optimum frequency that maximizes the outcome designed by the advertisers, such as sales, profits, or price level.

Databases that record sales as consumers' purchases of brands or quantity purchased on various occasions, typically also record the delivery of advertising in the form of advertising exposures. The analysis of consumers' choices presents unique problems and opportunities for understanding the effects of advertising. The major problem is that, since each consumer has a large number of purchases, the size and complexity of the database quickly increases with the sample size. However, a focus on choice provides a large number of advantages. The key advantages are greater insight into how advertising works and a freedom from bias that occurs if one aggregates data over consumers or exposures.

Like studies on advertising elasticity, studies on frequency also determine the effectiveness of advertising in terms of the shape of the response function. However, studies on advertising elasticity capture the response function of aggregate sales to aggregate advertising expenditure. In contrast, studies on advertising frequency capture the response function of disaggregate consumers' choices to disaggregate advertising exposures. Thus, such studies are far more specific in details and insight. At the same time, they are not immediately practical. Even if a manager knows the effective frequency, he or she still needs to know what advertising budget and scheduling will deliver that frequency to the appropriate consumers. So this stream of research by itself is insufficient to understanding how to optimally use advertising.

8.4.1 *History of important studies*

A pioneering study on advertising frequency was by McDonald (1971). He analyzed the diary records of a sample of 266 panelists in 9 product categories for 13 weeks. He took great care to avoid spurious causality when analyzing the data. In particular, he made sure that he did not interpret the pattern of loyal consumers of a brand being targeted with more ads, as one of the responses to advertising. First, McDonald (1971) found that panelists were 5% more likely to switch to than from a brand, when, in the interval between two purchases, they had seen two or more ads for the brand. Second, the above effect was stronger for ads seen less than four days before the purchase than for ads seen more than four days before the purchase. Third, subjecting panelists to 3 or more exposures did not seem to have a stronger effect than doing so with 2 exposures.

Tellis (1988a) did a choice analysis of panelists' purchases of toilet tissue in single source data. He was inspired by the well-known choice model of Guadagni and Little (1983) that modeled how consumers' choices respond to promotions. The latter authors did not have access to advertising data. Tellis (1988a) noted that despite the almost commodity status of this category, total advertising in the category amounted to about a hundred millions dollars. Tellis obtained the following results. First, the effects of advertising were small and quite difficult to identify. In contrast, the effects of sales promotions were strong, immediate, and hard to miss. Second, brand loyalty moderated the effects of ad exposure. Buyers responded more strongly to brands to which they were more loyal. Third, the response to ad exposure seemed non-linear. However, brand loyalty strongly moderated this non-linearity. The response for brands to which the consumer was loyal, occurred rapidly and peaked at 2 to 3 exposures. However, brands with which the consumer was not familiar, required many more exposures per week, but could achieve a higher peak. Fourth, advertising had a small effect in winning new buyers but a little stronger effect in reinforcing preference.

Pedrick and Zufryden (1991) studied the effectiveness of advertising in the yogurt category using single-source data. Three of the results that Pedrick and Zufryden (1991) obtained are similar to those of Tellis (1988a): the effects of advertising are relatively small, the effects of promotions are much stronger than those of advertising, and the response to ad exposure is non-linear. The most important result they obtained is that market share increases were much more responsive to increases in reach than to increases in frequency.

Deighton, Henderson, and Neslin (1994) carried out analysis of single-source data using econometric models similar to the two prior studies described in this sub-section. The authors studied the effect of exposure frequency on brand choice of the advertised brand. As in the prior two studies, the authors found that the effects of other promotional variables were much stronger than that of advertising. The effect of advertising was significantly different from 0 for two of the three categories. The authors' most important finding was that probability of a consumer buying a brand increased steadily with the number of exposures, even going up to exposure levels of 20. However, this effect went up at a declining rate. Also, the biggest increase occurred when going from an exposure level of 0 to 1.

Jones (1995) analyzed single-source data for 142 brands in 12 categories for 1991. All 12 were from packaged grocery products and included markets that were competitive and heavily advertised. He focused on the short-term effect of advertising that occurred in the 7 days just prior to purchase. Jones (1995) found that advertising does have short-term effects on household purchases of the advertised brands. However, the direction of the effect is not universal. About 50% of the brands have ad effects that are moderate to strong. About 30% have effects that are not clearly distinguishable, while 20% strangely have negative effects. Some fraction of the brands that have a short-term effect, also have long-term effects on sales. But long-term effects are much less pronounced than the short-term effects. The most important result from the Jones (1995) study is about advertising repetition. He finds that that in the 7 days just prior to purchase, the first exposure gets the most response. Additional exposures do not add much. Thus, the conclusion from this study is that "one exposure is enough."

A marketing consultant, Gibson (1996), found similar results from analyzing TRI-NET market experiments of 60 commercials at General Mills. He found that just one exposure of an ad was adequate to achieve big changes in attitude and coupon usage for that brand; multiple exposures were not necessary.

This last result has created some controversy and has led some researchers to question Jones' (1995) analysis and interpretation. Two issues that are most pertinent are the formation of the baseline sample and the identification of the 7-day period. First, the results of the study are valid only if advertisers do not target with heavier advertising households who buy their brands. If that is the case, then Jones (1995) might pick up an effect of advertising, which is merely due to targeting. McDonald (1971) took great pains to ensure that his analysis was free from such a spurious correlation. Second, Jones' (1995) analysis excludes households that may have received ads earlier than the 7-day period. Thus, any increase in response from those unmeasured exposures remains unaccounted.

In conclusion, Jones (1995) obtains some very important results. However, the validity and generalizability of the findings must await replication that is assuredly free of the above two problems.

8.4.2 *Generalizations*

This stream of research contains relatively few studies that have used relatively different models and designs for analyzing the effect of advertising exposure. As yet, no major generalizations have emerged. However, an informal consensus is emerging, and is as follows:

- The effect of advertising frequency on consumers choices is small relative to that of promotions.

- However, when effective, the effect of advertising on profits may be positive, while that of promotions may be negative.
- The optimum number of exposures of advertising varies widely by market, category, brand, and state of the consumer.

8.5 Stream 4: Models of advertising content

This stream of research focuses on how changes in the content of advertising affect sales or market share. Ironically, this is probably the most important aspect of advertising that marketers can vary in. However, most past research uses only measures of advertising expenditure, frequency, or GRP. In contrast, a vast literature in consumer behavior has addressed how the content of an ad must be configured to make the ad effective. However, most of these studies have been laboratory experiments conducted in highly artificial environments (Vakratsas and Ambler, 1999; Tellis, 2004). An emerging effort in market studies is to integrate these two streams of research by determining the effect of the content of ads on sales in real markets. There are only a few major studies in this stream of research.

8.5.1 *History of important studies*

Chandy *et al.* (2001) sought to determine the effectiveness of various ad appeals in real market situations. Their study was an extension of the one reported above for the referral service. The service started initially in only one city (market). Over a decade, it gradually expanded to cover over 23 markets. Thus, the markets varied in age from a few months to over 10 years. During that time, the service developed a set of 72 ads that it used with varying frequency and intensity across the various cities.

One important finding was that the effects of advertising on sales and profits varied substantially over markets, TV channels, and especially creative. Many creative executions were not effective in increasing sales while most were not profitable. A valuable part of the analysis was its specific findings about creative executions, media, and time slots that worked. The analysis pinpointed as to which creative executions the advertiser should pursue and which it should drop, which channels it should use and which it should drop, and the time slots in which media buys would be most productive.

The ads themselves used a variety of appeals. The authors measured these appeals on a rich set of behavioral variables. In particular, they assessed to what extent the ads used argument, emotion, or endorsement, how the message was framed, and how long the key message was on. With these measures, the authors were able to assess the effectiveness of various ad appeals depending on whether they were used in new versus old markets. A general finding was that advertising response was stronger in younger markets. The results of the study indicate that argument-based appeals, expert sources, and negatively framed messages are particularly effective in new markets. Emotion-based appeals and positively framed messages are more effective in old markets.

MacInnis, Rao, and Weiss (2002) report on a set of multistage experiments conducted in the 1990s. The authors developed a database of TV commercials that had been used in advertising weight tests for frequently purchased products. The database contained 47 ads, each tested in a different market experiment. Twenty-five of these ads produced statistically significant increases in sales, while 22 did not do so. The authors then recruited and trained a set of 22 paid judges to evaluate these ads on a scale of emotional to rational appeals. The results showed that emotional ads were significantly more likely to have produced increases in sales in the weight tests. On the other hand, ads that used heuristic-based or rational appeals were more likely to have not produced increases in sales in the weight tests. In a further experiment, the authors pursued whether these ads affected subjects in laboratory conditions. They found that ads that produced positive feeling and limited negative feelings were more likely to have produced increases in sales in the weight tests.

The message from these sets of experiments is that in frequently purchased mature product categories, emotional ads that create positive feelings and limit negative feelings can benefit from increased advertising.

This stream of research is as yet too small to draw generalizations.

8.6 Stream 5: Field experiments of the effects of advertising

This stream of studies focuses on the effect of aggregate advertising expenditure on sales or market between two comparable regions or time periods in a field experiment. The field experiments are also called weight studies, because many of them measure the intensity of advertising as the "weight" of advertising used in a particular region during a particular time period. The dependent variable in these tests typically is sales or market share. The goal of a weight test is to see whether the increase or decrease in the level of advertising has any effect at all on sales. If increases in advertising weight lead to increases in sales and profits that more than compensate for the additional cost of advertising, then the brand needs to stay with that increase. Similarly, if decreases in advertising weight do not lead to decreases in sales and profits that exceed the savings from the lower weight, then the brand needs to stay with the lower weight. Studies that have researched this issue have done so by testing various conditions of higher or lower advertising intensity or weights versus a control condition. Typically, the control condition has the level of advertising that the firm currently uses. In the spirit of good experimentation, all other factors are kept as similar as possible between the conditions. In addition to weight, other aspects of advertising that researchers also test are copy, media, audience, and schedule.

Studies in this stream do not give an estimate of advertising elasticity. However, they do measure the increases or decreases in sales or market share as one increases or decreases the intensity (weight) of advertising. As such, studies in this stream have immediate implications for marketing and advertising managers. These implications can be put to immediate use in determining the advertising budget for the period following the experiment.

8.6.1 *History of important studies*

Researchers have carried out over 450 market experiments to assess the effectiveness of advertising (Tellis, 2004). Six sets of experiments are especially instructive about the effects of advertising on sales. These experiments were associated with Anheuser-Busch, Grey, and D'Arcy Advertising, AdTel, Campbell Soup, and Information Resource Inc. In addition, two advertising researchers (Aaker and Carman, 1982) review the first three of these studies as well as several smaller experiments. Here, I describe key features of these studies and summarize their main findings.

Aaker and Carman (1982) summarized the results of 120 AdTel experiments in 3 cities during the 1960s and 1970s in which, AdTel controlled advertising by varying either ad-levels or ad-content to subgroups in each city. Of the 120 tests, 48 were weight tests and 36 were copy tests. Six of the 48 weight tests involved lower levels of advertising. However, none of these 6 tests showed any decline in sales. Of the 42 remaining tests (involving increased advertising), 30% showed sales changes that were different from the control groups. Most of the latter tests were for new products. In contrast, 47% of the copy tests showed significant differences in sales between test and control groups. Aaker and Carman (1982) report on a total of 11 experiments conducted by Grey Advertising and D'Arcy Advertising. Overall, this set of experiments showed that advertising increases were effective in about half the experiments, while an advertising decrease had no deleterious effect in sales in the one place it was tested. Aaker and Carman (1982) also analyzed a total of 69 other experiments. 11 of these tests involved a reduction in advertising, some for 2 years or more. Almost all (10 of 11) of these experiments indicated that such reductions in advertising had no deleterious effects on sales. Of the remaining 58 experiments, only a minority of the experiments showed that increases in advertising were sufficiently effective in increasing sales so as to justify an increase in the advertising budget for the tested brand.

Ackoff and Emshoff (1975) describe an interesting set of experiments at Anheuser-Busch, Inc, for the Budweiser brand of beer, in the mid 1960s. The experiments varied advertising levels, pulsing patterns, media, and other promotional activity. The most elaborate of these experiments involved changes in advertising weight of -100%, -50%, -25%, 0%, $+50\%$, $+100\%$, $+200\%$ relative to current expenditure. Each level was tried over 6 areas for greater confidence in the results. The experiments showed that in the short term, decreasing the level of advertising had no negative impact on sales. The authors attributed the response pattern to the over-saturation of primary segments with past advertising of the brand. They found that suspension for more than a year led to some deterioration in sales. In these situations, the sales levels and sales growth could be restored with just the previous (normal) advertising level. These results suggest the use of scheduling in which a firm staggers normal levels of advertising with periods of complete suspension of all advertising (also called flighting, see Chapter 4). Cost for advertising can be lower with the suspension, while advertising can be re-started as soon as sales seem to erode.

As regards the effectiveness of different media, they found no significant difference between radio, magazines, and newspapers. However, they found that television was slightly superior to the other media, while billboards were slightly inferior. They also found that promotional expenditure was close to the optimum. Careful implementation of their recommendations led to a decrease in advertising expenditure from US$1.89/barrel to US$0.8/barrel with a corresponding sales increase from 7.5 million to 14.5 million barrels.

Eastlack and Rao (1989) reported a series of 19 advertising experiments on the sales of six brands of the Campbell Soup Company in the mid-1970s. The experiments varied factors such as advertising weight (-50% to $+50\%$), scheduling, media, copy, and target market. The experiments show that changes in advertising weight had little or no impact on sales. However, changes in copy, media, and target markets did result in sales increases in some situations. Whenever sales increased significantly, the increase occurred early on rather than after prolonged repetition.

Abraham and Lodish (1989), Lodish *et al.* (1995a,1995b) summarized over 389 advertising tests conducted over the last 10 years of BehaviorScan Advertising Tests at Information Resources Inc. (IRI) (see Chapters 3–5). 49% of the weight tests that increased advertising yielded significantly higher sales at the 80% level of significance. The number of test results that would be significant at the 95% level is likely to be substantially lower, but the authors do not report that number. Even when the advertising was effective at this level of significance, it was found to be profitable (within the medium term of one year) in only 20% of the cases. An important finding, which echoes that from prior studies, was that massive increases in advertising weight were not more likely to yield better sales responsiveness than moderate increases. Increases in advertising were more likely to lead to increase in sales when the copy strategy is changed or the brand is in a growth stage. Advertising was much more effective for new products than for mature or established products. Most important, if advertising were not effective early on, then it would never be effective, even if it were repeated.

8.6.2 *Generalizations*

The review of experiments is important because of its scope. It covers 450 experiments by numerous investigators, using a variety of brands, contexts, and time periods. The review leads to the following generalizations:

- For many mature brands, advertising weight, or the level of TV advertising *per se* is not critical in influencing sales. More than half the time, increases in weight alone do not lead to an increase in sales. However, neither do decreases in weight lead to sales decline, at least in the short to medium term. On the other hand, changes in these latter factors (media, copy, product, segments, or scheduling) could influence the effectiveness of advertising. In general, novelty in any of these factors may lead to an increase in sales.
- Tests that involve a reduction in advertising, do not typically lead to a decrease in sales immediately. That could mean that past advertising has some carryover effect that does not decline immediately. Alternatively, it could mean that firms are over-advertising, and recent advertising was not effective at all. Prolonged cessation of advertising seems to have deleterious effects in some tests but no negative effects in others. What has not been studied is whether deleterious effects from cessation can be quickly corrected by fresh advertising. Thus, firms should be very careful about complete cessation of all advertising for prolonged periods of time. If they do so, they need to monitor the effects of such changes closely for a long period of time.
- Thus, the overall message from these studies is that advertisers may be over-advertising, at least in targeting the same segments with the same copy, media, schedule, and product. This situation would be exacerbated if advertisers resorted to further increases in advertising weight alone in these conditions.
- If advertising has any effect, that effect is visible early on. If it has no effect early on, then it is unlikely to have an effect with further repetition. On the other hand, when advertising is effective and maintained over a period of a year, its effects could last at least for two more years. In these cases, the effect in the latter two years could equal that in the first year.

8.7 Summary

The last 60 years of research have been rich, varied, and productive. We must acknowledge the contributions of five pioneers who have laid the foundation for much subsequent research: Koyck (1955), Palda (1964), McDonald (1971), Clarke (1976), Lambin (1976), and Aaker and Carman (1982).

- Koyck (1955) solved the problem of simply and conveniently estimating the carryover effects of advertising.
- McDonald (1961) showed how one could estimate the micro-effects of individual ad exposures on individual consumers.
- Palda (1964) laid the foundation for the econometric estimation of the effects of advertising.
- Clarke exposed the critical problem of data aggregation in estimating the dynamic effects of advertising.
- Lambin (1976) showed how estimating the effects of advertising in a variety of contexts enabled generalizations of its effectiveness. He then drew numerous generalizations, most of which stand even today.
- Aaker and Carman (1982) showed the importance and value of field experiments in estimating the effect of advertising.

Other researchers have built on this pioneering foundation. Some of the major problems that need to be researched are the following:

- What is the effect of new forms of advertising, such as e-mail, search, banner, and mobile ads?
- What are the roles of new media such as Internet, mobile, and social media?
- How do the ads in the various media complement or compete with each other?
- How long do the effects of advertising really last?
- If the effectiveness of advertising in traditional media is declining, what is its asymptotic value?

The field of research is vibrant and enriched by a new cadre of highly trained and motivated scholars. I remain hopeful that these and other problems will be suitably addressed in the coming years.

References

Aaker, D. A. and J. M. Carman (1982) Are you over advertising? *Journal of Advertising Research*, 22(4) (August/September), 57–70.

Abraham, M. and Leonard Lodish (1989). Advertising works: A study of advertising effectiveness and the resulting strategic and tactical implications. Chicago: Information Resources, Inc.

Ackoff, R. L. and J. R. Emshoff (1975). Advertising at Anheuser-Busch, Inc. (1963–1968), *Sloan Management Review*, 16(2), Winter 1975, 1–16.

Assmus, G., J. U. Farley, and D. R. Lehmann (1984). How advertising affects sales: Meta-analysis of econometric results, *Journal of Marketing Research*, 21(February), 65–74.

Blair, H. (2000). An empirical investigation of advertising wearin and wearout, *Journal of Advertising Research*, (November–December), 95–100.

Chandy, R., G. J. Tellis, D. MacInnis, and P. Thaivanich (2001). What to say when: Advertising appeals in evolving markets, *Journal of Marketing Research*, 38(4) (November), 399–414.

Clarke, D. G. (1976). Econometric measurement of the duration of advertising effect on sales, *Journal of Marketing Research*, 13(November), 345–357.

Deighton, J., C. Henderson, and S. Neslin (1994). The effects of advertising on brand switching and repeat purchasing, *Journal of Marketing Research*, 31(February), 28–43.

Dekimpe, M. G. and D. M. Hanssens (1995). The persistence of marketing effects on sales, *Marketing Science*, 14(1), pp. 1–21.

Eastlack, J. O., Jr. and A. G. Rao (1989). Advertising experiments at the Campbell Soup Company. *Marketing Science*, 8(Winter), 57–71.

Gibson, L. (1996). What can one exposure do? *Journal of Advertising Research*, (March/April), 9–18.

Guadagni, P. and J. D. C. Little (1983). A logit model of brand choice calibrated on scanner data, *Marketing Science*, 2, 3(Summer), 203–238.

Jedidi, K., C. F. Mela, and S. Gupta (1999). Managing advertising and promotion for long-run profitability, *Marketing Science*, 18(1), 1–22.

Jones, J. P. (1995). Single-source research begins to fulfill its promise, *Journal of Advertising Research*, (May/June), 9–15.

Lambin, J.-J. (1976). *Advertising, competition and market conduct in oligopoly over times*, Amsterdam: North Holland Publishing Company.

Leone, R. P. (1995). Generalizing what is known about temporal aggregation and advertising carryover, *Marketing Science* — 14(3), Part 2 of 2, G141–G149.

Lodish, L. M., M. M. Abraham, S. Kalmenson, J. Livesberger, B. Lubetkin, B. Richardson, and M. E. Stevens (1995a). How T.V. advertising works: A meta-analysis of 389 real world split cable T.V. advertising, *Journal of Marketing Research*, 32(May), 125–139.

Lodish, L. M., M. M. Abraham, J. Livelsberger, B. Lubetkin, B. Richardson, and M. E. Stevenson (1995b). A summary of fifty-five in-market experimental estimates of the long-term effect of TV advertising, *Marketing Science*, 14(3), Part 2 of 2, G133–G139.

MacInnis, D., A. G. Rao, and A. M. Weiss (2002). Assessing when increased media weight helps sales of real world brands, *Journal of Marketing Research*, 39(4), pp. 391–407.

Masterson, P. (1999). The wearout phenomenon, *Marketing Research*, 11(3)(Fall), 26–31.

McDonald, C. (1971). What is the short-term effect of advertising? *Marketing Science Institute Report No. 71-142*, Cambridge, MA: Marketing Science Institute.

Mela, C. F., S. Gupta, and D. R. Lehmann (1997). The long-term impact of promotion and advertising on consumer brand choice, *Journal of Marketing Research*, 34(May), 248–261.

Palda, C. (1964). *The measurement of cumulative advertising effects,* Englewood Cliffs, NJ: Prentice Hall.

Pedrick, J. H. and F. S. Zufryden (1991). Evaluating the impact of advertising media plans: A model of consumer purchase dynamics using single source data, *Marketing Science*, 10(2) (Spring), 111–130.

Sethuraman, R., G. J. Tellis, and R. Briesch (2011). How well does advertising work? generalizations from a meta-analysis of brand advertising elasticity, *Journal of Marketing Research*, XLVIII, June, 457–471.

Tellis, G. J. (1988a). Advertising exposure, loyalty and brand purchase: A two stage model of choice, *Journal of Marketing Research*, 15(2) (May), 134–144.

Tellis, G. J. (1988b). The price elasticity of selective demand, *Journal of Marketing Research*, 25(November), 331–341.

Tellis, G. J. (2004). *Effective advertising: How, when, and why advertising works*, Thousand Oaks, CA: Sage Publications.

Tellis, G. J. and P. H. Franses (2006). Optimal data interval for advertising response models, *Marketing Science*, 25(3) (May–June), 217–229.

Tellis, G. J., R. Chandy, and P. Thaivanich (2000). Decomposing the effects of direct advertising: Which brand works, when, where, and how long? (2000), *Journal of Marketing Research*, 37(February), 32–46.

The two reviews of econometric studies that are not covered here are Aaker and Carman (1982) *op. cit.*, and Leone and Schultz (1980), "A study of Marketing Generalization," *Journal of Marketing*, 44(Winter), 10–18.

Vakratsas, D. and T. Ambler (1999). How advertising works: What do we really know? *Journal of Marketing*, 63(1) (January), 26–43.

Vanhonacker, W. R. (1983). Carryover effects and temporal aggregation in a partial adjustment model framework, *Marketing Science*, 2(3) (Summer), 297–307.

Weinberg, C. B. and D. L. Weiss (1982). On the measurement of the duration of advertising effect on sales, *Journal of Marketing Research*, 19(November), 585–591.

Chapter 9

Branding and Brand Equity Models

Tulin Erdem and Joffre Swait

9.1 Introduction

Brands and their role in the marketplace have long been a central concern of the marketing discipline. A significant literature in both the marketing science and consumer behaviour branches of marketing has been built up over the past three decades addressing questions concerning how to manage brands, how to assess their extendibility, how to value brands financially, how consumers employ brands in their decision making, how experience with and advertising about a brand impact consumer behaviour, and so forth.

This chapter concerns itself with the development and evolution of marketing science models of branding, with particular emphasis on brand equity. Thus, its scope is necessarily limited to the modeling literature and its direct antecedents in economics. The chapter will review the history of the following topics on branding and brand equity in the marketing science literature:

(1) Economic signaling theory and its ramifications for branding and brand equity.
(2) Consumer-based brand equity measurement models, both static and dynamic in nature.

(3) The link between brand equity and the market performance of a brand and brand equity tracking models proposed in the literature.

We review papers chronologically within each sub-theme and attempt to sketch the historical evolution of research in each sub-area. Figure 9.1 presents an overview of the related streams of research, which we review in the remainder of the chapter.[1]

We conclude with an overview of the discipline's most important contributions to this point in time and then outline a proposed research agenda for the future.

9.2 Analytical models of strategic branding decisions and brand equity

The earliest analytical models that have a bearing for branding were proposed in the information economics literature. The importance of brand investments (Klein and Leffler, 1981) and brand reputation for high quality (Shapiro, 1983) to ensure commitment to high quality were stressed, and it was argued that if firms "cheat" on consumers by promising high quality but delivering low quality, firms would compromise the return on brand investments made and their reputation for high quality.

A related literature in information economics focused on signaling in product markets and studies marketing mix elements as quality signals. Spence (1974) defined signals as manipulable attributes or activities that convey information about the characteristics of economic agents (e.g., firms, consumers, job applicants). Not only do marketing mix elements such as packaging, advertising, and warranties provide direct product information, but also they convey indirect information about product attributes about which consumers are imperfectly informed, and may therefore serve as signals.

For example, advertising may demonstrate a firm's commitment to its brand via consumers' perceptions of advertisement costs (e.g., fly-by-night producers are much less likely to afford expensive endorsers and spend a lot of money on advertising) and serve as a quality signal (e.g., Kihlstrom and

---

[1]In Figure 9.1, the dotted lines represent the foundational influences on each stream of literature. The solid lines depict the historical influences of individual papers on later papers.

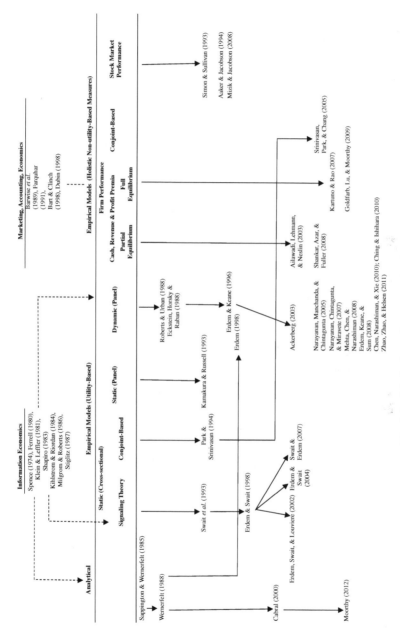

Fig. 9.1   Marketing science models of brand equity

Riordan, 1984; Milgrom and Roberts, 1986). A high price may convey demand- or supply-related quality information, and thus function as a quality signal (e.g., Gerstner, 1985; Stiglitz, 1987). More specifically, a high price may reflect either a high demand for superior quality or the high production costs associated with high quality (e.g., Spence, 1974; Tirole, 1990). Warranties may signal manufacturers' confidence in the quality of their products, since consumers often consider lower quality producers to be unable to match longer, more comprehensive warranties (Grossman, 1981; Lutz, 1989).

However, signals of quality are not always credible. Quality signals are credible only if sellers do not find it profitable to "cheat" by conveying false market signals, for example, by charging higher prices for lower quality. Sellers might refrain from cheating due to the desire for repeat sales or the presence of informed consumers (Farrell, 1980). For example, only high-quality firms may sustain a high price, because signaling high quality but offering low quality will not pay in the long run. When sellers do not find it profitable to cheat by conveying false market signals, and when low-quality and high-quality sellers find different strategies more profitable, buyers are able to differentiate between the sellers by observing their signals. In this case, these signals will be credible.

Nonetheless, sellers may find it profitable to "cheat" and may lack incentives to choose different strategies. In such markets, buyers will not be able to differentiate between the sellers by using their signals. For example, the high costs associated with producing high-quality products may outweigh the positive effect of high quality on generating repeat sales (Tirole, 1990). In this case, both low- and high-quality sellers may choose to advertise heavily. Consequently, consumers will not be able to differentiate between sellers using the advertising signal.

Some other signals may not be credible because they are subject to adverse selection or moral hazard problems (Philips, 1988). For instance, a full warranty offered by a contact lens firm may disproportionately attract consumers who know that they will likely lose them (adverse selection) or it may cause consumers to take less good care of their lenses (consumer moral hazard problem).

Finally, the signaling literature also studied whether a brand extension can signal the quality of existing and new products. Sappington and

Wernerfelt (1985) showed that brand associations are transferred in the case of brand extensions.[2] Wernerfelt (1988) showed that brand extension signals the quality of existing and new products if one assumes extension costs more than introducing a new brand. Cabral (2000) assumed cost neutrality and that old and new products are the same quality; he found (a) that a brand extension's signaling capacity is more limited than suggested in Wernerfelt (1988), but (b) that a brand extension's signaling capability does indeed increase the probability of the products being high quality. Moorthy (2012) changed five assumptions of the Wernerfelt's model and assumed that (1) the new brand costs more than the extension; (2) there may be positive, negative and zero correlation between the firm's old and new product, rather than zero; (3) instead of all consumers observing the firm introducing a new brand, some consumers do and some consumers do not; (4) firms in fact know the performance of their previous products; and (5) good products may occasionally perform poorly. Moorthy showed that a model with the first two assumptions mentioned above can yield Wernerfelt's signaling result, but that the existence of a separating equilibrium depends on various restrictions on the model, including an upper bound on brand extension's cost advantage and a ban on perfect positive correlation (the condition under which Cabral (2000) obtained his result).

This game-theoretic literature on brand reputation and brands and individual marketing mix elements as signals formed the theoretical bases of some of the empirical models of brand equity and branding, as we discuss in Secs. 9.3.1 and 9.3.2.

9.3 Empirical models

9.3.1 *Utility-theoretic empirical models of brand equity*

Owing in part to an impetus arising from the need to account for brand-based assets during a period of strong acquisition and merger activity,

---

[2]There is a large consumer behavior literature (that utilized lab studies) in marketing showing that such association transfer exists when there is a fit between the parent product and extension (e.g., Aaker and Keller, 1990). Sullivan (1990, 1992) showed such spillover effects to exist with secondary data, and Erdem (1998) found evidence for such spillover effects with individual-level transactional data.

interest in the concept of brand equity from both practitioners and academics accelerated markedly in the late 1980s and the early part of the 1990s. Farquhar (1989) introduced the notion that the brand created an "added utility" over and beyond that created by its physical and symbolic characteristics (i.e., attributes), which should be considered the brand's incremental contribution to the attractiveness of the product or service, to the consumer. This straightforward operational definition of consumer-based (as opposed to firm-based — Shocker and Weiss, 1988) brand equity proved to be a successful basis for the development of early measurement methods.

Consistent with this motivation (i.e., point-in-time financial valuation of brands) and definition (i.e., brand equity is the incremental utility to the individual consumer attributable solely to the brand, controlling for attributes), brand equity research efforts in the early 1990s began to explore means of measuring this quantity using cross-sectional data sources from surveys. Conceptually, these methods linked observed or hypothetical choice behavior (i.e., revealed and stated preferences) to the estimation of a latent (or random) utility measure, from which brand equity measures might be defined. One implication of this early approach of basing brand equity measures on consumer choice is that measurements become category-specific (e.g., the equity of Colgate in the toothpaste category), and thus raised the question of how to aggregate across categories.

Swait *et al.* (1993), in a special issue of the *International Journal of Research in Marketing (IJRM)* (1993, Volume 10) on brand equity, introduced the concept of the Equalization Price (EP) for a brand as a measure of its equity. Swait *et al.* argued that the effects of the brand permeated the entire random utility measure and were not limited to an isolated component (e.g., a brand-specific constant); this broadening of Farquhar's (1989) basic concept of brand equity as an isolated component of the utility function was also developed by Rangaswamy, Burke, and Oliva (1993) in the context of brand extensions. The EP expresses brand equity as the price equivalent that a brand would charge in a market where all brands have the same market share. The measure is, therefore, contextualized in a given competitive scenario, implying in turn that as the market evolves (brands enter, leave, change positioning, etc.) EP will also change. In this reference (equal share) market, strong brands are able to charge premia with respect to their current actual price, and weak brands are penalized by having lower EPs than their current actual price. EP is defined at the individual consumer level, and can be aggregated across consumers because it is scale-independent (we refer to the scale of the stochastic utility, see Swait and Louviere, 1993). The measurement of EP was conducted using discrete choice experiments and ancillary measures of symbolic attributes, as illustrated in Swait *et al.* (1993); however, the EP metric can also be obtained from revealed preference data, whether cross-sectional or panel in nature.

Kamakura and Russell (1993), in the same special issue of *IJRM* (1993, Volume 10), used scanner panel data to quantify a consumer-based brand equity measure. Though their data has a panel structure, the modeling approach employed did not recognize the dynamic nature of the represented choices, though it did recognize stochastic taste heterogeneity across households. The latent class choice model they specified was used to define a measure termed Brand Value (BV), as a weighted (using class membership weights) combination of class-level brand-specific constants α_{sj}, s a segment and j a brand. These constants were further decomposed additively into a tangible (i.e., attribute-based) and an intangible component, respectively BTV (Brand Tangible Value) and BIV (Brand Intangible Value). Similar to the EP measure, BV (and therefore its components) is contextualized within a specific market and set of conditions (e.g., advertising exposure and pricing history), which the authors referred to as "situational factors." BV, as implemented in Kamakura and Russell (1993), is not scale-independent (again, see Swait and Louviere, 1993), which makes aggregation across individuals somewhat troublesome.

By conceptualizing brand equity as the difference between the total utility of a branded product as perceived by a consumer and the total utility as measured by objectively measured attribute levels, Park and Srinivasan (1994) differentiated their work from previous brand equity measures. The measure was justified from the observation that various brands in a market differentially invest in brand-building activities (e.g., favorable associations, advertising investment levels, endorsements) that lead to utility that cannot be attributed directly to the product or service characteristics. The measurement framework formulated and tested by the authors involved obtaining the (1) objective product characterizations from laboratory measurements, experts, and/or blind consumer tests on which to base the total objective utility calculation, and (2) a consumer survey with three main components: (a) the total perceived utility, (b) attribute importance weights to combine with (1) to obtain objective utilities and (c) attribute perception ratings to be used for diagnostic purposes. The brand equity measure proposed using this method is a monetary equivalent elicited directly during the above-mentioned consumer survey (as opposed to the EP metric of Swait *et al.* (1993), which is the monetary equivalent of a utility function, i.e., EP is an implicit willingness-to-pay measure). Another contribution of the Park and Srinivasan (1994) work was the strong focus on managerial interpretability and usefulness of the brand equity measures for decision making.

This early work in brand equity measurement was, directly or indirectly, strongly influenced by what we term the cognitive-psychological view of brand equity (e.g., Aaker, 1991; Keller, 1993), though Swait *et al.* (1993) partially motivate their approach from the perspective of the signaling theory in economics. This latter view on brands as signals was formalized by Erdem and Swait (1998) through the testing of a structural equation model (SEM) focusing on brand credibility as the principal construct from which arise the benefits provided by the brand to the consumer during the choice process (see Sec. 9.2). Though not a random utility choice-based measurement approach, Erdem and Swait's SEM does nonetheless treat the impact of brand credibility as an additive component in a utility construct. The SEM models they estimated for the jeans and juice categories showed a significant impact of brand credibility on product utility via different pathways: through increased quality perception, reduced perceived risk, and reduced information/decision-making costs. Data were collected via a standard survey instrument involving ratings of brands along a number of relevant measurement items.

Erdem and Swait's (1998) signaling theory generates a set of testable propositions that can be embedded within a precise utility-theoretic framework. This precision of formulation resulted in a series of downstream tests of these propositions. First, Erdem, Swait, and Louviere (2002) motivated the proposition that price premia are one of the principal consequences of high brand equity, once brand credibility shifts to brand intercepts is accounted for. To elaborate, this proposition implies not only that the utility of a product rises or falls with increases or decreases in brand credibility, but also that its sensitivity to price decreases with brand credibility. This decreased price sensitivity is therefore the source of the price premium that a high equity (credibility) brand can charge in the market. Erdem, Swait, and Louviere (2002) defined a brand equity measure called the Value of Credibility (VOC), which is related to the EP of Swait *et al.* (1993). VOC expresses brand equity as a multiple of its market price, the multiple being a nonlinear function of brand credibility, current price, and price sensitivities. This measure is therefore individual to both consumer and brand, and contextualized in a given market structure; it is random-utility-scale independent, making it possible to aggregate over individuals, market regions and so forth.

A call for further research on brand equity was forthcoming from the 1998 Invitational HEC Choice Symposium in the form of a workshop report by Erdem *et al.* (1999). This workshop's perspective on brand impacts was on a much broader scale than prior literature: within a utility-theoretic perspective, brands were postulated to dynamically impact (a) transformations of raw attribute values to perceived values, (b) formation of tastes (or preferences) over time, (c) distribution of stochastic utilities, (d) selection of decision rules, and (e) formation of choice sets.

The broad scope of this call for further work in brand equity concep-tualization and measurement resulted in two papers testing some of these propositions using cross-sectional data. Erdem and Swait (2004) reported on the impact of brand credibility (the core construct from signaling theory) on brand consideration (i.e., consideration/choice set formation) and brand choice. While confirming previous results from Erdem and Swait (1998) that brand credibility impacts brand choice, they also demonstrated that brand consideration is strongly explained by brand credibility. This was an important result because it demonstrated the need for brand equity measurement to account for the impact of brand in the non-evaluative stages of the choice process, where the brand's role is non-compensatory. In their original theoretical development, Erdem and Swait (1998) had postulated that brand credibility was defined by two sub-constructs: trustworthiness, and expertise. Across the relatively wide range of product categories they tested, Erdem and Swait (2004) found that trustworthiness had a greater impact than expertise, particularly with respect to brand consideration.

From a cross-sectional perspective, however, it was Swait and Erdem (2007) who tested the most encompassing model of the impact of brand credibility on the choice process, with a representation containing several of the non-dynamic components mentioned in Erdem *et al.* (1999). Specifically, they tested for the impact of brand (a) on systematic utility, in the spirit of the earlier work in brand equity (e.g., Kamakura and Russell, 1993; Swait *et al.*, 1993; Park and Srinivasan; 1994); (b) on stochastic utility, by parameterization of its variance as a function of brand credibility (e.g., Swait and Louviere, 1993); and (c) on choice set formation, by modeling inclusion of a brand into the choice set as a function of credibility. The use of a two-stage model of the decision process, i.e., choice set formation followed by choice conditional on choice set, permitted Swait and Erdem (2007) to determine that brand credibility can have separate and identifiable effects on brand inclusion in the choice set, implying therefore that a high credibility brand receives a double benefit, first because the high credibility makes it more likely to be included in the choice set, and second because during the conditional evaluative/comparison process, high credibility favourably impacts both the average and variance of utility.

To close this section, we mention the work of Kim, Morris, and Swait (2008), who demonstrated the antecedent role of brand credibility in the formation and maintenance of brand loyalty. These authors used a SEM on cross-sectional survey data and found support for the hypothesis that brand credibility underlies both affective and cognitive convictions about a brand. High brand convictions create temporally stable attitudes, thus ultimately leading to brand loyalty. In Sec. 9.3.2, we turn our attention to dynamic measurement models of brand equity, so it is worthwhile to keep in mind this link between brand signal credibility, attitude stability and brand loyalty.

9.3.2 *Dynamic structural models to measure components of brand equity*

The preceding discussion showed that one very important way brands manifest their effects on consumer choice is through their impact on the evolution of constructs such as consumer perceptions of attributes, risk, and preferences, which underlie the formation of brand equity over time.

Dynamic structural choice models have explicitly modeled the processes through which these effects materialize.

Dynamic structural choice models estimated on individual-level disaggregate data with implications for brand equity formation, management and measurement date back to the late 1980s. These models are based on the random utility maximization framework, just as were the cross-sectional and static panel models of brand equity covered in the previous sections of this chapter. The main difference between these models is that they explicitly capture the dynamic processes that underlie brand equity formation. Roberts and Urban (1988), and Eckstein, Horsky and Raban (1988) were the two earliest groups of researchers who modeled explicitly how under quality uncertainty, learning about quality may reduce the variance of quality perceptions (which can be conceptualized as perceived risk), affect consumer mean quality perceptions, and hence, increase consumer-expected utility when consumers are risk-averse. In the Roberts and Urban model, consumers were assumed to be myopic and learn through word-of-mouth and test trials in the car market. Eckstein, Horsky, and Raban (1988) modeled brand choice in the context of frequently purchased product categories, where strategic sampling can be important. Thus, consumers were allowed to be forward-looking, maximizing expected utility over the planning horizon (rather than the immediate utility) by taking into consideration the impact of the information contained in the trial on future utilities.

The Eckstein, Horsky, and Raban (1988) model allowed learning to occur only through endogenous signals such as use experience. Erdem and Keane (1996) generalized the basic forward-looking learning model where consumers update their quality perceptions upon arrival of new information in a Bayesian manner by proposing a model in which consumers learn both through endogenous (e.g., use experience) and exogenous (e.g., advertising) signals. This latter model demonstrated how learning about quality through strategic sampling and use experience, as well as via marketing mix elements (advertising), may increase consumer utility in the long run by decreasing consumer uncertainty through reduction of the variance of consumer quality perceptions.

These forward-looking models explicitly capture the evolution of consumer perception (e.g., perceived quality) and perceived risk (the variance of quality perceptions). Brand equity can be measured by the mean and variance of quality perceptions, after controlling for price (and other variables like display, when appropriate). These models also explain how brand loyalty (defined as the repeated buying of a small subset of brands) is formed over time: brand loyalty occurs both due to a match between product offerings and consumer tastes (unobserved heterogeneity), as well as due to lower perceived risk associated with the familiar brand (state-dependence). Erdem and Keane (1996) found that learning models (both myopic and forward-looking) fit the data better than the reduced form approximations with a lagged purchase variable. They also found that consumer uncertainty exists and that consumers are risk-averse in the laundry detergent category. Their results implied that brand equity is formed by a combination of high mean and low variance of quality perceptions (perceived risk) achieved through use experience and information provided by advertising, which consequently leads to brand loyalty.[3]

Over the last 15 years, there have been a large number of models proposed both in economics and marketing, which enriched the Erdem and Keane (1996) set-up.[4] A number of models have represented the different roles advertising plays in brand choice and brand equity formation. Erdem and Keane modeled the direct information effect of advertising by allowing the advertising exposure to provide unbiased but noisy information about product quality. Ackerberg (2003) proposed another forward-looking dynamic structural model to account for the indirect informational role of advertising by allowing advertising intensity to signal product quality.[5] He also allowed for persuasive effects of advertising by allowing advertising frequency to shift consumer utility directly. Ackerberg found empirical evidence in the yogurt category for the indirect informational role of

---

[3]Osborne (2011) allowed for both forward-looking learning and switching costs (another force behind brand loyalty) and found that reduced risk associated with learning, as well as switching costs, lead to repeated buying of a small subset of brands in the detergent market.
[4]In some cases, researchers had to assume myopic consumers to be able to enrich other aspects of the learning model to overcome empirical identification or estimation feasibility issues.
[5]In Ackerberg's model, advertising frequency itself signals product quality, as in the theoretical literature where advertising is modeled as "burning money" (Kihlstrom and Riordan, 1984) which only high-quality brands can do if a separating equilibrium exists.

advertising but not for the persuasive role. Mehta, Chen, and Narashiman (2008) assumed myopic consumers and modeled the informative, persuasive and "transformative" effects of advertising, where advertising alters the consumption experience itself. They found that the informative effect dominates in the early life cycle of a brand, while the transformative effect becomes more important over time. Thus, this literature studied the long-term effects of advertising in brand building.

Another long-standing issue in the branding literature has been the potential adverse effects of price promotions on brand equity. Jedidi, Mela, and Gupta (1999) have shown that indeed promotions lead to increased price sensitivities and may erode brand equity. To explicitly model this possibility, Erdem, Keane, and Sun (2008) estimated a forward-looking model in which consumers learn about quality through use experience, advertising (both directly through information content, as well as indirectly through advertising intensity) and price. For brand equity to erode due to price promotions, consumers would need to also use price as a signal of quality. Indeed, results of Erdem, Keane, and Sun (2008) showed supporting evidence in the ketchup category for brand equity erosion due to price promotions; these increase sales in the short run but adversely affect quality perceptions in the long run since consumers infer quality from price. They also found that the impact of information on quality learning is greatest for use experience, followed by price, then by advertising content and last by ad frequency/intensity. The results of Erdem, Keane, and Sun are similar to those of Sriram and Kalwani (2007) who studied the optimal levels of advertising and promotion budgets in dynamic markets with brand equity as a mediating variable. Their state-space model based on the Kalman filter captured the dynamics of brand equity as influenced by its drivers, such as the brand's advertising and sales promotion expenditure. By integrating the Kalman filter with the random coefficients logit demand model and estimating the parameters of the demand model using store level data in the orange juice category, they determined the Markov perfect equilibrium advertising and promotion strategies. They found that sales promotion have a significant positive effect on consumers' utility and induce consumers to switch to the promoted brand. However, there is also a negative effect of promotions on brand equity that carries over from period to period.

Although a large number of learning models with implications for brand equity formation, management, and measurement have been proposed and implemented in the context of frequently purchased product categories, prescription drugs (e.g., Crawford and Shum, 2005; Narayanan, Manchanda, and Chintagunta, 2005; Ching, 2010) and tariff choice (Miravete, 2003; Narayanan, Chintgaunta, and Miravete, 2007), few learning models have been proposed for durables. An exception is Erdem *et al.* (2005), who modeled Apple/Mac versus Windows platform choices. For durable goods, there is both quality and price uncertainty since the prices of a given system drop over time due to technological progress. Thus, consumers have an incentive to wait to learn about the quality/price trajectory, but waiting involves a foregone utility of consumption. Erdem *et al.* (2005) modeled how consumers search for information sources, learn about quality and form both price and quality expectations in this setting. The results indicated that learning was the more important reason for purchase delay, stressing once again the importance of reduced uncertainty about quality being a main driver or purchase and brand equity.

Within the literature of dynamic structural models, researchers also developed a number of models to study specific issues related to brand equity. Erdem (1998) estimated a learning model of umbrella branding where consumers' priors about quality are correlated for umbrella brands and use experience with the brand in one category providing (noisy) information about the quality of the same brand in another category. She explicitly showed that in the complementary toothpaste and toothbrush categories, information spillover effects exist and brand equity dilutions occur when an extension is not well-received. Chan, Narashiman, and Xie (2010) showed how experience signals for different attributes, e.g., side effects and effectiveness of a branded prescription drug, can be correlated. They identified their model by combining stated and revealed preference data and found, for instance, that detailing visits are much more effective in reducing uncertainty about effectiveness than about side effects. Zhao, Zhao, and Helsen (2011) studied the Kraft Australia peanut butter product harm crisis case and its implications for brand equity by considering whether consumers who receive a very negative experience signal may change their perception of signal variance. They found evidence for the fact that consumers also update their perceptions of noisiness of information sources over time. Thus, the results based on these kinds of models have showed that standardization of quality and consistent provision of information through the marketing mix (advertising, price, and the like) is the key to successful brand equity management. This is in agreement with predictions of the Erdem and Swait (1998) signaling framework.

The models discussed thus far in this section all depicted partial equilibria, that is, they treated the supply side (i.e., firms' decisions) as exogenous. Ching and Ishihara (2010) allowed both consumers and firms to be uncertain about product quality in the prescription drugs market and estimated the demand model jointly with a pseudo-policy function for potential endogeneity of detailing, one source of information in such markets.

9.3.3 *Holistic measures of brand equity: Models linking customer-based brand equity and market performance of a brand*

9.3.3.1 *Modeling cash flow, revenue and profit premia due to brand equity*

Measuring the firm's intangible assets has been a research topic in accounting (e.g., Barth and Clinch, 1998), economics (e.g., Dubin, 1998) and marketing (e.g., Barwise *et al.*, 1989; Farquhar, Han, and Ijiri, 1991). Barwise *et al.* (1989) suggested past expenditure on brand development or royalty rates for comparable brands as measures of brand equity. Dubin (1998) proposed as an economic measure of a brand's value the difference between the profit of a brand and that of a generic (unbranded) product, consistent with Farquhar's (1989) idea of defining brand equity as the value that a brand endows a product. Similarly, Interbrand's (2011) valuation of brands hinges upon the estimation of brand-related share in future brand cash flows predicted by the analysts *vis-a-vis* the equivalent cash flow generated by a generic product.

Similar to the concept of cash flow premia, Ailawadi, Lehmann, and Neslin (2003) proposed revenue premium as an outcome measure of brand equity by defining the revenue premium as the difference in revenue between a branded good and a corresponding private label. Equilibrium revenue of a brand was assumed to be a function of sales, marketing mix, price, equity, pre-existing firm strength, and category characteristics. They applied their revenue premia model on two aggregate level datasets, the first covering 17 categories and 111 brands, and the second, 23 categories and 102 brands.

In the same spirit, and building on Park and Srinivasan (1994), Srinivasan, Park, and Chang (2005) defined brand equity as the incremental monetary contribution per year obtained by the brand in comparison to the underlying product (or service) with no brand-building efforts. The incremental contribution is driven by the individual customer's incremental choice probability for the brand in comparison to his choice probability for the underlying product with no brand-building efforts. The approach takes into account three sources of brand equity (brand awareness, attribute perception biases, and non-attribute preference) and reveals how much each contributes to brand equity. Thus, Srinivasan, Park, and Chang (2005) can be viewed as an important shift of focus from the cross-sectional, diagnostic interest in brand equity described in Sec. 9.3.1 to a dynamic, survey-based brand equity management system.

Kartuno and Rao (2007) and Goldfarb, Lu, and Moorthy (2009) estimated full equilibrium models to link customer-based brand equity derived from a utility maximization discrete choice framework to firm's decisions and profits. In Kartuno and Rao, the demand model captured the brand's physical characteristics (conceptualized as not being part of brand equity), its perceived quality, satisfaction with the brand and marketing mix variables. They also modeled firm competition in pricing and advertising and calculated profit and revenue premia due to brand equity. In Goldfarb, Lu, and Moorthy, the BV was defined as the difference between its equilibrium profit and its counterfactual unbranded equivalent on search attributes. Customer-based brand equity was then measured as the brand constants, after controlling for search attributes. An oligopoly model with a common retailer was used to describe the firms, but advertising decisions were assumed to be exogenous.

Shankar, Azar, and Fuller (2008) proposed a model to measure and track brand equity for multicategory brands based on customer survey and financial measures. BVs were computed from discounted cash flow analysis, and relative brand importance was computed from discrete brand choice models. They applied the model to estimate the brand equity of

Allstate, a leading insurance company, and of its main competitor, both of which compete in multiple categories.

9.3.3.2 *Modeling the link between customer-based brand equity and financial metrics*

Simon and Sullivan (1993) adopted a regression-based decomposition of a firm's market capitalization due to intangibles such as brand assets, while others tried to link individual components of customer-based brand equity to financial metrics (Aaker and Jacobson, 1994; Mizik and Jacobson; 2008). Aaker and Jacobson (1994) investigated whether movement in a firm's stock price, as a measure of firm value, is correlated with information contained in perceived quality, a component of customer-based brand equity (Erdem and Swait, 1998). In a model that also allowed for the effect of macroeconomic factors and a firm's return on investment, they found a positive relationship between stock returns and changes in quality perceptions. Mizik and Jacobson (2008) studied which brand asset metrics provide incremental information to accounting performance measures in explaining stock returns. The components of brand equity they used were the five "pillars of brand equity" that form the basis for the Young & Rubicam Brand Asset Valuator (BAV) model:[6] differentiation, relevance, esteem, knowledge, and energy. Their analysis showed that perceived brand relevance and energy provide incremental information to accounting measures in explaining stock returns while esteem and knowledge do not. Stahl *et al.* (2012) use the BAV measure to investigate the precursor role of brand equity, as characterized by four of the five components mentioned above (energy is not included in this analysis), to Customer Lifetime Value (CLV) which is the net present value of long-term profit contribution by a customer. They employ 10 years of BAV data for 39 brands, along with independent data sources for marketing activity, and find that BAV has a measurable impact on customer acquisition, retention, and profitability.

---

[6]Please see http://young-rubicam.de/tools-wissen/tools/brandasset-valuator/?lang=en for a detailed description of Brand Asset Valuator (BAV) model.

9.4 Discussion and conclusion

This chapter provided a brief historical overview of marketing science models of branding and brand equity since the 1980s. Both the analytical and empirical marketing science models have stressed the informational role that brands play when there is consumer uncertainty and imperfect and asymmetric information in the marketplace. Brands, of course, play non-informational roles: they can be foci for social identity formation or useful for signaling consumers' identity or self-image (e.g., Kleine, Kleine, and Kernan, 1993), they can be tools for self-expression (e.g., Chernev, Hamilton, and Gal, 2011; Escalas and Bettman, 2003) and can act as symbols (Aaker, 1991). Behavioral research has actively studied how these other brand roles play out in such contexts. Future research can incorporate these non-informational roles of brands in marketing science models of branding, both as extensions and as controls.

As our review demonstrates, only a handful of papers model both the demand side (consumer behavior with regard to firms' branding decisions) and the supply side (firm's positioning and marketing mix decisions). Empirical identification and computational challenges make estimating such models difficult. However, (1) the increased trend of combining different data sources (e.g., transactional data with consumer expectations data), which will alleviate empirical identification challenges, and (2) the availability and further development of new approximation techniques, which decrease the computational burden, will make such models more feasible to estimate. Combining the demand and supply sides will also help researchers to better link consumer-based measures of brand equity to firm performance metrics.

Indeed, there is also a pressing need to construct explicit links between these levels of aggregation of brand equity measures and more commonly understood financial and accounting measures (e.g., elements of balance sheets). In particular, marketing science models of brand equity can be further developed to be used as direct inputs to generate valuation figures-of-merit for brands. As Mizik and Nissim (2011) discuss, the accounting treatment of marketing activities and assets are not well understood by marketers and it is important for marketing academics and practitioners to recognize the importance of financial reporting as it pertains to marketing activities and assets. Companies like Interbrand and Brand Finance already have proprietary models in place and there are a number of methods based on the concepts of cash flow, royalties, and other accounting valuation practices, but the shortcomings of these models and practices are well-known (Kapferer, 2012). Indeed, the numbers generated differ vastly across different methods (e.g., Interbrand's vs. Brand Finance's approach).[7] Such approaches may be improved with input from marketing science models of brand equity to provide more reliable and consistent valuation numbers.

Finally, explicit models of brand and brand equity tracking need to be further developed to guide long-term brand asset management. Models that incorporate customer relationship management, marketing mix responsiveness, management SKUs of the same brand and multiple products that share the same brand can shed light on how to manage brands over time to improve market share, firm profitability, financial metrics, and BV.

References

Aaker, D. A. (1991). *Managing brand equity*, New York: The Free Press.

Aaker, D. A. and R. Jacobson (1994). The financial information content of brand equity, *Journal of Marketing Research*, 31(May), 191–201.

Aaker, D. A. and K. L. Keller (1990). Consumer evaluations of brand extensions, *Journal of Marketing*, 54(1), 27–41.

Ackerberg, D. (2003). Advertising, learning, and consumer choice in experience good markets: A structural empirical examination, *International Economic Review*, 44, 1007–1040.

Ailawadi, K. L., D. R. Lehmann, and S. A. Neslin (2003). Revenue premium as an outcome measure of brand equity, *Journal of Marketing*, 67(October), 1–17.

Barth, M. A. and G. Clinch (1998). Revalued financial, tangible, and intangible assets: Associations with share prices and nonmarket-based value estimates, *Journal of Accounting Research*, 30(3 Suppl.), 199–233.

Barwise, P., C. Higson, A. Likierman, and P. Marsh (1989). *Accounting for brands*, London: London School of Business.

Cabral, L. M. B. (2000). Stretching firm and brand reputation, *The RAND Journal of Economics*, 31(4), 658–673.

---

[7] Such differences and implications for marketers have been discussed at great length at the conference, "Brands and branding in accounting, law and marketing: Integrating strategies to maximize firm value" in Chapel Hill, North Carolina, April 12–13, 2012.

Chan, N. and Y. Xie (2010). An empirical model of physician learning on treatment effectiveness and side-effects, Working Paper, Washington University, St. Louis.

Ching, A. T. (2010). Consumer learning and heterogeneity: Dynamics of demand for prescription drugs after patent expiration, *International Journal of Industrial Organization*, 28(6), 619–638.

Ching, A. and M. Ishihara (2010). The effects of detailing on prescribing decisions under quality uncertainty, *Quantitative marketing and economics*, 8(2), 123–165.

Crawford, G. S. and M. Shum (2005). Uncertainty and learning in pharmaceutical demand, *Econometrica*, 73(4) (July), 1137–1173.

Dubin, J. A. (1998). The demand for branded and unbranded products: An econometric method for valuing intangible assets. *Studies in consumer demand: Econometric methods applied to market data*, Norwell, MA: Kluwer Academic Publishers, pp. 77–127.

Chernev, A., R. Hamilton, and D. Gal (2011). Competing for consumer identity: Limits to self-expression and the perils of lifestyle branding, *Journal of Marketing*, 75(May), 66–82.

Eckstein, Z., D. Horsky, and Y. Raban (1988). An empirical dynamic model of brand choice, Working Paper 88, University of Rochester.

Erdem, T. (1998). An empirical analysis of umbrella branding, *Journal of Marketing Research*, 35(3), 339–351.

Erdem, T. and M. P. Keane (1996). Decision-making under uncertainty: Capturing dynamic brand choice processes in turbulent consumer goods markets, *Marketing Science*, 15, 1–20.

Erdem, T. and J. Swait (1998). Brand equity as a signaling phenomenon, *Journal of Consumer Psychology*, 7(2), 131–157.

Erdem, T. and J. Swait (2004). Brand credibility, brand consideration and choice, *Journal of Consumer Research*, 31(June), 191–198.

Erdem, T., J. Swait, S. Broniarczyk, D. Chakravarti, J.-N. Kapferer, M. Keane, J. Roberts, J. B. Steenkamp, and F. Zettelmeyer (1999). Brand equity, consumer learning and choice, Special Issue on the 1998 HEC Choice Symposium, *Marketing Letters*, 10(3), 301–318.

Erdem, T., J. Swait, and J. Louviere (2002). The impact of brand credibility on consumer price sensitivity, *International Journal of Research in Marketing*, 19(1), 1–19.

Erdem, T., M. P. Keane, T. S. Öncü, and J. Strebel (2005). Learning about computers: An analysis of information search and technology choice, *Quantitative Marketing and Economics*, 3(3), 207–246.

Erdem, T., M. Keane, and B. Sun (2008). A dynamic model of brand choice when price and advertising signal product quality, *Marketing Science*, 27(6), 1111–1125.

Escalas, J. E. and J. R. Bettman (2003). You are what they eat: The influence of reference groups on consumers' connections to brands, *Journal of Consumer Psychology*, 13(3), 339–348.

Farquhar, P. H. (1989). Managing brand equity, *Marketing Research*, 1, 24–33.

Farquhar, P. H., J. Y. Han, and Y. Ijiri (1991). Recognizing and measuring brand assets, *Marketing Science Report*, 91–119 (July), Cambridge: Marketing Science Institute.

Farrell, J. (1980). *Prices as signals of quality*, PhD thesis, University of Oxford.

Gerstner, E. (1985). Do higher prices signal higher quality, *Journal of Marketing Research*, 22(May), 209–215.

Goldfarb, A., Q. Lu, and S. Moorthy (2009). Measuring brand value in an equilibrium framework, *Marketing Science*, 28(1), 69–86.

Grossman, S. (1981). The informational role of warranties and private disclosure about product quality, *Journal of Law and Economics*, 24, 461–483.

Interbrand (2011). Best global brands. Available at: www.interbrand.com.

Jedidi, K., C. F. Mela, and S. Gupta (1999). Managing advertising and promotion for long-run profitability, *Marketing Science*, 18(1) (Winter), 1–22.

Kamakura, W. and G. Russell (1993). Measuring brand value with scanner data, *International Journal of Research in Marketing*, 10, 9–22.

Kapferer, J. N. (2012). *The new strategic brand management*, 5th edn., London: Kogan Page.

Kartuno, B. and V. R. Rao (2005). Linking consumer-based brand equity to market performance: An integrated approach to brand equity management, Working Paper.

Keller, K. L. (1993). Conceptualizing, measuring, and managing consumer-based brand equity. *Journal of Marketing*, 57, 1–22.

Kihlstrom, R. E. and M. H. Riordan (1984). Advertising as a signal, *Journal of Political Economy*, 92, 427–450.

Kim, J., J. Morris, and J. Swait (2008). Antecedents of true brand loyalty, *Journal of Advertising*, 37(2), 99–117.

Klein, B. and K. B. Leffler (1981). The role of market forces in assuring contractual performance, *Journal of Political Economy*, 89(4), 615–639.

Kleine, R. E., S. S. Kleine, and J. B. Kernan (1993). Mundane consumption and the self: A social identity perspective, *Journal of Consumer Psychology*, 2(3), 209–235.

Lutz, N. A. (1989). Warranties as signals under consumer moral hazard, *RAND Journal of Economics*, 20(Summer), 239–255.

Mehta, N., X. Chen, and O. Narasimhan (2008). Informing, transforming, and persuading: Disentangling the multiple effects of advertising on brand choice decisions, *Marketing Science*, 27(3), 334–355.

Milgrom, P. and J. Roberts (1986). Prices and advertising signals of product quality, *Journal of Political Economy*, 94, 796–821.

Miravete, E. J. (2003). Choosing the wrong calling plan? Ignorance and learning, *American Economic Review*, 93, 297–310.

Mizik, N. and R. Jacobson (2008). The financial value impact of perceptual brand attributes, *Journal of Marketing Research*, 45(1), 11–32.

Mizik N. and D. Nissim (2011). Accounting for marketing activities: Implications for marketing research and practice, *MSI Working Paper Series, Report No. 11-103*.

Moorthy, S. (2012). Can brand extension signal brand quality, *Marketing Science*, 31, 756–770.

Narayanan, S., P. K. Chintagunta, and E. J. Miravete (2006). The role of self selection, usage uncertainty and learning in the demand for local telephone service, *Quantitative Marketing and Economics*, 5, 1–34.

Narayanan, S., P. Manchanda, and P. K. Chintagunta (2005). Temporal differences in the role of marketing communication in new product categories, *Journal of Marketing Research*, 42(3), 278–290.

Osborne, M. (2011). Consumer learning, switching costs, and heterogeneity: A structural examination, *Quantitative Marketing and Economics*, 9(1), 25–46.

Park, C. and V. Srinivasan (1994). A survey-based method for measuring and understanding brand equity and its extendibility, *Journal of Marketing Research*, 31(2), 271–288.

Philips, L. (1988). *The economics of imperfect information*, New York: Cambridge University Press.

Rangaswamy, A., R. Burke, and T. Oliva (1993). Brand equity and the extendibility of brand names, *International Journal of Research in Marketing*, 10, 61–75.

Roberts, J. H. and G. L. Urban (1988). Modeling multiattribute utility, risk, and belief dynamics for new consumer durable brand choice, *Management Science*, 34(2) 167–185.

Sappington, D. E. M. and B. Wernerfelt (1985). To brand or not to brand? A theoretical and empirical question, *The Journal of Business*, 58(3), 279–293.

Shankar, V., P. Azar, and M. Fuller (2008). BRAN*EQT: A multicategory brand equity model and its application at all state, *Marketing Science*, 27(4), 567–584.

Shapiro, C. (1983). Premiums for high quality products as rents to reputation, *Quarterly Journal of Economics*, 98, 659–680.

Shocker, A. and B. Weiss (1988). A perspective on brand equity principles and issues, in defining, measuring and managing brand equity: A conference summary, L. Leuthesser, ed., *Marketing Science Institute Report*, 88–104, 2–3.

Simon, C. J. and M. W. Sullivan (1993). The measurement and determination of brand equity: A financial approach, *Marketing Science*, 12(1) 28–52.

Spence, M. (1974). *Market signaling: Informational transfer in hiring and related screening processes*, Cambridge, MA: Harvard University Press.

Sriram, S. and M. V. Kalwani (2007). Optimal advertising and promotion budgets in dynamic markets with brand equity as a mediating variable, *Management Science*, 53(1), 46–60.

Srinivasan, V., C. S. Park, and D. R. Chang (2005). An approach to the measurement, analysis, and prediction of brand equity and its sources, *Management Science*, 51(9), 1433–1448.

Stahl, F., M. Heitmann, D. Lehmann, and S. Neslin (2012). The impact of brand equity on customer acquisition, retention, and profit margin, *Journal of Marketing*, 76(July), 44–63.

Stiglitz, J. (1987). The causes and consequences of the dependence of quality on price, *Journal of Economic Literature*, 25, 1–48.

Sullivan, M. (1990). Measuring image spillovers in umbrella-branded products, *The Journal of Business*, 63(3), 309–329.

Sullivan, M. (1992). Brand extensions: When to use them, *Management Science*, 38(June), 793–806.

Swait, J. and T. Erdem (2007). Brand effects on choice and choice set formation under uncertainty, *Marketing Science*, 26(5), 679–697.

Swait, J. and J. Louviere (1993). The role of the scale parameter in the estimation and comparison of multinomial logit models, *Journal of Marketing Research*, 30, 305–314.

Swait, J., T. Erdem, J. Louviere, and C. Dubelaar (1993). The equalization price: A consumer-perceived measure of brand equity, Special Issue on Brand Equity of *International Journal of Research in Marketing*, 10(1), 23–45.

Tirole, J. (1990). *The theory of industrial organization*, Cambridge, MA: MIT Press.

Wernerfelt, B. (1988). Umbrella branding as a signal of new product quality: An example of signaling by posting a bond, *The RAND Journal of Economics*, 19(3), 458–466.

Zhao, Y., Y. Zhao, and K. Helsen (2011). Consumer learning in a turbulent market environment: Modeling consumer choice dynamics after a product-harm crisis, 58(April), 255–267.

Chapter 10

Distribution Channels

Richard Staelin and Eunkyu Lee

10.1 Introduction

Channel management issues have been a central topic for marketing academics for many decades. Most of the initial research in this area was descriptive and/or managerial in nature and the emphasis was empirical and/or organizational. Of special concern in the 1970s and early 1980s were the issues of power and conflict. These issues were investigated within a variety of social science paradigms such as political economy (Stern and Reve, 1980), inter-organizational theory (Evan, 1965), Aldersonian functionalism (Alderson, 1957), and transaction cost theory (Williamson, 1975). There also existed a small number of researchers who adopted economic theories to look at different channel systems. Most of this work was found in the economics literature (e.g., Spengler, 1950; Pashigian, 1961; Machlup and Taber, 1960; Wu, 1964; White, 1971) with a focus on consumer welfare issues. The rest appeared in the management literature and was concerned with the organizational form best suited for a given environment (e.g., Baligh and Richartz, 1967; Baligh and Burton, 1976).

One notable exception was Bucklin's (1965, 1973) economic analyses of channel control, coordination, and structure published in the marketing literature. These publications signaled the potential of developing and establishing a major stream of quantitative research on distribution channels. However, it was only in the late 1970s that a new movement began in the field of marketing to study channel coordination mechanisms and channel structure design by employing a new quantitative approach. This new paradigm differed from the above literature in that it tended to use game theory and equilibrium analyses. The purpose of this chapter is to detail how this literature evolved and to discuss a number of the major insights derived from this field of inquiry.[1]

10.2   The (rocky) start

The first paper that appeared in the marketing literature using the new game-theoretic paradigm was Doraiswamy, McGuire, and Staelin (1979). It was an outgrowth of work done by Tim McGuire and Rick Staelin in the early 1970s concerning a lawsuit between an automobile manufacturer and one of its dealers. That work led to an academic paper on the optimal channel structure as a function of the level of competition within the industry. It was submitted to three economics journals between 1976 and 1978, but each time was rejected. The reaction to the Doraiswamy *et al.* paper was not much different. The discussant at the AMA conference pointed out that the paper used no data and was built entirely on (unsubstantiated) economic assumptions, and recommended that it should be ignored by the field. This reaction, coupled with the three prior rejections, led the authors to discontinue this line of analytic research. However, about the same time, two other events occurred that resulted in the 1983 publication of the original work of McGuire and Staelin. First, in 1982 the new journal, *Marketing Science*, was launched with the stated goal of publishing more quantitative papers. Second, another set of modelers, Abel Jeuland and Steve Shugan independently became interested in the general channel management area and submitted a paper on channel coordination mechanisms to *Marketing Science*. Fortuitously, one of the reviewers of the Jeuland and Shugan paper was Staelin. Seeing that *Marketing Science* might be open to pure game theory papers with no "data", he suggested to McGuire that they revise their paper and submit it to *Marketing Science*, too. These two papers were published in 1983, and the rest is history.

Over the next seven years, these four authors extended their basic set ups in book chapters that came out of two major special purpose conferences, one sponsored by Berkeley's Pete Bucklin and James Carman and the other

---

[1]We make no claim of providing an exhaustive list of all the work in a particular area. Instead our intent is to provide illustrative examples on how the field evolved.

by David Gautschi, a graduate of Berkeley (Jeuland and Shugan, 1983b; McGuire and Staelin, 1983b, 1986), in addition to a few additional journal articles (Jeuland and Shugan, 1988b; Shugan, 1985). Simultaneously, Anne Coughlan, as a Stanford economics PhD student, took a course from a former student of McGuire, and was exposed to the then unpublished version of McGuire and Staelin (1983). She extended their linear model in her thesis, which resulted in its publication in *Marketing Science* (Coughlan, 1985). She continued her work with two other co-authors to produce Anderson and Coughlan (1987) and Coughlan and Wernerfelt (1989). Another early researcher, Sridhar Moorthy, became interested in the area because of his expertise in game theory and the potential of this underdeveloped field of channel modeling. In 1987, he wrote a comment on the Jeuland and Shugan (1983a) paper (Moorthy, 1987), which resulted in a rejoinder (Jeuland and Shugan, 1988a), and the next year, he wrote a comment on the McGuire and Staelin (1983a) paper (Moorthy, 1988). Note, however, that none of these additional papers explored new channel management issues, but only extended the basic set-ups and insights of the two 1983 papers. It was not until the 1990s that researchers began exploring other channel management issues.[2]

The rest of this chapter discusses the development of the field starting with the two 1983 papers and the numerous insights that have flowed from this line of work. We start by looking at the different channel systems investigated and then discuss the two central components of all these papers, i.e., the specification of the demand function and the rules of the game. Our discussion of these methodological issues is summarized in Table 10.1. We then follow it with a discussion of substantive topics that have been investigated in this field, which are summarized in Figure 10.1.

10.3 Channel systems and industries studied

By definition a channel system must have at least two players, an upstream member (the manufacturer) and a downstream member (the retailer). This

---

[2]One other paper (Zusman and Etgar, 1981) using the analytic framework of game theory and economic modeling, appeared prior to these two papers. It used the somewhat different framework of a bargaining game.

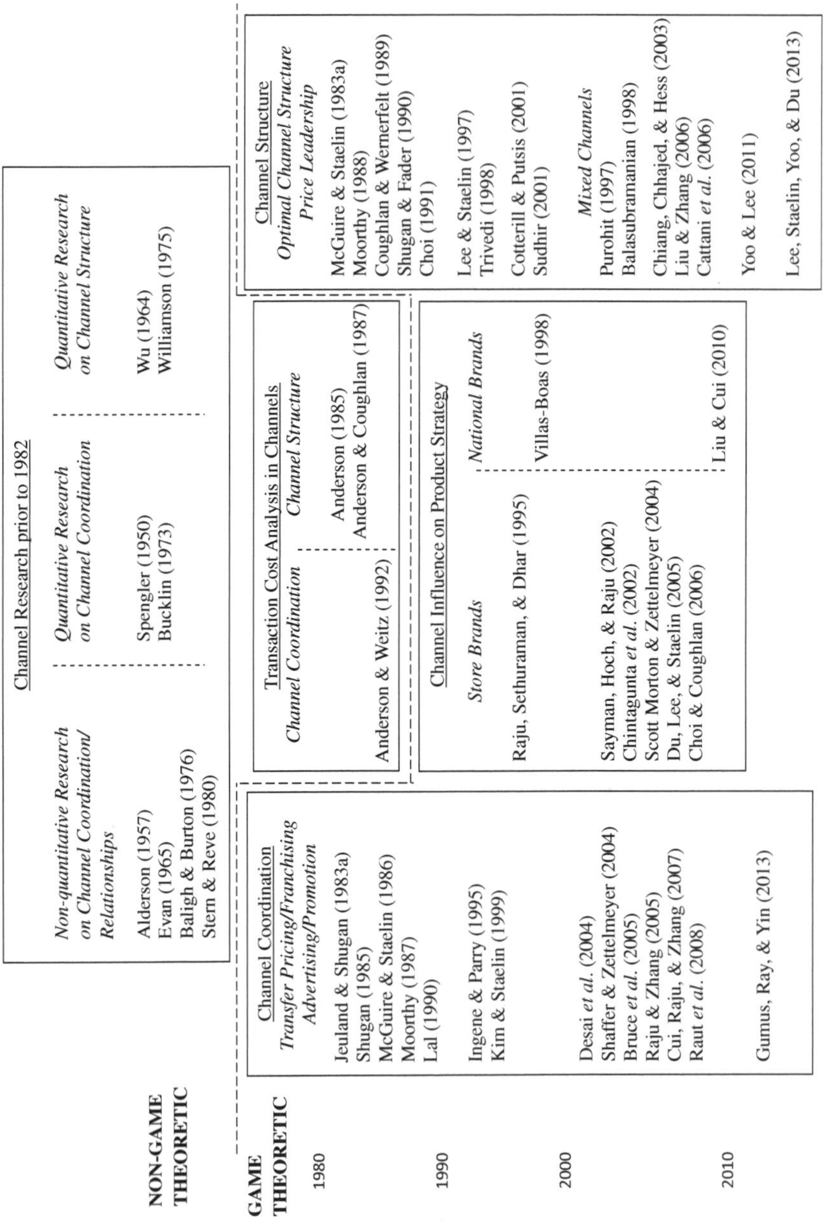

Fig. 10.1 Development of quantitative research on marketing channels

Table 10.1 Methodological approaches in game theoretic research on marketing channels

Available information	Demand functions	Sequence of moves	Solution identification
Full Information Almost all papers	*General* Jeuland & Shugan, 1983a Moorthy, 1987 Moorthy, 1988 Lee & Staelin, 1997	*Vertical Nash* Jeuland & Shugan, 1983a Shugan, 1985 Choi, 1991 Lee & Staelin, 1997	*Mathematical* Almost all papers deriving closed form solutions and/or providing mathematical proofs
Partial Information Jeck, 1990; Lal, 1990; Desai & Srinivasan, 1995; Dukes et al., 2006	*Assumed* McGuire & Staelin, 1983a Shugan & Jeuland, 1988 Choi, 1991 Ingene & Parry, 1995 Trivedi, 1998 Kim & Staelin, 1999 Sayman et al., 2002	*Manufacturer Stackelberg* McGuire & Staelin, 1983a McGuire & Staelin, 1983b McGuire & Staelin, 1986 Moorthy, 1988 Choi, 1991 Ingene & Parry, 1995 Lee & Staelin, 1997 Trivedi, 1998 Sayman et al., 2002 Yoo & Lee, 2011	*Numerical* Du, Lee, & Staelin, 2005 Raut et al., 2008 Lee et al., 2013
	Representative Consumer Choi & Coughlan, 2006 Ingene & Parry, 2007	*Retailer Stackelberg* Moorthy & Fader, 1990 Choi, 1991 Lee & Staelin, 1997	*Empirical* Kadiyali et al., 2000 Sudhir, 2001 Cotterill & Putsis, 2001 Chintagunta et al., 2002
	Based on Spatial Models Balasubramanian, 1998 Shaffer & Zettelmeyer, 2004 Du, Lee, & Staelin, 2005 Liu & Cui, 2010 Lee et al., 2013	*Bargaining Game* Zusman & Etgar, 1981 Scott Morton & Zettelmeyer, 2004 Dukes et al., 2006	

(Continued)

Table 10.1 (Continued)

Channel structure

Bilateral Monopoly	One Manufacturer and Multiple Retailers	Multi-Manufacturer and One Common Retailer	Multi-Manufacturer and Multi-Retailer Excusive Retailers	Other Structures Non-Spatial Channels
Jeuland & Shugan, 1983a	Jeuland & Shugan, 1983a	Choi, 1991	McGuire & Staelin, 1983a	Balasubramanian, 1998
Moorthy, 1987	Ingene & Parry, 1995	Raju et al., 1995	Coughlan & Wernerfelt, 1989	Chiang et al., 2003
Villas-Boas, 1998	Raju & Zhang, 2005	Du et al., 2005	Trivedi, 1998	Cattani et al., 2006
Ingene & Parry, 2007		Raut et al., 2008	Lee et al., 2013	Liu & Zhang, 2006
				Yoo & Lee, 2011
			Common Retailers	Lee et al., 2013
			Lee & Staelin, 1997	Other Systems
			Trivedi, 1998	Purohit, 1997
			Dukes et al., 2006	Calzada & Valletti, 2012
			Lee et al., 2013	

was the original structure analyzed by Jeuland and Shugan (1983a), who investigated the channel coordination problem in a bilateral monopoly, and suggested a variety of channel coordination mechanisms. However, such a structure ignores competition at both levels across the channels. In order to capture this competition, McGuire and Staelin (1983a) proposed a channel system with two exclusive retailers and two competing manufacturers where the retailers either were independent agents or controlled by the manufacturer. In this paper, their primary focus was on the optimal channel structure under different competitive conditions. Choi (1991) built upon this work by extending these two basic structures to a system where there were two manufacturers, each distributing their competing products through one common retailer. In this case, there was no competition at the retail level, and the retailer had the opportunity to do product line pricing. Conversely, Ingene and Parry (1995) introduced a structure composed of one manufacturer and two retailers, and extended Jeuland and Shugan's (1983a) work on channel coordination. Lee and Staelin (1997) proposed an extension of Choi's common retailer system by adding a second common retailer, thereby incorporating both inter- and intra-brand competition, and provided deeper insights into channel price leadership.

These five channel systems form the foundation for many of the subsequent channel management analyses. However, by the second half of the 1990s, these basic structures were expanded to look at more complex distribution systems. For example, Purohit (1997) looked at a mixed channel system where a manufacturer distributed its durable product through the dealer channel and the rental channel. The competition in this case comes from the used rental cars that compete with the new cars sold by the dealer in the second period. A similar situation was studied by Calzada and Valletti (2012) who analyzed the strategy of distributing the theater version and the DVD version of a movie through a mixed channel system. Other researchers, such as Balasubramanian (1998) and numerous others after him, investigated the implications of manufacturers using a direct non-spatial channel (e.g., the Internet or catalog sales) and independent brick-and-mortar retailers. Given the importance of this emerging channel structure, we discuss some of these papers in more detail later.

10.4 Demand functions

Channel management involves interactions among the consumer, the company, and the competitor. This interaction is captured in analytic channel research by applying strategic channel decisions to an environment captured by demand functions. There are three broad categories of approaches to modeling the demand: (i) general demand functions, (ii) assumed demand functions, and (iii) derived demand functions. Each of these approaches has distinct advantages and disadvantages for analyzing channel management issues, as discussed below.

General demand functions employ a bare minimum set of necessary assumptions, such as downward sloping in price and upward sloping in marketers' demand-enhancing activities (e.g., advertising, product quality improvement, retailer's service enhancement, etc.). This was the approach first used by Jeuland and Shugan (1983a). Moorthy (1987, 1988) used a similar general demand function as did Coughlan and Wernerfelt (1989) and Lee and Staelin (1997).

The advantage of the general demand function approach is obvious; the results of analyses using such demand functions are highly generalizable since they are not limited to particular functional forms. Thus, this is a powerful way of providing general proofs of the properties of fundamental strategic forces shaping channel management strategies. On the other hand, the incomplete specification of the demand functions keeps the analysis from being able to produce closed-form equilibrium solutions, thereby making it impossible to conduct comparative statics useful for deriving specific tactical conclusions. For this reason, this general approach has been used by only a few channel studies.

Reduced form (assumed) demand functions were first used by Doraiswamy, McGuire, and Staelin (1979), and expanded on by McGuire and Staelin (1983a) who specified a system of two linear demand functions for the two competing products using four parameters (out of a possible six parameters). They then rescaled this system into very simple demand functions with just one parameter. This makes their derivations and interpretations of the equilibrium solutions extremely efficient. Thus, it is not surprising that a multitude of studies have followed this approach by applying variations and extensions of this rescaled linear demand function (e.g., Choi, 1991, 1996; Ingene and Parry, 1995; Raju,

Sethuraman, and Dhar, 1995; Trivedi, 1998; Sayman, Hoch, and Raju, 2002).

Despite its clear advantage of superior mathematical tractability, the assumed demand function approach comes with a few inherent weaknesses. First, a complete specification of demand function inevitably involves certain properties that are chosen for mere analytical convenience without any theoretical significance. Therefore, the modeler must ensure that the key conclusions drawn from the equilibrium solutions are neither seriously affected by limited generalizability nor by spurious by-products of those convenience assumptions. Moorthy (1988) addresses this issue by showing that the necessary condition for McGuire and Staelin's (1983a) finding of channel decentralization being a Nash equilibrium is that the two products are horizontal strategic complements, i.e., when one player lowers its price the other player finds it optimal to also lower the price.[3] McGuire and Staelin's linear demand system satisfied such a condition, but a constant elasticity demand function does not. Choi (1991) highlights this issue by showing that the conclusion on the profitability of channel price leadership completely reverses when one switches from a linear demand to a nonlinear (constant elasticity) demand.

This "linear vs. non-linear" debate became a major issue in the mid-1990s causing many reviewers at that time to require authors using an assumed linear demand function to show that their results based on this linear assumption also hold for at least one assumed non-linear demand function. However, Lee and Staelin (1997) showed that the critical factor was not whether the demand functions were linear or not, but instead the type of vertical strategic interaction that occurred between the channel members. Thus, the emphasis is less on the shape of the demand function and more on the best reaction of a player to another channel member's action.

A second problem with assumed demand functions concerns the linkages between the demand parameters and the underlying market characteristics such as the number of product offerings or the degree of product differentiation. Some of these relationships might seem intuitively

---

[3] It is an empirical question whether players find it optimal to follow (not follow) their competition. What is important is that the modeler makes explicit that this is the industry setting being modeled.

obvious, but it is extremely difficult, if not impossible, to link all of the key market characteristics with demand parameters by intuition alone. For instance, consider the often used three-parameter demand function: $q_i = A - Bp_i + \theta p_j$ in which the cross-price sensitivity parameter, θ, is supposed to reflect product substitutability between product i and product j. While there is little doubt about the positive impact that product substitutability has on cross-price sensitivity, this demand formulation also implies that product substitutability has no impact on the demand intercept and the own-price sensitivity coefficient, which in many situations lacks face validity and results in conclusions that lack much external validity (e.g., a negative effect of product differentiation on prices and profits). A number of researchers (Shugan and Jeuland, 1988; Raju, Sethuraman, and Dhar, 1995; Kim and Staelin, 1999; initial four parameter model of McGuire and Staelin, 1983a) attempted to address this issue by linking product substitutability not only to cross-price sensitivity but also to own-price sensitivity, but still assumed no effect on the base demand (i.e., the intercept term), which, it turns out, could distort the derived results (Dixit and Stigtiz, 1977; Lee *et al.*, 2013).

The lack of clear linkage between demand parameters and the underlying market also presents problems in comparisons across situations associated with different sets of demand functions. For instance, consider a case of two competing manufacturers and one common retailer, where one of the manufacturers launches a direct Internet channel to compete with the retailer. The base case has only two offerings while the latter has three. A meaningful comparison between these two cases would require that the expanded demand equation system with 12 parameters (four for each of the three product offerings) reflects the same underlying market characteristics captured by the system of two demand functions with six parameters capturing the situation before the new direct channel entry. Such a task is virtually impossible without some explicit underlying consumer behavior model. This, along with the other above discussed issues, led some channel researchers to develop methods of deriving the appropriate demand functions from an underlying utility model of consumer demand. We discuss two different approaches next.

The representative consumer model approach, based on the work of Dixit and Stiglitz (1977), is reasonably new to the marketing literature, i.e., Choi and Coughlan (2006) and Ingene and Parry (2007). This approach models the aggregate behavior of the market based on a utility maximizing consumer, whose utility is a function of the quantity consumed of the two available product offerings. Maximizing this utility function subject to a budget constraint results in linear demand functions that are clearly linked to the underlying utility parameters, and convenient for mathematical analyses. The resulting demand functions imply that the utility parameter capturing product substitutability affects not only the cross-price sensitivity, but also the own-price sensitivity and the intercept terms in the demand function, which, as noted above, is not adequately reflected in the assumed demand formulations.

Despite these nice features, the representative consumer approach has two potential drawbacks that may limit its broader adoption. First, there is an ongoing debate in economics regarding what this "representative consumer" really represents. Does it imply that all consumers are completely homogeneous (not very interesting for marketing researchers)? If consumers are heterogeneous, does the representative consumer simply capture the behavior of an average consumer? Can diverse consumer behaviors and choices be correctly reflected by one aggregate utility maximization process? Second, the parameters of the representative consumer's utility function measure the effects of marginal utility of consumption for the representative consumer without an explicit link to the underlying industry structure characteristics such as product quality and product differentiation.

Spatial models first appeared in the marketing literature in the early 1990s as another way to link demand parameters to consumer heterogeneity and product/store positioning. The most typical and frequently used approach is Hotelling's (1929) linear city model (e.g., Lal and Rao, 1997; Shaffer and Zettelmeyer, 2004; Liu and Cui, 2010), in which consumer ideal points in product position or store location are assumed to be distributed over a line segment. We use the term "spatial model" in a broad way by including those models that represent the distribution of consumer willingness to pay for quality along a line segment (e.g., Purohit, 1997; Villas-Boas, 1998; Chiang, Chhajed, and Hess, 2003) as well as the circular city model (Salop, 1979; Balasubramanian, 1998), two-dimensional spatial models (e.g., Desai, 2001; Du *et al.*, 2005; Yoo and Lee, 2011), and three-dimensional spatial models (Lee *et al.*, 2013). The explicit link between the demand parameters and the consumer parameters allows the researcher to compare equilibrium solutions across different values for parameters of interest and across different channel structures while holding the remaining market characteristics constant.

Considering these advantages and the frequent application of Hotelling's (1929) linear city model to many other theoretical marketing analyses, it may seem surprising how few studies have used this model to investigate channel management issues. One main reason is that this model is typically used with the assumption of full market coverage, which directly implies inelastic aggregate demand and the cross-price sensitivity being equal to the own-price sensitivity. If such a model is applied to a simple channel structure including just one manufacturer or just one retailer, it gives that monopolist channel member complete power to extract the entire channel profit, resulting in trivial conclusions. For this reason, the early studies applying spatial models to channel-related issues focused exclusively on the retail level competition without considering a strategic manufacturer in the upstream (e.g., Lal and Rao, 1997; Balasubramanian, 1998). Even with multiple competing manufacturers, the full market coverage assumption fails to capture the channels' important strategic role of providing expanded access to the market. Given this disadvantage, channel researchers started proposing other spatial models that allowed for partial market coverage but still were mathematically tractable (Purohit, 1997; Villas-Boas, 1998; Desai, 2001; Chiang, Chhajed, and Hess, 2003; Du et al., 2005; Yoo and Lee, 2011). However, these models often produce kinked demand functions with multiple regions, requiring complicated comparisons of all the interior solutions and corner solutions across the multiple regions. When applied to more complex channel structures, this process often results in the loss of mathematical tractability so desired for equilibrium analysis. A few recent studies (Du et al., 2005; Raut et al., 2008; Yoo and Lee, 2011; Lee et al., 2013) still use the spatial model approach to generate the demand functions, but solve for equilibrium solutions using numerical analysis. It is an open question as to whether our field will accept this latter approach.

10.5 Rules of the game and available information

Channel management, by its very nature, involves the interaction of two or more agents. To study this interaction, the analyst must specify what each agent knows, what is the set of actions each agent can take, what are the agent's objectives of these actions, and in what sequence the agents decide on their actions. We next discuss how these topics evolved over the last 30 plus years of channel management research.

10.5.1 *Available information set*

The initial analytic channel management papers all assumed full information, i.e., that all the agents know the retail demand function and the actions of the other channel members. This is still a standard assumption for most analyses. However, a few papers have studied what happens if this assumption is relaxed. Jeck (1990) looked at situations where the agents observed only their own prices and profits, but had no knowledge of the demand function and thus were not able to infer their opponent's actions. He showed that the prices resulting from this incomplete information environment converged to the same Nash equilibrium solution found under the full information assumption. This line of research is encouraging since it implies that the full information assumption may not be as restrictive as one might perceive.

Others allowed agents at different levels to have different sets of knowledge. Thus, Lal (1990) had the retailer be more knowledgeable about the parameters of the demand function, whereas Desai and Srinivasan (1995), and Dukes, Gal-Or, and Srinivasan (2006) assumed the manufacturer to know more about the product quality. These analyses required the researchers to alter their analysis technique from the standard game theory approach. Lal (1990) uses a principle agent formulation while Srinivasan and his co-authors use a signaling model to derive their results. We suspect that more researchers will try to reflect asymmetric or incomplete information for distribution channels research. A good reference to possible approaches can be found in Narasimhan *et al.* (2005).

10.5.2 *Sequence of moves*

There are two different ways to model the interaction between the different players. In the first, each agent simultaneously decides on its action. This was the assumption used by Jeuland and Shugan (1983a). In effect, this means that no set of agents commits to actions before the other agents make their decisions. In the second, one firm moves first, but in doing so anticipates the response of the second mover, which conditions its response on the leader's action. This leader–follower assumption was used by McGuire and Staelin (1983a). The equilibrium solution coming from the first assumption is referred to as Vertical Nash (VN) and from the second as Manufacturer Stackelberg (MS) or Retailer Stackelberg (RS) depending on which channel member moves first. Not surprisingly, these assumptions can lead to different results. Shugan (1985) further explored this issue by analyzing a bilateral monopoly model and a constant elasticity demand function under various scenarios of price leadership in terms of the extent of foresight or "implicit understanding" utilized by one channel member regarding the other channel member's pricing behavior. His results show that higher levels of implicit understanding leads to greater channel profits, and that channel price leadership benefits the price follower more than the price leader. Interestingly, the latter finding counters McGuire and Staelin's (1983a) equilibrium solutions, which indicate that the presence of channel price leadership leads to a greater profit for the price leader than that for the price follower.

Choi (1991) extended this debate by using a different channel structure composed of two manufacturers and one or two retailers and allowing the retailer to move first. His analysis of the MS, VN, and RS games replicated the previous conflicting findings by showing that channel price leadership benefits the price follower more than the price leader under the constant elasticity demand function assumed by Shugan (1985), but it increases the price leader's profit and decreases the price follower's profit when the demand function is linear as in McGuire and Staelin (1983a). Moorthy and Fader's (1990) analysis of a bilateral monopoly and Lee and Staelin's (1997) later analysis of a broader set of channel structures resolved this debate by showing that the seeming discrepancy stems from the different types of vertical strategic interactions associated with the different functional forms used for the demand equations. Specifically, the primitive is what is the best response of one channel member when its other channel member increases its margin. Is the best response to reduce its margin (Vertical Strategic Substitutability or VSS), to increase its margin (Vertical Strategic Complementarity or VSC), or to keep its margin unchanged (Vertical Strategic Independence)? If the market environment is characterized by VSS, a channel member finds it more profitable to be a price leader than to be a price follower, but the opposite is true for the case of VSC, while VSI leaves channel members indifferent across different price leadership scenarios. The mixed results on the profitability of channel price leadership indicate that being a channel price leader does not automatically imply superior channel power.

In the early 2000s, the new empirical industrial organization approach emerged as a new method of analyzing vertical strategic interactions with empirical data. Kadiyali, Chintagunta, and Vilcassim (2000) allow for a continuum of possible channel pricing games beyond MS, VN, and RS, and report more diverse and complex pricing interactions between the manufacturers and the retailer than the three pricing games found in the theoretical literature. Cotterill and Putsis (2001) analyzed data for six product categories across 59 different local markets, and found that VN tends to be the more common pricing game than MS or RS for private label brands. In contrast, Sudhir's (2001) analysis found that his data exhibited the best fit with the MS game in a VSS environment. Chintagunta, Bonfrer, and Song (2002) show that store brand introductions lead to changes of the national brand manufacturers' pricing behavior, who take a "softer" stance in their interactions with the retailer.

10.6 Channel member objectives and channel coordination

Channel management ultimately is all about managing profits. Since the individual channel members are independent businesses, it seems natural to assume that each member's goal is to maximize its own profit, as found in many studies. However, there are channel systems where the manufacturer integrates forward or the retailer integrates backward. In this case the objective is to maximize total channel profits, since the organization gets profits from both levels. This objective is also found in the channel coordination literature. In this case, the problem is to devise some way of getting independent agents within a channel system to choose that set of actions that leads to the equilibrium solution associated with maximizing total channel profits. In effect, channel coordination and vertical integration both address the issue of overcoming the negative profit impact of double marginalization, i.e., the effects of each independent decision maker selecting the action that maximizes its own profits. The difference is that vertical integration solves the problem via organizational structure, while channel coordination solves the problem through some incentive scheme.

The issue of channel coordination via incentives or organizational structure was the topic of the two 1983 papers and the subsequent follow-ups by these authors and Moorthy (1987, 1988). Jeuland and Shugan (1983a), McGuire and Staelin (1986) and Moorthy (1987) showed that it is possible to devise transfer pricing incentive schemes such as quantity discounts or two-part tariffs that fully coordinate a bilateral monopoly channel by inducing the independent retailer to set a retail price that is identical to the retail price that would be set if the channel were vertically integrated, thereby maximizing total channel profits. However, McGuire and Staelin (1983a, 1986) and Moorthy (1988) show that if there is competition at both the manufacturer and retailer level, a decentralized channel may be more profitable than the fully coordinated vertically integrated channel. This is due to the fact that an additional layer of decentralized retailers provides a buffer from direct price competition. Coughlan and Wernerfelt (1989) generalized this insight by allowing the two competing manufacturers (retailers) to have multiple retailers (suppliers). They reproduce the previous findings by showing in this more general setting that if the channel partners have full information and use a transfer pricing scheme that allows the dominant channel member (i.e., either the manufacturer or the retailer) to acquire all the channel profits, the equilibrium channel structure will be a decentralized system. However, they next show that if the competing players cannot observe their opponents' channel coordinating contracts, then the unique equilibrium degenerates to the Nash equilibrium associated with the integrated (fully coordinated) channel system. Thus, even if the competing manufacturers (retailers) wanted to buffer themselves from direct competition by using a decentralized channel system and thus double marginalization, they cannot reach the desired equilibrium associated with a decentralized system unless they can fully observe all the contracts.

Lal (1990) addresses the channel coordination problem within a franchised system where one franchisee's actions affect the other franchisees' demand. He adds an error term to the linear demand function so that the manufacturer cannot directly infer the retailer's actions. Then using a principal-agent formulation and assuming an MS leader–follower game, he shows that the manufacturer can get coordination without fully monitoring the retailer by supplementing the standard two-part tariff suggested by Moorthy (1987) with the manufacturer giving a royalty payment to the retailer based on the retailer's sales.

Ingene and Parry (1995) add complexity to the coordination problem by having the monopolist manufacturer distribute its product through multiple retailers, each of which face a different demand function. Given these different demand functions, the manufacturer would normally like to charge a different price to each retailer. However, the 1936 Robinson–Patman Act generally prohibits such price discrimination. In this context, these researchers explore various incentive schemes for channel coordination, and find that a single, second-best tariff may lead to greater channel profits than a more complex menu of two-part tariffs. In 2004, Desai, Koenigsberg, and Purohit looked at the problem of solving the coordination problem in a durable goods market. In this setting, they recognize that sales that occur in the first period compete with new sales in the second period via the used-product market. They show that the manufacturer can increase its profits by inserting an independent retailer into the system and then instead of using the standard two-part tariff where the manufacturer sets its wholesale price to be its marginal cost, it sets this wholesale price to be higher. It does this in order to reduce the first period sales which in turn reduces the competition in the second period. This paper provides deeper insights into why we observe independent auto dealers and why a manufacturer may want to limit (reduce) sales in the first period in order to maximize profits over a longer horizon. More recently Gumus, Ray, and Yin (2013) study the influence of peer-to-peer used markets on the return policy for a durable goods manufacturer and how these two factors impact the ability of getting channel coordination.

Channel modelers have also investigated the channel coordination problem in the context of sales promotions. In a non-durable setting, Kim and Staelin (1999) look at the retailer pass-through of manufacturer allowances, and Dreze and Bell (2003) investigate retailer responses to trade promotions to demonstrate superior channel coordination achieved by scan-back trade deals, relative to off-invoice deals. Bruce *et al.* (2005, 2006) analyzed both dealer and consumer cash-back rebates in durable goods markets. Other researchers have looked at situations where the retailer is the dominant player within the channel. Raju and Zhang (2005) assume a structure with one manufacturer, one dominant retailer and a number of smaller retailers who follow the pricing lead of the dominant retailer. They use an MS game to solve for the equilibrium conditions. They put forth a number of channel-coordinating solutions and point out that one of them has the manufacturer paying a fixed fee to the retailer. They suggest that this fee should not be viewed as a slotting allowance, but instead as "street cash" that the manufacturer uses to coordinate the channel. Finally, Cui, Raju, and Zhang (2007) explore how the concept of fairness can affect channel coordination within a bilateral monopoly situation. They show if both parties are concerned about fairness, then the manufacturer can coordinate the channel with a simple wholesale pricing scheme where this price is above the manufacturer's marginal cost.

10.7 Product positioning in distribution channels

In the 1990s, the growth of private labels (or store brands) caught the attention of channel modelers. Raju, Sethuraman, and Dhar (1995) introduced the first theoretical model which was composed of two national brand manufacturers and a common retailer where the latter could introduce a store brand. Their model distinguishes a store brand from national brands by assuming that a store brand is supplied by a non-strategic manufacturer at this manufacturer's cost, while the national brands follow the standard MS game and thus are obtained at the national brand manufacturer's wholesale price. Applying an assumed linear demand system to this model, they compare the equilibrium solutions before and after the store brand launch, and conclude that store brands are more likely to increase retailer's category profits if the cross-price sensitivity among national brands is low and cross-price sensitivity between the national bands and the store brand is high. Sayman, Hoch, and Raju (2002) later analyzed a slightly generalized version of the same model to conclude that the most profitable strategy for the retailer is to position the store brand as close to the leading national brand as possible.

Three other sets of researchers also looked at this problem. Each still assumed two national brand manufacturers and one common retailer. However, they used different approaches to model demand and specify the rules of game. Scott Morton and Zettelmeyer (2004) applied a Nash bargaining game to a demand model derived from the spatial model approach. By making assumptions of two consumer segments and limited retail shelf space, they replicated Sayman *et al.*'s finding that store brand should be positioned as a close substitute to the leading national brand. Du, Lee, and Staelin (2005) analyzed a model that combines Scott Morton and Zettelmeyer's spatial model approach with Sayman *et al.*'s rules of the game. In the process, they found that there exist three distinct types of store brand positioning strategies depending on the quality levels and degree of differentiation of the different brands. These strategies were to position the store brand (a) close to the leading national brand, (b) close to the weaker national brand, or (c) at roughly the midpoint between the two national brand positions. Similar conclusions were found in Choi and Coughlan's (2006) paper using the representative consumer approach. These five different papers and conclusions point again to the importance of the demand functions, in this case whether they are assumed or derived, and the rules of the game in driving the results.

Other studies have looked at product positioning issues from the manufacturers' point of view. Villas-Boas (1998) analyzed a bilateral monopoly model for a market composed of two consumer segments differing in terms of willingness to pay for quality to investigate a manufacturer's product line design problem in the context of channel management. The analysis reveals that an independent retailer has an economic incentive to cannibalize the sales of the high-quality product with the low-quality product, which disrupts the manufacturer's targeting strategy and reduces its profit as well as total channel profits. To prevent such a problem in a decentralized channel, the manufacturer should set the low-end product's quality lower than what it would be in an integrated channel, thereby creating greater differentiation within the product line. Liu and Cui (2010) analyze the issue of product line length, by applying a Hotelling demand model to a bilateral monopoly channel. Interestingly, their analysis finds a condition under which channel decentralization leads to the more socially desirable solution of a longer product line compared to the optimal product line in a vertically integrated channel.

10.8 Determining the optimal channel structure

A major focus of the 1983 McGuire and Staelin paper was the determination of the manufacturer's optimal channel structure within a franchise channel system as a function of the level of differentiation of the two product offerings. They showed that the manufacturer was better off with a decentralized channel system when the level of differentiation of the two products was small. This four-player channel structure problem was addressed again in Coughlan's 1985 paper using a different demand function, and by Moorthy in 1988 using a more general demand function. Coughlan and Wernerfelt (1989) generalized it by looking at different number of players at both levels. Choi (1991) broadened the setting by added a common retailer into the channel system, and Trivedi in 1998 expanded the setting again by adding a second common retailer.

Roughly around the same time period, another stream of research was in progress by applying the transaction cost economics paradigm to issues related with channel structure. It started with Anderson's (1985) analysis of manufacturers' choice of using integrated or independent sales forces, and was soon extended to the development of theoretical frameworks for understanding the factors affecting the efficiency and sustainability of decentralized channels (Anderson and Weitz, 1989, 1992). These studies led to a series of empirical studies based on survey data collected from various distribution channel members, providing insights into the role of a broad set of socio-political factors that influence the behavior and performance of the members of decentralized channels, which cannot be explained by simple normative microeconomics models (Anderson and Coughlan, 1987; Anderson and Weitz, 1992; Fein and Anderson, 1997).

In the late 1990s, the focus of research on channel structure shifted to the issues involved in managing mixed channels composed of online and offline outlets. The first marketing channels paper to look at non-spatial outlets such as the Internet was Balasubramanian (1998). He modified the circular city model by placing the brick-and-mortar retailers along the periphery of a circle and the direct channel at the circle's center, and demonstrated that the entry of the direct channel can alter the patterns of retail competition so significantly that the traditional focus on retail entry equilibria may not adequately capture the new market environment with strong direct channels. Interestingly, the manufacturer does not have to generate a substantial (or any) sales through the direct online channel to benefit from it, since the mere competitive threat from the direct online channel can alter the offline retailer's behavior, leading to enhanced channel coordination and a superior manufacturer profit, as demonstrated by Chiang, Chhajed, and Hess (2003). Liu and Zhang (2006) and Cattani *et al.* (2006) also analyzed various strategic pricing issues using the same channel structure with one manufacturer using a direct online channel and an independent offline retailer. Yoo and Lee (2011) broadened the channel structure setting by recognizing that the vast majority of the leading online marketers were either the electronic arms of the brick-and-mortar retailers (e.g., BestBuy.com) or pure-play e-tailers (e.g., Amazon.com). Therefore, they analyzed multiple alternative structures of an online–offline mixed channel for a monopolist manufacturer, using a two-dimensional spatial model, and, in the process, identified five key strategic forces that shape the overall impact of the Internet channel introduction.

Lee *et al.* (2013) further extended the research on channel structure by proposing a three-dimensional spatial model that captures consumer heterogeneity in terms of spatial location, horizontal tastes, and Internet costs. They then apply this spatial model to 11 different online–offline channel structures to conduct a meta-analysis of simulated data. This analysis results in a general model that indicates three demand characteristics (*market coverage, inter-brand competition,* and *intra-brand competition*) and the degrees of utilization of three types of channel coordination mechanisms (*vertical integration, product line pricing,* and *multichannel coordination*) efficiently capture the profit impact of most of the channel structure models considered in previous studies as well as some new channel structures under various market conditions. Interestingly, their result also suggests that, if competing brands are carried by a common retailer, the addition of an Internet outlet reduces the intensity of inter-brand competition, and this effect becomes particularly pronounced when the two brands are highly substitutable.

10.9 Summary

Much has been done since the first two papers on channel management appeared in *Marketing Science* in 1983, but the new emerging channel systems and the associated managerial problems call for continued expansion of the field. Models reflecting complex new channel structures and emerging selling formats frequently lack the mathematical tractability of simpler channel models of the previous decades. With increased computing power, numerical analysis is a new viable way of deriving and analyzing equilibrium solutions for such complex models. In addition, the notable progress in research on online consumer behavior in the recent years, especially concerning social networks, online channels, and two-sided markets, points to the need to analyze the implications of these behavioral characteristics for channel strategies. Finally, we note that the majority of the analytic channel papers assume complete rationality and perfect information among channel members. Deviating from this standard paradigm to investigate the impact of the characteristics of managerial decision making on channel strategies can be a fruitful direction for future research.

References

Alderson, W. (1957). *Marketing behavior and executive action: A functionalist approach to marketing theory*, Homewood, IL: Richard D. Irwin.

Anderson, E. (1985). The salesperson as outside agent or employee: A transaction-cost analysis, *Marketing Science*, 4(3), 234–254.

Anderson, E. and A. T. Coughlan (1987). International market entry and expansion via independent or integrated channels of distribution, *Journal of Marketing*, 51(1), 71–82.

Anderson, E. and B. A. Weitz (1989). Determinants of continuity in conventional industrial channel dyads, *Marketing Science*, 8(4), 310–323.

Anderson, E. and B. A. Weitz (1992). The use of pledges to build and sustain commitment in distribution channels, *Journal of Marketing Research*, 29(1), 18–34.

Anderson, E., L. M. Lodish, and B A. Weitz (1987). Resource allocation behavior in conventional channels, *Journal of Marketing Research*, 24(1), 85–97.

Balasubramanian, S. (1998). Mail versus mall: A strategic analysis of competition between direct marketers and conventional retailers, *Marketing Science*, 17(3), 181–195.

Baligh, H. H. and R. M. Burton (1976). Organization structure and cooperative market relations, *Omega*, 4(5), 583–593.

Baligh, H. H. and L. E. Richartz (1967). *Vertical market structures*, Boston, MA: Allyn and Bacon, Inc.

Bruce, N., P. Desai, and R. Staelin (2005). The better they are, the more they give: Trade promotions of consumer durables, *Journal of Marketing Research*, 42(1), 54–66.

Bruce, N., P. Desai, and R. Staelin (2006). Enabling the willing: Consumer rebates for durable goods, *Marketing Science*, 25(4), 350–366.

Bucklin, L. P. (1965). Postponement, speculation and the structure of distribution channels, *Journal of Marketing Research*, 2(1), 26–31.

Bucklin, L. P. (1973). A theory of channel control, *Journal of Marketing*, 37(1), 39–47.

Calzada, J. and T. M. Valletti (2012). Intertemporal movie distribution: Versioning when customers can buy both versions, *Marketing Science*, 31(4), 649–667.

Cattani, K., W. Gilland, H. S. Heese, and J. Swaminathan (2006). Boiling frogs: Pricing strategies for a manufacturer adding a direct channel that competes with the traditional channel, *Production and Operations Management*, 15(1), 40–56.

Chiang, W. K., D. Chhajed, and J. D. Hess (2003). Strategic analysis of dual-channel supply-chain design, *Management Science*, 49(1), 1–20.

Chintagunta, P. K., A. Bonfrer, and I. Song (2002). Investigating the effects of store-brand introduction on retailer demand and pricing behavior, *Management Science*, 48(10), 1242–1267.

Choi, S. C. (1991). Price competition in a channel structure with a common retailer, *Marketing Science*, 10(4), 271–296.

Choi, S. C. (1996). Price competition in a duopoly common retailer channel, *Journal of Retailing*, 72(2), 117–134.

Choi, S. C. and A. T. Coughlan (2006). Private label positioning: Quality versus feature differentiation from the national brand, *Journal of Retailing*, 82(2), 79–93.

Cotterill, R. W. and W. P. Putsis. (2001). Do models of vertical strategic interaction for national and store brands meet the market test? *Journal of Retailing*, 77(1), 83–109.

Coughlan, A. T. (1985). Competition and cooperation in marketing channel choice: Theory and Application, *Marketing Science*, 4(2), 110–129.

Coughlan, A. T. and B. Wernerfelt (1989). On credible delegation by oligopolists: A discussion of distribution channel management, *Management Science*, 35(2), 226–239.

Cui, T. H., J. S. Raju, and Z. J. Zhang (2007). Fairness and channel coordination, *Management Science*, 53(8), 1303–1314.

Desai, P. (2001). Quality segmentation in spatial markets: When does cannibalization affect product line design?" *Marketing Science*, 20(3), 265–283.

Desai, P. and K. Srinivasan (1995). Demand signalling under unobservable effort in franchising: Linear and non-linear contracts, *Management Science*, 41(10), 1608–1623.

Desai, P., O. Koenigsberg, and D. Purohit (2004). Strategic decentralization and channel coordination, *Quantitative Marketing and Economics*, 2(1), 5–22.

Dixit, A. K. and J. E. Stiglitz (1977). Monopolistic competition and optimum product diversity, *The American Economic Review*, 67(3), 297–308.

Doraiswamy, K., T. W. McGuire, and R. Staelin (1979). An analysis of alternative advertising strategies in a competitive franchise framework, in N. Beckwith, *et al.*, eds., *1979 Educators' conference proceedings*, Chicago: American Marketing Association, pp. 463–467.

Dreze, X. and D. R. Bell (2003). Creating win-win trade promotions: Theory and empirical analysis of scan-back trade deals, *Marketing Science*, 22(1), 16–39.

Du, R., E. Lee, and R. Staelin (2005). Bridge, focus, attack, or stimulate: Retail category management strategies with a store brand, *Quantitative Marketing and Economics*, 3(4), 393–418.

Dukes, A. J., E. Gal-Or, and K. Srinivasan (2006). Channel bargaining with retailer asymmetry, *Journal of Marketing Research*, 43(1), 84–97.

Evan, W. M. (1965). Toward a theory of inter-organizational relations, *Management Science*, 11(10), 217–230.

Fein, A. J. and E. Anderson (1997). Patterns of credible commitments: Territory and category selectivity in industrial distribution channels, *Journal of Marketing*, 61(2), 19–34.

Gumus, M., S. Ray, and S. Yin (2013). Returns policies between channel partners for durable products, *Marketing Science*, 32(4), 622–643.

Hotelling, H. (1929). Stability in competition, *Economic Journal*, 39(153), 41–57.

Ingene, C. A. and M. E. Parry (1995). Channel coordination when retailers compete, *Marketing Science*, 14(4), 360–377.

Ingene, C. A. and M. E. Parry (2007). Bilateral monopoly, identical distributors, and game-theoretic analyses of distribution channels, *Journal of the Academy of Marketing Science*, 35(4), 586–602.

Jeck, J. (1990). *Channel of distribution dynamics under conditions of imperfect information*, unpublished doctoral dissertation, Duke University.

Jeuland, A. P. and S. M. Shugan (1983a). Managing channel profits, *Marketing Science*, 2(3), 239–272.

Jeuland, A. P. and S. M. Shugan (1983b). Coordination in marketing channels, in David A. Gautschi, ed., *Productivity and efficiency in distribution systems*, New York: North Holland, 17–32.

Jeuland, A. P. and S. M. Shugan (1988a). Reply to: Managing channel profits: Comment, *Marketing Science*, 7(1), 103–106.

Jeuland, A. P. and S. M. Shugan (1988b). Channel of distribution profits when channel members form conjectures, *Marketing Science*, 7(2), 202–210.

Kadiyali, V., P. Chintagunta, and N. Vilcassim (2000). Manufacturer-retailer channel interactions and implications for channel power: An empirical investigation of pricing in a local market, *Marketing Science*, 19(2), 127–148.

Kim, S. Y. and R. Staelin (1999). Manufacturer allowances and retailer pass-through rates in a competitive environment, *Marketing Science*, 18(1), 59–76.

Lal, R. (1990). Improving channel coordination through franchising, *Marketing Science*, 9(4), 299–318.

Lal, R. and R. Rao (1997). Supermarket competition: The case of every day low pricing, *Marketing Science*, 16(1), 60–80.

Lee, E. and R. Staelin (1997). Vertical strategic interaction: Implications for channel pricing strategy, *Marketing Science*, 16(3), 185–207.

Lee, E., R. Staelin, W. S. Yoo, and R. Du (2013). A 'meta-analysis' of multibrand, multioutlet channel systems, *Management Science*, 59(9), 1950–1969.

Liu, Y. and T. H. Cui (2010). The length of product line in distribution channels, *Marketing Science*, 29(3), 474–482.

Liu, Y. and Z. J. Zhang (2006). The benefits of personalized pricing in a channel, *Marketing Science*, 25(1), 97–105.

Machlup, F. and M. Taber (1960). Bilateral monopoly, successive monopoly, and vertical integration, *Economica*, 27(May), 101–119.

McGuire, T. W. and R. Staelin (1983a). An industry equilibrium analysis of downstream vertical integration, *Marketing Science*, 2(2), 161–191.

McGuire, T. W. and R. Staelin (1983b). The effects of channel member efficiency on channel structure, in D. Gautschi, ed., *Productivity and efficiency in distribution systems*, New York: North Holland, 1–16.

McGuire, T. W. and R. Staelin (1986). Channel efficiency, incentive compatibility, transfer pricing, and market structure: An equilibrium analysis of channel relationships, in L. P. Bucklin and J. M. Carman, eds. *Research in marketing: Distribution channels and institutions*, Volume 8, Greenwich, CT: JAI Press Inc., 181–223.

Moorthy, K. S. (1987). Managing channel profits: Comment, *Marketing Science*, 6(4), 375–379.

Moorthy, K. S. (1988). Strategic decentralization in channels, *Marketing Science*, 7(4), 335–355.

Moorthy, K. S. and P. Fader (1990). Strategic interaction within a channel, in S. K. Reddy and L. Pellegrini, eds., *Retail and marketing channels*, London: Routledge.

Narasimhan, C., C. He, E. T. Anderson, P. Desai, D. Kuksov, P. Messinger, S. Moorthy, J. Nunes, Y. Rottenstreich, R. Staelin, G. Wu, and Z. J. Zhang (2005). Incorporating behavioral anomalies in strategic models, *Marketing Letters*, 2005, 16(3/4), 361–373.

Pashigian, B. P. (1961). *The distribution of automobiles: An economic analysis of the franchise system*, Englewood Cliffs, NJ: Prentice Hall, Inc.

Purohit, D. (1997). Dual distribution channels: The competition between rental agencies and car dealers, *Marketing Science*, 16(3), 228–245.

Raju, J. S., R. Sethuraman, and S. K. Dhar (1995). The introduction and performance of store brands, *Management Science*, 41(6), 957–978.

Raju, J. S. and Z. J. Zhang (2005). Channel coordination in the presence of a dominant retailer, *Marketing Science*, 24(2), 254–262.

Raut, S., S. Swami, E. Lee, and C. B. Weinberg (2008). How complex do movie channel contracts need to be? *Marketing Science*, 27(4), 627–741.

Salop, Steven C. (1979), Monopolistic Competition with Outside Goods, *Bell Journal of Economics*, 10(1), 141–156.

Sayman, S., S. J. Hoch, and J. S. Raju (2002). Positioning of store brands, *Marketing Science*, 21(4), 378–397.

Scott Morton, F. and F. Zettelmeyer (2004). The strategic positioning of store brands in retailer-manufacturer negotiations, *Review of Industrial Organization*, 24(2), 161 –194.

Shaffer, G. and F. Zettelmeyer (2004). Advertising in a distribution channel, *Marketing Science*, 23(4), 619–628.

Shugan, S. M. (1985). Implicit understanding in channels of distribution, *Management Science*, 31, 435–460.

Shugan, S. M. and A. P. Jeuland (1988). Competitive pricing behavior in distribution systems, in T. M. Devinney, ed., *Issues in pricing: Theory and research*, Lexington, MA and Toronto: Health Lexington Books, pp. 219–237.

Spengler, J. (1950). Vertical integration and antitrust policy, *Journal of Political Economy*, 58, 347–352.

Stern, L. W. and T. Reve (1980). Distribution channels as political economies: A framework for comparative analysis, *Journal of Marketing Research*, 19(4), 517–524.

Sudhir, K. (2001) Structural analysis of manufacturer pricing in the presence of a strategic retailer, *Marketing Science*, 20(3), 42–60.

Trivedi, M. (1998). Distribution channels: An extension of exclusive retailership, *Management Science*, 44(7), 896–909.

Villas-Boas, J. M. (1998). Product line design for a distribution channel, *Marketing Science*, 17(2), 156–169.

White, L. J. (1971). *The automobile industry since 1945*, Cambridge, MA: Harvard University Press.

Williamson, O. E. (1975). *Markets and hierarchies: Analysis and antitrust implications*, New York: Free Press.

Wu, S. Y. (1964). The effect of vertical integration on price and output, *Western Economic Journal*, 2, 117–133.

Yoo, W. S. and E. Lee (2011). Internet channel entry: A strategic analysis of mixed channel structures, *Marketing Science*, 30(1), 29–41.

Zusman, P. and M. Etgar (1981). The marketing channel as an equilibrium set of contracts, *Management Science*, 27(3), 284–302.

Chapter 11

Customer Relationship Management (CRM)

Scott A. Neslin

11.1 Introduction

Customer relationship management (CRM) emerged as the fusion of relationship marketing and direct marketing. Relationship marketing was pioneered by Berry (1983) as the strategy of "attracting, maintaining, and, in multi-service organizations, enhancing customer relationships" (p. 25). Direct marketing, whose genesis can be traced to the beginning of the 20th century (Petrison, Blattberg, and Wang, 1993), was concerned with the use of customer databases to improve the efficiency of marketing through better targeting, for example, of direct mail and catalogs. Missing from direct marketing was the customer relationship; missing from relationship marketing was the use of customer data.

These notions came together in the 1990s. Blattberg and Deighton (1991, p. 5, Abstract) stated, "It's a marketer's dream — the ability to develop interactive relationships with individual customers. Technology, in the form of the database, is making this dream a reality." The concept of customer relationship was deepened by Fournier (1998), who showed that consumers developed rich, subjective perceptions of their relationships with brands. However, relationships in CRM are often measured by higher-order constructs such as customer satisfaction, loyalty, and mind-set brand equity. And ultimately,the relationship is manifested in enhanced acquisition, retention, and development of customers. We therefore define CRM as follows (see also Bolton and Tarasi, 2007):

> Customer relationship management (CRM) is the development of customer value through an enhanced relationship between the customer and the firm. This relationship is rooted in customer perceptions. However, it is ultimately manifested in superior customer acquisition, retention, and development, achieved by leveraging customer data to increase the productivity of marketing efforts.

Relationship marketing is concerned with the acquisition, retention, and development of the customers, and is the foundation for subjective customer perceptions; direct marketing is concerned with the use of customer data and emphasizes on marketing productivity.

A related concept, "database marketing (DBM)," can be seen historically as a bridge between direct marketing and CRM. Blattberg, Kim, and Neslin's (2008) definition of DBM (p. 4) entails acquisition, retention and the utilization of customer data, but does not include the role of customer perceptions. Another view is manifested in the title of the book by Kumar and Reinartz, *Customer Relationship Management: A Databased Approach* (2006). The relationship comes first, but the data are crucial. Finally, some use the phrase "analytical CRM." Our preference simply is to use the term CRM as defined above. As this chapter is about the history of CRM in marketing science, indeed there will be ample emphasis on the data and methodologies.

11.2 Framework

Figure 11.1 proposes a framework for tracing the historical development of CRM in marketing science. It consists of applications, predictive models, optimization, and marketing metrics. Applications is placed at the top of the framework to emphasize that CRM is about getting things done — developing a relationship, improving marketing productivity, etc. The bottom three boxes — predictive models, optimization, and marketing metrics — are the methods for bringing the applications to fruition.

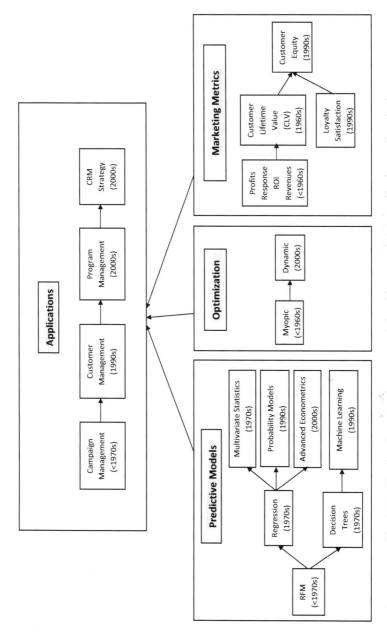

Fig. 11.1   The development of customer relationship management: applications and methods

A given application draws on a combination of methods. Probably the earliest example of CRM was improving the success of a direct mail campaign (campaign management application) by using RFM (predictive model) to maximize short-term profit (myopic optimization, profit metric). A more recent example would be a customer management system (application) that uses a selection regression (econometric predictive model) to specify the period-by-period marketing efforts (dynamic program optimization) to maximize customer equity (metric). First, we will discuss the development of each of the four components in Figure 11.1. Then, we will illustrate how they have been combined over time.

11.3   Historical development of the components of CRM

11.3.1   *Applications*

Figure 11.1 categorizes the applications of CRM by campaign management, customer management, program management, and CRM strategy. Campaign management focuses on the success of a short-term marketing effort such as direct mail or e-mail campaign. Customer management is concerned with managing the value of each customer on a long-term basis. Program management is concerned with the design and management of ongoing efforts such as loyalty programs and recommendation systems. Strategy involves big-picture issues such as customer privacy or how to organize the management team for implementing CRM. Campaign management has the longest history, originating before the 1970s. Customer management emerged in the 1990s. Program management and strategy became prominent in the 2000s.

11.3.1.1   *Campaign management*

Campaign management was the original focus of direct marketing. For example, a company might want to maximize profits from a single direct mail campaign. It could use an RFM model to identify the customers most likely to respond to that campaign, organize customers by profitability, and mail to whom the RFM model predicted to be profitable (see Hughes, 1996; pp. 164–171). Campaign management was and still is highly profitable. Importantly, the practice of campaign management has evolved from "non-personalized" to "personalized." In a non-personalized campaign, the direct mail piece or e-mail is specified and the best customers for that campaign are selected using a predictive model. In a personalized campaign, the direct mail piece or e-mail is personalized to each customer. The advantage of personalization is obvious — higher response rate. Whereas non-personalized campaigns are targeted based on customer, personalized campaigns are targeted based on customer *and* message.

11.3.1.2 *Customer management*

Campaign management can be so profitable that the company loses sight of its customers. The company jumps from one campaign to the next, maximizing immediate profits but not cultivating the customer relationship that leads to long-term profits. Perhaps as a reaction to this mentality, Blattberg and Deighton (1991) and the path-breaking work by Peppers and Rogers (1993, 1997) set the stage for customer management. The idea is to start with a prospect or customer and determine what actions to take to acquire, retain and develop that individual. Customer management might entail selecting customers based on their profitability *potential* to target for special treatment in a customer tier program (Blattberg, Kim, and Neslin, 2008, Chapter 23). It might involve a "customer base analysis" to identify the customers who are likely to be most valuable in the future and hence warrant particular attention (Fader and Hardie, 2009). It might entail decision rules for what marketing action to take with each customer at a particular point in time. These are called "dynamic customer optimization models" (Neslin, 2013; Blattberg, Kim, and Neslin, 2008, Chapter 28). Customer management inherently is long-term oriented; the objective is often to maximize customer lifetime value (CLV).

11.3.1.3 *Program management*

CRM programs can also be seen as a reaction to the one-shot nature of campaign management. CRM programs are ongoing efforts to develop the customer relationship. While these programs can be traced to the "frequent-flyer" programs started by airlines in the 1980s (Kopalle and Neslin, 2003), they have become more widespread and commanded more attention during the 2000s. The goal of these programs can be to cross-sell (for example, using recommendation systems; Ansari, 2013; Ansari, Essengaier, and

Kohli, 2000), enhance loyalty (loyalty programs; Bijmolt, Dorotic, and Verhoef, 2010; Dorotic, Bijmolt, and Verhoef, 2012; Kopalle *et al.*, 2012; Rust, Zeithaml, and Lemon, 2000), prevent churn (churn management programs, Neslin *et al.*, 2006a), improve service (call center management; Sun and Li, 2011), or make the best use of the firm's multiple channels (customer multichannel management; Neslin *et al.*, 2006b). These areas — loyalty programs, churn management programs, call center management, multichannel customer management, recommendation systems — are very fertile grounds for research.

11.3.1.4 *CRM strategy*

CRM has taken on a tactical quality at many companies. Companies use campaign management, customer management, and program management to improve metrics such as retention, CLV, acquisition, etc. This is all well and good, but in the 2000s, researchers started thinking about bigger-picture issues. One of the first areas to be investigated was whether management of customer data could be a competitive advantage (Chen, Narasimhan, and Zhang, 2001; Blattberg, Kim, and Neslin, 2008, Chapter 2). Other areas include organization (Reinartz, Krafft, and.Hoyer, 2004), privacy (Blattberg, Kim, and Neslin, 2008, Chapter 4), company valuation (Gupta, Lehmann, and Stuart, 2004), mind-set brand equity (Stahl *et al.*, 2012), and competitive channel strategy (Chu, Chintagunta, and Vilcassim, 2007).

Campaign management, customer management, program management, and CRM strategy build on each other. For example, customer management might entail deciding which campaigns should be targeted to the customer, or how to develop the customer through various ongoing CRM programs. Campaign management, especially non-personalized, has a solid track record in practice. Personalized campaign management, customer management and program management are less proven. Papers in this area show pro forma profit gains and sometimes implement field tests (e.g., see Simester, Sun, and Tsitsiklis, 2006; Knott, Hayes, and Neslin, 2002; Kumar, Venkatesan, and Reinartz, 2008a; Kumar *et al.*, 2008b), but more work is needed to establish that the personalized campaign, customer management, and program management methods developed over the last 15 years create a strategic competitive advantage.

11.3.2 *Predictive modeling*

Drawing on its direct marketing heritage, CRM usually requires a model to relate marketing actions to customer behavior. Accordingly, much CRM research has centered on predictive modeling — the use of customer data to develop statistical models that predict customer behavior.

The first predictive model was the RFM framework, where R stands for recency (how recently the customer has purchased), F is for frequency (how frequently the customer has purchased over a given time period), and M signifies monetary value (the total amount spent during a given time period, or the amount spent per purchase) (see Blattberg, Kim, and Neslin, 2008, Chapter 12). Petrison, Blattberg, and Wang (1993) credit Alden's catalog company with developing these concepts in the 1920s, although the Direct Marketing Association recognizes George Cullinan as the concept's champion (http://www.the-dma.org/awards/hofinductees.shtml#1989). The RFM model is simple. Customers from a test or a previous campaign are binned into RFM categories, and the response rate is calculated for each category (Hughes, 1996; p. 169).

The staying power of RFM is a testament to the power of previous behavior to predict future behavior. Many modern predictive models use RFM measures as independent variables, even if they are embedded within a sophisticated econometric framework (e.g., Khan, Lewis, and Singh, 2009). Fader, Hardie, and Lee (2005a) related RFM to CLV. This was a key contribution because it showed the continued relevance of RFM even with regard to today's foremost CRM metric — CLV.

Two significant predictive modeling methods made their entrance in the 1970s — regression and decision trees. Regression includes linear (Cremer, 1974) as well as logistic regression (Bult and Wansbeek, 1995). The dependent variable might be customer-level measures of response, quantity bought, profit, or CLV. The independent variables often involved RFM as well as demographics and previous marketing efforts. Decision trees (CHAID and CART, Haughton and Oulabi, 1993, David Shepard Associates, 1999) provided a more accessible and implementable view of the determinants of customer response.

While RFM, regression, and decision trees each had their strong points, predictive accuracy was the primary concern, because the ability to separate responders from non-responders, highly profitable from not highly profitable customers, etc., went straight to the bottom line (Blattberg, Kim, and Neslin, 2008, Chapter 10). The field now had three viable methods — RFM, regression, and decision trees — with many more to come. To evaluate new methods, the field established the tradition of a "horse race", i.e., apply the current and new methods on the same calibration data and test them on the same holdout ("validation") data. The accuracy of the best model could then be traded off versus other issues such as diagnostics, ease of use, etc.

Accuracy was measured most often using a decile chart or lift table (Blattberg, Kim, and Neslin, 2008, Chapter 10; David Shepard Associates, 1999, Chapter 24). Lift tables rank order customers according to their predicted response likelihood, profitability, etc., and then bin them into deciles. Often the focus is on top decile lift — performance of the top decile relative to the average performance for the entire sample. Top-decile lifts often range from 2-to-1 to 5-to-1, e.g., the response rate in the top decile is 10%, whereas it is 2% for the entire sample.

Regression methods were soon enhanced by three developments: (1) multivariate statistics such as factor analysis (Cremer, 1974), which has more recently been updated by singular value decomposition methods (Ansari, 2013), and cluster analysis (Cremer, 1974; David Shepard Associates, 1999), (2) probability models (Bayus, 1993; Rao and Steckel, 1995), and (3) a series of advanced econometric models. Factor analysis and cluster analysis often worked hand in hand to provide orthogonal regressors for regression models (Cremer, 1974) or segmentation schemes within which analysts could run separate regression models. Probability models were a more flexible way to represent 0-1 response or customer decisions, compared to logistic regression. For example, Bayus used the Weibull distribution; Rao and Steckel used the beta distribution. Probability models were also used to represent purchase counts (e.g., Schmittlein, Morrison, and Colombo, 1987).

Advanced econometric models include customer-level decision models (e.g., Ansari, Mela, and Neslin, 2008), panel data regression addressing selectivity (e.g., Reinartz, 2008; Reinartz, Thomas, and Kumar, 2005), dynamic learning models (e.g., Hauser et al., 2009; Sun and Li, 2011), and models with unobserved heterogeneity (e.g., Khan, Lewis, and Singh, 2009). For example, if the researcher was estimating a customer-level model of customer acquisition and subsequent profit, the potential selection bias is that unobserved factors that influence acquisition also influence profit (Greene, 2008). If the interest was in measuring the impact of customer contacts on profit, the coefficients from an ordinary regression would be biased unless corrected for selectivity. The other models had their purposes as well. Dynamic learning models are useful when there is not enough history for a set of customers, so their predictive model must be learned over time. The goal of unobserved heterogeneity was either to make sure that response to marketing was estimated without bias (e.g., through incorporating a random effect), or to derive customer-specific response parameters. This was facilitated by the growth and acceptance of Bayesian estimation methods.

Note the progression from prediction toward prediction *plus* diagnostics. RFM and standard regression models were all about accurate predictions; multivariate statistics, probability models, and especially advanced econometrics were much more about diagnostics. This does not mean that predictive modeling had lost its way, but reflects the movement from campaign management to customer and program management.

The decision tree approach to predictive modeling presaged the emergence of machine learning methods. Machine learning emerged mostly in the computer science field (see Coussement, De Bock, and Neslin, 2013). Decision trees can be viewed as a machine learning method, albeit an elementary one. For example, the technique of bagging and boosting can be used to combine several decision trees into one predictive model (see Salford Systems http://www.salford-systems.com/en/products/treenet). Machine learning methods that have worked their way into CRM include neural nets (Zahavi and Levin, 1997), support vector machines (Coussement and Van den Poel, 2008), Bayesian networks (Cui, Wong, and Lui, 2006; Guo, Lee, and Wong, 2013), genetic algorithms (Bhattacharya, 1999), ensemble methods (Ha, Cho, and Maclachlan, 2005; De Bock and Coussement, 2013), bagging and boosting (Quinlan, 1996; Lemmens and Croux, 2006), and text mining (Coussement and De Bock, 2013). See Coussement, De Bock, and Neslin (2013) for a more complete review. The emphasis of most of these techniques is predictive accuracy. For example, there are several papers focused on predicting customer churn (e.g., Lemmens and Croux, 2006).

From a historical perspective, one might observe that predictive modeling has bifurcated into two areas — advanced econometric models that emphasize diagnostics, and machine learning methods that emphasize prediction. This may be a bit over-stated. Indeed, econometric models with unobserved heterogeneity can claim higher predictive accuracy, and machine learning methods, Bayesian networks for example, can claim ample diagnostics. In fact, machine learning methods of rule extraction are aimed at deriving diagnostics (see Verbraken *et al.*, 2013). However, one is struck by the prediction orientation of machine learning, and the diagnostics orientation of modern econometric models.

11.3.3 *Optimization*

Campaign management emphasizes the maximization of immediate profits. For example, profits for a traditional direct mail campaign can be calculated using the following formula:

$$\Pi = M \times r \times N - c \times N, \tag{11.1}$$

where M = profit margin per response, N = total number of customers contacted, r = response rate, and c = contact cost per customer contacted. Equation (11.1) yields the following break-even response rate:

$$r > c/M. \tag{11.2}$$

Equation (11.2) can be used to decide which deciles to mail to for the campaign. The key requirement is that the response rate of a decile be large enough to cover the contact cost relative to the benefit of a response.[1] Profits are optimized by contacting only the profitable customers.

Interestingly, the same math applies today to modern campaigns, for example a search advertising campaign. Here we have (Rutz and

---

[1]One difficulty is the uncertainty in the prediction of r, an issue addressed by Bult and Wansbeek (1995).

Bucklin, 2013):

$$\Pi = I \times CTR \times (M \times CVR - CPC), \qquad (11.3)$$

where $I =$ the number of impressions delivered by the search ad campaign, $CTR =$ the click-through rate, i.e., the percentages of impressions resulting in a click through (see Ghose and Yang, 2009), $CVR =$ the conversion rate, i.e., the fraction of click-throughs that result in a sale generating M in profit, and CPC is the cost-per-click, i.e., how much the firm pays the search ad vendor for each click. Equation (11.3) yields following break-even requirement:

$$CVR > CPC/M. \qquad (11.4)$$

Note the isomorphism between Eqs. (11.2) and (11.4), although they are separated by decades.

The concern with the above analysis is that it is myopic. It does not consider whether it is worthwhile to contact a customer because even though this contact may not be profitable today, it may keep the customer's awareness high and set up a more profitable contact later (see Neslin *et al.* (2013) discussion of the "recency trap"). The myopically managed search campaign does not consider that companies run several campaigns, and what does not break even in the short run may in fact break even in the long run.

The above suggests the need for dynamic optimization, i.e., making decisions today that take into account the ramifications for the future. The appearance of dynamic programming in the CRM literature began with early sales force management models (e.g., Beswick, 1977), but was brought to the fore in CRM by Gönül and Shi (1998). Dynamic programming relies on a description of the "state" of each customer, and derives a set of decision rules for what marketing action should be taken depending on the state. Because different customers are in different states, dynamic programming derives customer management actions that maximize the long-term value of the customer, usually measured by CLV (see Neslin, 2013; Blattberg, Kim, and Neslin, 2008).

Dynamic programming has become *de rigueur* in recent customer management CRM papers. There are several methods for calculating optimal dynamic policies (Judd, 1998; Ross, 1983) and with current computational power, these computations are becoming feasible. Customer management and dynamic programming go hand-in-hand. There are however challenges in implementation. One is that dynamic programming can have difficulties incorporating many state variables (it has to resort to approximations as the number of states for describing the customer, e.g., RFM and other measures, increases). In addition, predictive models based on unobserved heterogeneity generate different parameters for each customer; requiring millions of dynamic programs for implementation. Clearly, this is difficult not only for reasons of computer power, but also because it is difficult to infer customer-specific parameters for the millions of customers not included in model estimation.

In summary, optimization of myopic criteria such as campaign profit or annual profit is easy to do and useful. However, the evolution from campaign to customer and program management arguably requires that the customer be treated differently over time, and this requires dynamic optimization. A large component of academic research has accordingly moved from myopic to dynamic optimization. However, there are methodological challenges in doing so, fertile ground for future research.

11.3.4 *Marketing metrics*

As Figure 11.1 shows, the criteria initially used in CRM were profits, response, ROI, and revenues. These can apply to a given period and are therefore particularly applicable for campaign management. We saw in the previous section that profits and break-evens are relatively easy to calculate.

Underlying these metrics are more specific quantities such as response rate, contribution margin, and contact cost. An emerging area of debate involves cost metrics, particularly the relevance of fixed costs. The question is whether fixed costs should be included in profit calculations. Fixed costs are those that do not change as a function of the number of customers, e.g., the acquisition of 1000 customers may not require a new call center. Including fixed costs (F) would change

Eq. (11.1) as follows:

$$\Pi = M \times r \times N - c \times N - F. \qquad (11.5)$$

The break-even becomes:

$$r > [c/M + F/(N \times M)]. \qquad (11.6)$$

The response rate now must achieve a higher hurdle, by an amount $F/(N \times M)$, in order to break even (cf. Eq. 11.2). The debate between "marginal costers" and "fixed (or full) costers" is whether fixed costs should be included in evaluating CRM efforts (Blattberg, Kim, and Neslin, 2008, pp. 145–155). The marginal-cost argument is that if the program contributes profit over and above the direct costs associated with that program, the program should be undertaken. However, the full-costers argue that fixed costs are real and are included in the company's P&L statement. In order to run a profitable business, the fixed costs have to be covered, and using Eq. (11.5) as the profit calculation makes sure that the CRM effort covers its "fair" share of those fixed costs. The fixed versus marginal cost debate did not originate in CRM, but has emerged perhaps because many firms have made significant fixed investments in CRM technology.

Aside from this thorny issue, marketers were content with the simple profit calculations shown in Eq. (11.1) or (11.5). But during the 1960s, the concept of long-term or lifetime value emerged (Petrison, Blattberg, and Wang, 1993). The concept was that profits should include not only the current revenues generated by an acquired customer, but also the future revenues. The underlying reasoning was that the action taken with respect to a customer may not pay off immediately, but will in the long term because the action affects not only the immediate term but the long term as well. Blattberg, Kim, and Neslin, (2008, p. 106) define CLV as:

> The net present value of the profits linked to a specific customer once the customer has been acquired, after subtracting incremental costs associated with marketing, selling, production, and servicing over the customer's lifetime.

CLV² can be seen as corporate finance capital budgeting applied to customers. Accordingly, two key notions appear immediately, that future returns are uncertain, and that future profits are not worth as much as current profits, so need to be discounted. This is captured by Blattberg, Kim, and Neslin's general formula for lifetime value:

$$CLV = \sum_{t=1}^{\infty} \frac{E[\tilde{V}_t]}{(1+\delta)^{t-1}},$$ (11.7)

where $\tilde{V}_t$ is the customer's profit contribution in period t (a random variable), and δ is the discount rate the firm applies to future profits. The appropriate discount rate is largely ignored in the CRM literature. Theoretically the discount rate is the opportunity cost of capital for the firm's investors (Blattberg, Kim, and Neslin, 2008), and in practice is usually assumed to be somewhere between 5 and 15%. More attention has been devoted to modeling uncertain future profits. Two fundamental models have emerged — the simple retention model and the customer migration model. The simple retention model, which appeared first in the literature (see Simon, 1975) assumes that the key uncertainty is whether the customer will still be a customer several periods after acquisition.

The simple retention model held its own for several years. However, from the 1980s, companies began to realize that customers would naturally move in and out of their customer base. For example, a customer may visit a retailer in January, skip February through May, come back in June, purchase again in July, and not purchase again until November. This gave rise to the migration model of lifetime value. While there are many ways to formulate this notion, a simple way is to view customer purchasing as a Markov process, where the probability of purchasing in a given period depends on how long it has been since the last purchase (notice the reference to the "R" in RFM).

Distinguishing between the simple and migration models of lifetime value was a major advance in CRM. Jackson (1985) discussed

---

[2]Of historical interest is the evolution of LTV (lifetime value) to CLV (customer lifetime value) as the acronym for customer lifetime value. This author's impression is that the field has moved from LTV to CLV. For example, Dwyer (1989) uses LTV, while Berger and Nasr (1998) use CLV.

the "always-a-share" versus the "lost-for-good" model for describing the customer relationship (this terminology is still used today for migration and simple CLV models (e.g., Gupta and Zeithaml, 2006)). These notions were formalized by three highly significant papers: Dwyer (1989) showed how to compute CLV using both models and spreadsheet-like calculations. Berger and Nasr (1998) put both the simple and migration models in algebraic form, generalizing the concepts. Pfeifer and Carraway (2000) placed the migration model in a Markov process framework and derived matrix formulas for CLV.

These models focused on whether the customer acquired in period t would still be a customer in period $+ t'$. This of course is very important, but another crucial uncertain issue is how much the customer will *spend* if indeed the customer is still a customer in period $t + t'$; less attention has been paid to this issue, but important exceptions can be found in Kumar *et al.* (2008b), Fader, Hardie, and Lee (2005a), and Khan, Lewis, and Singh (2009).

An important conceptualization of lifetime value arose from stochastic models of customer profitability, originated by Schmittlein, Morrison, and Colombo (1987).[3] These models implicitly assumed a simple retention model, and modeled two phenomena: (1) is the customer still "alive" (i.e., has the customer been retained), and (2) if so, how many purchases will the customer make? The models assume that the alive probability is distributed across customers, as is the buying rate. Different models emerge depending on the specific distributions assumed. If customer lifetimes follow an exponential distribution, and purchases follow a Poisson distribution, and the parameters for both these distributions are distributed gamma across customers, then the probability a randomly selected customer is alive is governed by a Pareto distribution, and the number of purchases made in a given time period is governed by a negative binomial distribution. This is the Pareto/NBD model. This model was extended in important ways by and Fader, Hardie, and Lee (2005b). As mentioned earlier, Fader, Hardie, and Lee (2005a) showed that the Schmittlein *et al.* model could be used to calculate CLV, *and* that the calculation related directly to RFM variables.

---

[3] See the chapter "Stochastic Models of Buyer Behavior" by Fader, Hardie, and Sen, in this book.

This important paper linked three key streams of literature: stochastic models of customer profitability, lifetime value of the customer, and RFM. In addition, there have been important extensions to Fader *et al.*'s work. For example, Abe (2009) relaxed the assumption that the alive and purchase rate distributions were independent, and incorporated observable covariates into the formulation for heterogeneity.

A key concept that built on CLV is customer equity (Blattberg and Deighton, 1996; Blattberg, Getz, and Thomas, 2001; Villanueva and Hanssens, 2007). Customer equity includes acquisition success as well as acquisition cost, thereby providing a framework for developing programs to allocate resources to acquisition versus customer retention and development. A simple way to express the concept is:

$$CE = a \times CLV - A, \qquad (11.8)$$

where *CE* stands for customer equity, *a* is the acquisition rate (the percentage of prospects who are converted to customers, i.e., acquired), and *A* is expenditure per prospect. One sees just at the first level shown in Eq. (11.8) the rich trade-offs involved for a firm. If a firm spends a lot on acquiring prospects, it needs either a very high acquisition rate or high value in the prospects it acquires. Since acquisition rate, acquisition costs, and CLV are all functions of marketing effort, this funnels down to a question of resource allocation, captured very nicely for example by Reinartz, Thomas, and Kumar (2005) (see also Blattberg, Kim, and Neslin, 2008, Chapter 26).

In summary, we see a clear evolution of CRM metrics over time, from calculating immediate profit, to incorporating the future value of acquired customers (CLV), to including acquisition cost and success as well as the future value of acquired customers (CE).

The above discussion is direct-marketing-oriented; it looks at hard numbers such as retention rates, purchase rates, acquisition costs, etc. Yet CRM is about customer *relationships*. Customer perceptions of loyalty, satisfaction, product attributes, and mind-set equity are important indicators of relationships, and are sometimes used as objectives in and of themselves. However, since CRM is ultimately about acquisition, retention, and development, it is crucial to link perceptions to concrete metrics such as retention, acquisition rate, etc. One of the first to do so was Bolton (1998) who linked customer satisfaction to customer lifetime (essentially the reciprocal of the retention rate). Most recently, Stahl *et al.* (2012) related mind-set measures of brand equity to acquisition and retention in the automobile industry.

The work that has most thoroughly integrated the hard and the soft numbers is Rust, Lemon, and Zeithaml, (2004), based on Rust, Zeithaml, and Lemon (2000). Rust, Lemon, and Zeithaml, (2004) utilize a migration model of CLV, and show how customer perceptions of attributes such as quality, price, and convenience relate to the migration probabilities ("switching" probabilities in their terminology). The authors do not explicitly model customer acquisition, considering it part of the migration model. They therefore calculate customer equity as the mean CLV per customer multiplied by the total number of customers. With this framework in hand, the authors calculate "return on marketing," relating specific improvements in quality, price, or convenience to customer equity. This is highly significant work, showing that the soft measures such as attribute perceptions that define a customer relationship, relate to the hard measures of migration switching probabilities, and ultimately to CLV and CE.

11.4 An illustrative history of CRM applications

Table 11.1 provides an illustrative list of CRM applications over the last four decades. We have discussed several of these papers in this chapter, so instead will focus on the trends we can discern from the table. Several emerge:

First, there is a trend toward advanced econometric and machine learning predictive models. The advantages of machine learning methods are their predictive accuracy and ease of implementation (the computer science field is particularly concerned with implementation). The disadvantage is that there are fewer diagnostics and hence the models are less oriented toward resource allocation. The advantages of the econometric models are rigorous estimation of response elasticity to marketing actions, often measured at the customer level. These models are particularly well-suited for resource allocation at the customer level, i.e., customer management applications. A perusal of Table 11.1 shows that indeed many of these models have been used for customer management. The downside of the econometric models is implementation. A Bayesian estimation of

Table 11.1   Illustrative list of CRM applications

Paper	Predictive model	Optimization method	Key metric	Application	Domain
Cremer, 1974	Regression	Decile Analysis	Profit	Campaign	Direct Mail
Hicks, 1975	Multivariate	NA	Penetration	Campaign	New Products
Gensch, 1984	Logistic	Search	Revenues	Program	Sales Force/Direct Mail
Haughton & Oulabi, 1993	Decision Tree	Top Decile	Profit	Campaign	Direct Mail
Schmittlein & Peterson, 1994	Probability	Search	CLV	Customer	Customer Selection
Bult & Wansbeek, 1995	Probability	Marginal Cost/Return	Profit	Campaign	Direct Mail
Rao & Steckel, 1995	Probability	Positive Profit	Profit	Campaign	Prospecting
Levin & Zahavim, 1998	Logistic, Tobit	Decile Analysis	Response Rate	Campaign	Direct Mail
Gönül & Shi, 1998	Econometric	Dynamic Program	CLV	Customer	Catalog Mailing
Reinartz & Kumar, 2000	Probability	Decile Analysis	CLV	Customer	Selection for Direct Mail
Knott et al., 2002	Neural Net	Decile Analysis	ROI	Campaign	Cross-Selling
Ansari & Mela, 2003	Econometric	Integer Program	Click-through	Campaign-P	Email
Thomas et al., 2004	Econometric	Search	CLV	Program	Customer Win-Back Pricing
Reinartz et al., 2004	Regression	NA	Profit	Strategy	Assessment of CRM Process
Gupta et al., 2004	Regression	NA	CLV	Strategy	Firm Valuation
Rust et al., 2004	Econometric	NA	Customer Equity	Program	Resource Allocation
Reinartz et al., 2005	Econometric	Search	CLV — Migration	Program	Acquisition & Retention

(Continued)

Table 11.1   (*Continued*)

Paper	Predictive model	Optimization method	Key metric	Application	Domain
Fader *et al.*, 2005	Probability	NA	CLV	Customer	Profit segmentation
Thomas & Sullivan, 2005	Econometric	NA	NA	Program	Multichannel Communications
Cui *et al.*, 2006	Machine Learning	Decile Analysis	Response Rate	Campaign	Catalog Mailing
Venkatesan *et al.*, 2007	Probability	Genetic Algorithm	CLV — Migration	Customer	Resource Allocation
Bodapati, 2008	Econometric	Search	Profit	Campaign-P	Product Recommendations
Kumar, Venkatesan, & Rreinartz, 2008	Econometric	NA	Revenues	Campaign-P	Cross-Selling
Kumar *et al.*, 2008	Econometric	Genetic Algorithm	CLV	Customer	Resource Allocation
Khan *et al.*, 2009	Econometric	Dynamic Program	CLV	Customer	Coupons, Free Shipping
Montoya *et al.*, 2010	Econometric	Dynamic Program	CLV	Customer	Pharmaceutical Promotion
Wiesel *et al.*, 2011	Regression	NA	Profit	Program	Multichannel Communications
Sun & Li, 2011	Econometric	Dynamic Program	Profit	Program	Call Centers
Kopalle *et al.*, 2012	Econometric	Search	Revenues	Program	Loyalty Program
Stahl *et al.*, 2012	Regression	NA	CLV	Strategy	Brand Equity
Braun & Moe, 2012	Probability	Search	Web Visits	Customer	Targeted Banner Ads

Note: "Campaign-P" means a personalized campaign application.

an in........ce/choice/quantity model will yield customer-level parameters relating marketing actions to incidence, choice, and quantity. However, this is for the sample of customers considered. In order to implement these models, one needs to obtain customer-specific parameters for all the millions of the firm's customers. Overall, the rise of econometric and machine learning models is a major development in CRM; the question is whether they will go their separate ways or by some means be integrated.

Second, dynamic programming is appearing more often in the literature, although it does not dominate it. Orthodoxy dictates that customer management requires dynamic programming, i.e., that the CRM manager deciding whether to take an action with a particular customer should consider where the customer has been (the customer's state) and where the customer will go as a result of the action. The question however is how much is lost by not considering the future. Neslin *et al.* (2009) compare their dynamic program to a myopic greedy algorithm. They find that for their field test, the greedy algorithm would have done just as well as the dynamic program. However, they then show that if the requirements of their field test were different, the greedy algorithm would have come up short. The key question is whether real applications require both backward and forward looking, or can get by just with backward looking.

Third, applications have clearly moved from an emphasis on campaigns to customer management. That is, rather than first specifying the campaign and then deciding which customers are good for the campaign, the emphasis now is considering the individual customer and deciding what to do for that customer. This is a promising development and exemplifies the move from direct marketing to CRM.

Fourth, applications to CRM strategy are sparse. Issues such as firm valuation, core competence, and discerning the components of successful CRM have not received the attention they should have, given the promising start of Reinartz, Krafft, and Hoyer (2004) and Gupta, Lehmann, and Stuart (2004).

Overall, the trend is toward sophisticated statistics — either econometric models or machine learning — coupled with customer management applications that may or may not directly incorporate CLV. Another trend, just emerging, is the application of CRM to the online domain. We mention one working paper in Table 11.1 (Braun and Moe, 2012), but there are other recent papers and surely more to come (see Moe, 2013; Rutz and Bucklin, 2013; Mayzlin, 2013; Ghose and Han, 2013).

11.5 Summary and what next

We have traced the origins and development of the CRM field in marketing science. There have been several key steps along the way, summarized as follows:

- CRM emerged as a fusion of direct marketing and relationship marketing.
- Applications have moved from campaign management to customer and program management.
- CRM applications draw on three methodological components: predictive models, optimization, and marketing metrics.
- The predictive modeling field has progressed from simple RFM models to regression and decision trees to sophisticated econometric and machine learning methods.
- Dynamic programming has seen more use, but this evolution is by no means complete.
- Key "hard" marketing metrics have moved from immediate-term profit, ROI, response rate, etc. to CLV and finally to the integrative concept of customer equity (CE). CLV and CE in turn have their own "sub-metrics" — retention rate (or its inverse, churn), migration probabilities, contribution margin, contact costs, acquisition rate, etc.
- The "soft" CRM metrics, which in fact define customer relationship, have received more attention over time, but are not standard in many CRM applications.
- The field is accelerating with many key contributions during the past decade.

What holds next for the field? There are several specific areas and we highlight a few:

- More work is needed on program management, particularly the *design and management* of loyalty programs, churn management programs, recommendation systems, and multichannel programs. Much work has been done on how customers respond to elements of these programs (Blattberg, Kim, and Neslin, 2008), but future work needs to develop decision support for program design and management (Gupta and Lehmann, 2005).

- We need to sort out the roles of econometric versus machine learning tools, and whether they can be combined into one application.
- We need to determine whether dynamic programs, which look both forward and backward, are *necessary* for customer management, or whether models that just look backward are sufficient. Another way of looking at this is, how necessary is it to explicitly maximize CLV? Or perhaps more specifically, *when* is it necessary?
- More work is needed to deepen our understanding of what a relationship really is from the perspective of the customer, and what role this relationship plays. For example, it may be that a recommendation program is working fine from a CLV perspective, but doing nothing to create a relationship in the sense that Fournier articulates it. A high CLV does not mean the customer perceives a *relationship* with that firm. Even positive customer perceptions of attributes such as quality and convenience are imperfect indicators of a true relationship with the firm. Also, there may be "relationship-prone" and "transactional" segments. What are the relative sizes of these segments? Can CRM manage the non-relationship-prone segment, or is this simply an oxymoron?
- Internet marketing is the next frontier for CRM. A strategic question is whether in fact relationships can be forged in an online environment. There are programmatic questions of how to leverage the online channel to complement or substitute for other channels. And finally, with the increasing ability of firms to identify customers in an online environment (see Singer, 2012; Moe, 2013), what tools and applications will be used to manage customer relationships in this environment?
- Do we need more methods, or do we have the methods we need and is it just a question of putting them together? For example, do we need new methods to extrapolate customer-specific response from sample to the full customer base?
- We need much more work on CRM strategy. How should firms organize to implement CRM? Is CE a reliable framework for valuing firms,

especially those not publically traded? How do we coordinate brand equity and customer equity? Most importantly, is CRM a source of competitive advantage, and if so, under what conditions?

- What role will privacy play? How can firms take a proactive stance with regard to privacy, perhaps through active use of opt-in? This is especially important in new channels such as mobile devices.
- More work is needed based on analytical models. While there has been some excellent analytical work in CRM (e.g., Chen, Narasimhan, and Zhang, 2001), we need to understand for example whether the multichannel movement is a prisoner's dilemma or a way for all firms to benefit. We need to understand under what conditions firms will rely more on search advertising, mobile devices, or banner ads — these differ in which stage of the customer's decision analysis stage they address.

The history of CRM has seen rapid and exciting development. Judging from what has been accomplished to date, coupled with what more needs to be done, and with the superior tools and data now available, there is every reason to believe that the next four decades will be as productive and impactful on the practice of management, as the previous four decades.

References

Abe, M. (2009). Counting your customers' one by one: A hierarchical Bayes extension to the Pareto/NBD model, *Marketing Science*, 28(3), 541–553.

Ansari, A. (2013). Hybrid models for recommender systems, in K. Coussement, K. W. De Bock, and S. A. Neslin, eds., *Advanced database marketing*, London: Gower Publishing.

Ansari, A. and C. F. Mela (2003). E-Customization, *Journal of Marketing Research*, 40(2), 131–145.

Ansari, A., C. F. Mela, and S. A. Neslin (2008). Customer channel migration, *Journal of Marketing Research*, 45(1), 60–76.

Ansari, A., S. Essengaier, and R. Kohli (2000). Internet recommendation systems, *Journal of Marketing Research*, 37(3), 363–375.

Bayus, B. L. (1993). The targeted marketing of consumer durables, *Journal of Direct Marketing*, 7(4), 4–13.

Berger, P. D. and N. I. Nasr (1998). Customer lifetime value: Marketing models and applications, *Journal of Interactive Marketing*, 12(1), 17–30.

Berry, L. L. (1983). Relationship marketing, in L. L. Berry, G. I. Shostack, and G. Upah, eds., *Emerging perspectives in services marketing*, Chicago, IL: American Marketing Association, pp. 25–28.

Beswick, C. A. (1977). Allocating selling effort via dynamic programming, *Management Science*, 23(7), 667–678.

Bhattacharya, S. (1999). Direct marketing performance modeling using genetic algorithms, *Journal of Computing*, 11(3), 248–257.

Bijmolt, T. H. A., M. Dorotic, and P. Verhoef (2010). Loyalty programs: Generalizing on their adoption, effectiveness, and design, *Foundations and Trends in Marketing*, 5(4), 197–258.

Blattberg, R. C. and J. Deighton (1991). Interactive marketing: Exploiting the age of addressability, *Sloan Management Review*, 83(1), 5–14.

Blattberg, R. C. and J. Deighton (1996). Manage marketing by the customer equity test, *Harvard Business Review*, 17(4), 136–144.

Blattberg, R. C., B. D. Kim, and S. A. Neslin (2008). *Database marketing: Analyzing and managing customers*, New York: Springer.

Blattberg, R. C., G. Getz, and J. S. Thomas (2001). *Customer equity: Building and managing relationships as valuable assets*, Boston, MA: Harvard Business School Press.

Bodapati, A. V. (2008). Recommendation systems with purchase data, *Journal of Marketing Research*, 45(1), 77–93.

Bolton, R. N. (1998). A dynamic model of the duration of the customer's relationship with a continuous service provider, *Marketing Science*, 17(1), 45–65.

Bolton, R. N. and C. O. Tarasi (2007). Managing customer relationships, in N. K. Malhotra, ed., *Review of marketing research*, Volume 3, Emerald Group Publishing Limited, pp. 3–38.

Braun, J. and W. Moe (2012). Online advertising response models: Incorporating multiple creatives and impression histories, Working Paper, Cambridge, MA: Sloan School of Management, MIT.

Bult, J. R. and T. Wansbeek (1995). Optimal selection for direct mail, *Marketing Science*, 14(4), 378–394.

Chen, Y., C. Narasimhan, and Z. J. Zhang (2001). Individual marketing with imperfect targetability, *Marketing Science*, 20(1), 23–41.

Chu, J., P. K. Chintagunta, and N. J. Vilcassim (2007). Assessing the economic value of distribution channels: An application to the personal computer industry, *Journal of Marketing Research*, 44(1), 29–41.

Coussement, K. and D. Van den Poel (2008). Churn prediction in subscription services: An application of support vector machines while comparing two parameter-selection techniques, *Expert Systems with Applications*, 34(1), 313–327.

Coussement, K. and K. W. De Bock (2013). Textual customer data handling for quantitative marketing analytics, in K. Coussement, K. W. De Bock, and S. A. Neslin, eds., *Advanced database marketing*, London: Gower Publishing.

Coussement, K., K. W. De Bock, and S. A. Neslin (2013). *Advanced database marketing*, London: Gower Publishing.

Cremer, R. (1974). How to find treasure in your customer file, *Direct Marketing*, 37(3), pp. 40, 42, 44, and 46.

Cui, G., M. L. Wong, and H. K. Lui (2006). Machine learning for direct marketing response models: Bayesian networks with evolutionary programming, *Management Science*, 52(4), 597–612.

David Shepard Associates, Inc. (1999). *The new direct marketing*, Boston: McGraw Hill.

De Bock, K.W. and K. Coussement (2013). Ensemble learning in database marketing, in K. Coussement, K. W. De Bock, and S. A. Neslin, eds., *Advanced database marketing*, London: Gower Publishing.

Dorotic, M., T. H. A. Bijmolt, and P. C. Verhoef (2012). Loyalty programmes: Current knowledge and future directions, *International Journal of Research in Marketing*, 14(3), 217–237.

Dwyer, F. R. (1989). Customer valuation to support marketing decision making, *Journal of Direct Marketing*, 3(4), 8–15.

Fader, P. S. and B. G. S. Hardie (2009). Probability models for customer-base analysis, *Journal of Interactive Marketing*, 23(1), 61–69.

Fader, P. S., B. G. S. Hardie, and K. L. Lee (2005a). RFM and CLV: Using iso-value curves for customer base analysis, *Journal of Marketing Research*, 42(4), 415–430.

Fader, P. S., B. G. S. Hardie, and K. L. Lee (2005b). Counting your customers the easy way: An alternative to the Pareto/NBD model, *Marketing Science*, 24(2), 275–284.

Fournier, S. (1998). Consumers and their brands: Developing relationship theory in consumer research, *Journal of Consumer Research*, 24(4), 343–373.

Gensch, D. H. (1984). Targeting the switchable industrial customer, *Marketing Science*, 3(1), 41–54.

Ghose, A. and S. P. Han (2013). Marketing in the new mobile economy, in K. Coussement, K., K. W. De Bock, and S. A. Neslin, eds., *Advanced database marketing*, London: Gower Publishing.

Ghose, A. and S. Yang (2009). An empirical analysis of search engine advertising: Sponsored search in electronic markets, *Management Science*, 59(10), 1605–1622.

Gönül, F. and M. Z. Shi (1998). Optimal mailings of catalogs: A new methodology using estimate structural dynamic programming models, *Management Science*, 44(9), 1249–1262.

Greene, W. H. (2008). *Econometric analysis*, 6th edn., Upper Saddle River, NJ: Pearson.

Guo, Y. Y., S. Y. Lee, and M. L. Wong (2013). Bayesian networks and their application to marketing, in K. Coussement, K. W. De Bock, and S. A. Neslin, eds., *Advanced database marketing*, London: Gower Publishing.

Gupta, S. and D. R. Lehmann (2005). *Managing your customers as assets*, Upper Saddle River, NJ: Wharton School Publishing.

Gupta, S. and V. Zeithaml (2006). Customer metrics and their impact on financial performance, *Marketing Science*, 25(6), 718–739.

Gupta, S., D. R. Lehmann, and J. A. Stuart (2004). Valuing customers, *Journal of Marketing Research*, 41(1), 7–18.

Ha, K., S. Cho, and D. Maclachlan (2005). Response models based on bagging neural networks, 19(1), 17–30.

Haughton, D. and S. Oulabi (1993). Direct marketing modeling with CART and CHAID, *Journal of Direct Marketing*, 11(4), 42–52.

Hauser, J. R., G. L. Urban, G. Liberali, and M. Braun (2009). Website morphing, *Marketing Science*, 28(2), 202–223.

Hughes, A. M. (1996). *The complete database marketer*, Revised edn., New York: McGraw-Hill.

Jackson, B. B. (1985). Build customer relationships that last, *Harvard Business Review*, November–December, 120–128.

Judd, K. L. (1998). *Numerical methods in economics*, Cambridge, MA: Massachusetts Institute of Technology.

Khan, R., M. Lewis, and V. Singh (2009). Dynamic customer management and the value of one-to-one marketing, *Marketing Science*, 28(6), 1063–1079.

Knott, A., A. Hayes, and S. A. Neslin (2002). Next-product-to-buy models for cross-selling applications, *Journal of Interactive Marketing*, 16(3), 59–75.

Kopalle, P. K. and S.A. Neslin (2003). The economic viability of frequency reward programs in a strategic competitive environment, *Review of Marketing Science* 1(1). Available at: http://www.degruyter.com/view/j/roms.2003.1.1_20120105044856/roms.2003.1.1/roms.2003.1.1.1002/roms.2003.1.1.1002.xml (accessed November 2012).

Kopalle, P. K., Y. Sun, S. A. Neslin, B. Sun, and V. Swaminathan (2012). The joint sales impact of frequency reward and customer tier components of loyalty programs, *Marketing Science*, 31(2), 216–235.

Kumar, V. and W. J. Reinartz (2006). *Customer relationship management: A databased approach*, Hoboken, NJ: John Wiley & Sons, Inc.

Kumar, V., R. Venkatesan, and W. Reinartz (2008a). Performance implications of adopting a customer-focused sales campaign, *Journal of Marketing*, 72(5), 50–68.

Kumar, V., R. Venkatesan, T. Bohling, and D. Beckmann (2008b). The power of CLV: Managing customer lifetime value at IBM, *Marketing Science*, 27(4), 585–599.

Lemmens, A. and C. Croux (2006). Bagging and boosting classification trees to predict churn, *Journal of Marketing Research*, 43(2), 276–286.

Levin, N. and J. Zahavi (1998). Continuous predictive modeling — A Comparative Analysis, *Journal of Interactive Marketing*, 12(2), 5–22.

Li, S. B. Sun and A. L. Montgomery (2011). Cross-selling the right product to the right customer at the right time, *Journal of Marketing Research*, 48(4), 683–700.

Mayzlin, D. (2013). Social media management, in K. Coussement, K. W. De Bock, and S. A. Neslin, eds., *Advanced database marketing*, London: Gower Publishing.

Moe, W. (2013). Targeting display advertising, in K. Coussement, K. W. De Bock, and S. A. Neslin, eds., *Advanced database marketing*, London: Gower Publishing.

Montoya, R., O. Netzer, and K. Jedidi (2010). Dynamic allocation of pharmaceutical detailing and sampling for long-term profitability, *Marketing Science*, 29(5), 909–924.

Neslin, S. A. (2013). Dynamic customer optimization models, in K. Coussement, K. W. De Bock, and S. A. Neslin, eds., *Advanced database marketing*, London: Gower Publishing.

Neslin, S. A., T. P. Novak, K. R. Baker, and D. L. Hoffman (2009). An optimal contact model for maximizing online panel response rates, *Management Science*, 55(5), 727–737.

Neslin, S. A., G. A. Taylor, K. D. Grantham, and K. R. McNeil (2013). Overcoming the 'recency trap' in customer relationship management, *Journal of the Academy of Marketing Science*, 41(3), 320–337.

Neslin, S. A., S. Gupta, W. Kamakura, J. Lu, and C. H. Mason (2006a). Defection detection: Measuring and understanding the predictive accuracy of customer churn models, *Journal of Marketing Research*, 43(2), 204–211.

Neslin, S. A., D. Grewal, R. Leghorn, V. Shankar, M. L. Teerling, J. S. Thomas, and P. C. Verhoef (2006b). Challenges and opportunities in multi-channel customer management, *Journal of Service Research*, 9(2), 95–112.

Peppers, D. and M. Rogers (1993). *The one to one future: Building relationships one customer at a time*, New York: Doubleday.

Peppers, D. and M. Rogers (1997). *Enterprise one to one: Tools for competing in the interactive age*, New York: Doubleday.

Petrison, L. A., R. C. Blattberg, and P. Wang (1993). Database marketing: Past, present, and Future, *Journal of Direct Marketing*, 7(3), 27–43.

Pfeifer, P. E. and R. L. Carraway (2000). Modeling customer relationships as Markov chains, *Journal of Interactive Marketing*, 14(2), 43–55.

Quinlan, J. R. (1996). Bagging, boosting, and C4.5, *Proceedings of the Fourteenth National Conference on Artificial Intelligence*, Menlo Park, CA: AAAI Press.

Rao, V. R. and J. H. Steckel (1995). Selecting, evaluating, and updating prospects in direct mail marketing, *Journal of Direct Marketing*, 9(2) 20–31.

Reinartz, W. J. and V. Kumar (2000). On the profitability of long-life customers in a noncontractual setting: An empirical investigation and implications for marketing, *Journal of Marketing*, 64(4), 17–35.

Reinartz, W., M. Krafft, and W. D. Hoyer (2004). The customer relationship management process: Its measurement and impact on performance, *Journal of Marketing Research*, 41(3), 293–305.

Reinartz, W., J. S. Thomas, and V. Kumar (2005). Balancing acquisition and retention resources to maximize customer profitability, *Journal of Marketing*, 69(1), 63–69.

Ross, S. (1983). *Introduction to stochastic dynamic programming*, New York: Academic Press.

Rust, R. T., K. N. Lemon, and V. A. Zeithaml (2004). Return on marketing using customer equity to focus marketing strategy, *Journal of Marketing*, 68(1), 109–127.

Rust, R. T., V. A. Zeithaml, and K. N. Lemon (2000). *Driving customer equity: How customer lifetime value is reshaping corporate strategy*, New York: The Free Press.

Rutz, O. J. and R. E. Bucklin (2013). Paid search advertising, in K. Coussement, K. W. De Bock, and S. A. Neslin, eds., *Advanced database marketing*, London: Gower Publishing.

Schmittlein, D. C. and R. A. Peterson (1994). Customer base analysis: An industrial purchase process application, *Marketing Science*, 13(1), 41–67.

Schmittlein, D. C., D. G. Morrison, and R. Colombo (1987). Counting your customers: Who are they and what will they do next, *Management Science*, 33(1), 1–24.

Scott, S.L. (2010). A Modern Bayesian Look at the Multi-Armed Bandit, *Applied Stochastic Models in Business and Industry*, 26(6), 639–658.

Simester, D. L., P. Sun, and J. N. Tsitsiklis (2006). Dynamic catalog mailing policies, *Management Science*, 52(5), 683–696.

Simon, J. (1975). How much is your customer worth to your firm's goal? *Direct Marketing*, 38(6), pp. 80, 82, 86, 88, 90, and 92.

Singer, N. (2012). Shoppers, meet your scorekeeper, *New York Times*, Sunday Business, pp. 1–4, Sunday, August 19, 2012.

Stahl, F., M. Heitmann, D. R. Lehmann, and S. A. Neslin (2012). The impact of brand equity on customer acquisition, retention, and profit margin, *Journal of Marketing*, 76(4), 44–63.

Sun, B. and S. Li (2011). Learning and acting on customer information: A simulation-based demonstration on service allocations with offshore centers, *Journal of Marketing Research*, 48(1), 72–86.

Thomas, J. S. and U. Y. Sullivan (2005). Managing marketing communications with multichannel customers, *Journal of Marketing*, 69(4), 239–251.

Thomas, J. S., R. C. Blattberg, and E. J. Fox (2004). Recapturing lost customers, *Journal of Marketing Research*, 41(91), 31–45.

Venkatesan, R., V. Kumar, and T. Bohling (2007). Optimal customer relationship management using Bayesian decision theory: An application for customer selection, *Journal of Marketing Research*, 44(4), 579–594.

Verbraken, T., V. V. Vlasselaer, W. Verbeke, D. Martens, and B. Baesens (2013). Advanced rule base learning: Active learning, rule extraction, and incorporating domain knowledge, in K. Coussement, K. W. De Bock, and S. A. Neslin, eds., *Advanced database marketing*, London: Gower Publishing.

Villanueva, J. and D. M. Hanssens (2007). Customer equity: Measurement, management and research opportunities, *Foundations and Trends in Marketing*, 1(1), 1–95.

Wiesel, T., K. Pauwels, and J. Arts (2011). Marketing's profit impact: Quantifying online and off-line funnel progression, *Marketing Science*, 30(4), 604–611.

Wikipedia (2012). Available at: http://en.wikipedia.org/wiki/John_Wanamaker (accessed November 2012).

Zahavi, J. and N. Levin (1997). Applying neural computing to target Marketing, *Journal of Direct Marketing*, 11(1), 5–22.

Chapter 12

Digital and Internet Marketing

Wendy W. Moe and David A. Schweidel

12.1 Introduction

Early research in Internet marketing took advantage of clickstream data to shed light on the consumer purchase process. Clickstream data, collected either from a website's server logs or a panel of participants managed by a third party research firm, tracked individual pageviews and actions across the Internet. For an e-commerce store, this means that each consumer's path to purchase can be carefully examined and studied. What does the sequence of pageviews tell us about the customer's motivations, preferences, etc.? Does a customer's search behavior help us predict his/her future purchasing behavior? What products did they view in the consideration stage and how does that relate to their final purchasing decision? Several researchers have developed models for clickstream data that answer these questions, and we will discuss these clickstream models in this chapter.

In a parallel stream of research, digital marketing also offered the promise of increased accountability in advertising. For the first time, we can expose individuals to advertisements and then track their purchase of the featured item. Consumers were also able to interact with the ads by clicking on them; when they did, they would be directed to the advertiser's website for more information, a behavior that was also tracked. Thus, advertisers began to measure the effectiveness of their online ads by monitoring how much consumers interacted with them (e.g., clickthrough) and how much they affected purchasing (e.g., purchase conversion). While the data available to online advertisers was superior to that available to offline advertisers from an accountability perspective, the online environment

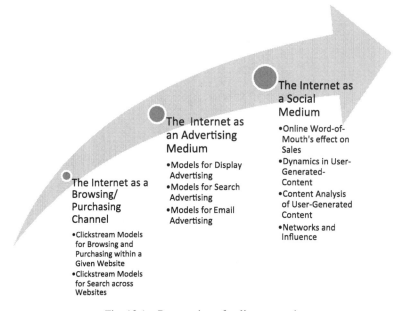

Fig. 12.1   Progression of online research

brought unique challenges that made researchers devise new advertising response models, which we discuss in this chapter.

Understanding the path to purchase and advertising response have been tried and true problems addressed in marketing science that were now being investigated in the online domain. Additionally, as the Internet evolved, the online environment moved from being a broadcast and commerce channel, in which sellers could reach consumers, to one in which consumers could also interact with one another. Thus, online researchers also began to investigate the Internet as a social medium, spawning further research into online word-of-mouth, user-generated content (UGC) and social network behaviors (Figure 12.1).

In this chapter, we discuss the models and methods developed by marketing scientists to investigate the unique research problems presented by the new digital environment. We start by discussing the clickstream models that have focused on consumer browsing and online buying. In other words, we focus on the models that helped marketing scientists better understand the Internet as a browsing/purchasing channel. We then turn to the research that examines the Internet as an advertising medium and discuss research into online advertising response. We also discuss how consumers use the Internet as a social medium and provide an overview of the growing social media research. We conclude by discussing key directions for future research.

12.2 The Internet as a browsing/purchasing channel

Clickstream research was initially seen by marketing scientists as a window into the consumer purchasing process. The Internet provided valuable clickstream data that recorded each and every page a consumer viewed and allowed researchers to link each sequence of pageviews to a purchasing decision. To take advantage of this data, researchers developed models that captured an individual's browsing behavior both within a website and across multiple websites. These models can be important tools for marketing scientists who need to better understand consumer behavior in this new environment. For example, Hoffman and Novak (1996) explore the concept of "flow," a state in which the consumer is fully immersed in online browsing, and its relation to consumption behavior.

12.2.1 *Clickstream models for browsing and purchasing within a given website*

Early research focused on an individual's browsing behavior at a single website, partly because the data were easy to obtain from each site's log files and third-party research firms. Each time a user visited the website and requested to view a page, the website's server log would record that activity. The result was an abundance of data on (1) when users visited a site and (2) what pages they viewed. Thus, initial clickstream models focused on these two behaviors.

One of the first efforts to examine website visit behavior was a study that analyzed the data from a panel of visitors across 36 different websites by Johnson, Bellman, and Lohse (2003). Specifically, they examined how the duration of an individual's visit to a website varied with the number of times that an individual visited the same site. Applying the power law of practice, they posited that consumers learn over time and become more efficient at using a given website to accomplish their goal, whether that goal is to gather information or to make a purchase.

In an effort to explicitly incorporate dynamics in visit behavior, Moe and Fader (2004a) developed a duration model in which the rate at which individuals visit the website evolved over time. Importantly, they allow for a multiplier that either accelerates or decelerates visiting rates to vary across visitors and visits. In their empirical context, visitation decelerated over time (i.e., visitors returned less frequently over time), a result that is consistent with the theory that visitors are learning to use the website more efficiently over time.

From the e-commerce site's perspective, there is clear value in understanding an individual's pattern of website visits if it related to their purchasing behavior at that site. Since purchasing conversion rates (i.e., the percentage of visits that included a purchase transaction) were notoriously low (e.g., according to Forrester Reports, the average conversion rate in 2009 was just 3.4%), it was important to understand how repeat visits contributed to subsequent purchasing. In other words, even if a given visit did not result in an immediate purchase, it may still have value and contribute to future purchasing. Moe and Fader (2004b) examined how past visiting may affect the likelihood of purchase conversion. They proposed an individual-level stochastic model of purchasing in a given visit, allowing the purchase probability to shift as more visits are made. To capture the dynamics in conversion behavior, Moe and Fader (2004b) assume that prior visits positively contribute to the likelihood of purchase and that customers' baseline purchasing tendencies may change as they make more purchases and gain experience at the site. While the authors find support for a positive effect of visits on the likelihood of purchasing consistent with Johnson, Bellman, and Lohse (2003), they also find that the baseline purchasing tendencies decline as customers make repeated purchases over time, the net effect being a decreased likelihood of purchase over time in this empirical application.

As researchers began to link website visiting behavior to purchase, the focus shifted from visits as the unit of analysis to pageviews. That is, rather than examining an individual's sequence of website visits over time, researchers began to model the specific pages each visitor viewed when they were at the website.

Bucklin and Sismeiro (2003) examined two aspects of an individual's browsing behavior: the decision of whether or not to continue viewing pages at the website and, conditional on viewing an additional page at the site, the amount of time spent on the page. The authors measured the effects of a number of covariates on each of these two component behaviors, including the number of pages previously viewed on the site during the session and the number of visits made to the website. These covariates allowed the authors to examine the extent of "within-site lock-in" and learning across sessions, the latter posited by Johnson, Bellman, and Lohse (2003). They find support for both of these behavioral phenomena. With regards to "within-site lock-in," the authors find that the time spent on pages increases with the number of pages previously viewed in the session. Consistent with learning across sessions, the authors also find that the duration spent on a website decreased over the course of subsequent visits. This decrease was attributed mainly to the decrease in number of pages viewed rather than any decrease in the duration of pageviews, suggesting that perhaps consumers were becoming more efficient in navigating the website.

In subsequent research, Sismeiro and Bucklin (2004) incorporated within-visit pageviews into a model of online purchasing. The authors employ a choice model for different stages that comprised the purchase process and modeled customers' progression through each stage of the process, with a purchase requiring the successful completion of each stage. By decoupling different stages of the purchase process, the work offers insights that could be employed for dynamically targeting customers based on their progress through the purchase process.

In an effort to better understand pageview data, Moe (2003) offered a typology of behavior that characterized visits based on their pages viewed in that visit. She distinguished between visits along two dimensions: search behavior and purchasing horizon. Search behavior could be characterized as goal-directed or exploratory. Whereas goal-directed search occurs when visitors have a particular purchase in mind, exploratory search is less deliberate. The second dimension focused on the likely purchasing horizon and differentiated between visitors who intend to make an immediate purchase and those with a longer purchase horizon.

This 2 × 2 typology (Table 12.1) yields four different online shopping strategies. *Directed buying* occurs when a visitor is goal-directed and plans on purchasing immediately. These visits tend to be short and focused around specific products and categories. *Search and deliberation* occurs

Table 12.1   Online shopper typology

Purchasing horizon	Search behavior	
	Directed	Exploratory
Immediate	Directed-Buying	Hedonic-Browsing
Future	Search/Deliberation	Knowledge-Building

when a goal-directed visitor plans on purchasing sometime in the future. These visits are focused on information gathering within a specific product category, perhaps involving the consideration and evaluation of multiple products within the category. *Hedonic browsing* visits are more exploratory in nature but may still result in purchases in the short-term horizon (e.g., impulse buying). However, these visits are likely to span multiple product categories and appear less focused, as they are exploratory in nature. Lastly, *knowledge building* trips allow visitors to gather the necessary information for a purchase that will be made farther in the future. Such trips are likely to be marked by a focus on informational pages rather than product or category pages.

To differentiate these different types of visits from clickstream data, Moe (2003) constructed a number of different metrics that described each visit: (1) general session measures (e.g., number of page views and average time spent on each page), (2) the allocation of time across different types of pages (e.g., percent of pages that were information-related, number of category pages viewed, number of product pages viewed), (3) variety measures (e.g., percent of brand pages that were unique, percent of product pages that were unique), (4) repeat product viewing and, ultimately, (5) purchasing. A cluster analysis based only on the pageview data (and excluding purchasing data) revealed distinct clusters that corresponded to the four types of browsing behaviors previously mentioned. The findings reveal notable variation in browsing activity across individuals over time for a given individual and related to the content of the website, providing the foundation for marketers to dynamically target customers.

Montgomery *et al.* (2004) also incorporate within-site browsing activities into their model of a visitor's path to purchase. The authors employ a dynamic multinomial probit model for the sequence of pages that a customer visits, allowing for a visitor's past behavior to affect the likelihood of visiting different types of pages and allude to the possibility of using path data to dynamically customize a website. Hauser *et al.* (2009) demonstrate the benefits of customizing the layout of a website to best suit a visitor's cognitive style and increase the likelihood with which they will make a purchase. By showing each visitor her "optimal" version of the website, the authors demonstrate increases in purchase intentions of approximately 20%.

Finally, models have also been developed to uncover consumer utility functions and decision rules based on pageview data. Specifically, Moe (2006a) modeled consumer purchasing at an online retailer as a two-stage process. The visitor chooses a set of products to view in the first stage and then chooses one product among this set to purchase (if they purchase anything at all) in the second stage. The two stages are linked by a single utility function that is determined by the consumer's value for various product attributes, but different attributes may affect each stage of the decision process. Consistent with offline behavioral decision theories, Moe (2006a) found that fewer attributes affected the decision as to which products to view when compared to the number of attributes that affected the final choice as to which product to purchase.

12.2.2 *Clickstream models for search across websites*

In addition to research investigating consumers' browsing behavior within a particular website, methods were also developed to understand consumers' activities across multiple websites. Johnson *et al.* (2004) explore the depths and dynamics of search behavior across multiple websites. The authors break the search process down into three underlying components: depth of search, dynamics of search, and activity of search and find that most consumers only search a limited number of websites, despite the lower search costs online (compared to offline search costs). The authors also find that the heaviest online shoppers tend to be more active searchers.

While Johnson *et al.* (2004) investigate search behavior across multiple websites, their analysis does not shed light on the individual-level process governing visits to different sites. Park and Fader (2004) do so using clickstream data that tracked consumers' browsing at two different websites in the same product category. The authors develop a duration model that allows for: (1) an individual's visiting rate at one website to be linked to that at another website and (2) coincidence in time at which visits to the websites occur. The authors find evidence of positive coincidence, with visitors more likely to visit one website if they have visited the other website in the recent past.

Understanding the patterns that exist in consumers' behavior across multiple websites is key for marketers interested in gauging the reach and frequency of online advertising. If those consumers who visit one website are very likely to visit another particular website, advertising on both websites may have a limited impact on the reach of an advertisement, but will increase the frequency with which visitors see the advertisement. Danaher (2007) builds on the work of Park and Fader (2004), generalizing the bivariate analysis to consider advertising on multiple websites. He shows that accounting for the correlation that exists in visiting behavior across multiple websites yields more accurate estimates of reach and frequency. Later, Danaher, Lee, and Kerbache (2010) demonstrate how this modeling approach can be put to use to optimize an online media schedule.

12.3   The Internet as an advertising medium

While the research discussed thus far investigated consumer behavior after the consumers visited websites, firms expend significant resources on advertising campaigns that drive traffic to their websites. A variety of ad formats are available to the online marketer. Display ads are the online equivalent of the traditional print ads we see offline, which appear on high-traffic web pages. Search ads appear when we use a search engine and usually target those who search for specific key words. Finally, e-mail ad campaigns are similar to direct mail campaigns that reach out to specific individuals on a targeted contact list. Models have been developed for each of these online ad formats, and we will discuss each of them in this chapter.

One notable challenge that has emerged in the online advertising environment is attribution. Given that most marketers employ multiple online ad formats in addition to offline advertisements, how do we attribute our successes across our different advertising outlets? How much of our sales lift is due to offline versus online advertising? How much of our sales lift is due to display ads versus search ads versus e-mail campaigns? And within each format, how much of our sales lift can be attributed to each ad impression?

Before we delve into the models that have been designed for specific ad formats, we discuss some of the efforts that have identified cross-channel effects. That is, how does offline advertising affect online behavior and vice versa? Ilfeld and Winer (2002) provide an investigation of how offline and online advertising drive awareness, online traffic and brand equity. The authors conclude that online advertising directly drives website traffic without necessarily contributing to increased awareness. The impact of offline advertising is to build awareness, which in turn contributes to website traffic. Dinner, van Heerde, and Neslin (2011) also found evidence of multi-channel advertising effects. In their study, not only did offline advertising impact online sales, but the reverse was also true.

12.3.1 *Models for display advertising*

In addition to the studies mentioned above, several other researchers have also documented significant effects of online display advertising. Chatterjee, Hoffman, and Novak (2003) find that an individual's likelihood of clicking through on an ad decreases (non-linearly) with repeated exposures to the ad if the additional exposures are within the same online browsing session. Across sessions, repeated exposures to the same ad increases click-through behavior.

Whereas Chatterjee, Hoffman, and Novak (2003) focus on advertising clickthrough, Manchanda *et al.* (2006) examine the efficacy of banner advertising on driving online purchasing. The authors use a hazard process to model the inter-purchase times of existing customers, allowing for banner advertising to affect the purchasing rate. They find that exposure to advertising, both the absolute number of exposures as well as the number of different sites on which these ads appear, accelerates purchasing.

One unique aspect of online advertising is the ability to target individuals with customized ads. Individuals who have exhibited an interest in cars would be shown a car ad whereas individuals who have exhibited an interest in travel would be shown travel ads. Several online algorithms have been developed by computer scientists and online ad networks to identify each individual's interest based either on the content of the webpage they are viewing or on their historical online browsing behavior (which is collected by tracking cookies). The former is often referred to as contextual targeting whereas the latter is referred to as behavioral targeting.

To investigate the effects of contextual targeting strategies, Goldfarb and Tucker (2011) distinguished between advertisements that complement the content of the website and obtrusive advertisements. Examples of such advertisements include pop-up or pop-under advertisements; advertisements with streaming content; advertisements that are interactive, or those that occupy the full screen. They find that either targeted advertising or obtrusive advertising contribute to increased purchase intent. However, the combination of these techniques is found to be ineffective. In a related study, Moe (2006b) examined the interruption effect of pop-up ads. Depending on when in the user's clickstream the pop-up ad was shown, these ads can interrupt the user's flow and browsing experience and, as a result, cause the visitor to exit the website sooner than he or she would have otherwise exited.

In a study of behavioral targeting (Beales, 2010), the National Advertising Initiative (NAI) found that behaviorally targeted ads experience significantly higher conversion rates (6.8%) compared to untargeted ads (2.8%). For example, Sherman and Deighton (2001) discuss how Avenue A used CHAID to identify an individual's *affinity* websites (i.e., those websites that were frequently visited and purchased from). When banner advertisements were placed on high-affinity rather than low-affinity websites, visitors were nine times more likely to make a purchase.

To further refine targeting practices, Braun and Moe (2013) develop an advertising response model that allows each ad impression to vary in effectiveness depending on the targeted individual's history of impressions. Their model follows the "leaky bucket" approach used in offline advertising response models where advertising goodwill accumulates with each additional ad exposure and decays over time as the consumer forgets (Nerlove and Arrow, 1962). By decomposing the advertising effect into an accumulated inventory of goodwill that decays over time and an instantaneous effect of a single ad impression, Braun and Moe (2013) are able to measure the differential effectiveness of each creative on an individual's subsequent visiting and purchasing behavior, effectively yielding an advertising attribution model. Furthermore, they allow the instantaneous effect to vary with the targeted individual's unique ad impression history, allowing the advertiser to target individuals with specific ads that will maximize response in the context of the other ads that the individual has already seen.

Banner advertisements have also been shown to affect the way in which we gather information online. Rutz and Bucklin (2012) investigate the impact of exposure to banner advertisements on visitors' clickstream behavior at a major commercial website in the automotive industry. Like Montgomery *et al.* (2004), the authors characterize the content of different pages of the website, distinguishing between pages that contain different vehicle makes and pages that do not contain vehicles, such as pages with financing information. The authors find that banner advertising affects the subsequent browsing behavior for one segment of visitors, while it does not have a significant impact on the browsing behavior of other customers.

12.3.2 *Models for search advertising*

In addition to display advertising, sponsored search advertising (sometimes also referred to as paid search advertising) has grown rapidly. Unlike display advertisements such as banner advertisements and pop-up advertisements, sponsored search advertisements appear above or along the side of the results returned by search engines. Ghose and Yang (2009) provide an integrated model in which they consider the clickthrough and conversion rates, the cost per click and the position of sponsored search advertising. When an individual is exposed to a sponsored search advertisement, the authors model the clickthrough probability as a function of the ordinal position of the advertisement and the specificity of the keywords entered in the search, allowing for an interaction between the factors. A similar approach is used in modeling the likelihood of conversion, conditional on clickthrough. The authors simultaneously model the firm's cost per click (CPC), which arises from an auction process, and the search engine operator's decision of what position to slot the firm's advertisement into. As one would expect, firms with advertisements that appear toward the top of the results have a higher clickthrough. Keywords mentioning a specific retailer have higher clickthrough rates, and those mentioning a brand or with longer search queries have lower clickthrough rates.

Yao and Mela (2011) develop a dynamic model of sponsored search advertising. In their structural model, the authors assume that advertisers act in such a way as to maximize their profits. The authors model the advertiser's optimal bid amount, akin to the CPC an advertiser is willing to pay, based on the expected revenue, expected costs, and prior performance. While higher bids are expected to increase revenue by placing the advertisement in a higher slot on the website, they come with a higher cost that can adversely affect revenue.

Several studies have also examined the effects of different keywords in paid search advertising. For example, Rutz and Bucklin (2011) differentiate between generic keywords (e.g., "hotels") and branded keywords (e.g., "Hilton Hotels") used by consumers in search engines. They show an asymmetric effect where generic keyword searches will affect subsequent branded keyword searches but not vice versa. For search engine advertisers, the implication is that advertising your brand when a generic keyword is searched may increase future searches for your specific branded keyword. Thus, benefits from paid search advertising are not limited to just clickthrough on the original ad.

Other indirect effects have also been documented. Rutz, Trusov, and Bucklin (2011) show that paid search advertising may cause consumers to visit the brand's website in the future by typing in the URL directly into their web browser. Again, the existence of these "direct type-in" visits results in paid search ad clickthrough rates understating advertising's overall value.

12.3.3 *Models for e-mail advertising*

Besides advertising on websites and search engines, e-mail advertising has also provided a means for companies to reach out to consumers. Just as direct marketing can be targeted, so too can e-mail campaigns. Ansari and Mela (2003) propose a modeling framework to develop customized communications for each individual. To calibrate the model, they use customers' responses to the e-mails that they have received previously from the website. They then use these results to optimize the content and layout of the emails to be sent to customers. In characterizing the probability with which individuals respond to emails, the authors include customer characteristics, variables that reflect the layout of e-mails received and variables that reflect the content of the website they visit. As the authors allow for heterogeneity across consumers in their analysis, they can assess how various consumers will respond to different e-mail configurations and send each the message to which they are most likely to respond. The authors estimate that their optimization of e-mail messages could increase clickthroughs by more than 60%.

In an effort to provide timely assessments of e-mail campaigns, Bonfrer and Dreze (2009) develop a framework that provides a rapid evaluation of the performance of e-mail marketing campaigns, effectively allowing for real-time management of the campaign. The authors model recipients' decisions of whether to open the e-mail and, if opened, when to open the e-mail as a split hazard process. Bonfrer and Dreze (2009) take advantage of how e-mail campaigns are administered, with e-mails in their dataset being sent sequentially in batches. As the model can be estimated in seconds (reducing the time needed to assess the likely success of e-mail campaigns by as much as 91%), managers can take corrective measures if a campaign appears to be unsuccessful.

In addition to optimizing the content of e-mails, firms can also optimize the timing of their e-mails. Specifically, Dreze and Bonfrer (2008) find that recipients respond more favorably, in terms of the likelihood of e-mail opening and clicking rates, when the frequency of promotional e-mails increase. However, the likelihood of retaining the customer improves with less frequent e-mails. In light of these mixed results, the authors suggest a more holistic measure of customer equity, incorporating a variety of short-term and long-term response metrics into a single measure that reflects the customer's overall value to the firm.

Neslin *et al.* (2013) further examine the effects of e-mail timing on purchase likelihood and compare them to the effects of direct mail activities. They find that e-mails have a greater impact when a customer has made a purchase recently while direct marketing exhibits a larger effect when more time has passed. The authors show that by optimizing the timing of both e-mail and direct marketing efforts, firms can substantially increase customer lifetime value.

12.4 The Internet as a social medium

Just as the Internet revolutionized the ease with which consumers' purchase processes could be tracked, it also opened the door to research aimed at understanding how consumers interact with one another. Several researchers have focused on user-generated content such as product ratings and reviews. Recommendation systems, such as those proposed by Ansari, Essegaier, and Kohli (2000) and Ying, Feinberg, and Wedel (2006), take advantage of user-provided product ratings to recommend products to others who share similar preferences, thereby using user-generated content to drive sales. In addition to fueling recommendation engines, user-generated content has also been employed to further our understanding of word-of-mouth (WOM) and its effects on sales.

12.4.1 *Online WOM's effect on sales*

Godes and Mayzlin (2004) conducted one of the early studies of electronic WOM activity, often dubbed eWOM. They identify two distinct dimensions of eWOM, volume and dispersion. Using television program ratings as their dependent variable, they investigate the impact of the volume and dispersion of eWOM postings and find that the dispersion of conversations across communities is a significant predictor of ratings.

In their seminal research, Chevalier and Mayzlin (2006) also investigate the impact of online product reviews, but in the context of books. Like Godes and Mayzlin (2004), the authors find that reviews impact sales, with negative reviews exhibiting a larger impact on a product's sales rank compared to positive reviews. Using datasets from two different retailers, the authors find that the reviews posted online are generally positive, as would other researchers who subsequently investigate user-generated content. This is one area in which eWOM was found to differ from offline WOM, where comments are predominantly negative (Anderson, 1998). The authors also find that product reviews declined over time at both websites. This empirical finding would be further investigated by researchers interested in the dynamics exhibited in user-generated content, which we will discuss next.

12.4.2 *Dynamics in user-generated content*

While not the focus on their research, Chevalier and Mayzlin (2006) identified empirical evidence suggesting ratings dynamics. This spawned a number of subsequent studies that were designed specifically to identify

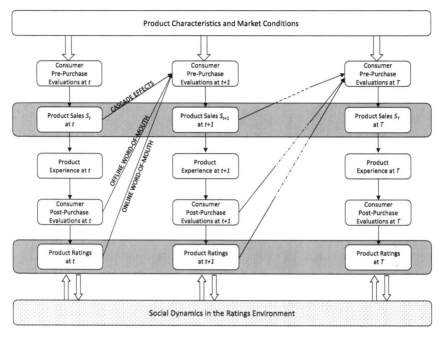

Fig. 12.2   The effects of ratings and dynamics on sales

Source: Moe and Trusov (2011).

and measure these dynamics. In continuing the study of how product ratings affect sales, Moe and Trusov (2011) decompose ratings metrics into a component that represented the consumers' unbiased product evaluations and a component that represented the effects of social dynamics. Their results provided some initial evidence that social dynamics among consumers can influence subsequent rating behavior and hence product sales (see Figure 12.2 for an illustration of how online ratings and dynamics in rating behavior affect sales).

Given the impact of user-generated content and the associated dynamics on sales, substantial interest in understanding the specifics dynamics at play began to develop. In particular, researchers sought to better understand the process that contributed to the observed decline in product ratings over time. To that end, Moe and Schweidel (2012) focused on behaviors of the individual consumers underlying the average ratings metrics. Specifically, they propose a model of the consumers' opinion expression behavior and break down each consumer's posted rating into two component decisions: (1) whether or not to post product ratings and (2) if so, how many stars the product was given. Building on the incidence and evaluation modeling framework employed by Ying, Feinberg, and Wedel (2006), the authors characterize the ratings environment based on the valence, volume and variance of previously contributed product ratings. They find that the most active posters tend to post lower ratings. Moreover, these "activists" post more negative evaluations when the ratings environment is characterized by higher variation in ratings and a large number of ratings. In contrast, "low involvement" posters tend to have higher ratings and avoid posting in environments that lack consensus. The authors show via simulations that, as time passes, activists become over-represented in the posting population, pulling down the observed average. Thus, one explanation offered for the decline in ratings is a shift in the composition of the posting population.

In a similar vein, Godes and Silva (2012) suggest that there are two distinct sources of dynamics that contribute to the decline in average product ratings. Consistent with Li and Hitt (2008), who posit that the decline in ratings is driven by a selection process in which later purchasers have a lower valuation for the product, the authors account for *sequential dynamics*, captured by the number of reviews that have been contributed previously. The authors also capture the *temporal dynamics* by taking the time since the first review into account. The authors find heterogeneity across reviewers in the evaluations that they provide, as well as support for both temporal and sequential dynamics in affecting the trajectory of a ratings environment.

12.4.3 *Content analysis of user-generated content*

While early marketing research involving user-generated content focused on quantitative data such as product ratings, user-generated content also takes the form of text. Whether user-generated content is sourced from tweets, product reviews, blog posts or forum discussions, content analysis is required to extract insights. With readily available user-generated content, it stands to reason that problems commonly investigated with traditional marketing research techniques could also be explored with user-generated content, yielding key insights more rapidly and more economically

(Schweidel and Moe, 2014). Lee and Bradlow (2011) demonstrate the benefits of using automated content analysis to understand market structure. In their approach, the authors scrape the web for product reviews and create a matrix that reflects which words occur in which product reviews. Using this matrix, the authors apply a clustering algorithm to group together those phrases that commonly co-occur. They demonstrate that their approach can work in conjunction with other methods of identifying product attributes to analyze market structure.

Netzer *et al.* (2012) employ a similar approach to examine market structure, using the co-occurrence of brand mentions and product attributes in the same forum posting as an indication that different car models compete with each other. They compare the inferred market structure from user-generated comments to the market structure inferred from brand switching behavior in transaction data and find strong correlation between the resulting inferences. They go on to demonstrate that the content analysis approach can be employed to understand shifts in market structure and examine the effectiveness of marketing campaigns.

12.4.4 *Networks and influence*

In addition to research investigating the nature by which user-generated content propagates and affects outcomes of interest, research has also examined the nature of the connection between individuals via social media. As with clickstream research that facilitated understanding the path to purchase, online social networks have made it easier to investigate how individuals affect each other's behaviors. Watts and Dodd (2007) examine the "influential hypothesis" that there exist a small number of individuals who exert influence over their peers. Using simulations, Watts and Dodd (2007) examine the "cascades" that are triggered by one individual affecting others' behaviors based on the likelihood that an initiator's action triggers an action by others and the susceptibility of others to his influence. They find that it is not the likelihood of an individual affecting others (i.e., his influence over them), but rather the susceptibility of the individuals to whom he is connected that ultimately affects the size of the cascades.

While Watts and Dodd raise the question of whether influence or others' susceptibility to influence is more pertinent, the question of how to assess an individual's influence remains. While one approach to understanding opinion leadership is to directly ask participants about who influences them, Trusov, Bodapati, and Bucklin (2010) develop a methodology to infer influence from behavioral data. The authors reason that an influential individual's actions will affect the actions of others. The authors examine the log-ins to a social networking site and identify those individuals whose own login rates will affect others' as influentials. They employ a hierarchical Bayesian model in which they estimate a latent measure of influence for each individual in the social network. In doing so, they provide a foundation by which researchers and firms can evaluate the extent to which consumers are affected by their social interactions.

12.5   Directions for future research

In this chapter, we discussed three key areas of digital marketing research. Researchers have studied the internet as (1) a channel for browsing and purchasing, (2) a medium for advertising and (3) a social medium. While we have made significant progress in a short amount of time, a number of challenges and areas for future research still remain.

Research to date on individuals' browsing behavior both within a website and across multiple websites has increased our understanding of consumers' path to purchase. Yet, this research only allows us to observe the online activities involved in the path to purchase. Realistically, though, the path to purchase encompasses both online and offline activities. While we may search for product information on a manufacturer's or retailer's website, we may also head to a brick and mortar store so that we can have a hands-on experience on the product. The eventual purchase may take place at the retail location or through a website. If we were able to monitor an individual's activities leading up to purchase regardless of whether those activities took place online or offline, a number of substantive problems can be addressed, including investigating the prevalence of "showrooming" (using retail stores to experience a product, but conducting a transaction online) and how it affects purchasing behavior.

A related challenge is the notion of attribution. That is, how do each of our marketing activities affect sales? While recent research has tackled slices of this problem (e.g., Braun and Moe, 2013; Neslin *et al.*, 2013), consider the multitude of ways in which firms' marketing messages may reach consumer in the online setting. Search engine results, search advertising, display ads and e-mail campaigns (whether originating with the firm or being passed on by connection) may all contribute to a customer's purchase. On top of these activities, direct marketing efforts and mass marketing activities may also affect a customer's transactional activity. Yet, individuals' exposures to mass marketing activities are difficult to monitor. Integrating the distinct marketing efforts into a unified framework for attribution analysis remains an outstanding issue for marketers to address. If this could be accomplished, firms could then optimize the mix of their marketing activities based on how an individual has previously responded to both online and offline marketing communications.

As our tracking of individuals' digital footprints improve, we also come one step closer to being able to answer the question of what is the ROI associated with social media. By linking the social media activity generated by an individual to both his own purchasing behavior and the purchasing behavior of those who were exposed to the social media message, we can assess the degree to which social media contributes to transactional activity and ultimately a customers' long-term value to the firm. Merging social media data with a firm's CRM database is not without its own challenges, particularly given the privacy concern that such data integration raises. Social media exposure would need to be incorporated into a broader attribution analysis, which could allow firms to assess customers' "social value."

As digital marketing expenditures do not (or, at the very least, should not) occur in a vacuum, additional research addressing how digital efforts fit with the other marketing expenditure remains an important issue that is under-researched. In both practice and academia, marketing has erected silos, often treating social and digital activities as distinct from other marketing efforts. As this area of research matures, these walls will gradually begin to give way to integrated marketing strategies in which digital and social media are seen simply as additional channels for communication and commerce.

References

Anderson, E. W. (1998). Customer satisfaction and word of mouth, *Journal of Service Research*, 1(1), 5–17.

Ansari, A. and C. F. Mela (2003). E-Customization, *Journal of Marketing Research*, 40(2), 131–145.

Ansari, A., S. Esegaier, and R. Kohli (2000). Internet recommendation systems, *Journal of Marketing Research*, 37(3), 363–375.

Beales, H. (2010). The value of behavioral targeting. Available at: http://www.networkadvertising.org/pdfs/Beales_NAI_Study.pdf.

Bonfrer, A. and X. Dreze (2009). Real-time evaluation of e-mail campaign performance, *Marketing Science*, 28(2), 251–263.

Braun, M. and W. W. Moe (2013). Online advertising campaigns: Modeling the effects of multiple ad creatives, *Marketing Science*, 32(5), 753–767.

Bucklin, R. E. and C. Sismeiro (2003). A model of web site browsing behavior estimated on clickstream data, *Journal of Marketing Research*, 40(3), 249–267.

Chatterjee, P., D. L. Hoffman, and T. P. Novak (2003). Modeling the clickstream: Implications for web-based advertising efforts, *Marketing Science*, 22(4), 520–541.

Chevalier, J. and D. Mayzlin (2006). The effect of word of mouth on sales: Online book reviews, *Journal of Marketing Research*, 43(3), 345–354.

Danaher, P. J. (2007). Modeling page views across multiple websites with an application to internet reach and frequency prediction, *Marketing Science*, 26(3), 422–437.

Danaher, P. J., J. Lee, and L. Kerbache (2010). Optimal internet media selection, *Marketing Science*, 29(2), 336–347.

Dinner, I. M., H. J. van Heerde, and S. Neslin (2011). Driving online and offline sales: The cross-channel effects of digital versus traditional advertising, Tuck School of Business Working Paper.

Dreze, X. and A. Bonfrer (2008). An empirical investigation of the impact of communication timing on customer equity, *Journal of Interactive Marketing*, 22(1), 36–50.

Ghose, A. and S. Yang (2009). An empirical analysis of search engine advertising: Sponsored search in electronic markets, *Management Science*, 55(10), 1605–1622.

Godes, D. and D. Mayzlin (2004). Using online conversations to study word-of-mouth communications, *Marketing Science*, 23(4), 545–560.

Godes, D. and J. C. Silva (2012). Sequential and temporal dynamics of online opinion, *Marketing Science*, 31(3), 448–473.

Goldfarb, A. and C. Tucker (2011). Search engine advertising: Channel substitution when pricing ads to context, *Management Science*, 57(3), 458–470.

Hauser, J. R., G. L. Urban, G. Liberali, and M. Braun (2009). Website morphing. *Marketing Science*, 28(2), 202–223.

Hoffman, D. L. and T. P. Novak (1996). Marketing in hypermedia computer-mediated environments: Conceptual foundations, *Journal of Marketing*, 60(3), 50–68.

Ilfeld, J. S. and R. S. Winer (2002). Generating website traffic, *Journal of Advertising Research*, 42(5), 49–61.

Johnson, E. J., S. Bellman, and G. L. Lohse (2003). Cognitive lock-in and the power law of practice, *Journal of Marketing*, 67(2), 62–75.

Johnson, E. J., W. W. Moe, P. S. Fader, S. Bellman, and G. L. Lohse (2004). On the depth and dynamics of online search behavior, *Management Science*, 50(3), 299–308.

Li, X. and L. M. Hitt (2008). Self-selection and information role of online product reviews, *Information Systems Research*, 19(4), 456–474.

Lee, T. Y. and E. T. Bradlow (2011). Automated marketing research using online customer reviews, *Journal of Marketing Research*, 48(5), 881–894.

Manchanda, P., J.-P. Dube, K. Y. Goh, and P. K. Chintagunta (2006). The effect of banner advertising on internet purchasing, *Journal of Marketing Research*, 43(1), 98–108.

Moe, W. W. (2003). Buying, searching, or browsing: Differentiating between online shoppers using in-store navigational clickstream, *Journal of Consumer Psychology*, 13(1&2), 29–39.

Moe, W. W. (2006a). An empirical two-stage choice model with decision rules applied to internet clickstream data, *Journal of Marketing Research*, 43(4), 680–692.

Moe, W. W. (2006b). A field experiment assessing the interruption effect of pop-up promotions, *Journal of Interactive Marketing*, 20(1), 34–44.

Moe, W. W. and P. S. Fader (2004a). Capturing evolving visit behavior in clickstream data, *Journal of Interactive Marketing*, 18(1), 5–19.

Moe, W. W. and P. S. Fader (2004b). Dynamic conversion behavior at E-commerce sites, *Management Science*, 50(3), 326–335.

Moe, W. W. and D. A. Schweidel (2012). Online product opinions: Incidence, evaluation and evolution, *Marketing Science*, 31(3), 372–386.

Moe, W. W. and M. Trusov (2011). The value of social dynamics in online product ratings forums, *Journal of Marketing Research*, 48(3), 444–456.

Montgomery, A. L., S. Li, K. Srinivasan, and J. C. Liechty (2004). Modeling online browsing and path analysis using clickstream data, *Marketing Science*, 23(4), 579–595.

Nerlove, M. and K. J. Arrow (1962). Optimal advertising policy under dynamic conditions, *Econometrica*, 29(114), 129–142.

Neslin, S. A., G. A. Taylor, K. D. Grantham, and K. R. McNeil (2013). Overcoming the 'recency trap' in customer relationship management, *Journal of the Academy of Marketing Science*, 41(3), 320–337.

Netzer, O., R. Feldman, J. Goldenberg, and M. Fresko (2012). Mine your own business: Market-structure surveillance through text mining, *Marketing Science*, 31(3), 521–543.

Park, Y.-H. and P. S. Fader (2004). Modeling browsing behavior at multiple websites, *Marketing Science*, 23(3), 280–303.

Rutz, O. J. and R. E. Bucklin (2011). From generic to branded: A model of spillover in paid search advertising, *Journal of Marketing Research*, 48(1), 87–102.

Rutz, O. J. and R. E. Bucklin (2012). Does banner advertising affect browsing for brands? Clickstream choice model says yes, for some, *Quantitative Marketing and Economics*, 10(2), 231–257.

Rutz, O. J., M. Trusov and R. E. Bucklin (2011). Modeling indirect effects of paid search advertising: Which keywords lead to more future visits? *Marketing Science*, 30(4), 646–665.

Schweidel, D. A. and W. W. Moe (2014). Listening in on social media: A joint model of sentiment and venue format choice, *Journal of Marketing Research*, forthcoming.

Sherman, L. and J. Deighton (2001). Banner advertising: Measuring effectiveness and optimizing placement, *Journal of Interactive Marketing*, 15(2), 60–64.

Sismeiro, C. and R. E. Bucklin (2004). Modeling purchase behavior at an e-commerce web site: A task-completion approach, *Journal of Marketing Research*, 41(3), 306–323.

Trusov, M., A. V. Bodapati and R. E. Bucklin (2010). Determining influential users in internet social networks, *Journal of Marketing Research*, 47(4), 643–658.

Watts, D. J. and P. S. Dodds (2007). Influentials, networks, and public opinion formation, *Journal of Consumer Research*, 34(4), 441–458.

Yao, S. and C. F. Mela (2011). A dynamic model of sponsored search advertising, *Marketing Science*, 30(3), 447–468.

Ying, Y., F. Feinberg, and M. Wedel (2006). Leveraging missing ratings to improve online recommendation systems, *Journal of Marketing Research*, 43(3), 355–365.

Chapter 13

New Products Research

Donald R. Lehmann and Peter N. Golder

New products have been a key focus of research in marketing for decades. As such, there is a huge literature associated with (and numerous books on) the subject, which makes it impossible to provide a comprehensive treatment in this short chapter. To provide some focus, this chapter concentrates on five streams of research: opportunity identification and concept generation, design and development, forecasting and testing, strategy and management, and valuation, including the evolution of these streams over the past 50 years.

Beyond this chapter, we encourage readers to see the seminal book in this area (Urban and Hauser, 1980, 1993) and an excellent review article (Hauser, Tellis, and Griffin, 2006). Moreover, an association (Product Development Management Association) and its journal (*Journal of Product Innovation Management*) are devoted to this topic. By emphasizing the marketing science literature, this chapter leaves out the large and important literatures on consumer behavior with respect to new products (e.g., Rogers, 2003). Diffusion models, based on Bass (1969), are dealt with in this book in the chapter by Muller.

13.1 Introduction

Marketing science scholars have made important contributions to the new products literature over the last 50 years. Most of these map directly into the typical new product development process where firms move from

341

identifying opportunities to generating concepts through designing and developing these concepts into actual products to testing and forecasting market response and finally to formally launching new products in the market. Across the sub-fields of new products research, these contributions have been especially strong and persistent in two areas — design and development and forecasting and testing. Contributions have been more recent or limited in three other areas — opportunity identification and concept generation, strategy and management, and valuation. The final two areas of research link most closely to the final stage of the new product development process — launching new products in the market.

We organize our discussion into these five areas of research (see Table 13.1 for an overview). By doing so, we seek to satisfy three key objectives:

(1) To introduce readers to the breadth of new products research in marketing.
(2) To give readers a sense of the historical evolution of this research.
(3) To elucidate emerging trends in research as well as overlooked opportunities for new research.

New product failure rates can range as high as 90%. Marketing science methods, models, and findings have consistently been shown to decrease failure rates and enhance success. Thus, application of current marketing science knowledge is vital. Moreover, many additional opportunities exist to build on existing research to further enhance new product success.

13.2   Opportunity identification and concept generation

The marketing science community has generated limited research on the front end of the new product development process. Perhaps this is because data are sparse and less in need of complex models. However, the current and potential future insights in these areas are tremendous. We highlight several noteworthy contributions across decades.

The 1980s initiated interest in focusing on "special" customers, i.e., those who had needs ahead of the overall market and in some cases actually began to develop solutions for those needs. "Lead users" (Von Hippel, 1988; Urban and Von Hippel, 1988) entered the lexicon as both a term

Table 13.1   New products research over time

Decade	Opportunity identification and concept generation	Design and development	Forecasting and testing	Strategy and management	Valuation
1960s		*Foundations of Conjoint Analysis:* Luce & Tukey, 1964	*Regression:* Fourt & Woodlock, 1960 Claycamp & Liddy, 1969 *Stochastic Models:* Kuehn, 1962 STEAM		
1970s		*Conjoint Analysis:* Green & Rao, 1971 Wind, 1973 Shocker & Srinivasan, 1979	*Stochastic Models:* Massy, Montgomery, & Morrison, 1970 Ehrenberg, 1972 *Consumer Flow Models:* Urban, 1970 SPRINTER; Urban, 1975 PERCEPTOR; Assmus, 1975 *Recursive Regression:* NEWPROD Blattberg & Golanty, 1978 TRACKER *Pre Test Market Composite Models:* Silk & Urban, 1978 ASSESSOR		

(*Continued*)

Table 13.1 (*Continued*)

Decade	Opportunity identification and concept generation	Design and development	Forecasting and testing	Strategy and management	Valuation
1980s	*Lead Users:* Von Hippel, 1986	*Adaptive Conjoint, Choice-based Conjoint, Self-explicated Conjoint* (see chapter by Rao) *House of Quality:* Hauser & Clausing, 1988	*Pre Test Market Composite Models:* Pringle, Wilson, & Brody, 1982 Urban & Katz, 1983	*Competitive Response:* Hauser & Shugan, 1983 Robinson, 1988a *Order of Entry:* Robinson & Fornell, 1985 Urban et al., 1986 Carpenter & Nakamoto, 1989	*Market Share:* Buzzell & Gale, 1987
1990s	*New Product Templates:* Goldenberg, Mazursky, & Solomon, 1999	*Voice of the Customer:* Griffin & Hauser, 1993 *Information Acceleration:* Urban et al., 1996 Urban et al., 1997	*Stochastic Models:* Fader & Schmittlein, 1992 *Sales Takeoff:* Golder & Tellis, 1997	*Order of Entry:* Golder & Tellis, 1993 Shankar, Carpenter, & Krishnamurthi, 1998 *Meta-analysis of Success Factors:* Montoya-Weiss & Calantone, 1994 *Organizational Issues:* Griffin & Hauser, 1996 Boulding, Morgan, & Staelin, 1997 Chandy & Tellis, 1998 Moorman & Miner, 1998	*Stock Price Impact:* Chaney, Devinney, & Winer, 1990

(*Continued*)

Table 13.1 (*Continued*)

Decade	Opportunity identification and concept generation	Design and development	Forecasting and testing	Strategy and management	Valuation
				Preannoucements: Heil & Robertson, 1991	
2000s	*Creativity:* Moreau & Dahl, 2005 *Incentives:* Toubia, 2006 *Listening In:* Urban & Hauser, 2004	*Web Morphing Technology Evolution:* Hauser et al., 2009 Sood & Tellis, 2005 *Precommercialization:* Golder, Shacham, & Mitra, 2009	*Stochastic Models:* Fader, Hardie, & Lee, 2005 *Online Word-of-Mouth:* Godes & Mayzlin, 2004 Mayzlin, 2006 Chevalier & Mayzlin, 2006 *Product Life Cycle:* Golder & Tellis, 2004	*Meta-analysis of Success Factors:* Henard & Syzmanski, 2001 *Alliances:* Rindfleisch & Moorman, 2001	*Stock Price:* Mizik & Jacobson, 2003 Sorescu & Spanjol, 2008 Srinivasan et al., 2009
2010s		*Adaptive Self-explication:* Netzer & Srinivasan, 2011	*Simulated Stock Market:* Dahan et al., 2011	*Competitive Entry:* Thomadsen, 2012	

and direction for action. These so-called lead users could be enticed to participate in the development process by testing beta versions, and then would be more likely to adopt new products early on once they were launched. Partnering with "lead users" can improve product design and expedite its development. These concepts were validated in a more recent study utilizing a natural experiment. Here, Lilien *et al.* (2002) found that 3M divisions implementing lead user projects achieved their highest rate of generating major product lines in the last 50 years and that sales from lead user projects were eight times those generated by contemporaneous projects developed along traditional lines.

More recent research focused on the product by identifying five "templates" that successful new products typically conform to Goldenberg, Mazursky, and Solomon (1999). These templates are based on certain sequences of six operators performed on product attributes or product components: inclusion, exclusion, linking, unlinking, joining, and splitting. Successful applications of these new product templates are described in Goldenberg *et al.* (2003) as well as Boyd and Goldenberg (2013). For example, Philips has generated numerous ideas using "Systematic Inventive Thinking," the technique developed by Jacob Goldenberg, Roni Horowitz, Amnon Levav, and David Mazursky (which follows on the work of Genrich Altscbeller). Specifically, they examined the complex DVD players at the time and via exclusion (subtraction) simplified the controls and produced the now-common handheld controller. Similarly Samsonite turned the weight of college back packs into a comfort benefit via "task unification" (linking), and subtracting the polymer from permanent markers led to the dry-erase marker. Interestingly, the basic idea behind a new product and the circumstances surrounding its emergence are useful predictors of new product success (Goldenberg, Lehmann, and Mazursky, 2001). For example, finding solutions to customers' problems works, while mimicking popular trends or developing new products in isolation does not. These determinants of success or failure allow early screening of new product concepts before moving on to the more expensive phases of development and testing.

The 2000s brought efforts to improve creative problem solving. Morreau and Dahl (2005) demonstrated, paradoxically, that idea quality is enhanced by placing constraints on the creative process. Toubia (2006) went further by showing how collaboration effectiveness was enhanced through an incentive system that rewards individual contributors for their own ideas as well as for the extent their ideas are utilized by others. Urban and Hauser (2004) demonstrated how "listening in" to conversations between customers and virtual advisors can uncover unsatisfied needs.

Of the five areas of research that we discuss, opportunity identification and concept generation has had the least amount of marketing science research to date and represents a fertile area for future research. Opportunity identification seems to be an area especially ripe for developing more structured processes.

13.3 Design and development

Decades ago, marketing scientists explored and developed conjoint analysis as a means of incorporating customer inputs into design decisions (Green and Rao, 1971; Wind, 1973; Green and Srinivasan, 1978; Shocker and Srinivasan, 1979; Green, Carroll, and Goldberg, 1981; Green and Srinivasan, 1990). This method decomposes overall preferences for multi-attribute options into utilities for various levels of each attribute, i.e., the "part-worths." We touch on conjoint analysis in this chapter because of its strong grounding in the new products literature; Rao's chapter in this volume presents a more complete discussion of conjoint analysis.

Conjoint evolved from simpler models that reflected preferences as either vectors or ideal points as was typically done in the literature on multi-attribute models and perceptual mapping. Conjoint analysis has had a tremendous impact on new product development. In fact, it has become one of the most well-established and accepted methods in all of marketing as demonstrated in applications by Green and colleagues to products such as Courtyard by Marriott (Wind *et al.*, 1989) and E-Z Pass. Over a thousand applications of conjoint analysis throughout the 1970s, 1980s, and 1990s in the United States and Europe are documented by Wittink and Cattin (1989) and Wittink, Vriens, and Burhenne (1994). The most common use of conjoint is for new product development, but the method has proved useful more broadly in competitive analysis, market segmentation, pricing, repositioning, etc. Applications of conjoint analysis have continued to grow.

The basic model underlying conjoint analysis is that the value of a product is the sum of the value of the levels in the product across attributes, dimensions, or characteristics:

$$\text{Value of Product} = \sum_i \text{Value of Product on Attribute } i.$$

The initial treatment for conjoint analysis was provided by Luce, a mathematical psychologist, and Tukey, a statistican (Luce and Tukey, 1964), which appeared as the lead article in the first issue of the *Journal of Mathematical Psychology*. That article provided an axiomatic (algebraic) basis for the method and related papers and presentations followed in the 1960s (see Green and Srinivasan, 1978). The foundational paper in the marketing literature is Green and Rao (1971).

Initial applications focused on either two attributes at a time — trade-off analysis (Johnson, 1974) or full profile ratings (Wind, 1973). However, complex products involving numerous attributes led to additional alternatives. One obvious approach was to treat the attributes separately and use "self-explicated" measures for determining the relative importance of all attributes (Green, Carroll, and Goldberg, 1981; Srinivasan, 1988). Another approach uses self-explicated weights as a starting point to cluster individuals who then provide input to incorporate taste heterogeneity. A third alternative is the so-called adaptive conjoint (Johnson, 1987). Here, individuals give initial estimates, which are then revised based on choices between pairs of options purposely selected by the researcher to provide the most useful additional information. This approach was popularized commercially by Sawtooth Software. A fourth alternative approach involving ideal points and linear programming, LINMAP, was developed by Shocker and Srinivasan (1974).

Recent developments in adaptive conjoint analysis use a polyhedral, choice-based design and estimation algorithms to quickly converge on a respondent's part-worth utilities with a limited number of questions (Toubia *et al.*, 2003, 2004). Nonetheless, work in the self-explicated tradition continues (Netzer and Srinivasan, 2011).

The late 1980s and early 1990s produced work targeted toward understanding how to systematically incorporate customer preferences into a firm's product design. Hauser and Clausing (1988) introduced one tool from the Quality Function Deployment (QFD) literature, the House of Quality, into marketing as a means of coordinating manufacturing, design, and marketing to create and deliver products aligned with customer preferences (Prasad, 1998). While conjoint analysis provides insights on the trade-offs customers make among product attributes, QFD explicitly links customer benefits with product attributes. As a result, these two approaches yield complementary insights to help optimize new product design. Following this line of research, Griffin and Hauser (1993) detailed procedures for incorporating the Voice of the Customer in order to identify, structure, and prioritize customer needs. These studies and related research enjoyed both academic and practical attention.

In the 1990s, advancing technology promoted the development of multi-media tools, including enhanced visual and interactive features, to assist in designing new products and forecasting their ultimate success. Rather than creating actual products and marketing stimuli, these "information acceleration" techniques created simulated products, advertisements, and salesperson interactions (Urban, Weinberg, and Hauser, 1996; Urban, *et al.*, 1997). Importantly, they moved beyond product design to the design of the overall customer experience. Such simulations can be especially valuable in designing radically new products.

In the 2000s, even more recent technology enabled development of real-time design modifications of digital products such as "web morphing" (Hauser, *et al.*, 2009). Here, not only is a website's content adjusted in real time, but also its look and feel and the way information is presented are modified to match each consumer's cognitive style. Consumers may be visual vs. verbal and analytic vs. holistic processors of information. These differences affect the extent and placement of text, graphics, and level of detail. Companies implementing website morphing have seen sales increases of 20% (Urban *et al.*, 2009).

Interestingly, in the 2000s, some research has moved in the opposite direction, away from adjusting a product's final design, to explore the origins of radical innovations and their underlying technologies. These studies expand marketing's traditional emphasis on commercializing finished products toward exploring the long period of pre-commercialization development and the set of advancing technologies on which these radical innovations are based (Sood and Tellis, 2005; Golder, Shacham, and Mitra, 2009).

The renewed interest in the S-shaped model of technology substitution can trace its roots to at least as early as Fisher and Pry (1971).

Overall, marketing scientists' research in the area of Design and Development has made meaningful and lasting contributions to new product development practice. Going forward, structured processes like conjoint analysis and QFD could be supplemented with less structured processes which are better suited to generating more radical innovations.

13.4   Forecasting and testing

This area of research has emphasized new product sales forecasting. Poor performance vs. sales forecasts may indicate design deficiencies that firms should correct. While many methods emphasize market testing, along with forecasting, others collect diagnostic information to help firms determine whether the product or marketing program should be modified.

Beginning with the 1960 paper by Fourt and Woodlock on grocery products, generations of marketing scientists have developed and improved models designed to forecast new product success early on. According to Fourt and Woodlock (1960, p. 31), "a reliable method for early selection of the most promising fraction of innovations would eliminate much of the loss now incurred on failures." Fourt and Woodlock concentrated on modeling the number of customers over time who bought a new product once, twice, three times, etc. and extrapolating these customer purchase rates into the future. Kuehn (1962), along with Massy, Montgomery, Morrison, and others, used stochastic processes to describe and model new product adoption. Massy's STEAM model (1969) incorporated purchase incidence as a Poisson process and concentrated on depth of repeat as a key success factor (see also Parfitt and Collins, 1968). Ehrenberg (1972) continued in this stochastic tradition, which still generates important work on product adoption and repeat purchase (Fader and Schmittlein, 1992; Fader, Hardie, and Lee, 2005).

From the late 1960s through the early 1980s, researchers proposed a stream of commercially applicable models for predicting new product sales. These models focused on nondurable goods using test market results to forecast market-wide sales. Seminal work on this topic emerged from MIT led by Glen Urban and his colleagues. Urban's (1970) Sprinter, published in *Operations Research*, offered three flow models (Mod I, Mod II, and Mod III) enabling managers to customize their analysis. This model was the forerunner of other models such as PERCEPTOR (Urban, 1975) and the widely used BASES model. This class of models tracks consumers as they flow through states of awareness, trial, purchase, and repurchase of own and others' brands. These models also provide valuable diagnostic information about where marketing activities are or are not having their desired effects. However, the cost of this information is such that it necessitates a large data collection effort. Assmus (1975) proposed an 11-state model, NewProd, which balances insights from flow models against the cost and complexity of collecting data and analyzing it.

An alternative, regression-based approach developed alongside the flow models. An early effort in this area includes Claycamp and Liddy (1969) who modeled advertising recall and trial purchase as a function of numerous factors. Notably, advertising recall was included as one factor in the trial purchase equation. Such recursive models were further developed in NewProd (Assmus, 1975) and Tracker (Blattberg and Golanty, 1978), which incorporates awareness and repeat sales among many features. Recursive models yield good predictions at a reasonable cost based on several months of test market data. However, they do not yield much insight into the behavioral process that consumers traverse before becoming loyal repeat purchasers. LITMUS (Blackburn and Clancy, 1980), NEWS (Pringle, Wilson, and Brody, 1982) NPD's ESP and other similar models used varying combinations of early test market results and survey data to forecast new product sales, provide diagnostic information on a new product's strengths and weaknesses, and feedback on a product's entire marketing mix.

Because relying on trial and repeat data required actually launching a product, at least in a meaningful test market, attention shifted to pretest market methods. Silk and Urban (1978) developed an approach consisting of two models — an awareness-trial-repeat model and a preference model that uses constant sum preference data across the consideration set as input. Their ASSESSOR model (see also Urban and Katz, 1983) proved to be accurate as well as commercially viable. Another approach which combines multiple-stages, predictive ability, diagnostic insights, and commercial success is NEWS (Pringle, Wilson, and Brody, 1982).

In the 2000s, data have become available to explore the impact of word-of-mouth on new product sales and have been exploited by marketing scientists. Godes and Mayzlin (2004) show that the dispersion of online word-of-mouth across user communities helps to explain new TV show ratings. Chevalier and Mayzlin (2006) demonstrate the relationship between books sales and both the number and average rating of online reviews. Similarly, Liu (2006) demonstrates the link between online word-of-mouth, primarily its volume, and movie box office revenue. Most recently, in the 2010s, Dahan *et al.* (2011) show how an online stock market can be used to aggregate consumer preferences about new product concepts. The primary benefits of this approach are cost-efficiency and scalability.

13.5 Strategy and management

This area of research has covered a wide range of topics. To guide the reader, we italicize the sub-areas within each paragraph. In general, the dominant paradigm for managing new products is the *stage-gate method* (Cooper, 1990, 1994), consisting of concept development, design, testing, and launch. Ding and Eliashberg (2002) investigate how to structure the new product development pipeline by selecting the appropriate number of projects to fund at each stage in order to have a successful product emerge in the end. Several authors have worked on ways to increase the speed and improve the chances of success in moving through this "funnel" (e.g., Griffin, 1997). Nonetheless, there is a trade-off between speed to market and both the quality of product offered and the readiness of a market to accept it. Importantly, recent research has found that a strictly applied stage-gate process may inhibit the development of really new products (Sethi and Iqbal, 2008).

Another focus of work has been on explaining *why new products are successful*. Some research has taken a conceptual approach by identifying the characteristics of products, potential adopters, and the broader social and competitive environments that contribute to or inhibit new product success (Gatignon and Robertson, 1985; Robertson and Gatignon, 1986). Other research has summarized empirical research through meta-analyses of the most common success factors (Montoya-Weiss and Calantone, 1994; Henard and Syzmanski, 2001).

Organizational issues have also been investigated as important determinants of new product success. One frequently studied topic is the role of cross-functional teams and coordination among R&D, design, marketing, operations, etc. For example, Sethi, Smith, and Park (2001) show that moving beyond functional boundaries to identify with the cross-functional team promotes the innovativeness of new products. More specifically, some attention has been devoted to the marketing–R&D interface (Griffin and Hauser, 1996), but many opportunities remain for delineating and expanding marketing's role at this early stage of the new product development process.

Another interesting perspective focuses on *managerial decision making*. Chandy and Tellis (1998) show how willingness to cannibalize prior investments may be more important than firm size as a driver of radical product innovation. However, firm size has also played a role in the introduction of radical innovations (Chandy and Tellis, 2000). While older radical innovations tended to be introduced by small non-incumbents, more recent radical innovations tended to be introduced by large incumbents. Ofek and Sarvary (2003) provide a framework for understanding how leaders and followers will invest in R&D versus advertising with next-generation technology products. They conclude that firm investments depend on whether current leadership is based on R&D competence or reputation. Research on organizational memory shows that greater memory dispersion increases new product creativity and performance (Moorman and Miner, 1997). Also, improvisation in the new product development process can have positive or negative effects depending on environmental and organizational factors (Moorman and Miner, 1998).

Other research on organizational decision making investigates *how well managers can shift away from a failing new product*. Boulding, Morgan, and Staelin (1997) demonstrate that managers remain committed to a new product launch even when confronted with strong evidence of failure. This commitment is lessened somewhat, although not overcome, by precommitment to a predetermined stopping rule or introducing a new decision maker. More recently, Byalogorsky, Boulding, and Staelin (2006) develop and test a more general conceptual framework that explains why new product managers maintain or escalate their commitment to a failing new product. They argue that it may not be possible to eliminate commitment bias at the individual level, and that organizational processes must be used instead. The roles of organizational norms and strategic orientations are further developed in Gatignon and Xuereb (1997). They find that different strategic orientations of a firm (customer, competitive, technological) are more useful in different new product contexts.

Research has also considered *organizational structures beyond a single firm*. For example, Rindfleish and Moorman (2001) report the different impacts of horizontal and vertical alliances on new product development. They find that alliances with higher overlap in firms' knowledge bases and higher quality relationships lead to higher new product creativity and faster new product development. In a related study, Ganesan, Malter, and Rindfleisch (2005) examine the geographic proximity of alliance partners and conclude that strong relational ties may be more important than simple geographic proximity and that e-mail communication, in contrast to face-to-face communication, enhances new product creativity and development speed.

Once new products are developed, firms must decide on their *entry strategy*. Optimal entry decisions have been studied from both theoretical and empirical perspectives. Work in game theory has focused on spatial competition, in a particular location on a horizontal (Hotelling) line. This literature draws heavily on the economic literature on sequential location of entrants (e.g., Rothschild, 1976; Prescott and Visscher, 1977; Lane, 1980; Bonanno, 1987). In marketing, studies of product pre-announcements (Heil and Robertson, 1991; Robertson, Eliashberg, and Rymon, 1995), as well as false pre-announcements or vaporware (Bayus, Jain, and Rao, 2001) have been a focus of investigation. Recently, Thomadsen (2012) demonstrates that competitive entry through an expanding product line can increase the profits of all firms in horizontally differentiated markets.

A broad and rich literature in marketing has concentrated on *order of entry* and the rewards associated with entry timing. Several papers from the mid-1980s to the early-1990s (Robinson and Fornell, 1985; Urban *et al.*, 1986; Robinson, 1988b; Kalyanaram and Urban, 1992) established empirical support for a pioneer or first mover advantage. This evidence is nicely summarized in Kalyanaram, Robinson, and Urban (1995). However, Golder and Tellis (1993) show that the advantage of pioneers is overstated due to a survival bias whereby a large number of firms enter early but then go out of business and hence are not included in most datasets. Moreover, successful later entrants can be misclassified as pioneers. Later, Boulding and Christen (2003) find that pioneers may suffer a long-term profit disadvantage.

Theoretical and normative work has helped broaden our understanding of how various contexts contribute to the *success or failure of early entrants.* While being first may have advantages in acculturating consumers to the specific attributes of the pioneer (Carpenter and Nakamoto, 1989), other work suggests disadvantages to pioneering under various conditions related to market uncertainty and firm heterogeneity (Narasimhan and Zhang, 2000). Carpenter and Nakamoto (1990) examined optimal strategy for a late entrant and concluded that a "me-too" positioning was often sub-optimal. Successful late entrant strategies were examined by Shankar, Carpenter, and Krishnamurhi (1998). Introducing new product features has important effects on brand choice (Nowlis and Simonson, 1996) and even irrelevant attributes can result in the meaningful differentiation necessary for product success (Carpenter, Glazer, and Nakamoto, 1994). Finally, pioneers may be relatively better off with incremental innovations and in markets where consumers value variety, and later entrants may be relatively better off with radical innovations and in markets where consumers value quality (Bohlmann, Golder, and Mitra, 2002; Min, Kalwani, and Robinson, 2006).

Beyond determining entry timing, firms must select the *appropriate marketing mix* to use in entering a new market. Papers on this topic have been relatively scarce outside of the *Journal of Product Innovation Management.* One important exception is Horsky and Nelson's (1992) paper on positioning and pricing. Similarly, Cooper (2000) discusses planning for radically new products and Hitsch (2006) explores optimal entry when demand is uncertain. At a more tactical level, Kopalle and Lehmann (2005) examine optimal advertised quality as well as actual quality and price. Channel acceptance has also received some attention (Luo, Kannan, and Ratchfood, 2007).

An interesting and related, yet relatively unresearched topic, is *how incumbents should respond to a new entrant.* Hauser and Shugan (1983) developed an analytical model that developed normative prescriptions for such defensive strategies. However, Robinson (1988a) finds that the most common response to a new entrant is either no response or response in a single marketing mix variable. Gatignon, Robertson, and Fein (1997) empirically examined defensive strategy effectiveness against new product entry and found that fast reaction was viewed as more successful whereas breadth of reaction (number of marketing mix variables used) was viewed as less successful. Bowman and Gatignon (1996) merge the literatures on competitive response and order of entry by showing that late entry impacts sensitivity to price, promotion, and quality.

13.6 Valuation

Initial work on valuing new products focused primarily on sales and market share, often using PIMS (Profit Impact of Market Strategy) data (Buzzell and Gale, 1987). More recently, attention has centered on financial consequences related to stock prices.

The explosion of work on metrics and linking marketing to financial performance occurred in the late 1990s and 2000s. However, prior work also addressed this topic. Chaney, Devinney, and Winer's (1991) paper on the value of new product introductions moved the focus from product market results (e.g., market share) to financial/stock market value. Across all stages of development, innovation projects have market returns of US$643 million (Sood and Tellis, 2009). Other work in this area has analyzed stock price movements to generate insights into the impact of marketing decisions and competencies (e.g., market orientation) on financial performance. This includes examining the trade-off between marketing and R&D (Mizik and Jacobson, 2003), rewards from radical innovations (Sorescu, Chandy, and Prabhu, 2003), the relationship between customers and stock price (Gupta, Lehmann, and Stuart, 2004), the impact of innovation on firm value and risk, (McAlister, Srinivasan, and Kim, 2007; Sorescu and Spanjol, 2008), the impact of product innovations and advertising on stock returns (Srinivasan, *et al.*, 2009), and total returns to innovation (Sood and Tellis, 2009). All of these studies use stock price as an outcome measure and relate it to these important marketing activities. Interestingly, one recent study finds that stock prices can predict the sales take-off of new products (Markovitch and Golder, 2008). Recently, research has begun to assess the reverse effect: how stock price and financial performance (e.g., ROA) impacts marketing decisions in general and innovation, R&D spending, and new product performance in particular.

13.7 Practitioner priorities

To assess the perspective of business, it is useful to focus on the research priorities of the Marketing Science Institute, developed through surveying its members. Somewhat surprisingly, new products or innovation was not identified as a high priority topic between 1974 and 1992, although developing business opportunities was the highest priority topic in 1984–1985. By contrast, since 1992, some variation on new products, innovation, and growth has consistently been a top priority.

Through the 1980s, the top priorities concentrated on improving (innovating) the marketing mix, with no special focus on new products. The 1992–1994 priorities spotlight improving the new product development process, i.e., efficiency, while for 1994–1996, the top priority was forecasting both new product sales and future environments. Next, attention centered on "really new" (discontinuous) innovations as well as on developing organizations capable of producing multiple new products over time.

For 1998–2000, attention focused on best practices. The specific topics identified as high priority were "breakthrough" product platforms (a.k.a. really new products) and the development of customer insights. The next set of priorities (2000–2002) showed a lessening concern about new products *per se* as attention shifted to the Internet and new media. However, interest in consumer (customer) insights, speed to market, and evaluating/selecting among products remained high.

The 2002–2004 priorities showed an important shift in emphasis. Growth was identified as the key aspect, with innovation and new products now (appropriately) thought of as means to this end/goal. In addition, the role of metrics in assessing product development, including the more qualitative aspects of idea generation, became more prominent, especially related to predicting success and failure.

Growth ascended to the top priority in 2004–2006, a position it held for three of the next four sets of priorities. Discontinuous growth strategies effectively combined the older emphasis on really new products with growth. The emphasis on organic growth signaled increased emphasis on internal versus external growth via mergers and acquisitions.

The 2006–2008 priorities combined innovation with growth and emphasized involving customers in the innovation and product development process while formally identifying design as a key focus. In addition, it returned to the topic of the organization, specifically a culture of innovation.

The 2008–2010 priorities identified other aspects worthy of exploration including services while retaining a focus on product development, co-creation, and technology. The 2010–2012 priorities again placed profitable growth at the top, highlighting the roles of information and technology.

Most recently, the 2012–2014 priorities shifted the focus slightly away from developing new products to designing customer experiences. In particular, emphasis moved toward identifying what firm practices are successful in designing positive experiences. This shift reflects a desire on MSI's part to incorporate knowledge from the services domain (i.e., retailing) where the consumption experience has always been paramount. Also, the shift reflects a return to the age-old marketing concept that people buy products for the benefits they deliver (Levitt, 1960).

Examining these priorities across time reveals an interesting progression. The focus has moved from innovation to improve the marketing mix in general to new products and then to really new products/discontinuous innovation. Innovation itself then emerged as a major theme, including idea generation, creativity, and design. Most recently, the focus has shifted to organic growth, with new products seen more as a means to this end, and finally how new products contribute to consumers' overall consumption experience and their resulting satisfaction.

As seen in Table 13.2, the number of award-winning papers on new products has increased over time. The strong interest of the managerial community has no doubt helped guide some researchers toward fruitful and important areas of new product research.

Table 13.2 Award-winning papers on new products.

1970s

1. Silk and Urban, *JMR* 1978 (O'Dell) Pre-Test-Market Forecasting of New Packaged Goods: A Model and Measurement Methodology.
2. Shocker and Srinivasan, *JMR* 1979 (O'Dell) Multi-Attribute Approaches for Product Concept Evaluation and Testing.

1980s

1. Urban and Katz, *JMR* 1983 (O'Dell) Pre-Test-Market Models: Validation and Managerial Implications.
2. Hauser and Shugan, *Marketing Science* 1983 (Little) Defensive Marketing Strategies.
3. Urban, Carter, Gaskin, and Mucha, *Marketing Science* 1986 (Little) Market Share Rewards to Pioneering Brands: An Empirical Analysis and Strategic Implications.
4. Robertson and Gatignon, *JM* 1986 (Maynard) Competitive Effects on Technology Diffusion.
5. Norton and Bass, *Management Science* 1987 (Little) A Diffusion Theory Model of Adoption and Substitution for Successive Generations of High-Technology Products.
6. Carpenter and Nakamoto, *JMR* 1989 (O'Dell) Consumer Preference Formation and Pioneering Advantage.

1990s

1. Sultan, Farley, and Lehmann, *JMR* 1990 (O'Dell) A Meta Analysis of Applications of Diffusion Models.
2. Mahajan, Muller, and Bass, *JM* 1990 (Maynard) Product Diffusion Models in Marketing: A Review and Directions for Research.
3. Horsky and Nelson, *Marketing Science* 1992 (Bass) New Brand Positioning and Pricing in an Oligopolistic Market.
4. Golder and Tellis, *JMR* 1993 (O'Dell) Pioneer Advantage: Marketing Logic or Marketing Legend?.
5. Carpenter, Glazer, and Nakamoto, *JMR* 1994 (O'Dell) Meaningful Brands from Meaningless Differentiation.
6. Raju, Sethuraman, and Dhar, *Management Science* 1995 (Little) The Introduction and Performance of Store Brands.
7. Nowlis and Simonson, *JMR* 1996 (O'Dell) The Effect of New Product Features on Brand Choice.
8. Urban, Weinberg, and Hauser, *JM* 1996 (Root) Premarket Forecasting of Really New Products.
9. Golder and Tellis, *Marketing Science* 1997 (Bass) Will it Ever Fly: Modeling the Takeoff of Really New Consumer Durables.

(Continued)

Table 13.1 (*Continued*)

2000s

1. Cooper, *JM* 2000 (Root) Strategic Marketing Planning for Radically New Products.
2. Amaldoss and Meyer, *Marketing Science* 2000 (Little) Collaborating to Compete.
3. Chandy and Tellis, *JM* 2000 (Maynard) The Incumbent's Curse: Incumbency, Size, and Radical Product Innovation.
4. Mittal and Kamakura, *JMR* 2001 (O'Dell) Satisfaction, Repurchase Intent, and Repurchase behavior: Investigating the Moderating Effect of Customer Characteristics.
5. Ofek and Sarvary, *Marketing Science* 2003 (Little, Bass) R&D, Marketing, and the Success of Next-Generation Products.
6. Bronnenberg and Mela, *Marketing Science* 2004 (Little) Market Roll-out and Retailer Adoption for New Brands.
7. Golder and Tellis, *Marketing Science* 2004 (Long-term Impact) Growing, Growing, Gone: Cascades, Diffusion, and Turning Points in the Product Life Cycle.
8. Chevalier and Mayzlin, *JMR* 2006 (O'Dell) The Effect of Word of Mouth on Sales: Online Book Reviews.
9. Biyalogorsky, Boulding, and Staelin, *JM* 2006 (Maynard) Stuck in the Past: Why Managers Persist with New Product Failures.
10. Hitsch, *Marketing Science* 2006 (Bass) An Empirical Model of Optimal Dynamic Product Launch and Entry under Demand Uncertainty.
11. Mayzlin, *Marketing Science* 2006 (Bass) Firm Created Word of Mouth Communication.
12. Luo, Kannan, and Ratchford, *Marketing Science* 2007 (Little) New product Development under Channel Acceptance.
13. Johnson and Tellis, *JM* 2008 (Root) Drivers of Success for Market Entry into China and India.
14. Gordon, *Marketing Science* 2009 (Little) A Dynamic Model of Consumer Replacement Cycles in the PC Processor Industry.

13.8 The future

Where will the future emphasis be in new products research? Recognizing the fallibility of forecasts, the following seem likely to be important.

Over time, the emphasis moved from the lone inventor as almost a mythical hero to teams/labs, e.g., Xerox PARC, Bell Labs, and GE (which has recently expanded its R&D spending). External collaborations have been emphasized, both alliances/partnerships with other companies and with customers via lead users and beta sites. More recently, attention has shifted to listening to "common folk" and customers, and incorporating their ideas and "duct tape" solutions to problems. Particularly interesting in this regard is the importing of designs that originate in less developed countries into industrialized countries (i.e., reverse exporting/innovation).

One area ripe for further development is structured creativity devices to identify growth options. Another is design, including design for efficient production in terms of cost and resource use, repair, easy upgrade, and disposal and/or re-purposing.

Another important area is implementation/execution. Areas such as cross-functional coordination, use of beta sites, and means for scaling up (and the ability and willingness to scale back in the face of weak demand) remain important and relatively understudied.

A third area, organic creation, is an extension of the first. Customer-developed and customer-refined (and evaluated) designs/products are increasingly recognized for their potential to drive organic growth. In effect, these recognize the "new normal," i.e., firms are no longer in charge of their products or reputations.

The final area is a less pleasant one. To many constituencies, new products are not seen as a mechanism for economic improvement but rather as a drain on resources (natural, financial, and human) and a means to encourage a more wasteful and less fulfilling lifestyle. Figuring out ways to incorporate both customer and environmental (sustainability) concerns in the design, evaluation, and marketing of new products is or at least should be a high priority.

References

Amaldoss, W., R. J. Meyer, J. S. Raju, and A. Rapaport (2000). Collaborating to compete, *Marketing Science*, 19(2) (Spring), 105–126.

Assmus, G. (1975). NEWPROD: The design and implementation of a new product model, *Journal of Marketing*, 39(1) (January), 16–23.

Bass, F. M. (1969). A new product growth model for consumer durables, *Management Science*, 15(5), 215–227.

Bayus, B. L., S. Jain, and A. G. Rao (2001). Truth or consequences: An analysis of vaporware and new product announcements, *Journal of Marketing Research*, 38(1), 3–13.

Biyalogorsky, E., W. Boulding, and R. Staelin (2006). Stuck in the past: Why managers persist with new product failures, *Journal of Marketing*, 10(2) (April), 108–121.

Blackburn, J. D. and K. J. Clancy (1980). LITMUS: A new product planning model, in Robert P. Leone, ed., *Proceedings: Market measurement and analysis*, Providence, R.I.: The Institute of Management Sciences, pp. 182–193.

Blattberg, R. and J. Golanty (1978). Tracker: An early test market forecasting and diagnostic model for new product planning, *Journal of Marketing Research*, 15(2), 192–202.

Bohlmann, J. D., P. N. Golder, and D. Mitra (2002). Deconstructing the pioneer's advantage: Examining vintage effects and consumer valuations of quality and variety, *Management Science*, 48(9), 1175–1195.

Bonanno, G. (1987). Location choice, product proliferation and entry deterrence, *The Review of Economic Studies*, 54(1), 37–45.

Boulding, W. and M. Christen (2003). Sustainable pioneering advantage? Profit implications of market entry order, *Marketing Science*, 22(3), 371–392.

Boulding, W., R. Morgan, and R. Staelin (1997). Pulling the plug to stop the new product drain, *Journal of Marketing Research*, 34(1), 164–176.

Bowman, D. and H. Gatignon (1996). Order of entry as a moderator of the effect of the marketing mix on market share, *Marketing Science*, 15(3), 222–242.

Boyd, D. and J. Goldenberg (2013). *Inside the box*, NY, NY: Simon and Schuster.

Buzzell, R. D. and B. T. Gale (1987). *The PIMS principles: Linking strategy to performance*, New York: The Free Press.

Bronnenberg, B. J. and C. F. Mela (2004). Market roll-out and retailer adoption for new brands, *Marketing Science*, 23(Fall), 500–518.

Carpenter, G. S., R. Glazer, and K. Nakamoto (1994). Meaningful brands from meaningless differentiation: The dependence on irrelevant attributes, *Journal of Marketing Research*, 31(3) (August), 339–350.

Carpenter, G. S. and K. Nakamoto (1989). Consumer preference formation and pioneering advantage, *Journal of Marketing Research*, 26(3) (August), 285–298.

Carpenter, G. S. and K. Nakamoto (1990). Competitive strategies for late entry into a market with a dominant brand, *Management Science*, 36(10) (October), Focused Issue on the State of the Art in Theory and Method in Strategy Research, 1268–1278.

Chandy, R. K. and G. J. Tellis (1998). Organizing for radical product innovation: The overlooked role of willingness to cannibalize, *Journal of Marketing Research* 35(4), 474–487.

Chandy, R. K. and G. J. Tellis (2000). The incumbent's curse? Incumbency, size, and radical product innovation, *Journal of Marketing*, 64(3) (July), 1–17.

Chaney, P. K., T. M. Devinney, and R. S. Winer (1991). The impact of new product introductions on the market value of firms, *Journal of Business*, 64(4), 573–610.

Chevalier, J. A. and D. Mayzlin (2006). The effect of word of mouth on sales: Online book reviews, *Journal of Marketing Research*, 43(3) (August), 343–354.

Claycamp, H. J. and L. E. Liddy (1969). Prediction of new product performance: An analytical approach, *Journal of Marketing Research*, 6(4) (November), 414–420.

Cooper, R. G. (1990). Stage-gate systems: A new tool for managing new products, *Business Horizons*, 33(3), 44–54.

Cooper, R. G. (1994). Perspective third-generation new product processes, *Journal of Product Innovation Management*, 11(1), 3–14.

Cooper, L. G. (2000). Strategic marketing planning for radically new products, *Journal of Marketing*, 64(1) (January), 1–16.

Dahan, E., A. J. Kim, A. W. Lo, T. Poggio, and N. Chan (2011). Securities trading of concepts (STOC), *Journal of Marketing Research*, 48(3), 497–517.

Ding, M. and J. Eliashberg (2002). Structuring the new product development pipeline, *Management Science*, 48(3), 343–363.

Ehrenberg, A. S. C. (1972). *Repeat-buying: Theory and application*, Amsterdam: North Holland Press.

Fader, P. S. and D. C. Schmittlein (1992). Excess behavioral loyalty for high-share brands: Deviations from the Dirichlet model for repeat purchasing, *Journal of Marketing Research*, 30(November), 478–493.

Fader, P. S., B. G. S. Hardie, and K. L. Lee (2005) Counting your customers the easy way: An alternative to the Pareto/NBD model, *Marketing Science*, 24(Spring), 275–284.

Fisher, J. C. and R. H. Pry (1971). A simple substitution model of technological change, *Technological Forecasting and Social Change*, 3, 75–88.

Fourt, L. A. and J. W. Woodlock (1960). Early prediction of market success for new grocery products, *Journal of Marketing*, 25(2), 31–38.

Ganesan, S., A. J. Malter, and A. Rindfleisch (2005). Does distance still matter? Geographic proximity and new product development, *Journal of Marketing*, 69(4), 44–60.

Gatignon, H. and T. S. Robertson (1985). A propositional inventory for new diffusion research, *Journal of Consumer Research*, 11(4), 849–867.

Gatignon, H., T. S. Robertson, and A. J. Fein (1997). Incumbent defense strategies against new product entry, *International Journal of Research in Marketing*, 14(2), 163–176.

Gatignon, H. and J.-M. Xuereb (1997). Strategic orientation of the firm and new product performance, *Journal of Marketing Research*, 34(1) (February), 77–90, Special Issue.

Gatignon, H. and T. S. Roberston (1985). A propositional inventory for new diffusion research, *Journal of Consumer Research*, 11(March), 849–867.

Godes, D. and D. Mayzlin (2004). Using online conversations to study word-of-mouth communication, *Marketing Science*, 23(4), 545–560.

Goldenberg, J., D. R. Lehmann, and D. Mazursky (2001). The primary of the idea itself as a predictor of new product success, *Management Science*, 47(1), 69–84.

Goldenberg, J., R. Horowitz, A. Levav, and D. Mazursky (2003). Finding your innovation sweet spot, *Harvard Business Review*, 81(3), 120–130.

Goldenberg, J., M. David, and S. Solomon (1999). Toward identifying the templates of new products: A channeled ideation approach, *Journal of Marketing Research*, 36(2) (May), 200–210.

Goldenberg, J., R. Horowitz, A. Levav, and D. Mazursky (2003). Finding your innovation sweet spot, *Harvard Business Review*, 81(3) (March), 120–130.

Golder, P. N. and G. J. Tellis (2004). Growing, growing, gone: Cascades, diffusion, and turning points in the product life cycle, *Marketing Science*, 23(2) (Spring), 207–218.

Golder, P. N., R. Shacham, and D. Mitra (2009). Innovations' origins: When, by whom, and how are radical innovations developed? *Marketing Science*, 28(1), 166–179.

Golder, P. N. and G. J. Tellis (1993). Pioneer advantage: Marketing logic or marketing legend? *Journal of Marketing Research*, 30(May) 158–170.

Golder, P. N. and G. J. Tellis (1997). Will it ever fly: Modeling the takeoff of really new consumer durables, *Marketing Science*, 16(3), 256–270.

Gordon, B. R. (2009). A dynamic model of consumer replacement cycles in the PC processor industry, *Marketing Science*, 28(5) (September–October), 846–867.

Green, P. E. and V. Srinivasan (1978). Conjoint analysis in consumer research: issues and outlook, *Journal of Consumer Research*, 5(2), 103–123.

Green, P. E. and V. Srinivasan (1990). Conjoint analysis in marketing: New developments with implications for research and practice, *Journal of Marketing*, 54(4), 3–19.

Green, P. E., J. D. Carroll, and S. M. Goldberg (1981). A general approach to product design optimization via conjoint analysis, *Journal of Marketing*, 45(Summer), 17–37.

Green P. E. and V. R. Rao (1971). Conjoint measurement for quantifying judgmental data, *Journal of Marketing Research*, 8(August), 355–363.

Griffin, A. (1997). PDMA research on new product development practices: Updating trends and benchmarking best practices, *Journal of Product Innovation Management*, 4(6), 429–458.

Griffin, A. and J. R. Hauser (1996). Integrating R&D and marketing: a review and analysis of the literature, *Journal of Product Innovation Management*, 13(3), 191–215.

Griffin, A. and J. R. Hauser (1993). The Voice of the Customer, *Marketing Science*, 12(1) (Winter), 1–27.

Gupta, S., D. R. Lehmann, and J. Ames-Stuart (2004). Valuing customers, *Journal of Marketing Research*, 41(1) (February), 7–16.

Hauser, J. R. and D. Clausing (1988). The house of quality, *Harvard Business Review*, 66(3) (May–June), 63–73.

Hauser, J. R. and S. M. Shugan (1983). Defensive marketing strategies, *Marketing Science*, 2(4) (Autumn), 319–360.

Hauser, J., G. J. Tellis, and A. Griffin (2006). Research on innovation: A review and agenda for marketing science, *Marketing Science*, 25(6), 687–717.

Hauser, J. R., G. L. Urban, G. Liberali, and M. Braun (2009). Website morphing, *Marketing Science*, 28(2), 202–223.

Heil, O. and T. S. Robertson (1991). Toward a theory of competitive market signaling: a research agenda, *Strategic Management Journal*, 12(6), 403–418.

Henard, D. H. and D. M. Szymanski (2001). Why some new products are more successful than others, *Journal of Marketing Research*, 38(3), 362–375.

Hitsch, G. A. (2006). An empirical model of optimal dynamic product launch and exit under demand uncertainty, *Marketing Science*, 25(1) (January–February), 25–50.

Horsky, D. and P. Nelson (1992). New brand positioning and pricing in an oligopolistic market, *Marketing Science*, 11(2) (Spring), 133.

Johnson, R. M. (1974). Tradeoff analysis of consumer value, *Journal of Marketing Research*, 11(2) (May), 121–127.

Johnson, R. M. (1987). *Adaptive conjoint analysis.* Paper presented at the Sawtooth Software Conference.

Johnson, J. and G. J. Tellis (2008). Drivers of success for market entry into China and India, *Journal of Marketing*, 72(3) (May), 1–13.

Kalyanaram, G., W. T. Robinson, and G. L. Urban (1995). Order of market entry: Established empirical generalizations, emerging empirical generalizations, and future research, *Marketing Science*, 14(3 Suppl.), G212–G221.

Kalyanaram, G. and G. L. Urban (1992). Dynamic effects of the order of entry on market share, trial penetration, and repeat purchases for frequently purchased consumer goods, *Marketing Science*, 11(3), 235–250.

Kopalle, P. and D. R. Lehmann (2006). Setting quality expectations when entering a market: What should the promise be? *Marketing Science*, 25(1) (January–February), 8–24.

Kuehn, A. A. (1962). Consumer brand choice as a learning process, *Journal of Advertising Research*, 2, 10–17.

Lane, W. J. (1980). Product differentiation in a market with endogenous sequential entry, *The Bell Journal of Economics*, 11(1), 237–260.

Levitt, T. (1960). Marketing myopia, *Harvard Business Review*, 38(4), 24–47.

Lilien, G. L., P. D. Morrison, K. Searls, M. Sonnack, and E. V. Hippel (2002). Performance assessment of the lead user idea-generation process for new product development, *Management Science*, 48(8), 1042–1059.

Liu, Y. (2006). Word of mouth for movies: Its dynamics and impact on box office revenue, *Journal of Marketing*, 70(3), 74–89.

Luce, D. R. and J. W. Turkey (1964). Simultaneous conjoint measurement: A new type of fundamental measurement, *Journal of Mathematical Psychology*, 1, 1–27.

Luo, L., P. K. Kannan, and B. T. Ratchford (2007). New product development under channel acceptance, *Marketing Science*, 26(2) (March–April), 149–163.

Mahajan, V., E. Muller, and F. M. Bass (1990). New product diffusion models in marketing: A review and directions for research, *Journal of Marketing*, 54(1) (January), 1–26.

Markovitch, D. G. and P. N. Golder (2008). Using stock prices to predict market events: Evidence on sales takeoff and long-term firm survival, *Marketing Science*, 27(4), 717–729.

Massy, W. F. (1969). Forecasting the demand for new convenience products, *Journal of Marketing Research*, 6(4), 405–412.

McAlister, L., R. Srinivasan, and M. Kim (2007). Advertising, research and development, and systematic risk of the firm, *Journal of Marketing*, 71(1), 35–48.

Min, S., M. U. Kalwani, and W. T. Robinson (2006). Market pioneer and early follower survival risks: A contingency analysis of really new versus incrementally new product-markets, *Journal of Marketing*, 70(1), 15–33.

Mittal, V. and W. A. Kamakura (2001). Satisfaction, repurchase intent, and repurchase behavior: Investigating the moderating effect of customer characteristics, *Journal of Marketing Research*, 38(1) (February), 131–142.

Mizik, N. and R. Jacobson (2003). Trading off between value creation and value appropriation: The financial implications of shifts in strategic emphasis, *Journal of Marketing*, 67(1) (January), 63–96.

Montoya-Weiss, M. M. and R. Calantone (1994). Determinants of new product performance: A review and meta-analysis, *Journal of Product Innovation Management*, 11(5) (November), 397–417.

Moorman, C. and A. S. Miner (1997). The impact of organizational memory on new product performance and creativity, *Journal of Marketing Research*, 34(1), 91–106.

Moorman, C. and A. S. Miner (1998). Organizational improvisation and organizational memory, *Academy of Management Review*, 23(4), 698–723.

Moreau, C. P. and D. W. Dahl (2005). Designing the solution: The impact of constraints on consumers' creativity, *Journal of Consumer Research*, 32(1), 13–22.

Narasimhan, C. and Z. J. Zhang (2000). Market entry strategy under firm heterogeneity and asymmetric payoffs, *Marketing Science*, 19(4), 313–325.

Netzer, O. and V. Srinivasan (2011). Adaptive, self-explication of multiattribute preferences, 48(1) (February), 140–156.

Norton, J. A. and F. M. Bass (1987). A diffusion theory model of adoption and substitution for successive generations of high-technology products, *Management Science*, 33(9) (September), 1069–1086.

Nowlis, S. M. and I. Simonson (1996).The effect of new product features on brand choice, *Journal of Marketing Research*, 33(1), 36–46.

Ofek, E. and M. Sarvary (2003). R&D, marketing and the success of next-generation products, *Marketing Science*, 22(3) (Summer), 355–370.

Parfitt, J. H. and B. J. K. Collins (1968). Use of consumer panels for brand-share prediction, *Journal of Marketing Research*, 5(2) (May), 131–145.

Prasad, B. (1998). Review of QFD and related deployment techniques, *Journal of Manufacturing Systems*, 17(3), 221–234.

Prescott, E. C. and M. Visscher (1977). Sequential location among firms with foresight, *The Bell Journal of Economics*, 8(2), 378–393.

Pringle, L. G., R. D. Wilson, and E. I. Brody (1982). News: A decision-oriented model for new product analysis and forecasting, *Marketing Science*, 1(1) (Winter), 1–29.

Raju, J. S., R. Sethuraman, and S. K. Dhar (1995). The introduction and performance of store brands, *Management Science*, 41(6) (June), 957–978.

Rindfleisch, A. and C. Moorman (2001). The acquisition and utilization of information in new product alliances: A strength-of-ties perspective, *Journal of Marketing*, 65(2), 1–18.

Robertson, T. S. and H. Gatignon (1986). Competitive effects on technology diffusion, *Journal of Marketing*, 50(July), 1–12.

Robertson, T. S., J. Eliashberg, and T. Rymon (1995). New product announcement signals and incumbent reactions, *Journal of Marketing*, 59(3), 1–15.

Robinson, W. T. (1988a). Marketing mix reactions to entry, *Marketing Science*, 7(4), 368–385.

Robinson, W. T. (1988b). Sources of market pioneer advantages: The case of industrial goods industries, *Journal of Marketing Research*, 25(1), 87–94.

Robinson, W. T. and C. Fornell (1985). Sources of market pioneer advantages in consumer goods industries, *Journal of Marketing Research*, 22(3) (August), 305–317.

Rogers, E. M. (2003). *Diffusion of innovations*, (5th ed.), New York: Free Press.

Rothschild, R. (1976). A note on the effect of sequential entry on choice of location, *The Journal of Industrial Economics*, 24(4), 313–320.

Sethi, R. and Z. Iqbal (2008). Stage-gate controls, learning failure, and adverse effect on novel new products, *Journal of Marketing*, 72(1), 118–134.

Sethi, R., D. C. Smith, and C. W. Park (2001). Cross-functional product development teams, creativity, and the innovativeness of new consumer products, *Journal of Marketing Research*, 38(1), 73–85.

Shanker, V., G. S. Carpenter, and L. Krishnamurthi (1998). Late mover advantage: How innovative late Entrants Outsell Pioneers, *Journal of Marketing Research*, 35(February), 54–70.

Shocker, A. D. and V. Srinivasan (1974). A consumer-based methodology for the identification of new product ideas, *Management Science*, 20(6), 921–937.

Shocker, A. D. and V. Srinivasan (1979). Multi-attribute approaches for product concept evaluation and generation: A critical review, *Journal of Marketing Research*, 16(May), 159–180.

Silk, A. J. and G. L. Urban (1978). Pre-test-market forecasting of new packaged goods: A model and measurement methodology, *Journal of Marketing Research*, 15(2) (May), 171–191.

Sood, A. and G. J. Tellis (2005). Technological evolution and radical innovation, *Journal of Marketing*, 69(3), 152–168.

Sood, A. and G. J. Tellis (2009). Do innovations really pay off? Total stock market returns to innovation, *Marketing Science*, 28(May–June), 442–456.

Sorescu, A. B. and J. Spanjol (2008). Innovation's effect on firm value and risk: Insights from consumer packaged goods, *Journal of Marketing*, 72(2) (March), 114–132.

Sorescu, A. B., R. K. Chandy, and J. C. Prabhu (2003). Sources and financial consequences of radical innovation: Insights from pharmaceuticals, *Journal of Marketing*, 67(4), 82–102.

Srinivasan, V. (1988). A conjunctive-compensatory approach to the self-explication of multiattributed preferences, *Decision Sciences*, 19(2), 295–305.

Srinivasan, S., K. Pauwels, J. Silva-Risso, and D. Hanseens (2009). Product innovations, advertising, and stock returns, *Journal of Marketing*, 73(1) (January), 24–43.

Srinivasan, S. and A. D. Shocker Allan (1973). Estimating the weights for multiple attributes in a composite criterion using pairwise judgments, *Psychometrika*, 38(4) (December), 473–493.

Sultan, F., J. U. Farley, and D. R. Lehmann (1990). A meta analyses of applications of diffusion models, *Journal of Marketing Research*, 27(1) (February), 70–77.

Thomadsen, R. (2012). Seeking an expanding competitor: How product line expansion can increase all firms' profits, *Journal of Marketing Research*, 49 (June), 349–360.

Toubia, O. (2006). Idea generation, creativity, and innovation, *Marketing Science*, 25(5) (September–October), 411–425.

Toubia, O., D. I. Simester, J. R. Hauser, and E. Dahan (2003). Fast polyhedral adaptive conjoint estimation, *Marketing Science*, 22(3), 273–303.

Urban, G. L. and J. R. Hauser (1980). *Design and marketing of new products*, Englewood Cliffs, NJ: Prentice-Hall.

Urban, G. L. and J. R. Hauser (2004). "Listening in" to find and explore new combinations of customer needs, *Journal of Marketing*, 68(2), 72–87.

Urban, G. L., J. R. Hauser, G. Liberali, M. Braun, and F. Sultan (2009). Morph the web to build empathy, trust and sales, *MIT Sloan Management Review*, 50(Summer), 53–61.

Urban, G. L., J. R. Hauser, W. J. Qualls, B. D. Weinberg, J. D. Bohlmann, and R. A. Chicos (1997). Validation and lessons from the field: Applications of information acceleration, *Journal of Marketing Research*, 34(February), 143–153.

Urban, G. L., B. D. Weinberg, and J. R. Hauser (1996). Premarket forecasting of really new products, *Journal of Marketing*, 60(1) (January), 47–60.

Urban, G. L. and J. R. Hauser (1993). Design and marketing of new products, Englewood Cliffs, NJ: Prentice Hall.

Urban, G. L. and E. Von Hippel (1988). Lead user analysis for the development of new industrial products, *Management Science*, 34(5) (May), 569–582.

Urban, G. L. and N. Dholaria (1987). *Essentials of new product management*, Englewood Cliffs, NJ: Prentice Hall.

Urban, G. L., T. Carter, S. Gaskin, and Z. Mucha (1986). Market share rewards to pioneering brands: An empirical analysis and strategic implications, *Management Science*, 32(June), 645–659.

Urban, G. L. and G. M. Katz (1983). Pre-test-market models: Validation and managerial implications, *Journal of Marketing Research*, 20(3) (August), 221–234.

Urban, G. L. (1975). PERCEPTOR: A model for product positioning, *Management Science*, 21(8), Application Series (April), 858–871.

Urban, G. L. (1970). SPRINTER MOD III: A model for the analysis of new frequently purchased consumer products, *Operations Research*, 18(5) (September–October), 805–854.

Von Hippel, E. (1986). Lead users: A source of novel product concepts, *Management Science*, V32(7), 791–805.

Von Hippel, E. (1988). *The sources of innovation*, New York: Oxford University Press.

Wind, Y. (1973). A new procedure for concept evaluation, *Journal of Marketing*, 37(4) (October), 2–11.

Wind, J., P. E. Green, D. Shifflet, and M. Scarbrough (1989). Courtyard by Marriott: Designing a hotel facility with consumer-based marketing models, *Interfaces*, 19(1), 25–47.

Wittink, D. R. and P. Cattin (1989). Commercial use of conjoint analysis: An update, *Journal of Marketing*, 53(3), 91–96.

Wittink, D. R., M. Vriens, and W. Burhenne (1994). Commercial use of conjoint analysis in Europe: Results and critical reflections, *International Journal of Research in Marketing*, 11, 41–52.

Chapter 14

Organizational Buying Behavior

Gary L. Lilien

14.1 Introduction

It is quite common to differentiate between models of consumer behavior and models of organizational buying that result from some key differences in the way individuals and organizations buy. First, organizational demand is derived demand. Products are purchased by organizations to meet the needs of their customers. Impulse buying is far less common in organizational buying and is clearly stated. Objective criteria such as meeting production needs and schedules with a minimum cost product (or "offering" to include the combination of physical product and surrounding service) often drive the choice process.

Second, because more than one and often many individuals are involved in the purchasing decision process, purchasing managers rarely make a buying decision independent of the influence of others (stakeholders) in the buying organization. In addition, individuals outside the organization (in supplier firms, in other firms in the industry, in the supply chain and elsewhere) may influence the decision. Hence, the purchasing decision is made by a group, which is, in turn, embedded in a network of individual and organizational relationships.

Third, because of the (1) high dollar volume of the purchase, (2) the number of stakeholders involved and (3) the often complex, technical nature of the offerings under consideration, the purchasing process often takes a long time and may involve extensive bargaining and negotiations. The extended nature of the organizational purchase process (which can take months or years in some cases) and its interactive nature (involving multiple individuals within both the buying and selling organizations) make it difficult to develop a functional relationship between the marketing effort of a supplier and the response of the buyer.

Fourth, as organizational buyers are more interested in satisfying a total need than in buying a specific product, the resulting offering can be quite complex, including such items as training, technical support, financing, delivery terms and the like, with neither the buyer nor the seller easily able to determine what offer is the best for the buyer.

Yet organizational buying and consumer buying have two attributes in common — a purchase is the usual outcome of the process and there is some form of process that leads to that outcome, and the consumer/organizational buying border is not at all clear. Hence, the marketing science developments in choice models and stochastic models of buyer behavior discussed in other chapters of the book (Fader, Hardie, and Sen, 2013; Russell, 2013) apply here as well. For example, Gensch (1984) used a multinomial logit model to determine the switchability (or customer loyalty) in the market for electrical equipment aimed at electric utility customers.

In this chapter, we will trace several streams of research on models of organizational buying behavior: large system models, models of group choice, bargaining and negotiation models, and relationship and network models. The developments in these domains have taken place largely in parallel, and independently as show in the development timeline in Figure 14.1.

14.2   Large system and group choice models

The 1960s and 1970s displayed great interest in large scale system models of organizational buying behavior. The *BUYGRID* framework (Robinson, Faris, and Wind, 1967) serves as a seminal starting point for models of organizational buying. The authors divided the buying process into straight rebuy, modified rebuy and novel purchases. The more novel the purchase, the greater the degree of uncertainty and the more people involved in the purchase decision (the buying center). The buygrid framework, a conceptual model, has three key dimensions: (1) the buying situation (straight or modified rebuy and novel or new task), (2) the stages of the decision process (needs identification, establishment of specifications, search, evaluate

Relationship and network models		Relationships dyadic marketing concept Bonoma & Johnston (1978)	Relationship models and networks Hutt & Reingen (1987); Turnbull & Valla (1986)	Integrative relationship models Cannon & Perreault (1999); Iacobucci & Ostrom (1996)	Network models with incomplete data, multiplexity, dynamics Van den Bulte & Wuyts (2007)
Bargaining models	Economic/equilibrium Models — two party/single issue Nash (1950)	Multi-issue/ multi-agent models Keeney & Raiffa (1976)	Behavioral economic models Raiffa (1982); Neslin & Greenhalgh (1983)	Process models of negotiations Balakrishnan & Eliashberg (1995)	Agenda strategies with buying teams Patton & Balakrishnan (2012)
System and group choice models	Arrow's impossibility theorem Arrow (1963) Buygrid Framework (Robinson, Farris, & Wind, 1967)	Large system models Sheth (1973); Webster & Wind (1972)	Operational and group choice models Choffray & Lilien (1980); Corfman & Lehmann (1987); Corfman & Gupta (1993); Steckel (1990); Rao & Steckel (1991); Wilson, Lilien, & Wilson (1991)	Large system model expansion Johnston & Lewin (1996); Spekman & Gronhaug (1986)	Extension of buying center — across firm functions and across the supply chain (Johnston & Chandler, 2013)
Timeline (rough)	1960s and earlier	1970s	1980s	1990s	2000 and later

Fig. 14.1   A rough time trend of major themes in organizational buying models

alternatives, negotiate, buy, use and feedback) and (3) the roles of buying center participants (purchasing, user, specifier, finance, top management, etc.).

The 1970s saw publication of more than a dozen major articles on organizational buying (see Reid and Plank, 2000). Webster (1984) cited three that he felt were applicable to a wide spectrum of organizational buying contexts as they identified the most important variables in the process and the relationships between them: The Sheth (1973) model, the Webster–Wind Model (1972) and the Choffray–Lilien Model (1980).

Sheth (1973) adapted the Howard and Sheth (1969) model of consumer buying behavior for organizational contexts. The model posits three major elements in the organizational buying process: (1) the psychological world of the individuals involved, (2) the conditions that precipitate joint decision making and (3) the conflict resolution process for joint purchasing decisions. The model also identifies situational factors that influence the final choice of supplier or brand.

Webster and Wind (1972) view organizational buying as a special case of organizational decision making. They view the decision process as involving environmental factors (legal, cultural and economic that constrain action), organizational characteristics (technology, structure, goals and factors that determine the decision process and the actors involved), interpersonal characteristics (that describe the relationships between the actors in the buying center and individual characteristics (the personality and role-based variables that drive individual action). They also posit that many different decision models — conjunctive, disjunctive, lexicographic and compensatory — can be used in making multi-attribute decisions in a group context.

Building on this work, Choffray and Lilien (1980) develop an operational model that deals with three major elements of organizational buying once a set of feasible alternatives has been identified: (1) the elimination of alternatives that do not meet organizational requirements, (2) the preference formation process for individuals in the buying center and (3) the formation of an organizational preference and choice function. Their model also deals with basic market identification (including macro and micro-segmentation to identify organizations most likely to find an offering attractive) and forecasting and diffusion models to project long term sales (Figure 14.2).

The Choffray–Lilien model is comprised of five submodels: an awareness model, a feasibility model, an individual choice model, a group choice model and a growth model. Stated analytically, the probability that a product a_0 in evoked set A is an organization's choice at time t (given that the organization is in the market to purchase a product in the class) can be written as

$$p(a_0 = \text{organizational choice})$$

$$= p(a_0 = \text{group choice} \mid \text{interaction, feasible, evoked})$$

$$\times p(a_0 = \text{feasible} \mid \text{evoked}) \times \ p(a_0 = \text{evoked}).$$

Johnston and Lewin (1996) integrated the perspectives of Robinson, Faris, and Wind (1967), Webster and Wind (1972), and Sheth (1973) and added some additional variables, including decision role and role stress (see Figure 14.3). However, the development of large scale, largely

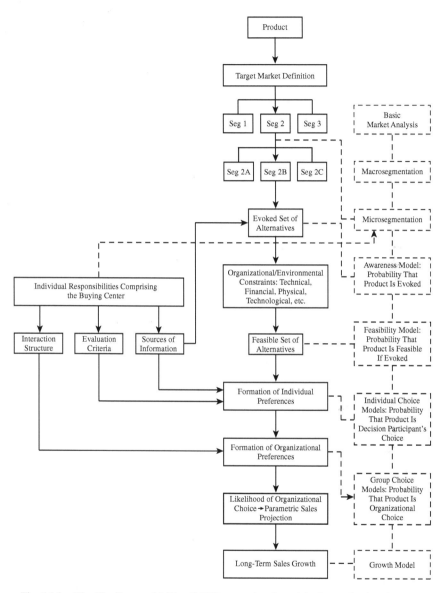

Fig. 14.2   The Choffray and Lilien (1980) operational model of organizational buying

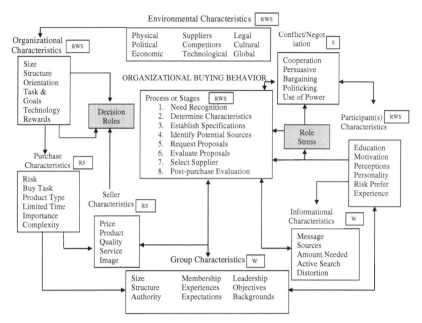

Fig. 14.3   Johnston and Lewin's (1996) summary of issues associated with organizational buying behavior models

Notes:
R indicates constructs contained in the Robinson *et al.* (1967) model.
W indicates constructs contained in the Webster and Wind (1972) model.
S indicates constructs contained in the Sheth (1973) model.
New constructs not contained in any of the original three models.

Source: Johnson and Lewin (1996).

conceptual models of organizational buying appears to have been largely abandoned by then in favor of more operational, empirical work as noted below. [See Reid and Planck (2000) for a comprehensive review up to that date and Johnston and Chandler (2013) and Spekman and Thomas (2011) for more recent reviews].

The large system models above all highlighted group choice (within a buying center) as a key modeling issue for organizational buying. Economists have focused on the important social welfare question: How *should* individuals with different preference structures put their preferences together to form a group rank ordering of alternatives (group social welfare function). Arrow (1963) proved that, in general, no such group ordering, consistent with five reasonable assumptions, exists. That result has been used to conclude that knowledge about group structure (hierarchy, dictatorship, power levels and communication patterns) is needed to develop a group welfare function. Hence, predicting group choice from individual measurements (what buying centers actually do, not what they should do) requires models calibrated to the specifics of the actors and the situation the group faces.

There was a flurry of work in the late 1980's and early 1990's looking at various group decision models and when they could be most appropriately applied (Corfman and Lehmann, 1987; Steckel, 1990; Rao and Steckel, 1991; Corfman and Gupta, 1993). Most of these models fall into one of three categories: (1) *non-quota schemes*, where there is no pre-specified minimum number of group members who must favor an alternative for it to be selected (weighted probability model, equi-probability model, voting model and preference perturbation model), (2) *agreement quota schemes*, where the group deliberates until a (pre-specified) number or proportion of the group selects a given choice (majority rule model and the unanimity model) and (3) *an individual decision scheme* (autocracy model), where one group member chooses for the group. These models are specified as follows:

In the *weighted probability model*, the assumption is that the group, as a whole, is likely to adopt a given alternative, say a_j in the choice set A, proportionally to the relative importance to the members who choose it. Let

$P_G(a_j; A)$ = probability that the group chooses a_j, $j = 1, \ldots, k$ alternatives, and

w_i = relative importance, on the average, of decision participant i, $i = 1, \ldots, r$ in the choice process.

Hence

$$\sum_{i=1}^{r} w_i = 1.$$

Then the weighted probability model postulates that

$$P_G(a_j; A) = \sum_{i=1}^{r} w_i P_i(a_j; A), \quad j = 1, \ldots, k. \tag{14.1}$$

The *equiprobability model* takes follows from Eq. (14.1) with $w_i = 1/r$ for all i.

The *voting model* states that the probability that the group will choose alternative a_j is equal to the probability that a_j is selected by the largest number of decision participants. Let

$$X_{ij} = \begin{cases} 1 & \text{if individual } i \text{ chooses } a_j \\ 0 & \text{otherwise} \end{cases}.$$

Then,

$$Pr(X_{ij} = 1) = P_i(a_j; A).$$

Let,

$$Z_j = \sum_{i=1}^{r} X_{ij},$$

then

$$P_G(a_j; A) = Pr[Z_j = \max(Z_k)]. \tag{14.2}$$

In the *preference perturbation model*, the assumption is that if a group does not reach unanimous agreement, it is most likely to choose the alternative that "perturbs" individual preference structures least. Let,

θ_{iw} = event that individual i has preference ordering w, $i = 1, \ldots, r$; $w = 1, \ldots, k!$, where a preference ordering means, e.g., $a1 \gg a2 \gg a3$ and $\gg$ means "is preferred to";

λ_μ = set of preference ordering across decision participants = $\{\theta_{1w1}, \theta_{2w2}, \ldots, \theta_{rwr}\}$ where $w_i = 1, \ldots, k!$ for $i = 1, \ldots, r$ and, hence, $\mu = 1, \ldots, rk!$;

$Q(a_j \mid \lambda_\mu)$ = "perturbation" associated with the set of preference ordering λ_μ; i.e., the sum of the number of preference shifts that are required to make option a_j the first choice of all decision participants.

To see how Q evolves, consider a two-person, three-product decision, with

$$\lambda_\mu = (\theta_{1w1}, \theta_{2w2}) = [a_0 \gg a_1 \gg a_2; a_2 \gg a_0 \gg a_1].$$

Here $Q(a_0 \mid \lambda_\mu) = 1$, $Q(a_1 \mid \lambda_\mu) = 3$, $Q(a_2 \mid \lambda_\mu) = 2$ (i.e., a_0 must move from second to first choice for participant 2 to give $Q(a_0 \mid \lambda_\mu) = 1$; a_1 must move from second to first for participant 1 and move from third to first for participant 2 for $Q(a_1 \mid \lambda_\mu) = 3$, and so on).

Assuming that individual preference distributions are mutually independent,

$$Pr(\lambda_\mu) = Pr(\theta_{1w1}, \theta_{2w2}, \ldots, \theta_{rwr})$$

$$= \prod_{i-1}^{r} Pr(\theta_{iwi}), \quad \mu = 1, \ldots, rk!, \qquad (14.3)$$

where the $\{i, w_i\}$ are suitably mapped to the appropriate μ. The model postulates that the ratio of probability of group choice equals the ratio of needed preference perturbation to achieve first preference within the group

$$\frac{P_G(a_j \mid \lambda_\mu)}{P_G(a_e \mid \lambda_\mu)} = \frac{Q(a_e \mid \lambda_\mu)}{Q(a_j \mid \lambda_\mu)}. \qquad (14.4)$$

Moreover, if $Q(a_e \mid \lambda_\mu) = 0$, then $P_G(a_e \mid \lambda_\mu) = 1$ and $P_G(a_j \mid \lambda_\mu) = 0$ for $j \neq e$ (this is a case of unanimous first preference).

As the total number of possible preference shifts is fixed, these conditional probabilities are uniquely determined. Hence, the unconditional probabilities of group choice are given by

$$P_G(a_j; A) = \sum P_G(a_j \mid \lambda_\mu) Pr(\lambda_\mu). \qquad (14.5)$$

The *majority rule model* is a special case of the voting model when a quota (say 50% or more) of the group is required to agree for an alternative to be chosen. Formally, we have

$$P_G(a_j; A) = Pr[Z_j = \max(Z_k \mid Z_k > r/2)]. \qquad (14.6)$$

The *unanimity model* is another special case of the voting model with

$$P_G(a_j; A) = Pr[Z_j = \max(Z_k \mid Z_k = r)]. \qquad (14.7)$$

The autocracy model uses the most influential decision participant's preferences as those of the group

$$P_G(a_j; A) = Pr_{i*}(a_j; A), \qquad (14.8)$$

where $_{i*}$ is the index representing that individual for whom $w_{i*} = \max(w_i)$.

The group choice or organizational buying model challenge, then, became to determine which of these models (or others) best predicts group choice under what circumstances. Wilson, Lilien, and Wilson (1991) found that a "key informant" (an individual whose preferences could be used to predict organizational preferences and choice) only exists in what Robinson, Faris, and Wind (1967) called a straight rebuy situation. That finding — that the way individuals combine individual preferences to form a group preference depends on the type and riskiness of the task (at least) — has proven to be both an opportunity and a challenge for researchers and practitioners alike. As with Arrow's impossibility theorem, it appears that no single combining rule from individual preferences exists that will be robust in predicting group or organizational choice. As noted below, this domain is in need of additional modeling and empirical generalizations.

14.3 Bargaining and negotiation models

Given the central nature of bargaining in organizational buying process, it should not be surprising to find much research on the topic. The early work in the area was mainly normative, relying on equilibrium concepts (Nash, 1950) with utility maximizing agents on both sides (Keeney and Raiffa, 1976). Yet as Eliashberg, Lilien, and Kim (1995) report in a review of 293 academic research articles and 97 real cases, there was (and remains) a large gap between theory and practice. The very messy nature of real bargaining situations within an organizational buying context (Raiffa, 1982) involves multiple participants, multiple issues and unclear or evolving preference structure amongst buying team members. Hence, normative concepts like the Nash Bargaining solution have had limited predictive ability (Neslin and Greenhalgh, 1986).

Eliashberg, Lilien, and Kim (1995) provided a time trend of issues addressed in academic articles on business marketing negotiations, beginning pre-1970 and continuing through the 1990s, showing more work emerging on multiple party, multiple agent, repeated multiple issue negotiations. That work involves bargaining models that are more realistic representations of real organizational buying behavior. Yet, through the 1990s at least, the amount of work involving, personality, power, venue, culture and learning was vanishingly small and with no noticeable upward trends.

In addition, most of the early analytical work focused on equilibrium outcomes, while (in line with the discussions above) models were needed for the negotiation process. A pioneering model of this type by Balakrishnan and Eliashberg (1995), building on Pruitt's (1981) work, incorporates power, concession points, aspiration level and timer pressure and is able to predict likelihood of agreement and the pattern of offers and counter-offers.

Analytically, their model has a seller ($i = 1$) making price offers in periods with an odd index and the buyer ($i = 2$) making (counter) offers in periods with an even index. The seller's problem is to maximize the price offer, X_t subject to

$$\rho_1(X_t) - \phi(X_t) = 0, \tag{14.9}$$

(resistance curve, ρ is in balance with concession curve ϕ) and

$$\mu_1 \leq X_t \leq \tau_1, \tag{14.10}$$

(offer must be between the reservation price μ and aspiration level τ).

Similarly, the buyer tries to minimize his buying price offer, Y_t is subject to

$$\rho_2(Y_t) - \phi_2(Y_t) = 0, \tag{14.11}$$

$$\tau_2 \leq Y_t \leq \mu_2, \tag{14.12}$$

where

X_t, Y_t = offers made by seller/buyer, respectively, in period t
$\quad \phi$ = party i's concession curve ($i = 1$ is the seller, $i = 2$ is the buyer)
$\quad \rho_i$ = party i's resistance curve
$\quad \tau_i$ = aspiration level for party i (target point)
$\quad \mu_i$ = reservation price for party i.

The authors propose the following functional forms for the ρ_i and ϕ_i curves:

$$\rho_{1,t} = \Pi_1(\tau_1 - X_t), \tag{14.13}$$

$$\rho_{2,t} = \Pi_2(Y_t - \tau_2), \tag{14.14}$$

$$\phi_1 = \alpha_1(X_t - \beta_{1,t}), \tag{14.15}$$

$$\phi_2 = \alpha_2(\beta_{2,t} - Y_t). \tag{14.16}$$

Equations (14.13)–(14.16) introduce the focal point, $\beta_{i,t}$ for both the buyer and seller. The authors interpret this quantity as $\beta_{2,t} =$ party i's projection of j's ultimate offer, given what has occurred up until time t and model it recursively as

$$\beta_{1,2t} = \beta_{1,2t-2} + \theta_1(Y_{2t-1} - Y_{2t-3}), \tag{14.17}$$

$$\beta_{2,2t+1} = \beta_{2,2t-1} + \theta_2(X_{2t} - X_{2t-2}), \tag{14.18}$$

where

$\theta_i =$ the coefficient of party i's tendency to reciprocate ($-1 \leq \theta_t \leq 1$) and
$Y_{2t-1} - Y_{2t-3}; X_{2t} - X_{2t-2} =$ most recent concessions made by the buyer and seller, respectively.

Note that if $\theta_i < 0$, the bargainer is acting in a reciprocative manner (tit-for-tat) while if $\theta_i > 0$, the bargainer is attempting to exploit concessions of the other party.

Note also that the time indices in Eqs. (14.17) and (14.18) suggest that party 1 acts during period with an even-t index while party 2 acts during periods with an odd-t index. After some algebra, Eqs. (14.13)–(14.18) yield

$$X_{t'+2} - (K + 1)X_{t'+1} + KX_{t'} = 0, \tag{14.19}$$

where

$$K = \frac{\alpha_1\alpha_2\theta_1\theta_2}{(\Pi_1 + \alpha_1)(\Pi_2 + \alpha_2)}. \tag{14.20}$$

Equation (14.19) is a second order difference equation with solution

$$X_{t'} = \frac{X_1 - KX_0}{(1 - K)} + K^t \left[\frac{X_0 - X_1}{1 - K} \right], \qquad (14.21)$$

where X_0 and X_1 are the seller's first and second offers, respectively.

An equation similar to (14.21) holds for $Y_{t'}$, and an agreement is said to occur at the first time, t, where $Y_{t+1} > X_t$ (that is, where the buyer is willing to meet the seller's demanded price). By studying the individual — and dyadic — level dynamics associated with Eq. (14.21), the model predicts if and when an agreement will take place and what the pattern of offers and counter offers looks like.

The Balakrishnan and Eliashberg (1995) model allows predictions of (a) the conditions under which offers oscillate, (b) when no agreement will take place, (c) what the agreement point is likely to be and (d) when (at what iteration in the bargaining process) that agreement will take place. The authors report encouraging results on the predictive validity of the model in a lab experiment and a field study. The model and empirical analysis suggests that it is possible to model and at least partially control the nature and dynamics of the bargaining process.

During the last decade and a half, researchers have focused on addressing issues associated with multiple issues and multiple agents. Multiple issue negotiations can be categorized into two types: independent issues and dependent issues. Independent issue negotiations are simple extensions of single issue negotiations with a unique optimal solution. Interdependent issues the utility functions for buyers and sellers can be quite complex, with multiple local optima. Hence, research has focused on mechanisms to address the interdependency issue, including the possible role of a mediator. For example, Ehtamo, Kettunen, and Hamaleinen (2001) propose a model with the mediator (human or machine) which learns buyer and seller preferences from previous offers and suggests offers closer to the efficient frontier.

An important problem with multiple issue negotiations is the procedure for determining how the issues will be settled. Fatima, Wooldridge, and Jennings (2006) model three types of processes: package deals, simultaneous (where issues are settled simultaneously but independently) and sequential. They show how time constraints and the form of utility functions lead to different optimal procedures.

Particularly with the advent of team buying in the 1990s, more and more firms began readjusting their organizational structures to formalize cross-functional team buying procedures. Morgan (2001) found that over 70% of the firms he sampled used team buying and sourcing methods. This observation has begun to spawn modeling and analysis focusing on agenda strategies with buying teams dealing with multiple issues. (See Patton and Balakrishnan, 2012, for an example.) Yet it is clear that there is potential for far more work in this important area.

14.4 Relationship and network models

While this chapter focuses on organizational buying models, the nature of business marketing suggests that a relationship or network focus (looking at linkages that cross-organizational boundaries) may be most appropriate. Nearly 10% of the more than 2100 articles on business marketing that Reid and Planck (2000) reviewed covered relationships in some manner. Research in this domain has used different theoretical perspectives including agency theory (Bergin, Dutta, and Walker, 1992), transactional cost analysis (Lothia and Krapfel, 1994), equity theory (Lucas and Bush, 1983), social psychology (Bonoma and Johnston, 1978), and network theory (Hutt and Reingen, 1987).

Bonoma and Johnston (1978) argued that a dyadic or systems approach to examining organizational buying behavior would provide more insight into the process and likely outcome of an organizational buying process than segregated view of buyers and sellers. They also argued that previous research had overlooked critical social variables in models of organizational buying. Wilson (1978) provided a dyadic model and argued that in order to understand buying centers, one must understand the interactions within the buying center as well as interactions with sellers. Other authors such as Bonoma, Bagozzi, and Zaltman (1978), Hakansson and Wootz (1979), and LaGarce and Prell (1978) provided alternative dyadic models.

Research in this domain has provided considerable insight into the factors that promote continuity in a given relationship, such as social and structural bonds (Berry, 1995), relationship quality (Crosby, Evans, and Cowles, 1990), satisfaction (Fornell, 1992), and service quality (Ostrom and Iacobucci, 1995). Different variables are conjectured and integrated to contribute to successful relationships. Morgan and Hunt (1994) argued that commitment and trust are the major variables that affect the relationship between different parties involved in marketing exchanges. Wilson (1995) developed an integrative relationship model in which more variables are included: commitment, trust, cooperation, mutual goals, interdependence and power, performance satisfaction, structural bonds, comparison level of alternatives, adaptation, non-retrievable investments, shared technology, and social bonds.

While more recent work on buyer–seller relationship still focuses on the factors that affect the dynamics of buyer–seller relationships, much of that work (e.g., Heide, Wathne, and Rokkan, 2007; Palmatier, Dant, and Grewal, 2007; Jap and Haruvy, 2008; Wang, Kayande, and Jap, 2010) has adopted longitudinal study designs (more appropriate for modeling dynamics than historical cross-sectional approaches). In addition, some of the work has focused on new marketing issues such as online auctions, customizing complex products, and service management from the perspective of buyer–seller relationships (Ghosh, Dutta, and Stremersch, 2006; Jap and Haruvy, 2008; Roels, Karmarkar, and Carr, 2010).

Critics of basic relationship models argue that, while those models focus on two business partners (e.g., buyer–supplier), they neglect the environment (the network of personal and business connection) in which the relationship is housed (Achrol, 1997; Snow, 1997; Walker, 1997; Ehret, 2004; Kamp, 2005; Johanson and Vahlne, 2011). In spite of the challenges of using a network perspective to study organizational buying behavior, the approach allows researchers to examine the interdependencies of the firms and individuals in a scope beyond dyads (Wasserman and Iacobucci, 1988; Wuyts *et al.*, 2004; Freytag and Ritter, 2005).

At the firm level, buying firms form alliances and collaborative relationships with suppliers, channel members and clients and even competitors. Hence, there are interfirm networks in which a buying firm and its connections form a small part of a complex and dynamic network: within the buying firm, a cross-functional intrafirm network of managers and the members of buying center are embedded in the network of the entire buying firm and they all interact with the networked sales team from the selling firm. The complexity of the network and the associated measurement difficulties provide formidable research challenges (Borders, Johnston, and Ridgon, 2001).

One challenge of the network paradigm is to account for the effects of agents not directly connected to the focal firm. One approach to address this challenge involves modeling techniques to analyze the (incomplete) dyadic network data, such as exponential random graph models, latent space models and the multiple regression quadratic assignment procedure (Ansari, Koenigsberg, and Stahl, 2011). Another approach is to expand the unit of analysis to be triads. Wuyts *et al.* (2004) investigate buyer–vendor–supplier triads and test how buyer's preferences on vendors are affected by second-order ties. Wathne and Heide (2004) investigate customer–manufacturer–supplier triads and show how governance mechanisms (supplier qualification and incentive design) affect the nature and uncertainty of the manufacturer–supplier relationship. Choi and Wu (2009) consider triads of one buyer and two suppliers and model relationship dynamics under conditions of both balanced and unbalanced triadic states and triads with structural holes. These studies show the importance that network structure and the location of the buyer (and its agents) in that network plays in understanding organizational buying behavior.

A second challenge in applying network concepts to organizational buying involves relationship multiplexity: the number of diverse types of ties between two firms arising from different modes of interaction or because of different roles firms/individuals play within a network setting (Van den Bulte and Wuyts, 2007). Much the same way that traditional organizational buying models viewed the buying center as composed of numerous roles (gatekeeper, purchasing agent, financial analyst, etc.), the nature of the relationship between various agents in the buying and selling firm (joint problem-solving/R&D links, price negotiation links, service management links, etc.) should be considered to properly characterize the interfirm relationships. Multiplexity not only contributes to the total strength of a tie but also increases the number of ways in which resources flows through the networked firms (Van den Bulte and Wuyts, 2007).

Tuli, Bharadwaj, and Kohli (2010), shows that multiple types of ties between a buyer and a supplier are valuable resources for increasing multiplexity in relationships, leading to an increase in sales and to a decrease in sales volatility.

A third challenge in applying network concepts to organizational buying arises from the dynamics of relationships and the individual linkages that comprise those relationship, necessitating the collection of associated data and analytic procedures. Dwyer, Schurr, and Oh (1987) proposed a fixed order life-cycle theory of the development of relationships between organizational buyers and organizational sellers. They proposed that a relationship passes through five stages: awareness, exploration, expansion, commitment and dissolution; relationships without high overall dependence are either at early stage or about to dissolve. Ring and Van de Ven (1994) proposed a cyclical theory of relationship development where the steps (negotiation, commitment to an agreement, execution of the agreement, assessments, terminating the relationship) repeat within each of the five phases. Due to the challenges of tracing ongoing relationship, there has been limited empirical work to analyze relationship life-cycle theories. Jap and Anderson (2007), test the propositions in Dwyer Schurr and Oh (1987) and Ring and Van de Ven (1994), beginning the process of putting dynamic relationship and network ideas into practice. Although the unit of analysis in relationship life-cycle studies and longitudinal relationship studies has been independent dyads to date, the findings from these studies suggest that both the types and the strength of the ties connecting firms change over time; different ties are driven by different forces and exhibit different evolutionary properties.

The application of network models (especially those that involve dynamic, evolving networks) should be a fruitful research domain for organizational buying modelers in the years to come.

14.5 Looking ahead

The complexities of organizational buying noted above have limited the amount of attention marketing scientists have paid to the area. Indeed, it seems that interest in some of what once appeared to be quite promising areas for marketing science has waned. To a large degree, marketing scientists, like academic researchers in many fields, suffer from the "search under the lamp-post" syndrome,[1] researching where there is a large volume of readily accessible data. Organizational buying behavior takes place in domains that often do not readily generate large amounts of data (far fewer, more complex transactions of much higher economic size than in the consumer marketplace) and hence has seen far less scrutiny by marketing scientists than have consumer behavior models.

To put things into perspective consider the following (US-centric) facts:

1. According to the most recent Department of Commerce Statistics (www.census.gov/econ/estats/2010), BtoB transactions account for US$10.7 trillion of the US$25.7 trillion or over 40% of the transactions that comprise the US economy. All those BtoB transactions involve organizational buying.
2. According to the same Department of Commerce report, 89.7% of all electronic transactions take place on the BtoB side, which means that organizational buying accounts for the overwhelming majority of all electronic transactions, a major and under researched area of organizational buying;
3. The 2013 budget for the US Department of Defense (http://comptroller. defense.gov/budget.html) amounts to more than $600 Billion. And that amount is a small fraction of the total spending for federal, state and local governments. Hence, governments, non-profits and non-government organizations (NGO's) account for an enormous amount and variety of organizational buying activity, yet there is minimal research into how these organizations buy.

---

[1]A drunken man is crawling around on his hands and knees under a lamp-post. His friend asks him "what are you doing crawling around under that lamp-post?" The drunk responds that he has lost his keys and is looking for them. His friend responds "your car is over here, you have not been near that lamp-post". The drunk responds "it is very dark and this is the only place where there is some light".
Source: http://www.physicsforums.com/showthread.php?t = 249522.

These US facts are representative of situations elsewhere in the world and lead to the following five domains in need of more attention from marketing scientists[2]:

1. *Better predictive models of organizational choice.* In spite of the work of Wilson, Lilien, and Wilson (1991) and others cited above, standard organizational buying research still involves seeking a "key informant" who will complete some questionnaire and/or trade-off task to assess organizational preferences. We need robust, operational models of the organizational buying process that can be calibrated in a cost-effective manner, can predict what organizations will buy and what the key factors are that will influence those purchases. This topic was also one of the two most pressing issues cited by Wiersema (2012) in the recent, inaugural report of the B2B Leadership Board.

2. *Models of government buying.* Governments at all levels make purchases using rules and processes that have different objectives and constraints. As Krug and Weinberg (2004) point out in the context of non-profits, the different goals, objectives and constraints of non-profits lead to drastically different optimal behaviors that for profits. Hence, both descriptive and normative models of organizational buying applied to governments and non-profits are sorely needed.

3. *Operational network models of organizational buying.* The previous section noted a number of benefits and key challenges associated with applying network models and methods to organizational buying problems. Challenges at least include dealing with incomplete data on network structure, mulitiplexity and the dynamics of network provide rich avenues for research and methodological advances.

4. *Models of electronic ecommerce in the B2B domain.* While not a traditional organizational buying topic, given that nearly 90% of the economic value of electronic transactions takes place between organizations, it is surprising that the domain has not attracted researchers. Following Rust (1997), we need a theory and models of computer buying behavior in the context of organizational purchasing.

---

[2] See Johnston and Chandler (2013) and Spekman and Thomas (2011) for other look-aheads in this field.

5. *Realistic models of bargaining and negotiations.* As noted above, the gap between academic research in bargaining and negotiations and its practice in an organizational buying context is large. There is need for marketing science work seeking empirical generalizations about bargaining processes and strategies and work that does not assume away the complexity of bargaining in a multi-agent, multi-attribute environment.

While there are more challenges in the organizational buying domain, those cited above have great managerial relevance and provide fertile ground for scholars wishing to tackle difficult but important problems.

Acknowledgments

I would like to thank Huanhuan Shi, a PhD student at Penn State, who provided outstanding support in compiling and helping to summarize the material in this chapter.

References

Achrol, R. S. (1997). Changes in the theory of interorganizational relations in the marketing paradigm, *Journal of the Academy of Marketing Science*, 25(1), 56–71.

Arrow, K. J. (1963). *Social Choice and Individual Values*, 2nd edn., New York: John Wiley.

Ansari, A., O. Koenisberg, and F. Stahl (2011). Modeling multiple relationships in social networks, *Journal of Marketing Research*, 48(4), 713–728.

Balakrishnan, P. V. and J. Eliashberg (1995). An analytic process model of two party negotiations, *Management Science*, 41(2), 226–242.

Bergin, M., S. Dutta, and O. C. Walker (1992). Agency relationships in marketing: A review of the implications and applications of agency and related theories, *Journal of Marketing*, 56(3), 1–24.

Berry, L. L. (1995). Relationship marketing of services — growing interest, emerging perspectives, *Journal of the Academy of Marketing Science*, 23(4), 236–245.

Bonoma, T., R. Bagozzi, and G. Zaltman (1978). The dyadic paradigm with specific application toward industrial marketing, in T. V. Bonoma and G. Zaltman, eds.,

Organizational Buying Behavior, Chicago: American Marketing Association, pp. 49–66.

Bonoma, T. and W. J. Johnston (1978). The social psychology of industrial buying and selling, *Industrial Marketing Management*, 17, 213–224.

Borders, A. L., W. J. Johnston, and E. E. Rigdon (2001). Beyond the dyad: Electronic commerce and network perspectives in industrial marketing management, *Industrial Marketing Management*, 30(2), 199–205.

Cannon, J. P. and W. D. Perreult, Jr. (1999). Buyer–seller relationships in business markets, *Journal of Marketing Research*, 36(4), 439–460.

Choffray, J.-M. and G. L. Lilien (1980). *Market Planning for New Industrial Products*, New York: John Wiley.

Choi, T. Y. and Z. Wu (2009). Triads in supply networks: Theorizing buyer–seller relationships, *Journal of Supply Chain Management*, 45(1), 8–25.

Corfman, K. and D. R. Lehmann (1987). Models of comparative group decision making and relative influence, *Journal of Consumer Research*, 14, 1–13.

Corfman, K. P. and S. Gupta (1993). Mathematical models of group choice and negotiations, in J. Eliashberg and G. L. Lilien, eds., *Handbooks in operations research and management science: marketing*, Volume 5, Amsterdam, Netherlands: North-Holland, pp. 83–142.

Crosby, L. A., K. R. Evans, and D. Cowles (1990). Relationship quality in services selling: An interpersonal influence perspective, *Journal of Marketing*, 54, 68–81.

Dwyer, F. R., P. H. Schurr, and S. Oh (1987). Developing buyer–seller relationships, *Journal of Marketing*, 51(2), 11–27.

Ehret, M. (2004). Managing the trade-off between relationships and value networks. Towards a value-based approach of customer relationship management in business-to-business markets, *Industrial Marketing Management*, 33(6), 465–473.

Ehtamo, H., E. Kettunen, and R. Hamalainen (2001). Searching for joint gains in multi-party negotiations, *European Journal of Operational Research*, 130(1), 54–69.

Eliashberg, J., G. L. Lilien, and N. Kim (1995). Searching for generalizations in business marketing negotiations, *Marketing Science (Special Issue on Empirical Generalizations in Marketing)*, 14(3), G47–G60.

Fader, P., B. Hardie, and S. Sen (2013). Stochastic models of buyer behavior, in R. Winer and S. Neslin, eds., *History of marketing science*, Hanover, MA: Now Publishers.

Fatima, S. S., M. Wooldridge, and N. R. Jennings (2006). Multi-issue negotiation with deadlines, *Journal of Artificial Intelligence Research*, 27, 381–417.

Fornell, C. (1992). A national customer satisfaction barometer: The Swedish experience, *Journal of Marketing*, 56, 6–21.

Freytag, P. V. and T. Ritter (2005). Dynamics of relationships and networks — creation, maintenance and destruction as managerial challenges, *Industrial Marketing Management*, 34(7), 644–647.

Gensch, D. H. (1984). Targeting the switchable customer, *Marketing Science*, 3(1) (Winter), 197–207.

Ghosh, M., S. Dutta, and S. Stremersch (2006). Customizing complex products: When should the vendor take control? *Journal of Marketing Research*, 43(4), 664–679.

Hakansson, H. and B. Wootz (1979). A framework of industrial buying and selling, *Industrial Marketing Management*, 8(1), 28–39.

Heide, J. B., K. H. Wathne, and A. I. Rokkan (2007). Interfirm monitoring, social contracts, and relationship outcomes, *Journal of Marketing Research*, XLIV(3), 425–433.

Howard, J. A. and J. Sheth (1969). *The Theory of Buyer Behavior*, New York: John Wiley.

Hutt, M. H. and P. Reingen (1987). Social network analysis: emergent versus prescribed patterns in organizational buying behavior, *Proceedings, Association for Consumer Research*, 14, 259–265.

Iacobucci, D. and A. Ostrom (1996). Commercial and interpersonal relationships: Using the structure of interpersonal relationships to understand individual-to-individual, individual-to-firm, and firm-to-firm relationships, *International Journal of Research in Marketing* 13(1), 53–72.

Jap, S. D. and E. Anderson (2007). Testing a life-cycle theory of cooperative interorganizational relationships: Movement across stages and performance, *Management Science*, 53(2), 260–275.

Jap, S. D. and E. Haruvy (2008). Interorganizational relationships and bidding behavior in industrial online reverse auctions, *Journal of Marketing Research*, 45(5), 550–556.

Johanson, J. and J.-E. Vahlne (2011). Markets as networks: Implications for strategy-making, *Journal of the Academy of Marketing Science*, 39(4), 484–491.

Johnston, W. J. and J. D. Chandler (2013). The organizational buying center: Innovation, knowledge management and brand, in G. Lilien and R. Grewal, eds., *Handbook of Business to Business Marketing*, Northhampton, MA: Edward Elgar, pp. 386–399.

Johnston, W. J. and J. E. Lewin (1996). Organizational buying behavior: Toward an integrative framework, *Journal of Business Research*, 35(1), 1–15.

Kamp, B. (2005). Formation and evolution of buyer–supplier relationships: Conceiving dynamism in actor composition of business networks, *Industrial Marketing Management*, 34(7), 658–668.

Keeney, R. and H. Raiffa (1976). *Decisions with multiple objectives: Preferences and value tradeoffs*, Reading, MA: Addison Wesley.

Krug, K. and C. B. Weinberg (2004). Mission, money, merit: strategic decision-making by nonprofit managers, *Nonprofit Management & Leadership*, 14(2), 325–342.

LaGarce, R. and A. E. Prell (1978). Transactional marketing: An understanding of the industrial marketing process, *Industrial Marketing Management*, 7(1), 54–59.

Lothia, R. and R. Krapful (1994). The impact of transaction specific investments on buyer–seller relationships. *Journal of Business and Industrial Marketing*, 9(1), 6–17.

Lucas, G. H. and A. J. Bush (1983). An examination of equity theory in the organizational buyer–seller dyad, *Proceedings of the American Marketing Association*, 49, 301–304.

Morgan, J. P. (2001). Cross functional buying: Why teams are hot, *Purchasing*, 130(7), 27–32.

Morgan, R. M. and Hunt, S. D. (1994). The commitment–trust theory of relationship marketing, *Journal of Marketing*, 58, 20–38.

Nash, J. (1950). The bargaining problem, *Econometrica*, 18(2), 155–162.

Neslin, S. A. and L. Greenhalgh (1986). The ability of Nash's theory of cooperative games to predict the outcome of buyer-seller negotiations: A dyadic level test, *Management Science*, 32(4), 480–498.

Ostrom, A. and D. Iacobucci (1995). Consumer trade-offs and the evaluation of services, *Journal of Marketing*, 59, 17–28.

Palmatier, R. W., R. P. Dant, and D. Grewal (2007). A comparative longitudinal analysis of theoretical perspective of interorganizational relationship performance, *Journal of Marketing*, 71(4), 172–194.

Patton, C. and P. V. Balakrishnan (2012). Negotiating when outnumbered: Agenda Strategies for bargaining with buying teams, *International Journal of Research in Marketing*, 29(3), 280–291.

Pruitt, D. C. (1981). *Negotiation behavior*, New York: Academic Press.

Raiffa, H. (1982). *The art and science of negotiation*, Cambridge, MA: The Harvard University Press.

Rao, V. H. and J. H. Steckel (1991). A polarization model for describing group preferences, *Journal of Consumer Research*, 18(1), 108–118.

Reid, D. A. and R. E. Plank (2000). Business marketing comes of age: A comprehensive review of the literature, *Journal of Business-to-Business Marketing*, 7(2), 9–186.

Ring, P. S. and A. H. Van de Ven (1994). Developmental processes of cooperative interorganizational relationships, *Academy of Management Review*, 19(1), 90–118.

Roels, G., U. S. Karmarkar, and S. Carr (2010). Contracting for collaborative services, *Management Science*, 56, 849–863.

Robinson, P. J., C. W. Faris, and Y. Wind (1967). *Industrial buying and creative marketing*, Boston: Allyn & Bacon.

Russell, G. (2013). Brand choice models, in R. Winer and S. Neslin, eds., *History of marketing science*, Hanover, MA: Now Publishers.

Rust, R. T. (1997). The dawn of computer behavior, *Marketing Management*, 6(Fall), 31–33.

Sheth, J. N. (1973). A model of industrial buyer behavior, *Journal of Marketing*, 37(4), 50–56.

Snow, C. C. (1997). Twenty-first-century organizations: Implications for a new marketing paradigm, *Journal of the Academy of Marketing Science*, 25(1), 72–74.

Spekman, R. E. and R. J. Thomas (2011). Organizational buying behavior: Where we have been and where we need to go, SSRN No: 1993207.

Spekman, R. E. and K. Gronhaug (1986). Conceptual and methodological issues in buying centre research, *European Journal of Marketing*, 20(7), 50–63.

Steckel, J. H. (1990). Committee decision making in organizations: An experimental test of the core, *Decision Sciences*, 21(Winter), 204–215.

Tuli, K. K., S. G. Bharadwaj, and A. K. Kohli, (2010). Ties that bind: The role of relationship multiplexity in increasing sales and reducing volatility, *Journal of Marketing Research*, XLVII, 36–50.

Turnbull, P. and J. P. Valla (1986). Strategic planning in industrial marketing: An inter-action approach, *European Journal of Marketing*, 20(7), 5–20.

Van den Bulte, C. and S. Wuyts (2007). Social networks and marketing, *Marketing Science Institute*.

Walker, O. C., Jr. (1997). The adaptability of network organizations: Some unexplored questions. *Journal of the Academy of Marketing Science*, 25(1), 75–82.

Wang, Q., U. Kayande, and S. Jap (2010). The seeds of dissolution: Discrepancy and incoherence in buyer–supplier exchange, *Marketing Science*, 29(6), 1109–1124.

Wasserman, S. and D. Iacobucci (1988). Sequential social network data, *Psychometrika*, 53, 261–282.

Wathne, K. H. and J. B. Heide (2004). Relationship governance in a supply chain network, *Journal of Marketing*, 68, 73–89.

Webster, F. E., Jr. (1984). *Industrial marketing strategy*, 2nd edn., New York: Wiley.

Webster, F. E., Jr. and Y. Wind (1972). A general model for understanding organizational buying behavior, *Journal of Marketing*, 36(2), 12–19.

Wiersema, F. (2012). The B2B agenda: The current state of B2B marketing and a look ahead, ISBM Report.

Wilson, D. T. (1978). Dyadic interactions: Some conceptualizations, in T. V. Bonoma and G. Zaltman, eds., *Organizational buying behavior*, Chicago: American Marketing Association, pp. 31–48.

Wilson, D. T. (1995). An integrated model of buyer–seller relationships, *Journal of the Academy of Marketing Science*, 23(4), 335–45.

Wilson, E., G. L. Lilien, and D. T. Wilson, (1991). Developing and testing a contingency paradigm of group choice in organizational buying, *Journal of Marketing Research*, 28, 452–466.

Wuyts, S., S. Stremersch, C. Van den Bulte, and P. H. Franses (2004). Vertical marketing systems for complex products: A triadic perspective, *Journal of Marketing Research*, 41(4), 479–487.

Chapter 15

Pricing

Russell S. Winer

15.1 Introduction

The theory of price has been studied for as long as economists have been writing about supply and demand. Classic books such as those by Stigler (1987) and chapters in various economics handbooks such as that written recently by Stole (2007) covering price discrimination demonstrate the centrality of pricing to economic theory.

In this chapter, however, the focus is on the contributions that marketing scholars have made to pricing. Unlike most economists, marketing academics are interested in applied topics that are relevant to marketing managers such as pricing new products and brand-level analysis. Good reviews of the marketing science literature on pricing have appeared previously (Rao, 1984, 1993; Gijsbrechts, 1993). In addition, pricing research in marketing is voluminous; there are 26 chapters in the recent *Handbook of Pricing Research in Marketing* (Rao, 2009). Like the other chapters in this book, however, the purpose of this chapter is not to review the entire marketing literature on price but rather to focus on the most important marketing science contributions in the central areas of research on pricing.

15.2 Empirical price elasticity research

One of the basic concepts in pricing is the price elasticity of demand. Typically, this is expressed as the following:

$$\epsilon_{ij} = [\partial S_i/\partial P_j] \times P_j/S_i, \tag{15.1}$$

where ϵ_{ij} is the sales change of brand i with respect to the price change of brand j, and S and P are the prices of brands i and j respectively. When $i \neq j$, this is called the cross-elasticity; when $i = j$, it is the brand's own price elasticity of demand.

The estimation of price elasticities has, of course, a long tradition in economics due to the fundamental nature of the construct to the field. By its nature, understanding the price elasticity of demand is equally important to marketing academics and practitioners. While the concept itself is straightforward, the calculation of price elasticities is not (see Telser, 1962 and Simon, 1966, for example) due to different levels of aggregation (e.g., category, brand, store, market share), data availability, and other issues.

There are four strands of research in this area. First, a few papers present some basic empirical results pertaining to elasticities. A second stream of research describes some unconventional approaches to estimating the elasticities. A number of papers have demonstrated significant differences in price elasticities between market segments and alternative industry structure variables. Finally, some research has been conducted examining how price elasticities evolve over time.

15.2.1 Some basic results

A few key papers in the marketing literature have provided important empirical evidence pertaining to price elasticities (see also the summary in Hanssens, Parsons, and Schultz, 2001). The earliest paper was published by Massy and Frank (1965). They used a double-log model with a Koyck error structure to estimate price elasticities for a frequently-purchased product. Lambin (1976) was the first to develop a comprehensive set of price elasticities across a large number of product categories using European data. Hoch *et al.* (1995) estimate category and brand-level elasticities for 18 product categories at each of 83 stores. Two studies performed meta-analyses of price elasticity studies. Tellis (1988) found that the mean price elasticity across 367 elasticities found in the literature was -1.76, eight times higher than the average advertising elasticity found in an earlier advertising meta-analysis (Assmus, Farley, and Lehmann, 1984). Following up on Tellis's study, Bijmolt, van Heerde, and Pieters

(2005) analyzed 1,851 price elasticities from 81 studies and found a mean of −2.62.

15.2.2 *Estimating price elasticities*

While many papers utilize conventional approaches to estimating price elasticities with allowances for the aggregation level of the data or other unique aspects of the study, a few papers have made contributions to the literature through their unique estimation approaches. Weiss (1969) developed an early model he termed the MATE ("Marketing Analysis Training Exercise") model which accounted for competitive interactions and buyer switching behavior. He estimated the parameters of the model using a least-squares approach and then calculated the price elasticities based on the non-linear structure of the model. Mahajan, Green, and Goldberg (1982) adapted the traditional conjoint analysis structure to enable the estimation of own and cross-elasticities. Neslin and Shoemaker (1983) utilize the results of a natural experiment to estimate the price elasticity for the ready-to-eat cereal market. Guadagni and Little (1984) showed how to estimate price elasticities from the parameter estimates of the logit random utility model. Russell and Bolton (1988) incorporated assumptions about the market share structure of sub-markets in estimating price elasticities. Their ACREP (aggregate constant ratio elasticity pattern) model hypothesizes that price elasticities are functions of market shares; they use this model to explain both sales and market share elasticities.

15.2.3 *Explaining differences in elasticities*

The interesting questions are whether estimated price elasticities vary over consumer segments and when multiple product category data are available, if there are explanations based on industry or category structure variables that explain heterogeneity in the elasticities. A number of papers including some already cited explored these issues.

In their analysis of the price elasticity for a frequently-purchased product, Massy and Frank (1965) examined three categories of descriptor variables: degree of brand loyalty, package size purchased, and store type (chain vs. independent stores). As would be expected, loyal customers to the brand were half as price sensitive as non-loyals; the results for the other two sets of variables were unclear. Hagerty, Carman, and Russell (1988) studied differences in price elasticities (and other marketing mix variables) for the companies in the PIMS (Profit Impact of Market Strategy) dataset. Their analysis found that the elasticities were higher for low search vs. high search products, for companies where less than 20% of their sales were from new products, and for products with interpurchase times of one month or less. Bolton (1989) analyzed data for four product categories with three brands each at 12 stores. Her covarying variables were category price activity, brand market share, and a number of promotional variables. She found that high share brands are more price inelastic and that promotional activities such as displays and features significantly impact price elasticities, displays negatively and features positively. Kamakura and Russell (1989) develop a probabilistic approach to aggregating consumers into segments (latent class). Their application is to price elasticities and show that there are a number of underlying segments based on price sensitivity in a frequently-purchased food category. In the Hoch *et al.* (1995) paper previously cited, the authors analyzed a number of demographic and store-level factors on the 18 product categories and 63 stores to see if there was a relationship between the factors and the price elasticities. They found that education and house value in a store's trading area reduced price sensitivity, the percentage of African–American and Hispanic consumers, the average family size, and the percentage of working women in the household increased price sensitivity, and increased distance to the nearest warehouse store reduced price elasticity. In the Bijmolt, van Heerde, and Pieters (2005) meta-analysis previously referenced, the authors found, among a number of factors, that durable goods had higher price elasticities than non-durables.

15.2.4 *Life cycle differences*

It is logical that price elasticities will vary over the product life cycle given the varying numbers of competitors, customer product knowledge, and a number of other factors. Simon (1979) was the first to explore this. He focused on the brand life cycle for 43 German products rather than product category life cycles. He found that the price elasticity for these brands, in general, declined from introduction through maturity and then increased in the decline stage. Tellis (1988) found similar results in his meta-analysis.

Parker (1992) studied 17 durable goods categories for product life cycle dynamics. His null hypothesis was that product life cycle price elasticities should increase over the life cycle. He found mixed results as the patterns varied over product categories.

These strands of research are found in Figure 15.1.

15.3 Willingness-to-Pay research

Marketing managers have been using manufacturing costs and competitors' prices to set their own prices for many years. Recently, more emphasis is being placed on a third factor in the price setting process: customer value. Many books (e.g., Anderson, Kumar, and Narus, 2007) have emphasized the importance of understanding customers' willingness-to-pay (WTP) when determining a price to charge. Consequently, the literature in this area is very large to which recent reviews attest (e.g., Jedidi and Jagpal, 2009).

Definitions of customer value vary. A commonly-used definition is the economic term, reservation price, or the maximum amount a customer is willing to pay for a good (more precisely, the price at which the good leaves the choice set). However, this is not necessarily the customer's WTP at any given point in time. A customer may have a reservation price of US$100 for a good but is only willing to pay US$75 at a given point in time due to a temporary budget constraint. Jedidi and Jagpal (2009) provide an extensive set of alternative definitions of WTP.

In this section, the main contributions to different approaches to measuring WTP are listed. These include survey approaches, adaptations of conjoint analysis, and newer, incentive-compatible approaches based on the work of Becker, DeGroot, and Marschak (1964). A final area for discussion is the comparison of different measurement approaches. It should be noted that auctions will not be covered in this section. While auctions are an obvious way of eliciting reservation prices, the literature is so vast and emanates from economics rather than marketing which led to the decision to exclude this stream of literature.

15.3.1 *Survey approaches to estimating WTP*

The earliest approaches to measuring WTP used survey methods to ask consumers directly how much they would be willing to pay for the products

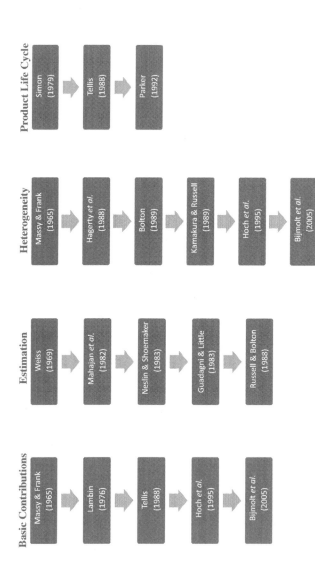

Fig. 15.1   Price elasticity research

being tested. The idea was similar to work by Gabor and his colleagues who were looking for thresholds above which consumers would not purchase a given product. Stoetzel (1954) was among the first to take this approach. His innovation was to also measure a lower price threshold assuming that there is a price below which the consumer would feel the perceived quality would be too low to warrant a purchase. The typical implementation of this approach would be to give a respondent a product concept and then a card with a list of prices on it. The respondent would then be asked to mark the price on the card at the point where s/he would not purchase it ("too expensive"). Likewise, the respondent would be asked to mark the price at the point below which s/he would not purchase due to suspect quality ("too cheap"). The distributions of the responses to the two questions would be utilized to determine an appropriate price. Gabor and Granger's questions (1966, Appendix 2) were similar although somewhat more indirect.

A very popular approach that is extensively used in practice was developed by Van Westendorp (1976) and is called the Price Sensitivity Meter (PSM). The approach is similar to those developed by Stoetzel and Gabor in that it includes the two questions about "too expensive" and "too cheap". However, the PSM also includes two other questions about the price at which the product is "starting to get expensive" and the price at which the product is a "bargain". Again, the resulting distributions of responses are used to formulate a price.

Economists use an approach to value natural resources called contingent valuation (see Mitchell and Carson, 1989). A typical question would be the following (Mitchell and Carson, 1989, p. 5):

> Would you be willing to pay a $1 per day family fee to prevent Situation C from occurring, thus preserving Situation A? $2 per day? (increment by $1 per day until a negative response is obtained, then decrease the bid by $.25 per day until a positive response is obtained).

15.3.2 *Conjoint analysis*

Kohli and Mahajan (1991) and Jedidi and Zhang (2002) utilize the framework of conjoint analysis to estimate consumer reservation prices although they have somewhat different definitions of reservation price. The former defines reservation price for a product as the maximum price a consumer is willing to pay to switch away from the most preferred choice in the choice set of the product in question. Jedidi and Zhang (2002) define it as the maximum WTP, a somewhat more typical definition as noted above. Jedidi and Zhang (2002) show that the reservation price for a product profile P can be stated as follows:

$$r_i(P) = [1/\beta_{ip}]\Sigma_k \beta_{ik} A_k, \tag{15.2}$$

where β_{ip} is a function of the price of an outside or composite good of all other goods consumer i purchases and $\Sigma_k \beta_{ik} A_k$ is the utility consumer i receives from all non-price attributes of product profile P. In both papers, applications of the methods are demonstrated with experimental choice-based data.

15.3.3 Incentive-compatible approaches

A common complaint about survey-based approaches to estimating WTP is that the respondents have little incentive to tell the truth. Wertenbroch and Skiera (2002) adapt Becker, DeGroot, and Marschak's (BDM) (1964) approach for assessing the utility of lotteries to estimating WTP at point-of-purchase. While the exact application of the procedure is shown in the paper, the BDM method involves (1) eliciting an estimate of WTP from a respondent, (2) having the respondent draw a price randomly from a distribution of prices, and (3) the outcome is determined as follows: if the price drawn is higher than the stated WTP, the respondent cannot purchase the product; if it is lower, the respondent can buy the product at the price drawn from the urn. Thus, the respondent has a disincentive to specify a price that is too low (will not be able to purchase) or too high (may wind up paying a higher price than desired). An important result from their experimental studies is that when compared to a direct elicitation approach, the BDM method produced lower estimates of WTP. Wang, Venkatesh, and Chatterjee (2007) extend the Wertenbroch and Skiera paper to create a range for the reservation price (ICERANGE, Incentive Compatible Elicitation of a RANGE) rather than a point estimate. In addition, the BDM procedure has been adapted to understanding reservation prices in a conjoint analysis context (Ding, 2007).

15.3.4 *Comparing methods*

Given the wide variety of approaches to estimating WTP, it is not surprising that there are a number of studies that attempt to compare them. The most comprehensive comparison study was conducted by Miller *et al.* (2011). They compared four different approaches to estimating WTP: survey-based, conjoint, BDM, and incentive-based conjoint. The problem, of course, is what is the "truth" against which these methods are compared? In this study, the authors compared the estimated WTPs against a "real" criterion which was a stated WTP in an online shop where the participants were committed to buy a product at the price stated. The results showed that the incentive-based methods (BDM and incentive-based conjoint) had much lower bias against the "real" criterion than the "hypothetical" methods.

Figure 15.2 shows these strands of research.

15.4 Dynamic pricing

While easier to say in theory than to do in practice, optimal pricing in a static environment follows directly from basic microeconomics: set the price where marginal costs equal marginal revenues. However, in marketing, we know that pricing problems have an important dynamic component, particularly for durable goods where the cost structure follows the famous Boston Consulting Group model of the experience curve. In addition, the popularity of the Bass model of dynamic demand (see Chapter 4) lends itself well to enhancements involving price. In this section, we cover three strands of dynamic pricing research: basic contributions, models which incorporate competition, and models that also account for consumer price expectations.

15.4.1 *Basic contributions*

What is generally considered to be the first dynamic pricing paper in marketing-related literature is the model proposed by Robinson and Lakhani (1975). They developed a dynamic programming model based on introducing price multiplicatively into the classic Bass (1969) durable goods diffusion model. While they did not produce any analytical results, their numerical simulation showed that the myopic price path is

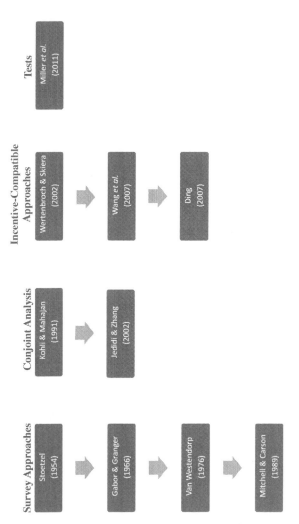

Fig. 15.2 Willingness-to-Pay research

monotonically declining over time while the optimal policy is more like the S-shaped Bass model, that is, lower initial prices to develop the market, increasing over time, and then declining (they assumed a five-year horizon). This produces much greater profits than the static policy. Bass (1980) extended this early work to incorporate experience curve effects. Thus, the resulting dynamic price path was monotonically declining. He also assumed that firms maximize current period profits rather than discounted profits over a planning horizon.

Building on this first work, Dolan and Jeuland (1981) studied both durables and non-durable goods. In the case of non-durable goods, when the discount rate is zero and when the repeat purchase rate is higher than the "conversion" rate (the rate at which non-triers become triers), the optimal price path is to start low and then increase over time (penetration policy). For durable goods, the results depend upon the size of the imitation effects in the Bass model. If they are high, then a penetration policy is optimal. If they are low, then a skimming strategy (high initial prices and then declines) is optimal. Kalish (1983) finds similar results under more general functional form assumptions.

Several papers have extended these basic models in a variety of ways. Kalish (1985) included advertising as a vehicle for increasing awareness of a durable good over time. Dhebar and Oren (1985) consider a monopolist for a product or service characterized by network externalities, that is, where the utility of purchase increases with the number of other adopters or those on the network. Their results point to low initial prices to build the network, with prices increasing monotonically over time. Bayus (1992) examines the case of durable goods with overlapping replacement cycles (e.g., color TV replacing black and white TV). He characterizes two different scenarios: one where a household accelerates its replacement of the first generation product ("discretionary" replacement) and the other where normal replacement occurs for an old version of the first-generation product. When replacements are discretionary, his analytical results show monotonically decreasing prices of the second-generation product and increasing prices of the first-generation product. When replacements are normal, both prices are monotonically decreasing over time. Krishnan, Bass, and Jain (1999) utilized the Generalized Bass Model to show that incorporating price into the diffusion process does not necessarily lead to a pricing policy that follows the sales curve over time. Jing (2011) adds social learning to a two-period monopoly model. The pricing tradeoff for the firm is that penetration pricing promotes early adoption and word-of-mouth. Alternatively, the firm can price higher so fewer buy in Period 1 and thus pay a higher price in Period 2, as the true quality is revealed by buyers in Period 1.

15.4.2 *Models with competition*

The papers previously cited only consider the monopoly situation. While these results are normatively instructive, it is clear that this is a serious limitation. Clarke and Dolan (1984) present results of a simulation model of a Stackelberg game where a competitor enters following a market leader. While they do not produce any general analytical results, the paper certainly does more than hint that adding competitive effects to dynamic models matters.

Both Wernerfelt (1985) and Rao and Bass (1985) incorporated competition into dynamic pricing models at an early stage of the literature development. Wernerfelt's analysis of a duopoly market shows that firms should invest in market share early in the life cycle and that prices will decline early and might increase later. This is true for both large and small firms. Rao and Bass's analysis studies three separate cases: (1) demand saturation, (2) demand diffusion, and (3) cost learning (i.e., experience effects). The authors examine their model analytically, using simulation, and with an empirical illustration. They find that, in equilibrium, prices will decline for the cases of market saturation and cost-learning and increase for demand-diffusion. Eliashberg and Jeuland (1986) analyze three cases for a monopolist: (1) a non-myopic monopolist who perfectly predicts when a competitor will enter, (2) a myopic monopolist who ignores the periods after the competitor enters, and (3) a "surprised" monopolist who does not foresee the competitive entry. They find that the non-myopic firm will price its products higher than the myopic firm; they also show conditions under which the "surprised" monopolist will price too high during the monopoly period.

Two papers examine dynamic pricing using consumer-level models as foundations. Chintagunta and Rao (1995) start with a logit model of choice, aggregate across consumers, and build a differential game based on consumers' evolving preferences over time. The authors find that brands with higher levels of preferences charge higher prices over time. They also add consumer heterogeneity to the analysis and find that, under certain conditions, ignoring heterogeneity cause an upward bias in dynamic prices. Seetharaman and Che (2009) develop a two-period duopoly model based on a consumer utility specification including variety seeking behavior. They find that prices in both periods are higher than they would be in an identical market without variety seeking.

15.4.3 *Incorporating price expectations*

Some dynamic pricing models incorporate future price expectations into the model. A key reference for this work was the seminal research by Coase (1972) in economics. His theory was that for durable goods, even though a monopolist would like to skim by taking advantage of different consumer reservations prices, prices would quickly converge to marginal cost as consumers would anticipate the later price declines. In marketing, we know that this does not necessarily hold because the consumers with high reservation prices also have high utility for owning the product earlier which more than offsets the loss in utility from paying a higher price.

Yoo, Dolan, and Rangan (1987) published the first paper to incorporate future price expectations into a dynamic pricing model. They utilized the Bass diffusion model and three assumptions about how consumers form the future price expectations: myopic (only current price), full expectations (incorporating the total utility consumers obtain at time t), and partial expectations, as well as three different functional forms representing the heterogeneity of the future price expectation across the population. In their empirical work and simulations, they found the optimal price path to be constant for a few periods and then declining. Narasimhan (1989) assumes that consumers have rational expectations (perfect foresight) and a diffusion process with consumers entering the market every period. He finds the dynamic price path to be cyclical with prices being highest at the beginning of the cycle. Interestingly and realistically, he also finds that if consumers enter the market by reservation price (the highest entering the earliest), then prices will decline monotonically over time with no cycling.

These three strands of research are shown in Figure 15.3.

15.5 Product line research

The previous areas of research have largely focused on the pricing of a single good whether in a monopoly or competitive situation. Clearly, most companies are multi-product; the problem of how to price a line of related products is thus an important managerial problem. It is also difficult to model due to the interdependencies of the prices. A good recent review of this area can be found in Chen (2009). He summarizes the product line pricing problem nicely by indicating that the firm's problem for pricing m products is the following:

$$Max\ \pi = \sum_{i=1}^{m} \pi_i = \sum_{i=1}^{m} D_i(p_i, P_i, P_c, X, X_c)p_i - \sum_{i=1}^{m} C_i(D_i, D_{-i}),$$

(15.3)

where π is the total profit of the line, π_i is the profit of the ith product in the line, D_i is the demand of the ith product, D_{-i} is the demand of the products other than the ith product in the line, p_i is the price of the ith product, P_{-i} is the vector of prices of the products other than the ith, P_c is the vector of prices from competing brands, X is a set of marketing mix variables, and C_i is the cost of selling D_i units of the ith product. The research areas are divided into empirical and theoretical work. A third section briefly covers a related area, bundling (see Venkatesh and Mahajan, 2009).

15.5.1 *Empirical research*

The first empirical work in marketing on product line pricing was the paper by Urban (1969). He developed a multiplicative demand structure allowing for cross-elasticities within and between different product groups within a category as well as a profit function to be optimized. He applied the model using data from a food category demonstrating that the prices of the products in one company's line should be changed. Reibstein and Gatignon (1984) also use a multiplicative demand structure with cross-elasticities but with multiple equations for the different brands and different assumptions about error terms. They estimate their model with store-level branded egg data

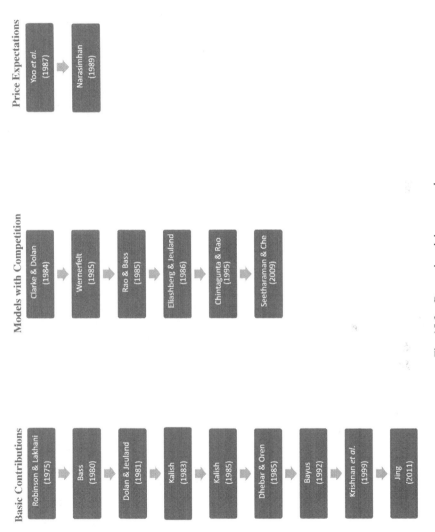

Fig. 15.3   Dynamic pricing research

with eight variants by size and color and a private label brand. Kadiyali, Vilcassim, and Chintagunta (1996) introduce competition into the product line pricing problem by introducing the use of a fully structural model of demand and costs at the firm level. They study the liquid detergent market and find a leader–follower-type pricing structure for the two leading manufacturers, Procter & Gamble and Unilever. Sudhir (2001) uses a model of competitive interactions following the literature in New Empirical Industrial Organization economics (NEIO) to study the pricing policies in the automobile market. His model not only permits competitive interactions but also for a large number of brands. He finds different pricing policies depending upon the product segment (e.g., subcompact vs. compact). Draganska and Jain (2006) tackle the problem of a product line (yogurt) that is differentiated both vertically (e.g., fat/sugar content) and horizontally (e.g., flavor) and investigate the opportunities for price discrimination across the horizontal dimension. Using a model of both supply and demand similar to Sudhir (2001), they find that, in the yogurt category, no horizontal price discrimination (i.e., pricing the flavors similarly) is the optimal product line pricing policy.

15.5.2 *Theoretical work*

Little and Shapiro (1980) offered an early paper on product line policy at the supermarket level rather than for the manufacturer. They assume that both customers and stores are optimizing — the customers are maximizing their utility and the stores are maximizing profit. Oren, Smith, and Wilson (1984) developed a monopoly model in the context of nonlinear pricing where the basic idea is that different elements of the product line allow price discrimination among different segments with different product valuations. Moorthy (1984) makes a contribution to both market segmentation and pricing by developing a model that permits third-degree price discrimination, i.e., customer self-selection by market segment. Dobson and Kalish (1988) extend this literature by taking a mathematical programming approach to the product line pricing problem. Gerstner and Hess (1989) address the question of why products come in different package sizes and prices per unit. This research can be viewed as a product line pricing decision.

15.5.3 *Bundling*

Many manufacturers and service providers offer bundles of products to customers. In some cases like the classic McDonald's Happy Meal, the bundle offers more utility to consumers than the separate items. Schmalensee (1984) categorizes bundles into two types: (1) pure bundles where only bundles are offered, and (2) mixed bundles where both a bundle and the individual "components" are available for sale. A conceptual integrative framework for bundling is offered by Stremersch and Tellis (2002) and a recent review is provided by Venkatesh and Mahajan (2009).

Although pricing is not the focus, the early work by Farquhar and Rao (1976) shows how consumers could use multi-attribute valuations to "balance" a subset of items from a larger set. Schmalensee (1984) follows up a seminal paper in economics by Adams and Yellen (1976) by showing that for a monopolist with two products and symmetric Gaussian demand, mixed bundling is optimal. Goldberg, Green, and Wind (1984) advance the bundling literature by demonstrating how conjoint analysis can be used to construct bundles of hotel amenities. Hanson and Martin (1990) used mixed integer linear programming which they find to be useful for a monopolist in a situation where there are a large number of possible product bundle combinations. Venkatesh and Mahajan (1993) developed a model with two dimensions of consumer decision-making in an arts context: time to attend performances and reservation price. They develop a profit-maximization model and show, similarly to Schmalensee's earlier results, that mixed bundling is optimal. Bakos and Brynjolfsson (1999) develop a bundling model in the context of Internet information goods where marginal costs of production and distribution are very low. Jedidi, Jagpal, and Manchanda (2003) developed a new approach for measuring reservation prices in the context of bundles. Their experimental data show that reservation prices for a bundle are less heterogeneous than those for individual bundle components.

These strands of research are shown in Figure 15.4.

15.6 Reference price research

The concept of a reference price results from a stream of earlier research on the psychophysics of price (see, for example, Monroe, 1973).

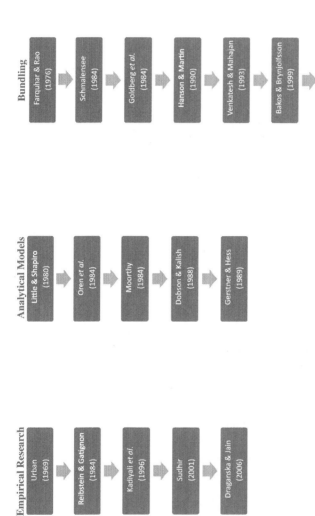

Fig. 15.4   Product line research

A variety of psychological theories including adaptation-level theory, the Weber–Fechner law, assimilation-contrast theory, and a number of others posit that decision-makers utilize some threshold that demarcates the line between response and no-response to a stimulus such as price. Due to the various underlying psychological theories, different reference prices have been posited in the literature (Winer, 1988) including perceived, expected future, fair, price usually paid, and others. In this section, research on reference price will refer to the modeling of consumer response to a comparison of actual to any definition of reference price.

Four strands of research on reference prices are considered in this section. One strand covers basic contributions to the reference price modeling literature. A second strand has added consumer heterogeneity to the analysis. A third area takes an analytical approach to reference prices. Finally, some work has attempted to distinguish between difference reference price formulations.

15.6.1 *Basic contributions*

The first formal modeling of psychological price thresholds began with the work of Gabor and his colleagues. This work is summarized in Gabor (1977) but actually started in the mid-1960s. The basic building block is what they termed the buy response curve (see also Sec. 15.3). Based on a set of hypothetical questions about WTP, the authors sketched this curve to represent the percentage of consumers who would purchase a product at a given price. Plotted against the actual prices paid for products, the buy response curve was shown to peak at a similar price indicating that there is a price point beyond which consumers would show purchasing resistance. The peak of the buy response curve was incorporated into a conceptual market share model but not estimated directly (see Gabor, 1977, Appendix 2).

The basic reference price model was developed by Winer (1985, 1986). The 1985 paper focused on applications to frequently-purchased products while the latter focused on durable goods. The basic model is the following:

$$P_i = f[Loyalty, (PR^r - PR^o), PR^o, \text{ marketing mix variables}], \quad (15.4)$$

where P_i is the probability of purchase of brand i, Loyalty is some formulation of state dependence, PR^r is the reference price, and PR^o

is the observed price at point-of-purchase. The theory is that observed prices above reference prices contribute negatively to utility (probability of purchase) as an unpleasant "surprise" or "sticker shock" while those below contribute positively. Empirical work supported the basic model.

A number of papers extended the basic model. Lattin and Bucklin (1989) added reference effects for price promotions in terms of both depth and frequency. Kalwani *et al.* (1990), Mayhew and Winer (1992), and Krishnamurthi, Mazumdar and Raj (1992) added loss aversion by splitting the reference price term into gains ($PR^r > PR^o$) and losses ($PR^o > PR^r$). The empirical results from the studies were consistent with Kahneman and Tversky's Prospect Theory (1979) in that the coefficient on the loss term was greater in absolute value than the coefficient on the gain term. Krishnamurthi Mazumdar and Raj (1992) also analyzed both the brand choice and purchase quantity decisions. Hardie, Johnson, and Fader (1993) added product quality to reference effects as well as defining reference price and quality based on a "reference product." Rajendran and Tellis (1994) developed the concept of an external reference price based on a consumer's observation of prices in the store or "contextual" prices to supplement internal or perceived prices. Rather than using just the absolute different of a reference and observed price, Kalyanaram and Little (1994) construct a latitude of acceptance around the reference price, i.e., a range of price insensitivity.

15.6.2 *Adding heterogeneity*

Most of the preceding research did not account for heterogeneity of the parameter estimates between consumers. Krishnamurthi, Mazumdar, and Raj (1992) allowed for differences in consumer brand loyalty in the loss aversion estimates noted above. Chang, Siddarth, and Weinberg (1999) argue that promotion effects on purchase timing can create biased estimates of reference price parameters for households that are price sensitive. Bell and Lattin (2000) find that a more general specification of consumer heterogeneity can confound loss aversion estimates in reference price models; they find weaker effects of loss aversion than in prior empirical work. Mazumdar and Papatla (2000) find differences between households in terms of their responsiveness to internal vs. external (contextual) reference prices.

15.6.3 *Analytical models*

The previously-cited papers were all empirical studies of the reference price effect utilizing mainly frequently-purchased categories and scanner datasets. The models are reduced-form models rather than developed from first principles using an underlying economic or other disciplinary structure. A few papers have taken a different tack on the problem by developing models based on economic theory. Putler (1992) incorporates loss aversion around a reference point directly into a microeconomic model of the consumer. The resulting model has kinked demand curves where actual price equals the reference price. He empirically tests his model with egg demand data. Greenleaf (1995) incorporates reference prices into a dynamic model of price promotions and shows that the optimal pricing policy for a monopolist can be cyclical. Kopalle, Rao, and Assunção (1996) extend Greenleaf's work to the duopoly and oligopoly situations and find different optimal pricing policies depending upon the assumptions of the reference price formation process and how customers behave with respect to loss aversion.

15.6.4 *Testing for reference price formulations*

A number of different formulations for the formation of reference price have been specified in the literature. Three different formulations have been popular: reference price formed by some combination of past prices and other information, past prices alone, and current prices. While a number of papers have tested different formulations (e.g., Winer, 1986), only three papers have performed a comprehensive test of the different approaches for estimating reference prices. Jacobson and Obermiller (1990) found that a serial correlation model based on past prices and a serially correlated error was the most consistent with experimental data examining future price expectations. Briesch *et al.* (1997) found that memory-based formulations, that is, those based on past prices alone, fit data from a number of frequently-purchased brands the best. Erdem, Katz, and Sun (2010) develop a test for distinguishing between different theoretical justifications for using past prices as a reference price mechanism.

These four strands of research are shown in Figure 15.5.

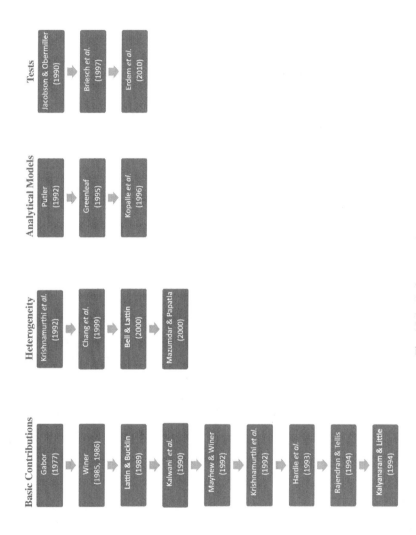

Fig. 15.5 Reference price research

15.7 Directions for future research

An examination of the five figures points to areas where more research is needed. While there has been substantial research on price elasticities, the area of changes over the life cycle needs to be updated, particularly given the recent study by Sethuraman, Tellis, and Briesch (2011) on advertising elasticities during periods of recession. For example, as more years pass since the recession of 2007–2009, more opportunity will exist for quasi-experiments to be conducted about price sensitivity prior, during, and after economic contractions. New approaches to measuring WTP are sorely needed. Incentive-compatible methods are a big step forward, but they are somewhat unwieldy to apply. Particular focus should be placed on online approaches that are low-cost and provide fast turnaround to companies. In addition, work applying WTP to non-traditional areas such as socially responsible products (see, for example, Tully and Winer, 2014) are needed. Dynamic pricing has seen a considerable amount of work already; as can be seen from Figure 15.4, more work incorporating price expectations is warranted. Given that this is such an important area for e-commerce companies, more data should be available as well. Empirical work on product line decision-making is a good area for more work particularly incorporating both online and offline products and services. Finally, reference price research has been popular and continues to be so. As a result, seminal findings will be hard to come by. However, partnered with the substantial increase in dynamic pricing as noted above, the importance of understanding how customers process price information and update their reference prices will only increase.

Overall, pricing remains one of the largest areas of research in the field of marketing science and will continue to be so given its critical nature to business and marketing.

References

Adams, W. J. and J. L. Yellen (1976). Commodity bundling and the burden of monopoly, *Quarterly Journal of Economics*, 90(8), 475–498.

Anderson, J. C., N. Kumar, and J. A. Narus (2007). *Value merchants*, Boston: Harvard Business School Press.

Assmus, G., J. U. Farley, and D. R. Lehmann (1984). How advertising affects sales: Meta-analysis of econometric results, *Journal of Marketing Research*, 21(2), 65–74.

Bakos, Y. and E. Brynjolfsson (1999). Bundling information goods: Pricing, profits, and efficiency, *Management Science*, 45(12), 1613–1630.

Bass, F. M. (1969). A new product growth model for consumer durables, *Management Science*, 15(1), 125–127.

Bass, F. M. (1980). The relationship between diffusion rates, experience curves, and demand elasticities for consumer durable technological innovations, *Journal of Business*, 53(7), S51–S67.

Bayus, B. L. (1992). The dynamic pricing of next generation consumer durables, *Marketing Science*, 11(Summer), 251–265.

Becker, G. M., M. H. DeGroot, and J. Marschak (1964). Measuring utility by a single-response sequential method, *Behavioral Science*, 9, 226–232.

Bell, D. R. and J. M. Lattin (2000). Looking for loss aversion in scanner panel data: The confounding effect of price response heterogeneity, *Marketing Science*, 19(Spring), 185–200.

Bijmolt, T. H. A., H. J. van Heerde, and R. G. M. Pieters (2005). New empirical generalizations on the determinants of price elasticity, *Journal of Marketing Research*, 2(5), 141–156.

Bolton, R. N. (1989). The relationship between market characteristics and promotional price elasticities, 8(Spring), 153–169.

Briesch, R. A., L. Krishnamurthi, T. Mazumdar, and S. P. Raj (1997). A comparative analysis of reference price models, *Journal of Consumer Research*, 24(9), 202–214.

Chang, K., S. Siddarth, and C. B. Weinberg (1999). The impact of heterogeneity in purchase timing and price responsiveness on estimates of sticker shock effects, *Marketing Science*, 2, 178–192.

Chen, Y. (2009). Product line pricing, in V. R. Rao, ed., *Handbook of pricing research in marketing*, Cheltenham, UK: Edward Elgar, Chapter 10.

Chintagunta, P. K. and V. R. Rao (1996). Pricing strategies in a dynamic duopoly: A differential game model, *Management Science*, 42(11), 1501–1514.

Clarke, D. G. and R. J. Dolan (1984). A simulation analysis of alternative pricing strategies for dynamic environments, *Journal of Business*, 57(1), S179–S200.

Coase, R. (1972). Durability and monopoly, *Journal of Law and Economics*, 15, 143–149.

Dhebar, A. and S. S. Oren (1985). Optimal dynamic pricing for expanding networks, *Marketing Science*, 4(Fall), 336–351.

Ding, M. (2007). An incentive-aligned mechanism for conjoint analysis, *Journal of Marketing Research*, 44(5), 214–223.

Dobson, G. and S. Kalish (1988). Positioning and pricing a product line, *Marketing Science*, 7(Spring), 107–125.

Dolan, R. J. and A. P. Jeuland (1981). Experience curves and dynamic demand models: Implications for optimal pricing strategies, *Journal of Marketing*, 45(Winter), 52–73.

Draganska, M. and D. C. Jain (2006). Consumer preferences and product-line pricing strategies: An empirical analysis, *Marketing Science*, 25(3–4), 164–174.

Eliashberg, J. and A. P. Jeuland (1986). The impact of competitive entry in a developing market upon dynamic pricing strategies, 5(Winter), 20–36.

Erdem, T., M. L. Katz, and B. Sun (2010). A simple test for distinguishing between internal reference price theories, *Quantitative Marketing and Economics*, 8(9), 303–332.

Farquhar, P. H. and V. R. Rao (1976). A balance model for evaluating subsets of multiattributed items, *Management Science*, 22(1), 528–539.

Gabor, A. (1977). *Pricing: Principles and practices*, London: Heinemann Education Books.

Gerstner, E. and J. D. Hess (1989). Why do hot dogs come in packs of 10 and buns in 8s or 12s? A demand-side investigation, *Journal of Business*, 60(10), 491–517.

Gabor, A. and C. W. J. Granger (1966). Price as an indicator of quality: Report on an enquiry, *Economica*, 33(2), 43–70.

Gijsbrechts, E. (1993). Prices and pricing research in consumer marketing: Some recent developments, *International Journal of Research in Marketing*, 10, 115–151.

Goldberg, S., P. E. Green, and Y. Wind (1984). Conjoint analysis of price premiums for hotel amenities, *Journal of Business*, 57(1), S111–S132.

Greenleaf, E. A. (1995). The impact of reference price effects on the profitability of price promotions, *Marketing Science*, 14(Winter), 82–104.

Guadagni, P. M. and J. D. C. Little (1983). A logit model of brand choice calibrated on scanner data, *Marketing Science*, 2(Summer), 203–238.

Gurumurthy, K. and J. D. C. Little (1994). An empirical analysis of latitude of price acceptance in consumer package goods, *Journal of Consumer Research*, 21(12), 408–418.

Hagerty, M. R., J. M. Carman, and G. J. Russell (1988). Estimating elasticities with PIMS data: Methodological issues and substantive implications, *Journal of Marketing Research*, 25(2), 1–9.

Hanson, W. and R. K. Martin (1990). Optimal bundle pricing, *Management Science*, 36(2), 155–174.

Hanssens, D., L. J. Parsons, and R. L. Schultz (2001). *Market response models: Econometric and time series analysis*, 2nd edn., Boston, MA: Kluwer Academic Publishers.

Hardie, B. G. S., E. J. Johnson, and P. S. Fader (1993). Modeling loss aversion and reference dependence effects on brand choice, *Marketing Science*, 12(Fall), 378–394.

Hoch, S. J., B.-D. Kim, A. L. Montgomery, and P. E. Rossi (1995). Determinants of store-level price elasticity, *Journal of Marketing Research*, 32(2), 17–29.

Jacobson, R. and C. Obermiller (1990). The formation of expected future price: A reference price for forward-looking consumers, *Journal of Consumer Research*, 16(3), 420–432.

Jedidi, K. and S. Jagpal (2009). Willingness to pay: Measurement and managerial implications, in V. R. Rao, ed., *Handbook of pricing research in marketing*, Cheltenham, UK: Edward Elgar, Chapter 2.

Jedidi, K., S. Jagpal, and P. Manchanda (2003). Measuring heterogeneous reservation prices for product bundles, *Marketing Science*, 22(Winter), 107–130.

Jedidi, K. and Z. J. Zhang (2002). Augmenting conjoint analysis to estimate consumer reservation prices, *Management Science*, 48, 1350–1368.

Jing, B. (2011). Social learning and dynamic pricing of durable goods, *Marketing Science*, 30(9–10), 851–865.

Kadiyali, V., N. J. Vilcassim, and P. K. Chintagunta (1996). Empirical analysis of competitive product line pricing decisions: Lead, follow, or move together? *Journal of Business*, 69(10), 459–487.

Kahneman, D. and A. Tversky (1979). Prospect theory: An analysis of decision under risk, *Econometrica*, 47, 263–291.

Kalish, S. (1983). Monopolist pricing with dynamic demand and production costs, *Marketing Science*, 2(Spring), 135–160.

Kalish, S. (1985). A new product adoption model with price, advertising, and uncertainty, *Management Science*, 31(12), 1569–1585.

Kalwani, M. U., C. K. Yin, H. J. Rinne, and Y. Sugita (1990). A price expectations model of customer brand choice, *Journal of Marketing Research*, 27(8), 251–262.

Kamakura, W. A. and G. J. Russell (1989). A probabilistic choice model for market segmentation and elasticity structure, *Journal of Marketing Research*, 26(11), 379–390.

Kohli, R. and V. Mahajan (1991). A reservation-price model for optimal pricing of multiattribute products in conjoint analysis, *Journal of Marketing Research*, 28(8), 347–354.

Kopalle, P. K., A. G. Rao, and J. L. Assunção (1996). Asymmetric reference price effects and dynamic pricing policies, *Marketing Science*, 15(Winter), 60–85.

Krishnamurthi, L., T. Mazumdar, and S. P. Raj (1992). Asymmetric response to price in consumer brand choice and purchase quantity decisions, *Journal of Consumer Research*, 19(12), 387–400.

Krishnan, T. V., F. M. Bass, and D. C. Jain (1999). Optimal pricing strategy for new products, *Management Science*, 45(12), 1650–1663.

Lambin, J. J. (1976). *Advertising, competition and market conduct in oligopoly over time*, Amsterdam: North-Holland Publishing Company.

Lattin, J. M. and R. E. Bucklin (1989). Reference effects of price and promotion on brand choice behavior, *Journal of Marketing Research*, 26(8), 299–310.

Little, J. D. C. and J. F. Shapiro (1980). A theory for pricing nonfeatured products in supermarkets, *Journal of Business*, 53(7), S199–S209.

Mahajan, V., P. E. Green, and S. M. Goldberg (1982). A conjoint model for measuring self- and cross-price/demand relationships, *Journal of Marketing Research*, 19(8), 334–342.

Massy, W. F. and R. E. Frank (1965). Short-term price and dealing effects in selected market segments, *Journal of Marketing Research*, 2(5), 171–185.

Mazumdar, T. and P. Papatla (2000). An investigation of reference price segments, *Journal of Marketing Research*, 2(May), 246–258.

Mayhew, G. E. and R. S. Winer (1992). An empirical analysis of internal and external reference prices, *Journal of Consumer Research*, 19(6), 62–70.

Miller, K. M., R. Hofstetter, H. Krohmer, and Z. J. Zhang (2011). How should consumers' willingness to pay be measured? An empirical comparison of state-of-the-art approaches, *Journal of Marketing Research*, 48(2), 172–184.

Mitchell, R. C. and R. T. Carson (1989). *Using surveys to value public goods: The contingent valuation method*, Washington, DC: Resources for the Future.

Monroe, K. B. (1973). Buyers' subjective perceptions of price, *Journal of Marketing Research*, 10(2), 70–80.

Moorthy, K. S. (1984). Market segmentation, self-selection, and product line design, *Marketing Science*, 3(Fall), 288–307.

Narasimhan, C. (1989). Incorporating price expectations into diffusion models, *Marketing Science*, 8(Autumn), 343–357.

Neslin, S. A. and R. W. Shoemaker (1983). Using a natural experiment to estimate a price elasticity: The 1974 sugar shortage and the ready-to-eat cereal market, *Journal of Marketing*, 47(Winter), 44–57.

Oren, S., S. Smith, and R. Wilson (1984). Pricing a product line, *Journal of Business*, 57(1), S73–S99.

Parker, P. M. (1992). Price elasticity dynamics over the adoption life cycle, *Journal of Marketing Research*, 29(8), 358–367.

Putler, D. S. (1992). Incorporating reference price effects into a theory of consumer choice, *Marketing Science*, 3(Summer), 287–309.

Rajendran, K. N. and G. J. Tellis (1994). Contextual and temporal components of reference price, *Journal of Marketing*, 58(1), 22–34.

Rao, R. C. and F. M. Bass (1985). Competition, strategy, and price dynamics: A theoretical and empirical investigation, *Journal of Marketing Research*, 22(8), 283–296.

Rao, V. R. (1984). Pricing research in marketing: The state of the art, *Journal of Business*, 54, S39–S60.

Rao, V. R. (1993). Pricing models in marketing, in J. Eliashberg and G. Lilien (eds.), *Handbooks in OR & MS*, Vol. 5, Amsterdam: Elsevier, Chapter 11.

Rao, V. R. (ed.) (2009). *Handbook of pricing research in marketing*, Cheltenham, UK: Edward Elgar.

Reibstein, D. J. and H. Gatignon (1984). Optimal product line pricing: The influence of elasticities and cross-elasticities, *Journal of Marketing Research*, 21(8), 259–267.

Robinson, B. and C. Lakhani (1975). Dynamic price models for new-product planning, *Management Science*, 21(6), 1113–1122.

Russell, G. J. and R. N. Bolton (1988). Implications of market structure for elasticity structure, *Journal of Marketing Research*, 25(8), 229–241.

Schmalensee, R. (1984). Gaussian demand and commodity bundling, *Journal of Business*, 57(1), S211–S230.

Seetharaman, P. B. and H. Che (2009). Price competition in markets with consumer variety seeking, *Marketing Science*, 28(5–6), 516–525.

Sethuraman, R., G. J. Tellis, and R. A. Briesch (2011). How well does advertising work? Generalizations from meta-analysis of brand advertising elasticities, *Journal of Marketing Research*, 48(6), 457–471.

Simon, H. (1979). Dynamics of price elasticity and brand life cycles: An empirical study, *Journal of Marketing Research*, 16(11), 439–452.

Simon, J. L. (1966). The price elasticity of liquor in the U.S. and a simple method of determination, *Econometrica*, 34(1), 193–205.

Stigler, G. J. (1987). *The theory of price*, New York: Macmillan.

Stoetzel, J. (1954), Le prix comme limite, in P. L. Reynaud, ed., *La Psychologie Economique*, 184–188.

Stole, L. A. (2007). Price discrimination and competition, in M. Armstrong and R. Porter, eds., *Handbook of industrial administration*, Volume 3, Amsterdam: Elsevier, Chapter 34.

Stremersch, S. and G. J. Tellis (2002). Strategic bundling of products and prices: A new synthesis for marketing, *Journal of Marketing*, 66(1), 55–72.

Sudhir, K. (2001). Competitive pricing behavior in the auto market: A structural analysis, *Marketing Science*, 20(Winter), 42–60.

Tellis, G. J. (1988). The price elasticity of selective demand: A meta-analysis of econometric models of sales, *Journal of Marketing Research*, 25(11), 331–341.

Telser, L. G. (1962). The demand for branded goods as estimated from consumer panel data, *The Review of Economics and Statistics*, 44(8), 300–324.

Tully, S. M. and R. S. Winer (2014). The role of the beneficiary in willingness to pay for socially responsible products: A meta-analysis, Working Paper, New York University.

Urban, G. L. (1969). A mathematical modeling approach to product line decisions, *Journal of Marketing Research*, 6(2), 40–47.

Van Westendorp, P. (1976). NSS-Price Sensitivity Meter (PSM): A new approach to study consumer perception of price, *Proceedings of the ESOMAR Congress*, 139–167.

Venkatesh, R. and V. Mahajan (1993). A probabilistic approach to pricing a bundle of products and services, *Journal of Marketing Research*, 30(11), 494–508.

Venkatesh, R. and V. Mahajan (2009). The design and pricing of bundles: A review of normative guidelines and practical approaches, in V. R. Rao, ed., *Handbook of pricing research in marketing*, Cheltenham, UK: Edward Elgar, Chapter 11.

Wang, T., R. Venkatesh, and R. Chatterjee (2007). Reservation price as a range: An incentive-compatible measurement approach, *Journal of Marketing Research*, 44(5), 200–213.

Weiss, D. L. (1969). An analysis of the demand structure for branded consumer products, *Applied Economics*, 1, 37–49.

Wernerfelt, B. (1985). The dynamics of prices and market shares over the product life cycle, *Management Science*, 31(8), 928–939.

Wertenbroch, K. and B. Skiera (2002). Measuring consumers' willingness to pay at the point of purchase, *Journal of Marketing Research*, 39(5), 228–241.

Winer, R. S. (1985). A price vector model of demand for consumer durables: Preliminary developments, *Marketing Science*, 4(Winter), 74–90.

Winer, R. S. (1986). A reference price model of demand for frequently purchased products, *Journal of Consumer Research*, 13(9), 250–256.

Winer, R. S. (1988). Behavioral perspectives on pricing: Buyer's subjective perceptions of price revisited," in T. M. Devinney, ed., *Issues in pricing: Theory and research*, Lexington, MA: Lexington Books, Chapter 2.

Yoo, P. H., R. J. Dolan, and V. Kasturi Rangan (1987). Dynamic pricing strategy for new consumer durables, *Zeitschrift für Betriebwirtschaft*, 57(10), 1024–1043.

Chapter 16

Sales Force Productivity Models

Murali K. Mantrala

16.1 Introduction and overview

Among the various forms of marketing communications, personal selling has perhaps the longest history. There is evidence of personal selling activities by peddlers and traders going back to the Classical Age (e.g., Powers *et al.*, 1987). In more modern times, personal selling has contributed to the economic growth and high standard of living of the United States and other Western nations (see, e.g., Bartels, 1976). Powers *et al.* (1988) document how personal selling and sales force management, enabled by the advances in automobile transportation and telephone communications occurring at the time, became vital functions for businesses in the first decades of the 20th century. Since then, sales forces have continued to grow in both size and importance even as the industrial revolution has given way to the information revolution, and firms' orientation has moved from product-centric to customer-centric (e.g., Sheth and Sharma, 2008). While these developments may be transforming the selling process in many business markets, they have not obviated the need for sales forces (e.g., Mantrala and Albers, 2012). Personal selling remains one of the most effective marketing instruments for many businesses (Albers, Mantrala, and Sridhar, 2010) but sales force expenditures are among the highest in firms' marketing budgets and continue to rise as selling environments become more complex (Jones *et al.*, 2005; Zoltners, Sinha, and Lorimer, 2006). Consequently, managing and enhancing sales force productivity and profitability, remains a major challenge and priority for firms today (e.g., Ledingham, Kovac, and Simon, 2006).

Sales force productivity-related decisions were in fact among the earliest problems addressed by marketing scientists. Initially "scientific sales management" research in the 1920s focused on the selling process and how managers could make salespeople more effective in personal selling to take advantage of burgeoning economic opportunities at that time (e.g., Hoyt, 1918). Subsequently, however, with the extreme swings in the economy and business fortunes during the Great Depression, World War II, and post-WW II years of the 1930s, 1940s, and 1950s, sales managers' attention focused on problems of better sizing, allocation, and control of sales resources. In response, several notable papers with an operations research (OR) orientation were published in this time period, e.g., Wellman (1939), Nordin (1943), Waid *et al.* (1956), Semlow (1959). However, such papers were few and far between, hardly meeting the need for solutions to many pressing sales productivity management questions (e.g., Montgomery and Webster, 1968). Two seminal sales force modeling research papers did appear in the early 1960s (Talley, 1961; Farley, 1964), and the decade culminated in the publication of the 1971 special issue of *Management Science* (MS) that included influential papers by Davis and Farley (1971), Hess and Samuels (1971), Lodish (1971), and Montgomery, Silk, and Zarazoga (1971). Montgomery (2001) has described this special issue as marking the moment when marketing science research finally "arrived" in the broader OR and MS community.

Following this event, a major surge in sales force research with a "marketing engineering" flavor (Steckel and Brody, 2001) occurred through the 1970s and the early 1980s. However, toward the mid-1980s, modeling research with a more theoretical orientation, i.e., providing more explanations and normative guidelines for sales management, especially in the domain of sales force compensation, e.g., Basu *et al.* (1985), began to emerge. Such research also led to more empirical studies of theoretical propositions (e.g., Coughlan and Narasimhan, 1992) as distinct from field applications and tests of decision support models (e.g., Fudge and Lodish, 1977) that had appeared in the earlier literature. Moreover, as richer archival transactions and standardized market data (e.g., physician-level prescription-detailing data from IMS Health, etc.) became available and accessible, there was a shift from the decision calculus-based sales response parameterization of the 1970s to econometric estimation of sales response functions between the 1980s and first decade of the new millennium (e.g., Parsons and Abeele 1981, Leeflang, Mijatovic, and Saunders, 1992). Much of this research, however, focused on effectiveness and allocation of detailing effort in pharmaceutical markets where there was better access to such data than in other industries (see, e.g., Manchanda and Honka, 2005). That is, econometric models of sales–selling effort relationships suitable for addressing sales force productivity problems in non-pharmaceutical industries have remained relatively sparse in the literature (Albers, Mantrala and Sridhar, 2010). Overall, the surge in sales force model-based research papers seen in the 1970s and 1980s abated significantly in the next two decades (e.g., Williams and Plouffe, 2007) as marketing scientists turned their attention to other topic domains, e.g., brand advertising and retail price promotions, where standardized data for sophisticated econometric model-building were more readily available (e.g., Bronnenberg, Kruger, Mela, 2008). As evidence of this shift, no "sales"-related keyword appears in Mela, Roos, and Deng's (2013) tabulation (Table 1, p. 9) of the top 25 most frequently used keywords in *Marketing Science* over the 1982–2011 time period!

Regardless of this abatement in related scholarly research, however, sales force management questions remain of critical importance and consequence in practice, especially in business markets. Therefore, it is heartening to see signs of an uptick in research on outstanding sales force productivity questions in very recent years, utilizing a variety of sources of data including surveys (Lo, Ghosh, and LaFontaine, 2011), trade association data (e.g., Mantrala *et al.*, 2007), firms' internal records (e.g., Misra and Nair, 2011), and economic experiments (e.g., Lim, Ahearne, and Ham, 2009). Interestingly, however, the latest research on some of the longstanding questions of sales force deployment is actually being done by scholars in disciplines other than marketing such as computer science and systems engineering (e.g., Golalikhani and Karwan, 2013; Ríos-Mercado and López-Pérez, 2013) and by industry analytics groups (e.g., Lawrence *et al.*, 2010, Baier *et al.*, 2012).

Against this backdrop, this chapter's goal is to trace the history of developments in sales force productivity decision models and related empirical studies in marketing science since about the second quarter of the 20th century — in four of the most salient streams of research in this domain (see e.g., Mantrala *et al.*, 2010): (1) *sales force sizing and effort allocation* (Table 16.1, Column 1); (2) *sales territory alignment*[1] (Table 16.1, Column 2); (3) *integrated sales force deployment*[2] (models and/or studies that simultaneously address two or more decisions such as sales force sizing, resource allocation, territory alignment, structuring, planning, hiring, or training, Table 16.1, Column 3[3]); and (4) *sales force compensation and incentives use and design* (Tables 16.2 and 16.3). Given this purpose, this paper only briefly discusses the themes/contributions of the works listed in Tables 16.1–16.3. Readers interested in more comprehensive and detailed treatments of the models in these and other papers should refer to other review articles, e.g., Vandenbosch and Weinberg (1993), Albers and Mantrala (2008). The chapter concludes with comments on some discernible trends in current research and directions for future research.

---

[1]Sales territory alignment is known by various names, including: sales force alignment, territory design, or territory re-alignment. In the alignment process, geographical boundaries (or account listings independent of geography) are created to assign work to sales representatives.

[2]In this chapter, we use the term sales force "deployment" to refer to any one, subset, or all of the following sales management decisions: sales force *sizing* (determining the sales force size or budget), *structuring* (determining how many sales forces and how they should be organized, e.g., specialized by product, customer, or geography), sales effort or resource allocation (across products, customers, or markets), sales territory alignment, and salesperson selection and location (who should be in the sales force and where should they be located).

[3]By "integrated" models we are referring to models for simultaneously improving/optimizing two or more sales force deployment decisions. In principle, all deployment decisions are interrelated within a selling effort "decisions complex" (Albers and Mantrala, 2008). However, these interdependencies considerably complicate the development of models for globally optimizing sales force decisions. Not surprisingly, therefore, sales force research has largely progressed by solving one or two deployment decision problems at a time, assuming other parts of the selling effort decisions complex are fixed. Indeed only three decision models in our history have attempted to integrate and simultaneously solve three or more deployment decisions, namely, Beswick and Cravens (1977), Rangaswamy, Sinha and Zoltners (1990), Drexl and Haase (1999). However, as pointed out by Skiera and Albers (2007), such models have had limited success in actual applications because of the differing organizational groups, levels, and time horizons of stakeholders involved in these decisions.

Table 16.1   Sales force deployment research streams

Sales resource allocation and sizing models	Sales territory alignment models	Integrated deployment models
Wellman (1939): Introduced concepts of nonlinear sales-effort response functions for determining optimal sales effort allocations.	**Talley (1961)**: Described systematic approach for computing calls (workload) required to cover customer accounts of varying sales potentials, and determining 'equal workload' territories' number and alignment.	**Lodish (1975)**: Proposed mathematical programming model and heuristic solution procedure for simultaneously determining a profit-maximizing sales territory alignment and optimal account sales call frequencies.
Lodish (1971): Introduced decision calculus approach to estimating S-shaped sales-effort response functions for sales call planning (CALLPLAN).	**Hess and Samuels (1971)**: Proposed linear programming-based algorithm for determining maximally compact and equal territories on some single activity measure (GEOLINE).	**Beswick and Cravens (1977)**: Proposed multistage dynamic programming-based model for improving interrelated sales force sizing, sales effort allocation, and sales territory alignment decisions.
Zoltners and Sinha (1980): Proposed comprehensive framework for modeling and solving sales resource allocation and sizing optimization problems using integer programming.	**Zoltners and Sinha (1983)**: Proposed integer programming-based model for developing sales territory alignments with contiguous (connected) sales coverage units (SCUs) that are balanced relative to one or more 'activity' measures, and compatible with geographic considerations.	**Rangaswamy, Sinha, and Zoltners (1990)**: Proposed mathematical programming model using market segment- and sales force structure-dependent product sales response functions for simultaneously optimizing number of sales forces, sizes, and effort allocations across product-markets.

(Continued)

Table 16.1   (*Continued*)

Sales resource allocation and sizing models	Sales territory alignment models	Integrated deployment models
Horsky and Nelson (1996): Proposed assessment of optimal sales force size and allocation using efficient frontier benchmarking.	***Skiera and Albers (1998)***: Proposed contribution optimizing sales territory alignment model (COSTA) based on SCU-level response functions.	***Drexl and Haase (1999)***: Proposed nonlinear mixed-integer programming model for optimizing sales force sizing, salespeople's locations, territory alignment, and effort allocations.
Manchanda, Rossi, Chintagunta (2004): Presented approach for econometric estimation of sales response models with nonrandom selling effort.	***Zoltners and Sinha (2005)***: Described evolution of sales territory alignment modeling and implementation at 500 firms over 30 years and the need for both "high tech and high touch" approach.	***Godes (2003)***: Presented game-theoretic model-based insights into optimal type, number, organization, and training of salespeople in selling environments of varying task complexity.
Montoya, Netzer, and Jedidi (2010): Proposed hidden Markov model of heterogeneous customers' responses to selling and sampling efforts for determining their dynamically optimal allocations and budgets.	***Rios-Mercado and Lopez-Perez (2013)***: Presented mixed-integer LP model for compact and contiguous territories, balanced on multiple activity measures, allowing for required disjoint assignments of SCUs.	***Golalikhani and Karwan (2013)***: Proposed multistage model for optimal allocation of customer acquisition and retention efforts, sizing of "hunters" and "farmer" sales force, and hiring, relocating, firing strategies.

Table 16.2   Theoretical-normative sales force compensation and incentives research streams

Commissions and/or salary	Sales quotas, bonuses, and menus	Multiperson incentives
Farley (1964): Presented the first analysis for optimal sales compensation, assuming a deterministic sales setting; showed that paying equal commission rates on gross margins of products simultaneously meets income-maximizing salesperson and profit-maximizing firm's objectives.	***Davis and Farley (1971)***: Introduced sales quota-based commission systems and product cost interdependence into Farley's (1964) problem and showed that (a) Farley's original result does not hold; and (b) a decentralized system of quotas and commission setting works better in this environment.	***Kalra and Shi (2001)***: Developed and analyzed a tournament theory-based model to determine the optimal number of prizewinners in a rank-order (closed-ended) sales contest with logistically distributed sales outcomes.
Berger (1972), (1975): Showed how introducing sales response uncertainty and salesperson risk-aversion into optimal multiproduct sales commission-setting problem changes Farley's (1964) results.	***Lal and Staelin (1986)***: Introduced information asymmetry and sales force heterogeneity into the Basu *et al.* (1985) problem and showed that offering a menu of quota-based compensation plans rather than a single nonlinear commission plan is optimal in such settings.	***Murthy and Mantrala (2005)***: Developed a model to determine the optimal division of an integrated marketing communications (IMC) budget between advertising and sales contest prizes as well as the optimal number and amounts of prizes using Gumbel distributed sales.
Weinberg (1978): Showed that, in a deterministic sales environment, Farley's results continue to hold for a salesperson maximizing income subject to a minimum return per unit time.	***Rao (1990)***: Derived explicit solutions to menu design within the Lal and Staelin (1986) framework, but assuming risk-neutral salespeople; showed a menu of linear quota-based contracts is frequently optimal.	***Caldieraro and Coughlan (2009)***: Investigated and compared performance under piece-rate plans versus contests when territory sales are positively (negatively) correlated.

(Continued)

Table 16.2 *(Continued)*

Commissions and/or salary	Sales quotas, bonuses, and menus	Multiperson incentives
Srinivasan (1981): Considering utility rather than income maximizing fixed total time sales rep as in Farley (1964), showed latter's results no longer hold.	**Mantrala et al. (1994)**: Proposed a practical agency-theoretic approach for multiproduct sales quota-bonus planning for a heterogeneous sales force.	**Syam et al. (2012)**: Investigated whether sales contests or quota systems are superior incentive mechanisms when territories have unequal sales potentials.
Basu et al. (1985): Introduced formal agency-theoretic model allowing for sales uncertainty and showed that a salary plus nonlinear commission plan, rather than straight commission form assumed by Farley (1964), is optimal.	**Raju and Srinivasan (1994)**: Showed via simulation analyses that a common salary plus commission plan with tailored sales quotas is nearly optimal and simpler to implement than the Basu et al. (1985) plan.	—
Lal and Srinivasan (1993): Investigated optimal linear salary plus multiproduct commission plan parameters based on model of Holmstrom & Milgrom (1987).	**Misra and Nair (2009)**: Built a dynamic structural model of sales reps' response to quota-based commission scheme to identify profit improving changes.	

Table 16.3 Theoretical-empirical sales force compensation and incentives research streams

Commission and/or salary	Sales quotas, bonuses, contests
John and Weitz (1989): Conducted survey data-based study that did not find support for agency-theoretic (AT) prediction that greater sales uncertainty is associated with more salary-weighted compensation plans.	*Gaba and Kalra (1999)*: Showed experimentally how risk behavior of sales reps is affected by payoffs in quota-bonus systems and contests they face.
Coughlan and Narasimhan (1992): Tested and found mixed support for AT predictions of effects of various sales force, firm, product, and market factors on salary to incentive pay ratio and total pay using aggregate industry survey data (from Dartnell Corporation).	*Steenburgh (2009)*: Analyzed archival data on monthly sales and quotas of salespeople at a firm and found that lump-sum bonuses primarily motivate reps to put in more effort than play strategic sales timing games.
Joseph and Kalwani (1995): Test and find mixed support for AT prediction that higher salesperson risk-aversion will lead to more salary-weighted plans using industry survey data.	*Chung, Steenburgh, and Sudhir (2013)*: Use dynamic structural modeling on Steenburgh's (2009) data to show that annual quotas are not effective in the absence of quarterly quotas.
Ghosh and John (2000): Did experimental economics tests of AT predictions, finding mixed support.	*Lim, Ahearne, and Ham (2009)*: Performed economic experiments to test and find mixed support for Kalra and Shi's (2001) predictions regarding optimal number and values of prizes in rank-order contests.
Krafft, Albers, and Lal (2004): Surveyed chief executives of German sales organizations and found no support for AT prediction of higher salary in the presence of higher sales uncertainty.	*Lim (2010)*: Conducted two incentive-aligned lab experiments to find, contrary to conventional wisdom, that a contest with more winners than losers is more effective than one with fewer winners than losers.
Misra, Coughlan, Narasimhan (2005): Extended classical AT model to include firm size and find support for their predictions on firm size effects on salary:pay ratio and total pay using updated Dartnell survey data.	*Kishore et al. (2013)*: Conducted a natural field-based experiment of the effects of a switch from a quota-bonus to commission plan at a pharmaceutical firm and found that commission (bonus) plans are more effective for small (diverse) sales task portfolios.

(Continued)

Table 16.3   *(Continued)*

Commission and/or salary	Sales quotas, bonuses, contests
Rouzies et al. (2009): Tested and found positive support for AT prediction and find a positive relationship between total (take-home) pay and variable to fixed pay ratio.	—
Lo, Ghosh, and LaFontaine (2011): Predicted and used data from a cross-sectional survey of managers to show that firms design their pay plans to *select* salespeople as well as provide them with the right level of incentives.	—
Misra, Nair, and Daljord (2012): Used dataset from Misra and Nair (2011) to show that a firm may use a partially uniform plan for the sake of agent selection even if it implies loss in incentives.	—

16.2 Sales force resource allocation and sizing models

The fluctuating economic conditions between the 1920s and 1950s brought to the fore, issues of how to optimally size and allocate limited and expensive selling effort, over various competing sales entities and activities such as products geographic areas, prospective ("hunting") and current customers ("farming"). As shown in Table 16.1 (Column 1), the chronology of significant scholarly contributions in this stream commences with Wellman's (1939) paper focused on the allocation of selling effort across geographic areas. This paper was perhaps the first to formally propose nonlinear aggregate sales–selling effort response relationships exhibiting decreasing returns to selling effort as the bases for optimal selling effort allocation. Since then, aggregate sales response functions of this form have remained a central concept of sales force decision modeling (e.g., Albers, 2012). Considering sales entities characterized by such sales–effort relationships, Wellman noted that optimal (revenue-maximizing) allocations of effort were those at which marginal sales responses in all entities were equalized subject to their sum being equal to the total effort or budget constraint. Wellman also discussed the more complex conditions for optimal allocations when sales are part concave and part convex, i.e., S-shaped, over the range of effort (an issue revisited in later decades by Lodish (1971), Rao and Rao (1983) among other scholars). Last but not least, Wellman noted the problems of sub-optimization in using entities' relative sales potentials — as suggested by contemporaries like Brown (1937) — rather than responsiveness as a basis for allocation decisions — an issue extensively treated five decades later by Mantrala, Sinha, and Zoltners (1992).

Following Wellman (1939), a few more papers addressing similar problems appeared in the next three decades, e.g., Nordin (1943), Brown *et al.* (1956), Waid *et al.* (1956) (see, e.g., Zoltners and Sinha, 1980 for a review). However, the next significant advances in this stream came at the beginning of the 1970s in the form of decision calculus-based models led by Lodish's (1971) CALLPLAN model (concerned with allocation of sales representative's call time to accounts) and Montgomery, Silk, and Zarazoga's (1971) DETAILER model (concerned with the allocation of salesperson details across products). The decision calculus approach had been previously introduced to marketing scientists by Little (1970). CALLPLAN utilized Little's (1970) flexible ADBUDG functional form that allowed for account sales response functions to be concave or S-shaped while DETAILER used a flexible, polynomial (cubic) functional form. Subsequently, Fudge and Lodish (1977) reported a validation of the CALLPLAN decision calculus approach in a field study at United Airlines.

A stream of decision model-based solutions to variants of the sales call or time allocation problem, employing subjectively parameterized response functions followed CALLPLAN in the 1970s. In a major article, Zoltners and Sinha (1980) reviewed and integrated these developments in an overarching general model of sales resource allocation problems. This framework accommodates complications such as the allocation of multiple sales resources over multiple time periods, accounting for dynamic carryover effects and sales response uncertainty, solvable using integer programming methods. The other notable contribution in that year was Lodish's (1980) extension of Montgomery Silk, and Zarazoga's (1971) DETAILER model to determine optimal sales force size and effort allocation across products and markets simultaneously. Eight years later, a variant of this model was applied at Syntex Corporation and led the firm to significantly increase its sales force size along with deployment changes that led to a continuing US$25,000,000, 8% annual sales increase (Lodish *et al.*, 1988).

While many more applications of the subjectively parameterized decision models occurred in practice (see, e.g., Lodish, 2001; Sinha and Zoltners, 2001), few new sizing and selling effort allocation decision models were proposed in the marketing science literature in the 1980s and 1990s. One notable exception was the novel approach proposed by Horsky and Nelson (1996) to assess optimal sales force size and allocation (across sales districts) using an efficient frontier benchmarking methodology. However, by the time the 1990s ended, marketing scientists' attention had largely shifted from decision model optimization and implementation to response model estimation using objective rather than subjective judgmental data that was the hallmark of the decision calculus approach. Specifically, as disaggregate (product- or physician-) level standardized panel data from sources such as IMS Health and ImpactRx for pharmaceutical markets become increasingly available, especially in the United States, marketing modelers focused on developing increasingly sophisticated econometric assessments of detailing-sales response functions that can assist in more refined detailing allocation and targeting decisions. Notable papers in this vein within the last decade include those by Manchanda and Chintagunta (2004), Manchanda, Rossi, and Chintagunta (2004), Dong, Manchanda, and Chintagunta (2009), and Montoya, Netzer, and Jedidi (2010). Unfortunately, however, such fine data are not available in many industries or, for that matter, pharmaceutical markets outside of the United States. In such situations, Albers (2012) reminds us that simpler but robust response models that are also optimizable and usable in decision-making are still useful and needed.

16.3 Models for sales territory alignment

Every firm with a geographically specialized sales force faces the challenge of aligning sales territories that enhance efficiency and effectiveness in salespeople's coverage of their markets, as well as promise fair rewards and boost the morale of salespeople. Like sales resource allocation models, issues of sales territory alignment also have a long history. An early modern text on the subject was that of Aspley (1930). However, the first article in a major marketing research journal (see Table 16.1, Column 2) is that of Talley (1961). Talley's (1961) "workload model" aggregates smaller geographic or "sales coverage" units (SCUs) to build up sales territories that are balanced (equalized) in terms of workload (sales calls or hours) required to cover the present and potential customers in each territory. Workload required is computed by classifying accounts according to their present dollar sales or potential; setting a call frequency for each type of account; and multiplying and summing the products of these numbers to determine the total calls required in each SCU. In the final step, SCUs are accumulated into territories such that each territory's workload is equal to each (or average) rep's call capacity. Talley's equal workload territories, however, may be quite imbalanced or unequal on other important criteria, e.g., sales potentials, travel costs and time etc., which can affect a salesperson's earning opportunity and motivation. Subsequent sales territory alignment algorithmic models starting with Hess and Samuels (1971) GEOLINE model attempted to address this limitation. Like Talley's (1961) model, GEOLINE aims to create territories that are balanced on some "activity measure" (sales potential, workload etc.) of importance to management. GEOLINE attempts to attach SCUs of known "activity value," to trial territory centers (headquarter locations) so as to maximize across-territory balance (equalization) as well as within-territory *"compactness"* with respect to the selected activity measure. Here, "compactness" is the squared "distance" between the control unit and the territory center. Hess and Samuels determined the optimal solution using linear programming (LP).

As a LP's solution is non-integer, and SCUs can only be assigned in their entirety to one territory or another, GEOLINE had to work with a rounding procedure that leads to differences of activity across territories of up to 15%. Subsequently, Shanker, Turner, and Zoltners (1975) presented integer programming approaches for the alignment task that did not have this limitation. In that same year, Lodish (1975) presented a model with the objective of maximizing anticipated profit generated by the sales force rather than simply creating territories that were equalized on some selected activity measure. The Lodish (1975) procedure also simultaneously considered the interrelated problem of account-specific call frequency determination and attempts to equate the marginal profit contributions across territories. Zoltners (1976) then proposed two more easily implementable integer programming models as alternatives to Lodish's (1975) mathematical programming model and heuristic solution procedure.

Next, Zoltners and Sinha (1983) provided a generalization of the previous models by allowing for any objective function and almost achieving equality for potential or other balancing criteria through the introduction of lower and upper bounds. This model also offered other important enhancements from the viewpoint of implementation, namely, (a) avoiding territories encompassing natural boundaries like mountain ranges and rivers that complicate travel; and (b) ensuring contiguous territories. Two decades later, the work of Zoltners and Sinha (2005) won the *Marketing Science* Practice Prize for its summarization of the insights gathered from over "1500 (territory alignment) project implementations for 500 companies with 500,000 territories", many by the consulting firm, ZS Associates Inc., founded by them in 1983.

After Zoltners and Sinha (1983), no major territory alignment modeling advances appeared in the marketing science literature until Skiera and Albers' (1998) COSTA (contribution optimizing sales territory alignment) model. This model was aimed at reviving the stream of research in the 1970s that had profit maximization as the territory alignment objective. Skiera and Albers (1998) argued that Lodish's (1975) procedure that attempts to make the marginal profit contribution equal at the territory-level was still sub-optimal. Instead, marginal profit contribution values need to be equalized at the SCU-level within territories to maximize total profits. COSTA, therefore, uses SCU-level sales-selling effort response function (where selling effort includes calling time as well as travel time) that permit simultaneous solution of the call planning problem and the assignment of SCUs to territories to maximize overall profit.

The debate about the relative merits of the balancing and profit-maximizing approaches to territory alignment still continues (see, e.g., Albers and Mantrala, 2008). However, in the decade following COSTA, no significant new territory alignment models have been proposed in the marketing science literature. This is not to say that there were no refinements of existing models in practical applications. For example, Zoltners and Sinha (2005, Table 16.3) document over a dozen such refinements in the evolution of the sales territory alignment model, system, and process in their practice at ZS Associates. More recently, however, several new territory alignment problems and models to solve them are emerging — interestingly, led by scientists in fields other than marketing. Notable here is the work of Ríos-Mercado and colleagues (2009, 2013).

16.4 Integrated deployment models (sizing, resource allocation, territory alignment, selection)

The first paper in this stream, Lodish (1975), shown in Table 16.1 (Column 3) provides for integrated allocation and territory alignment solutions. Subsequently, Beswick and Cravens' (1977) multistage decision model provides a framework for improving (rather than optimizing) the allocation of selling effort along with sales force size determination as well as sales territory alignment. Similarly, Glaze and Weinberg (1979) presented a procedure "TAPS" which seeks to maximize sales for a given sales force size while also attempting to achieve equal workload between salespersons and, in addition, minimize total travel time. Although these models provide useful frameworks for considering multiple sales management decisions, they can be hard to implement because of the need to calibrate numerous control unit response functions.

Over a decade later, there were two novel contributions in this research stream in the 1990s. Rangaswamy, Sinha, and Zoltners (1990) focused on integrated sales force allocation, size, and *structure* (rather than territory alignment) decisions, e.g., whether a firm should deploy a single or multiple product line sales forces. To solve these interrelated decision problems, Rangaswamy Sinha, and Zoltners (1990) propose a mathematical programming model which incorporates product sales response functions by market segment *and* sales force structure, allowing for product-line interdependencies. The model is solved via evaluation of all partitions of the firm's product line corresponding to the feasible set of sales force structures and thereby determines optimal values for the number of sales forces, product assignments to sales forces, size of each sales force, and effort allocations for each product-market-structure combination. Toward the end of the decade, Drexl and Haase (1999) inspired by some of the features of Skiera and Albers' (1998) COSTA model, proposed a novel nonlinear mixed-integer programming model to solve the four sub-problems of sales force sizing, location, alignment, and allocation of effort simultaneously utilizing fast approximation methods capable of solving large-scale, real-world problems.

In the next decade, Godes (2003) contributed a notable paper which is one of the few in this domain that takes a theoretical economics, specifically game-theoretic perspective, rather than OR orientation. Godes commences with a model of the *selling process* at a micro-level (similar to Wernerfelt, 1994). This model enables examination of the interaction between selling ability and task complexity and leads to the finding that highly skilled reps should sell better products when the task is very complex and worse products when the task is very simple. With this result in hand, Godes is able to shed light on the optimal type, number, organization, and training of salespeople by firms in selling environments of differing complexity, including the intriguing insight that the firm that has the biggest sales force does not always have the best.

Later in the decade, Skiera and Albers (2007) focused on the important issue of how a firm can prioritize investments to be made in the several productivity-enhancing sales resource deployment decisions including selling effort allocation, sizing, territory alignment and training. To do this, Skiera and Albers (2007) assert that management must assess the outcomes of investments on the basis of a common metric, namely, profit. They then propose, specify, and estimate a "core" sales response function that drives all these decisions and show how it can be used to quantify the profits derived from each possible action in an actual case study.

No further significant contributions to this stream have been made by marketing scientists since 2007. However, the related problems facing firms have not gone away and are being addressed by scholars in other disciplines or in-house by firms. In this vein, the works of Lawrence *et al.* (2010) at IBM that won the INFORMS Franz Edelman Award, Baier *et al.* (2012), and Golalikhani and Karwan (2013) are noteworthy. (We revert to these developments outside the academic marketing field in the concluding section.)

16.5 Sales force compensation and incentives

Historically, the importance of compensation and incentives in "indirect control" of sales forces (see, e.g., Albers and Mantrala, 2008) has been recognized for many centuries. According to Powers *et al.* (1988), commissioned salespeople and paid agents were a common sight in the Roman Empire. By the beginning of the 20th century, a variety of sales force compensation and incentive elements such as salaries, commissions, quotas, bonuses, and contests had become prevalent. Despite periodic questions and concerns about their efficacy and deleterious consequences (e.g., Kohn, 1993; Zoltners, Sinha, and Lorimer, 2012), the use of sales incentives remains popular, e.g., it is estimated that US spending on sales force financial incentives totaled more than US$200 billion in 2006 showing no signs of abatement (Zoltners, Sinha, and Lorimer, 2006). Not surprisingly, therefore, there has been continuing interest in the optimal design of sales force compensation plans over the last half-century. The core question is how to set up a compensation structure that aligns the salesperson's and firm's objectives. Due to paucity of space, we cannot go into the details of the numerous models and studies. Rather, the focus here is on the major mileposts in this domain of research. Readers may see Coughlan (1993), Albers (1996), Coughlan and Joseph (2012) for more comprehensive reviews of works in this field.

For convenience in exposition, this historical view is divided into two broad categories: (1) *Theoretical–Normative Research*; and (2) *Theoretical–Empirical Research*. Further, we classify this research according to the compensation element that is the main focus of inquiry, i.e., (i) commissions and/or salary compensation; (ii) sales quota-bonuses & menus of quota-based contracts; (ii) multiperson incentive mechanisms, i.e., sales contests and team incentives. (Tables 16.2 and 16.3 outline the chronologies of major developments in these streams.)

16.5.1 *Theoretical–normative research*

16.5.1.1 *Commissions and/or salary compensation*

Considering the multiple product sales forces that were prevalent across the industrial landscape, the seminal paper by Farley (1964) addressed two key questions: First, when the firm's goal is to maximize profits, what should be the *basis*, e.g., product sales or gross margins for commission payments and, second, how should the multiple products commission rates be set relative to each other? Through a simple and elegant analysis of the firm's and rep's first-order conditions for profit and maximization respectively, Farley established that the optimal policy was to set commission rates tied to gross margins that were equal across the set of products in the rep's selling portfolio. The result was not only counterintuitive (typically, business students think that higher commissions should be set on "harder to sell" products) but also administratively appealing (setting one commission rate rather than juggling with multiple rates). In a later paper, Farley and Weinberg (1975) showed how the commissions could be derived. However, Farley's work made a number of restrictive assumptions such as income-maximizing salespeople with fixed total selling time who operated in a deterministic environment. This stimulated a number of papers investigating whether Farley's result held up when his assumptions were relaxed.[4]

Berger (1972, 1975) was the first to introduce sales response uncertainty in conjunction with salespeople's risk attitude into Farley's problem and showed that Farley's original result did not hold when sales variance was proportional to selling effort and salespeople are risk-averse. Later, Weinberg (1978) reverted to a deterministic setting but considered salespeople maximizing income subject to a minimum return per unit time, and shows that Farley's result still holds in such circumstances. Next, Srinivasan (1981) considered utility maximizing individuals in a deterministic setting who pay attention to both the payoff from and the cost of their selling effort when deciding their investment and allocation of effort across products. Considering such agents, Srinivasan (1981) showed that in the case of the utility maximizing rep, Farley's result does not hold.

---

[4]As our subsequent discussion suggests, Farley (1964) addressed a very restricted sales compensation design problem and his basic result regarding optimality of equal commission rates on gross margins do not hold, once a number of restrictive assumptions are relaxed. However, the Farley (1964) is still termed as "seminal" in this history because it was the first paper in marketing to analytically treat the compensation design problem as an economic 'game' between the firm and the sales representative, an analytical approach and paradigm that triggered a long line of papers that advanced the field while systematically relaxing one or more of Farley's model assumptions.

By the time Srinivasan's (1981) work appeared, the agency-theoretic literature in economics introducing the concepts of moral hazard and adverse selection (e.g., Holmstrom,1979) was rapidly developing and soon shifted the attention of marketing scientists from the more OR orientation of past compensation research (i.e., how to set the parameters of commission plans) to theoretical models aimed at explaining the variety of commission plus salary compensation plans seen in practice (e.g., Joseph and Kalwani, 1998). Unlike Farley (1964), the basic agency-theoretic perspective assumed (a) stochastic sales response functions; (b) expected utility maximizing agents with minimum expected utility requirements; (c) "leader–follower" (Stackelberg) game between a risk-neutral principal who is the leader and risk-averse agent/s, who is the follower.

Using the agency-theoretic approach, Basu *et al.* (1985) derived the optimal form of the compensation plan for a homogeneous, risk-averse sales force and risk-neutral principal and showed that this solution was tantamount to a salary plus nonlinear commission pay plan. Basu (1985) also examined how the different parameters of the problem would impact the fixed (salary) to variable (commission) pay ratio of the plan, providing theoretical support for Smyth's (1968) guidelines for setting salary and/or commission plans in practice. However, many combination compensation plans seen in practice take a simpler linear form. Basu and Kalyanaram (1990) investigated this issue and showed that a linear sales compensation plan is almost as profitable as the optimal nonlinear plan for highly risk-averse salespeople. Moreover, economists Holmstrom and Milgrom (1987) had provided a rationale for linear compensation plans assuming an agent characterized by a constant absolute risk aversion utility function who engages in dynamic effort optimization behavior. Exploiting these results, Lal and Srinivasan (1993) show that the commission income as a fraction of total compensation goes up with an increase in selling effectiveness or base sales, while the salary component goes up with increases in uncertainty, absolute risk aversion, marginal cost of production, perceived cost of effort, and/or alternative job opportunities for the salesperson.

Although the Basu *et al.* (1985) model went much beyond Farley (1964), they too made some restrictive assumptions such as assuming a homogeneous sales force and symmetric information between the firm and the salesperson. In reality, salespeople are heterogeneous with respect to abilities, utility and sales response functions they face in their respective territories, and asymmetric information between agent and principal also exists. In particular, sales managers in central locations are not as well informed about local conditions as are individual salespeople. Compensation plans that involve quotas and menus of contracts can serve to handle these complications.

16.5.1.2 Sales quotas, bonuses, and menus

The first analytical marketing paper (Table 16.2, Column 1) providing a rationale for the use of sales quotas was by Davis and Farley (1971) who address the same problem as Farley (1964) except that they allow (a) quantity-dependent product production cost functions and (b) sales quota-based commission systems. Davis and Farley show that under such circumstances involving product cost interdependencies, Farley's (1964) original result does not hold. They also show that a decentralized system of setting quotas and commissions based on iterative exchanges between the salespeople and the firm would work better in this situation. (Note that the proposed exchanges are effectively a means of reducing the asymmetry in information between the firm and the reps.)

Fifteen years later, Lal and Staelin (1986) formally relaxed the assumptions of homogeneity and symmetric information in the Basu *et al.* (1985) model and showed that in these conditions it can be advantageous for a profit maximizing firm to offer each salesperson the opportunity to self-select a plan from a *menu of quota-based compensation plans* (thereby revealing his/her private information). They noted that although such contractual arrangements are not common, they do exist, e.g., one such mechanism was implemented by IBM (Gonik, 1978). Subsequently, Mantrala and Raman (1990) showed that the Gonik scheme is nothing but a specific form of the "New Soviet Incentive Model" (see. e.g., Weitzman, 1976), useful for inducing truthful sales forecasts from salespeople (by way of a self-selected sales quota or forecast). Mantrala and Raman (1990) derive specific guidelines for setting the parameters of the Gonik-type plan for risk-neutral and risk-averse salespeople and also provide directions for implementation. At the same time, Rao (1990) derived explicit solutions to menu design within the Lal and Staelin (1986) framework, by assuming salespeople are also risk-neutral like the principal. Specifically, Rao (1990) showed that a menu of *linear* quota-based contracts — i.e., a scheme in which payout is linear in the sales relative to the quota — is optimal for sales environments characterized by commonly encountered sales response functions, and a large class of frequency distributions of selling skills in the sales force.

However, menu design and implementation are clearly complicated, especially for multiproduct salespeople. In reality, firms are prone to use uniform bonus plans with individual or customized quotas for their salespeople (i.e., partially uniform plans) that adjust for territories that are imbalanced or unequal in terms of sales potential. Setting up such plans requires firms to gain knowledge of their reps' utility and sales response functions and then solve for the optimal quota-bonus plan accounting for the rep's utility-maximizing actions and his/her minimum expected utility constraint. This problem was addressed and solved for a heterogeneous multiproduct sales force by Mantrala, Sinha, and Zoltners (1994), utilizing estimates of reps' utilty for income (bonus pay) and disutility for the effort required to achieve specified quotas obtained via conjoint measurement. (Darmon, 1979, 1987) had previously suggested conjoint analysis for quota planning but his methodology was not consistent with the agency-theoretic framework nor considered multiproduct bonus plans.)

While Mantrala, Sinha, and Zoltners (1994) focused on optimally structuring a quota-based plan, Raju and Srinivasan (1996) examined whether and when plans of such forms would be optimal or near optimal relative to Basu *et al.*'s (1985) agency-theoretic solution. Based on a numerical simulation analysis, Raju and Srinivasan (1996) concluded that the non-optimality in using quota-based salary plus bonus commission plans is slight while they have the benefit of being easily adapted for new salespeople assignments (by changing the quota without having to change the common salary or commission parameters). A further advantage of a periodic quota-based compensation scheme shown by Mantrala, Raman, and Desiraju (1997) in a dynamic framework is that it enables a manager to learn about a new salesperson's ability or territory potential by observing how his/her sales respond to periodic changes in his/her quota.

After this work, a decade passed before the appearance of the next significant contributions of marketing science to the optimal use and design of sales quota-based schemes. Specifically, Misra and Nair (2011) develop a sophisticated dynamic structural econometric model of agent behavior in response to a quota-based commission scheme utilizing a rich dataset consisting of complete details of sales and compensation plans for a US contact lens manufacturer's sales force. Using the estimated model, Misra and Nair (2011) recommend profit-improving changes to the extant compensation plan that were actually implemented by the firm, achieving predicted changes in agent behavior and output and yielding a 9% improvement in overall revenue. More recently, Jain (2012) highlights another and heretofore overlooked explanation for firms' use of multiperiod sales quota-bonus schemes. Specifically, Jain analytically shows that multiperiod quotas that have the effect of delaying the bonus payment help to reduce the negative consequences of their employees' present-biased preferences, i.e., self-control problems.

16.5.1.3 *Multi-person incentive schemes — sales contests and team incentives*

Sales contests are very popular in practice but their design and use can be fairly arbitrary (e.g., Murphy and Dacin, 1998). A competitive multiperson sales contest is a short-term incentive program where salespeople can win prizes for performing better than, i.e., "beating" other salespeople. Such rank-order contests have been extensively studied under tournament theory in economics (e.g., Lazear and Rosen, 1981; Green and Stokey, 1983). As shown in Table 16.2, Column 3, the normative literature on this issue in marketing is limited with the first notable paper contributed by Kalra and Shi (2001). Assuming the sales outcome is logistically distributed and the contest budget is set high enough, Kalra and Shi find the total number of winners in a closed-ended sales contest should not exceed half the number of contestants. However, under the assumption of uniformly distributed sales, they find a single-prize "Winner-Take-All" contest is best. In contrast, Murthy and Mantrala (2005) take an integrated marketing communications (IMC) perspective and build and analyze a model aimed at finding the optimal allocation of a fixed promotion budget between media advertising and sales contest prizes. Assuming the sales outcome has a Gumbel distribution, Murthy and Mantrala (2005) find the total number of winners in the contest should not exceed approximately 63% of the participants.

Aside from questions of optimal sales contest design, there is also the basic question of when are contests superior to individual piece-rates or quota-based incentive systems in selling contexts? Caldieraro and Coughlan (2009) compare piece-rate compensation to contests and find that tournaments are favored over piece-rate plans when territories are highly positively correlated, territory sales potentials are similar, salespeople are not very risk-averse and have a low disutility for effort. A piece-rate plan conversely dominates a tournament when these conditions are reversed.

All the previous papers assumed salespeople worked in equal potential territories. However, territories are more often than not heterogeneous in sales potentials. This led Syam, Hess, and Yang (2011) to examine whether sales contests or quota systems are superior incentive mechanisms to use in such situations. Syam Hess, and Yang (2011) major result is that territory imbalance in terms of sales potential has a differential effect and affects performance in a contest more adversely than under a quota system. Handicapping the contest to correct for territory potential imbalances overcomes its disadvantage vis-à-vis the quota plan, but this is seldom incorporated into sales contests.

Lastly, sales contests are competitive multi-person compensation schemes. But firms that employ selling teams may be more interested in fostering multi-person coordination rather than competition (e.g., Brown *et al.*, 2005). Surprisingly, however, the marketing science literature on group incentives is sparse despite the prevalence of sales teams. One notable exception is the analysis by Caldieraro and Coughlan (2009) that shows the positive role of a group commission pay incentive in improving performance of salespeople assigned to territories with negatively correlated uncertainties.

16.5.2 *Theoretical-empirical research*

16.5.2.1 *Commissions and salary components*

In this section we confine our attention to the history of focused empirical tests of agency-theoretic (AT) predictions with respect to the sales force compensation elements of salary and commissions. Table 16.3, Column 1 shows the chronology of this research stream. In this chronology, the early empirical studies of the validity of AT's basic prediction that greater variability in sales leads to more salary-weighted plan compensation models, produced equivocal results: *nonsupportive* (John and Weitz, 1989), *supportive* (Lal, Outland, and Staelin, 1994), and *opposite* (Coughlan and Narasimhan, 1992). Similarly, the one test of the AT prediction that higher risk aversion leads to salary-weighted plans found support only among a subset of relatively higher risk-averse agents (Joseph and Kalwani, 1995). These studies were all survey-based. The next study by Ghosh and John (2000) followed an experimental economics approach and its basic result was a "persistent and striking lack of support for the agency model outside of the circumstance in which risk-averse agents undertake *nonverifiable* effort".

In a cross-sectional survey of chief sales executives of German sales organizations, Krafft, Albers, and Lal (2004) also did not find support for the AT prediction that compensation plans should emphasize salary with increasing uncertainty. Subsequently, Misra, Coughlan, and Narasimhan (2005) empirically test the predictions of an extension of the classic AT model that includes firm size and allows for risk-averse principals using two survey datasets from the Dartnell Corporation — one collected in 1996 and the other ten years earlier that had been used by Coughlan and Narasimhan (1992). Misra Coughlan, and Narasimhan (2005) find support for their analytical prediction that firm size is positively associated with the ratio of total to incentive pay and also substantiate the past findings of Coughlan and Narasimhan (1992). In the most recent in this line of research on leverage in the pay plan, Rouziès *et al.* (2009) analyze a unique multicountry European dataset measured at the salesperson level and find a positive relationship between total (take-home) pay and the variable to fixed pay ratio. This is consistent with the AT prediction that if the compensation plan makes the salesperson bear more risk, then his/her total pay should be higher.

The novelty of the next study in this chronology, by Lo, Ghosh, and LaFontaine (2011), is that it is the first to posit and show that firms design their pay plans to both discriminatingly *select* (i.e., attract and retain) salespeople as well as provide them with the right level of incentives. The data for the study were collected via a cross-sectional survey of sales managers of industrial equipment manufacturers wherein the survey questions were specific to a particular salesperson that these sales managers were currently supervising. The theme of endogenizing sales force composition (selection) rather than treating it as fixed when designing optimal compensation contracts is also sounded by the latest study in this stream by Misra, Nair, and Daljord (2012). Using the same dataset as Misra and Nair (2011) to identify primitive agent parameters (cost of effort, risk aversion, productivity), Misra, Nair, and Daljord (2012) shed light on how the ability to choose agents makes up for the loss of incentives when companies use partially uniform rather than customized incentive pay plans as is quite common, e.g., Mantrala, Sinha, and Zoltners, 1994).

16.5.2.2 *Sales quotas, bonuses, and contests*

The chronology of empirical research on this topic in marketing science is shown in Table 16.3, Column 2. Gaba and Kalra (1999) show theoretically and experimentally that the risk behavior of sales representatives is influenced by the payoff structure of quota-systems or contests set for them. Specifically, they predict that when salespeople are set high (low) quotas or compete in rank-order contests with few (many) prizes they will opt to work on high (low)-risk sales prospects. They find strong support for their predictions in a series of economic experiments.

Other interesting questions about how salespeople respond to quota-based compensation are investigated in two later econometric studies. Steenburgh (2008) conducts a study of whether lump-sum bonuses induce salespeople to work harder or play timing games with their order submissions (a concern expressed in earlier economics literature by Jensen, 2003 and Oyer, 1998). Steenburgh utilizes a unique longitudinal dataset consisting of monthly sales and quotas of 2,570 salespeople over a three year period at a large durable goods company. The elements of this sales force's incentive contract include quarterly and annual lump-sum bonuses along with overachievement commission payments. Based on his analysis, Steenburgh concludes that lump-sum bonuses primarily motivate salespeople to work harder rather than play timing games. Chung, Steenburgh, and Sudhir (2013) utilize the same dataset as Steenburgh (2008), and build a dynamic structural model of sales force response to the quota-based compensation plan. Interestingly, they find that annual quotas are not effective in enhancing productivity in the absence of quarterly quotas.

The next two studies in the empirical compensation research chronology (Table 16.3, Column 2) are two experimental economics studies of agent response to sales contests. Lim, Ahearne, and Ham (2009) test two extant theoretical predictions made by Kalra and Shi (2001), specifically: (1) The number of prizewinners in a rank-order contest should be greater than one, and (2) prize values should be unique and rank ordered. The findings from two lab experiments and two field experiments lead Lim, Ahearne, and Ham (2009) to conclude that the number of prizewinners in a sales contest should indeed be greater than one. However, introducing rank-ordered prizes into contests with multiple prizewinners does not boost performance. More recently, Lim (2010) conducted two incentive-aligned lab experiments to investigate the impact of the proportion of contest winners to losers has on agent performance. Lim finds the experimental results support his prediction that a contest with a higher proportion of winners than losers can yield greater effort than one with fewer winners than losers, if the degree of social loss aversion in the contestants is sufficiently strong. This runs counter to the prevailing marketing theory that fewer winners than losers is better for stimulating performance.

Most recently, Kishore et al. (2013) conducted a natural field-based experimental study at a pharmaceutical firm, based on monthly observations spanning three years and 458 sales territories, to investigate the effects of a switch from a quota-bonus plan to an equivalent commission plan. Interestingly, they found that the bonus plan was strictly inferior to the implemented commission plan with respect to short-term revenues and timing games. In contrast, the commission plan induced greater neglect of non-incentivized tasks (tasks not directly affecting observable output).

16.6 Conclusion and directions for future research

This chapter has recounted the history of four major streams of sales force productivity-related research in marketing science. As the chronologies of these streams of research indicate, great progress has been made in developing OR-oriented models for optimal sales resource allocation, sales territory alignment, and regular sales force compensation design. These subjects, especially incentives design, have also been the focus of important theoretical-normative and theoretical-empirical research efforts. However, over the last 25 years, the overall attention given to sales force productivity questions by marketing scientists has not been proportionate to its importance in marketing management, especially in business markets. This is undoubtedly related to the difficulty of accessing adequate quantitative data for conducting the kinds of rigorous empirical analyses expected today by journals such as *Marketing Science*. However, while the pursuit of rigor is commendable, it has come in the way of timeliness in tackling some outstanding sales force questions of great relevance to sales managers (see, e.g., Mantrala *et al.*, 2010). Some problems can benefit from better even if not "perfect" solutions. This was demonstrated decades ago by Lodish (1974) who famously wrote that being "vaguely right was better than being precisely wrong"!

For example, sales forces everywhere are being transformed by more informed and demanding customers and the forces of globalization, creating new challenges in areas like sales force sizing, territory alignment, structuring, specialization, and compensation. Some interesting questions, longstanding as well as emerging, demanding research include: (1) How should sales forces be structured, i.e., the optimal number, sizes, and types of specialized sales forces in the new environment? (2) How should key account management and supporting teams be optimally organized and compensated? (3) Can incentives play a role in integrating marketing and sales force activities more closely? How? (4) How can "Big Data" be harnessed to develop new analytics-driven implementable solutions for improved customer targeting, sales force specialization, and territory alignment? (5) How should salespeople's social networks be leveraged in sales prospecting efforts? (6) Should salespeople's social networks be integrated into territory alignment decisions and how? (7) How should B2B marketers allocate sales resources between face-to-face meetings vs. call centers vs. e-mail exchanges vs. Skype meetings etc., in buyer-driven selling cycles that are taking shape in the Internet Age (e.g., Mantrala and Albers, 2012)?

As we have noted before, solutions to some of the above questions are being pursued today — but in disciplines like system engineering and

OR rather than in marketing. Undoubtedly, those disciplines house experts in many research methods, e.g., mathematical programming, dynamic optimization, data mining and analytics, numerical simulation etc., that are becoming increasingly necessary to apply to sales force problems today in the face of growing marketplace complexity and Big Data availability. However, at the core, most of these issues are about how can a firm effectively and efficiently create, satisfy, serve, keep, and grow its customers. In other words, they are all fundamentally "marketing" problems which presumably are best understood by marketers and marketing scholars. Moreover, the sales force is an important but not the only marketing instrument that firms can employ in designing and executing customer-centric marketing strategies. Other instruments such as price, advertising, and promotions of various kinds all play a critical role in achieving marketing and sales objectives. Increasingly, it is how well the sales force is integrated with the rest of the marketing program that will drive sales force success. Marketing scientists are very knowledgeable about marketing mix effects on targeted customers and segments. Logically, therefore, they are in the best position to lead and advance rigorous and relevant research in the sales force domain and should do so. As the research chronologies detailed in this chapter indicate, there are some heartening signs that the sales force is moving back to center stage in marketing science as it was in the early years of the field and it is hoped that this trend will intensify in the coming years.

References

Albers, S. (1996). Optimization models for sales force compensation, *European Journal of Operational Research*, 89, 1–17.

Albers, S. (2012). Optimizable and implementable aggregate response modeling for marketing decision support, *International Journal of Research in Marketing*, 29(2), 111–122.

Albers, S. and M. K. Mantrala (2008). Models for sales management decisions, in Berend Wierenga, ed., *Handbook of marketing decision models*, Springer: Berlin, pp. 163–210.

Albers, S., M. K. Mantrala, and S. Sridhar (2010). Personal selling elasticities: A meta-analysis," *Journal of Marketing Research*, 47(10) (October), 840–853.

Aspley, J. C. (1930). Managing a sales territory, *Dartnell Corp.*

Baier, M., J. E. Carballo, A. J. Chang, Y. Lu, A. Mojsilovi, M. J. Richard, M. Singh, M. S. Squillante, and K. R. Varshney (2012). Sales force performance analytics and optimisation, *IBM Journal of Research and Development*, 56(6) (November–December), 1–10.

Bartels, R. (1976). *The history of marketing thought*, Grid, Inc., p. 71.

Basu, A. K. and G. Kalyanaram (1990). On the relative performance of linear versus nonlinear compensation plans, *International Journal of Research in Marketing*, 7, 171–178.

Basu, A. K., R. Lal, V. Srinivasan, and R. Staelin (1985). Salesforce compensation plans: An agency theoretic perspective, *Marketing Science*, 4(4), 267–291.

Berger, P. D. (1972). On setting optimal sales commissions, *Operations Research Quarterly*, 23(2), 213–215.

Berger, P. D. (1975). Optimal compensation plans: The effect of uncertainty and attitude toward risk on the salesman effort allocation decision, in E. H. Mazze, ed., *Marketing educator's conference*, American Marketing Association, Chicago, pp. 517–520.

Beswick, C. A. and D. W. Cravens (1977). A multistage decision model for salesforce management, *Journal of Marketing Research*, 14(2), 135–144.

Bronnenberg, B. J., M. W. Kruger, and C. F. Mela (2008). Database paper — The IRI marketing data set, *Marketing Science* 27(4), 745–748.

Brown, L. O. (1937). Quantitative market analysis: Scope and uses, *Harvard Business Review*, 15(2), 233–234.

Brown, A. A., F. T. Hulswit, and J. D. Kettelle (1956). A study of sales operations, *Operations Research*, 4(3) (June), 296–308.

Brown, S. P., K. R. Evans, M. Mantrala, and G. Challagalla (2005). Adapting motivation, control, and compensation research to a new environment, *Journal of Personal Selling & Sales Management*, 25(2), 155–167.

Caldieraro, F. and A. T. Coughlan (2009). Optimal sales force diversification and group incentive payments, *Marketing Science*, 28(6) (November–December), 1009–1026.

Chung, D., T. Steenburgh, and K. Sudhir (2013). Do bonuses enhance sales productivity? A dynamic structural analysis of bonus-based compensation plans, Working Paper, Harvard Business School, pp. 13–66.

Coughlan A. T. (1993). Salesforce compensation: A review of MS/OR advances, Jehoshua Eliashberg and Gary L. Lilien, eds., *Marketing, Handbooks in operations research and management science*, Volume 5, North Holland, Amsterdam, pp. 611–651.

Coughlan A. T. and K. Joseph (2012). Sales force compensation: Research insights and research potential, in Gary L. Lilien and Rajdeep Grewal, eds., *Handbook* on *business-to-business marketing*, Chapter 26, Edward Elgar Publishing, pp. 473–495.

Coughlan, A. T. and C. Narasimhan (1992). An empirical analysis of sales-force compensation plans, *Journal of Business*, 65(1) (January), 93–122.

Darmon, R. Y. (1979). Setting sales quotas with conjoint analysis, *Journal of Marketing Research*, 16(1), 133–140.

Darmon, R. Y. (1987). QUOPLAN: A system for optimizing sales quota-bonus plans, *Journal of the Operational Research Society*, 38(12), 1121–1132.

Davis, O. A. and J. U. Farley (1971). Allocating sales force effort with commissions and quotas. *Management Science* 18(4), Part II, 55–63.

Dong, X., P. Manchanda, and P. K. Chintagunta (2009). Quantifying the benefits of individual-level targeting in the presence of firm strategic behavior, *Journal of Marketing Research*, 46(2), 207–221.

Drexl, A. and K. Haase (1999). Fast approximation methods for sales force deployment, *Management Science*, 45(10), 1307–1323.

Farley, J. U. (1964). An optimal plan for salesmen's compensation, *Journal of Marketing Research*, 1(2), 39–43.

Farley, J. U. and C. B. Weinberg. (1975). Inferential optimization: An algorithm for determining optimal sales commissions in multiproduct sales forces. *Operational Research Quarterly*, 26(2), 413–418.

Fudge, W. K. and L. M. Lodish (1977). Evaluation of the effectiveness of a model based salesman's planning system by field experimentation, *Interfaces*, 8(1), Part 2, 97–106.

Gaba, A. and A. Kalra (1999). Risk behavior in response to quotas and contests, *Marketing Science*, 18(3), 417–434.

Ghosh, M. and G. John (2000). Experimental evidence for agency models of salesforce compensation, *Marketing Science*, 19(4), 348–365.

Glaze, T. A. and C. B. Weinberg (1979). A sales territory alignment model and account planning system (TAPS), in Richard P. Bagozzi, ed., *Sales management: New developments from behavioral and decision model research*, Cambridge, MA: MSI, pp. 325–342.

Godes, D. (2003). In the eye of the beholder: An analysis of the relative value of a top sales rep across firms and products, *Marketing Science*, 22(2), 161–187.

Golalikhani, M. and M. H. Karwan (2013). A hierarchical procedure for multi-skilled sales force spatial planning, *Computers & Operations Research*, 40(5), 1467–1480.

Gonik, J. (1978). Tie salesmens' bonuses to their forecasts, *Harvard Business Review*, 56(3), 116–123.

Green, J. R. and N. L. Stokey (1983). A comparison of tournaments and contracts, *Journal of Political Economy*, 91(3), 349–364.

Hess, S. W. and S. A. Samuels (1971). Experiences with a sales districting model: Criteria and implementation, *Management Science*, 18(4), Part II, 41–54.

Hölmstrom, B. (1979). Moral hazard and observability, *The Bell Journal of Economics*, 10(1) (Spring), 74–91.

Holmstrom, B. and P. Milgrom (1987). Aggregation and linearity in the provision of intertemporal incentives, *Econometrica*, 55(2), 303–328.

Horsky, D. and P. Nelson (1996). Evaluation of salesforce size and productivity through efficient frontier benchmarking, *Marketing Science*, 15(4), 301–320.

Hoyt, C. W. (1918). *Scientific sales management: A practical application of the principles of scientific management to selling*. GB Woolson & Co.

Jain, S. (2012). Self-control and incentives: An analysis of multiperiod quota plans, *Marketing Science*, 31(5), 855–869.

Jensen, M. C. (2003). Paying people to lie: The truth about the budgeting process, *European Financial Management*, IX, 379–406.

John, G. and B. Weitz (1989). Salesforce compensation: an empirical investigation of factors related to use of salary versus incentive compensation, *Journal of Marketing Research*, 26(1), 1–14.

Jones, E., S. P. Brown, A. A. Zoltners, and B. A. Weitz (2005). The changing environment of selling and sales management, *Journal of Personal Selling & Sales Management*, 25(2), 105–111.

Joseph, K. and M. U. Kalwani (1995). The impact of environmental uncertainty on the design of salesforce compensation plans, *Marketing Letters*, 6(3), 183–197.

Joseph, K. and M. U. Kalwani (1998). The role of bonus pay in salesforce compensation plans, *Industrial Marketing Management*, 27(2) (March), 147–159.

Kalra, A. and M. Shi (2001). Designing optimal sales contests: A theoretical perspective, *Marketing Science*, 20, 170–193.

Kishore, S., R. S. Rao, O. Narasimhan, and G. John (2013). Bonuses versus commissions: A field study, *Journal of Marketing Research*, 1(June), 317–333.

Krafft, M., S. Albers, and R. Lal (2004). Relative explanatory power of agency theory and transaction cost analysis in German salesforces, *International Journal of Research in Marketing*, 21(3), 265–283.

Kohn, A. (1993). Why incentive plans cannot work, *Harvard Business Review*, 71(5), 54–63.

Lal, R. and V. Srinivasan (1993). Compensation plans for single- and multi-product salesforces: An application of the Holmstrom-Milgrom model, *Management Science*, 39, 777–793.

Lal, R., D. Outland, and R. Staelin (1994). Salesforce compensation plans: An individual-level analysis, *Marketing Letters*, 5, 117–130.

Lal, R. and R. Staelin (1986). Salesforce compensation plans in environments with asymmetric information, *Marketing Science*, 5, 179–198.

Lawrence, R., C. Perlich, S. Rosset, I. Khabibrakhmanov, S. Mahatma, S. Weiss, M. Callahan, M. Collins, A. Ershov, and S. Kumar (2010). Operations research improves sales force productivity at IBM, *Interfaces*, 40(1) (January–February), 33–46.

Lazear, E. P. and S. Rosen (1981). Rank-order tournaments as optimum labor contracts, *Journal of Political Economy*, 89, 841–864.

Ledingham, D., M. Kovac, and H. L. Simon (2006). The new science of sales force productivity, *Harvard Business Review*, 9, 124–133.

Leeflang, P. S. H., G. M. Mijatovic, and J. Saunders (1992). Identification and estimation of complex multivariate lag structures: A nesting approach. *Applied Economics*, 24(2), 273–283.

Lim, N. (2010). Social loss aversion and optimal contest design, *Journal of Marketing Research*, 47(4), 777–787.

Lim, N., M. J. Ahearne, and S. H. Ham (2009). Designing sales contests: Does the prize structure matter? *Journal of Marketing Research*, 46(June), 356–371.

Little, J. D. C. (1970). Models and managers: The concept of a decision calculus, *Management Science*, 16, B466–B485.

Lo, D. (Ho-Fu), M. Ghosh, and F. Lafontaine (2011). The incentive and selection roles of sales force compensation contracts, *Journal of Marketing Research*, 48(4), 781–798.

Lodish, L. M. (1971). CALLPLAN: An interactive salesman's call planning system, *Management Science*, 18(4), Part II, P25–P40.

Lodish, L. M. (1974). Vaguely right approach to salesforce allocations, *Harvard Business Review*, 52(January–February), 119–125.

Lodish, L. M. (1975). Sales territory alignment to maximize profit, *Journal of Marketing Research*, 12, 30–36.

Lodish, L. M. (1980). A user oriented model for sales force size, product and market allocation decisions, *Journal of Marketing*, 44(Summer), 70–78.

Lodish, L. M. (2001). Building marketing models that make money, *Interfaces*, 31(3), 45–55.

Lodish, L. M., E. Curtis, M. Ness, M. K. Simpson (1988). Sales force sizing and deployment using a decision calculus model at Syntex laboratories, *Interfaces*, 18(1), 5–20.

Manchanda, P. and P. K. Chintagunta (2004). Responsiveness of physician prescription behavior to salesforce effort: An individual level analysis, *Marketing Letters*, 15(2–3), 129–145.

Manchanda, P., P. E. Rossi, and P. K. Chintagunta (2004). Response modeling with nonrandom marketing-mix variables, *Journal of Marketing Research*, 61(November), 467–478.

Manchanda, P. and E. Honka (2005). The effects and role of direct-to-physician marketing in the pharmaceutical industry: An integrative review, *Yale Journal of Health Policy, Law and Economics*, 5, 785–822.

Mantrala, M. K. and S. Albers (2012). Impact of the internet on B2B sales force size and structure, in G. Lilien and R. Grewal, eds., *Handbook of business-to-business marketing*, ISBM, Pennsylvania State University, Edward Elgar Publishing, Inc: Northampton, MA.

Mantrala, M. K., S. Albers, K. Joseph, M. Krafft, C. Narasimhan, F. Caldieraro, O. Jensen, S. Gopalakrishna, R. Lal, A. Zoltners, and L. Lodish (2010). Sales force modeling: State of the field and research agenda, *Marketing Letters*, 21(3) (March), 255–272.

Mantrala, M. K., P. A. Naik, S. Sridhar, and E. Thorson (2007). Uphill or downhill? Locating your firm on a profit function, *Journal of Marketing*, (April), 26–44.

Mantrala, M. K. and K. Raman (1990). Analysis of a sales force incentive plan for accurate sales forecasting and performance, *International Journal of Research in Marketing*, 7, 189–202.

Mantrala, M. K., K. Raman, and R. Desiraju (1997). Sales quota plans: Mechanisms for adaptive learning, *Marketing Letters*, 8, 393–405.

Mantrala, M. K., P. Sinha, and A. A. Zoltners (1992). Impact of resource allocation rules on marketing investment-level decisions and profitability, *Journal of Marketing Research*, 29, 162–175.

Mantrala, M. K., P. Sinha, and A. A. Zoltners (1994). Structuring a multiproduct sales quota-bonus plan for a heterogeneous sales force: A practical model-based approach, *Marketing Science*, 13, 121–144.

Mela, C. F., J. Roos, and Y. Deng (2013). A keyword history of *Marketing Science*, *Marketing Science*, 32(1) (January–February), 8–18.

Misra, S., A. T. Coughlan, and C. Narasimhan (2005). Salesforce compensation: An analytical and empirical examination of the agency theoretic approach, *Quantitative Marketing and Economics*, 3, 5–39.

Misra, S. and H. Nair (2011). A structural model of sales-force compensation dynamics: estimation and field implementation, *Quantitative Marketing and Economics*, 9(3) (September), 211–257.

Misra, S., H. Nair, and O. Daljord (2012). Homogenous contracts for heterogeneous agents: aligning salesforce composition and compensation, Working Paper, GSB Stanford University.

Montgomery, D. B. (2001). Management science in marketing: prehistory, origin, and early years of the INFORMS marketing college, *Marketing Science*, 20(4) (Autumn), 337–348.

Montgomery, D. B., A. J. Silk, and C. E. Zaragoza (1971). A multiple-product sales force allocation model, *Management Science*, 18, P3–P24.

Montgomery, D. B. and F. E. Webster, Jr. (1968). Application of operations research to personal selling strategy, *Journal of Marketing*, 32(1) (January), 50–55.

Montoya, R., O. Netzer, and K. Jedidi (2010). Dynamic allocation of pharmaceutical detailing and sampling for long-term profitability, *Marketing Science*, 29(5), 909–924.

Murphy, W. H. and P. A. Dacin (1998). Sales contests: A research agenda, *Journal of Personal Selling & Sales Management*, 18(Winter), 1–16.

Murthy, P. and M. K. Mantrala (2005). Allocating a promotion budget between advertising and sales contest prizes: An integrated marketing communications perspective, *Marketing Letters*, 16(1), 19–35.

Nordin, J. A. (1943). Spatial allocation of selling expense, *Journal of Marketing*, 7(3) (January), 210–219.

Oyer, P. (1998). Fiscal year ends and nonlinear incentive contracts: The effect on business seasonality. *The Quarterly Journal of Economics*, 113(1), 149–185.

Parsons, L. J. and P. V. Abeele (1981). Analysis of sales call effectiveness, *Journal of Marketing Research*, 18, 107–113.

Powers, T. L., W. S. Martin, H. Rushing, and S. Daniels (1987). Selling before 1900: A historical perspective, *The Journal of Personal Selling and Sales Management*, 7(3) (November), 1–7.

Powers T. L., W. F. Koehler, and W. S. Martin (1988). Selling from 1900 to 1949: A historical perspective, *The Journal of Personal Selling and Sales Management*, 8(3) (November), 11–21.

Raju, J. S. and V. Srinivasan (1996). Quota-based compensation plans for multiterritory heterogeneous salesforces, *Management Science*, 42, 1454–1462.

Rangaswamy, A., P. Sinha, and A. A. Zoltners (1990). An integrated model-based approach for sales force structuring, *Marketing Science*, 9, 279–298.

Rao, A. G., and M. R. Rao (1983). Optimal budget allocation when response is S-shaped. *Operations Research Letters*, 2(5), 225–230.

Rao, R. C. (1990). Compensating heterogeneous salesforces: Some explicit solutions, *Marketing Science*, 10, 319–341.

Ríos-Mercado, R. Z. and E. Fernández (2009). A reactive GRASP for a commercial territory design problem with multiple balancing requirements. *Computers & Operations Research*, 36(3), 755–776.

Ríos-Mercado, R. Z. and J. F. López-Pérez (2013). Commercial territory design planning with realignment and disjoint assignment requirements, *Omega*, 41(3), 525–535.

Rouziès, D., A. T. Coughlan, E. Anderson, and D. Iacobucci (2009). Determinants of pay levels and structures in sales organizations, *Journal of Marketing*, 73(6), 92–104.

Semlow, W. (1959). How many salesmen do you need? *Harvard Business Review*, 38(May–June), 126–132.

Shanker, R. J., R. E. Turner, and A. A. Zoltners (1975). Sales territory design: An integrated approach, *Management Science*, 22, 309–320.

Sheth, J. N. and A. Sharma (2008). The impact of the product to service shift in industrial markets and the evolution of the sales organization, *Industrial Marketing Management*, 37(3), 260–269.

Sinha, P. and A. A. Zoltners (2001). Sales-force decision models: Insights from 25 years of implementation, *Interfaces*, 31(3), Part 2 of 2, S8–S44.

Skiera, B. and S. Albers (1998). COSTA: Contribution optimizing sales territory alignment, *Marketing Science*, 18, 196–213.

Skiera, B. and S. Albers (2007). Prioritizing sales force decision areas for productivity improvements using a core sales response function, *Journal of Personal Selling and Sales Management, Special Issue on Enhancing Sales Force Productivity*, 28(2), 145–154.

Smyth, R. C. (1968). Financial incentives for salesmen, 46(January–February), 109–117.

Srinivasan, V. (1981). An investigation of the equal commission rate policy for a multi-product salesforce, *Management Science*, 27, 731–756.

Steenburgh, T. J. (2008). Effort or timing: The effect of lump-sum bonuses, *Quantitative Marketing and Economics*, 6(3), 235–256.

Steckel, J. H. and E. Brody (2001). 2001: A marketing odyssey, *Marketing Science*, 20(4) (Fall), 331–336.

Syam, N. B., J. D. Hess, and Y. Y. Yang, (2011). Sales contests versus quotas with imbalanced territories, *Marketing Letters*, 1–16.

Talley, W. (1961). How to design sales territories, *Journal of Marketing*, 25(3), 7–13.

Vandenbosch, M. B. and C. B. Weinberg (1993). Salesforce operations, in J. Eliashberg and G. L. Lilien, eds., *Marketing, handbooks in operations research and management science 5*, North Holland, Amsterdam, pp. 653–694.

Waid, C., D. F. Clark, and R. L. Ackoff (1956). Allocation of sales effort in the lamp division of the general electric company, *Operations Research*, 4(6), 629–647.

Weinberg, C. B. (1978). Jointly optimal sales commissions for nonincome maximizing sales forces, *Management Science*, 24, 1252–1258.

Weitzman, M. L. (1976). The new soviet incentive model, *The Bell Journal of Economics*, 60(4), 251–257.

Wellman, H. R. (1939). The distribution of selling effort among geographic areas, *Journal of Marketing*, 3(3) (January), 225–239.

Wernerfelt, B. (1994). On the function of sales assistance, *Marketing Science*, 13(1), 68–82.

Williams, B. C. and C. R. Plouffe (2007). Assessing the evolution of sales knowledge: a 20-year content analysis, *Industrial Marketing Management*, 36(4), 408–419.

Zoltners, A. A. (1976). Integer programming models for sales territory alignment to maximize profit, *Journal of Marketing Research*, 13, 426–430.

Zoltners, A. A. and P. Sinha (1980). Integer programming models for sales resource allocation, *Management Science*, 26, 242–260.

Zoltners, A. A. and P. Sinha (1983). Sales territory alignment: A review and model, *Management Science*, 29, 1237–1256.

Zoltners, A. A. and P. Sinha (2005). Sales territory design: Thirty years of modeling and implementation, *Marketing Science*, 24, 313–331.

Zoltners, A. A., P. Sinha, and S. E. Lorimer (2006). Match your sales force structure to your business cycle, *Harvard Business Review*, 84(July–August), 81–89.

Zoltners, A. A., P. Sinha, and S. E. Lorimer (2012). Breaking the sales force incentive addiction: A balanced approach to sales force effectiveness, *Journal of Personal Selling and Sales Management*, 32(2), 171–186.

Chapter 17

Sales Promotions

Kusum L. Ailawadi and Sunil Gupta

17.1 Introduction

Sales promotions are marketing events designed to create short-term excitement in the marketplace and have a direct and immediate impact on consumers' purchase behavior. Examples include temporary price discounts, buy-one-get-one free offers, in-store displays, free samples, coupons, mail-in rebates, contests and sweepstakes. Promotions are broadly classified into three types. Manufacturers offer *trade promotions* to retailers in forms ranging from temporary off-invoice discounts and bill-backs to cooperative advertising allowances and lump-sum payments if the retailers achieve a sales target. These retailers in turn can offer *retail promotions*, such as price discounts and weekly features, to consumers. Finally, manufacturers can also offer *consumer promotions* such as coupons and mail-in rebates directly to consumers.

Why is it rational for manufacturers and retailers to offer promotions? Blattberg and Neslin (1990) offer a concise categorization of the economic explanations that have been proposed in the literature. One set of arguments is based on differential costs of search and information processing, inventory-carrying, and time, across consumers. Varian (1980) showed that if consumers have different search costs and ability to process information, it would lead to a two-price equilibrium, which can be implemented through promotions. Blattberg, Eppen, and Lieberman (1981) showed that promotions allow a retailer to shift the cost of carrying inventory to those consumers who have lower inventory holding costs and will therefore forward buy. Narasimhan (1984) showed how coupons exploit differences in the opportunity cost of consumers' time. Another set of arguments relates to *brand loyalty*. Narasimhan (1988) showed that, given the existence of brand loyal and brand switching consumers, in equilibrium, manufacturers who are competing for the brand switchers will promote. Rao (1991) showed that, as long as there is a sizeable segment of switchers, a national brand manufacturer will promote to compete with a private label. Raju, Srinivasan, and Lal (1990) also linked the promotional strategy of competing firms to their brand loyalties. A third argument relates to *competitive equilibria*. Lal (1990) argued that promotions are a pure strategy equilibrium in which national brand manufacturers collaborate to combat private labels, though subsequent work made the case that competitive promotions are a mixed equilibrium (Rao, Arjunji, and Murthi, 1995). A common theme underlying all the above arguments is the notion that promotions can be used as a price discrimination tool because there are consumer segments in the market that differ in their costs and/or preferences. Another, very different, rationale for promotions relates to *demand uncertainty*. Lazear (1986) showed that it is optimal for a firm to first charge a high price and subsequently promote in situations with high demand uncertainty.

Given all these reasons for companies to offer promotions, it is no surprise that they have not only persisted but grown as a percentage of the total marketing budgets of consumer goods companies. In 2012, US spending on sales promotions is estimated to be US$68 billion, compared to US$62 billion on TV advertising (Zenith OptiMedia, 2012). Nor is it any surprise that promotions research dominated marketing science for several decades. What may be surprising to some is the fact that, as early as the 1960s, researchers introduced many of the key substantive issues associated with promotions that have been studied well into subsequent decades.

Massy and Frank (1967) discussed how and why response to promotions varies across consumers, brands, and stores; the immediate versus longer term impact of deals; and the importance of competitive reaction in the longer term effects of promotions. Schwartz (1966) discussed how coupon redemption rates vary across media and over time and the advertising versus monetary value of coupons. Of course, the early discussions of these topics exposed just the tip of the iceberg and empirical analysis was often restricted to simple regressions using small datasets.

Subsequent analyses dug into these issues in-depth, with the benefit of more sophisticated methods as well as larger scanner datasets spanning multiple categories. Indeed, the availability of scanner data starting in the eighties, jump-started empirical research on promotions that has lasted into the current decade.

Figure 17.1 lists four themes that, in our view, summarize marketing science research in the promotions area, and documents how each of them has evolved over the decades. We use this figure as a guiding framework for this chapter, devoting a section to each theme. The first two themes deal with market response to promotions, but separate immediate response from longer term effects. A very significant and important body of promotions research deals with the decomposition of the promotional bump and sits at the intersection between immediate and longer term effects. For convenience, we discuss this topic under long-term response. The third theme relates to trade promotions and how retailers respond to them. The fourth is about how manufacturers and retailers can evaluate, optimize, and profitably target promotions.

17.2   Immediate market response

In this section, we discuss research on the type of consumer who uses promotions, the magnitude of the immediate promotional lift, and the immediate impact of a promotion on other brands, stores, and categories.

17.2.1   *Deal proneness*

Webster (1965) was among the first to try characterize deal prone consumers using 45 different demographic and shopping behavior variables from a diary panel. Other researchers like Montgomery (1971), Teel, Williams and Bearden (1980) performed similar exploratory analyses. Blattberg *et al.* (1978) took an important step forward by proposing a theoretical basis for study of deal proneness. They modeled a household's inventory decision based on storage, stock-out and other costs, and used it to predict how characteristics like home and car ownership, income, and family size should be associated with deal proneness.

Work on deal and coupon prone consumers continued through the eighties and nineties, becoming more theoretically driven and distinguishing

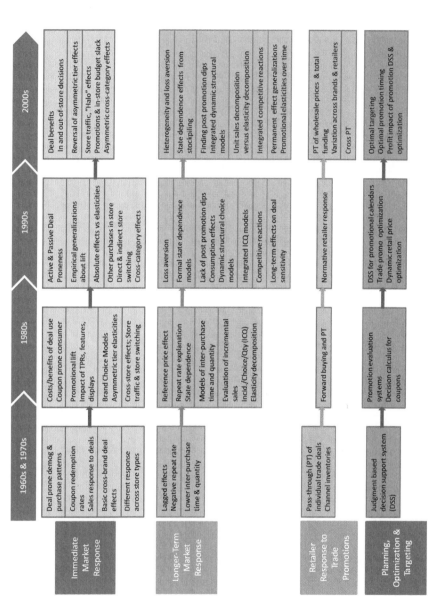

Fig. 17.1 Genealogy of sales promotion research

between different types of deals. Shimp and Kavas (1984) identified some of the costs and benefits to a household of using coupons, including the cost of having to switch to a less preferred brand and the benefit of feeling like a "smart shopper". Bawa and Shoemaker (1987) developed a consumer utility model incorporating fixed and variable costs as well as benefits of coupon usage and derived household characteristics that should be related to coupon usage across multiple categories. Schneider and Currim (1991) distinguished between active and passive deal proneness, where the former refers to coupons and features which require significant effort, and the latter to in-store displays.

In 2000, Chandon, Wansink, and Laurent expanded the cost-benefit framework, proposing that promotions differ in the utilitarian and hedonic benefits they provide and showing that consumers respond more positively to promotions when there is a benefit congruency between the type of promotion and the promoted product. Ailawadi, Neslin, and Gedenk (2001) brought together the costs and benefits of promotions with the distinction between active "out of store" and passive "in-store" promotions, in their investigation of consumers who seek value in store brands versus different types of promotions. Gauri, Sudhir, and Talukdar (2008) also used a cost-benefit framework to distinguish between deal seekers who search spatially (across stores) versus temporally (over time). A series of recent papers on unplanned purchases (Inman, Winer, and Ferraro, 2009; Bell, Corsten, and Knox, 2011) in the store also study how such purchases are related to in-store versus out-of-store promotions and consumer characteristics.

17.2.2 *Promotional lift*

The next logical question after who buys on deal is what the effect of deals is on sales. Most of the work on sales response to promotions has studied either coupons or retail promotions like TPRs, features, and displays. Coupons can lift sales through an advertising exposure effect or through redemption. The earliest work on coupons focused on redemption rates. Schwartz (1966) documented differences in redemption rates across coupons distributed by direct mail, newspapers, and magazines. He also emphasized the importance of redemption timing and the advertising value of coupons. Ward and Davis (1978) built on this by explaining variation in redemption rate as a function of distribution medium, availability of the couponed product in the store, competitive activity, and time since distribution. Other researchers also showed that discount value and market share of the couponed brand increases redemption rates (Reibstein and Traver, 1982; Neslin and Clarke, 1987). Other research evaluated incremental sales and profit from coupons which we discuss under longer term market response. During the 1990s, a few papers examined the advertising exposure effect (Leclerc and Little 1997; Srinivasan, Leone, and Mulhern, 1995) and sales impact of different types of coupons (Raju, Dhar, and Morrison, 1994) but the popularity of coupons, and therefore research on them, ebbed.

That the immediate promotional sales bump is large, significant, and varies across brands and stores was shown in early work by Massy and Frank (1967), Chevalier (1975), and Moriarty (1985) among others and was reinforced in subsequent analyses through the eighties and nineties, both through disaggregate models of brand choice and aggregate store sales models. With the advent of scanner data, Guadagni and Little's (1983) brand choice model was the seminal paper in disaggregate analysis, while Wittink *et al.*'s (1988) Scan*Pro model and Abraham and Lodish's (1993) PromotionScan model were the seminal papers in aggregate store level analysis. By the mid-1990s, the large magnitude of the immediate promotional bump was an empirical generalization (Blattberg, Briesch, and Fox, 1995); it was known to be high as 500% in some product categories; and Narasimhan, Neslin, and Sen (1996) analyzed how promotional elasticities vary across product categories.

In the late 1980s and 1990s, researchers also examined how price cuts, features and displays affect promotional response by themselves and in combination. In aggregate analyses, both features and displays showed a positive effect on sales over and above the effect of a pure price cut (Wittink *et al.*, 1988; Narasimhan, Neslin, and Sen, 1996). However, when price cuts were interacted with features or displays in disaggregate brand choice models, Gupta (1988) and Papatla and Krishnamurthi (1996) found negative interactions. Zhang (2006) reconciled previous findings by integrating two mechanisms by which features and displays can work — as a proxy for a price cut (Inman, McAlister, and Hoyer, 1990) or as a way to bring the brand into the consumer's consideration set (Fader and McAlister, 1990). Another stream of research examined how limit and multiple unit promotions affect sales through their impact on purchase incidence, brand choice, and purchase quantity (Inman, Peter, and Raghubir, 1997; Wansink, Kent, and Hoch, 1998; Foubert and Gijsbrechts, 2007).

17.2.3 *Cross-brand effects*

If promotions had only immediate effects, then the promotional lift for a given brand in a given store would have to come from other brands, other stores, or higher consumption. Frank and Massy (1971) allowed for cross-brand price and deal effects in estimating brand sales models but imposed equality constraints on the cross effects for model parsimony. A decade later, the logit brand choice models estimated by Guadagni and Little (1983) and McAlister (1986) imposed the implicit assumption of proportional share draw.

However, other researchers (Batsell and Polking, 1985) found that cross effects did not follow simple patterns. Blattberg and Wisnewski (1989) documented a specific type of asymmetry, whereby higher (price and quality) tier brands, when promoted, draw from their own tier competitors and from lower tiers but when lower tier brands offer a promotion price cut, they do not draw from higher tier brands. This asymmetry was noted enough times to be labeled an empirical generalization by Blattberg, Briesch, and Fox (1995). However, Sethuraman, Srinivasan, and Kim's (1999) meta-analysis showed that asymmetric price effects favoring higher tier brands are exhibited in elasticities but not in absolute magnitudes. Sethuraman and Srinivasan (2002) went on to document a reversal of the asymmetric tier effect when absolute magnitude effects are considered instead of elasticities. We refer the interested reader to the chapter by Shugan in this book for more details on cross brand effects and market structure.

17.2.4 *Store effects*

From a retailer's perspective, the store traffic, store switching, and cross-category effects of promotions are important. Chevalier and Curhan (1976) noted the potential negative impact of a promotion in one category on sales of another category in the store. Walters and Mackenzie (1988) studied the impact of loss leader promotions on store traffic and store profit and found little evidence of a positive effect, especially on store traffic. Kumar and

Leone (1988), in one of the first papers on the topic, examined how brand sales in one store were affected by promotions in the same category in competing stores. They found evidence for switching, but only between stores that were in close proximity. Walters (1991) also found support for some cross-store effects. In addition, he found some evidence that a promotion in one category increased sales in a complementary category. Bucklin and Lattin (1991) distinguished between direct and indirect store-switching and found support only for the latter. Indirect switching occurs because consumers regularly shop at more than one store. So a promotion in a store they happen to be visiting can spur them to buy the product there instead of in the store where they usually buy it.

Given these mixed findings and the importance of determining how promotions affect retailers, research on this issue has continued into the last decade, albeit sporadically. Lam *et al.* (2001) built a comprehensive model of the impact of different types of promotions on consumers' store entry, purchase incidence, and spending decisions, and estimated it with data from two non-CPG stores. Gijsbrechts, Campo, and Goossens (2003) examine the effect of weekly store flyer characteristics on store traffic and sales. Ailawadi *et al.* (2006) estimated the "halo effect" of promotions in a store — the extent to which a promotion on one item affects sales of other categories in the store. Stilley, Inman, and Wakefield (2010) combine survey data on planned items on the consumers' shopping list and their mental budgets, with grocery receipt information to provide a more in-depth look at the effect of promotions and "budget slack" on planned and unplanned purchases in the store.

Since the late 1990s, researchers have delved in-depth into cross-category effects. Erdem (1998) modeled brand spillover effects across categories. Manchanda, Ansari, and Gupta (1999) built a multivariate probit model to disentangle complementarity from co-incidence in cross-category effects. Russell and Peterson (2000) also confirmed cross-category effects by building a multivariate logistic model for basket selection. Duvvuri, Ansari, and Gupta (2007) examined patterns of correlation in consumers' price sensitivity across pairs of complementary products and showed how these patterns can be used to design promotions for complementary products. Niraj, Pabmanabhan, and Seetharaman (2008) found that cross-category promotion spillover effects are asymmetric.

17.3 Longer-term market response to promotions

Starting with the distributed lag models of Massy and Frank (1967), researchers recognized and modeled the fact that the effect of promotion on sales is not only immediate, but continues into subsequent weeks. In this section, we discuss the progression of research on these effects which led to models for decomposing the immediate promotional lift and determining incremental sales. We also discuss long-term and permanent promotion effects, which include changes in consumer deal sensitivity, competitive reaction, and other feedback effects.

17.3.1 *Reference price effect*

Reference prices are an important phenomenon underlying the potential negative effect of promotions on repeat rates and longer term deal sensitivity. Simply put, consumers form expectations of the price of a product and evaluate the actual price in relation to this reference point. Their choice is influenced by the discrepancy between the actual and reference price. Winer (1986) developed the basic reference price model. Lattin and Bucklin (1989) showed that the reference effect exists for both regular price and promotions. Exposure to frequent price promotions lowers the reference price and therefore, subsequent choice at the higher regular price. Mayhew and Winer (1992) and others, distinguished between losses and gains in the reference price effect and showed that, consistent with prospect theory (Kahneman and Tversky, 1979), losses loom larger than gains. While Bell and Lattin (2000) and other researchers subsequently (see Chapter 15) showed that controlling for consumer heterogeneity reduces the loss aversion effect, the impact of promotions on reference prices and therefore, on longer term consumer response has remained an important area of work.

17.3.2 *Repeat rates and state dependence*

Buying on promotion can affect the consumer's repeat rate for the brand bought on promotion. Self perception theory (Dodson, Tybout, and Sternthal, 1978) and reference prices (Winer, 1986) suggest a negative effect on repeat rates while behavioral learning theory suggests a positive effect. Shoemaker and Shoaf (1977) documented a negative repeat rate effect by separating promotional from non-promotional purchases and comparing repeat rates for the two types. Neslin and Shoemaker (1989) provided an alternative explanation for this result based on cross-sectional heterogeneity and argued that there may be no repeat rate effect. Davis, Inman, and McAlister (1992) provided similar evidence.

Starting with the brand choice model of Guadagni and Little (1983), researchers started modeling state dependence (also referred to as purchase event feedback by some researchers). The simplest way to do so was to include a lagged purchase term in the brand choice model, and this variable was consistently found to be positive. Guadagni and Little found that state dependence was less positive when the previous purchase was on promotion, versus a regular purchase. Subsequently, other researchers modeled the effect of promotion on state dependence in different ways (Papatla and Krishnamurthi, 1996; Gedenk and Neslin, 1999). Seetharaman (2004) distinguished between four sources of state dependence and found "structural state dependence", i.e., the effect of previous brand choice, to be the most important. Ailawadi et al. (2007) showed that promotion-induced purchase acceleration results in positive state dependence because, the household consumes more of the brand over a continuous period of time.

It was recognized early on that state dependence could be confounded with cross-sectional differences in brand preferences (Kuehn, 1962). During the 1990s, researchers used better methods to control for preference heterogeneity, from latent class models (Kamakura and Russell, 1989) to random effects (Chintagunta, Jain, and Vilcassim, 1991) to Bayesian methods (Rossi, McCulloch, and Allenby 1996), but continued to find positive, albeit smaller, state dependence effects (Allenby and Rossi, 1991; Keane 1997; Seetharaman, Ainslie, and Chintagunta, 1999).

17.3.3 *Purchase acceleration, stockpiling, and consumption*

Shoemaker (1979) and Blattberg, Eppen, and Lieberman (1981) provided early evidence that promotional purchases are quicker (less time since the last purchase) and bigger (higher quantity). Neslin, Henderson, and Quelch (1985) formalized this purchase acceleration in a model of purchase quantity and inter-purchase time, finding that coupons increase purchase quantity but do not affect inter-purchase time, while featured price cuts accelerate both timing and quantity. Some researchers used hazard models to specify inter-purchase time (Jain and Vilcassim, 1991; Seetharaman and Chintagunta, 2003), but models of category purchase incidence (rather than inter-purchase time), often integrated with the brand choice and purchase quantity decisions, had the most staying power (e.g., Gupta, 1988; Chiang, 1991; Bucklin and Gupta, 1992; Chintagunta, 1993). These models confirmed the purchase acceleration effect of promotion.

However, if consumers accelerate their purchases and stockpile for future consumption, one should see post-promotion dips in aggregate sales, which researchers did not observe (e.g., Moriarty 1985; Wittink *et al.*, 1988; Abraham and Lodish, 1993). Krishna (1992) and Neslin and Stone (1996) offered some explanations for this. Subsequently, however, van Heerde, Leeflang, and Wittink (2000) and Macé and Neslin (2004) were able to find both post- and pre-promotion dips with careful time series analysis with large samples.

The question that arose was — does purchase acceleration only result in stockpiling or does it also increase consumption? Scanner data do not provide information on inventory and consumption, so researchers through the 1990s had assumed a constant household usage rate. However, Ailawadi and Neslin (1998) modeled usage rate as a function of inventory, even though both are unobserved, and embedded this function in their incidence-choice-quantity model. They showed that promotion induced stockpiling can significantly increase consumption. Bell, Chiang, and Padmanabhan (1999) provided evidence for consumption effects in several categories. Sun (2005) estimated a dynamic structural model of endogenous consumption in the presence of uncertain promotions and Chan, Narasimhan, and Zhang (2008) developed a dynamic structural model of when, what, and how much to buy, and how much to consume.

In general, several studies recognized that consumers may anticipate future promotions and adjust their purchase behavior. Assunção and Meyer (1993), and Krishna (1994) examined how promotion uncertainty influenced consumers' optimal forward-buying behavior. Gönül and Srinivasan (1996) found that given sufficient inventory, consumers can shift their purchase time to coincide with a promotion schedule. More recently, Erdem, Imai, and Keane (2003) developed a structural dynamic model where consumers form price expectations to decide when, what and how much to buy. Sun, Neslin, and Srinivasan (2003) showed that brand-switching elasticities derived from a logit model are biased upwards, compared to those derived from a dynamic structural model where, consumers adjust purchases based on expectations of future promotions.

17.3.4 *Decomposition of the promotional bump and incremental sales*

Since the promotional bump can borrow sales from other brands, other stores, and future purchases, in addition to increasing consumption, decomposing the bump into its components is critical to understanding whether the promotion results in incremental sales. Further, some components, e.g., brand switching, are incremental for the manufacturer but not the retailer, and others, e.g., store switching, are incremental for the retailer but not the manufacturer. So, an analysis of incremental sales depends on whose perspective is being taken (van Heerde and Neslin, 2008).

Since, coupons were traditionally offered by manufacturers, analyses of the incremental sales and profitability of coupons were conducted from the manufacturer's perspective. Klein (1985) and Irons, Little, and Klein (1983) found in "Couponlab" experiments that the cumulative effect of coupons is much as eight share points over a 12-week period. In a field experiment, Bawa and Shoemaker (1989) found that coupons generate substantial incremental sales but these vary with household characteristics suggesting the value of targeting coupons, and that coupons lead to incremental sales even among those who do not redeem them, supporting the advertising or exposure effect noted by Schwartz (1966). Neslin (1990) developed a model of coupon response making a key distinction among brand loyal and brand switching coupon users, and estimated incremental sales per redeemed coupon.

Abraham and Lodish (1987) developed a promotion evaluation system for a single brand called PROMOTER, which used some judgmental input, but also estimated baseline sales using shipment and consumer sales data. Later they used scanner data to develop expanded PROMOTIONSCAN evaluation systems covering all brands and relating incremental sales to various discount levels, feature, and display activity (Abraham and Lodish, 1993).

The development of integrated models of incidence, choice, and quantity helped quantify the incremental sales effect of promotions from the manufacturer's perspective since, the overall sales increase could be decomposed into sales increase due to brand switching, purchase acceleration and stockpiling. Gupta (1988) was one of the first papers to do this decomposition. He showed that the total sales elasticity could be expressed as a sum of brand choice, purchase time, and purchase quantity elasticities, and found that, of the total sales increase due to promotion for a coffee brand, more than 84% was due to brand switching. Analyses by Chiang (1991), Chintagunta (1993), and Bucklin, Gupta, and Siddarth (1998) showed similar results with some variation across categories. Bell, Chiang, and Padmanabhan (1999) analyzed almost 200 brands and found that 75% of the promotion elasticity is due to secondary demand effects (i.e., brand switching) and 25% due to primary demand effects (i.e., stockpiling and consumption).

van Heerde, Gupta, and Wittink (2003) challenged this elasticity interpretation and argued that decomposition of unit sales, and not elasticity, is the way to look at incremental effects of promotions. They found that 75% of incremental sales of a brand are due to primary demand and only 25% are due to brand switching. van Heerde, Leeflang, and Wittink (2004) reported similar results when they decomposed the bump for four types of promotional discounts: without feature or display, with feature only, with display only, and with both. Other studies confirmed their findings (Pauwels, Hanssens, and Siddarth, 2002; Nair, Dube, and Chintagunta, 2005; Chan, Narasimhan, and Zhang, 2008).

Steenburgh (2007) tried to reconcile the difference between elasticity and unit sales decompositions by explaining what each measures and argued that both contribute to a complete picture of how promotions work. He noted that unit-based decomposition, measures stolen business by the decrease in demand of *competing goods*, while elasticity decomposition measures the relative influence of changes in consumers' decisions on the increase in *own-good demand.* van Heerde and Neslin (2008) provided a nice summary of empirical generalizations that can now be made about the promotional bump decomposition.

Two exceptions to this incremental sales research from the manufacturer's perspective are Srinivasan *et al.* (2004) and Ailawadi *et al.* (2006, 2007), who study the retailer's perspective. The former use Vector

Autoregressive (VAR) models to quantify the effect of promotions on a retailer's category revenue, margin, and store traffic in additional to the effect on manufacturer revenue. The latter analyze all promotions offered by a drug store chain during a year, estimate the percentage of the promotional bump that is due to switching within the store, acceleration of future sales in the store and incremental sales for the retailer, and compute the profitability of each promotion. Neither paper paints a rosy picture of the impact of promotions on retailer revenue and margins. A different approach examined the profitability of price searchers for a retailer. Gauri, Sudhir, and Talukdar (2008) found that consumers who search for promotions both spatially and temporally are less profitable for a retailer than those who do only one, but even the former have a positive contribution to the retailer's profit. Talukdar, Gauri, and Grewal (2010) found that loss leader promotions benefit the retailer's bottom line despite the negative profit from extreme cherry picking consumers.

17.3.5 *Competitive reactions*

Massy and Frank (1967) noted that the longer term impact of promotions depends not only on a retailer or brand's own decisions and consumer response but also on how competitors react. In a series of papers, Leeflang and Wittink (1992, 1996, 2001) used store level weekly scanner data to estimate self- and cross-share elasticities for marketing mix variables as well as reaction elasticities of competing brands. They showed that competitive response is often, but not always, "simple", i.e., a change in one marketing variable by a brand may evoke a change by a competing brand in a different marketing variable. They also showed that firms may over- or under-react but do take into account consumer response to their own and competitors' actions. Subsequently, researchers used VAR models to estimate competitive reactions. Steenkamp *et al.* (2005) studied the frequency and nature of competitive reactions across several categories and related it to brand and category characteristics. Pauwels (2007) used a similar methodology but distinguished between competing manufacturer and retailer reactions. Horvath *et al.* (2005) and Pauwels (2004) evaluated the importance of competitor reaction versus other feedback effects in determining longer-term promotions response.

More recently, researchers argued that competitor reactions to major policy changes may be quite different from interactions in ongoing marketing mix activity. Ailawadi, Lehmann, and Neslin (2001) studied competitor and consumer response to P&G's value pricing move, which was initiated and widely publicized during the early 1990s. Ailawadi, Kopalle, and Neslin (2005) subsequently estimated a dynamic Manufacturer–Retailer Stackelberg model to study competitor and retailer reactions to the same move. van Heerde, Gijsbrechts, and Pauwels (2008) examined the consequences of a widely publicized price war between Dutch grocery retailers.

17.3.6 *Long-term and permanent effects*

Although several researchers had discussed and measured the immediate and medium-term impact of promotions (i.e., in the weeks following a promotion), multiple years of scanner data became available in the 1990s and allowed researchers to study the impact of promotions over the long term. Krishna, Currim, and Shoemaker (1991) argued that frequent exposure to promotions can change consumer behavior in the long term. Mela, Gupta, and Lehmann (1997) empirically quantified the change in consumers' promotion sensitivity in one product category over a period of several years. They found that price promotions make consumers more deal sensitive. Jedidi, Mela, and Gupta (1999) also found that promotions were associated with increased price sensitivity. They showed that the long-term effect of promotions on sales is negative and about two-fifths the magnitude of their positive short-term effects. Mela, Gupta, and Jedidi (1998) examined the long-term impact of promotions on market structure and found that promotions reduced differentiation between brands. Later work generalized some of these findings. In a meta-analysis of over 1,800 price elasticities reported over four decades, Bijmolt, van Heerde, and Pieters (2005) found that average price elasticity increased from −1.8 to −3.5, a trend that was confirmed by van Heerde *et al.* (2013). Ataman, van Heerde, and Mela (2010) studied 70 brands across 25 categories over a five-year period and confirmed a positive association between discounting and price sensitivity over time. We note, though, that these papers do not rule out the possibility of reverse causality, i.e., that firms may be promoting more because consumers have become more price sensitive, due to factors like tight economic conditions, intensive distribution, and lower brand differentiation.

A separate body of research has examined whether the effects of promotions are permanent. Using VAR models, these studies separate the transient and permanent effects of promotions on sales and account for competitive reaction and feedback loops. Across more than 400 product categories, Nijs *et al.* (2001) and Steenkamp *et al.* (2005) found no permanent effects of promotion on category and own-brand sales respectively. Pauwels, Hanssens, and Siddarth (2002) examined immediate, transient, and permanent effects in brand choice, category incidence and purchase quantity. They found negative transient effects for brand choice but not for purchase incidence, and confirmed the lack of permanent effects for the top brands in a category. However, Slotegraaf and Pauwels (2008) included a broader set of brands in their analysis and reported a sizeable percentage of permanent effects, generally for small brands.

17.4 Retailer response to trade promotions

Since the manufacturer must depend largely on retailers to offer promotions to end consumers, and can only motivate them through trade promotions, retailer response to trade promotions has always been an important issue.

17.4.1 *Forward buying and pass-through*

One of the first articles was by Magee (1953) who estimated the number of cases ordered by a dealer with and without promotion. It was in 1976, however, that Chevalier and Curhan provided the first empirical analysis of retailers' response to trade deals and reasons for variation in this response. They analyzed almost 1,000 trade deals offered by various manufacturers to a retail chain during a 24-week period. This early evidence showed that many deals were not passed through at all but among those that were, retailers often passed through more than 100%.

Curhan and Kopp (1987) examined how retailer self-reported acceptance and pass-through of trade deals is influenced by the type of deal, and item, category, and manufacturer characteristics. Blattberg and Levin (1987) used a four-equation model to estimate the effect of trade promotions on shipments, retailer inventory, retail promotions, and consumer sales. They documented retailer forward-buying and found that the trade deal was not profitable for the manufacturer. Abraham and Lodish (1987) also quantified retailer response in their brand level PROMOTER model and documented retailer forward buying. Armstrong, Gerstner, and Hess (1994) analyzed data on all trade deals in four products categories offered over two years to a grocery chain, reported patterns similar to Chevalier and Curhan (1976), and proposed an analytical model to explain them.

During the 1990s and early 2000s, unprofitable trade deals for manufacturers were often attributed to retailers' incentive to forward buy and attention focused on the type of trade deals that could alleviate this problem. Dreze and Bell (2003) compared off-invoice deals preferred by retailers, with scan-back deals preferred by manufacturers and showed how deals could be re-designed to make retailers no worse off and manufacturers better off by reducing the dead weight costs of forward bought inventory. Gomez, Rao, and McLaughlin (2007) showed that large retailers and those with successful private label brands have greater power and are therefore, able to increase the allocation of promotional funds to off-invoices and decrease allocation to performance-based trade promotions such as scan-backs.

Yet, manufacturers continue to offer trade promotions. Lal, Little, and Villas-Boas (1996) showed analytically that retailers' forward buying behavior can in fact benefit manufacturers, by decreasing manufacturer competition. Kim and Staelin (1999) identified conditions under which manufacturers will give lump sum trade allowances to retailers even when pass-through is low. Cui, Raju, and Zhang (2008) argued that since large retailers have an inventory cost advantage over smaller retailers and can forward buy more easily, manufacturers may use trade promotions as a price discrimination tool between dominant retailers and smaller independents.

During the last decade, access to wholesale price data has allowed researchers to quantify pass-through across many brands and categories. Besanko, Dubé, and Gupta (2005) examined pass-through by the Dominicks grocery chain by regressing weekly retail price on wholesale price. They found that own-brand pass through rates were, on average, more than 60% for most categories. Using a similar model, Nijs *et al.* (2010) analyzed pass-through for one category across several wholesalers and retailers and found mean pass-through of 0.71, 0.59, and 0.41 for the wholesaler, retailer, and total channel respectively. Pauwels (2007) used the same data source as Besanko, Dubé, and Gupta (2005) but extended the analysis in a VAR model to allow for dynamic longer-term effects, and found similar pass-through rates.

In 2009, Ailawadi and Harlam argued for a different measure of pass-through as trade deals shifted from off-invoice price discounts to various types of lump-sum and pay-for-performance offers. Using data across all products sold by a major US retailer, they compared the total annual funding provided by manufacturers with the retailer's total annual spending on promoting the manufacturers' products. They found that this retailer passed through *more* than 100% of manufacturer funding it received in aggregate (some manufacturers, and private label, were promoted without any funding), but among manufacturers who provided some funding and received some promotional spending, the median pass-through rate was 75%. All these investigations also studied the determinants of pass-through and consistently found that variables related to the manufacturer versus the retailer's power, e.g., market share, strongly influence pass-through.

17.4.2 *Cross pass-through*

Theoretical models predicted that retailers, e.g., those who maximize category rather than brand profit, should engage in cross brand pass-through, i.e., promote products of a competing brand when they receive trade deals from another brand in the same category (Besanko, Gupta, and Jain 1998; Moorthy, 2005). However, empirical research until 2005 had only examined own brand pass-through. Besanko, Dubé, and Gupta (2005) allowed for cross pass-through by regressing a brand's weekly retail price not only on its own wholesale price but also on wholesale prices of competing brands in the category. They documented significant cross-brand effects in two-thirds of the cases analyzed. If valid, this finding meant that a retailer would take a wholesale price reduction offered by one brand in a given week and use it to reduce the retail price of a competing brand in the same category. However, McAlister (2007) showed that these significant cross-brand pass-through effects were an artifact of an inadvertent inflation of sample size in the work by Besanko *et al.* After a further round of analyses and comments on the original work (Dubé and Gupta, 2008; Duan, McAlister, and Shameek, 2011), the take-away seems to be that week-to-week cross pass-through of the type described by Besanko *et al.* does not exist in the Dominicks data.

But this does not mean that retailers only spend the trade allowances they receive from a manufacturer on promoting that manufacturer's products. As noted earlier, over the years, several researchers have found that some manufacturers get no or very little pass-through and others get more than 100% pass-through or get promoted even without providing funding (Chevalier and Curhan, 1976; Armstrong, 1991; Ailawadi and Harlam, 2009). However, this type of cross pass-through occurs not just within a product category but also across product categories, as shown by Ailawadi and Harlam (2009) and Pancras, Gauri, and Talukdar (2013).

17.5 Promotion planning, optimization, and targeting

Based on their understanding of consumer, competitor, and retailer response, manufacturers must decide whether, when, how much to promote directly to consumers (often through coupons) as well as to retailers. Similarly, retailers need to make similar decisions for their promotions to consumers. Little (1966) introduced a model of adaptive control where he used a quadratic response function that was updated based on the results of an experiment. Promotion rate was then chosen to maximize expected profits in the next period and the process was repeated. Paucity of data in the 1970s prompted Little to propose decision-support systems where managerial input could be used to estimate some or all the parameters of a model (Little, 1975, 1979). The goal of these models was to help managers make better decisions rather than worry about parameter estimates and econometric specifications. In a similar spirit, Neslin and Shoemaker (1983) developed a decision calculus model for coupon profitability. The promotion evaluation systems of Abraham and Lodish (1987, 1993) were also used not just to quantify incremental sales from individual promotions but to improve them by discontinuing the unprofitable ones.

As more data became available and richer models of consumer response were developed in the 1990s, normative models took these into account.

Neslin, Powell, and Stone (1995) moved from evaluation to optimization, developing a dynamic optimization model for trade promotions that took into account manufacturer, retailer, and consumer response. In the same year, Tellis and Zufryden (1995) developed an optimization model of promotion depth and timing from a retailer's perspective, using an integrated incidence-choice-quantity model as the basis. Greenleaf (1995) and Kopalle, Rao, and Assunção (1996) incorporated reference prices into a dynamic model of price promotions to obtain optimal pricing policies in a monopoly and oligopoly respectively. Subsequent normative work developed promotional calendars for manufacturers (Silva-Risso, Bucklin, and Morrison, 1999) and dynamic pricing schedules for both manufacturers and retailers (Kopalle, Mela, and Marsh, 1999).

During the 2000s, loyalty program data became available and, retailers started offering targeted coupons and other promotional offers; researchers began to optimize and evaluate targeted promotions. Lam *et al.* (2001) and Heilman, Nakamoto, and Rao (2002) studied the impact of targeted and in-store coupons on store traffic, total sales, and unplanned sales in the store. Venkatesan and Farris (2012) examined the effectiveness of targeted retailer coupons in increasing store trips, revenue, and redemptions, while controlling for endogenous targeting. They found a substantial advertising exposure effect and also showed the value of targeted over FSI coupons.

Zhang and Krishnamurthi (2004) took another step forward by optimizing customized promotions for each household shopping at an online retailer. Subsequently, Zhang and Wedel (2009) demonstrated the profit impact of optimizing promotions both online and off-line. They also investigated the return on targeting promotions and found that the additional benefit from individually targeted promotions over segment level targeting is small, especially offline. Most recently, Divakar, Ratchford, and Shankar (2005) and Natter *et al.* (2007) have developed dynamic decision support systems for a manufacturer and a retailer respectively and demonstrated the bottom line benefit of implementing these systems.

17.6 Directions for future research

Sales promotion is a mature area with hundreds of published articles over 40 years. However, it still has many opportunities for research and the internet is propelling it into another period of sustained growth. We conclude this chapter with some suggestions.

17.6.1 *Knowledge gaps*

Based on almost 30 years of work on short- and long-term promotion response, we believe it is fair to conclude that promotions do generate incremental sales for manufacturers, though it is still difficult to make a generalization about the magnitude. While there is evidence for a negative longer term impact, this is outweighed by the immediate and medium-term benefit. More research is definitely needed before we can make a statement about incremental profit. Also, while many scholars have examined the long-term effects of promotions, there is still an opportunity to examine how frequent promotions may depress baseline sales, which in turn may make short-term effects of promotions look even more attractive. Relatedly, have consumers become more price sensitive because of promotions, or have promotions become more prevalent in response to increasing consumer price sensitivity?

For retailers, it is unclear whether the net effect of promotions is positive, not only on profit, but even on sales. In general, while manufacturer-oriented issues, such as brand choice, have received a lot of attention in our literature, retailer-oriented issues such as store traffic and in-store decision making, need more research. The availability of new technologies like RFID, GPS, and mobile eye tracking are making it possible to get much deeper insight into not just whether but how consumers engage with promotions in the store. The recent work by Hui *et al.* (2013) is a good example of the opportunities and insights that these technologies can provide.

There is also an opportunity to bridge the gaps in understanding between academic work and industry practice. Attempts to do so have been intermittent over the decades, with the ScanPro and PromotionScan models of the 1980s and early 1990s, the work by Bucklin and Gupta (1999), and more recently, the implementation of promotion evaluation and planning models for retailers by Ailawadi *et al.* (2006) and Natter *et al.* (2007). More and closer collaboration is needed between academics and practitioners, especially since, as we discuss below, the type of promotions being used in practice are undergoing a sea-change.

17.6.2 *Loyalty program-based promotions*

In the last decade or so, retailers have become much more data savvy and are using their loyalty programs to target promotions, both on- and off-line. Instead of offering the usual promotional discounts on manufacturers' products, these retailers offer deals whereby purchasing a given product allows consumers to earn discounts that can be used on any products in their stores. Zhang and Breugelmans (2012) analyzed the effectiveness of such promotions for an online retailer but more work is needed to assess their profitability for both the retailer and the manufacturers who provide trade funds for such promotions. More work is also needed on the type of targeted promotions that have the highest returns.

17.6.3 *New media*

First, the internet and then mobile commerce have led to the introduction of many new forms of deals. For example, coupons range from the traditional ones that are now available online to Groupons. The former are inexpensive to distribute, but they are also easily found and redeemed, leaving open the question of their incremental profitability. The latter bring revenue to Groupon but research is needed on the incremental sales and profit they provide to the vendor paying for the coupons. Similarly, flash deal sites have proliferated online. Because these deals have a short time fuse and are only open to registered users, they have an exclusivity element that may spur incremental sales. But they can also take store visits and sales away from a wide group of other retailers through which the manufacturer sells. So, evaluating the manufacturer's incremental sales and profitability is both important and more difficult. Additionally, from the point of view of the flash deal site, returns are an important element in profitability. Return rates are significantly higher online especially as many companies offer free shipping, exchanges, and even returns. Indeed, in some markets like China, these deal sites also offer unique payment options whereby the consumer is charged only when the product is received by them. There is an opportunity to develop dynamic structural models of consumer purchase behavior that account for all of these phenomena. Finally, the impact of location-based and other mobile promotional offers is another exciting research opportunity.

17.6.4 *Non-grocery purchases*

Most of academic work on sales promotion has been done for frequently purchased supermarket products like coffee, ketchup, and tuna. There is an opportunity to understand how promotions work for other industries such as travel, apparel, durables, etc. Apart from contextual differences, these categories have different purchase cycles, promotion frequency and data availability, which will require new models and methods. Although researchers cannot expect to get long time series of purchase data for these categories, there is an opportunity to collect and analyze data from field experiments as more marketers are willing to conduct them, especially online where the risk and the expense of experimenting is considerably lower. Not to mention the opportunity afforded by natural experiments when companies like JC Penney etc., make promotional policy changes and reversals.

References

Abraham, M. M. and L. M. Lodish (1987). PROMOTER: An automated promotion evaluation system, *Marketing Science*, 6(2) (Spring), 101–123.

Abraham, M. M. and L. M. Lodish (1993). An implemented system for improving promotion productivity using store scanner data, *Marketing Science*, 12(3), 248–269.

Ailawadi, K. L. and S. Neslin (1998). The effect of promotion on consumption: Buying more and using it faster, *Journal of Marketing Research*, 35, 390–398.

Ailawadi, K. L., D. R. Lehmann, and S. A. Neslin (2001). Market response to a major policy change in the marketing mix: Learning from Procter & Gamble's value pricing strategy, *The Journal of Marketing*, 44–61.

Ailawadi, K. L., S. Neslin, and K. Gedenk (2001). Pursuing the value conscious consumer: Store brands versus national brand promotions, *Journal of Marketing*, 65(1) (January), 71–89.

Ailawadi, K. L., B. A. Harlam, J. Cesar, and D. Trounce (2006). Promotion profitability for a retailer: The role of promotion, brand, category, and store characteristics, *Journal of Marketing Research*, 43(4), 518–535.

Ailawadi, K. L., P. Kopalle, and S. Neslin (2005). Predicting competitive response to a major policy change: Combining normative and empirical analysis *Marketing Science*, 24(1) (Winter), 12–24.

Ailawadi, K. L., K. Gedenk, C. Lutzky, and S. A. Neslin (2007). Decomposition of the sales impact of promotion-induced stockpiling, *Journal of Marketing Research*, 44(3) (August), 450–467.

Ailawadi, K. L. and B. A. Harlam (2009). Retailer promotion pass-through: A measure, its magnitude and its determinants, *Marketing Science*, 28(4) (July–August), 782–791.

Allenby, G. M. and P. E. Rossi (1991). Quality perceptions and asymmetric switching between brands, *Marketing Science*, 10(Summer), 185–204,

Armstrong, M. K. S. (1991). *Retail response to trade promotion: An incremental analysis of forward buying and retail promotion*, unpublished doctoral dissertation, University of Texas at Dallas.

Armstrong, M., E. Gerstner, and J. Hess (1994). Pocketing the trade deal, *Proceedings from the Nec-63 Spring Conference*, (Spring), 105–112.

Assunção, J. L. and R. J. Meyer (1993). The rational effect of price promotions on sales and consumption, *Management Science*, 39(5), 517–535.

Ataman, M. B., H. J. van Heerde, and C. F. Mela (2010). The long-term effect of marketing strategy on brand sales, *Journal of Marketing Research*, 47(5), 866–882.

Batsell, R. R. and J. C. Polking (1985). A new class of market share models, *Marketing Science*, 4(3) (Summer), 177–198.

Bawa, K. and R. W. Shoemaker (1987). The coupon-prone consumer: Some findings based on purchase behavior across product classes, *Journal of Marketing*, 51(4) (October), 99–110.

Bawa, K. and R. W. Shoemaker (1989). Analyzing incremental sales from a direct mail coupon promotion, *Journal of Marketing*, 53(3) (July), 66–78.

Bell, D. R., J. Chiang, and V. Padmanabhan (1999). The decomposition of promotional response: An empirical generalization, *Marketing Science*, 18(4), 504–526.

Bell, D. R. and J. M. Lattin (2000). Looking for loss aversion in scanner panel data: The confounding effect of price response heterogeneity, *Marketing Science*, 19(Spring), 185–200.

Bell, D., D. Corsten, and G. Knox (2011). From point of purchase to path to purchase: How preshopping factors drive unplanned buying, *Journal of Marketing*, 75(January), 31–45.

Besanko, D., S. Gupta, and D. Jain (1998). Logit demand estimation under competitive pricing behavior: An equilibrium framework, *Management Science*, 44(11, Part 1 of 2), 1533–1547.

Besanko, D., J. P. Dubé, and S. Gupta (2005). Own-brand and cross-brand retail pass-through, *Marketing Science*, 24(1), 123–137.

Bijmolt, T. H. A., H. J. van Heerde, and R. G. M. Pieters (2005). New empirical generalizations on the determinants of price elasticity, *Journal of Marketing Research*, 42(May), 141–156.

Blattberg, R. C., T. Buesing, P. Peacock, and S. Sen (1978). Identifying the deal prone segment, *Journal of Marketing Research*, XV(August), 369–377.

Blattberg, R. C., G. A. Eppen, and J. Lieberman (1981). A theoretical and empirical evaluation of price deals for consumer nondurables, *Journal of Marketing*, 45(1) (Winter), 116–129.

Blattberg, R. C. and A. Levin (1987). Modelling the effectiveness and profitability of trade promotions, *Marketing Science*, 6(2) (Spring), 124–146.

Blattberg, R. C. and K. Wisnewski (1989). Price induced patterns of competition, *Marketing Science*, 8(4) (Fall), 291–309.

Blattberg, R. C. and S. A. Neslin (1990). *Sales promotion: Concepts, methods and strategies*, Englewood Cliffs, NJ: Prentice Hall.

Blattberg, R. C., R. Briesch, and E. Fox (1995). How promotions work, *Marketing Science*, 14(3), G122–D132.

Bucklin, R. E. and J. M. Lattin (1991). A two-state model of purchase incidence and brand choice, *Marketing Science*, 10(1), 24–39.

Bucklin, R. E. and S. Gupta (1992). Brand choice, purchase incidence, and segmentation: An integrated modeling approach, *Journal of Marketing Research*, 29(2), 201–215.

Bucklin, R. E., S. Gupta, and S. Siddarth (1998). Determining segmentation in sales response across consumer purchase behaviors, *Journal of Marketing Research*, 189–197.

Bucklin, R. E. and S. Gupta (1999). Commercial use of upc scanner data: Industry and academic perspectives, *Marketing Science* 18(3), 247–273.

Chan, T., C. Narasimhan and Q. Zhang (2008). Decomposing promotional effects with a dynamic structural model of flexible consumption, *Journal of Marketing Research*, 45(4), 487–498.

Chandon, P., B. Wansink, and G. Laurent (2000). A benefit congruency framework of sales promotion effectiveness, *Journal of Marketing*, 64(October), 65–81.

Chevalier, M. (1975). Increase in sales due to in-store display, *Journal of Marketing Research*, 12(4), 426–431.

Chevalier, M. and R. C. Curhan (1976). Retail promotions as a function of trade promotions: A descriptive analysis, *Sloan Management Review*, 18(3), 19–32.

Chiang, J. (1991). A simultaneous approach to the whether, what and how much to buy questions, *Marketing Science*, 10(4), 297–315.

Chintagunta, P. K., D. C. Jain, and N. J. Vilcassim (1991). Investigating heterogeneity in brand preferences in logit models for panel data, *Journal of Marketing Research*, 28(4), 417–428.

Chintagunta, P. K. (1993). Investigating purchase incidence, brand choice and purchase quantity decisions of households, *Marketing Science*, 12(2), 184–208.

Curhan, Ronald and R. Kopp (1987). Obtaining retailer support for trade deals, *Journal of Advertising Research*, (December–January), 51–60.

Cui, T., J. S. Raju, and Z. J. Zhang (2008). A price discrimination model of trade promotions, *Marketing Science*, 27(5) (September–October), 779–795.

Davis, S. J., J. Inman, and L. McAlister (1992). Promotion has a negative effect on brand evaluations — or does it? Additional disconfirming evidence, *Journal of Marketing Research*, 29(1), 143–148.

Divakar, S., B. T. Ratchford, and V. Shankar (2005). CHAN4CAST: A multichannel multiregion forecasting model for consumer packaged goods, *Marketing Science*, 24(3), 333–350.

Dodson, J., A. Tybout, and B. Sternthal (1978). Impact of deals and deal retraction on brand switching, *Journal of Marketing Research*, 15(1) (February), 72–81.

Dreze, X. and D. Bell (2003). Creating win–win trade promotions: Theory and empirical analysis of scan-back trade deals, *Marketing Science*, 22(1), 16–39.

Duan, J., L. McAlister, and S. Sinha (2011). Reexamining Bayesian model — Comparison evidence of cross-brand pass-through, *Marketing Science*, 30(3), 550–561.

Dubé, J.-P. and S. Gupta (2008). Cross-brand pass-through in supermarket pricing, *Marketing Science*, 27(3), 324–333.

Duvvuri, S. D., A. Ansari, and S. Gupta (2007). Consumers' price sensitivities across complementary categories, *Management Science*, 53(12) (December), 1933–1945.

Erdem, T. (1998). An empirical analysis of umbrella branding, *Journal of Marketing Research*, 35(August), 339–351.

Erdem, T., S. Imai, and M. P. Keane (2003). Brand and quantity choice dynamics under price uncertainty, *Quantitative Marketing and Economics*, 1(1), 5–64.

Fader, P. S. and L. McAlister (1990). An elimination by aspects model of consumer response to promotion calibrated on UPC scanner data, *Journal of Marketing Research*, 27(August), 322–332.

Foubert, B. and E. Gijsbrechts (2007). Shopper response to bundle promotions for packaged goods, *Journal of Marketing Research*, XLIV(November), 647–662.

Frank, R. E. and W. F. Massy (1971). The effect of retail promotional activities on sales, *Decision Sciences*, 2(4), 405–431.

Gauri, D., K. Sudhir, and D. Talukdar (2008). The temporal and spatial dimensions of price search: Insights from matching household survey and purchase data, *Journal of Marketing Research*, XLV(April), 226–240.

Gedenk, K. and S. A. Neslin (1999). The role of retail promotion in determining future brand loyalty: Its effect on future purchase event feedback, *Journal of Retailing*, 75(4), 433–459.

Gijsbrechts, E., K. Campo, and T. Goossens (2003). The impact of store flyers on store traffic and store sales: A geo-marketing approach, *Journal of Retailing*, 79, 1–16.

Gomez, M. I., V. R. Rao, and E. W. McLaughlin (2007). Empirical analysis of budget and allocation of trade promotions in the US. supermarket industry, *Journal of Marketing Research*, XLIV(August), 410–424.

Gönül, F. and K. Srinivasan (1996). Estimating the impact of consumer expectations of coupons on purchase behavior: A dynamic structural model, *Marketing Science*, 15(3), 262–279.

Greenleaf, E. A. (1995). The impact of reference price effects on the profitability of price promotions, *Marketing Science*, 14(Winter), 82–104.

Guadagni, P. M. and J. D. C. Little (1983). A logit model of brand choice calibrated on scanner data, *Marketing Science*, 2(3), 203–238.

Gupta, S. (1988). Impact of sales promotions on when, what, and how much to buy, *Journal of Marketing Research*, 25(November), 342–355.

Heilman, C., K. Nakamoto, and A. Rao (2002). Pleasant surprises: Consumer response to unexpected in-store coupons, *Journal of Marketing Research*, XXXIX(May), 242–252.

Hui, S. K., J. J. Inman, Y. Huang, and J. Suher (2013). The effect of in-store travel distance on unplanned spending: Applications to mobile promotion strategies, *Journal of Marketing*, 77(March), 1–16.

Horvath, C., P. S.H. Leeflang, J. E. Wiering, and D. R. Wittink (2005). Competitive reaction and feedback effects based on VARX models of pooled store data, *International Journal of Research in Marketing*, 22, 415–426.

Inman, J. J., L. McAlister, and W. D. Hoyer (1990). Promotion signal: Proxy for a price cut? *Journal of Consumer Research*, 17(June), 74–81.

Inman, J. J., A. C. Peter, and P. Raghubir (1997). Framing the deal: The role of restrictions in accentuating deal value, *Journal of Consumer Research*, 24(1), 68–79.

Inman, J. J., R. S. Winer, and R. Ferraro (2009). The interplay among category characteristics, customer characteristics, and customer activities on in-store decision making, *Journal of Marketing*, 73(September), 19–29.

Irons, K. W., J. D. C. Little, and R. L. Klein (1983). Determinants of coupon effectiveness, in Fred Zufryden, ed., *Proceedings of the 1983 ORSA/TIMS marketing science conference*, USC, Los Angeles, CA, 157–164.

Jain, D. C. and N. J. Vilcassim (1991). Investigating household purchase timing decisions: A conditional hazard function approach, *Marketing Science*, 10(1), 1–23.

Jedidi, K., C. F. Mela, and S. Gupta (1999). Managing advertising and promotion for long-run profitability, *Marketing Science*, 18(1), 1–22.

Kahneman, D. and A. Tversky (1979). Prospect theory: An analysis of decision under risk,*Econometrica*, 47, 263–91.

Kamakura, W. A. and G. J. Russell (1989). A probabilistic choice model for market segmentation and elasticity structure, *Journal of Marketing Research*, 379–390.

Keane, M. P. (1997). Modeling heterogeneity and state dependence in consumer choice behavior, *Journal of Business and Economic Statistics*, 15(3), 310–327.

Kim, S. Y. and R. Staelin (1999). Manufacturer allowances and retailer pass-through rates in a competitive environment, *Marketing Science*, 18(1), 59–76.

Klein, R. L. (1985). How to use research to make better sales promotion marketing decisions in Stanley Ulanoff, ed., *Handbook of sales promotion*, New York: McGraw Hill, 457–466.

Kopalle, P. K., A. G. Rao, and J. L. Assunção (1996). Asymmetric reference price effects and dynamic pricing policies, *Marketing Science*, 15(Winter), 60–85.

Kopalle, P., C. F. Mela, and L. Marsh (1999). The dynamic effect of discounting on sales: Empirical analysis and normative pricing implications, *Marketing Science*, 18(3), 317–332.

Krishna, A., I. S. Currim, and R. W. Shoemaker (1991). Consumer perceptions of promotional activity, *Journal of Marketing*, 55, 4–16.

Krishna, A. (1992). The normative impact of consumer price expectations for multiple brands on consumer purchase behavior, *Marketing Science*, 11(3), 266–286.

Krishna, A. (1994). The impact of dealing patterns on purchase behavior, *Marketing Science*, 13(4), 351–373.

Kuehn, A. A. (1962). Consumer brand choice as a learning process, *Journal of Advertising Research*, 2, 10–17.

Kumar, V. and R. P. Leone (1988). Measuring the effect of retail store promotions on brand and store substitution behavior, *Journal of Marketing Research*, 25(May), 178–185.

Lal, R. (1990). Price promotions: Limiting competitive encroachment, *Marketing Science*, 9(3) (Summer), 247–262.

Lal, R., J. D. C. Little, and M. Villas-Boas (1996). A theory of forward buying, merchandising, and trade deals, *Marketing Science*, 15(1) (Winter), 21–37.

Lam, S. Y., M. Vandenbosch, J. Hulland, and M. Pearce (2001). Evaluating promotions in shopping environments: Decomposing sales response into attraction, conversion, and spending effects, *Marketing Science*, 20(2), 194–215.

Lattin, J. M. and R. E. Bucklin (1989). Reference effects of price and promotion on brand choice behavior, *Journal of Marketing Research*, 26(August), 299–310.

Lazear, E. P. (1986). Retail pricing and clearance sales, *American Economic Review*, 76(1) (March), 14–32.

Leclerc, F. and J. D. Little (1997). Can advertising copy make FSI coupons more effective? *Journal of Marketing Research*, 34, 473–484.

Leeflang, P. S. H. and D. R. Wittink (1992). Diagnosing competitive reactions using (aggregated) scanner data, *International Journal of Research in Marketing*, 9, 39–57.

Leeflang, P. S. H. and D. R. Wittink (1996). Competitive reaction versus consumer response: Do managers overreact? *International Journal of Research in Marketing*, 13(2), 103–120.

Leeflang, P. S. H. and D. R. Wittink (2001). Explaining competitive reaction effects, *International Journal of Research in Marketing*, 18, 119–137.

Little, J. D. C. (1966). A model of adaptive control of promotional spending, *Operations Research*, 14(6), 1075–1097.

Little, J. D. C. (1975). BRANDAID: A marketing-mix model, part 1: Structure, *Operations Research*, 23(4), 628–655.

Little, J. D. C. (1979). Decision support systems for marketing managers, *Journal of Marketing*, 9–26.

Macé, S. and S. A. Neslin (2004). The determinants of pre-and postpromotion dips in sales of frequently purchased goods, *Journal of Marketing Research*, 41(3), 339–350.

Magee, J. F. (1953). The effect of promotional effort on sales, *Operations Research*, 1(2), 64–74.

Manchanda, P., A. Ansari, and S. Gupta (1999). The "shopping basket": A model for multi-category purchase incidence decision, *Marketing Science*, 18(2), 95–115.

Massy, W. F. and R. E. Frank (1967). Short term price and dealing effects in selected market segments, *Journal of Marketing Research*, 2(2) (May), 171–185.

Mayhew, G. E. and R. S. Winer (1992). An empirical analysis of internal and external reference prices, *Journal of Consumer Research*, 19(June), 62–70.

McAlister, L. (1986). The impact of price promotions on a brand's market share, sales pattern, and profitability, *Marketing Science Institute Report*, 86–110.

McAlister, L. (2007). Cross-brand pass-through: Fact or artifact? *Marketing Science*, 26(6), 876–898.

Mela, C. F., S. Gupta, and D. R. Lehmann (1997). The long-term impact of promotion and advertising on consumer brand choice, *Journal of Marketing Research*, 34(May), 248–261.

Mela, C., S. Gupta, and K. Jedidi (1998). Assessing long-term promotional influences on market structure, *International Journal of Research in Marketing*, 15(2), 89–107.

Montgomery, D. B. (1971). Consumer characteristics associated with dealing: An empirical example, *Journal of Marketing Research*, 8(1), 118–120.

Moorthy, S. (2005). A general theory of pass-through in channels with category management and retail competition, *Marketing Science*, 24(1), 110–122.

Moriarty, M. M. (1985). Retail promotional effects on intra- and inter-brand sales performance, *Journal of Retailing*, 63(3), 27–47.

Nair, H., J. P. Dubé, and P. Chintagunta (2005). Accounting for primary and secondary demand effects with aggregate data, *Marketing Science*, 24(3), 444–460.

Narasimhan, C. (1984). A price discrimination theory of coupons, *Marketing Science*, 3(2) (Spring), 128–146.

Narasimhan, C. (1988). Competitive promotional strategies, *Journal of Business*, 61(4), 427–449.

Narasimhan, C., S. A. Neslin, and S. K. Sen (1996). Promotional elasticities and category characteristics, *Journal of Marketing*, 60(April), 17–30.

Natter, M., A. Mild, T. Reutterer, and A. Taudes (2007). An assortment-wide decision-support system for dynamic pricing and promotion planning in DIY retailing *Marketing Science*, 26(4), 576–583.

Neslin, S. A. and R. W. Shoemaker (1983). A model for evaluating the profitability of coupon promotions, *Marketing Science*, 2(4) (Fall), 361–388.

Neslin, S. A., C. Henderson, and J. Quelch (1985). Consumer promotions and the acceleration of product purchases, *Marketing Science*, 4(2), 147–165.

Neslin, S. A. and D. G. Clarke (1987). Relating the brand use profile of coupon redeemers to brand and coupon characteristics, *Journal of Marketing Research*, 27(1) (February–March), 23–32.

Neslin, S. A. and R. W. Shoemaker (1989). An alternative explanation for lower repeat rates after promotion purchases, *Journal of Marketing Research*, 26(2) (May), 205–213.

Neslin, S. A. (1990). A market response model for coupon promotions, *Marketing Science*, 9(2) (Spring), 125–145.

Neslin, S. A., S. G. Powell, and L. G. S. Stone (1995). The effects of retailer and consumer response on optimal manufacturer advertising and trade promotion strategies, *Management Science*, 41(5), 749–766.

Neslin, S. A. and L. S. Stone (1996). Consumer inventory sensitivity and the post-promotion dip, *Marketing Letters*, 7(1), 77–94.

Nijs, V., M. G. Dekimpe, J. B. Steenkamp, and D. M. Hanssens (2001). The category demand effects of price promotions, *Marketing Science*, 20(1), 1–22.

Nijs, V., K. Misra, E. T. Anderson, K. Hansen, and L. Krishnamurthi (2010). Channel pass-through of trade promotions, *Marketing Science*, 29(2) (March–April), 250–267.

Niraj, R., V. Padmanabhan, and P. B. Seetharaman (2008). A cross-category model of households' incidence and quantity decisions, *Marketing Science*, 27(2), 225–235.

Pancras, J., D. Gauri, and D. Talukdar (2013). Loss leaders and cross-category retailer pass-throughs: A Bayesian multilevel analysis, *Journal of Retailing*, 89(2), 140–157.

Papatla, P. and L. Krishnamurthi (1996). Measuring the dynamic effects of promotions on brand choice, *Journal of Marketing Research*, 33(February), 20–35.

Pauwels, K., D. M. Hanssens, and S. Siddarth (2002). The long-term effects of price promotions on category incidence, brand choice, and purchase quantity, *Journal of Marketing Research*, 39, 421–439.

Pauwels, K. (2004). How dynamic consumer response, competitor response, company support, and company inertia shape long-term marketing effectiveness, *Marketing Science*, 23(4) (Fall), 596–610.

Pauwels, K. (2007). How retailer and competitor decisions drive the long-term effectiveness of manufacturer promotions for fast moving consumer goods, *Journal of Retailing*, 83(3), 297–308.

Raju, J. S., S. K. Dhar, and D. G. Morrison (1994). The effect of package coupon on brand choice, *Marketing Science*, 13(2) (Spring), 145–164.

Raju, J. S., V. Srinivasan, and R. Lal (1990). The effects of brand loyalty on competitive price promotional strategies, *Management Science*, 36(3), 276–304.

Rao, R. (1991). Pricing and promotions in asymmetric duopolies, *Marketing Science*, 10(2) (Spring), 131–144.

Rao, R., R. Arjunji, and B. P. S. Murthi (1995). Game theory and empirical generalizations concerning competitive promotions, *Marketing Science*, 14(3) Part 2 of 2, G89–G100.

Reibstein, D. J. and P. A. Traver (1982). Factors affecting coupon redemption rates, *Journal of Marketing*, 46(4) (Fall), 102–113.

Rossi, P. E., R. E. McCulloch, and G. M. Allenby (1996). The value of purchase history data in target marketing, *Marketing Science*, 15(4), 321–340.

Russell, G. J. and A. Petersen (2000). Analysis of cross category dependence in market basket selection, *Journal of Retailing*, 76(3), 367–392.

Schneider, L. and I. Currim (1991). Consumer purchase behaviors associated with active and passive deal-proneness, *International Journal of Research in Marketing*, 8, 205–222.

Schwartz, A. (1966). The influence of media characteristics on coupon redemption, *Journal of Marketing*, 30(January), 41–46.

Seetharaman, P. B., A. Ainslie, and P. K Chintagunta (1999). Investigating household state dependence effects across categories, *Journal of Marketing Research*, 36(4), 488–500.

Seetharaman, P. B. and P. K. Chintagunta (2003). The proportional hazard model for purchase timing, *Journal of Business & Economic Statistics*, 21(3), 368–382.

Seetharaman, P. B. (2004). Modeling multiple sources of state dependence in random utility models: A distributed lag approach, *Marketing Science*, 23(2) (Spring), 263–271.

Sethuraman, R., V. Srinivasan, and D. Kim (1999). Asymmetric and neighborhood cross-price effects: Some empirical generalizations, *Marketing Science*, 18(1), 23–41.

Sethuraman, R. and V. Srinivasan (2002). The asymmetric share effect: An empirical generalization on cross-price effects, *Journal of Marketing Research*, 39(3) (August), 379–386.

Shimp, T. and A. Kavas (1984). The theory of reasoned action applied to coupon usage, *Journal of Consumer Research*, 11(3) (December), 795–809.

Shoemaker, R. and F. R. Shoaf (1977). Repeat rates of deal purchases, *Journal of Advertising Research*, 17(2), 47–53.

Shoemaker, R. W. (1979). An analysis of consumer reactions to product promotions, in N. Beckwith, M. Houston, R. Mittelstaedt, K. Monroe, and S. Ward, eds., *Educators' Conference Proceedings*, Chicago, IL: American Marketing Association, 244–248.

Silva-Risso, J. M., R. E. Bucklin, and D. G Morrison (1999). A decision support system for planning manufacturers' sales promotion calendars, *Marketing Science*, 18(3), 274–300.

Slotegraaf, R. and K. Pauwels (2008). The impact of brand equity and innovation on the long-term effectiveness of promotions, *Journal of Marketing Research*, XLV(June), 293–306.

Srinivasan, S. S., R. P. Leone, and F. J. Mulhern (1995). The advertising exposure effect of free standing inserts, *Journal of Advertising*, 24, 29–40.

Srinivasan, S., K. Pauwels, D. M. Hanssens, and M. G. Dekimpe (2004). Do promotions benefit manufacturers, retailers, or both? *Management Science*, 50(5), 617–629.

Steenburgh, T. J. (2007). Measuring consumer and competitive impact with elasticity decompositions, *Journal of Marketing Research*, 44(4), 636–646.

Steenkamp, J. B. E. M., V. R Nijs, D. M. Hanssens, and M. G. Dekimpe (2005). Competitive reactions to advertising and promotion attacks, *Marketing Science*, 24(1), 35–54.

Stilley, K. M., J. J. Inman, and K. L. Wakefield (2010). Spending on the fly: Mental budgets, promotions, and spending behavior, *Journal of Marketing*, 74(3), 34–47.

Sun, B., S. A. Neslin, and K. Srinivasan (2003). Measuring the impact of promotions on brand switching when consumers are forward looking, *Journal of Marketing Research*, 40(4), 389–405.

Sun, B. (2005). Promotion effect on endogenous consumption, *Marketing Science*, 24(3), 430–443.

Talukdar, D., D. Gauri, and D. Grewal (2010). An empirical analysis of the extreme cherry picking behavior of consumers in the frequently purchased goods market, *Journal of Retailing*, 86(4), 336–354.

Teel, J. E., R. H. Williams, and W. O. Bearden (1980). Correlates of consumer susceptibility to coupons in new product grocery product introductions, *Journal of Advertising*, 9(3), 31–46.

Tellis, G. J. and F. S. Zufryden (1995). Tackling the retailer decision maze: Which brands to discount, how much, when and why? *Marketing Science*, 14(3, Part 1 of 2), 271–299.

van Heerde, H. J., P. S. H. Leeflang, and D. R. Wittink (2000). The estimation of pre- and post promotion dips with store-level scanner data, *Journal of Marketing Research*, 37(3), 383–395.

van Heerde, H. J., S. Gupta, and D. R. Wittink (2003). Is 75% of the sales promotion bump due to brand switching? No, only 33% is, *Journal of Marketing Research*, 40(November), 481–491.

van Heerde, H. J., P. S. H. Leeflang, and D. R. Wittink (2004). Decomposing the sales promotion bump with store data, *Marketing Science*, 23(3), 317–334.

van Heerde, H., E. Gijsbrechts, and K. Pauwels (2008). Winners and losers in a major price war, *Journal of Marketing Research*, XLV(October), 499–518.

van Heerde, H. J. and S. A. Neslin (2008). Sales promotion models, in B. Wierenga, ed., *Handbook of marketing decision models*, New York: Springer Publishers, 107–162.

van Heerde, H., M. Gijsenberg, M. Dekimpe, and J. B. Steenkamp (2013). Price and advertising effectiveness over the business cycle, *Journal of Marketing Research*, L(April), 177–193.

Varian, H. (1980). A model of sales, *American Economic Review*, 70(4), 651–659.

Venkatesan, R. and P. W. Farris (2012). Measuring and managing returns from retailer-customized coupon campaigns, *Journal of Marketing*, 76(January), 76–94.

Walters, R. G. and S. B. Mackenzie (1988). A structural equations analysis of the impact of price promotions on store performance, *Journal of Marketing Research*, 25(1), 51–63.

Walters, R. G. (1991). Assessing the impact of retail price promotions on product substitution, complementary purchase, and interstore sales displacement, *Journal of Marketing*, 55(April), 17–28.

Wansink, B., R. Kent, and S. Hoch (1998). An anchoring and adjustment model of purchase quantity decisions, *Journal of Marketing Research*, 35(1), 71–81.

Ward, R. W. and J. E. Davis (1978). A pooled cross-section time series model of coupon promotions, *American Journal of Agricultural Economics*, 60(November), 393–401.

Webster, F. E. (1965). The 'deal-prone' consumer, *Journal of Marketing Research*, 11(May), 186–189.

Winer, R. S. (1986). A reference price model of brand choice for frequently purchased products, *Journal of Consumer Research*, 13(2), 250–256.

Wittink, D. R., M. Addona, W. Hawkes, and J. Porter (1988). SCAN* PRO: A model to measure short-term effects of promotional activities on brand sales, based on store-level scanner data, Working Paper, AC Nielsen, Schaumburg IL.

Zhang, J. and L. Krishnamurthi (2004). Customizing promotions in online stores, *Marketing Science*, 24(4), 561–578.

Zhang, J. (2006). An integrated choice model incorporating alternative mechanisms for consumers' reactions to in-store display and feature advertising, *Marketing Science*, 25(3) (May–June), 278–290.

Zhang, J. and E. Breugelmans (2012). The impact of an item-based loyalty program on consumer purchase behavior, *Journal of Marketing Resarch*, 49(1), 50–65.

Zhang, J. and M. Wedel (2009). The effectiveness of customized promotions in online and offline stores, *Journal of Marketing Research*, XLVI(April), 190–206.

Zenith Optimedia (2012). *Advertising Expenditure Forecast* September 2012.

Index